Thinking and deciding

Thinking and deciding

JONATHAN BARON

University of Pennsylvania

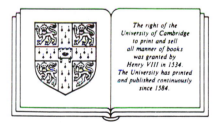

The right of the
University of Cambridge
to print and sell
all manner of books
was granted by
Henry VIII in 1534.
The University has printed
and published continuously
since 1584.

CAMBRIDGE UNIVERSITY PRESS

Cambridge

New York   New Rochelle   Melbourne   Sydney

Published by the Press Syndicate of the University of Cambridge
The Pitt Building, Trumpington Street, Cambridge CB2 1RP
32 East 57th Street, New York, NY 10022, USA
10 Stamford Road, Oakleigh, Melbourne 3166, Australia

First published 1988

Printed in the United States of America

Library of Congress Cataloging-in-Publication Data
Baron, Jonathan, 1944–
Thinking and deciding.
Bibliography: p.
Includes indexes.
1. Thought and thinking.   2. Decision-making.
I. Title.
BF441.B29   1988   153.4′2   87–35238
ISBN   0   521   34253   8 hard covers
ISBN   0   521   34800   5 paperback

British Library Cataloguing in Publication Data applied for

Contents

Preface

Many people have been saying that schools ought to do a better job of teaching students how to think. These critics believe that students, and the adults they become, are deficient in making personal decisions, participating intelligently in public affairs, solving technical problems, and writing reflectively and creatively. Articles and books have appeared proposing new ways to remedy these deficiencies. Often lacking in these proposals, however, is a clear statement of what the problem is and why it should be solved one way rather than another.

The underlying issues that need to be dealt with before such statements can be made are these: What *is* thinking, anyway? How *should* individuals go about making decisions and evaluating beliefs? When do we think as we should, when do we err, and in what ways do we err? Can our errors be cured or prevented with the right kind of instruction?

The importance of these questions for educating our children is reason enough to concern ourselves with them, but they also affect other parts of our lives. Government agencies rely upon the new field of decision analysis for help in making policy decisions, and businesses increasingly rely on it for management decisions. Computer analysis enhances human judgment in fields such as medicine, where computer programs are now being used to diagnose diseases and select treatments. Psychotherapists have designed new therapies intended to help clients improve the way in which they think about personal problems.

As this listing suggests, knowledge about thinking and decision making has been scattered among a number of different fields. Philosophers, psychologists, educators, economists, decision scientists, and computer scientists all have different approaches to the theory of thinking and decision making. The approach represented in this book represents my own effort to draw together some of the key ideas about thinking from these different disciplines into a unified theory. Much of this theory is not original or new: If it were either of these, I would not be so confident that it is basically correct.

I argue, in this book, that all goal-directed thinking and decision making can be described in terms of what I call the *search-inference framework*: Thinking can be described as inferences made from possibilities, evidence, and goals that are discovered through searching. The main problem with our thinking and decision making is that much of it suffers from a lack of *active*

ix

open-mindedness: We ignore possibilities, evidence, and goals that we ought to consider, and we make inferences in ways that protect our favored ideas.

In the course of this book, I apply these ideas to the major concepts and theories in the study of thinking. I begin, in part I, with general considerations: the nature of rationality; methods for studying thinking; the theory of problem solving; learning; intelligence; creativity; and logic. Part II is concerned with belief formation, which is a form of thinking in which the goal of thinking is held constant. In this part, I introduce probability theory as a formal standard. Part III concerns decision making, including the making of decisions about personal plans and goals, and decisions that affect others, such as those that involve moral issues or matters of public concern. This part introduces utility theory, which formalizes many of the ideas that run throughout the book. Part IV draws together the lessons of the rest of the book for education.

This book was written to serve as a text in undergraduate (and beginning graduate) psychology courses in thinking and decision making. The early drafts have been used as a primary text (with additional reading and laboratory assignments) in a one-semester course entitled "Thinking and Decisions," taught in the Psychology Department of the University of Pennsylvania. Most of the students are psychology majors who have taken one or more courses in psychology. Many such courses are being taught elsewhere, but without texts that cover the full range of relevant topics in depth. I hope this book will encourage other courses of this type.

Although the approach is broad, some things are left out. I deal here with thinking as a purposive activity – as a way of choosing actions, beliefs, and personal goals – not as an experience. I also exclude such highly skilled behavior as speaking and understanding language. Such skills can help us think, and thinking well can help us to acquire them, but these skills in themselves do not fit into the framework.

This book overlaps with the subject matter of cognitive psychology, but it leaves out many topics in that field, such as attention and skilled performance, and it includes several topics that are not traditionally part of cognitive psychology, such as moral thinking. It is therefore possible for psychologists to teach both a course that uses this book and a more traditional course in cognitive psychology without substantial overlap.

Students and scholars in related fields, such as philosophy, education, decision sciences, and social psychology, should find this book useful in gaining perspective about the relation of their fields to the psychology of thinking and decision making. Prospective teachers and psychotherapists can also benefit. More generally, this book is addressed to anyone who is disturbed by irrationality and poor thinking, both individual and collective, and wants to understand and correct it. It may also be helpful to those who want to improve their own thinking or decision making and who are puzzled about how to do that.

I have tried to give sufficient background to permit further reading in primary sources. The chapters on utility theory (chs. 16 and 17) are probably the farthest from achieving that goal: The study of decision theory has now become very mathematical, and research in this field moves so quickly that summaries are rapidly outdated. Students who want to pursue that topic should supplement this text with recent reviews. (I have cited some of these, but others will undoubtedly appear shortly.)

Parts of chapters 1, 3, and 6 are taken from my earlier book *Rationality and Intelligence* (1985b), and a few passages in chapter 16 are taken from my paper "Tradeoffs among Reasons for Action" (1986).

Judy Baron, Kathie Galotti, and anonymous reviewers each gave useful advice about several chapters. Other chapters or sections were helpfully read by George Ainslie, Dorrit Billman, Colin Camerer, Allan Collins, Deborah Frisch, John R. Hayes, John C. Hershey, Joel Kupperman, David Messick, and David Perkins. Several students provided helpful comments on drafts used in my course: Sarah Pantelias, Heather Shay, Mark Spranca, and others who chose anonymity. My recent thinking about matters in this book has been informed by several colleagues, particularly Colin Camerer, John C. Hershey, David Perkins, and John Sabini, and by my students, particularly Jane Beattie, Deborah Frisch, and Mark Spranca. Christie Lerch, as an editor for Cambridge University Press, provided the final, most demanding, most detailed, and most helpful set of criticisms and constructive suggestions concerning all levels of writing and organization.

Part I

Thinking in general

Part 1 is about the basics, the fundamentals. Chapters 1 through 3 present the concepts that underlie the rest of the book. Chapter 1 defines thinking, introduces the main types of thinking, and presents what I call the search-inference framework for describing thinking. Chapter 2 introduces the *study* of thinking and decision making, including the three types of questions we shall ask:

1. The *normative* question: What is good thinking, ideally?
2. The *descriptive* question: How do we think? What prevents us from doing our best thinking?
3. The *prescriptive* question: What can we do to improve our thinking and decision making, both as individuals and as a society?

These three questions define the contents of the book: We can ask them about every topic. The third chapter introduces a theory of the nature of *good* thinking and of how we tend to think poorly. By comparing our actual thinking to the thinking specified by the normative theory, we can evaluate it with a view to improving it if it is found wanting. In this way, we can learn to think more *rationally*, that is, in a way that helps us achieve our goals.

Chapters 4 through 10 present the traditional subjects in the psychology of thinking: problem solving (ch. 4), the learning of simple and complex material (chs. 5 and 6), intelligence and creativity (chs. 7 and 8), and logic (chs. 9 and 10). These topics have been part of modern psychology since it began in the late nineteenth century. There would have been much to say about them 30 years ago, and little to say about psychological approaches to the topics covered in the rest of the book. Of course, there is even more to say about these topics now than there was 30 years ago, because they are still active fields of research. I shall review and reassess these traditions from the point of view introduced in chapters 1 through 3.

1   What is thinking?

Thinking is important to all of us in our daily lives. The way we think affects the way we plan our lives, the personal goals we choose, and the decisions we make. Good thinking is therefore not something that is forced upon us in school: It is something that we all want to do, and want others to do, to achieve our goals and theirs.

This approach gives a special meaning to the term "rational." Rational does not mean, here, a kind of thinking that denies emotions and desires: It means, *the kind of thinking we would all want to do, if we were aware of our own best interests, in order to achieve our own goals*. People want to think "rationally," in this sense. It does not make much sense to say that you do not want to do something that will help you achieve your goals: Your goals are, by definition, what you want to achieve.

The main theme of this book is the comparison of what people do with what they should do, that is, with what it would be rational for them to do. By finding out where the differences are, we can help people – including ourselves – to think more rationally, in a way that helps us achieve our own goals more effectively.

This chapter discusses three basic types of thinking that we have to do in order to achieve our goals: *thinking about decisions, thinking about beliefs*, and *thinking about our goals themselves*. It also describes what I call the *search-inference framework*, a way of identifying the basic elements in all of these thinking processes.

Types of thinking

We think when we are in doubt about how to act, what to believe, or what to desire. In these situations, thinking helps us to resolve our doubts: It is purposive. We have to think when we *make decisions*, when we *form beliefs*, and when we *choose our personal goals*, and we will be better off later if we think well in these situations.

A *decision* is a choice of action – of what to do or not do. Decisions are made to achieve goals, and they are based on beliefs about what actions will achieve the goals. For example, if I believe it is going to rain, and if my goal is to keep dry, I will carry an umbrella. Decisions may attempt to satisfy the goals of others as well as the selfish goals of the decision maker. I may carry

3

an extra umbrella for a friend. Decisions may concern small matters, such as whether to carry an umbrella, or matters of enormous importance, such as how one government should respond to a provocation by another. Decisions may be simple, involving only a single goal, two options, and strong beliefs about which option will best achieve the goal, or they may be complex, with many goals and options and with uncertain beliefs.

Decisions depend on beliefs and goals, but we can think about beliefs and goals separately, without even knowing what decisions they will affect. When we think about *belief*, we think to decide how strongly to believe something, or which of several competing beliefs is true. When we believe a proposition, we tend to act as if it were true. If I believe it will rain, I will carry my umbrella. We may express beliefs in language, even without acting on them ourselves. (Others may act on the beliefs we express.) Many school problems, such as those in mathematics, involve thinking about beliefs that we express in language only, not in actions. Beliefs may vary in strength, and they may be quantified as probabilities. A decision to go out of my way to buy an umbrella requires a stronger belief that it will rain (a higher probability) than a decision to carry an umbrella I already own.

When we decide on a *personal goal*, we make a decision that affects future decisions. If a person decides to pursue a certain career, the pursuit of that career becomes a goal that many future decisions will seek to achieve. When we choose personal goals by thinking, we also try to bind our future behavior. Personal goals of this sort require self-control.

Actions, beliefs, and personal goals can be the results of thinking, but they can also come about in other ways. For example, we are born with the personal goal of satisfying physical needs. It may also make sense to say that we are born holding the belief that space has three dimensions. The action of laughing at a joke does not result from a decision. If it did, it would not be a real laugh.

The search-inference framework

Thinking about actions, beliefs, and personal goals can all be described in terms of a common framework, which asserts that thinking consists of search and inference. We search for certain objects and then we make inferences from and about the objects we have found.

Let us take a simple example of a decision. Suppose you are a college student trying to decide which courses you will take next term. Most of the courses you have scheduled are required for your major, but you have room for one elective. The question that starts your thinking is simply this: Which course should I take?

You begin by saying to a friend, "I have a free course. Any ideas?" She says that she enjoyed Professor Smith's course in Soviet–American relations. You think that the subject sounds interesting, and you want to know more about modern history. You ask her about the work, and she says that there is a lot of reading and a 20-page paper. You think about all the computer-science assignments you are going to have this term, and, realizing that you were hoping for an easier course, you resolve to look for something else. After thinking about it yourself, you recall hearing about a course in American history since World War II. That has the same advantages as the first course – it sounds interesting and it is about modern history – but you think the work might not be so hard. You try to find someone who has taken the course.

Clearly, we could go on with this imaginary example, but it already shows the main characteristics of thinking. It begins with doubt. It involves a search directed at removing the doubt. Thinking is, in a way, like exploration. In the course of the search, you have discovered two possible courses, some good features of both courses, some bad features of one course, and some goals you are trying to achieve. You have also made an inference: You rejected the first course because the work was too hard.

There are three kinds of objects we search for: possibilities, evidence, and goals.

Possibilities are possible answers to the original question, possible reso-lutions of the original doubt. (In the example just given, they are the two possible courses.) Notice that possibilities can come from inside yourself or from outside. (This is also true of evidence and goals.) The first possibility in this example came from outside: It was suggested by someone else. The second came from inside: It came from your memory.

Goals are the criteria by which you evaluate the possibilities. Three goals have been mentioned in our example: your desire for an interesting course; your feeling that you ought to know something about recent history; and your desire to keep your work load manageable. Some goals are usually present at the time that thinking begins. In this case, only the goal of finding a course is present, and it is an insufficient goal, because it does not help you to distinguish among the possibilities, the various courses you could take. Ad-ditional goals must be sought.

Evidence consists of any object that helps you determine the extent to which a possibility achieves some goal. In this case, the evidence consists of your friend's report that the course was interesting and her report that the work load was heavy. The example ended with your resolution to search for more evidence about the work load of the second possibility, the American history course. Such a search for evidence might initiate a whole other episode of thinking, the goal of which would be to determine where that evidence can be found.

In addition to these search processes, there is a process of *inference*, or *use of evidence*, in which each possibility is strengthened or weakened as a choice on the basis of the evidence, in the light of the goals. Goals determine the way in which evidence is used. For example, the evidence about work load would be irrelevant if having a manageable work load was not a goal.

The importance of that goal, which seems to be high, affects the importance of that evidence, which seems to be great.

The objects of thinking are represented in our minds. We are conscious of them. If they are not in our immediate consciousness, we can recall them when they are relevant, even after an episode of thinking resumes after an interruption. The processes of thinking – the search for possibilities, evidence, and goals and the use of the evidence to evaluate possibilities – do not go on in any fixed order. They overlap. The thinker alternates from one to another.

Why just these phases: the search for possibilities, evidence, and goals, and the use of evidence? *Thinking is, in its most general sense, a method of choosing among potential possibilities, that is, possible actions, beliefs, or personal goals.* For any choice, there must be purposes or goals, and goals can be added to or removed from the list. I can search for (or be open to) new goals; therefore, search for goals is always possible. There must also be objects that can be brought to bear on the choice among possibilities; hence, there must be evidence, and it can always be sought. Finally, the evidence must be used, or it might as well not have been gathered. These phases are "necessary" in this sense.

The term *judgment* will be important in this book. By judgment, I mean the *evaluation of one or more possibilities with respect to a specific set of evidence and goals*. In decision making, we can judge whether to take an option or not, or we can judge its desirability relative to other options. In belief formation, we can judge whether to accept a belief as a basis of action, or we can judge the probability that the belief is true. In thinking about personal goals, we can judge whether or not to adopt a goal, or we can judge how strong it should be relative to other goals. The term "judgment" therefore refers to the process of inference.

Let us review the main elements of thinking, using another example of decision making, the practical matter of looking for an apartment. "Possibilities" are possible answers to the question that inspired the thinking: here, they are possible apartments. Possibilities (like goals and evidence) can be in mind before thinking begins; you may already have seen one apartment you like before you even think about moving. Or possibilities can be added, as a result of active search (through the newspaper) or suggestions from outside (tips from friends).

Goals are criteria used for evaluating possibilities. In the apartment-hunting example, goals include factors such as rent, distance from work or school, safety, and design quality. The goals determine what evidence is sought and how it is used. It is not until you think that safety might be relevant that you begin to inquire about building security or the safety of the neighborhood. When we *search for goals*, we ask, "What should I be trying to do?" or "What is my purpose in doing this?" Can you think of other criteria for apartments aside from those listed? In doing so, you are searching for goals. We also

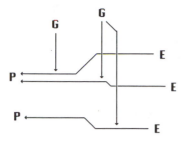

Figure 1.1. Diagram of thinking, showing the relation between possibilities (*P*), the evidence for and against them (*E*), and the goals that determine the weight of the evidence (*G*).

often have a *subgoal*, a goal whose achievement will help us achieve some other goal. In this example, "good locks" would be a subgoal for "safety."

Each possibility has what I shall call its *strength*, which represents the extent to which it is judged by the thinker to satisfy the goals. In decision making, the strength of a possibility corresponds to its overall desirability as an act, taking into account all the goals that the decision maker has in mind.

Evidence is sought – or makes itself available. Evidence can consist of simple propositions such as "The rent is $300 a month," or it can consist of arguments, imagined scenarios, or examples. One possibility can serve as evidence against another, as when we challenge a scientific hypothesis by giving an alternative and incompatible explanation of the data. Evidence, in other words, is defined by its function, which is to increase or decrease the strengths of the possibilities.

Each piece of evidence has what I shall call a *weight* with respect to a given possibility and set of goals. The weight of a given piece of evidence determines how much it should strengthen or weaken the possibility as a means of achieving the goals. The weight of the evidence by itself does not determine how much the strength of a possibility is revised as the possibility is evaluated; the thinker controls this revision. Therefore a thinker can err by revising the strength of a possibility too much or too little.

The *use of the evidence* to revise (or not revise) strengths of possibilities is the end result of all of these search processes. This phase is also called *inference*. It is apparent that inference is not all of thinking, although it is a crucial part.

The relationship among the elements of thinking is illustrated in Figure 1.1. The evidence (*E*) affects the strengths of the possibilities (*P*), but the weight of the evidence is affected by the goals (*G*). Different goals can even reverse the weight of a piece of evidence. For example, if I want to buy a car and am trying to decide between two different ones (*possibilities*), and one of the cars is big and heavy (*evidence*), my concern with safety (a *goal*) might make the size a virtue (*positive weight*), but my concern with mileage (another *goal*) might make the size a detriment (*negative weight*).

The following story describes the situation of a person who has to make an important decision. As you read it, try to discover the goals, possibilities, evidence, and inferences:

A corporate executive is caught in a dilemma. Her colleagues in the Eastern District Sales Department of the National Widget Corporation have decided to increase their expense accounts without informing the central office (which is unlikely to notice). When she hears about the idea, at first she wants to go along, imagining the nice restaurants she could take her clients to, but then she has an uneasy feeling about whether it is right to do this. She thinks that not telling the central office is a little like lying.

When she voices her doubts to her colleagues, they point out that other departments in the corporation are allowed higher expense accounts than theirs and that increased entertainment and travel opportunities will benefit the corporation in various ways. Nearly persuaded to go along at this point, she still has doubts. She thinks of the argument that any other department could do the same, cooking up other flimsy excuses, and that if all departments did so, the corporation would suffer considerably. (She makes use here of a type of moral argument that she recognizes as one she has used before, namely, "What if everyone did that?") She also wonders why, if the idea is really so harmless, her colleagues are not willing to tell the central office.

Now in a real quandary, because her colleagues had determined to go ahead, she wonders what she can do on her own. She considers reporting the decision to the central office, but she imagines what would happen then: her colleagues might all get fired, but if not, they would surely do their best to make her life miserable. And does she really want them all fired? Ten years with the company have given her some feelings of personal attachment to them, as well as loyalty to the company. But she cannot go along with the plan herself either, for she thinks it is wrong, and, besides, if the central office does catch them, they could *all* get fired. (She recalls a rumor that this happened once before.) She finally decides not to go above the company's stated limit for her department's expense accounts herself and to keep careful records of her own actual use of her own expense account, so that she can prove her innocence if the need arises.

In this case, the *goals* were entertaining clients in style, following moral rules, serving the interests of the corporation, being loyal to colleagues, and avoiding punishment. The *possibilities* were going along, turning everyone in, not going along, and not going along plus keeping records. The *evidence* consisted of feelings and arguments, sometimes arguments of others, sometimes arguments that our executive thought of herself.

Initially the executive saw only a single possibility – to go along – but some evidence against that possibility presented itself, specifically, an intuition or uneasy feeling. Such intuitions are usually a sign that more evidence will be found. Here, the executive realized that withholding evidence was a form of lying, so a moral rule was being violated. With this piece of evidence came a new *goal* that was not initially present in the executive's mind, the goal of being moral or doing the right thing. She sought more evidence by talking to her colleagues, and she thought of more evidence after she heard their arguments. Finally, another possibility was considered: turning everyone in. Evidence against this possibility also involved the discovery of other relevant goals – in particular, loyalty to colleagues and self-protection.

The final possibility was a compromise, serving no goals perfectly. It was not as "moral" as turning everyone in or trying to persuade them to stop. It might not turn out to be as self-protective either, should the whole plot be discovered, and it is not as loyal to colleagues as going along. This kind of result is typical of many difficult decisions.

This example clarifies the distinction between *personal goals* and *goals for thinking*. The goals for thinking were drawn from our executive's personal goals. She had adopted these personal goals sometime in the past. When she searched for goals for her thinking, she searched among her own personal goals. Many of her personal goals were not found in her search for goals, in most cases because they were irrelevant to the decision. Each person has a large set of personal goals, only a few of which become goals for thinking in any particular decision.

The examples presented so far are all readily recognizable as decisions, yet there are other types of thinking – not usually considered to be decision making – that can be analyzed as decision making when they are examined closely. For example, any sort of inventive or creative thinking can be analyzed this way. When we create music, poetry, paintings, stories, designs for buildings, scientific theories, essays, or computer programs, we make decisions at several levels. We decide on the overall plan of the work, the main parts of the plan, and the details. Often, thinking at these different levels goes on simultaneously. We sometimes revise the overall plan when problems with details come up. At each level, we consider possibilities for that level, we search for goals, and we look for evidence about how well the possibilities achieve the goals.

Planning is decision making, except that it does not result in immediate action. Some plans – such as plans for a Saturday evening – are simply decisions about specific actions to be carried out at a later time. Other, long-term plans produce personal goals, which then become the goals for later episodes of thinking. For example, a personal career goal will affect decisions about education. Thinking about plans may extend over the period during which the plans are in effect. We may revise our plans on the basis of experience. Experience provides new evidence. The goals involved in planning – the criteria by which we evaluate possible plans – are the personal goals we already have. We therefore create new goals on the basis of old ones. We may also decide to give up (or temporarily put aside) some personal goals.

We may have short-term plans as well as long-term plans. When we solve a math problem, we often make a plan about how to proceed, which we may revise as we solve the problem.

Thinking about beliefs

The search-inference framework applies to thinking about beliefs as well as thinking about decisions. When we think about beliefs, we make decisions to strengthen or weaken possible beliefs. One goal is to bring our beliefs into line with the evidence. (Sometimes we have other goals as well – for example, the goal of believing certain things, regardless of their fit with the evidence.) Roughly, beliefs that are most in line with the evidence are beliefs that correspond best with the world as it is. They are beliefs that are most likely to be *true*. If a belief is true, and if we hold it because we have found the right evidence and made the right inferences, we can be said to *know* something.[1] Hence, thinking about beliefs can lead to knowledge.

Examination of a few types of thinking about belief will show how the search-inference framework applies. (Each of these types is described in more detail in later chapters.)

Diagnosis. In diagnosis, the goal is to discover what the trouble is – what is wrong with a patient, an automobile engine, a leaky toilet, or a piece of writing. The search for evidence is only partially under the thinker's control, both because some of the evidence is provided without being requested and because there is some limitation on the kinds of requests that can be obeyed. In particular, the import of the evidence cannot usually be specified as part of the request (for example, a physician cannot say, "Give me any evidence *supporting a diagnosis of ulcers*," unless the patient knows what this evidence would be). In the purest form of diagnosis, the goal is essentially never changed, although there may be subepisodes of thinking directed toward subgoals such as obtaining a certain kind of evidence.

Scientific thinking. A great deal of science involves testing hypotheses about the nature of some phenomenon. What is the cause of a certain disease? What causes the tides? The "possibilities" are the hypotheses that the scientist considers: germs, a poison, the sun, the moon. Evidence consists of experiments and observations. Pasteur, for example, inferred that several diseases were caused by bacteria, after finding that boiling contaminated liquid prevented the spread of disease – an experiment. He also observed bacteria under a microscope – an observation.

---

[1] For a more complete introduction to these concepts, see Scheffler, 1965. We shall also return to them throughout this book.

Science differs from diagnosis in that the search for goals is largely under the thinker's control, and the goals are frequently changed. Scientists frequently "discover" the "real question" they were trying to answer in the course of trying to answer some other question. There is, in experimental science, the same limitation on control over the evidence-search phase: The scientist cannot pose a question of the form "Give me a result that supports my hypothesis." This limitation does not apply when evidence is sought from books or from one's own memory.

Reflection. Reflection includes the essential work of philosophers, linguists, and others who try to arrive at general principles or rules on the basis of evidence gathered largely from their own memories rather than from the outside world. Do all words ending in "-ation" have the main stress on the syllable "a"? Does immoral action always involve a kind of thoughtlessness? In reflection, the search for evidence is more under the control of the thinker than in diagnosis and experimental science; in particular, thinkers can direct their memories to provide evidence either for or against a given possibility (in this case, a generalization). One can try to think of words ending in "-ation" that follow the proposed rule or words that violate it. One can try to recall, or imagine, immoral actions that do or do not involve thoughtlessness. In reflection (and elsewhere), new possibilities may be modifications of old ones. For example, after thinking of evidence, a philosopher might revise the rule about immorality: "All immorality involves thoughtlessness, except ———— ." Reflection lies at the heart of scholarship, not just in philosophy but also in the social sciences and humanities.

Insight problems. Much of the psychology of thinking concerns thinking of a very limited sort, the solution of puzzle problems. For example, why is any number of the form ABC,ABC (for example, 143,143 or 856,856) divisible by 13?[2] These are problems whose solution usually comes suddenly and with some certainty, after a period of apparently futile effort. Many are used on intelligence tests. Essentially, the only phase under the thinker's control at all is the search for possibilities. Often, it is difficult to come up with any possibilities at all (as in the 13 problem). In other cases, such as crossword puzzles, possibilities present themselves readily and are rejected even more readily. In either case, search for evidence and inference (acceptance or rejection) are essentially immediate, and the goal is fixed by the problem statement. It is this immediate, effortless occurrence of the other phases that gives insight problems their unique quality of sudden realization of the solution.

Prediction. Who will be the next president of the United States? Will the

---

[2] Hint: What else are such numbers also divisible by? Another hint: What is the smallest number of this form? Another hint: A and B can both be zero. Another hint: Is it divisible by 13?

stock market go up or down? Will student X succeed if we admit her to graduate school? Prediction of likely future events is like reflection, in form, although the goal is fixed. The evidence often consists of memories of other situations the thinker knows about, which are used as the basis of analogies, for example, student Y, who did succeed, and who was a lot like X.

Behavioral learning. In every realm of our lives – in our social relationships with friends, families, colleagues, and strangers, and in our work – we learn how our behavior affects ourselves and others. Such learning may occur without thinking, but thinking can also be brought to bear. When it is, each action is a search for evidence, an experiment designed to find out what will happen. The evidence is the outcome of this experiment. Each possibility we consider is a type of action to take in some type of situation.

This kind of learning can have much in common with science. Whereas science is a "pure" activity, with a single goal, behavioral learning has two goals: learning about the situation and obtaining immediate success or reward in the task at hand. These goals frequently compete (Schwartz, 1982). We are often faced with a choice of repeating some action that has served us reasonably well in the past or taking some new action, hoping either that it might yield an even better outcome or that we can obtain evidence that will help us decide what to do in the future. Some people choose the former course too often and, as a result, achieve adaptations less satisfactory to them than they might achieve if they experimented more.

An example of behavioral learning with enormous importance for education is the learning of ways of proceeding in thinking tasks themselves – for example, the important strategy of looking for reasons why you might be wrong before concluding that you are right. The effectiveness of thinking may depend largely on the number and quality of these thinking strategies. This, in turn, may (or may not) depend on the quality of the thinking that went into the learning of those heuristics.

The results of behavioral learning are beliefs about what works best at achieving what goal in what situation. Such beliefs serve as evidence for the making of plans, which, in turn, provide personal goals for later decisions. For example, people who learn that they are admired for a particular skill, such as telling jokes, can form the goal of developing that skill and seeking opportunities to display it.

Learning from observation. This includes all cases in which we learn about our environment from observation alone, without intentional experimentation. As such, it can include behavioral learning without experimentation – namely, learning in which we simply observe that certain actions (done for reasons other than to get evidence) are followed by certain events. It also includes a large part of the learning of syntax, word meanings, and other culturally transmitted bodies of knowledge.

The distinctive property of learning by observation is that the evidence is not under the thinker's control, except for the choice of whether we attend to it or not. By contrast, Horton (1967, pp. 172–173) has suggested that one of the fundamental properties of *scientific* thinking is active experimentation: "The essence of the experiment is that the holder of a pet theory does not just wait for events to come along and show whether or not [the theory] has a good predictive performance. He bombards it with artificially produced events in such a way that its merits or defects will show up as immediately and as clearly as possible."

How do search processes work?

All of these types of thinking involve search. Search for possibilities is nearly always present, and search for evidence or goals is often included as well. The critical aspect of a search process is that the thinker has the goal of finding some sort of mental representation of a possibility, a piece of evidence, or a goal.

Search is directed by the goals, possibilities, and evidence already at hand. Goals provide the most essential direction. If my goal is to protect the walls in my house from my child's scribbling, I seek different possibilities than if my goal is to teach my child not to scribble on walls. Possibilities direct our search for evidence for them or against them, and evidence against one possibility might direct our search for new ones.

There are two general ways of finding any object: *recall* from memory, and use of *external aids*, such as other people, written sources (including our own notes), and computers. External aids can help us overcome the limitations of our own memories, including the time and effort required to get information into them. As I write this book, for example, I rely extensively on a file cabinet full of reprints of articles, my own library, the University of Pennsylvania library, and my colleagues and students. I rely on my memory as well, including my memory of how to use these tools and of who is likely to be able to help with what.

Thinking is not limited to what we do in our heads. The analogy between thinking and exploration is therefore not just an analogy. When an explorer climbs up a hill to see what lies beyond, he is actually seeking evidence. Moreover, libraries, computers, and file cabinets make us truly more effective thinkers. When we try to test people's thinking by removing them from their natural environment, which may include their tools and other people they depend on, we get a distorted picture (however useful this picture may be for some purposes).

Because thinking involves search, there must be something for the search to find, if thinking is to succeed. Without *knowledge*, without beliefs that correspond to reality, thinking is an empty shell. This does not mean, however, that thinking cannot occur until one is an expert. One way to become an expert is to think about certain kinds of problems from the outset. Thinking helps us to learn, especially when our thinking leads us to consult outside sources or experts. As we learn more, our thinking becomes more effective. If you try to figure out what is wrong with your car (or your computer, or your body) every time something goes wrong with it, you will find yourself looking up things in books and asking experts (repair-people, physicians) as part of your search for possibilities and evidence. You will then come to know more and to participate more fully in thinking about similar problems in the future. It is often thought that there is a conflict between "learning to think" and "acquiring knowledge"; in fact, these two kinds of learning normally reinforce each other.

What we recall (or get from an external aid) may be either an item itself or a rule for producing the item we seek. For example, the "What if everybody did that?" rule is not by itself evidence for or against any particular action, but it tells the thinker how to arrive at such evidence. When we solve a problem in physics, we recall formulas that tell us how to calculate the quantities we seek. Rules can be learned directly, or we can invent them ourselves through a thinking process of hypothesis testing or reflection. (The use of rules in thinking can be distinguished from the use of rules to guide behavior. We may *follow* a rule through habit without representing it consciously.)

Recall or external aids may not give us exactly what we want, but sometimes an item suggests something else more useful. We may transform what we get in a variety of ways to make it applicable to our situation (Bregman, 1977). This is the important mechanism of *analogy*. To see the role of analogies in thinking, try thinking about a question such as "Can a goose quack?" or "How does evaporation work?" (Collins & Gentner, 1986; Collins & Michalski, in press). To answer the first question, you might think of ducks. To answer the second, some people try to understand evaporation in terms of analogies to things they already know. The escape of a molecule of a liquid might be analogous to the escape of a rocket from the earth. The conclusion drawn from this analogy is that a certain speed is required to overcome whatever force holds the molecules in the liquid. Some people conclude that the force to be overcome is gravity itself. (Although gravity plays a role, other forces are usually more important.)

Notice that analogies can sometimes be used straightforwardly to support the same possibility, but sometimes they require modification. If the possibility under consideration is to "fight communism" in Nicaragua, an analogy with the United States's experience in Vietnam might argue against it. Here, the possibility is essentially the same, fighting communism. On the other hand, an analogy with the appeasement of Hitler at Munich would argue for it, but here the enemy was not communism but fascism, so the possibility supported is not quite the same.

When an analogy requires modification, the person may need to think about how to make the relevant modification. For example, the lesson of

Munich may be that fascists should not be appeased, or it could be that one's enemies should not be appeased. Likewise, if you know how to find the area of a rectangle, how should you apply this knowledge to finding the area of a parallelogram? Do you multiply the base by the length of the sides next to it, or do you multiply the base by the height? For rectangles, both yield the same result. Evidence can be brought to bear about which of these possibilities serves the goal.

Conclusion

Thinking can help us to make decisions that achieve our personal goals, to adopt beliefs about which courses of action are most effective, and to adopt goals that are most consistent with our other goals (including the general goal of being satisfied with our lives). In the rest of this book, we shall be concerned primarily with the properties of thinking that make it useful for these purposes. Like any goal-directed activity, thinking can be done well or badly. Thinking that is done well is thinking of the sort that achieves its goals. When we criticize someone's thinking, we are trying to help them achieve their own goals. When we try to think well, it is because we want to achieve our goals.

2   The study of thinking

Descriptive, normative, and prescriptive

Here is a problem: "All families with six children in a city were surveyed. In 72 families, the *exact order* of births of boys (B) and girls (G) was G B G B B G. What is your estimate of the number of families surveyed in which the *exact order* of births was B G B B B B?"

Many people give figures less than 72 as their answers, even if they believe that boys and girls are equally likely (Kahneman & Tversky, 1972). Apparently they feel that the second sequence, which contains only one girl, is not typical of the sequences they expect. In fact, if you believe that boys and girls are equally likely, your best guess should be exactly 72. This is because the probability of each sequence is ½ · ½ · ½ · ½ · ½ · ½ or ¼₆₄, the same in both cases. In other words, the two sequences are equally likely. (If you do not believe this, consult a textbook of probability theory.) What makes this problem tricky is that the first sequence looks more like the kind of sequence you might expect, because it has an equal number of boys and girls, and the sexes alternate fairly frequently within the sequence.

This problem can help us illustrate three general "models,"[1] or approaches to the study of thinking, which I shall call descriptive models, prescriptive models, and normative models.

Descriptive models are theories about how people normally think – for example, how we solve problems in logic or how we make decisions. Many of these models are expressed in the form of *heuristics*, or rules of thumb, that we use in certain situations. In the probability problem that I just described, the heuristic used is to judge probability by asking "How similar is this sequence to a typical sequence?" (see ch. 12). Because he sequence G B G B B G is more similar to the typical sequence than B G B B B B, the former is judged more likely. Another heuristic is the "What if everyone did that?" rule for thinking about moral situations, and another is the use of analogies in making predictions.

Unlike many other fields of psychology, such as the study of perception,

---

[1] The term "model" comes from the idea that one way to understand something is to build a model of it. In this sense, the game of Monopoly is a model of real estate investment. In this book, the term "model" is used loosely to mean "theory" or "proposal." Sometimes, however, the models will be more detailed – for example, computer models or mathematical models.

16

where the emphasis is on finding out "how it works," much of the study of thinking is concerned with how we *ought* to think, or with comparing the way we usually think with some ideal. This difference from other fields is partly a result of the fact that we have a considerable amount of control over how we think. That is not so with perception: Except for going to the eye doctor once in a while, we have very little control over how our visual system works. To answer the question "How do we think?", we also have to answer the question "How do we *choose* to think?" The way we think is, apparently, strongly affected by our culture. Such tools as probability theory, arithmetic, and logic are cultural inventions. So are our attitudes toward knowledge and decision making. Thus, the way we think is a matter of cultural design. To study only how we happen to think in a particular culture, at a particular time in history, is to fail to do justice to the full range of possibilities.

Part of our subject matter is therefore the question of how we *ought* to think. If we know this, we can compare it to the way we *do* think. Then, if we find discrepancies, we can ask how they can be repaired. The way we ought to think, however, is not at all obvious. Thus, we shall have to discuss models or theories of how we ought to think, as well as models of how we do think. Models of how we ought to think will fall, in our discussion, into two categories: prescriptive and normative.

Prescriptive models are simple models that "prescribe" or state how we ought to think. Teachers are highly aware of prescriptive models and try to get their students to conform to them, not just in thinking but also in writing, reading, and mathematics. For example, there are many good prescriptive models of composition in books on style. There may, of course, be more than one "right" way to think (or write). There may also be "good" ways that are not quite the "best." A good teacher encourages students to think (or write) in "better" ways rather than "worse" ones.

Prescriptive models may consist of lists of useful heuristics, or rules of thumb, much like the heuristics that make up many descriptive models. Such heuristics may take the form of "words to the wise" that we try to follow, such as "Make sure each paragraph has a topic sentence" or (in algebra) "Make sure you know what is 'given' and what is 'unknown' before you try to solve a problem." In studying probability, one might learn the general rule "All sequences of equally likely events are equally likely to occur." Knowing this heuristic would have saved you the effort of calculating the answer to the problem about the families with six children.

To determine which prescriptive models are the most useful, we apply a *normative model*, that is, a standard that defines the best thinking for achieving the thinker's goals. For probability problems like the one concerning the birth order of boys and girls, the normative model is the theory of probability. By using the theory of probability, we could prove that the heuristic "All sequences of equally likely events are equally likely to occur" always works.

For thinking and decision making in general, normative models are designed to achieve the personal goals of the thinker. For decision making, the normative model consists of that policy that will, in the long run, achieve these personal goals to the greatest extent. Such a model takes into account the probability that a given act (for example, leaving my umbrella at home) will bring about a certain outcome (my getting wet) and the relative desirability of that outcome according to the decision maker's personal goals (see ch. 16). It is not enough simply to say that the normative model *is* the decision that leads to the best outcome (carrying an umbrella only when it will rain). Such a statement would not tell us how to reach that decision, even under ideal circumstances.

One personal goal that most people have is to minimize the time they spend thinking and making decisions. Because of this goal, prescriptive models usually differ from normative models. A normative model of decision making may require elaborate calculations of probabilities and desirabilities of various outcomes. (For example, in deciding whether to take an umbrella, I would have to determine the probability of rain and the relative undesirability of carrying an umbrella needlessly and getting wet.) For most practical purposes, however, people can do better by using some simple heuristics (for example, "When in doubt, carry the umbrella") than by making these calculations. Even if the calculations sometimes yielded a better choice than the choice that the heuristics would yield, the difference between the two choices in desirability would usually be too small to make calculation worthwhile as a general policy.

In short, normative models of thinking specify the ideal. The idea is to figure out what kind of thinking would, under ideal conditions, bring us as close as possible to achieving our personal goals, or the personal goals we would have "on reflection" – that is, after thinking about them carefully and well. Descriptive models specify what people in a particular culture actually do, and how they deviate from the normative models. Prescriptive models are designs or inventions, whose purpose is to bring the results of actual thinking into closer conformity to the normative model. If prescriptive recommendations derived in this way are successful, the study of thinking can help people to become better thinkers.

Development of descriptive models

If we want to improve our thinking, we need to know what is wrong with it. To discover this, we do not merely speculate or generalize from our experience. We observe and conduct experiments, and we try to make sense out of these experiments by developing descriptive models. These models, in turn, guide the design of new experiments. The development of descriptive models is the scientific side of the study of thinking.

We cannot observe thinking directly, unless it is our own thinking, and then we are too busy doing it to make the kinds of systematic observations that science requires. To study thinking scientifically, we must use indirect methods, such as asking people to talk aloud as they think, to explain how they reached some conclusion. We can also make inferences about people's thinking by observing how they respond to carefully designed tasks. These methods for studying thinking have become a topic of study in their own right. Each method has advantages and disadvantages.

Process tracing

Many methods attempt to describe thinking by tracing the *process* of thinking as it occurs. These methods are not concerned with the subject's conclusion, but with how the conclusion was reached, that is, the steps or "moves" that led to it. Ideally, it would be nice to have a mind-reading machine that displays the subject's thoughts on a television screen, in color and stereophonic sound. Until such a device is invented, we must make do with less direct methods.

One method in this category involves the use of computers and other apparatus to record everything that subjects look at, and for how long, during a task (e.g., Payne, Bettman, & Johnson, in press). This method has been used for studying decisions about apartments. The subject is asked to read a table giving data on various apartments. Each column represents an apartment and each row gives figures on matters such as rent, size, and distance from work. If the subject scans across the rent row first and then seeks no other information about the apartments with the highest rent, we can infer that he has eliminated those apartments on the basis of their high rent. To use this method effectively, the experimenter must be clever in setting up the experiment so that such inferences can be made.

Another method for process tracing is the use of historical records of decisions made by groups. Janis (1982), for example, studied group decision making by reading historical records of how President Kennedy and his advisers made the policy decisions that led to the fiasco of the Bay of Pigs invasion of Cuba in 1961. This method is useful when the records are very thorough, as they were in this case.

Perhaps the simplest and most direct method for process tracing is to give a subject a task that requires thinking and ask the subject to "think aloud," either while doing the task or as soon afterward as possible. What the subject says is then a *verbal protocol*, which a researcher can analyze in many ways. This method has been in almost continuous use since the nineteenth century (see Woodworth & Schlosberg, 1954, ch. 26, for some examples).

To get a feeling for this method, try reading the following puzzle problem; then stop reading, and think aloud to yourself as you try to work out the answer. Remember that your task is to do the problem and to say out loud, at the same time, what is going on in your mind, *as it happens*.

Problem: Examine the following three-by-three matrix. Notice that the lower right-hand corner of the matrix is blank. What symbol belongs in that corner?

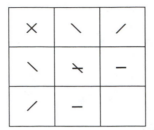

Here is an example of a verbal protocol in which someone is thinking about this problem. (The different moves are numbered for later reference):

1. Let's see. There's an X, a tilted X, and a bunch of lines – diagonal lines along the top and left side, and horizontal lines in the lower right.
2. It looks like there ought to be another horizontal line in the lower right.
3. That would make a nice pattern.
4. But how can I be sure it's right?
5. Maybe there's a rule.
6. I wonder if the X has something to do with the diagonals. The X is really just the two diagonals put together.
7. That doesn't help me figure out what goes in the lower right.
8. Oh, another idea. Maybe there's two of each thing in each row.
9. Yes, that works. The X is there because there have to be two left diagonals and two right diagonals in the top row. And it works for the columns too.
10. So I guess there has to be a dash and a right diagonal together in the bottom right.

This example is fairly typical. It reveals to us that the thinker is making a search for possibilities, evidence, and goals. Now here is an analysis of the same verbal protocol, describing each step in terms of the search-inference framework:

1. The subject spends some time simply seeking evidence, without any idea about the answer (that is, without being aware of any possibilities for it).
2. A possibility is found for the answer.
3. Evidence is found in favor of the possibility. (Some subjects would stop here, making an error as a result of failing to search further.)
4. Further search for evidence.
5. The subject sets up a subgoal here. The original goal was to say simply what kind of symbol went in the lower right-hand corner. The new goal is to find a rule that will produce the pattern. The search for goals and subgoals – as if the subject said to himself, "Exactly what should I be trying to do?" – is an important, and often neglected, part of thinking.
6. Here is a possibility about the rule, suggested by the evidence that "X is two diagonals put together." It is not a complete possibility, however, for the idea that X has something to do with the diagonals does not say exactly what it has to do with the other diagonals in the matrix. So this possibility, because it is incomplete, sets up a subgoal of making it complete.
7. In this problem, the possibility and the subgoal are put aside because the

subject cannot find a way in which they help to satisfy the goal of finding a rule. This failure is a kind of evidence, and the subject uses this evidence to weaken the possibility in question.

8. Another possibility for the rule is found (not unrelated to the first).
9. Evidence for this possibility is sought and found.
10. The subject returns to the original goal of figuring out what goes in the lower right, a task quickly accomplished once the subgoal of finding the rule is achieved.

This analysis shows how the search-inference framework enables us to categorize the moves that a thinker makes in the course of thinking. Notice that a given move can belong to two different categories, because the move may have two different functions; for example, in move 6, the same object is both a possibility and a new subgoal. A given phase in an episode of thinking can contain other episodes of thinking, which can contain others, and so on. For example, the task of searching for the goal might involve trying to understand the instructions, which might involve searching for possibilities and for evidence about the meaning of words such as "matrix" (if one did not know the meaning already). As an exercise, you might find it useful to generate another verbal protocol of your own thinking about some problem and analyze it in this way.

A great variety of other methods for analyzing thinking-aloud protocols has been developed (see Ericsson & Simon, 1980, for a review of some of these). Different approaches use different *units of analysis*. Some investigators allow the system of analysis itself to define the unit: I did this in the example just given, using as units the categories of the search-inference framework. Other investigators divide the protocol into linguistic units, such as sentences. Others use time measurements, dividing the protocol into 5- or 10-second units and analyzing what is happening (or not happening) in each unit. Approaches also differ in the categories used. The method of analysis is closely linked with the investigator's own goals and the theoretical or practical questions that led to the work.

Thinking aloud has (as already noted) been used in education, as well as in psychological research (see Ericsson & Simon, 1980; Lytle, 1982). By asking a student to think aloud while writing, reading, or solving a problem in mathematics, a teacher may discover aspects of the student's approach to these activities that the student could try to change to improve school performance.

Despite the extensive use of this method, many doubts have been raised over the years about its adequacy:

> Some mental processes do not produce much that is accessible for conscious report. Suppose you are given the word "table" and asked to produce the first related word to come to mind. Most people think of "chair." Can you report the process that led to your response? Some people say they see a mental image of a table, but others say the response just popped into their heads. The inability of subjects to describe the processes in-

volved in tasks like this was one of the findings that encouraged the rise of behaviorism (Humphrey, 1951).

Subjects may not report everything that they think, especially if they think faster than they can talk, or if their verbal abilities are limited. In the extreme, if subjects are *unable* to verbalize their thoughts, as with young children and animals, verbal protocols are useless. For articulate adults, there are ways to minimize the impact of the reporting problem. An interviewer can ask the subject to explain steps that seemed to be left out, or the subject could listen (or watch) a recording of his own thinking in order to add comments about what was omitted.

The instruction to think aloud may induce subjects to think differently than they ordinarily would. For example, they could think less quickly because of the need to verbalize everything. Verbalization could interfere with thinking, or it could help by forcing thinkers to be more careful. Both of these results have been found, but it has also been found that in many tasks verbalization has no apparent effect (Ericsson & Simon, 1980).

Verbal protocols might be misleading with respect to the underlying determinants of the subjects' behavior. For example, suppose that you are deciding whether to buy a used television set, and you say, "The picture is nice, but the sound isn't very good, and $200 is too expensive. I'll keep looking." One might infer from this that you are following a rule that you should not pay more than $200, no matter what. Although this may be true, it may instead be true that you would be willing to pay more if the sound quality were good enough; you may be trading off quality against price, even though you do not express this in your verbalizations (Einhorn, Kleinmuntz, & Kleinmuntz, 1979).

Subjects may be unable to explain how they reached a certain conclusion. For example, in an experiment done by Nisbett and Wilson (1977), passersby in a shopping mall were asked to compare four nightgowns and rate their quality. Most subjects gave the last nightgown they examined the highest rating, regardless of which of the four it was, but all subjects attributed their rating to some property of the nightgown itself rather than its position in the sequence.

Ericsson and Simon (1980) argue that this last sort of demonstration does not shed any light on the validity of verbal reports, because there is a difference between reporting *what* one is thinking (as in the matrix problem) and explaining the *causes* of one's conclusions. Asking subjects to infer a cause requires that the subjects take the role of scientists, which they may not be able to do. If the subjects simply report their experiences instead of inferring causes, then they cannot be accused of making an error.[2]

Ericsson and Simon argue that verbal reports are sometimes quite reliable methods for discovering how thinking proceeds. In particular, they assert, "thinking" aloud may be useful when there is useful information to be reported that is in the subject's "working memory" (that is, the subject's immediate consciousness; see ch. 5). An example would be the information

---

[2] It is not even clear that the subjects in Nisbett and Wilson's experiments made an error at all. If a subject said she liked the last nightgown she examined because of its texture, she could be correct, even though it is also true that she liked it because it was the last: The fact that it was the last might have caused her to like its texture.

reported in the matrix-problem example. In such cases, performance is found not to be affected by the requirement to think aloud, and what subjects do is consistent with what they say.

On the other hand, Ericsson and Simon point out that verbal reports are less useful in other situations, such as when

> Subjects are asked to remember what they thought, rather than report their thoughts as they happen (because forgetting and distortion occur over time).
>
> Subjects are asked to explain the causes of their behavior or draw general conclusions about how they do a certain kind of task (because this is asking them to do the job of the researcher).
>
> The information of interest is not accessible to consciousness (because, for example, it concerns processes that happen too quickly).

Whether these problems are considered serious drawbacks will depend on the goals of our study and on the alternative methods available. If, for example, our goal is to discover why a student has difficulty in understanding a challenging text, asking the student to think aloud while reading may be useful, despite the imperfections of the method. If we are studying individual or group differences, the decision whether or not to use the method may depend on what sort of differences we are studying. For example, if we are studying the effect of education on thinking, we must be especially sensitive to the possible effect of education on the ability to verbalize one's thoughts; we would then reject the thinking-aloud method, because we would not be able to distinguish effects of education on thinking from effects on verbalization.

More generally, as Ericsson and Simon point out, verbal reports are just one kind of investigative method. Any method of investigation has defects, and these defects are more serious in some cases than in others. When possible, a good investigator will try to use a variety of methods to check the results from one against the results from another.

Methods based on conclusions

Another way to learn how people think or make decisions is to observe the conclusions that people draw or the decisions they make. The investigator then makes inferences from the effects of various variables on these responses. (A "variable" is anything that we can measure, label, or manipulate.) Investigators strive both to capture the phenomenon of interest and to control the effective variables, so that they may determine which variables do what.

Many studies of decision making (for example, those described in ch. 17) ask subjects what they would do in hypothetical situations. The disadvantage of hypothetical questions is that the results may not tell us much about what people would actually do in the real world. For example, in answering the hypothetical question, people may tell us that they would do what they think *we* (the researchers) would *want* them to do – not what they would really do. This is called a "social desirability" effect. (This is not a serious problem if the experimenter is *interested* in the subjects' views about what the best decision is.)

An advantage of using hypothetical situations for a study is that the researchers can extensively manipulate the situation to find out what variables are affecting the subject's responses. Another advantage is that the experimenter can ask subjects for justifications or explanations. Justifications and explanations can suggest new hypotheses for study, provide evidence bearing on other hypotheses, and provide evidence that subjects understand (or fail to understand) the situation as the experimenter intended. Hypothetical situations are also useful in telling us how subjects would respond to situations that are novel for them.

When the investigator is interested in decision making of a type familiar to the subjects, decision making can be studied in its natural setting. Keren and Wagenaar (1985), for example, studied gambling behavior by observing blackjack players in an Amsterdam casino over a period of several months, recording every play of every game. Observations of behavior in real-life situations obviously do not encounter the problem of the social desirability effect; however, there are other problems. Goals in the real world are often complex, and it is difficult to "purify" the situation so as to determine how a subject would pursue a single goal. For example, a subject in a hypothetical gambling experiment can be instructed to imagine that his goal is to win as much as he can, but Keren and Wagenaar (1985) found that in real life gamblers were often as concerned with making the game interesting as with winning.

The main problem with observation in natural settings, however, is that it is often impossible to carry out manipulations that will allow us to find out which aspects of the situation control the subject's behavior. Sometimes investigators have constructed real situations in which we can both observe and manipulate behavior. For example, Lichtenstein and Slovic (1973) studied gambling behavior by setting up experiments in a Las Vegas casino, with real money and real gamblers who had come to the casino to gamble. Such experiments may be expensive, if the experimenter is unlucky. Another problem is that of informing subjects about the experiment. If subjects understand that they are in an experiment, the social desirability effect may play a role. If they are not told, ethical objections can arise: People may feel that surreptitious observation of their behavior by scholars is an invasion of their privacy. (This is actually a moral dilemma worth thinking about.)

In some cases, the responses of interest are the justifications for decisions rather than the decisions themselves. For example, Kohlberg (1970) gave subjects a moral dilemma, like the one concerning the ethics of surreptitious observation, except with more details of a particular case, and asked what ought to be done. Then the subject is asked "Why?" She is also asked how she would respond if the situation were modified (for example, if the research concerned a possible cure for schizophrenia rather than the psychology of gambling), and why. The idea is not to get a record of the subject's thinking, as in a verbal protocol, but rather to determine just what fundamental moral principles the subject uses to make difficult judgments. The problem with this method (Shweder, Mahapatra, & Miller, 1988) is that it is dependent on the subject's ability to verbalize and to discover the true reasons for her judgments (problems that arise for verbal protocols as well).

Computer models and artificial intelligence

Some of the most important contributions to the descriptive theory of thinking have come not from any kind of observation of people thinking, but rather from attempts to make computers think. Simon (1969) has argued that much of the conduct of thinking is not determined by the peculiarities of human psychology but rather by the nature of the task. If, for example, we want to understand how people play chess, we would do well to try to build a chess-playing computer. It may not play chess exactly the way that people do, but it will tell us a lot about what kind of thinking is possible.

Such attempts have two different goals. One is to try to program the computer to do the task in the way that people do it. The computer program then becomes an embodiment of a particular theory about thinking.[3] The purpose of such an effort is to find out whether a certain type of theory can possibly account for a certain kind of behavior and to refine the theory itself by observing the difficulties that arise when we try to make it work.

Another goal is to forget about trying to make the computer perform as we do, but simply try to make it do its best. At first it may seem surprising that this approach has also yielded important insights about human thinking. It is less surprising when we reflect on Simon's view about the importance of the task itself in determining how thinking is done.

There are no perfect methods for development of descriptive theory. On the other hand, imperfect methods may be informative enough. Medical scientists who develop new treatment methods often proceed on the basis of imperfect research. Similarly, educators and decision scientists can develop new ways to improve thinking and decision making on the same basis.

Development of normative models

The study of thinking, as we have seen, involves the comparison of actual judgments and decisions to some normative standard of what they ought to be. The question of what they "ought" to be, if we were to do our best thinking, cannot be answered simply by observing what they are, through

[3] This is the approach taken by Newell and Simon (1972) and by J. R. Anderson (1976).

gathering descriptive information. The "ought" question must be answered by philosophical reflection – by trying to find normative principles, by criticizing these principles, and by modifying them in response to these criticisms. We shall see this kind of reflection in operation throughout this book.

One kind of evidence for a principle is that it agrees with our intuition. (By intuition, I mean an unanalyzed and unjustified belief.) For example, in our moral thinking, we often begin with intuitions that certain things are wrong – killing, stealing, breaking promises, telling lies, neglecting duties, and so forth. We then look for a broad moral theory to fit these intuitions, to explain why they are true. For example, the theory that right and wrong have to do with helping or hindering other people in achieving their goals can do fairly well in explaining these intuitions. In general, the acts just listed hinder rather than help. If we find a good theory that accounts for these intuitions, we can extend it to deal with cases about which we are less sure, such as how the costs of medical care should be borne.

On the other hand, our intuitions are not infallible. A conflict between intuition and principle does not always mean that the principle is wrong, for there may be other relevant arguments, or there may be no better alternative. Although most of our intuitions about thinking and decision making are probably held for good reason, some of them probably are not. They could simply be the results of exposure to certain cultural standards, or they could have been formulated by individuals and used uncritically for so many years that they have come to be accepted as truth. Although most people in our culture agree that killing and stealing are wrong, for example, we disagree strongly about whether premarital sex, abortion, or euthanasia are. When there is disagreement, somebody's intuition must be wrong.[4]

Often, as in the trick problem presented at the beginning of the chapter, intuition gives way easily to convincing arguments such as those based on mathematics. These arguments frequently concern the purpose of the normative model in question, for example, the purpose of achieving personal goals. In other cases, the argument for some principle is more difficult to understand, or less compelling, than are, say, mathematical arguments about probability theory, but these arguments may still be correct. Intuitions are often useful evidence in philosophical reflection, but they are not the last word.

Development of prescriptive models

If the basis of descriptive models is observation and the basis of normative models is reflection, then the basis of prescriptive models is design. Methods of thinking – such as logic, legal argumentation, and scientific method – were

[4] I speak here of intuitions about what is right and wrong for *everyone*. As explained in chapter 19, some people may think these questions are matters of taste or opinion, but these people cannot consistently apply their intuitions to others, and they are not at issue here.

invented and are now passed along as part of our culture. The normative and descriptive findings discussed in this book point to the need for other methods to bring our thinking closer to the normative standard. As new methods are invented, ways of spreading them through a society must be invented as well. The most direct way of doing this is through schools.

New methods can be designed for computers as well as people. Computers are powerful tools that can extend our powers of thinking and decision making. In order to use them to improve our thinking, however, we need to know just how our thinking needs to be improved.

Conclusion

The study of thinking goes back at least to Aristotle and other Greek philosophers, who attempted to codify the rules of good thinking (in the form of logic), to describe what went wrong with our thinking in daily life, and to propose ways in which we could guard against the errors we tend to make. In the last century, this speculative approach has been supplemented with the scientific study of thinking. We no longer have to rely on our experience alone. We must not, however, let ourselves get carried away with the power of science. It cannot tell us how we ought to think ideally, nor how we can best approximate this ideal. A scientist cannot "discover" what *good* thinking is. This is still a matter for philosophy and design. In this spirit, the next chapter puts forward a general prescriptive model based on the search-inference framework.

3   Good thinking: the nature of rationality

A normative view

The purpose of this chapter is to introduce a coherent normative model for thinking. I shall design the model to reflect what we want it to do: help us think in the way that best achieves our personal goals. I shall then make some assumptions about where thinking most often departs from this normative model, descriptively. These assumptions lead to a general prescriptive theory of thinking.

The best kind of thinking, which we shall call *rational* thinking, is whatever helps us fulfill our personal goals. If it should turn out that following the rules of logic leads to eternal happiness, then it is "rational thinking" to follow the laws of logic. If it should turn out, on the other hand, that carefully violating the laws of logic at every turn leads to eternal happiness, then it is these violations that we shall call "rational." When I argue that certain kinds of thinking are most rational, I mean that these help people fulfill their goals. Such arguments could be wrong. If so, some other sort of thinking is most rational.

Using the search-inference framework of chapter 1, let us consider how our best thinking is done. Take decision making. We do not achieve our goals best if we neglect some of them in evaluating possibilities. If, for example, in choosing a college course to take as an elective, we forget to consider the difficulty of the course, we might choose a course that is too hard. Other things being equal, the more goals we consider, the better our decision is likely to be.[1] (Of course, other things usually are not equal. Time may be short, and it takes time to search for goals. Let us come back to that later.)

Likewise, we do not achieve our goals best if we neglect possibilities that might achieve them better than the one we adopt. Even if Political Science 101 would serve my goals best, I cannot choose it if I do not think of it. Good thinking requires a thorough search for possibilities – other things being equal.

For the same reason, we must search thoroughly for evidence. The more we find out about the college courses we are considering, the more likely we are to pick one that does in fact satisfy our goals. We must also seek evidence in a way that is most helpful in finding the possibility that best achieves our

---

[1] In the case of thinking about beliefs, the goal is usually fixed (as described in ch. 1), so search for goals is less important.

goals. We must not seek evidence for any other reason. In particular, we should not seek evidence because we know it will turn out to favor possibilities that are already strong in our minds. If we seek evidence about the good qualities of the course we are thinking of taking – because we want our initial hunch to be right, for example – we will miss the evidence about its bad qualities.

We must use evidence in a way that best achieves our goals, not in any other way. Again, we should not use evidence in a way that favors possibilities that are already strong, just because we want them to be the ones ultimately chosen. We should be willing to change if the evidence points that way.

There is a problem with the idea that more search is always better. The search for possibilities, evidence, and goals takes time and effort. Eventually a point is reached at which the effort is not worthwhile in terms of achieving our goals. One of our goals is not to spend our whole life lost in thought. Sometimes, when a quick decision is required, our goal is to think quickly. If registration ends tomorrow, we must pick a course now, making do with the possibilities and evidence at hand. Thus, we must balance the need for thorough search against the cost of search itself. Ordinarily, search is most useful at the beginning of thinking, and there is a "point of diminishing returns" beyond which search is no longer useful (Baron, Badgio, & Gaskins, 1986).

In sum, good decision making involves *sufficient search* for possibilities, evidence, and goals, and *fairness* in the search for evidence and in the use of evidence (Baron, 1985b, in press a). Search is "sufficient" when it best serves the thinker's personal goals, including the goal of minimizing the cost of thinking. Search and inference are "fair" when they not influenced by other factors than the goals of the thinking itself.

This normative model of thinking is not very helpful as a practical, prescriptive model. In order to arrive at a prescriptive model, we ought to find out where people depart from the normative model. Then we can give practical advice to correct these departures, as well as whatever other advice will help people do their best thinking.

One comment before going on. It is possible to reflect on one's goals in life. Therefore, what achieves one's goals as they *are* may not achieve them as they *will be* after one thinks about them. We can still call the thinking good, though, if it takes into account a person's goals as they are.

Another thing we should note is that rational thinking can be defined relative to a person at a given time, with a given set of beliefs and goals. People may think rationally on the basis of irrationally formed beliefs. For example, if I believe (a delusion) that the Mafia is pursuing me, I might still make rational decisions for coping with that situation. Similarly, people who pursue irrational goals may do poor thinking about their goals, but, given their goals, they may still do good thinking about how to achieve them. If my goal is to escape from the Mafia, I may pursue it well or badly.

Toward a prescriptive model

The search-inference framework implies that thinking can go wrong for three reasons.

1. Our search misses something that it should have discovered.
2. We seek evidence and make inferences in ways that prevent us from choosing the best possibility.
3. We think too much.

The second of these problems seems to be the most serious. People tend to seek evidence, seek goals, and make inferences in a way that favors possibilities that already appeal to them. For example, we often ignore evidence that goes against a possibility we like.

The same favoritism for a particular possibility may cause us to prematurely cut off our search for alternatives to our first idea or for reasons why it might be wrong. This favoritism therefore leads to *insufficient* thinking – the first reason for poor thinking. In general, we tend to think too little, especially when thinking is important and time is available. Of course, in many situations quick thinking is itself important or thorough thinking is not worth the effort, yet on some of the most important questions of our lives, such as the choice of our personal goals or our moral beliefs, these constraints do not generally apply. It is in these situations that people tend to think too little.

Poor thinking, therefore, tends to be characterized by too little search and – most important – by biases in favor of the possibilities that are favored initially. In contrast, good thinking consists of (1) search that is thorough in proportion to the importance of the question, and (2) fairness to other possibilities than the one we initially favor.

These two principles – thorough search and fairness – are also the standards we apply when we criticize each other in academic settings. When I read a student's paper, or a colleague's, or sometimes even my own, the things I look for are omissions of relevant evidence, omissions of statements about goals or purposes, and omissions of alternative possibilities, other answers to the question at issue. I also look for partiality to the thesis of the paper, partiality that may itself cause the omissions just mentioned. When students take these kinds of criticisms to heart and try to become more thorough and more impartial, they are becoming more intelligent thinkers. They are acquiring abilities – in the form of habits and values – that will increase their effectiveness just as surely as would an improvement in their memory or their mental speed.

Thinking that follows these principles can be called *actively open-minded thinking*. It is "open-minded" because it allows consideration of new possibilities, new goals, and evidence against possibilities that already seem strong. It is "active" because it does not just wait for these things but seeks them out. These are the features of what I regard as "good thinking." (Remember, though, that this is simply a *theory* of what good thinking is. We must remain open to other possibilities about this as well.)

A good prescriptive model of thinking, I shall argue, is one that advises and helps people to become more actively open-minded. It counteracts the major biases in thinking, and it serves as a reminder of the normative theory. Advice of this type is an important part of a good prescriptive model. The rest of a prescriptive model consists of many detailed heuristics, or rules of thumb, some of which will be discussed in this book.

Here is an example of actively open-minded thinking. Students in a class on thinking and decision making were asked to think about the following dilemma and transcribe their thoughts. The dilemma concerned the "best" way to allocate, among the nations of the world, the mining rights to minerals on the ocean floor, a resource not yet developed. One student's transcribed verbal protocol read as follows:

Wealth must be divided among nations fairly. What does "fairly" mean? Should allocation be based on the *size* of the country? Some nations are significantly larger than others. But some countries have more people per unit area. Should allocation be based on overall population size? It would be *very* difficult to get all nations concerned to agree their shares were fair. Wait, the United Nations has a certain number of representatives from each country. They would be the ideal group to handle this. Total wealth should be divided by overall number of representatives, then allocated according to number of representatives per country. *But* some nations would be better able to *use* the mineral wealth. These would be nations with greater technology. Therefore, underdeveloped nations would be unable to benefit as well as nations that are financially more secure. That would be unfair. [The protocol continues for several more pages.]

This student (who earned an A+ in the course) searched for goals, considered several possibilities. After each possibility, she looked for counterevidence and then tried to modify or replace the possibility to meet the objection she had thought of.

By contrast, the following protocol, handed in by another student, shows no evidence of actively open-minded thinking (although it is always possible that some such thinking went on beforehand):

I believe that the most logical way of allocating the mineral wealth beneath the ocean is to allocate the ocean floors by extending national borders outward along the ocean floors. In effect, this plan would treat the ocean floor in the same way as exposed land surfaces. The water above the floor should still remain international territory, except where it is already considered national property. . . Establishing boundaries in this manner is fairly simple, but it will favor nations with long coastlines along large bodies of water, but is no less fair than the rules for establishing national air space. [This protocol also went on for a page or two.]

It must be remembered that this kind of prescriptive model advises moderation, a middle course. More thinking, as we have already noted, is not always better. The search for counterevidence and alternative possibilities reaches a point of diminishing returns – often quite quickly. We can compare active open-mindedness to a virtue such as thriftiness. Thriftiness, too, must be practiced in moderation. We think of thriftiness as a virtue because most people usually do not have enough of it, but some people are *too* thrifty, penny-pinchers unable to enjoy the fruits of their labor. Similarly, active open-mindedness is a virtue because most people do not have enough of it, but too much of it can lead to intellectual paralysis.

Rationality

The meaning of rationality

Rationality concerns the methods of thinking we use, not the conclusions of our thinking. Rational methods are those that are generally best in achieving the thinker's goals. It is true that when we say someone is "ir-rational," we usually disagree with this person's conclusion – but we disagree in a particular way: We think that better methods ought to have been used in reaching that conclusion. When we call someone "irra-tional," we are giving advice (to this person or anyone else who listens) about how he ought to have thought.

Rationality is, therefore, not the same as accuracy, and irrationality is not the same as error. We can use good methods and reach erroneous conclusions, or we can use poor methods and be lucky, getting a correct answer. There are even cases – such as thinking about one's life goals – where, although there is no reasonable standard of "correctness," we can still speak of ra-tionality and irrationality.

Rationality is a matter of degree. It makes sense to say that one way of thinking is "more rational" or "less rational" than another. Also, there may be no single "best" way of thinking. There may be several ways of thinking that are indistinguishable in terms of their value in helping people achieve their goals, but still better than many other ways of thinking.

A useful theory of rational thinking, such as the one I have begun to outline here, ought to provide advice to people that they can follow. It does no good to try to teach people by saying, "Be correct!" or "Make good decisions!" That is like telling investors to buy low and sell high: This advice only tells people what their goals are, not how to achieve them. An appropriate re-sponse to such advice is, "Gee, thanks."

Rationality and luck

In discussing rational decision making, we must distinguish between good decision making and good outcomes. A good *decision* is one that makes effective use of the information available to the decision maker at the time the decision is made. A good *outcome* is one that the decision maker likes. Such an outcome can result from a good decision, but it can also result from good fortune, following a bad decision. Of course, the whole point of good thinking is to increase the probability of good decisions (and true conclusions), but many other factors affect outcomes aside from good thinking. Some of these have to do with good thinking on earlier occasions. Others have to do with luck – factors beyond the person's control (hence, beyond any general advice we could give).

If we want to promote good decision making, we should ensure that people do the best they can with what is knowable. We cannot insist on clairvoyance. Prudently made investment decisions can lead to surprising losses. A decision to perform surgery could have been a rational one, even if the patient is the one in a thousand who dies on the operating table from that operation. In offering advice or instruction on good decision making, it does not do much good to say, "Do whatever achieves a good outcome." When we think a decision was badly made, we try to learn some lesson from it for our future decisions. If we think a decision was well made but turned out badly, there is no lesson to be learned. In such a case, we may need to make special efforts to emphasize the quality of the decision, lest the unfortunate outcome dissuade us from our good decision-making practices.

Similarly, when we judge how well a decision was made, we must bear in mind the possibility that well-made decisions turn out badly. Of course, when a decision turns out well, it is more likely to have been well made than if it turned out badly. (We do not appoint commissions of inquiry to study the causes of good outcomes.)

The comments made here apply to belief formation as well as to decision making. In general, good thinking leads us to true beliefs: But it can mislead us, and poor thinkers can hit on the truth by chance.

Objections to rationality

The definition of rationality as the kind of thinking that helps us achieve our goals answers a number of objections to the concept of rationality as a guide and dispenses with some caricatures of the concept.

First, rationality is not the same as cold calculation of self-interest. Many people think of rationality as exemplified by Dr. Strangelove (in the Stanley Kubrick film), whose single-minded devotion to winning a nuclear war enabled him to think quite coolly about the annihilation of most of the rest of humanity.

Rational thinking need not be cold. Emotions, in fact, are one type of evidence. A bad feeling about a choice is a reason not to make it – although not an overriding reason. Often, bad feelings are signals that some more tangible reason will reveal itself with further search. Even when the more tangible reason does not reveal itself, it may be rational to give uneasy feelings some weight, for the reason may still be there even though we do not know what it is.

The seeking of pleasant emotions and the avoidance of unpleasant ones are surely goals that most people have (and would want to have after thinking about their goals). Because these goals are things we want, we often think about how to achieve them.

Moreover, rationality need not be self-interested. Moral goals, including concern for the feelings of others, surely are among the goals we have and ought to have. More generally, rationality does not need to be single-minded; single-mindedness corresponds to the failure to search for more than one goal. The political leader who worries only about maximizing the Gross National Product is not the one who is rational. The rational leader is, rather, the one who worries about such things as people's feelings, the satisfaction of their desires, in all their variety (and in the long run).

Nor is rational thinking the same as thinking too much. When people really think rationally, the amount of thinking that they do is appropriate to the situation, insofar as possible. Rational thinkers, we have said, are moderate.

A more serious objection to rationality, some claim, is that it stands in the way of commitment. Take war, for example. If soldiers were rational (this argument goes), wars would never be won: The soldiers would either lose themselves in reflection and fail to act, or they would lose their singleness of purpose and become cowards. If our enemies are irrational in their hatred for us, then our own defense may require a similar irrationality. (Not necessarily, however: The Allied soldiers in World War II seemed to do a good enough job without being brainwashed; if anything, the anti-Nazi propaganda films they were shown turned out to underestimate the true gravity of the situation.) In such situations it may not be sufficient for us to bluff, *pretending* that we are irrational, because the behaviors needed to preserve our lives – true courage in battle, for example – may require more complete self-deception.

Another way to state this objection more generally is to argue that the ultimate objectives of rational decision making (decisions that best serve our goals) are not achieved by *trying* to make rational decisions but by trying to achieve some other goal – such as patriotism – which, by itself, is not necessarily always rational. In some cases, that is, rational thinking is *self-defeating* (Parfit, 1984). Like trying to "be spontaneous," trying to be rational may ensure that we cannot succeed in doing so. This objection does not undercut the idea of rationality as such. It does, however, imply that people might be better off not *knowing* about rationality and not trying to achieve it.

This approach, in my view, endangers the survival of rationality in a society. If rational thought is useful at all, then it must be maintained as a practice. Parents must teach it to their children, teachers must teach it to their students, and people must respect each other for their rationality. If the practice of rational thought is not to be lost, some group of people, at least, will have to maintain it. If that group is not to be an entire society, then it will have to be some sort of elite that perpetuates itself from generation to generation. This is not a foolish idea. It has been tried before in history, and it is still being tried. It is clearly inconsistent, however, with the ideal of an open society, in which all are given the tools and the opportunity to participate in decisions that affect them. Suppression of the teaching of rationality can therefore interfere with the existence of an open society itself. Without an elite that makes all important decisions, there is no way to ensure that people will make decisions that serve their own goals except by teaching them to think rationally.

A final objection to the concept of rationality is the claim that rational thinkers cannot be happy. By this argument, happiness requires a certain amount of self-deception. If one questions one's beliefs too closely, one may discover that one is not as successful, competent, or well-liked as one thought. This is consistent with Alloy and Abramson's finding (1979; discussed in this volume, ch. 14) that depressives correctly perceive their lack of control. Perhaps if we all correctly perceived the world, we would all be depressed.

It is true that some of us maintain an overly rosy view of ourselves through a kind of irrationality, in which we ignore the evidence against our rosy views. We convince ourselves that everything is just dandy, without asking whether it could be better. Many people may live their entire lives this way, happy as clams. If rational thinking were defined as whatever led to happiness, we might well have to change our view of what rational thinking is. Instead of respect for evidence, neglect of evidence might turn out to be rational.

In my view, happiness does not require such irrationality. Often, the happiness that results from irrationally formed beliefs goes along with irrationally formed goals. For example, people who think (irrationally) that they are universally liked often have the goal of being liked by everyone. Although it is surely rational to want to be liked, it is, for most people, hopeless to try to be liked by *everyone*. A balanced, rational view of how things actually are needs to be combined with a balanced, realistic view of how they ought to be, if we are not to be disappointed. If one's goals are as rationally formed as one's beliefs about how well one's goals are being achieved, accurate beliefs need not be disappointing. If I desire to be liked by *most* of the people I meet, I probably will not need to deceive myself in order to convince myself that this goal is being achieved reasonably well.[2]

Rationally formed beliefs have other advantages. On reflection, the combination of accurate beliefs and realistic goals may be more desirable than the combination of irrational beliefs and unrealistic goals, even though both combinations are capable of making us happy for the moment (and perhaps for longer, if we are lucky).

---

[2] Practically all of the "irrational beliefs" mentioned by Ellis (for example, 1987) as causes of psychological disturbance take the form of goals that are impossible to achieve.

Rationality and emotion

Rationality is often contrasted with emotion. If we think of "emotion" as a way of making decisions *without thinking*, then this contrast is reasonable. Sometimes it pays to think. We have already seen, however, that emotions enter into thinking itself in a variety of ways. In particular, we noted that emotions can serve as evidence and that the creation or avoidance of certain emotions can serve as goals of behavior, and therefore as goals of thinking. Let us look a little further into the relation between emotion and rationality.

What is emotion? Roughly, we can take it to be a mental state that is induced by a certain kind of situation. Anger is induced by unfair treatment (sometimes by unfair treatment of others); fear is induced by danger. Emotions also have certain effects on our desires, beliefs, and behavior, including our physiological responses. In extreme anger, our muscles tighten and our hearts pound; we are more inclined to strike out; we want to hurt certain people or to see them hurt. Fear can increase our belief that danger is present. The situations that induce emotions, as well as the effects of these emotions, may differ from person to person.

Emotions may be desirable or undesirable in themselves. Much of our behavior seems to be designed to let us feel desirable emotions. The way we do this is often indirect. The first parachute jump, researchers tell us, evokes terror followed by relief; after a few jumps, however, the terror decreases, and the relief becomes euphoria that may last for days (Solomon & Corbit, 1974). A single extremely positive experience such as winning the state lottery, on the other hand, can *reduce* the capacity to experience future pleasures, and vice versa (Brickman, Coates, & Janoff-Bulman, 1978). Direct attempts to induce pleasant emotions, then, are sometimes self-defeating. Many desirable emotions are essentially by-products of actions taken for other reasons (Elster, 1983).

Although emotions can serve as goals, then, they are certainly not the *only* goals we strive to achieve in our behavior. If you find this hard to believe, consider the fact that many people strive for goals that will not be reached until after their own deaths, and thus cannot possibly give them any future emotional experience. They put money aside for their children's inheritance, or they work for long-term causes in their old age, perhaps even knowing that their death is near. It may even be that the desire for emotional experiences plays a very unimportant role in the major goals of most people. Some Buddhists systematically strive to eliminate emotions, on the grounds that, on the whole, they are just not worth it (Kolm, 1986).

Emotions are to some extent unavoidable, but they are also partly under our control. Many actors can induce or suppress emotions in themselves almost on cue. Some people try to reshape their character – often with the help of therapists – so that their emotional responses change. Moreover, emotions often have undesired effects; for example, teachers who get angry at their students may fail to teach well, as a result. Emotions can also have desired effects, as when athletes' emotions make them try harder.

Are emotions rational? To the extent to which emotions are *not* under our control, this question makes no more sense than asking whether the knee-jerk reflex is rational; even if we decide that we do not like this reflex, there is nothing we can do about it, so the question is empty. If emotions are partly under our control, however, we can at least think about whether we should try to control them. The decision whether or not to try may be made well or badly, like any decision. In thinking about whether to try to control our emotions, we must consider the cost of the effort, which may be substantial. It could be better to live with a slightly mixed-up emotional system than to spend years in therapy trying to fix it. On the other hand, therapy for some kinds of undesirable emotional responses, such as phobias, could be well worth the effort involved (see Beck, 1976).

Our knowledge of our emotions can become part of our thinking itself. For example (ch. 17), in thinking about risky choices such as buying stock, we could take into account the regret we would feel if the value of the stock were to go down after we bought it. We could think of this emotion of regret as a risk we take *in addition to* the financial loss itself. If we know that we usually cannot control this emotion but are bothered by it, our unwillingness to feel so much regret could give us a good reason not to buy the stock, even if we were willing to take the risk on financial grounds alone. On the other hand, we may know that we can control this emotion. If the stock goes down, some people are able to avoid the feeling of regret by telling themselves (truthfully, perhaps) that the risk was worth taking, even though the venture did not work out. Control of emotion, therefore, can be a rational choice in its own right.

Can emotions *make* us think irrationally? Janis and Mann (1977) present a number of cases in which this seems to occur. They show, for example, that people experiencing fear often do not think effectively about how they can deal with the real danger that causes the fear. It may be misleading, though, to call such an effect "irrational." Once the emotion is present, its effect on thinking could be unavoidable. If there is nothing to be done about the effect, it is empty to call it irrational. If there is any irrationality, it may be in failing to control the emotion itself, or in failing to shape one's character so that panic does not easily occur.

Rationality and belief

Rational belief formation

When we form beliefs, we generally have the goal of believing what is true. We therefore look for beliefs that fit the evidence we have. When we have time to think thoroughly and openly, we look for evidence against beliefs we are considering – that is, evidence that they are not true – and we seek alternative beliefs. In general, then, actively open-minded thinking is most likely to lead to true beliefs. In addition, when we cannot be sure that a belief is true, good thinking will ensure that our *confidence* in the belief is in proportion to the evidence available. Appropriate confidence is, in most cases, a more realistic goal than certainty.

The main advantage of true beliefs, or beliefs that we hold with appropriate confidence, is that they allow us to make better decisions, decisions more likely to achieve our goals. This is illustrated most clearly in the discussion of probability and utility theory in chapters 11 and 16, where we shall see that coherent and consistent probability judgments are the ones most likely to give us good results. The same point may be made more generally, even when numerical probabilities are not at issue. If our confidence depends appropriately on the evidence we have, we will take the calculated risks that we ought to take, and when action requires certainty, we shall hold back if we cannot be certain.

There may well be other reasons to have rationally formed beliefs. We could have the goal of pursuing truth "for its own sake," regardless of the help it gives us in making decisions. There is surely nothing irrational about having such a goal.

Self-deception

Although our goal in belief formation is usually to believe the truth (or to have appropriate confidence), sometimes it would seem better to believe what is false. It might therefore be more rational sometimes to think in a way that leads to false beliefs. This amounts to self-deception. Although self-deception can at times be best, at other times it lies behind the most insidious forms of irrationality, as when people convince themselves that some idea of theirs is right, despite the evidence against it.

What is self-deception? To some, the idea implies that we really have two selves – the "deceiver" (perhaps the unconscious), who knows the truth, and the "deceived." The deceiver must have some reason to carry out his deception. For example, he might want the deceived to feel that she has been right all along. (The deceived might find changing her mind to be painful, and the deceiver might be sympathetic.)

Although this idea of a dual self has its appeal, it is not needed to explain self-deception. All I need to do to deceive myself is to do something in order to control my belief, without being aware that I have done it. For example, the philosopher Pascal argued (see ch. 16) that one ought to try to believe in God, since if God exists and one does not believe, one might be damned, and this is too big a risk to take. Pascal felt that someone who understood this argument could voluntarily become a believer by honestly trying to live the Christian life. In doing this, one would eventually, through studying the Bible and associating with other Christians, come to believe in Christianity and in the Christian God. Eventually one would very likely forget that the whole thing was inspired by the ulterior motive of avoiding eternal damnation.

All that is necessary for self-deception, then, is that when we form our belief we do not take account of the fact that self-deception has occurred. If we do, it will not work. If we keep in our minds the fact that we began to go to church only because we were afraid of hell, we will not be so easily persuaded by what we hear there.

Our beliefs are manipulated more frequently than Pascal's rather extreme example suggests. If you go to law school and become a lawyer, you will very likely come to believe that lawyers are good people who serve a valuable function in society (even if you go to law school for some other reason, without believing this at the outset). Similarly, if you have a child, you will very likely come to believe in the frivolity of those who voluntarily remain childless. Any course of life you choose, in other words, is likely to affect your beliefs. If you want to control your beliefs, then, you can do so by choosing your course of life for that purpose. On a more mundane level, some people set their clocks 5 minutes fast, in order to get to work on time – hoping to deceive themselves, if only for a panicky moment, into thinking that time is short, so they will get off to work quickly.

Can self-deception ever be rational? On the one hand, self-deception seems to be one of the major means we have for maintaining (at times with great confidence) false and harmful beliefs. If we want to believe that smoking is harmless, for example, we can make ourselves believe this by seeking evidence in favor of our belief and ignoring evidence against it. We must be sure not to fully take into account the fact that we have done these things however, for, if we do, we will see that the evidence we use was as good as useless, "cooked" to order: It might as well have been made up.

This kind of biased search can become so much a matter of habit for some people that they do not know that they behave this way. Perhaps they formed the habit unconsciously, because it was more comfortable: If they never questioned their beliefs, they never had to suffer the pain of changing them.

It is difficult to know how many of our beliefs are maintained in this way. If you wonder about a particular belief, try to think about it in an actively open-minded way over a period of time. This is the only cure for self-deception, and it is a cure that has few undesirable side-effects, even for those who did not really have the disease.

Self-deception is thus clearly irrational, in some cases. It is almost necessarily a part of poor thinking. If people *know* that their thinking is poor, they will not believe its results. One of the purposes of a book like this is to make recognition of poor thinking more widespread, so that it will no longer be such a handy means of self-deception.

On the other hand, in certain cases we can be reasonably sure that the benefits of self-deception outweigh the costs:

1. We can sometimes manipulate our own behavior to our benefit through self-deception. A simple case is one already described, setting one's clock ahead in order to get to work on time. Similarly, the behavior of liars may be more convincing if they believe the lies they tell. If they can make themselves believe their lies, they will be more effective. Actors, of course, deliberately try to deceive themselves in order to act more convincingly. Loyal spouses may maintain their belief that their spouse is the best one for them by never "experimenting" with other possibilities.
2. Beliefs can affect goals, particularly the strength of the goals; therefore, we may deceive ourselves in order to control our goals. Athletes may convince themselves that they are likely to win, in order to make themselves undergo the rigors of training or take the risks that they must take in playing. The potential cost here is that the effort and risk will be futile and hopeless, but again, the benefits might outweigh this. On the other hand, some people convince themselves that their goals are unattainable in order to avoid the anguish of trying to attain them (Elster, 1983).
3. Beliefs themselves can make us happy or unhappy, and sometimes the beliefs that make us unhappy have no compensating advantages. It can be reasonable not to want to be told that one is dying from an incurable disease, especially if one would only continue to live one's life as best one could. Workers who are subject to occupational hazards sometimes convince themselves that the risks are minor (Akerlof & Dickens, 1982), avoiding the stress of worrying about them. In general, it seems reasonable not to want to know bad things that we cannot do anything about.

From a normative point of view, it might be possible to calculate the advantages and disadvantages of a given case of self-deception before carrying it out. From a prescriptive point of view, it may be wise to try to seek the truth as a general rule. First, self-deception is often unnecessary. There are other ways of getting to work on time besides setting the clock ahead. Marital fidelity and bliss do not necessarily require the belief that one's spouse was the best possible choice.

Second, self-deception can have harmful effects. For every athlete who can win by "psyching herself up" for an important match, there are countless other average athletes who convince themselves that they will make it to the Olympics and waste years trying. (They may then tell themselves it was all somehow worthwhile, thus continuing the deception.)

Finally, if we get the idea that it is OK to deceive ourselves, we may well overdo it, because cases in which self-deception is irrational can be hard to recognize. When we overdo it, we are prevented from knowing the truth even when we want to. A person who has been ill but who has said to his doctor, "If it's really bad, don't tell me," may not be able to be truly reassured if his doctor tells him that he will indeed recover. In extreme cases, habitual self-deceivers may wake up one day in terror, not knowing which of their beliefs are real. Those who set out on the path of self-deception should proceed with caution.

Are people ever really irrational?

Much of the research described in this book involves attempts to show that people do not follow normative or prescriptive models – that is, they do not think in the best way. We are tempted, when reading about such studies, to come to the defense of the researcher's subjects. After all, calling someone "irrational" is not nice, especially if it is a false accusation.

Sometimes we attempt to defend these subjects by arguing that the behavior in question is functional – that it serves some purpose other than "rationality." If people are illogical, for example, perhaps it is because they "want" to be and feel better when they behave this way, or because illogic leads them to a "deeper" truth.

There are indeed many situations in which people can be rational while appearing to be irrational. The theory of rationality being used to judge their thinking might be wrong, or some important goal (such as the subject's feelings of self-esteem) might have been neglected in applying the theory of rationality.

On the other hand, we cannot assume that people always have good reasons for appearing to be irrational. People can really be irrational sometimes. Moreover, in this book I shall assume that the "burden of proof" is not on one side or the other. This is because I shall also assume that our main interest is in helping people to think better (or to maintain those aspects of good thinking that they already use). Therefore, the two kinds of mistakes that we can make – deciding falsely that others are or are not irrational – are both costly ones. If we falsely conclude that people are *irrational* in some way, we may waste our effort in trying to help them – and we may even make them worse. If we falsely conclude that people are rational when they are not, we lose an opportunity to help them. (Of course, to paraphrase Pogo, "them" is "us.")

For every argument of the form "If we're so irrational, how did we ever get to the moon?", there is another argument of the form "If we're so rational, how come we [pick your favorite complaint about the world situation or about people]?" It is, in a way, optimistic to discover biases and irrationalities, for we can teach people to avoid them. If the errors of humanity – collective and individual – cannot be prevented, our future is precarious.

To conclude, the purpose of the research discussed in this book is not to give grades to the human race or to Western culture: History gives the grades. Our job is to try to figure out *why* the human race is getting C's rather than A's and whether anything can be done about it.

Conclusion

The idea of rationality presented in chapters 2 and 3, and developed in the rest of the book, is not an arbitrary standard that some dictator of the mind is trying to impose on the world. It is a standard that we would all want to meet because we want to achieve our own goals. If you think I am wrong, you must argue that the standards I propose do not help us achieve our goals. All of this follows from the idea that the purpose of thinking is to achieve our goals.

4   Problem solving

Any thinking task may be viewed as solving a problem. The psychological study of "problem solving" as a topic, however, has traditionally emphasized experiments in which the goal is provided by the investigator, only one possibility is counted as achieving the goal, and the main difficulty is in finding that possibility.

The resulting theory of problem solving is concerned mostly with the search for possibilities. This theory has provided us with a rich characterization of search processes. Early concern with the question of whether search proceeded by trial and error or by insight has given way to the study of the methods that people use for directing their search. One fruitful view of problem solving sees it as a search through a "problem space." Each "state" in the space is reached by rule from some other state. Each possible move out of a given state can be seen as a possibility, to be evaluated by evidence, for example, evidence about whether the goal is any closer. Many heuristics can be seen as ways to improve the search for possibilities – for example, by looking for analogies in problems previously solved.

The study of problem solving has been fueled by its relation to education. Problems of the traditional sort – with a given goal and one "right" answer – are used on intelligence tests (which are used for educational placement), and many of the tasks given to students consist of problems of this type, particularly in mathematics and the natural sciences. A prescriptive theory of problem solving – emphasizing the concept of heuristics – has developed.

Trial and error versus insight

A problem (in the sense of a thinking task) arises when a person has a goal to achieve and does not know immediately how to achieve it. One natural way to proceed is to first try one thing, then another. For example, when a rat is first placed in a maze, there is not much it can do except to push ahead, trying one alley, then another, striving to remember which alleys turned out to be dead ends, so that it does not have to go down them again.

In a sense, all problem solving is trial and error, because all problem solving is thinking, and all thinking involves a search for possibilities, each of which is evaluated in terms of evidence and goals. When a possibility is first thought of, it is a "trial" possibility, and possibilities that are rejected are "errors."

43

Those who say that problem solving is trial and error, however, usually say that it is "blind" trial and error. The idea is that the thinker simply tries things at random. In the choice of possibilities for evaluation, the searcher has no foresight about what would work and what would not; hence the blindness.

Lloyd Morgan (1894) introduced the idea of trial and error into the study of problem solving in animals. He described the process by which his dog learned to open a gate (by raising the latch with his muzzle) as exactly one involving this sort of blind trial and error. The process was blind because the dog seemed to have no understanding of cause and effect.

Thorndike (1898) reported more systematic observations of problem solving in animals, mostly cats, using puzzle boxes, in which the animal had to discover how to get out of the box. Cats first placed in the box would typically claw or bite at parts of the box. After some time, the cat would by chance operate the latch and succeed in opening the box. The next time, the cat would exhibit the same sort of behavior, but it would take less time. The time needed for the cat to escape gradually decreased. Thorndike attributed this decrease to the gradual disappearance of behaviors that did not lead to success and the strengthening of the behavior that did lead to success.

Köhler (1917) argued that trial and error is used when insight is impossible. He presented chimpanzees with problems (of a sort used earlier by Hobhouse, 1901) in which it was easier (than in Thorndike's problems) for the animal to perceive the relationship between certain means and the ends they achieved. For example, he hung a banana from the top of a cage, too high for the chimp to reach, but placed a box in the cage. Sultan (the brightest of the chimps) first tried to reach the banana by jumping, then stopped, paced back and forth, as if lost in thought, and then shoved the box under the banana and stood on the box to grasp the banana.

Köhler was one of the founders of the movement called Gestalt psychology. (*Gestalt* is the German word for "form" or "shape.") Gestaltists were concerned mostly with perception and the principles by which forms are perceived as unitary wholes. They tended to view problem solving as a kind of *perceptual* process, in which the problem solver ultimately perceived the relationship between means and end. A problem was thus like a gap that needed to be filled, and the solution was the thing that filled the gap. Once the person paid attention to the solution and the problem simultaneously, the relevance of the solution would be perceived and insight could occur. It was as though the solution made the problem into a coherent whole.[1]

It has become generally accepted that both trial and error *and* insight are used in problem solving. The distinction between them can be seen as a matter

[1] I cannot do justice to the Gestalt position here. It must be understood not only as a reaction to behaviorism but also as an attempt to incorporate certain philosophical positions of the time into psychology (see especially Duncker, 1945). Woodworth and Schlosberg (1954) provide a good introduction.

of degree. Trial and error is never completely blind. When the cat tried to escape from Thorndike's puzzle box, it did not try rolling its eyes in various directions, or pointing its tail toward the moon; rather, it had sufficient "insight" to know that clawing at various parts of the box itself were more likely to get it out. Duncker would describe this as "partial insight." The cat has had the insight that it must do something to the box, but this was not enough to get it out.

In addition, trial and error can occur in the head. Even if the cat thought of rolling its eyes, it probably would not actually try it, since the cat could predict that eye rolling probably would not work.

What is the nature of insight? When we experience insight, the solution to a problem enters our minds suddenly, and, most important, the relevance of the solution is immediately apparent. Subjectively, insight is much like the sudden recalling of something that we have been trying to remember but have been unable to recall immediately. Duncker (1945, ch. 6, p. 75) offers the following account:

I look for a pencil on the table before me. My glance wanders around until it is finally "caught" on the pencil. We must thus distinguish between the signal or "model of search" (such as the approximate [mental] representation of the pencil) and a "region of search" (such as the table). Of course the region of search need not be in the perceptual field. Some memory field may be perused instead (with the "inner eye").

One day I myself was looking around the house for an organic solvent to use in removing 10-year old stickers from some dishes (received as wedding presents) that were being unpacked for the first time. I realized immediately that we did not have any of the usual solvents, such as benzene or xylene. I searched my memory field of "things in the house," with "organic solvent" as a model of search. Eventually, "charcoal lighter fluid" popped into my head. (I tried it on the labels, and it worked.) Nothing else came into my head in the several seconds between the onset of the search and its success. How did this happen? How did I think of the lighter fluid without thinking of anything else first?

The Gestaltists gave us several analogies to answer this question. One analogy is based on the perception of pairs. "Organic solvent" and "charcoal lighter fluid" formed a pair, because they would be perceived as similar if presented together. Recall often involves the use of one member of a pair as a cue for the entire pair; this amounts to use of a part as a cue for the whole.

Duncker suggests another analogy. Recall occurs by a process of "resonance." If you place your mouth next to a guitar (preferably one with nylon strings) and sing the note corresponding to one of the strings, the string will vibrate by physical resonance. Likewise, the recall of a solution involves resonance between the search model (the cue you give yourself, here, "organic solvent") and the solution ("lighter fluid").

My own alternative theory (1985b, ch. 5) is that what occurs in these cases is a very rapid, *unconscious*[2] search of the memory field "things in my house."[3] The search is unconscious because it is too fast to allow the individual elements to enter consciousness. Possibly several elements are even searched simultaneously. Because the search is so fast, it is also subject to error, and it often yields items that are not solutions. It is still a random search – that is, its order is unaffected by the problem, once the search field is defined. By this view, we could conclude that there is no true insight: What appears to be insight is a rapid, unconscious process of trial and error.

It is difficult to determine whether my alternative theory is correct. To see the difficulty, try the following problem. There are many words that have two or more meanings. "Rose" is a flower, a female name, and the past tense of a verb. Try to think of a male name that is also a verb. (There are several.)[4] Many people report that a few men's names enter their mind before a solution finally does. Are these names the result of a fallible unconscious search process or an imperfect operation of resonance?[5]

The critical feature of insight is the immediacy with which a solution is recognized once it is available. A good example of this is in doing crossword puzzles. Many times, when the right answer pops into our head, we know immediately that it is correct. This does not always occur, even in working crossword puzzles; more typically in thinking (for example, in decision making), a possibility is not recognized as the one required until some conscious search for evidence has occurred. The fact that recognition is sometimes immediate, however, indicates that in some kinds of thinking the search for possibilities is the only problem. Once the correct possibility is found (for instance, the right word in a crossword puzzle), the search for evidence and the use of evidence occur with practically no effort at all.

The existence of immediate recognition of solutions makes possible another way of reaching solutions, which Duncker (1945, ch. 1, p. 11) called *suggestion from below*, in which the solution (or something that resembles it) suggests itself *as* a solution. In suggestion from below, the solution is already present in the perceptual field (or has already been recalled from memory) before it is recognized as the solution. By contrast, in *suggestion from above*, when we try to think of something, we have a mental model of what we are looking for, in the form of a concrete subgoal, and the model calls forth, from "above," the memory of what is sought.

An example of suggestion from above is found in one of Duncker's problems. The task given to the subject was to think of a way of destroying a human stomach tumor with rays (like X rays), without destroying the sur-

---

[2] My use of the term "unconscious" has no implication about the role of motivational factors.

[3] By this theory, in contrast to the resonance theory, search times should be proportionate to the total contents of the memory field searched.

[4] Rob is one. There are others.

[5] Perhaps the right question has not yet been asked. (See Baron, 1985b, pp. 190–205, for some suggestions about other questions.)

rounding tissue as well. One idea that occurred to some subjects is to use the esophagus as a free path to the stomach. (This solution turns out to be difficult to implement.) Sometimes subjects discovered this idea by first forming a subgoal of finding a free path to the stomach and then, using this model of search, thinking of the esophagus.

The same idea could occur, however, by suggestion from below: "During a relatively vague, planless inspection of what is given in the situation, one 'stumbles on the esophagus.' Then the latter – so to speak, from below – suggests its functional value 'free path to the stomach.' " Similarly, Duncker suggests, when one of Köhler's chimps thinks of using a stick to reach a banana hanging out of reach, the stick itself may suggest the solution, without the chimp's first undertaking a search for something to use to reach the banana. In the terms of the search-inference framework, evidence, in the form of the stick, suggests a possibility, in this case, using the stick to reach a banana.

Perhaps the most famous example of suggestion from below is the story of how the Greek scientist Archimedes thought of a way to measure specific gravity. Hiero, the king of Syracuse, asked Archimedes to determine whether Hiero's new crown was solid gold or whether the gold had been mixed with silver. Archimedes knew that equal volumes of gold and silver had different weights, but he did not know how to measure the volume of the crown. On going to the public bath, Archimedes noticed that he displaced water as he entered the tub, and he realized immediately that this solved his problem; the volume could be measured by displacement of water. All Archimedes needed to do was to immerse the crown in a vessel full to the brim with water and then measure the amount of water that spilled. Archimedes, it is said, was so excited by his idea that he ran naked through the streets of Syracuse, shouting "Eureka!", which means (in Greek) "I have found it!"

Functional fixedness and mechanization

Duncker (1945, ch. 7, pp. 86 ff.) gave subjects a problem in which they were asked to attach three small candles to a wall. "On the table lie, among many other objects, a few tacks and the crucial objects: three little pasteboard boxes." The solution is to attach the boxes to the wall with the tacks, so that the boxes can serve as platforms for the candles. In one condition (that is, one version of the procedure), the boxes contained candles, tacks, and matches, respectively. In the other condition, the boxes were empty, and the candles, tacks, and matches were on the table. Subjects solved the problem more quickly in the condition in which the boxes were empty.

Duncker interpreted this result (and several others like it) as an indication of "functional fixedness." When the boxes were used as containers, he theorized, this inhibited the subject from perceiving their possible function as platforms. Duncker suggested (ch. 7, pp. 92–93) that this inhibition occurs

Table 4.1. *Luchins's water jar problems*

Problem	A	B	C	Solve
1	29	3	—	20
2	21	127	3	100
3	14	163	25	99
4	18	43	10	5
5	9	42	6	21
6	20	59	4	31
7	23	49	3	20
8	15	39	3	18
9	28	76	3	25

only when the problem is solved by suggestion from below – that is, when the box itself suggests the idea of a platform. The box was less likely to suggest the idea of a platform when it was already serving the function of a container. If the subject was already looking for a platform, the box would be found equally easily, whether it was full or empty.[6]

Another type of experiment performed by Luchins (1942) suggests a similar phenomenon. High school students were asked to solve a series of water jar problems (see Table 4.1). In each problem, the task was to use some combination of the jars labeled A, B, and C to get a certain quantity of water into one of the jars. For example, the solution to problem 1 is subtract 3 B jars from A, or $A - 3B$: that is, fill jar A, then use jar B to remove 3 units from A, three times. Try to solve the rest of the problems before reading on.

Problems 2 through 6 can all be solved by the rule $B - A - 2C$. Luchins found that subjects typically solved problems 7 and 8 that way too, even though there is a much simpler solution.[7] Many subjects were unable to solve problem 9 at all, even though other subjects who had not solved problems 2 through 6 could solve it easily.

Luchins argued that a habit may cease to be "a tool discriminantly applied" but rather become "a procrustean bed to which the situation must conform ... In a word, instead of the individual mastering the habit, the habit masters the individual" (p. 93). Problem solving repeated over and over, as in the drills used to teach elementary arithmetic, may cause a person to lose flexibility. Luchins and Luchins (1959) found the same kind of mechanization effect with other materials: for example, anagrams in which the letters were scrambled in a certain order.

Repeating the water jar experiment, they were able to eliminate this mech-

[6] Although the work of Weisberg and Suls (1973) casts doubt on Duncker's account of fixedness in the candle problem, other experiments reported by Duncker are not affected by this work. Also, Birch and Rabinowitz (1951) provide a convincing demonstration of functional fixedness in apes.
[7] The solution for 7 is $A - C$; for 8, $A + C$.

anization by telling subjects, before the critical problem (no. 7), "Don't be blind." When this was done, the subjects solved the remaining problems straightforwardly, the simplest way. The researchers concluded that the blinding effects of habit and experience are remediable.

The findings concerning functional fixedness and mechanization have inspired (or helped to justify) a number of applications. For example, Gordon (1961) suggested the idea of "making the familiar strange" as a way of solving problems in business, engineering, and design. Although Gordon does not refer to the work of the Luchinses or of Duncker, it is clear that he regards our blindness to novel solutions as a major obstacle to problem solving. In one of Gordon's examples (1961, pp. 49–50), a group of engineers succeeds in coming up with an idea for a device to use as a vapor-proof closure for space suits through a kind of group fantasy in which they discuss such possibilities as a row of trained insects locking their feet together to make a zipper, and a spider that stitches loops together. Gordon, and others such as Osborn (1953), argue that effective problem solving requires a kind of intentional loosening of the constraints that usually bind us.[8]

Clearly, it is right to encourage broad search – for possibilities, evidence, and subgoals – when we are trying to solve very difficult but important problems, on which we are willing to spend a great deal of time. Many examples from the history of science and invention suggest that perseverance can pay off, even after the first 10, or 100, possibilities have been rejected. We can see creativity training programs that are based on these ideas as encouraging perseverance. The various analogy mechanisms are ways of keeping the search going.

It is not so clear whether something more is going on here than extensive search – specifically, any kind of intentional loosening of the constraints of mechanization and functional fixedness. Let me be clear. I do not question the fact that solutions may be suggested by evidence that first appears irrelevant. Therefore, thorough search requires a *willingness* to entertain ideas that may seem bizarre at first. What is at issue is whether there is any point in *trying* to be crazy or unusual.

To answer this question, it might help us to go back to the original experiments of Duncker and Luchins. First, we must remember that Duncker's explanation was limited to cases in which the problem was solved "from below." There may be little we can do to affect whether we will see a clue (such as the box in Duncker's experiment) in a useful way when we do not even know what the clue will be. To my knowledge, no experiments have asked whether we can do anything to facilitate suggestion from below.

Weisberg and Alba (1981) have examined the more general case in which we appear to be prevented from finding a solution because of some limitation

[8] In a similar vein, Kris (1952), a psychoanalyst, spoke of the creative process as requiring "regression in the service of the ego." Regression is understood as a return to a childlike state of mind.

that we impose on ourselves. For example, consider the following classic problem: Connect the nine dots shown in the following figure with four straight lines without lifting your pencil from the paper.

Try the problem before reading the next paragraph.

If you have not gotten the answer yet, here is a hint: In order to solve the problem you will have to let the lines go outside the square. This hint ought to help, if people fail to solve the problem because they assume that the lines cannot go outside the square.

Weisberg and Alba found that this hint (given after 10 unsuccessful attempts had been made) did not help much. Very few subjects solved the problem after being given the hint. The finding is important because this very problem, and others like it, have been used to argue that our implicit assumptions often inhibit our problem solving (Scheerer, 1963) and that we must get rid of these assumptions to succeed. At least in this case, the assumption in question did not seem to be the main problem. (Subjects given the hint did come up with a few solutions, but they might have tried lines outside the square even without the hint.) These findings question the importance of self-imposed assumptions for the very phenomena that suggested their existence.

Let us turn now to the mechanization effect, as illustrated in the water jar experiment. As many have pointed out, this effect can be looked at in a different way. Suppose that the experiment were described as one in which we were interested in subjects' ability to learn a rule. Good learners would be those who discover the rule and apply it consistently. Why should the same rule apply, after all, in problems 2 through 6, if the experimenter did not intend us to learn that rule and continue to apply it? When the rule does not work, in problem 9, it is natural for us (the subjects) to be at a loss. Why, all of a sudden, did the experimenter change the rules? Of course, if we are told, "Don't be blind," we suspect a trick, and we are open to the possibility that the rules have changed. In sum, it is not at all clear that the subjects have done anything *wrong* in trying very hard to apply the rule that they have learned before they go on to consider why it might not work. It is not at all clear that any normative or prescriptive model has been violated. Put more simply, Luchins played a trick on his subjects, and they fell for it.

Of course, rules sometimes do change, and we should keep an open mind about this possibility – but how open? Should we check our electric clocks every morning, to make sure that the electricity has not gone off and come back on again overnight? Surely, such things happen, but there is cost in worrying about them, and there is good reason to trust, most of the time, in the regularities we observe.

It appears, therefore, that neither telling ourselves to question our assumptions – in order to avoid functional fixedness – nor telling ourselves not to be blinded by habit – to avoid mechanization – is the royal road to success in problem solving. Both methods can occasionally help us to persevere in our search for possibilities, but it is the continuation of that search (by any means) that is probably our best hope.

Search processes and the structure of problems

Task environments and problem spaces

In the 1950s, computer scientists started programming computers to play chess and solve other problems that involved manipulation of symbols as well as numerical calculations. The term "artificial intelligence" (AI) was applied to some of these efforts, although it is only in the last few years that programs worthy of such a name have been written. One of the early discoveries of workers in AI (first reflected, perhaps, in the work of Newell, Shaw, & Simon, 1958) was that the programs they wrote seemed to mimic, in many ways, the methods that people use to solve problems, even though the goal of the programmers was simply to write the best program possible for the task. It is of course conceivable that the imaginations of the programmers were limited by the methods they themselves used, but there is another, more interesting, account. It is possible that the way we solve problems is limited by the problems themselves.

Herbert Simon (1969, pp. 24-25) expresses this view dramatically:

Suppose we undertook to design . . . an automaton with the approximate dimensions of an ant, similar means of locomotion, and comparable sensory acuity. Suppose we provided it with a few adaptive capabilities: when faced with a steep slope, try climbing it obliquely; when faced with an insuperable obstacle, try detouring; and so on . . . How different would its behavior be from that of the ant?

These speculations suggest a hypothesis . . . :

An ant, viewed as a behaving system, is quite simple. The apparent complexity of its behavior over time is largely a reflection of the environment in which it finds itself.

Simon goes on to propose that the word "man" (in the sense of "human being") could be substituted for "ant" with little loss of plausibility of the basic hypothesis. In a later paper with Newell, Simon describes the rules that constrain human problem solving:

The system operates essentially serially, one process at a time, not in parallel fashion. Its elementary processes take tens or hundreds of milliseconds. The inputs and outputs of these processes are held in a small short-term memory with a capacity of only a few symbols. The system has access to an essentially infinite long-term memory system, but the time required to store a symbol is of the order of seconds or tens of seconds. (Simon & Newell, 1971, p. 149)

The short-term memory to which Simon refers is what you use when you hold a new phone number in mind between the time you look it up and the time you dial it. When you memorize the number, it goes into the long-term memory.

This account has been modified since 1971 (see Simon, 1978), and it can still be disputed as an account of human information processing in general. Newell and Simon (1972), however, examine verbal protocols in a variety of tasks and find that they can explain subjects' behavior on the assumption that the subjects are merely doing the task in a reasonable way, given the very simple assumptions of the theory. The complexity of problem-solving behavior must be seen as inherent in the problem itself, rather than in the problem solver.

Newell and Simon propose some concepts that are useful for understanding the complexity inherent in problem solving. The concept of the *task environment* is a standard way of representing the problem itself. Abstractly, it consists of a set of *states*, one of which is designated as the starting state and another as the *goal*, and a set of allowable *moves* between possible states. For example, try the following problem (from Thomas, 1974, p. 259) before reading on:

Three missionaries and three cannibals stand on one side of a stream, with a boat capable of carrying just two people. All six people are to be transported to the other side. At least one person must be in the boat during each crossing. Cannibals must never outnumber missionaries on either side of the river.

Figure 4.1 shows the simplest way of representing the task environment. The figure represents the task environment, the states and the transitions between them that are allowed by the rules given. Each state is represented by a three-digit code, in which the three digits represent, respectively, the number of missionaries on the top (starting) side of the stream, the number of cannibals there, and the position of the boat. The letter *b* represents the boat, and $\approx$ represents the stream. The lines represent transitions between two states, the possible moves. State 331, near the upper left, is the start state, and state 000 is the goal state.

A problem solver does not work directly with the task environment; rather, she forms a new representation, based on her perception of the task environment and other knowledge. This new representation is called the *problem space*. This too is a set of states and moves, but it must also contain a way of *evaluating* moves. For example, in the missionaries-and-cannibals problem, one method of evaluation is to ask whether each crossing either brings the boat back to the first side or moves one more person to the second side. The problem space may be identical to the one in the figure, except that moves are evaluated according to this criterion. If so, subjects will have trouble on

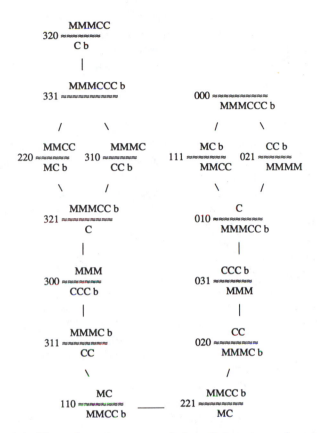

Figure 4.1. The task environment of the missionaries and cannibals problem. ($\approx$ represents the river; b, the boat; C, cannibals; and M, missionaries).

the move from state 110 to 221, because this seems to move away from the goal. Did you have trouble here? (Most people do; see Thomas, 1974.)

The states and transitions in the problem space may differ from those in the task environment. For example, in the figure, no illegal states (in which cannibals outnumber missionaries) are shown. A subject might solve the problem with a problem space in which illegal states are considered but in which the rule about outnumbering was part of the evaluation. We can tell what kind of a problem space the subject used by asking her to think aloud. We would infer that she used this kind of space if (for example, in state 110) she said things such as "Well, I could move one cannibal back, but that won't work, because then there would be two cannibals and one missionary." The problem space corresponds to what the subject actually does, not to the problem as stated.

An interesting thing about this problem is that it appears so simple when the problem space is laid out. It appears simple because it is possible to look ahead several moves. Such looking ahead is very difficult without the diagram, because of our limited short-term memory; we cannot hold more than a couple of states in mind at once. We must therefore use the problem space described, in which we evaluate one move at a time, rather than a problem space in which we evaluate several moves at once.

Problem-solving methods

The work of Newell and Simon on problem spaces has inspired a number of ideas about the kinds of methods that people or computers can use to solve problems. These ideas apply to problems of all types, and they therefore represent a set of abstract generalizations about problem solving by people or computers. Each problem-solving method is suited to a certain kind of problem. The suitability of a method depends on the task environment. As we shall see, the best method to use is not always obvious (to person or machine), and enormous improvement can result from a change in methods. Let us consider some of these methods.

Trial and error. The weakest method of all assumes that you have no knowledge except concerning how to make moves and whether you have reached your goal. It is the weakest method, the one to be used when you can use no other. You make moves, or sequences of moves, one after the other, until you reach your goal or until you give up. The rat in a maze can use only this method, because all that the rat can see is paths that it might take; the rat cannot tell where any path leads without trying it. Thorndike's cats may have been using this method in trying to escape from the box. Many calculus students are reduced to this sort of behavior when they try to differentiate or integrate a new expression. Notice, however, that trial-and-error problem solving is never completely "blind," because you always have some definition in your problem space of what is a legal move. For example, when you try to differentiate a new expression in calculus, you do not try writing it upside down.

Hill climbing. Suppose your goal is to get to the top of a hill, blindfolded (and wearing special shoes to prevent you from feeling the slope of the hill with your feet). You begin somewhere on the side of the hill. What would you do? There is not much you *can* do. You would take a step in some direction. If this step takes you down the hill, you would undo the step, going back to where you were and trying another direction next time. (You can still feel whether your body goes up or down.) If the step takes you up the hill, you would take it.

The term "hill climbing" has come to refer to a problem-solving method like this. Hill climbing differs from trial and error in that you have a way of evaluating whether you are *closer* to the goal or not. Thus, you can get closer and closer. Hill climbing is sometimes used by physicians in finding the optimal dosage of a drug for a patient with a chronic disease. One increases or decreases the dosage and observes whether the patient's health is better or worse. The method that most subjects use in the missionaries-and-cannibals problem can also be described as hill climbing. One can evaluate whether each *left-to-right* move takes one closer to the goal or not by increasing the number of people on the right side (making it higher than the number that were there the last time the boat was on that side). If one relies completely on this method, however, one will get stuck at position 221.[9]

A problem with hill-climbing methods is that they can lead to the top of a small knoll on the hill rather than to the real summit. To return to the example of the doctor and patient, as the dose of the drug increases, the patient's health may improve up to some dosage, then get worse with higher doses, but finally improve to the highest level with still higher doses. If we start with the lowest dose, we will end up with a small dose that is more effective than the next dose level above it but not as effective as the optimal dose. One way to attempt to avoid this is to try starting over at different points on the side of the hill, for example, starting with a high dose as well as a low one. If you reach the same point, you can be more certain that you have really reached the top.

Means–ends analysis. Suppose that you could characterize the *way* in which you needed to move in order to reach your goal and that you also knew which kind of move to take in response to the type of difference between where you are and where you want to be. This method would be more efficient than hill climbing, because there would be many steps that you would not need to try. Your "trial and error" would be even less "blind." In terms of the search-inference framework, you know which possibility can achieve which goal (or subgoal). Clearly, when you have this kind of knowledge, you should use it, rather than attempt hill climbing or pure trial and error.

Some people use means–ends analysis, for example, in adjusting the controls on their television sets to improve a bad picture. You could, of course, just turn the knobs at random and look to see whether the picture is better or worse. (This would be hill climbing.) The means–ends analyzers, though, look at the picture and try to figure out what is wrong with it. If the picture is too bright, they turn the "brightness" control to the left. If the picture has diagonal stripes, they turn the horizontal-hold control, and so on. (On the other hand, adjusting a rabbit-ears antenna *is* a matter of hill climbing, because the picture tells you nothing about which way to move the antenna.)

Means–ends analysis was the main method of problem solving incorporated

[9] We can avoid this problem by applying the hill-climbing method to larger groups of moves. Although the moves from 110 to 221 to 020 do not increase the number of people on the right side, there is an increase with the entire sequence 110, 221, 020, 031, 010. Another way to say this is that the problem solver must "look ahead."

in two well-known computer programs: Logic Theorist (Newell, Shaw, & Simon, 1958) and General Problem Solver (GPS) (Ernst & Newell, 1979). Logic Theorist was capable of solving problems in symbolic logic, and GPS was capable of solving any problem that could be represented formally in terms of a problem space, using means–ends analysis.

Means–ends analysis is a method of moving through a problem space in which we look for differences between the present state and the goal state. Once such a difference is found, we look for an operator – a type of transition between states – that we believe is likely to reduce the difference. If we reduce all of the differences, we have reached the goal. Again, the important thing here is that we must have knowledge about which operators reduce which differences.

To illustrate means–ends analysis, let us take an example from a more familiar domain, the simplification of expressions in algebra – for example, in solving equations for x. The goal here is to use only certain legal moves so as to get x on one side of the equation and everything else on the other side. For example, solve the following equation for x:

$$\frac{5}{10} = \frac{x-10}{x+5}$$

We note right away that there are several differences between this expression and the goal: For example, there are two x's rather than one, and there is an x in the denominator of a fraction. The latter difference can be eliminated by multiplying through by $(x+5)$, yielding

$$\frac{5(x+5)}{10} = x-10$$

The general rule here might be "When the goal is to get something out of a denominator, multiply both sides by the denominator." The next problem is that there is an x on both sides of the equation. Algebra students usually know several "means" that can be used to reach the "end" of getting all the x's on one side. They might be tried, one at a time. Here, it is clear that the one that works is to subtract x from both sides, yielding

$$\frac{5(x+5)}{10} - x = 10.$$

We proceed in the same way, multiplying through the terms of the parentheses in order to get the x out of the parentheses; multiplying all terms by 10, in order to get rid of fractions; adding terms with x, in order to get rid of the two values of x; and finally subtracting 25 from both sides, to get all non-x terms onto the right. (Other orders are of course possible.)

Algebraic simplification is a domain where means–ends analysis can be quite effective. At each step of problem solving, the solver – person or machine – looks for some *difference* between the current state and the goal, such as *x*'s being on both sides rather than one. Next the problem solver looks up the difference in a kind of mental "dictionary" – a list of all the differences there might be. After each type of difference, the dictionary tells the problem solver what *operator* to apply. Several operators might be listed after each difference type. For example, in order to get all the *x*'s on one side, one can either add the terms with *x*'s to both sides, multiply both sides by them, or divide both sides by them. It may be possible to provide rules about when to do which, but it may not. It may sometimes be necessary to try one operator after another. Operators may be rejected either because they fail to reduce the original difference or because the conditions for their application are not met.

Trial and error, hill climbing, and means–ends analysis form a kind of sequence. Each of the three requires that the problem solver have a certain knowledge of the problem domain (algebra, if the problem concerns algebra) that the earlier ones in the sequence do not assume. Trial and error requires only recognition of the goal; hill climbing requires information about closeness to the goal, as well; and means–ends analysis requires information about the type of difference between the present state and the goal, as well. Other methods are not so easily classified.

Subgoals and working backward. One important variant of means–ends analysis involves the use of subgoals. If we start from the goal and derive a subgoal that would lead to it, and then a sub-subgoal, and so on, it can be said that we *work backward* from the goal of the problem rather than from the given. Each subgoal is also a partial possibility (possible solution), except that the last "subgoal" is actually the possibility that is sought. For example, in trying to solve Duncker's tumor problem, some subjects thought of trying to weaken the rays as they passed through the tissue surrounding the tumor. "Weakening the rays" is a possible solution, but it is incomplete, because it does not say how the rays will be weakened. It therefore sets up a new goal, a subgoal. Duncker described the normal process of problem solving as a search for partial solutions or mediating phases, each of which, "in retrospect, possesses the character of a solution, and, in prospect, that of a problem" (1945, p. 9).

Newell and Simon (1972) give the following example of the use of subgoals and working backward. A father thinks about what he must do to get his son to nursery school:

I want to take my son to nursery school. What's the difference between what I have and what I want? One of distance. What changes distance? My automobile. My automobile won't work. What is needed to make it work? A new battery. What has new batteries? An auto repair shop. I want the repair shop to put in a new battery; but the shop doesn't know I need one. What is the difficulty? One of communication. What allows communication? A telephone. (p. 416)

Each step in the means–ends analysis involves the creation of a new subgoal, the achievement of which will permit the achievement of the goal that gave rise to it: the telephone, the battery, the car, and so forth.

Let us look at one classic toy puzzle where hill climbing fails completely but the use of means–ends analysis with subgoals saves the day: the Towers of Hanoi. The puzzle consists of three round pegs with a number of disks, in graduated sizes, on each peg:

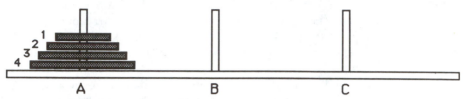

The problem is to move all of the disks from peg *A* to peg *C*. You must pick up only one disk at a time, and you can never put a disk on top of a smaller disk (for example, you cannot put disk *2* on top of disk *1*). If you want to try it, you can use four coins of different sizes and stack them in one of three places as shown above. The original version of this problem was said to be based on a similar problem with 64 disks (Ball, 1939). It was said that some priests in Benares were working on it and that when they finished it, the world would end. In my experience, however, doing it with four disks is quite safe.

As an exercise to see how well you understand the idea of problem spaces, try drawing a diagram of the problem space for this problem with two disks; then for three disks; then for four disks. Figure 4.2 is a diagram of the beginning of the space for the four-disk problem. This diagram shows that you can begin by moving disk *1* to either peg *B* or peg *C*, and you can move legally between these two states.

Consider what would happen if you approached the Towers of Hanoi problem using a means–ends analysis without subgoals. On the first move, you might notice that disk *1* was on peg *A* rather than peg *C*. You could reduce this difference by moving disk *1* to peg *C*. On the next move, transferring disk *2* to peg *C* would be illegal, because disk *2* is larger than disk *1*, which is already on the peg. So, you might move disk *2* to peg *B*. You will find that if you continue this way, you will reach a blind alley.

A more sophisticated version of such an analysis is "thinking ahead." The idea here is to develop a general plan for moving a *pair* of disks. For example, in the first-move group, one could move *both* disks 1 and 2 to peg *C* by moving disk *1* to *B*, disk *2* to *C*, then disk *1* to *C*. This method, however, leads to a blind alley again.

At this point, I am going to reveal the elegant solution, so if you want to try to discover it yourself, stop reading and try. The solution involves subgoals. Think of your goal: to move the whole stack. If you could move disk *4*, the

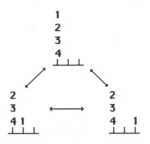

Figure 4.2. Part of the problem space for the Towers of Hanoi problem.

largest disk, which has to be on the bottom, then you would have the simpler problem of moving only the three smaller disks, so moving disk *4* is your first subgoal. What must you do to accomplish that? Move disks *1* through *3* out of the way – specifically, to peg *B*. You wind up with the following list of moves:

> Goal: disks *1–4* to *C*
> Subgoal: disk *4* to *C*
> Sub-subgoal: disks *1–3* to *B*
> Sub-sub-subgoal: disk *3* to *B*
> Sub-sub-sub-subgoal: disks *1–2* to *C*
> Sub-sub-sub-sub-subgoal: disk *2* to *C*
> Sub-sub-sub-sub-sub-subgoal: disk *1* to *B*

Now you know the solution. Begin by moving disk *1* to *B*, then disk *2* to *C*, disk *1* to *C*, disk *3* to *B*, disk *1* to *A*, disk *2* to *B*, disk *1* to *B*, disk *4* to *C*, and so on. The problem of moving four disks to *C* reduces to the problem of moving three disks to *B*, which reduces to moving two disks to *C*, which reduces to moving one disk to *B*. Each time that you solve a simpler problem, you return to the goal or subgoal that gave rise to it. Once you try this a few times, so that you see how it works, you will be able to solve a problem with any number of disks, although the number of moves required may become rather large.

When we use subgoals to solve a problem like this, our problem space is different from the earlier case where we use means–ends analysis without subgoals. In that case, each move was chosen to reduce a difference between the current state and the goal state. In the subgoal method, a whole series of moves operates on the goal itself, replacing it with subgoals, before any movement of disks actually begins.

Working backward is useful when the problem space is shaped a certain way – specifically, when there are many states that can be reached immediately from the present state, but only one (or a few) states leading directly to the goal state. In this case, it is difficult to tell which state to go to next from the present state but easy to figure out how to get *to* the goal.

The game of Nim presents a problem that illustrates this principle. In one form of this game, intended for two players, you start with a row of 10 pennies. Players alternate picking up pennies. Each player can pick up 1, 2, or 3 pennies on each turn. The object is to make the other player pick up the last penny. Try it yourself by laying out some pennies and playing the game with a real or imagined opponent.

From each state you are in, there are three possible other states you can go to, and from each of those, three others for your opponent, and so on. If you were to search ahead in this way, you would have to consider an enormous number of possible sequences, only a few of which could lead to a win.

To solve the problem by working backward, think of how you could get *to* the last state in which your opponent must pick up 1 penny. The answer is that you must have 2, 3, or 4 pennies on your last move. (You pick up 1, if you have 2; 2, if you have 3; and 3, if you have 4.) How do you get there? Answer: Your opponent must have 5 pennies on his turn before that. (There will then be 4 left, if he picks up 1, 3, if he picks up 2, and 2, if he picks up 3 – leading, in any case, to a winning situation for you.) How do you get him to have 5? Well, you can get him to 5 if you have 6, 7, or 8 on the turn before, and to get to that point, your opponent needs to have 9 on the turn before that. If you go first, pick up 1 penny. Otherwise, hope that your opponent does not know the winning strategy, and try to get him to have 5 before he does it to you. Figure 4.3 is a diagram of the solution, with you going first (the solid arrows are your moves, the broken ones your opponent's).

So far in this discussion, I have drawn certain general conclusions about when each method will be useful: trial and error, when we can recognize the goal; hill climbing, when we can tell whether we are closer to the goal after taking a step; means–ends analysis, when we know something about which operator will reduce which difference; and subgoals, when a subgoal can tell us more about how to get to the goal than a current state can tell us about where to go next. These are not the only methods; courses and textbooks in artificial intelligence (such as Nilsson, 1971) are full of others, and other ways of looking at these.

We can see in this analysis the beginning of a study of problem solving that concerns itself with the abstract form of problems and that therefore applies to machines and people alike. The appropriateness of each method to a problem is determined by the knowledge available, not by any other property of the problem solver. This knowledge is a property of the problem itself; it can be put into a computer as well as a person. We are therefore seeing the fruits of Simon's idea that the solving of problems has a lot to do with the problems themselves. The beast that solves them does not seem to matter much, provided that it is capable of learning what it needs to learn in order to set up the appropriate problem space (such as the associations between means and ends).

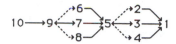

Figure 4.3. How to win at the game of Nim.

Expert versus novice problem solving

The analysis of problem solving in terms of methods for finding one's way through a problem space has been useful in understanding the difference between novice problem solvers, such as students in a college physics class, and experts in the same domain, such as their professors. Studies of experts' and novices' verbal protocols have found that novices tend to work backward from the goal, but experts solving problems of a familiar type tend to work forward (Larkin, McDermott, Simon, & Simon, 1980).

For example, both groups were given this problem (from Larkin, 1981, p. 313):

A block of mass m moves from rest down a plane of length l, tilted at angle θ. If the coefficient of friction between block and plane is μ, what is the block's speed as it reaches the bottom of the plane?

A typical novice first tried to think of a formula from which she could compute the speed (the goal), and realized that she could compute it from the time and the acceleration. She then looked for ways to compute time and acceleration, and so on, working backward from the goal. A typical expert, by contrast, immediately began to compute the acceleration of the block from the forces of gravity and friction, knowing that she would need the acceleration to compute the final speed.

It seems that experts have learned how to classify problems with respect to the type of solution required. In the absence of such learning, novices may do better by working backward than they would do by trying to blunder blindly ahead. Ultimately, by learning which "chapter heading" a problem fits under, they will be able to solve it more efficiently.

To demonstrate the role of problem classification, Chi, Feltovich, and Glaser (1981) asked physics students and physics professors to sort a collection of textbook-type physics problems into categories. Professors tended to sort the problems according to the physical principle that you need in order to solve them – for example, the principle of conservation of energy, balance of forces, or time, rate, distance, and acceleration. Students tended to sort the problems on the basis of superficial features such as the kinds of objects mentioned in the problems – for example, wheels, pulleys, or inclined planes. The students' classifications are essentially useless for deriving a method of solution for each problem. By contrast, the professors' classifications lead directly to a solution. It is as though they said to themselves, "Oh, this is a problem of type _____," recognizing it as a type of problem they already know how to solve, using a method that they knew very well from previous experience. These classifications allowed the professors to work forward directly from the givens, knowing that they would reach the goal, because they already knew that the problem was of a certain type.

Sweller, Mawer, and Ward (1983) have asked how the transition from goal-oriented, means–ends problem solving to working forward occurs (see also Sweller & Gee, 1978). Working forward, as we have seen, requires that we classify new problems according to the appropriate method of solution. People learn to work forward through experience in solving related groups of problems. They learn to classify new problems on the basis of their own previous *history* of solving similar problems. By contrast, means–ends analysis (and possibly working backward) require no special experience; these methods just require an understanding of the rules needed to solve the problem (the task environment). A given problem, then, can be solved either by thinking about the past history of solutions to similar problems or by applying means–ends analysis to the problem at hand. If means–ends analysis is encouraged, we would expect learners to pay less attention to the similarities and differences among related problems. Therefore, we would expect reliance on means–ends analysis to impede learning to work forward, by comparison to a condition in which subjects are asked only to work forward from the givens.

To test this hypothesis, Sweller, Mawer, and Ward gave physics problems (involving acceleration of bodies from a resting state) to two groups of students. One group, the *specific-goal group*, was told to calculate a certain quantity (such as the velocity of a body at some point in time, the average velocity, the acceleration, or the total time). A second group, the *nonspecific-goal group*, was told simply to calculate everything they could from the given information. In fact, both groups calculated the same quantities. Each problem allowed only two quantities to be calculated, and when one of these was the goal, the other was needed anyway in order to reach it.

An example from the more familiar domain of automobile trips may help to make the researchers' manipulation clear. Suppose that one subject were given the time (duration) of a car trip and the speed and miles per gallon of the car and was asked to calculate whatever he could. This is the working-forward, or nonspecific-goals condition. Another subject might be asked to figure out the number of gallons of gas used. This would be the specific-goal condition; and it would encourage means–ends analysis. In fact, both subjects would end up computing the same quantities: the distance and the number of gallons. (The distance is needed for computing the number of gallons, so the subjects using means–ends analysis would recognize right away that it was required.)

At the end of the experience at solving the problems in different ways, both groups were given problems with specific goals (the usual situation for problem solving). On these problems, the nonspecific-goal group tended to work forward from the given information, whereas the specific-goal group tended to work backward from the goal. For example, in the automobile trip problem, nonspecific-goal subjects would know immediately that they needed to compute distance first; they would not have to stop to ask themselves what they needed in order to find the number of gallons. Sweller and his colleagues argue that trying to reach the goal distracts subjects from the "history" of related problems, and it is that history that teaches the categorization needed for working forward.

We pay a price for this learning, however. Subjects taught with nonspecific goals are also more subject to the "mechanization" effect, of the sort shown in the water jar experiment described earlier. That is, they would apply the same methods even when a shortcut was available. The group that had learned with specific goals availed themselves of the shortcut, as indeed both groups had done with similar problems before they had practiced at all.

There is thus a tradeoff between the costs and benefits of the two methods. Working backward from the goal is often a more effective method for solving new problems. Working forward, although less efficient at the outset, encourages us to learn to classify problems so that we can solve them more effectively when they fall into the categories we have learned. However, because we then learn habits that are controlled by givens rather than goals, we are subject to mechanization effects. We will use a tried and trusted method even when a quicker or better one is available. Perhaps this is the cost of expertise in general.

Heuristics

Heuristics as general methods

These studies of expertise concern knowledge of specific domains, such as physics. It is possible that some people become expert at solving mathematical or scientific problems *in general*. (Perhaps some people are expert at solving *any* kind of problem, once they understand the facts. We might call these people good thinkers.) Schoenfeld (1985) gives an example of a mathematics professor's solving a problem in geometry, a field that the professor had not worked in since high school. The problem was this: Construct a line parallel to the base of a triangle of altitude A so as to divide the area of the triangle in half. (Try the problem before reading on, if you are brave.)

Although the professor makes several false starts (particularly in constructing a line of length $A/\sqrt{2}$, which is the distance of the desired line from the base), he monitors his own progress, gives up the unproductive approaches quickly, and solves the problem. Other subjects – mathematics students more familiar with the geometry than the professor – fail to solve the problem because they get sidetracked on "wild-goose chases." Schoenfeld argues that successful problem solving is in part the result of the use of general *heuristics*.

Heuristics, or heuristic methods, are methods that are sometimes useful in solving a problem – useful enough to try even when it is not clear that they will help.

Our modern concept of heuristic methods was devised by George Polya, an eminent mathematician born in Hungary in 1887, who moved to Stanford University in 1940. There he began the task of trying to set down what he had learned over the years about the *methods* of mathematics, as distinct from its content. His first book on this subject, *How to Solve It* (1945), brought into common use the term "heuristic," an adjective originally meaning "serving to discover." The term is often used in the expression "heuristic method" or simply as a noun meaning "heuristic method." The use of heuristics, or heuristic methods, constitutes "heuristic reasoning," which Polya defines (p. 115) as "reasoning not regarded as final and strict but as provisional and plausible only, whose purpose is to discover the solution of the present problem." Heuristic methods are likely to help solve many different problems, but no one can specify exactly when each method will help.

Polya's list of heuristics is a good example of a prescriptive theory for thinking in a specific field. Heuristics can be understood as suggestions to facilitate more extensive search for useful possibilities and evidence. They encourage active open-mindedness in mathematical problem solving. Many (but not all) of Polya's heuristics are included in an outline (given here in abbreviated form) in which he describes his method of solving a problem in mathematics (from Polya, 1945, pp. xvi–xvii):

> Understanding the problem
> *What is the unknown? What are the data? What is the condition?*
> Is it possible to satisfy the condition? . . .
> Draw a figure. Introduce suitable notation.
> Separate the various parts of the condition.
> Devising a plan
> Have you seen [the problem] before? . . .
> *Do you know a related problem?* . . .
> *Look at the unknown!* And try to think of a familiar problem having the same or a similar unknown. . . .
> Could you restate the problem? Could you restate it still differently? Go back to definitions. . . .
> Could you imagine a more accessible related problem? A more general problem? A more special problem? An analogous problem? Could you solve a part of the problem? Keep only a part of the condition; drop the other part; how far is the unknown then determined, how can it vary? Could you derive something useful from the data? . . .
> Carrying out the plan
> . . . *check each step.* . . .
> Looking back
> Can you *check the result*? . . .
> Can you derive the result differently? Can you see it at a glance?
> Can you use the result, or the method, for some other problem?

To see how Polya's heuristics work, try the following three problems.

Problem 1. Solve this equation:

$$x^4 - 13x^2 + 36 = 0$$

If you use the heuristic "Do you know a related problem?", the attempt to think of a related problem might make you think of an ordinary quadratic equation, which (let us suppose) you know how to solve. An attempt to "restate the problem" might lead you to think of letting $y = x^2$, which changes the equation into an ordinary quadratic equation in y. Once the values of y are found, the values of x can be determined.

Problem 2. Find the length of the diagonal of a room of length A, width B, and height C (that is, the distance from one corner on the floor to the opposite corner on the ceiling).

When you try to think of a related problem or a problem with a similar unknown, or if you try to "solve a simpler problem," you might think of finding the diagonal of a rectangle or the diagonal of a right triangle. If you try to solve a simpler problem, you might try finding the diagonal of the floor (or ceiling) alone, which is $\sqrt{A^2 + B^2}$. If you try to "use the result" of *this* problem, you might find that this diagonal is itself one side of a right triangle, the other sides of which are C and the quantity you seek.

Problem 3. Try the geometry problem that began this section again, if you did not get the answer the first time.

It is a curious fact that Polya's heuristic methods are always admired by computer scientists but rarely used (except for working backward). Alan Newell, one of the inventors of General Problem Solver (GPS) and other successful computer programs, finds it especially curious, because as an undergraduate at Stanford in the late 1940s he took every one of Polya's courses, even though they were not required for his major. As he put it (Newell, 1983, p. 196), "I was clearly majoring in Polya," yet Polya's ideas had no apparent influence on even Newell's work. Why is this? The answer is that most of Polya's heuristics are ways of "tickling memory" (Newell, 1983, p. 201). If you look at a problem in a variety of ways, it is more likely to remind you of the critical information that you need to solve it. But computers' memories – as most computers and programs are now designed – are not helped by tickling. If you ask them the right question, they answer it. If you ask the wrong question, they do not. They are, for better or worse, perfectly reliable.

This explains the distinction between the heuristics recommended by Polya and the methods discussed earlier in this chapter, such as hill climbing and working backward. Those methods *can* be used by computers as well as by people. They do not involve "tickling memory." Although they do not guarantee an answer they specify precisely what is to be done.

Polya's work and Newell's article (1983), are well worth further study, especially for the student of mathematics or computer science. Polya's methods never leave us without any idea about how to go about solving a mathematical problem: We always have something to *try*, at least, even if it does not work – and sometimes it does work. The possibility of failure is not a weakness of Polya's method but a characteristic of heuristics. It is in the nature of heuristics that we cannot tell just when they will succeed and when they will fail.

A course in problem solving

Alan Schoenfeld (1985) has developed a course in problem solving based partly on Polya's methods. In addition to heuristics, Schoenfeld emphasizes what he calls "control" and "beliefs."

Control refers to the allocation of time and effort to approaches. Good control involves asking oneself (or otherwise knowing) what goal one is trying to achieve with a certain approach, how likely one is to succeed, and whether other approaches might also be appropriate. Students often undertake difficult calculations or constructions without knowing how they will use the result or whether some alternative approach might be easier. Not all such "wild-goose chases" can be prevented, but it may help to ask whether there is some alternative to a lengthy calculation before attempting it.

Beliefs concern a student's working assumptions. For example, many students attempt to solve geometry constructions empirically, by asking whether their *drawing* meets the required conditions. They fail to ask whether the construction would work for other figures of the same type, and they fail to use deductive mathematical argument (of the sort used in proofs) for the purpose of discovery. They tend to think of deduction as something done only after one knows the truth and that the purpose of deduction is merely to satisfy the teacher or "play the game," rather than to discover the truth or to check a conjecture. Schoenfeld admits that there are other relevant beliefs. I suggest that beliefs about the efficacy of thinking in general, and one's own thinking in particular, are important in mathematics and elsewhere.

In one of Schoenfeld's studies, both experimental and control groups were shown how to solve the same problems. The experimental group was given explicit instruction in the heuristics that were used in the solutions. Subjects in this group transferred at least some of these heuristics to new problems. (To prevent wild-goose chases in the transfer test, subjects in both groups were reminded to ask themselves whether they were on a productive track.)

In the second study, the experimental group was given an intensive course in problem solving whereas the control group had a course in "structured" computer programming (a method that is supposed to facilitate organized thinking). Again, the experimental group improved in the use of the heuristics taught. They also improved in subjective measures of control: For example, when asked, "Did you plan your solution or just plunge into it?", they tended to answer that they planned. Analysis of verbal protocols corroborated these responses, showing objective evidence of improved control: experimental subjects were indeed less likely to "plunge in" without evaluation.

Schoenfeld concludes that heuristics are an important part of generally expert problem solving but that other factors, such as attention to the use of time, as well as beliefs about appropriate approaches, are required as well.

Heuristic methods in artificial intelligence

D. B. Lenat (1983) has made ingenious use of heuristics in a computer system. His system, called EURISKO, not only uses heuristics but also constructs and modifies its own heuristics – using those very same heuristics. An early version of EURISKO, called AM, succeeded in discovering many of the principles of elementary arithmetic simply by "playing around" with sets. It discovered the idea of natural numbers through the idea of sets that are the "same size as" each other. It defined addition, multiplication, exponentiation, prime numbers, and ultimately the "unique-factorization theorem," which holds that any natural number can be factored into primes in only one way.

EURISKO itself has been able to carry its heuristics from one domain to another, including such abstruse problems as the design of integrated circuits and the playing of a complex game based on naval warfare. (This computer system won the national tournament for this game by discovering a novel strategy. The next year, the rules were changed to disallow this strategy, but EURISKO won again.)

Lenat's heuristics do not "tickle memory." Rather, they are *operations* that can be used for experimenting with the *concepts* in the system's memory. Each concept (for example, that of prime numbers, or "Primes") has an elaborate representation, consisting of a nearly complete record of everything that has been done with the concept: its definition (for Primes, Numbers with two divisors); its specializations (Odd primes); generalizations (Positive integers); examples (2, 3); nonexamples (0, 1); and *worth*, a number representing how worthwhile it is to examine this concept further, as opposed to other concepts.

Each operation (for example, Compose, for making one operation out of two others) is represented much like a concept. Each operation has a condition for attempting its use. The condition may refer to the worth of various concepts and operations. Heuristics are themselves operations. For example, one heuristic is (in simplified form) "If the range of one operation has a large intersection with the domain of a second, and they both have high worth, . . . , then compose them and study the result." The "if" part of each operation is the condition. When the condition has many requirements, the heuristic is said to have a narrow range; when there are few requirements, the range is broad.

EURISKO constantly monitors the worth of its heuristics and attempts to improve them by changing their conditions or their actions. Heuristics can be modified in many ways: For example, by weakening the condition (making it broader); by adapting the condition so that it applies to a new situation (making an analogy); by narrowing the condition; by splitting one heuristic into two for different situations; or by modifying the action.

Each heuristic has a certain chance of helping in each situation. Lenat conjectures that those heuristics with the broadest range (most general application) are the least likely to pay off. Perhaps this is just a way of saying that it is most difficult to foresee whether these heuristics will help. They have broad conditions because it is impossible to specify when they will help, but they help often enough so that it is worthwhile to try them.

I cannot take the time to describe EURISKO in more detail here, but Lenat's enterprise is clearly of interest to students of problem solving. His system is one of the few for which the term "artificial intelligence" is unquestionably appropriate; indeed, in some ways, EURISKO may be smarter than we are. How many of us, after all, constantly monitor our own heuristics to determine which are most worthwhile and which need to be modified? Perhaps we would do better if we did.

Conclusion

Problem solving requires the use of knowledge that is already acquired. Heuristic methods allow us to search our memories for possibilities and evidence that are already there. Of course, we also learn from solving problems. Heuristics such as "Do you know a related problem?" require that memories of previous problems are available. However, aside from Lenat's idea of self-modifying heuristics, the study of problem solving has been largely separate from the study of learning, which is concerned with the *acquisition* of knowledge. Of course, knowledge is used in all thinking, not just problem solving in the specific sense discussed in this chapter.

5   Learning: basic processes

Experience is a dear teacher, and only fools will learn from no other.
Benjamin Franklin (*Poor Richard's Almanac*)

When possibilities, evidence, or goals are generated internally, they are based on information in our memories. In general, the more information that our memories contain, the more effective our thinking will be in helping us to achieve our goals. Learning, the acquisition of knowledge from experience, makes thinking more effective. This is true not only in school but also in all the domains of our lives: We learn our language; our cultural practices and social behavior; and how to do our jobs. We learn about the lives of the people close to us (and distant from us) and we learn about our own individual lives. When we think about any of these things, we use what we have learned.

The nature of learning and memory has been the subject of debates within psychology that are, in turn, closely tied to educational debates about how learning should occur. The early psychology of learning accepted implicitly the view that learning was the accumulation of knowledge and skill. This view has been under challenge from various directions. Recent research has emphasized the active role of the learner and the analogy between learning and the revision of scientific theories. There has been a revival of interest in the distinction between learning with understanding and learning by rote.

The present chapter concerns the basic mechanisms that subserve all learning. This chapter discusses the nature of memory, and the relation between learning and retrieval of information. We shall then review the evidence that learning is affected by what we do as we learn: The strategies that we use for learning can be affected by the thinking we do about what we learn and about how to learn.

The next chapter concerns the learning of complex material of the sort that requires understanding rather than memorizing. Active learning of such material often involves questioning familiar ideas and making major changes in our "naive" theories about the domain being learned. Learning with *understanding* – as opposed to learning by rote – requires learning the reasons why things are true: the goals of the knowledge in question and the evidence that it achieves those goals. Understanding can result from actively open-minded thinking. A crucial question for education is to find out what motivates

69

people to learn with active open-mindedness, in a way that brings about understanding.

The nature of memory

Let us begin with a quick overview of what is known about human memory. As I pointed out in chapter 1, we depend on memory for all kinds of thinking.

Primary memory

When you look up a telephone number, you sometimes hold it in your mind for a few seconds until you dial it or write it down. You are holding the number in what psychologists call *primary memory*, or *working memory*. This is a temporary storage space, like a blackboard that must be erased when it is filled up in order to fit more on it. When we think, we often hold possibilities, evidence, and goals in this temporary store.

If you look up the same phone number repeatedly, or if you make a special effort to remember it, you will not have to look up the number when you need to dial it. The number will be in your *secondary memory* or *long-term memory*. In humans, this memory seems to be limited only by the time and effort required to get things into it. No matter how much is stored in it, there is always room for more. Secondary memory is like a library. There is always room for new books, but old books can get lost. (The analogy breaks down, in that real libraries sell off their old books as well as lose them, whereas people seem to be unable to forget things intentionally from secondary memory.)

Primary memory is limited. Most people can remember only about seven digits at once – a few more if they read them slowly, but fewer if they read them quickly. In the *digit span* test, the tester reads a list of random digits at the rate of one per second, and the subject takes as long as necessary to try to recall the list. Each item of the test is a new list. In one version of the test, the tester increases the length of the list by one after each item, until the subject makes an error. The longest list that the subject can repeat back reliably is this subject's span. The digit span test is a part of many IQ tests (see ch. 7). The size of the span seems to be related to the *speed* at which subjects can repeat back the digits that they are given (Standing, Bond, Smith, & Isely, 1980). It appears that any given digit will be forgotten within a fixed time – about 2 seconds – if it is not rehearsed or repeated. The faster that subjects can rehearse the digits (silently) as the digits are being presented, then, the longer the sequence that they can rehearse repeatedly without any of the digits in the sequence reaching its 2-second limit.[1]

It also takes effort to maintain information in primary memory. It takes

---

[1] See Baddeley (1983) for more recent complications in the view presented here.

longer to do a reasoning problem when primary memory is busy rehearsing a few digits (Baddeley, 1976). Because of this need for effort, it is possible to erase information from primary memory; one simply stops trying to retain it (Reitman, Malin, Bjork, & Higman, 1973). The intentional maintenance of information is perhaps the most useful defining feature of primary memory, the criterion by which we recognize it.

Information in primary memory can be *recoded* or bundled into *chunks* (Miller, 1956), so that it can be maintained more easily. Consider a simple example (from Miller, pp. 93–96). The digit span for numbers consisting of the digits 1 and 0 is about ten in most people. The span can be increased dramatically, though, by learning to group the digits into threes and assigning one new digit to each old group of three (by the "octal" system): 000 is 0; 001 is 1; 010 is 2; 011 is 3; 100 is 4; 101 is 5; and so forth. The number 101110100111011 is thus recoded as 56473, which is much easier to remember. An expert in a certain field can develop all sorts of ways to represent complex ideas in terms of a word or two, a mathematical symbol, or a visual image such as a graph.

Newell and Simon (1972) have suggested that behavior in thinking, including problem solving, judgment, and decision making, is largely determined by the contents of primary memory. Specifically, before it can be used, anything you know must first be recalled from secondary memory and placed in primary memory. If this claim were true, it would imply that our thinking and decisions can be affected by only a few factors at a time, unless we found some conscious way to summarize the impact of some of the factors that we could not hold in memory at one time. If we assume that everything in primary memory is also in consciousness, it would imply as well that our choices are affected only by factors that we are conscious of at the time.

Although this claim is difficult to evaluate conclusively, it seems to be true, at least approximately. To the extent that it is true, the limitations on primary memory place an important constraint on thinking, especially in novel situations where we have not developed extensive methods for "chunking" information.

Secondary memory

Let us return to the analogy between secondary memory and a library. In a large library, one uses a card catalog to find books. When a new book comes in, the librarian makes up various cards for it for the card catalog, one alphabetized by title, one by author, and perhaps one or two others by subject. Only through the card catalog is it possible to find that particular book directly. Similarly, when we store something in memory, there seems to be something analogous to the cards for getting it out.

An experiment by Tulving and Thomson (1973) illustrates this point. Subjects were asked to study a list that contained pairs of items, such as GLUE–

CHAIR. They were told that the first item in each such pair (GLUE) would be presented later as a cue for the second item (CHAIR). Later, subjects did quite well at recalling that the word CHAIR was in the original list when they were given the word GLUE as a cue. In fact, the word GLUE was a better reminder of the word CHAIR than a word that is ordinarily a strong associate of CHAIR, such as TABLE. (To test the power of TABLE, subjects were given the word TABLE, asked to produce four associates of it, and then asked to choose one as the most likely to have occurred in the original list.) To return to the library analogy: It would seem that the best way to look up the "book," or locate the occurrence of the word CHAIR in the list was with the "card" GLUE. The word TABLE might be associated with other occurrences of the word CHAIR but not with the one at issue. The "card" that we use to retrieve something from memory can be called a *retrieval cue*. The principle that retrieval cues must be set up at the time of learning is called the principle of *encoding specificity* (Tulving & Thomson, 1973). The parallel principle for librarians would be "The way the card is listed in the catalog is (just about) the only way you'll ever find it again."

An experiment by Spyropoulis and Ceraso (1977) makes the point a different way. Subjects were not asked to learn anything but were simply requested to sort each of 10 cards into one of 10 boxes. Five of the boxes were labeled with a geometric shape (triangle, square, and so forth), and 5 were labeled with a color (red, green, and so forth). In one condition, each card had a different shape and was printed in a different color. The experimenter told the subjects whether to sort each card by shape or by color into the corresponding box. Five of the cards were sorted by shape (the 5 corresponding to the boxes labeled with shapes), and 5 were sorted by color. After the sorting, subjects were then given the shape of each card and asked to recall the color, and vice versa. Recall was excellent when the given dimension (color or form) had been used for sorting but poor when it had not; for example, when cards were sorted by color, subjects could recall the form when given the color but not recall the color when given the form. Sorting on a dimension created, like making up a library card, a retrieval cue. Notice that the intention to learn was not required.

In another condition, instead of a red triangle the subject would see the outline of a triangle next to a red patch. In this condition the redness and triangularity were no longer *unitary*. Subjects sorted the cards on the basis of one attribute or the other, just as in the original condition. In this condition, recall was poor, no matter which dimension was given as the cue. This indicates that unitary stimuli are easier to learn as pairs than nonunitary ones (as previously found by Asch, Ceraso, & Heimer, 1960).

In this nonunitary condition, recall was also *equally* poor no matter which cue was given, the one used as a basis for sorting or the one not used. This finding illustrates what Asch and Ebenholz (1962) called the *principle of associative symmetry*. Under certain conditions (not fully known) recall of associations can be accomplished *backward* just as easily as forward. Asch and Ebenholz showed that this occurred with intentional learning as well. When subjects learned associations between pairs of highly familiar words, expecting to recall the second word in each pair when given the first, they were just as good at recalling the first word when given the second as they were at doing what they had expected.[2]

The principle of associative symmetry – when it holds – is apparently a direct contradiction of the principle of encoding specificity. It is as though the librarian made up only a title card for each book and the author card magically appeared in the card catalog without any assistance. It is equally easy to find the book by title or author, and therefore easy to retrieve the name of the author, given the title, or of the title, given the author.

All these findings together lead to a certain view of how information is put into memory and gotten out (Asch, 1969). The fundamental process, according to Asch, is the laying down of a memory trace, which, in turn, is something like a record of an organized perception. Recall occurs when a new stimulus makes contact with part or all of the trace. Activation of a part leads to "redintegration" – that is, reactivation of the whole. Other parts of the whole can then be "read off," if they are sufficiently familiar. When we learn an association of the sort that we are given in a memory experiment (or, in real life, when we memorize foreign-language vocabulary or multiplication tables), we seem to form an organized perceptual representation of the whole association, with each element being a part. Presentation of one part activates the whole, and we may then be able to read off the other parts.

This view contrasts with the view that associations are based on connections between stimuli and responses, for that view is inconsistent with findings of associative symmetry. If a response can just as easily be a stimulus, the term "response" does not seem to mean much. We shall see that skill learning may be more like learning responses to stimuli.

The implication of this view for thinking is that it is possible to learn things in a way that enables us to retrieve them in a flexible way. Learning is not just a matter of learning what responses to make to what stimuli. Under certain conditions, we can access a library card by any of its parts (author, title, or subject), even if the card is out of alphabetical order. The important thing is to "see" the parts in their proper relation to one another at the time of learning. (Such "seeing" can result from a kind of thinking that psychologists call "understanding," discussed later in this chapter.)

Forgetting, interference, and transfer

Suppose you learn a list of paired associates – for example, a list of associations between courses you are taking and classroom numbers: Psychology–Room

---

[2] When the words are not familiar, this symmetry is not found, because the subjects may have difficulty recalling the words themselves, aside from their associations.

56, Economics–Room 113, and so on. Let us call the courses the *A* list and the numbers the *B* list. Thus, you have learned a list of *A–B* associations. Now suppose you learn a second list with the same first terms and different second terms, Psychology–Room 79, Economics–Room 14, etc. We shall call this an *A–C* list. (Imagine that all the rooms were changed in the middle of the term.) Let us suppose that you are tested, at various points, on your ability to recall the numbers in response to the course names. Several things will happen (see Baddeley, 1976, for further details).

First, the *A–C* list will be harder to learn than it would have been if you had not learned the *A–B* list first. This is called *negative transfer*. The learning of the *A–B* list transfers negatively to the learning of the second; that is, *A–B* learning makes the *A–C* learning more difficult. Part of the reason seems to be that you recall the *B*'s (old numbers) when you are trying to learn the *C*'s (new ones). For example, when you try to learn Psychology–Room 79, you will recall Psychology–Room 56.

Second, after you learn the *A–C* list you will have difficulty recalling the *B* terms of the first list in response to the *A*'s. After you finally learn Psychology–Room 79, you will have trouble recalling Psychology–Room 56. This is called *retroactive interference*. The new learning interferes "retroactively" with the memory of what has been learned before. This kind of interference may be one of the chief causes of forgetting as it occurs in everyday life. We forget things because we learn new things. (As one ichthyology professor put it, when asked why he never learned his students' names, "Every time I learn the name of a student, I forget the name of a fish.")

Retroactive interference and negative transfer occur mostly when the retrieval cue for the new material is the same as that for the old material. If the names of courses in the second list in our example were completely different from those in the first, there would be no difficulty. The problem results from the use of the same retrieval cue for different things. Therefore, retroactive interference is not the same as a fixed limit on the capacity of memory. (The ichthyology professor has no need to worry, unless he is teaching a school of fish.)

Now let us suppose we wait a while – a few days – after you learn the *A–C* list before we test your recall. Two more things will happen. First, you will forget the *A–C* list (assuming that you have not practiced it in the meantime). This forgetting will occur much more quickly than it would have if you had learned the *A–C* list without having learned the *A–B* list first. This effect is called *proactive interference*; it is an effect of the first list on the *memory* of the second. Note that proactive interference is not the same as negative transfer, because it occurs even after negative transfer has been overcome through extra learning of the *A–C* list. Proactive interference is an affect on the *forgetting* of the *A–C* list once it has been learned.

Second, you will be able to recall the *B* responses that you had forgotten as a result of the retroactive interference. This is called *spontaneous recovery*.

It is as though the retroactive interference temporarily suppressed the *B* responses, but they pop back up if you wait. Memories that appear to be lost are not always lost forever.

There is nothing to make spontaneous recovery occur except the passage of time. It is possible that the *A–C* learning, once it has occurred, *decays* as a result of time alone, allowing the *A–B* responses to reassert themselves. Therefore, interference may not be the only cause of forgetting. Forgetting may occur as the result of the effects of time alone, regardless of what is learned during that time. It is, however, very difficult to demonstrate such decay directly (Baddeley, 1976).

Sometimes we experience *positive transfer*, instead of negative transfer. Positive transfer is defined as a beneficial effect of some learning on later learning. In the learning of paired associates, positive transfer occurs when the stimuli and responses in the new list are similar or identical to those in the old list, for example, if each new room number were either one number higher or one number lower than the old room number (Psychology–Room 57, Economics–Room 112, and so forth). In this case, if you recall the old room number, it can help you to recall the new one.

Positive transfer is of enormous importance in education. Many people used to study Latin for the sole reason that it transfers positively to the learning of many modern languages such as French, Spanish, and Italian. (Such transfer does apparently occur, although it can occur as readily from Spanish to French as from Latin to French.) Much of the school curriculum is based on the idea that learning one thing will help you to learn another: for example, that learning arithmetic will help you to learn algebra and that learning to read will help you to learn to write. The order may matter less than is usually supposed. Learning some kinds of mathematics may help you learn other kinds, regardless of the order, and recently the value of teaching writing along with, or even before, reading has been widely discussed.

Learning to categorize

A basic kind of transfer is found in our ability to identify members of categories such as "dog" or "chair." After we have seen a number of dogs, we acquire some sort of knowledge that allows us to identify dogs we have never seen before as members of the category. We therefore transfer our knowledge to new cases. The learning of categories is clearly important in learning language, since many of the words we use refer to categories.

Psychologists who study categorization often ask subjects to learn to classify instances as members or nonmembers of some category. Experiments of this kind have distinguished three general mechanisms that seem to be used in learning to classify new instances: *learning of defining features and characteristic features; prototype abstraction*; and *exemplars*.

The *learning of defining features* of categories is illustrated in a type of experiment first made popular by Bruner, Goodnow, and Austin (1956). In one version of the experiment, a subject is shown an array of cards that varies along four dimensions: number of forms (1, 2, or 3); number of borders (1, 2, or 3); form (cross, square, or circle); and color (green, red, or black). Some subjects were asked to discover a rule that described a particular category, a subset of the 81 cards. For example, a category might be "black crosses" or simply "black." As the experimenter pointed to cards (randomly), the subject guessed whether each card was in the category or not and then received feedback from the experimenter. In this sort of experiment (which we shall run into again in chapter 13), the subject seems to proceed by thinking of hypotheses about the rule (for example, "black"). Hypotheses are maintained as long as the feedback supports them, and they are changed when it does not. The subject's guess is always based on the current best hypothesis.

The procedure, and the explanation of what subjects do, is easily extended to the case in which features are only probabilistically related to the category; that is, each relevant feature may occur in both category members and non-members, but the feature is *more likely* to occur in members than in non-members. In this case, features are called *characteristic features* (of the category) as opposed to *defining features*. Characteristic features are common in real categories; for example, the ability to fly is more common among birds than among nonbirds, but some birds cannot fly, and some nonbirds can. Likewise, in North America, short hair is a probabilistic cue for men (as opposed to women), because, although most men have short hair, some men have long hair. In a laboratory experiment, the rule might be that 80% of black cards and 20% of red cards are in the category.

When probabilistic cues are used in experiments like that of Bruner and his colleagues, subjects are reluctant to consider probabilistic hypotheses (Brehmer, 1980). Subjects seem to assume that experimenters would not try to trick them like this. (It is not clear that people assume the same of people in the real world.) When the experimenter says that the category might be somewhat or totally unpredictable, subjects are more willing to entertain this possibility (Peterson, 1980).

A curious phenomenon may result from the reluctance of subjects to consider probabilistic rules. When subjects are rewarded for guessing correctly, and when the rule is probabilistic, their best strategy is to act as though the rule was deterministic. For example, if the rule were that 80% of black cards and 20% of red ones were in the category, the best strategy would be to guess "yes" (the card is in the category) for every black card and "no" for every red one; however, subjects generally do not do this. Instead, they seem to look for hypotheses – almost endlessly. Even when hypothesis after hypothesis has been disconfirmed, hope springs eternal, and the subject seems to prefer the latest brainstorm to the hypothesis that things are less than completely predictable (Coombs, Dawes, & Tversky, 1970, pp. 286–287; Levine, 1971).

The fact that subjects have great difficulty learning probabilistic rules by testing hypotheses in the laboratory suggests that there must be other ways to learn categories, for even young children can learn to identify members of such categories as "bird" with little difficulty. A second method of learning to identify categories has been called *prototype abstraction*. The idea is that people form a sort of stereotype, or *prototype*, of the ideal member of each category. They then classify new items on the basis of their similarity to the prototype (Smith & Medin, 1981). When using a prototype, subjects classify some items more easily than others. For example, people are faster at judging that a robin is a bird than they are at judging that an ostrich is a bird (Rosch, 1973), presumably because the robin is more similar to the prototypical bird.

The mechanism of prototype abstraction perhaps resembles a composite (multiple-exposure) photograph. If you photograph the faces of all of the members of a family on the same piece of film, one at a time, each looking straight into the camera from a fixed distance, you will get a picture that we could say represents the "prototypical" member of that family. More abstractly, a prototype of a category forms in our minds if we remember most of the features of each example of the category but forget which feature goes with which example. This leads to a strong memory of the most common features among members of the category and a weaker memory of less common features.

Something like this may occur even when we are not trying to learn at all, as long as we are given only members of the category (and no nonmembers to confuse us). Reber (1969, 1976) asked subjects simply to memorize strings of letters, such as MRMRVTX (in groups of 3 at a time). The subjects thought the experiment was about memorizing, not rule learning or classification. Unknown to the subjects, the strings of letters were all formed according to a complex rule that specified what letters could follow what other letters. For example, the first letter could be M or V; if it were M, it could be followed by M or R, and so on. The effect of the rule was to make all the strings somewhat similar. (There might even have been a prototypical string, or prototypical pieces of a string.) After this sort of exposure, Reber informed the subjects that the strings had been constructed according to a rule, and he asked them to classify new cases as either following the rule or not. Subjects were able to do this with some accuracy. Reber suggested that subjects had learned part of the rule "implicitly," that is, without trying to learn it at all.

It is possible that subjects truly learned a rule (or some sort of abstract prototype) in this experiment, but Brooks (1978) reports some experiments that suggest another explanation. In one experiment, subjects were asked to memorize a list of associations, each between a string of letters and the name of an animal or a city. For example, XMMTVR might be associated with Boston, XXXMTTR with coyote, RMSSTTL with Paris, and RRMMSL with elephant. After the subjects were able to give each animal or city in response to its corresponding letter-string, the experimenter asked whether the subjects had noticed that the responses fell into two categories. All subjects had noticed the distinction between animals and cities. No subject noticed another distinction that cut across this one, that between the New World (Boston, coyote) and the Old World, including Africa (Paris, elephant). In fact, the letter-strings associated with Old World responses were made up according to one rule, and those associated with New World responses according to another. For example, the New World stimuli might start with X, which is followed either by other X's or by an M, and so forth.

After subjects were told about the Old World–New World distinction, they were asked to classify new letter strings, such as XXMMMTR. Subjects were able to do this fairly well, even though they did not have the original stimuli in front of them and even though they could not have consciously set about to learn a rule for a category they did not know was there.

How did this happen? The answer from this experiment and many others like it (see Smith & Medin, 1981) is that subjects do not need to learn a rule at all. Instead, they make judgments on the basis of similarity of new instances to old *exemplars*, or remembered examples. The use of exemplars is sometimes quite conscious; a subject might say that the string XXMMMTR reminds him of the string associated with Boston, so he will guess "New World." The subject need not remember the entire string associated with Boston in order for this mechanism to work. As yet, we do not know whether this mechanism can work without any awareness of the particular exemplars at all.

Transfer, rules, and analogy

Positive transfer occurs in problem solving as well as in memorizing and in categorization. More generally, whenever the learning of one thing helps us learn something else, that is positive transfer.

Problem solving is easier when we have previously learned to solve analogous problems. For example, Thorndike (1898) found that cats that had learned to escape from one puzzle box were helped in learning to escape from another, similar box. More recently, Reed (1986) found that students' ability to solve one mathematical problem was greatly improved when they had previously learned how to solve a related problem. Take this problem, for example: "A nurse mixes a 6% boric acid solution with a 12% boric acid solution. How many pints of each are needed to make 4.5 pints of an 8% boric acid solution?" After learning how to solve this problem, students were more likely to solve this one: "Mr. Smith receives 5% interest from his checking account and 14% interest from treasury bonds. How much money is in each account if he averages a 12% return on $4,500?"

For such analogies to be useful, the thinker must figure out which terms of the new problem correspond to which terms of the old one. This may require thinking. We may need to consider several possibilities for each term, and we may need to seek evidence as to which possibility is best.

Of course, effects of thinking about previous problems can hurt when the present problem is dissimilar, so that the analogy is misleading. Sometimes, too, we fail to note analogies, even when we have just solved a related problem (Gick & Holyoak, 1980).

Analogies are related to our formulation of rules for problem solving, based on experience with individual problems (or, indeed, rules of any sort). The discovery (or invention) of a rules can, in fact, begin with our noticing an analogy between two cases. If we ask what the two cases have in common, we may develop a memory of just the common features, with the "irrelevant" details removed. As new cases are presented, further "irrelevant" details may be dropped, until only a very abstract rule is retained (Gick & Holyoak, 1983).

For example, suppose that a person learning to play chess avoids making a bad move one time by asking herself, before she moves, what her opponent is likely to do on the next move. Later on in the game, she might be reminded of this precaution and use it again. Eventually she might formulate the general rule, "Always ask yourself what your opponent will do, before you make a move." (Later, she might qualify this rule: ". . . unless you have already figured it out.")

To see analogies at work, try to read the following nonsense words (from a 1977 paper of mine) out loud, thinking about how best to pronounce each one: "yaugh, yongue, yeart, yopy, yoth." Most people pronounce at least one of these words by analogy with words that happen to be the only examples in English of that spelling's pattern being pronounced that way[3] (exceptions to the ordinary pronunciation rules).[4] Because such analogies are based on single examples, they cannot be based on knowledge of rules.

Skill

When we learn how to *do* things, we can usually improve the quality of our performance by practicing. We often become faster, and, if our task requires precision, more precise. For example, practicing the violin helps violinists to play pieces faster and to play the notes more in tune. This type of learning – the learning of *skill* – is different from the learning of facts about what happened or what is true. It seems more related to the learning of motor patterns.

For example, certain brain disorders seem to produce a serious condition, known as Korsakov's syndrome, which inhibits the learning of new facts. This same disorder, however, often leaves the learning of skills and motor patterns virtually intact. A skilled pianist who has developed Korsakov's syndrome, for example, may be able to learn to play a new piece on the piano from the written music. When shown a copy of the score later on and asked to play

---

[3] Laugh, tongue, heart, copy, and both.
[4] The rules would yield: yaw, young-ue, yert, yopey, and yawth.

it, she may say she has never played the piece before. Once she starts to play it from the written music, however, the score may be removed, and she will continue to play the piece from memory. Apparently, she does have a memory of the finger movements and the sound of the music but not of the experience of learning it. She will still insist that she has not seen the piece before, and she will be puzzled by her ability to play it. Cohen and Squire (1980) and Moscovitch, Winocur, and McLachlan (1986) have demonstrated this phenomenon more formally in laboratory experiments.

Another piece of evidence for the distinction between skill learning and other learning is an experiment of Waugh's (1970), based on the idea of associative symmetry. Subjects learned paired associates and then practiced recalling the associates in one direction. After the initial learning, subjects were equally good in recalling the associates in either direction – a replication of Asch and Ebenholz's work. After practice at recalling the associations in one direction, however, subjects were much *faster* at recalling in this direction than in the opposite direction. Associative symmetry does not seem to work for skill. It may be that the idea of stimulus-response connections is an appropriate one for skills, even though it is not appropriate for memories in general.

When we learn a skill, we get faster and more precise, and something else seems to happen as well: The skill seems to require less effort; it becomes *automatic*. The beginning driver cannot (safely) carry on a conversation while driving or even listen to the news. An experienced driver can do these things.

There is much that is not understood about automatization. Possibly it is simply a consequence of doing things more quickly, so that one can (for example) handle the various demands of the road in the fractions of a second that are left over from the performance of the other tasks (talking, listening to the news). It is also possible, however, that attention is required less and less as practice increases. With sufficient practice, tasks may get done without any conscious effort at all. A phenomenon consistent with this view is the *Stroop effect*, named after J. Ridley Stroop, one of its early investigators (Stroop, 1935). If people are presented with the names of colors printed in different colors – "red" printed in green, "blue" printed in red, and so forth – and are asked to *name the colors* in which the words are printed, there is a strong tendency to read the words instead, because reading is such a well-practiced skill. We tend to read the words automatically, whether we intend to or not. As a result, people are likely to make many errors in this exercise (especially that of reading the word instead of naming the color) and tend to name colors less rapidly than if the stimuli were rows of X's or random letters. You can experience the difficulty yourself in a different way. Try counting the number of symbols in each group of symbols in the following list. For example, if you see XXX, respond "3," and if you see 2222, respond "4":

XX XXX X 22 333 44 111 222 33 4 22 11 333 2222 44 1111 3 222

Whatever the explanation of automatization, it seems to be very important in the learning of complex skills such as reading or playing the piano. By a "complex skill," I mean one that involves several levels of "translation." In reading, for example, the understanding of sentences depends on the recognition of words, which depends on the recognition of letters. Similarly, in translating Morse code skilled receivers may understand phrases and sentences just as they would in reading ordinary writing, and they also need to recognize words and "letters" (dot-dash patterns) (Bryan & Harter, 1899). Bryan and Harter, in a paper that is still worth reading even though it was published in 1899, suggested that automatization of the lower levels of a skill is necessary in order to free attention for the higher levels. In beginning reading, for instance, some automaticity with reading words is required before fluent reading of sentences can occur. Readers lacking such automaticity tend to "bark at print" – that is, read words separately, as though they were in a list of random words rather than part of a meaningful sentence. Bryan and Harter studied telegraphers who were learning to receive Morse code and actually did find that some learners, observed early in the learning process, were not able to "receive," or translate, strings of words that potentially conveyed meaningful messages any faster than they could receive random lists of words. These students, the researchers concluded, were essentially listening word by word. With further practice, however, there was such a great improvement in their ability to receive meaningful messages that those messages became much easier for them to receive than random words; reception of the random lists improved very little. Bryan and Harter suggested that this effect was the result of automatization of the "lower-level habits" (the reception of words), so that the telegraphers' attention was free to concentrate on the meaning of the message. They went on to suggest that such automatization is part of almost any kind of expert knowledge, including most of the professions and the arts. As they put it: "Automatism is not genius. It is the hands and feet of genius" (p. 375).

Practice may be good for learning some things, but it is not good for learning everything. Take physical exercise for example. We constantly are told about the benefits of regular, sustained exercise: better fitness, prevention of various diseases, and so forth. Moreover, it does not seem to matter much what kind of exercise it is, as long as we get out of breath doing it. If, for example, we run every day, we are probably well prepared for shoveling snow. The particular muscles are different, and we might get sore in the snow-shoveling muscles if we overdo it, but running offers substantial benefits that *transfer* to other very different physical activities. Exercise has *general* benefits.

We tend to think that practicing mental tasks must also have some sort of general benefits beyond the particular tasks being practiced. At present, however, one of the few well-supported conclusions of cognitive psychology is that this simply does not happen, however much we would like to believe that it does (Woodworth & Schlosberg, 1954; Baron, 1985c). The specificity of practice effects has been known to psychologists (and ignored by everyone else) since Thorndike and Woodworth first discovered it in 1901. They found, for example, that practice at discriminating M's from N's makes people faster at discriminating M's from N's, but no faster at discriminating A's from B's.

A more dramatic demonstration comes from an experiment by Ericsson, Chase, and Faloon (1980). They found a subject who was willing to practice at improving his digit span for several months. Starting with a span of 7 digits (and a span of 6 letters), he got up to a span of 79 digits by learning – and presumably automatizing – a recoding scheme based on times for track events. (No practice was done with letters.) He even demonstrated his skill on a network television show. At the end of all of this practice, what was his span for letters? Six, just what it had been at the beginning. There was no transfer. Practice at memorizing one thing does not by itself make you better at memorizing other things.

This conclusion about the specificity of practice applies only to skills, that is, whatever it is that improves in speed and accuracy as a result of practice. Such improvement seems to occur even when the person apparently does not learn how to do anything differently. Itzhak Perlman (the well-known violinist) can tell us how to hold the bow, where to put our fingers on the violin, and he can even help us to develop our taste for what sounds good and what does not, but his skill itself is not something that he can consciously communicate, or even understand. The lesson is this: We cannot improve the "condition" of the mind through *rote practice* the way we can condition the body through exercise; however, there may well be other things we *can* do for the mind. Practice is also extremely useful in the learning of particular skills such as reading, but we must make sure that the practice is given on exactly what the learner needs to do. Practice at discriminating Hebrew letters will not help a child learn to read English.

Strategies for learning

Memory experiments over the years have shown that children get better at memorizing things as they get older, although mentally retarded children remain considerably behind the others. It used to be thought that the ability to learn was a fixed property of the brain; therefore, older children must have better brains than younger ones, and retardates' brains are not so good. These conclusions may be true, but they are not the whole story. The ability to learn can itself be learned. Children *learn* how to learn more effectively: They learn strategies for learning. The learning of these strategies is an example of behavioral learning (discussed in ch. 1), and I suggest that it results from the application of thinking to the problem of how to learn better.

John Flavell (1970) and Ann Brown (1975) are largely responsible for calling to our attention the implications of the fact that learning – even the learning of lists of words in memory experiments – is not a passive activity.

When we are trying to learn, we do certain things with the explicit intention of making our memories work a certain way. When children learn multiplication tables, for example, they often write down the items on cards, rehearse them over and over, test themselves, rehearse the ones that they find difficult, and make up ways of helping themselves remember. When we learn foreign vocabulary, one learning strategy is to think of ways of relating the foreign words to English. (For example, the German word *Zeitung*, which means "newspaper," reminds me of the old English word "tiding," which sounds like *Zeitung* and which means "news," as in "tidings of comfort and joy.")

Flavell, Brown, and others found that young children and retardates sometimes do not even use the simplest of these strategies when they are trying to learn something (see Flavell, 1977, and Baron, 1978, for reviews). Young children, when instructed to memorize the order in which they are shown 10 pictures, for example, do not behave any differently from the way they behave when they are simply instructed to look at the pictures. Older children rehearse the order, to the point of moving their lips visibly. Moreover, if the young children are instructed to rehearse, they can do so, and their memory performance improves. The same kinds of experiments work with retardates, and with other methods besides rehearsing, such as self-testing.

One way of describing these experiments is to say that the older children use certain *strategies* (methods, heuristics) for learning that the younger children do not use. When the children are taught the strategies, learning improves.

Other experiments (Craik & Tulving, 1975) suggest that the *intention to learn*, by itself, does nothing. If adult subjects are instructed to perform a task that by itself helps with the particular learning objective – such as (if the objective is learning a list of words) judging whether a word they are given fits into a particular sentence – learning is equally good whether or not the subject is told that memory for the words will be tested. It seems that the intention to learn something helps us to learn it only because this intention leads to certain activities that themselves affect learning.

Can memory strategies transfer? Brown, Campione, and Barclay (1979) studied educable retarded children who had been taught to test themselves as they learned a list of common objects (shown in pictures). Six months after the initial training, the older children still remembered what they had been taught, and they were even able to *transfer* the strategy to a different task, in which they were asked to recall the gist of stories after studying each story as much as they wanted.

Brown, Campione, and Barclay and others point out that many psychological experiments have failed to show transfer of memory strategies. They suggest that in order for transfer to occur, the subject must *understand* the relevance of the strategy to the new situation. Someone must explain to the subject (or student), at the time when the strategy is taught, that the strategy could be valuable elsewhere. Woodrow (1927) reached a similar conclusion.

Even intelligent adults do not use all of the strategies for remembering that they could. "Mnemonists" (such as the digit memorizer studied by Ericsson and his colleagues) are people who become expert at such strategies. They have a variety of methods, many of which involve the use of visual images as memory clues (Luria, 1968; Neisser, 1982). Such methods rarely work, except on the stage. Although many students think that they would do better in school if they could memorize more, memory is not usually their problem.

I myself use visual imagery to avoid one kind of "forgetting" – forgetting to carry out a plan. Suppose I plan to pick up the new commuter train schedule at the station on my way home from work. By the end of the day, that plan may have completely slipped my mind as I hurry through the station, anxious to catch my train and get home. To help myself remember, I use the following method. When I form the plan – say, in the morning – I think about where I will be before I come home – for example, at a meeting with colleagues in the university hospital. I form a vivid visual image connected with the hospital (and my plan) – such as an Amtrak train rumbling down the hall that I will pass through as I leave my meeting. When I walk down that hall as I leave the hospital, the memory of the image recurs, and I am reminded to carry out my plan.

In sum, one reason people do not use optimal memory strategies is that they have not learned to do so. Training in memory strategies may help us memorize. (Later in this chapter we shall examine strategies for *understanding*, as opposed to memorizing.) Familiarity with the *strategies* themselves, however, may not be the only determinant of whether we use them. Familiarity with the *material* can also be important. Chi (1985) studied the strategy of grouping items together by category at the time of recall. This strategy has been found to be helpful in recalling lists of words. If a word list is composed of several categories (for example, furniture – chair, table, bookcase; birds – robin, bluejay, canary; professions – doctor, lawyer, teacher), subjects recall the word list better if they recall it one category at a time. Young children generally do not use this strategy for recalling ordinary lists of words. Chi found that even preschool children do use this strategy when they try to recall the names of their classmates, categorizing by seating section. A preschool child who was an "expert" on dinosaurs (after his parents had read dinosaur books to him for over a year) also used this categorization strategy when recalling dinosaurs. It would appear that children's failure to use this strategy for ordinary word lists is (in part) the result of their unfamiliarity with the categories themselves.

Conclusion

The strategies discussed in this chapter applied only to the memorization of lists of items and other simple material. What about the kinds of complex material that we learn in school and in our lives outside of school? Are there strategies for learning this material too? In the next chapter, we shall find that such "strategies" (if we still wish to call them that) often amount simply to thinking about what is being learned in a way that considers goals, evidence, and alternative possibilities – in short, in a way that is actively open-minded.

6   Learning: complex material

So far we have been concerned with the learning of essentially simple material. What about the learning of more complex material, such as academic subjects, the practices and beliefs of our culture, and the circumstances of individual lives (including our own)? Can the learning of these subjects be understood through the processes discussed so far?

It is indeed true that the basic principles of memory storage, retrieval, and transfer apply as much to memories of our insights into poems and mathematical proofs as they apply to memories of paired associates. These basic principles are not sufficient for the kind of useful understanding that we seek, however, just as the laws of physics alone will not get us to first base in understanding the game of baseball (even though the movements of the ball and the players surely obey those laws).

Most complex material is *organized*: That is to say, it is not simply a bundle of arbitrary associations. A field of knowledge is governed by general rules specific to that subject – in French, for example, the rules of French grammar; in geometry, Euclid's axioms. Pieces of knowledge within such bodies of knowledge are interrelated in that they refer to one another. We use our knowledge of such interrelations constantly in daily life. For example, in our culture we know that a collie is more than just a thing that barks and has long hair; we know that a collie is a kind of dog, which is a kind of mammal, which is a kind of animal, and so on. Because knowledge is organized, the learning of one piece affects the learning of others. Again, such effects very likely follow the laws of transfer of learning; however, there probably is more to the learning of particular bodies of knowledge than that.

Restructuring

Development of knowledge

One extreme view, which we shall pass over quickly, is that of the psychological theorist Jean Piaget and his followers. According to this view, children, as they develop intellectually, go through a number of stages. In each stage, they are capable of learning only certain kinds of bodies of knowledge. For example, Piaget argues that a very young child is incapable of understanding the rules of set theory or logic, or even certain kinds of moral reasoning such as the Golden Rule. Piaget asserts that the transition from one stage to another is a completely general, albeit gradual, *reorganization* or *restructuring* of the child's knowledge. Although this view still has its adherents, it has come under serious attack in recent years from myself and others (see Baron, 1973, 1978; Carey, 1985; Gelman & Baillargeon, 1983; Osherson, 1974). Our general criticisms are that (1) whenever the theory is made clear enough to permit an empirical test, the test fails to support the theory, and (2) we can give more plausible explanations of the data that seem to support Piaget's theory.

One of the more plausible accounts of some of the data is that although knowledge *is* restructured, this restructuring is not completely general; rather, it occurs within specific domains. By this view, reorganization is simply a form of learning that occurs in particular domains. Other forms are more gradual and do not require radical unlearning of what has already been learned (Rumelhart & Norman, 1981).

For example, some children seem to hold a view of astronomy much like that of some of the ancients (Vosniadou & Brewer, 1987). They say, if asked, that the earth is flat, the sun rises and passes through the sky, perhaps pushed by the wind, and so on. Unless the children have been specifically instructed otherwise, these are natural views to hold. They correspond to the way things appear, and this is the reason the ancients held them as well.

When the wonders of modern astronomy are first revealed to them, these children will at first modify their structure as little as possible so as to accommodate the new information. For example, one child (according to an anecdote I heard) learned dutifully in school that the earth went around the sun. When asked later where the earth was, he pointed upward, answering, "Up there, going around the sun." This earth he had learned about could not be the same earth he already knew, which, after all, was obviously flat and stationary. Another child (described by Piaget, 1929, p. 236) had been taught about the cycle of night and day and the rotation of the earth. She had been told that when it was night in Europe (where she lived), it was day in America. Not wanting to give up her idea of a flat earth, she now reported, when asked, that there was a flat-earth America underneath the flat-earth Europe, and that at night the sun dropped below the European layer to shine on the American layer.

Vosniadou and Brewer (1987) point out that when the modern view is finally adopted, the change is truly radical. First, the concepts themselves are replaced with new concepts: For example, whereas some young children believe that the sun is alive, sleeps at night, and could stop shining if it wanted to, older children learn that the sun is a star like the others that shine at night. Second, the relationships among the child's concepts change: The earth is no longer physically at the center of the universe; the light from the moon is understood as related to the positions of the earth and sun. Finally, the new system explains different phenomena: the relationship between sun, moon, and stars, but *not* the relationship between sun, clouds, and wind (which might have been understood as being interrelated in the old system). This last point is of interest because it suggests that something is lost by adopting the new system – not just the innocence of childhood, but also a way of understanding certain things. The appearance of the earth as being flat and of the sun as being much smaller than the earth now become mysteries. Eventually, these things too will be explained, of course. In sum, there are changes of belief that are as radical as those that have occurred in history, from the system of ancient astronomy to the system of Copernicus.

Naive theories

Just as children have naive theories of astronomy, children and adults seem to have naive theories in other subject areas, such as physics, which must be replaced, sometimes with great difficulty, in order for a person to learn a modern scientific theory. Often these naive theories correspond to systems proposed by early scientists such as Aristotle. (In chs. 12 and 17, we shall see that there may also be naive theories of statistics and probability, theories held by most adults.)

Clement (1983), for example, found that students who had taken a physics course held a theory (sometimes even after they had finished the course) about forces that was similar to one held by Galileo in his early work but was later questioned (first by Galileo himself, and ultimately by Newton). They believed that a body in motion always requires a force to keep it in motion. In contrast, we now find it more useful to suppose that a body keeps going unless it is stopped or slowed by some force. Of course, wagons and cars *do* require force to keep them going, but that is because they would otherwise be slowed down by friction.

Clement asked his subjects what forces were acting on a coin thrown up into the air, during the time it was rising but after it had left the thrower's hand. Most students (even after taking the course) said that there was a force directed upward while the coin was rising, in addition to the force of gravity pulling the coin down. This view fitted in with the "motion implies force" theory that the students held. Physicists find it more useful to suppose that there is only one force, the force of gravity, once the coin is released.

Clement also asked the students about the forces acting on the bob of a pendulum while the pendulum was swinging. Many students said that there were three forces: (1) the force of gravity pulling the bob straight down; (2) the force of the string pulling the bob directly toward the point where the string was attached; and (3) a force acting in the direction in which the bob was moving, as shown in Figure 6.1. A modern physicist would say that the third force is unnecessary to explain the motion of the bob.

In another series of studies, McCloskey (1983) asked undergraduates, some of whom had studied physics, to trace the path of a metal ball shot out of a curved tube at high speed, as shown in Figure 6.2. The tube is lying flat on

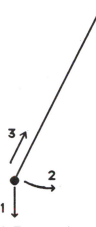

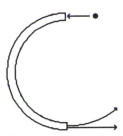

Figure 6.1. Forces acting on the bob of a pendulum, according to some of Clement's subjects.

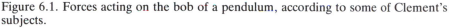

Figure 6.2. Which path does a ball take when shot out of a curved tube? Adapted from M. McCloskey, "Naive Theories of Motion," in D. Gentner & A. L. Stevens (Eds.), *Mental Models* (Hillsdale, NJ: Erlbaum (1983), p. 301.

top of a surface; therefore the effect of gravity can be ignored. Many of the subjects, including some who had studied physics, said that the path of the ball would be curved. In fact, it would be straight. McCloskey argues (on the basis of interviews with subjects) that his subjects held a theory in which the ball acquires some sort of "impetus," a concept something like the mature concept of momentum, except that the impetus can include the curvature of the path. A similar theory was apparently held during medieval times.

Another of McCloskey's studies involved asking subjects to trace the path of a ball after it rolls off the edge of a table. One incorrect answer is shown in Figure 6.3, along with the correct answer. Subjects seem to think that the impetus from the original force takes a little time to dissipate, but that once it does, gravity takes over and the ball falls straight down (much like movie cartoon characters, who usually look first, then fall). In fact, the momentum from the original push keeps the ball moving at the same speed in the hori-

Figure 6.3. Which path does a ball take when it rolls off the edge of a table?

zontal direction, and the path changes direction only because the downward speed increases.

McCloskey (pp. 321–322) argues that these naive theories are not entirely harmless in the real world:

An acquaintance of ours was recently stepping onto a ladder from a roof 20 feet above the ground. Unfortunately, the ladder slipped out from under him. As he began to fall, he pushed himself out from the edge of the roof in an attempt to land in a bush about three feet out from the base of the house . . . However, he overshot the bush, landing about 12 feet from the base of the house and breaking his arm. Was this just a random miscalculation, or did our acquaintance push off too hard because of a naive belief that he would move outward for a short time and then fall straight down?

It is also possible that naive theories have some advantages. Kempton (1986) has found that people in the United States tend to hold two different theories of home heat control. The physically correct theory for the vast majority of homes in the United States is the *feedback theory*. By this theory, the thermostat simply turns the heat on and off, depending on the temperature. As one Michigan farmer put it, "You just turn the thermostat up, and once she gets up there [to the desired temperature] she'll kick off automatically. And then she'll kick on and off to keep it at that temperature." By this theory, it does no good to turn the thermostat way up to warm up the home quickly. People who hold this theory tend to leave the thermostat set at a fixed value during the day.

Many people hold a different view, the *valve theory*. By this view, the thermostat is like the gas pedal of a car. The higher you turn it up, the more heat goes into the house, and the faster the temperature changes. People who hold this theory turn the thermostat way up when they come into a cold house, and then, if they remember, turn it down after the house warms up. The valve theory may well lead to wasted fuel, but it does give people a simple reason why they ought to turn the thermostat down when they are out of the house: less fuel will be used when the setting is lower.

The feedback theory is technically correct, as can be ascertained by looking inside a thermostat; however, it has some serious drawbacks. First, the valve theory does a better job than the basic feedback theory of explaining certain phenomena. In many homes, thermostats do need to be set higher to maintain the same feeling of warmth when it is very cold outside. This is easily explained by the valve theory, but in the feedback theory other concepts must be invoked, such as the fact that some rooms are less well heated than others and that some of the feeling of warmth may come from radiant heat from the walls and ceiling. Likewise, it may be necessary to turn the thermostat up higher than normal when entering a cold room, because the walls and furniture take longer to come to the desired temperature than the air does, and the room will still feel cold even after the air (which affects the thermostat) has reached the desired temperature.

Second, the feedback theory does not easily explain why it is a good idea to turn the heat down when one is out of the house. One valve theorist felt that the heat should be turned down when one is out, but, she said, "My husband disagrees with me. He, he feels, and he will argue with me long enough, that we do not save any fuel by turning the thermostat up and down . . . Because he, he feels that by the time you turn it down to 55°, and in order to get all the objects in the house back up to 65°, you're going to use more fuel than if you would have left it at 65 and it just kicks in now and then." Now the husband's reasoning here is physically incorrect. The use of fuel is directly proportionate to the flow of heat out of the house, and this, in turn, depends only on the temperature difference between the inside of the house and the outside. Thus, the house loses less heat, and uses less fuel, when it is at 55 degrees Fahrenheit than when it is at 65 degrees; but, as Kempton notes, the physically correct argument requires a more abstract understanding than most people typically achieve. If they act according to the valve theory, they may actually save more energy than if they act in terms of a rudimentary feedback theory such as that held by the husband in this example.

We might be tempted to suppose that the valve theory is maintained by its functional value in saving fuel rather than by the ready availability of analogies with other valves (accelerators, faucets) and by its explanatory value (as just discussed). This conclusion does not follow. To draw it, we would need to argue that the functional value of the valve theory *causes* the theory to be maintained (Elster, 1979). Are people really sensitive to the amount of fuel they use? People's beliefs sometimes are for the best, but, as Mc-Closkey argues, sometimes they are not.

This example is a particularly good illustration of naive theories, because it seems likely that the subjects have actually thought about how thermostats work. They have had to face the issue in learning how to use them. In the previous examples from college physics, it is not clear that the subjects really "had" any theories before they were confronted with the problems given them by the experimenters. They may simply have constructed answers to the problems on the spot. The fact that their answers often correspond to traditional theories simply reflects the fact (as it would on any account) that these theories explain the most obvious phenomena and are based on the most obvious analogies. After all, balls thrown with spin on them keep spinning; why should not balls shot out of a curved tube keep curving as well?

The home heat-control theories seem to provide yet another example of restructuring (assuming that some people change from the valve theory to the feedback theory). Like the Copernican theory of astronomy, the fully correct theory requires new concepts, such as the concept of heat flow over a temperature difference and that of radiant heat. The theory establishes new relationships among concepts, such as thermostat settings and heat flow. It also explains different phenomena, such as the fact that the house temperature stays roughly at the setting on the thermostat.

Is restructuring the rule or the exception in the acquisition of complex knowledge? The data that we reviewed in chapter 4 concerning the difference between expert and novice problem solving do not show any evidence of radical restructuring – although the investigators did not go out of their way to look for it. Novice behavior seemed not to be characterized by naive theories so much as by incomplete mastery, so that novices need to use different, more conservative, methods of search (means–ends analysis). The question of whether restructuring is the exception or the rule cannot be answered unless we know just what kinds of domains we are talking about, so that we can sample them and count. There may be little point in even trying to answer such questions. We should simply be aware that restructuring is sometimes required.

Another question is whether knowledge of naive theories helps or hurts the learning of mature theories. It is difficult to imagine an argument that the naive theories help.[1] Unlike Piaget's theory of general restructuring, the new theory of domain-specific restructuring no longer provides an argument that certain concepts cannot be learned at certain ages.

Understanding

Students and their teachers often make a distinction between *understanding* something and "just memorizing it" (or perhaps just not learning it at all). Everyone wants to learn with understanding and teach for understanding, but there is a lot of misunderstanding about what understanding is. The issue has a history worth reviewing.

Wertheimer and Katona

Max Wertheimer (1945/1959), one of the founders of Gestalt psychology in the early part of this century, is the psychologist who called our attention most forcefully to the problem of understanding. Wertheimer's main example was the formula for finding the area of the parallelogram, $A = b \cdot h$, where A is the area, b is the base, and h is the height (Figure 6.4). Wertheimer

---

[1] Of course, other knowledge may help, and by the time children acquire this other knowledge they may also have acquired naive theories, but this does not mean that the naive theories themselves are helpful.

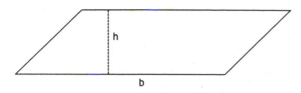

Figure 6.4. Parallelogram.

examined a group of students who had learned this formula to their teacher's satisfaction. On close examination, though, they turned out not to understand it. They could apply it in cases that they were familiar with (such as Figure 6.4) but refused to apply the formula to new cases, such as a parallelogram depicted standing on its side (Figure 6.5), which had not been among the original examples that they had studied. They also were given other new cases (which Wertheimer called "*A* problems") that followed the same principle: A rectangle was made into another figure by removing a piece from one side and attaching to the opposite side, just as a parallelogram can be made into a rectangle by cutting a triangle from one side and moving it to the other side (without changing *A*, *b*, or *h*) (Figure 6.6). Some students did indeed apply the formula to such cases, multiplying the base by the height to get the area, but these same students usually also applied the formula to other problems showing figures that could *not* be turned back into rectangles by moving a piece around (*B* problems). In sum, learning without understanding was characterized either by lack of transfer of the principle to cases where it applied or by inappropriate transfer to cases where it did not apply.

In contrast to these students, Wertheimer reported other cases of real understanding, some in children much younger than those in the class just described. Most of the time, these children solved the problem for themselves rather than having the formula explained to them. They figured out for themselves that the parallelogram could be converted into a rectangle of the same area without changing *b* or *h*. One child bent the parallelogram into a belt

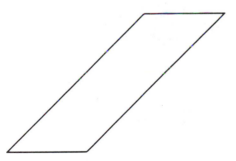

Figure 6.5. Parallelogram on its side.

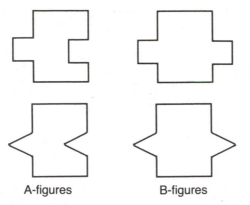

A-figures   B-figures

Figure 6.6. Wertheimer's "A problems" and "B problems."

and then made it into a rectangle by cutting straight across the middle. Wertheimer does not insist that understanding arises only from personal problem solving, but he implies that there is a connection. When one solves a problem oneself, one usually understands why the solution is the solution.

Learning with understanding is not the same as discovery by induction. Wertheimer (pp. 27–28) made this philosophical point concretely by giving the class the values of a, b, and h from each of the following problems (with parallelograms drawn) and asking the students to compute the area of each parallelogram:

a	b	h	Area to be computed
2.5	5	1.5	7.5
2.0	10	1.2	12.0
20.0	1⅓	16.0	21⅓
15.0	1⅞	9.0	16⅞

Wertheimer describes what happened:

The pupils worked at the problems, experiencing a certain amount of difficulty with the multiplication.

Suddenly a boy raised his hand. Looking somewhat superciliously at the others who had not yet finished, he burst out: "It's foolish to bother with multiplication and measuring the altitude. I've got a better method for finding the area – it's so simple. The area is $a + b$."

"Have you any idea why the area is equal to $a + b$?" I asked.

"I can prove it," he answered. "I counted it out in all the examples. Why bother with $b \cdot h$. The area equals $a + b$."

I then gave him a fifth problem: $a = 2.5$, $b = 5$, $h = 2$. The boy began to figure, became somewhat flustered, then said pleasantly: "Here adding the two does not give the area. I am sorry; it would have been so nice."

"*Would it?*" I asked . . .

I may add that the real purpose of this "mean" experiment was not simply to mislead. Visiting the class earlier, I had noticed that there was a real danger of their

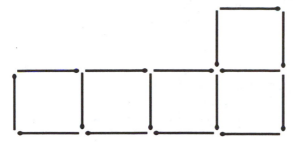

Figure 6.7. One of Katona's matchstick problems.

dealing superficially with the method of induction. My purpose was to give these pupils – and their teacher – a striking experience of the hazards of this attitude.

Wertheimer also pointed out that it is difficult or impossible to understand a principle that is "ugly" – that is, not revealing of certain important relationships in the matter to which it refers. An example would be a formula for the area that reduced to the simple formula only by some algebraic manipulation:

$$A = \frac{a-h}{1/h - 1/a}$$

Another way to put this, perhaps, is that the process that leads to understanding will fail to learn what cannot be understood. This process is unlikely to accept falsehood, even when propounded by authority, because falsehood is usually incomprehensible.[2] Of course, many facts are essentially arbitrary, so that "understanding," in the sense in which we are using the term, is impossible. A statement such as this – "The Battle of Hastings was fought in 1066" – must be accepted without understanding.

Katona (1940), a follower of Wertheimer, made several additional observations concerning the relation between understanding and learning. Katona taught subjects how to solve different kinds of problems under various conditions, some designed to promote understanding and others designed not to do so. Certain of his problems concerned rearranging squares made of matchsticks so that a different number of squares could be made from the same number of matchsticks with a minimal number of moves. For example, in Figure 6.7, make the 5 squares into 4 squares by moving only 3 sticks. The "no understanding" groups simply learned the solutions to a few such problems. The "understanding" groups were given a lesson in the relationship between number of matches, number of squares, and the number of matches that served as the border between two squares. The most efficient way to decrease the number of squares is to eliminate squares that share sides with other squares, so that the resulting squares touch only at their corners. For

[2] Scheffler (1965) makes related arguments.

example, the square in the lower right is a good one to remove. You can then build a new square on top of the second by using the bottom of the second square for the top side of the new one. Groups that learned with understanding of the common-side principle were able to transfer better to new problems, and they even "remembered" the solutions to example problems more accurately after a delay, even though these examples were not part of the lesson itself. The difference between Katona's demonstrations and Wertheimer's is mainly in the fact that subjects could see immediately whether they had solved Katona's problems or not, so they did not propose false solutions; hence, Katona did not observe inappropriate transfer of the sort observed by Wertheimer.

Katona also pointed out that learning with understanding was not the same as learning with "meaning." Two groups were given the number 581215192226 to memorize. One group was given a meaning for the figure: They were told that it was the number of dollars spent in the previous year by the federal government. This group recalled the figure no more accurately than a group told nothing about the figure's meaning. A third group, however, which discovered the inner structure of the number (a series starting with 5, 8, 12, and so forth) did recall it more accurately.

What is understanding?

Katona suggested that his results were due to the material's *organization*. The rule for the series gave subjects an organizing principle that they could use to aid memory. Hundreds of memory experiments since Katona's time have confirmed the fact that organized material is easier to learn than unorganized material, but organization does not seem to be what is most important. It is possible to organize material that we learn without understanding, as when chemistry students memorize the periodic table of the elements by grouping it into meaningless nonsense words. (One that sticks in my mind is "scati-vacrmnfeconicuznga.") I could just as well use this method to memorize mathematical formulas (or moral doctrines) that were false as those that were true.

What does understanding mean? Can we reduce understanding to knowing certain kinds of things? If so, what kinds?

Wertheimer suggested that understanding was the perception of "ρ relations." (ρ is the Greek letter "rho.") It is not clear what these relations are, except that they represent the "inner structure" of the problem. One possible explication of this theory rests on the work of Duncker (1945, discussed in ch. 4). Recall that Duncker described normal problem solving as a search for partial solutions or mediating phases. To use the more modern terms proposed by Newell and Simon (1972), we may think of the original tumor problem (ch. 4) as a *goal* (or end), and the discovery of the idea of weakening the rays as they pass through the surrounding tissue as a *means* to achieve that goal and simultaneously as a *subgoal* to be achieved through other means not yet discovered. Similarly, the parallelogram problem can be solved through the subgoal of making any nonrectangular parallelogram into a rectangle.

Perhaps a "ρ relation" is simply the relation between a goal and its subgoal, a relationship in which the subgoal serves the *purpose* of achieving the goal. Duncker suggests as much (p. 5): "[Knowledge of] the functional value of a solution is indispensable for the understanding of its being a solution." (By "functional value," Duncker means exactly this means–end, or subgoal–goal, relationship.)

The idea that understanding involves knowledge of purpose goes far toward explaining understanding. It helps us, for example, to see why the term "understand" is relative to some context, purpose, or goal. We can have partial understanding of some idea when we know the relationship of the idea to some goals but not others. For example, before I read a revealing article by Van Lehn and Brown (1980), I thought that I fully understood decimal addition. I found, however, that I was unable to answer a rather obvious question about decimal addition, "Why do we carry (regroup) rather than simply add up the numbers in a column whatever the sum (possibly putting commas between columns)?" Why do we not write the sum of 15 and 17 as 2,12? The reason given by Van Lehn and Brown is that, if we wrote totals in this way, we would violate the "cardinal rule" of our number system, the requirement that each quantity have a unique representation. This rule can be seen as a major goal – or purpose – that we have imposed on ourselves in the design of our number system. Even before I learned this, however, my understanding of some of the purposes of carrying was complete; for example, I did know that one reason for carrying, as opposed to simply writing a single digit and forgetting about the rest, was to "conserve quantity" – another (more crucial) goal imposed in the design of the number system.

Wertheimer, however, did not say that a ρ relation was just a relationship of purpose. Perhaps he was concerned that students might simply memorize that "the purpose of moving the triangle from one end to the other is to make the parallelogram into a rectangle," and so on, without knowing why each move serves its purpose. Perhaps, in order to understand something, we need to know more than the purpose of a particular idea. In an important recent work, Perkins (1986) suggests what else it is that we need to know. Understanding, Perkins states, involves knowing three things: (1) the structure of what we want to understand; (2) the purpose of the structure; and (3) the arguments about why the structure serves the purpose.

First, we must know the *structure* of the thing to be understood, the piece of knowledge, or what we shall (for reasons given shortly) call the *design*. We must know a general description of the design. Typically, this description refers to other concepts already known (or understood) for the relevant purpose. For example, $A = b \cdot h$ may be described *with reference to* the concepts "formula" (presumably already understood), "equality," and "variable." A full description would also indicate that *b* represents the base and *h* the height. Appropriate interpretation of the description is, practically always, facilitated by the use of at least one *model* or example in which the interpretation is given for a specific case.[3]

Second, we must know the *purpose*, or purposes, of the design: for example, to find the area of the parallelogram. The purpose also refers to still other concepts, such as "area" and the concept of "purpose" itself. So far, Perkins's theory fits well with the idea that the critical part of understanding is knowing purposes.

The third part of understanding, and the part that is new, is the group of *arguments* that explain how the design in fact serves the purpose. These arguments consist of other facts and beliefs. For example, in the case of the parallelogram, one argument explaining why the formula gives the area is that the parallelogram has the same area as a rectangle of the same base and height. Subsidiary arguments are relevant to each of these points: sameness of area, sameness of base, and sameness of height.

Perkins originally developed his theory for designs in general rather than knowledge in particular. A "design," as Perkins uses the term, is anything whose structure serves a purpose. It may be invented by people or it may evolve. In Perkins's theory, buttons, forks, and hands are designs; rocks and rainbows are not. Consider a pencil. One of its *purposes* is to write. Perhaps you have a wooden pencil with you (a *model*) that you can use to examine the *structure* of a pencil. What are the *arguments*? The pencil is soft, so that it can be sharpened (another purpose). The wooden shaft is (usually) hexagonal, so that the pencil does not roll off the table when you put it down (still another purpose). The pencil has an eraser on the end, so that . . . What other purposes might be served by the pencil's design? With this question, we can also criticize the ordinary pencil. It wears out. How can we change the design to prevent this? (The mechanical pencil.) Keep at it, and you will be an inventor, a designer.

Perkins's important insight was that *his* design – his theory of design – applied to knowledge as well: Hence the title of his book, *Knowledge as Design*. We can think of just about any kind of knowledge this way. The decimal system that we all labor over in elementary school is quite an impressive design – far superior, for example, to the Roman system of calculation. The theories and concepts discussed in this book, and in many other academic subjects, are also designs. Often the purpose of such designs is to explain something. In mathematics, designs often have the purpose of helping us to measure something.

The nature of arguments may be understood by thinking of them as *evidence*

---

[3] The danger here is that the interpretation will be too closely associated with a single model. The students described earlier who could not apply the formula to a parallelogram turned on its side might have been suffering from such an overly narrow description of the design, rather than from a more complete failure of understanding.

(defined as part of the search-inference framework). In thinking about the area of the parallelogram, for example, a student might simultaneously search for possibilities (possible formulas – perhaps ones already known that might be applied); evidence (properties of the figure that might provide a clue); and goals (actually subgoals, assuming that our student does not question the utility of the basic task itself). She might discover the formula for the rectangle (a possibility); the evidence that the parallelogram is visually similar to a rectangle (which would increase the strength of this possibility – for some students, perhaps increasing it enough that search would stop here); and the subgoal of making the parallelogram into a rectangle. This subgoal would in turn initiate a new process of thinking, inside, as it were, the main process.

By this account, a student understands the formula $A = b \cdot h$ when he has learned the following facts:

> The *purpose* is to find the area.
> The *design* is to use the rectangle formula, replacing one side of the paral-lelogram with the height.
> One *argument* is based on the subgoal (subpurpose) of making the parallel-ogram into a rectangle.
> The *design* for this subpurpose is to move the triangle from one side to the other.
> An *argument* for this subdesign is that when we do this, the area is unchanged.
> Another *argument* is that the base is unchanged and the height is unchanged.

This kind of analysis can be applied to other sorts of understanding, in-cluding the theory of actively open-minded thinking. If you understand this theory, you know that one *purpose* of the theory is to provide a standard for rational thinking, that is, the kind of thinking that will help us achieve our goals (or the goals we would have after reflection). The theory's *structure* is its description of thinking in terms of the search-inference framework and its prescription that search should be sufficient and that thinking should be fair to all possibilities. One *argument* was that thinking is often biased away from fairness and toward possibilities that the thinker already favors. Other ar-guments are being explicated as we proceed. *Models* of good and poor thinking were provided.

This analysis of understanding fits well with Wertheimer's and Katona's findings and with Wertheimer's arguments. Students who learn by solving a problem for themselves achieve understanding because the process of problem solving leaves just the knowledge sketched here. The "purpose" is the goal of the problem. The "design" is the possibility that is ultimately chosen. The "arguments" are the pieces of evidence discovered that support the possibility adopted.

Perkins's theory also suggests what *strategies* are the most useful for study-ing material in school and in the workplace: In general, it is useful to think of a piece of knowledge as a design and to ask about the purpose of the design, its structure, and the arguments that relate the structure to the purpose. The use of this strategy involves thinking about what one is learning, that is, searching for goals (purposes), for evidence (arguments), and for alternative possibilities (designs), and making inferences about the extent to which the evidence supports each possibility. Sometimes, the things we are asked to learn are not well supported and can be improved or replaced. The strategy of thinking as we learn is likely to encourage the discovery of such deficiencies. Students who insist on understanding do not learn simply because they are told that such and such is the truth: They resist false dogma. If they are given a questionable generalization to learn (such as the claim that all Communist states are aggressive), they will think of their own counterexamples (such as Yugoslavia).

Understanding plays an important role in problem solving, memory, and transfer. When a student solves a problem, she begins with a knowledge of the purpose, the goal of the problem. She seeks designs (possibilities) that will serve that purpose, and she also seeks arguments (evidence) for and against each design. When a student has understood the solution to an old problem with a purpose similar to the new one she is working on, the new purpose will evoke the memory of the old design and arguments. For example, a student who had understood the parallelogram problem will transfer appropriately to the *A* problems used by Wertheimer. The link between purpose and design serves as an appropriate retrieval cue for remembering the design. The subgoal of making the *A* figure into a rectangle may remind the student that the triangle was moved, which in turn may "tickle memory" enough to suggest moving the odd part. It is an interesting fact about problems in some areas of knowledge that the best retrieval cues are often purposes.

In solving the problems in Wertheimer's *B* group, the use of the goal as a retrieval cue may call forth the same knowledge as in solving the problems in the *A* group, but the search for arguments (evidence) will not succeed. The earlier arguments (about being able to move the part and not change the area) may be found, but they will not apply.

When students are asked to *recall* a solution to a problem that they already solved, they may be helped by trying to *solve* the problem as well as to recall it. If they understood the solution to the problem, they can solve it more easily than if they had learned the solution by rote. The purpose evokes the memory of the design and the arguments, just as in transfer to a new problem. In this way, understanding improves recall (as Katona found).

Perkins's analysis of understanding in terms of purposes, designs (and models), and arguments has several implications. First, this theory calls attention to the relationship between understanding and the use of evidence. Understanding involves knowing what a good argument is; we must have certain standards for this, and these standards are likely to change as we become more educated. A young child often accepts an argument if it is merely consistent with the possibility being argued for. An older child, in accepting the argument, often also insists that the argument be *more* consistent with this possibility than with some other possibility. It appears that understanding must be renewed as we become more sophisticated about arguments. There seem to have been no child prodigies in philosophy. This domain, by its nature, insists on the highest standards of evidence and therefore cannot be understood at all in an immature way.

Perkins's theory, like Wertheimer's, is also a remedy for a common misconception about the nature of understanding that is exemplified in the work of Ausubel (1963) and many others. The essence of Ausubel's theory is the idea that new knowledge becomes meaningful when relationships are established between new knowledge and old. Although Ausubel specifies that relationships must not be arbitrary in order for learning to count as meaningful, he fails to define "arbitrary relationships" with sufficient clarity to rule out mnemonically learned relationships (that is, relationships learned through special memorization techniques) that might hinder the acquisition of true understanding in Wertheimer's sense. Relationships of the sort indicated by Ausubel, for example, can just as easily be used to learn a falsehood (such as a formula stating that the area of a parallelogram is the sum of the lengths of the sides) as to learn the correct formula. Ausubel omits any consideration of purpose or evidence that a given element serves a purpose. These latter restrictions, as we have seen, seem to be required to account for Wertheimer's demonstrations – particularly his argument that the process of learning with understanding resists the learning of falsehoods.

To take another example, I once memorized a friend's phone number (545–1166) by finding "elaborative relationships" with "existing cognitive structures." After all, 1166 is 100 years after the Battle of Hastings, and 545 contains 55, which is the difference between 11 and 66 (and so forth – if I go on much longer, *you* will never forget the number either). Did I "understand" the number? Not unless my friend was a descendant of William the Conqueror and the phone company knew this. I just used some mnemonic tricks.

The neglect of purpose and arguments by Ausubel and others has important consequences for education and culture. Different theories suggest different kinds of education. Ausubel's theory suggests repeatedly asking the student such questions as "What does this remind you of? What is the similarity between this new concept and the old one? What is the difference?"

By contrast, Perkins's theory (and presumably Wertheimer's) suggests asking, "What is the *purpose*? What is the *design*? Can you give me a *model* or an *example*? What are the *arguments* for this design?" Asking these questions amounts to an effective strategy for understanding, a strategy useful to both students and teachers. The most important question here is perhaps, "What is the purpose?" It is one we should all ask more often than we do.

Rewards and goals

The cognitive psychology of learning is concerned largely with the acquisition of new knowledge and abilities: learning *that* such and such occurred; learning *that* such and such is true; learning *why* it must be true; and learning *how* to do something that we could not do before. When we have succeeded in such learning, we have additional tools, which we can use or not use at our discretion. A different kind of learning is learning *to* do things that we already know how to do: for example, learning to remember to be careful in our thinking, to take an interest in academic material, to be good citizens, or to be thoughtful of others. The real problem in learning to behave in these ways is usually that of developing the necessary goals and habits, rather than that of acquiring new abilities. Thoughtfulness is, before anything else, a matter of caring about the feelings of others and acting habitually in ways consistent with that caring. If a child does not learn to care about this, or does not develop such a habit of action, all the specific training in rules of manners or morals will be for naught.

Psychology currently provides some insight into the way in which such goals and habits are acquired, although we are far from having all the answers. We do know that behavior is sensitive to reward: Praise a child for some action, and the child is likely to repeat it. B. F. Skinner and others have tried to use this principle to explain all behavior. The idea that behavior is motivated by the desire for reward is indeed a powerful principle, hard to refute in any given case, because we can usually imagine some reward that could be operating as a motivation even when we cannot be sure that it is.

The desire for reward, however, does not seem to be the sole motivation for human behavior. We know, for example, that people often exert great effort to help others (chs. 19 and 20) or to study and develop their abilities in the absence of any apparent tangible reward. Of course, we could claim that such people are "rewarded" by the "satisfaction" of helping others or learning; in that case, rewards are still their motivation. If we say this, however, we are extending the concepts of "reward" and "satisfaction" so far that it becomes impossible to refute the claim that behavior is always motivated by reward. If this claim must be defended by making up some sort of "satisfaction" whenever the claim is challenged, the claim becomes empty. The sensible approach, I think, is to say that people have many personal *goals*, including the goal of helping others and the goal of learning, and that we do things because we believe they will help us to achieve some of our goals (Irwin, 1971). Some of our personal goals involve the pursuit of rewards (such as money, respect, and power), but other personal goals do not.

The use of reward as a motivation for learning has hidden costs. Lepper and Greene (1978) review a number of studies that show this. In a typical study, some nursery school children were given a chance to play with large felt-tipped pens, a new and intriguing activity for them. Some children were offered an "extrinsic" reward for drawing with the pens – a reward beyond the intrinsic pleasure of drawing with them. They were told that by drawing with the markers they would have a chance to win a "good-player award," a fancy paper certificate with a blue ribbon and a gold seal. Children in a control condition were not told this. All children were given an opportunity to use the markers, and each child in the experimental group was given the expected reward. (Half of the control subjects were given the certificate as well.) Two weeks later, the markers were again made available, along with other toys. The children in the experimental group, who had been told in advance about the reward before the first experience with the markers, used the markers the second time only half as much as the other subjects did. Most children enjoy the markers and, having played with them once, will play with them again. Those who were promised a reward, however, seem to have concluded that they did the original drawing in order to earn the certificate. This conclusion weakened their belief that they did the drawing out of intrinsic interest, and the motivation (personal goal) of drawing out of intrinsic interest was thereby reduced. This kind of study has been replicated extensively, and the general conclusions have been supported (Deci & Ryan, 1987).

The use of rewards in educational settings can undermine the intrinsic interest of the material. Traditionally, educators have used grades as incentives to get students to do desirable things such as reading books. We all know how this strategy has backfired for many students, who never develop real interest in intellectual work. As a general rule, the research on intrinsic motivation implies that educators should use the *minimum* extrinsic reward necessary to induce students to engage in the desired behavior.

Conclusion

Real knowledge is more than true belief. People cannot know things simply by memorizing them and believing them. When possible, students must try to understand why the truth is what it is. To do this, they must know not only the structure of the ideas to be learned but also their purpose, and the arguments for why the structure serves its purpose. Perkins's theory, which emphasizes purposes and arguments, provides a framework for learning and teaching that can be applied to all academic topics, including those discussed in this book.

The next two chapters are about two ideas of mental ability that many of us assume cannot be learned or taught: intelligence (ch. 7) and creativity (ch. 8). Intelligence is often discussed as though it is an inner quality that certain people are simply born with. If you do have intelligence, the theory goes, you will never get A's. The same goes for creativity: The creative artist, scientist, or thinker is supposed to be born with a certain special quality, or "genius," that results in great achievements like Shakespeare's or Einstein's. Creativity, this view says, is different from intelligence. It is a kind of emotional inspiration that comes from the subconscious mind, and too much thinking can be bad for it.

The research that psychologists have done on intelligence and creativity produces a different picture: What distinguishes creative "geniuses" from ordinary intelligent people is, in large part, their personal goals, their devotion to the creative tasks they have set for themselves. Intelligence itself is a function of personal goals and the kind of thinking we do, to a much greater extent than the "inner quality" idea implies. If this new view is true, then intelligence and creativity can, to a considerable extent, be taught and learned.

> Genius is rare because the means of becoming one have not been made commonly available.
>
> Luis Alberto Machado (1980)

The study of intelligence by psychologists has had tremendous influence on the way we conceive of good thinking and education. What is the relation between intelligence and actively open-minded thinking? Can good thinking increase intelligence? Let us first look at one of the central concepts of this field, the idea of the "intelligence quotient," or IQ.

Many of us grow up thinking that each person has a certain IQ that more or less represents that person's potential for intellectual achievement and effective thinking. We rank our acquaintances on this dimension; those with high IQs, we say, are "smarter" than others. If our own IQ scores are low, we conclude that we are not smart (and never can be). We assume that experts know exactly what IQ is and that certain tests can measure it. We know that individual test results can be misleading – that people who do not sleep well the night before the test or who are upset on the day of the test may not score as high as they could – but we still think that if we could create the perfect conditions for testing IQ such error would disappear.

None of these common ideas about intelligence is quite accurate. We need to rid ourselves of them and demystify the concept of intelligence. As a start, let us take a look at the history of the intelligence quotient (see Fancher, 1985).

The design(s) of IQ tests

Early attempts

Although all cultures seem to have some concept of intelligence, the systematic study of intelligence first began in England, in the nineteenth century. Sir Francis Galton (1822–1911), a cousin of Charles Darwin (and, ironically, a child prodigy who never seemed to live up to his own intellectual potential), was interested in the measurement of intelligence because he hoped to increase it through selective breeding of human beings, which he called *eugenics*.

105

If we had a good intelligence test, Galton thought, we could use it to pick out people who ought to be encouraged to reproduce (for example, by giving them prizes for having large families). In a few generations, the intelligence of the species, or at least of the nation where this plan had been adopted, would increase, to the benefit of all.

In his own work, Galton did little more than simply measure and tabulate individual differences in a variety of mental functions, such as reaction time and memory span. (In the memory span test described earlier in this book, in the section on primary memory in ch. 5, the subject is read a list of digits at a measured pace; the "span" is the number of digits that the subject can repeat back immediately without error.) Galton's ideas caught hold, however, and were pursued by others.

James McKean Cattell (1860–1944) was an American who followed Galton in gathering data on mental-test performance, including speed of color naming and judgment of the duration of a 10-second time interval. One of his students, Clark Wissler (1901) found that scores on such tests failed to correlate with class standing among Columbia University undergraduates. That is, students who did well on such tests received no better grades than students who did poorly (relative to others). Wissler took only a few measurements from each subject, and it is likely that his failure to find a correlation was partly the result of his measures being inaccurate. Charles Spearman (1904) found that simple tests, using more measurements for each subject, did correlate with teacher ratings of children's intelligence; however, Wissler had already convinced most workers that tests based on such simple processes were impractical.

The Binet Test

When Alfred Binet (1857–1911) set out to develop a practical intelligence test, he tried a different approach (Binet & Simon, 1905). His design also had a different purpose. Instead of selecting for intelligence, his test selected children who needed special remedial teaching. After compulsory schooling was instituted in France, it was noticed that many children were failing in the regular schools, some because they seemed mentally incapable of doing the work. Binet was a member of a commission charged by the government with making recommendations about how to educate such apparently retarded children in the public schools. Binet and Simon put together a test – made up partly out of other tests previously used by Binet to study intellectual development – for the purpose of distinguishing what we now call mild retardation from other possible causes of school failure. The structure of Binet's design was to use a test to select children who could not keep up in the regular classes but who might be able to benefit from other specially planned instruction.

Because Binet and Simon were convinced by Wissler's work that measurement of simple processes alone was insufficient, they tried to make up items to measure higher-level abilities, such as memory, judgment, the ability to maintain a set for a task (that is, a state of readiness to do the task as required), the ability to follow instructions, and the ability to check one's answers. Their criterion for a good test item was that it be able to distinguish older children from younger children; they thus assumed that intelligence, or at least its measurable products, increased with age. In order to meet this criterion, it may have been necessary to choose items that were largely dependent on the knowledge of specific facts, despite Binet's avowed aim of avoiding too much dependence on schooling and cultural background. Their final test included such items as identifying body parts, the memory-span test (again), finding rhymes, interpreting pictures, comparing the meanings of words, filling in missing words in a story, and answering questions about relative lengths of lines. Each item took less than a minute to give, and all could be scored relatively objectively, with very little judgment exercised by the tester.

The items were grouped so that the average child of a given age would pass most items in one group and fail most in the next group. Intelligence was therefore expressed in terms of level of development, corresponding roughly to the typical age at which a test would be passed (much as we now classify children by grade in reading and arithmetic). Binet recommended that a child who was 2 years behind be considered as subnormal.

Stern (1912) in Germany and Terman (1916) at Stanford University improved Binet's test by gathering more data on the youngest ages at which items are typically solved (allowing more accurate grouping of items) and defined the "intelligence quotient" (IQ) as the ratio of mental age to chronological age, multiplied by 100. Some new types of items were added, but the spirit was not changed. Terman's test, the Stanford Binet Test, after several more revisions, is still widely used.

Binet developed and partially implemented a program of "mental orthopedics" for those diagnosed by his test as lagging behind. This program included exercises intended to increase attention span - such as maintaining a "frozen" physical position for successively longer periods – and to increase speed. Binet's program was one of the first attempts to increase intelligence – to "teach children how to learn" - before asking them to do the real thing. This, of course, was part of his "design," which was quite different from Galton's.

Although Binet's methods of remediation were not evaluated, we now know that Binet's basic design was remarkably successful. First, IQ scores correlate well with school performance (Snow & Yalow, 1982).[1] More important, the IQ test is almost the *only* test that is useful for assigning children

---

[1] Of course, Spearman's perceptual tests did this too, but somehow they were forgotten, perhaps because Spearman himself was not concerned with this purpose.

to different educational programs (Cronbach & Snow, 1977; Snow & Yalow, 1982). Children who do poorly on the test actually learn more efficiently in a class that moves more slowly than the normal class, leaving nothing to be assumed, than they do in a regular classroom. Children who do very well on the test learn more efficiently in a class that moves quickly, letting the students fill in the gaps, than they do in a normal class. Appropriate use of the IQ test for such educational tracking, therefore, can benefit all students who are singled out for special education, whether that is slower or faster than the norm.[2]

When the IQ test took hold in the United States, it was widely assumed that it measured innate intelligence. One psychologist wrote, for example, "Intelligence tests have done much to show that all children are not created free and equal with respect to their mental abilities. A child's abilities are determined by his ancestors, and all that environment can do is to give opportunities for the development of his potentialities" (Pintner, 1931, pp. 520–521; quoted by Carroll, 1982). As far as I can determine, there was no empirical basis for this belief except for the finding that intelligence was correlated among family members, and the fact that environments are similar within families does not seems to have been given much consideration (see, however, the exchange between Lippman and Terman that appeared in the *New Republic*, 1922 and 1923, reprinted in Block & Dworkin, 1976, pp. 4–44). It was as though the Americans decided that Binet's test, which was developed for the purpose of selection for special education, could really serve Galton's purpose of selecting for intelligence.

In the last 70 years, several other kinds of tests have been devised, including some that do not depend on language and some that can be given to groups of people using pencil and paper alone. New kinds of items were developed for these tests, such as geometric analogies, mazes, and puzzles. "Aptitude" tests (tests designed to predict performance in a specific occupation or educational program) are also similar to IQ tests except that they make no effort to avoid material explicitly taught in school. Like IQ tests, they use many short items and objective questions that can be easily scored. Like most IQ tests, these tests measure the products of previous learning rather than learning itself.

Despite these modifications, most of our current tests are rather direct descendants of Binet's test and the conceptions behind it. As a result, practically all of them suffer from certain limitations. For one thing, Binet's test was designed to provide as much information as possible in as short a time as possible. It therefore consisted of items that could all be answered in a

---

[2] On the other hand, I know of no evidence that the use of tests allows us to improve on the judgments of teachers, when these are available, which can also be used for purposes of tracking. Also, there is reason to think that even better selection of students is possible with tests in which the students are actually asked to learn something during the course of testing (Campione, Brown, & Ferrara, 1982).

few seconds. It excluded difficult problems that might take an hour (or a week) to solve, or tests of actual learning and recall of material of the sort learned in school. Another constraint is imposed by the need for easy objective scoring: The test contains no items that require the subject to form a belief or make a decision in any sort of realistic context, even though such items might be useful in measuring what Binet called "judgment," which at times he regarded as the heart of intelligence. For example, the test contains no requests for moral reasoning or personal decision making. The selection of items was therefore dictated by practical needs first, and only secondarily by any clear theory of intelligence.

Factor analysis and the g factor

In the absence of a theory of intelligence, attempts were made to derive a theory from empirical study of IQ tests themselves. This effort has been largely associated with a single method of investigation: factor analysis, a statistical technique for inferring underlying causes from a pattern of correlations. Indeed, factor analysis, a method that is useful in other sciences (see Gould, 1981, ch. 6), developed largely in connection with the study of intelligence.

The roots of factor analysis go back to Spearman's 1904 paper, the same one in which he showed that perceptual measures correlated well with teachers' ratings of children's intelligence. The main point of that paper was to present and explain Spearman's finding that every measure correlated with every other measure. The ability to discriminate pitches of tones had a correlation of about .31 with ability to discriminate weights; sensory discrimination in general had a correlation of about .38 with teacher-rated intelligence; and so on.[3] (These particular correlations would be much higher if they are corrected, as Spearman recommended, for errors of measurement.) Spearman proposed that such correlations are the result of a general factor, g, or general intelligence. The tests are correlated with each other because they are all correlated with g. If the effect of g is removed from the correlations, most of the correlations fall to around zero. The methods of factor analysis, applied to this situation, allow us to postulate an underlying source of individual differences, a *factor* (such as g), and ask about the correlation between that factor and each subtest score within a test. This correlation is called a *loading* of that subtest on that factor. If the loading of two tests on a given factor is

[3] Correlation is measured on a scale ranging from 1, representing *perfect* correlation, to 0, representing *no correlation* at all, to −1, representing *perfect negative correlation*. If there a correlation of 1 between two variables, the highest ranked person on the first variable is the highest ranked for the second variable, and all the other rankings correspond perfectly. If there is a correlation of −1, the highest ranked person on the first variable is the *lowest* on the second. If there is a correlation of 0, the ranking on the first variable tells us nothing about the ranking on the other. A correlation of .38 indicates a modest but real relationship.

known, the effect of that factor on the correlation between the two tests can be removed by the technique of partial correlation.

Spearman and others applied the new technique to tests of the Binet type when these new tests appeared. The *g* factor was still found; that is, every item correlated with every other item. When the effect of the *g* factor was removed, *groups* of items correlated with each other.

For example, on the Wechsler tests (a popular series of IQ tests), items measuring knowledge of general information, ability to explain similarities, and vocabulary correlate with one another after *g* is removed, as do items measuring ability to do block puzzles, assemble objects, and code digits. It was proposed that these correlations could be explained by "group" factors, factors that characterized groups of tests. For example, the former correlations could be accounted for by a factor that we might call "verbal comprehension"; the latter might be accounted for by a "perceptual speed" factor. Names such as these did not come from any theory but from examination of the list of loadings on each factor found in the analysis.

Once it became apparent that a pattern of correlations among tests could be analyzed into several factors, a disturbing fact emerged. It turned out that there is more than one way to discover the factors and that different methods of analysis yield different results. Factor analysts do not necessarily have to begin by extracting the *g* factor and then go on to look for remaining group factors. Instead, as proposed by Thurstone (1938), they can seek a *set* of factors, in such a way as to maximize the number of zero or near-zero loadings in the entire table of loadings. This criterion, called "simple structure," would result in an analysis in which each factor had high loadings for a few tests and essentially zero loadings for others. It could then be said that those tests were the ones that measured that factor. When Thurstone applied this criterion to his own tests, he found seven major factors, which he called "verbal," "number," "spatial," "word-fluency," "memory," "perceptual speed," and "reasoning."

Given this sort of analysis, one could ask about the correlations among the factors themselves. Most studies indicate that the factors still intercorrelate, suggesting that there is a *g* factor in addition to the primary factors arising from a simple-structure analysis. The factors themselves, however, also seemed to fall into groups forming higher categories, such as "verbal" versus "performance" (a term used to include spatial, perceptual, and mathematical tasks). Each of these higher factors was thought to account for a group of correlations among lower factors. Vernon (1950) proposed a general factor at the top of the hierarchy. Below this, he thought, there were two factors - "verbal-educational" and "practical"; that is, the general underlying factor accounted for the correlation between these two factors. The verbal-educational factor was subdivided into a purely verbal factor, a number factor, and so on; the practical factor was subdivided into mechanical information, spatial ability, manual ability, and so on. Each of these factors could contain others; for example, the verbal factor contained a vocabulary factor, which could contain separate factors for different domains of vocabulary. In models such as this, the *g* factor sometimes disappeared. Whether one finds a *g* factor or not depends on the assumptions one makes.

A related problem is that the results one gets depend on the tests one chooses to analyze. Many factor analyses are based on test batteries in which all of the items are to be done in a limited time (Carroll, 1982, p. 102). In these cases, there will probably be a general factor that can be explained in terms of individual differences in speed of working. If some tests in the battery are untimed, however, their scores probably will not correlate at all with the others, so there will be two factors, one for the time-limited tests and one for the untimed tests.

An interesting example of this phenomenon comes from the work of Raymond Cattell (1963). He proposed a distinction between "fluid" and "crystallized" intelligence, which, under appropriate conditions, show up as superordinate factors. Fluid intelligence is measured by tests of speed, energy, and quick adaptation to new situations: for example, tests of memory span, copying symbols, and solving abstract problems (as in Raven's Progressive Matrices). Crystallized intelligence is measured by tests of vocabulary, social reasoning, and problem solving that depends on knowledge. Scores on fluid tests decline with age after adolescence, whereas scores on crystallized intelligence tests continue to increase throughout the life span. (Total score remains approximately the same over the life span, on the average, but this must be seen as a coincidence. If more of the crystallized items were used, IQ would increase with age, if fewer, IQ would decrease; we do not have a principle for deciding on the appropriate mixture.) Performance on fluid items, but not on crystallized items, is improved by administration of stimulant drugs (Gupta, 1977). Cattell suggests that crystallized intelligence is the result or product of prior fluid intelligence, since the former represents abilities useful in learning and the latter measures what has been learned. Although this seems to be an attractive conception of test design, as yet we do not possess a sufficiently developed theory to allow us to make up items that we know in advance will measure one type of intelligence or the other.

With all this, what happens to the idea that intelligence is a single thing that can be accurately measured (except for the error resulting from nonideal testing conditions)? Can Spearman's idea of general intelligence still be maintained? If there is such a thing, can it be measured?

Those who still believe in general intelligence (and many people do) point out that various intelligence tests all correlate highly with one another. Therefore, it is argued, some sort of true intelligence comes through, despite the variety of measures. But is the variety really that great? The various IQ tests, because of their ancestry, share many assumptions, which, together, lead to considerable overlap in the kinds of items used in different tests. Consider once again the kinds of tasks that are not usually included in IQ tests: learning new material of the sort taught in school; inventing or creating a novel product such as a poem or a machine; making moral arguments; memorizing large amounts of arbitrary material; or solving a real interpersonal problem. The evidence that we have suggests that correlations are not particularly strong when very different kinds of tasks are intercorrelated. For example, Wallach (1976) points out that measures of real-world creativity (such as ratings by critics, or number of awards, poems published, or inventions patented) do not correlate that highly with measures of academic performance or IQ. Similarly, Dörner and Kreutzig (1983) report essentially zero correlations between intelligence measures and success in very complex problem solving (such as governing an imaginary town successfully in a computer model). Ceci and Liker (1986) have found that IQ does not correlate with the ability to predict the odds on horses at the track among men with experience at making such predictions almost every day for several years.

It is quite possible, therefore, that the *g* factor is a statistical feature of IQ tests, resulting from a lack of variety in the selection of tasks. Most are short tasks that require some general knowledge, but not of specific school subjects, and that can be timed and easily scored for quality. There is no reason for use of such items other than tradition and convenience. (See Baron, 1985b, pp. 38–39, for other criticisms of the *g* factor.)

Is IQ inherited?

Most of the early workers who made up intelligence tests – except Binet – thought that intelligence was largely inherited. Furthermore, inherited abilities were assumed to be unaffected by styles of education or child rearing. A good IQ test, therefore, was designed to measure abilities that we could not easily imagine teaching. Of course, some abilities, such as verbal ability, were thought to be measured most easily by testing knowledge of material that everyone supposedly has a chance to learn, such as vocabulary. In the case of vocabulary, one could teach students the vocabulary to be tested. This is often done, but teachers have always considered it a subversion of the purpose of the test, because it is assumed that one is not teaching the underlying ability that leads to large vocabulary but is only coaching them on the specific test words. (The attitude of teachers is less clear when they try to convince their students to learn vocabulary on the grounds that "vocabulary is the best measure of IQ," to quote my 10th-grade English teacher. I wonder what his motive for saying this was. Did he really think that learning vocabulary increases intelligence, or did he just want to help us to do well on the IQ tests that would be so important to our academic careers?) For the same reason, extensive practice at items of the type used on a test is thought to make the test invalid.

Given this conception of what the test is supposed to measure, it is not surprising that much effort has been expended on finding out whether test scores are genetically determined. (Scarr & Carter-Saltzman, 1982, provide a review.) It is very hard to do good genetic research on human beings. In research on animals, we can separate littermates at birth, and we can compare littermates and other unrelated animals of the same species in identical environments. In humans, we cannot hold environment constant, and genetically related people tend to live in similar environments, no matter what pains we take to avoid this. Nor can we try to measure the relevant environmental differences and take account of their effect, because we do not know what these differences are. The evidence that we have concerning identical twins separated at birth suggests that IQ is somewhat heritable. Perhaps half of the variation in IQ is genetic; some say more, some say less. Of course, we must remember that IQ is not the same as intelligence, so the heritability of IQ and the heritability of intelligence itself are not necessarily the same.

Arguments about the inheritance of IQ have always been bitter (Block & Dworkin, 1976) because they get caught up in larger controversies concerning social issues. A particularly bitter one developed recently when it became known that American blacks score 10 to 15 points lower on IQ tests than whites, on the average, even though today most blacks attend school. Jensen (1969) suggested that this difference accounted for the overall failure of special education programs – designed to compensate for the disadvantages of living in poor neighborhoods – to raise the average IQs of blacks to the level of whites in the United States. Jensen argued that the difference in IQ between blacks and whites is itself genetically based and is therefore not something that compensatory education can correct. Now if IQ is not heritable at all, it follows that this difference in IQ is not genetic. If IQ is partly heritable, however, then the difference may or may not be genetic. The best guess about the heritability of IQ (Scarr & Carter-Saltzman, 1982) is that IQ *is* partly genetically determined but that average differences in IQ between different races are not genetically determined. The difference between the IQ scores of blacks and whites in the United States is probably due to such factors as low expectations of blacks for themselves; low expectations of others for them; prejudice; the effects of economic factors on intellectual development; poor nutrition and medical care; and the perpetuation of cultural and linguistic patterns that lead to low performance on academic tasks.

Even if intelligence is highly heritable, it might still be increased by education, nutrition, and other environmental influences. Measures of heritability tell us about the contribution of genes and environment to *differences* among people. If environments do not vary much, then the differences are due to genes; if environments vary a lot, then environment contributes to differences as well. Even if intelligence is now highly heritable, we might still increase it through education. High heritability does not mean that an ability cannot be changed, only that the things that could change it have not been put into effect for many people.

Sometimes we are tempted to assume that true intelligence is really a matter of biology. If the tests are affected by environment or education, we reason, well, they just are not perfect tests; better tests will not be affected that way. But why think this? Why do we want to have a single concept of intelligence as something purely biological? I see no good reason.

Other uses of the IQ test

The IQ test helps us predict which children will benefit most from which kind of instruction. Is there anything else it is good for? Some people would answer that it is a research tool, to be used for such purposes as making sure that two groups of subjects are equal in "general ability." Clearly, from what I have said, the IQ test cannot legitimately be used in this way. Two groups – for example, dyslexics and normal readers – may have identical scores on the same IQ test only because they excel or fail on different parts of the test. A different mixture of items in the test, one that included more of the strengths of one group and the weaknesses of the other, would show the groups to be unequal – and there is no well-founded basis for choosing any particular mixture of items.

In some situations, IQ tests can be used as stand-ins for cognitive tasks in general. For example, IQ tests have been used to study the fact that cognitive abilities among siblings decline with birth order (Zajonc & Markus, 1975); here, any measure of cognitive skills would do, and IQ happens to be available.

It has become clear that intellectual functioning is affected not only by genetics but also by other *biological* influences, such as childhood and fetal malnutrition; drugs of all sorts, including those taken by pregnant mothers; alcohol; environmental pollutants, such as lead; degenerative diseases such as Alzheimer's disease; normal aging; and possibly even physical exercise. In the study of such effects, we need a measure of that component of intelligence that is affected by current brain functioning.

IQ tests have been used for this purpose, but they are not entirely satisfactory. Parts of many IQ tests measure vocabulary and general knowledge, both of which are often preserved even in cases of fairly serious brain degeneration. More useful for testing current brain functioning are the sorts of simple measures that Jensen (1982) and others are now exploring, which deal with basic mental functions such as speed and accuracy of simple judgments and decisions. These measures have already proved their worth in medical research, even if they have not found a place elsewhere. A battery of such tests should be designed, because it is now clear that different biological manipulations affect different measures. For example, diazepam, or Valium (a tranquilizing drug), seems to affect our ability to learn but not our ability to recall what we have already learned (Clark, Glanzer, & Turndorf, 1979).

Beyond these research uses, IQ seems to play much the same role in our thinking as do many indices in economics, such as the Gross National Product

(GNP) and the Dow-Jones Industrial Average. We monitor rises and falls of test scores (including aptitude tests) as though they were some sort of measure of our national intelligence. These measures are proxies for things that are of real interest. Just as our real interest in economics does not concern the GNP but rather the material quality of the lives of our people, now and in the future, so our interest in a nation's intellect should not focus on test scores. Better measures are impractical or theoretically beyond our reach, so we use what we have, for the time being. The danger, in psychology as in economics, is that we may come to think of the measures themselves as representing our real concerns.

Cross-cultural research

It is generally found that people who grow up in cultures without Western-style schooling perform poorly on IQ tests and similar tasks, even when efforts are made to exclude tasks that the subject might have done in school. Recently, with increased but as yet not universal schooling in many cultures, it has become possible to ask whether these cultural differences are due to schooling itself or to other aspects of the cultures in question. In every case I know of in which this question has been asked, the answer is that the effects are due primarily to schooling. For example, Wagner (1974, 1978) found that rural Mexican children and both rural and urban children in Morocco showed no improvement with age in a serial memory task, unless the subjects had attended school. (The subjects had to remember the order in which the experimenter pointed to a series of pictures.) The schooled subjects showed the same age trends that had been found in other studies in the United States, trends of the sort usually explained in terms of increasing use of strategies such as rehearsal. Sharp, Cole, and Lave (1979) found that years of schooling, in contrast to age and sex, was also the main determinant of performance on most of the subtests of Thurstone's Test of Primary Mental Abilities (a kind of IQ test) and on a set of problems from Raven's Progressive Matrices (another IQ test). (Stevenson, Parker, Wilkinson, Bonnevaux, & Gonzalez, 1978, reached similar conclusions.)

It is noteworthy that most of these effects of schooling are on tasks that are not directly taught in school and that do not depend in any obvious way on the learning of reading, arithmetic, or other so-called basic skills. Whatever is responsible for these effects is, therefore, somewhat general. In some cases, as in Wagner's memory experiments, pains were taken to make sure that the materials were familiar to the unschooled subjects. Testing was often done by members of the subjects' cultural group.

The simplest interpretation of these results is that schooling teaches something more general than reading and arithmetic - something like thinking in a way that is more careful, thorough, and open to alternatives. This is not to say that the schooled children were marvelous thinkers, but that they may have been better thinkers than the unschooled children.

Critics of this interpretation have argued that the tasks used for the research are not representative of anything important, such as "intelligence," and that they reflect no more than arbitrary cultural biases. The results therefore have no more force than would a demonstration that Texans usually fail a test devised by Eskimos, in which most of the items consist of fine discriminations of different kinds of snow. Sharp and his colleagues (1979), for example, admit that their results are consistent with the claim that education fosters "the development of flexible problem-solving routines and rules for their application," but they feel that this impression is "an illusion produced by the narrow range of tasks, all of them derived from school contexts" (p. 82). Cole, in his reply to comments, indicates that more valid tasks would sample domains of work that are relevant to the culture. "Do rural Yucatecans who have been to school more rapidly adopt advantageous strains of corn?" (p. 112).

What Sharp and his colleagues seem to mean when they say that the tasks are "derived from school contexts" is that the tasks are abstract and novel. These researchers would grant that schooling might help people perform such tasks. They would argue, however, that the ability to solve abstract, novel problems, though an ability highly valued by our own culture, may not be seen as of particular value in other cultures (Laboratory of Comparative Human Cognition, 1982, p. 688 and n. 11). They seem to deny the possibility of a cross-culturally valid conception of intelligence. In particular, they seem to deny the possibility that people can learn to think in a way that will help them to achieve their own goals.

At issue is what we take intelligence to be. Many cross-cultural psychologists and others (for example, Sternberg, 1985) seem to take intelligence to be a matter of adaptation to one's environment: hence the emphasis on tasks that the culture does. Any other emphasis, it seems to these workers, puts us in the position of using our own cultural standards to make judgments about the value of other people.

In reply, I note that making a judgment about the level of intellectual abilities in a certain group is not the same as making a judgment of the value of the people in that group in any other sense – although we must of course be wary of slipping into this error. In fact, formulating such judgments may be a necessary part of any program to help people make the most of their capacities to achieve their own rational goals and therefore, in the end, may be a sign of respect for humanity rather than arrogance.

Further, intelligence has to include more than the ability to adapt to one's environment. We know, after all, that we cannot prepare people fully to cope with their environments by giving them specific knowledge, because we cannot fully anticipate their environments. If people are to be able to perform un-anticipated tasks that life presents to them, they will need some sort of general intellectual abilities. This is certainly as true today for members of rural societies throughout the world as it is for our own. The use of abstract and novel tasks as criteria is therefore partly justified by the role of these tasks as proxies for unanticipated tasks that people will be called on to do, such as (I hope) to decide among political candidates on the basis of abstract statements that the candidates make or to decide whether to adopt new agricultural methods.

The whole idea of adaptation, to tasks that are anticipated or not anticipated, is, I think, a stand-in for some other concept, such as goodness of life. The idea of adaptation seems sufficiently neutral and noncommittal to allow us to talk about other cultures without worrying much that we are imposing our own values on them; however, this is an illusion. It is simply not clear that the average Yucatecan, made aware of other possibilities, would want nothing more than to be "adapted" within the culture of Yucatán – that is, to have a good corn crop, or whatever else is considered desirable there. To assume that only the current values of foreign cultures are relevant to their people's personal decisions about the value of intellectual abilities and traits is, I think, as presumptuous as it is to assume that only our own current values are relevant. All people, whatever their culture, must in the end face squarely the question of what it is rational to want both in themselves and in others as thinking beings.

What is intelligence?

Defining intelligence

The confusion about the meaning of intelligence that we have noted in our examination of the debate concerning IQ shows that we need to define intelligence carefully before we try to argue about it. We also need to ask ourselves, as I noted earlier, why we want such a concept at all, or, in other words, what is the purpose of the design we call "intelligence." Let us begin with the problem of definition.

In ordinary speech, we use the word "intelligence" to describe several different sorts of things. Sometimes we speak of intelligence as a property of the way something is done: "He acted with great intelligence"; "She handled that problem in a really smart way." In such contexts, we are using the word "intelligence" much as we use the word "grace": "They handled that awkward situation with grace." In such contexts, intelligence and grace are both being thought (and spoken) of as *properties of behavior*.

Sometimes, instead of focusing on behavior, we speak of *results* as revealing intelligence, meaning (roughly) that the result is a "good idea," something that seems to have been *arrived at* intelligently. We might say, for example, "This is an intelligent book." This is really a derived sense of the term, since it still depends on the concept of intelligence as a property of behavior. The result (book) is intelligent because the author behaved intelligently when he wrote it. Intelligence as a property of behavior is still the underlying concept in statements like these.

Finally, we sometimes speak of intelligence as a property of people: "She's so intelligent!" Intelligence as a property of people is what the IQ test tries to measure, and, as we saw earlier, we tend to assign this property to people on the basis of IQ scores. Speaking of people as "being intelligent" is also using the term in a derived sense; the underlying concept is, again, that of intelligence as a property of behavior. Nobody can behave intelligently all the time, because we all make mistakes, so none of us possesses the property of intelligence in an unvarying, permanent way, in the same sense as that we are tall or short. It probably makes better sense to say that people behave intelligently in some situations but not in others. (Indeed, this is probably true of most people.) If we are discussing how people's intelligence differs, then we are really talking about differences in behavior. One person is more intelligent than another only if the former behaves consistently more intelligently than the latter.

Let us now return to the other question posed at the beginning of this discussion: What is the purpose of the concept of intelligence? What do we want to use it for?

One reason we need a definition of intelligent behavior is the cultural debate itself. If we find that a particular cultural change, such as schooling, affects certain abilities, we want to know whether those abilities are worth improving. Intelligence involves standards, but not just for our own society.

I described one way of defining intelligence for this purpose in my book *Rationality and Intelligence* (1985b, p. 13), where I said that, roughly speaking, intelligence consists of *those general abilities that help people to achieve their goals, whatever those goals may be, in any real environment.*

"General" means definable in any environment, for any person. (For example, the ability to discriminate among musical pitches is not "general," because it is not definable in the deaf.) This definition therefore excludes a great many abilities that by their very nature are restricted to certain domains, such as many of the abilities discussed by Gardner (1983), particularly those he calls "linguistic intelligence," "musical intelligence," "spatial intelligence," and "bodily-kinesthetic intelligence." Gardner shows how special talents often result from development in only one of these domains. I prefer not to regard them as part of intelligence but as more specific abilities. If such abilities were counted as parts of intelligence, it seems to me that there would be no need for a concept of intelligence at all, because intelligence would then be the same as "all human abilities." Such special abilities seem to have more to do with *expertise* (discussed in ch. 4).

I think we can say that certain abilities that constitute intelligence, such as mental speed, are fixed, at any one time, in individuals. Let us call these "fixed" abilities *capacities*. Capacities can be contrasted with *dispositions*, which are not fixed, at any one time, in individuals, but are learned tendencies to behave in certain ways. The tendency to search thoroughly, when there is sufficient time, and the tendency to be fair to all possibilities, which I have identified as so important to good thinking, help us to avoid errors in any environment. If schooling inculcates these dispositions, then schooling can be said to "increase intelligence" by making people *think more rationally* - that is, in closer conformity with a prescriptive model of thinking. Good thinking is part of intelligence because it helps people to achieve their goals. Capacities, such as a good memory or a high level of mental speed, also help people achieve their goals and are also part of intelligence, but they are not the only part.

In thinking about the question of what intelligence *is*, it is helpful to distinguish two different kinds of answers to that question: an answer that provides a criterion and an answer that provides an explanation. A *criterion* is a rule for distinguishing intelligence from other things (such as knowledge, skills, and character). This is what I have given so far in my "definition" of intelligence. An *explanation* is an answer to a question about how something works. In the case of intelligence, an explanatory theory will tell us just what the relevant general abilities are and how they improve the chances of success in achieving rationally chosen goals.

We must be careful to distinguish criteria from explanations. Many accounts of intelligence or creativity are criteria masquerading as explanations. For example, to say that an intelligent person is good at "sifting out relevant from irrelevant information" (Sternberg, 1985, ch. 11) does not tell us much about how the person does it. By analogy, we might define success at investing in the stock market as "buying low and selling high." Surely this is a reasonable criterion, but as we noted earlier, it does not tell us the specifics of how a good investor operates.

Capacities and dispositions

Psychologists have some ideas about the answer to the explanatory question. Cognitive psychologists have identified a number of apparent capacities that seem to differ from person to person. They have also found some suggestive evidence about dispositions. Because this is an active area of research, I shall not attempt a complete account but shall only give an example of each type (but see Baron, 1985b).

One characteristic of intelligent people is that they can think of things. They can recall things that they look for in their memories. Such an ability is obviously relevant to the success of any kind of search process that involves memory.

Psychologists have found some evidence that people differ in the speed with which they can discover items in their memories – even very familiar items such as the names of printed letters. For example, Hunt (1978) selected two groups of subjects from among University of Washington undergraduates; one group had relatively high scores on an admissions test similar to the Scholastic Aptitude Test (SAT), and the other group had relatively low scores. These subjects did an experiment in which they had to say whether two letters of the alphabet were the same or different in *name* – a "name-match" task. The high scorers had faster reaction times in this task. The two groups did not differ, however, in the reaction time for matching letters *physically*. In the physical-match task, the letters *A* and *a* would be responded to as "different," although they would be the same in the name-match task. The simplest explanation of this result is that the groups differ in the speed of retrieving the names (or identities) of the letters from memory in the name-match condition. In the physical-match condition, no memory of letter names is required: Chinese people who did not know the English letters could presumably do the task nearly as well as the subjects. (See Baron & Treiman, 1980, for other explanations of these results.)

Such capacities are very likely determined by genetic and physiological factors rather than by learning. They seem to be affected by drugs (see, for example, Gupta, 1977). Most important, it seems that they *cannot* be improved by practice *in general*. As we saw in chapter 5, skills do not seem to improve in general. They improve only in the situations in which practice is provided.

What about dispositions? It may help to think of these as *cognitive styles*. We may each have a distinctive "style" of thinking, or doing tasks. There may be properties of these styles that are relevant to intelligence. Moreover, some styles may be learned, and under our control.

The style dimension called *reflection-impulsivity* (Kagan, Rosman, Day, Albert, & Phillips, 1964), studied mostly in children, is an example. "Reflective" children are those who choose to be careful at the expense of speed. Impulsive children do things quickly but make many errors. One task used to measure this dimension is the Matching Familiar Figures Test (MFFT). Figure 7.1 shows a typical item from this test. The task is to pick the one figure of the six on the bottom that exactly matches the standard figure on top. In this task, children who answer very quickly (within 4 to 10 seconds) tend to make many errors (one or two per item) before getting the right answer, and children who answer slowly (within 30 to 40 seconds) tend to make few errors (less than one per item). There is a negative correlation between speed and accuracy. The "impulsives" are the children whose answers are fast and inaccurate; the "reflectives" are the children whose answers are the reverse.

Reflectives are more likely to be actively open-minded thinkers than impulsives. Reflectives reduce their error rate by searching thoroughly for possibilities other than the first one that looks like the standard and for evidence that possibilities that seem to match actually do not. The task itself, however, is not one that is closely related to most people's personal goals. Impulsivity may therefore result from lack of desire to give correct answers in the task

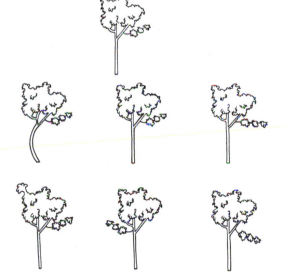

Figure 7.1. Sample items from Matching Familiar Figures Test. Reprinted with permission from Jerome Kagan.

rather than from a general tendency not to search thoroughly when the task is important. The task is perhaps best seen as measuring habits of thinking that are so general that they manifest themselves even when personal goals are not involved.

Reflectives tend to be older, to score higher on IQ tests (even when the tests are timed, but especially when they are not), and to be less prone to disruptive behavior in the classroom (Messer, 1976). These results are consistent with my theory that most people search too little rather than too much in their thinking. That would explain why greater search generally improves performance.

Children can be trained to be more reflective (see, for example, Baron, Badgio, & Gaskins, 1985), and such training seems to improve performance in school tasks. Part of this effect may result from the children's being taught the value of actively open-minded thinking. Such thinking takes time, but it does reduce errors.

Conclusion

We have seen how the IQ concept has distorted our understanding of thinking. It has encouraged us to believe that the only general determinants of good thinking are capacities, and this attitude has led to the neglect of general dispositions. It has limited our attention to those abilities concerned with answering questions that require no more than a minute or two of thought and that can be objectively scored. Although IQ tests must be considered a practical success in some of their uses, they have not provided us with a theory of what they are trying to measure or why we should be interested. The development of such a theory is a more reflective enterprise. Data cannot give us the answer.

I have suggested a definition of intelligence that reflects the purpose of the concept: Intelligence consists of those general abilities that help people achieve their goals. When we define intelligence in this way, we see that it includes abilities that lead to understanding, rational beliefs, and good decisions. Actively open-minded thinking is therefore part of intelligence – a teachable part – even though IQ tests are not designed to measure it.

What about creativity? Is it totally different from this, or does it, too, have something to do with actively open-minded thinking?

Actively open-minded thinking – search and inference that are thorough and fair – is part of intelligence because it helps us to achieve our goals. Creativity, we tend to assume, is different from intelligence – inborn, mysterious, unanalyzable, unteachable. To see if this is true, let us look at what psychologists have learned about creativity by studying the work of artists, inventors, and scientists and by studying creativity in the laboratory.

What distinguishes creative invention from other kinds of thinking? Before we can answer this, we must answer two other questions. First, what do we *mean* by invention? Second, what accounts for it? With respect to the definition, Perkins (1981) argues that creative products are *novel* and *successful* in achieving their purpose. Novelty is what makes creative problem solving different from ordinary problem solving. When a student solves a problem in Calculus 1, it is a problem that has been solved many times before by other students, yet Newton (or Leibniz) was considered a genius partly for having originally thought of and solved the very same problem for the first time.

Note that "novelty" is a relative term. The wheel may have been invented by several different cultures, independently of each other. From the point of view of humanity, only the first invention was novel, but from the point of view of each culture all of them were. Children – almost as a rule – "discover" many ideas on their own, without knowing that the ideas are already part of their culture (for example, the fact that one gets the same answer by counting objects from left to right as from right to left). These ideas are novel for the children.

Still, the true inventor is one who *tries* to be novel within a certain social context. Newton, Leibniz, Pasteur, Beethoven, Shakespeare, and Edison were not simply trying to do their lessons well. They were all trying very hard to do something new and different from anything known in their world. Perkins suggests that the *effort* to do something novel is in fact the main feature that distinguishes creative genius from ordinary intelligence. Invention is not something that just happens without making the effort, and most of us do not make the effort very often.

Novelty usually involves the pursuit of a novel goal. Therefore the "search for goals" is critical in invention. Alexander Graham Bell invented the idea of the telephone, as well as the telephone instrument itself. Each poet and composer takes on a task, in each work of art, that is at least slightly different from any task attempted before.

Novelty by itself is not enough, for pure novelty without success is nothing but playfulness or madness. True invention must be successful as well as novel. Even composers who have written music by sitting down at the piano blindfolded and hitting keys at random were at least successful in their purpose of making music in a new way or, perhaps, of shocking their audience (the first few times, at any rate).

Personal testimony and the role of the unconscious

What accounts for invention? Many writers on the subject have suggested that great and unusual ideas result from great and unusual thought processes, frequently involving the unconscious mind. It is often claimed (or implied) that the unconscious mind is aware of possibilities or evidence that the conscious mind is not yet aware of. It is as though there were, in the creative person, two different people, both working on the same problem, but one of them (the unconscious) sometimes doing it more quickly. Of course, it is the conscious mind that must ultimately produce the solution. Such writers conclude that the use of the unconscious in problem solving requires not only that it be given free rein but also that, after it has done its work, it is somehow encouraged to communicate its results to the conscious mind. This communication could occur through dreams or reveries or through direct messages: "We now interrupt this broadcast to give you the solution to the problem you were working on yesterday!"

When great creators describe how their ideas came to them, they provide some support for the idea of unconscious work. For example, in 1865 the chemist Friedrich August von Kekulé had been attempting to discover the chemical structure of benzene. He fell asleep and had a strange dream about snakes twisting and turning and, ultimately, chasing their own tails. This gave him the idea of a ring, which he immediately recognized (apparently in the dream) might be the solution to his problem. In fact, he was correct; the benzene molecule contains a ring of six carbon atoms. Many have concluded from this that Kekulé's unconscious mind discovered the solution to the problem and gave it to him in the form of a symbol.

The most celebrated example is the discovery by Poincaré, the French mathematician, of the theory of "fuchsian" groups and functions, a discovery that he described at length in a lecture to the Société de Psychologie in Paris (Poincaré, 1913; see also Hadamard, 1945, for an excellent discussion). (For present purposes you do not need to know what fuchsian groups and functions are, except that mathematicians consider this an important discovery.) Poincaré had been working on the problem intensely for some time. He describes how the solution came to him:

One evening, contrary to my custom, I drank black coffee and could not sleep. Ideas rose in crowds; I felt them collide until pairs interlocked, so to speak, making a stable combination . . . It seems, in such cases, that one is present at his own unconscious work, made partially perceptible to the over-excited consciousness, yet without having changed its nature.

During this night, he succeeds in building up one class of the functions he seeks.

Just at this time, I left Caen, where I was living, to go on a geologic excursion under the auspices of the School of Mines. The incidents of the travel made me forget my mathematical work. Having reached Coutances, we entered an omnibus to go some place or other. At the moment when I put my foot on the step, the idea came to me, without anything in my former thoughts seeming to have paved the way for it, that the transformations I had used to define the Fuchsian functions were identical with those of non-Euclidean geometry. I did not verify the idea; I should not have had time, as, upon taking my seat in the omnibus, I went on with a conversation already commenced, but I felt a perfect certainty. On my return to Caen, for conscience' sake, I verified the result at my leisure.[1]

Hermann von Helmholtz, the great nineteenth-century psychologist, physicist, and physiologist, described his own good ideas as "happy thoughts." In his experience, these happy thoughts

never came to a fatigued brain and never at the writing desk. It was always necessary, first of all, that I should have turned my problem over on all sides to such an extent that I had all its angles and complexities "in my head" and could run through them freely without writing. To bring the matter to that point is usually impossible without long preliminary labor. Then, after the fatigue resulting from this labor had passed away, there must come an hour of complete physical freshness and quiet well-being, before the good ideas arrived . . . The smallest amount of alcohol seemed to frighten them away. (Quoted in Woodworth & Schlosberg, 1954, p. 838)

Several nineteenth-century inventors, artists, and poets also noticed that their good ideas tended to come after they had spent an interval of time away from the problem they were working on (Carpenter, 1876). Wallas (1926), summarizing these accounts, suggested four stages of creative thought: *preparation, incubation, illumination*, and *verification*. The *preparation* is the extensive, usually fruitless, work mentioned by both Poincaré and Helmholtz. *Incubation* is the period away from the problem. *Illumination* is of course the insight itself, and *verification* is the checking that is done afterward. Patrick (1935, 1937) found that poets and pictorial artists also commonly report a stage of incubation. Patrick noticed, however, many reports that the problem or idea returns during the period of incubation, so it cannot clearly be said that all of the work done during this time is unconscious.

In experiments on incubation (such as that by Olton, 1979) subjects were asked to take long breaks during the solving of some problem, such as a chess problem. They were asked not to work on the problem during the break, and in some experiments they were even given another task to do in order to

[1] The translation of these passages is from Newman (1956, pp. 2044–2045).

prevent such work. Most experiments have shown no beneficial effect of incubation; the subjects take just as long to solve the problem after they return as do other subjects who continued working instead of being interrupted. Some experiments have shown small beneficial effects. If unconscious work occurs during the break, we conclude, it is not often very useful.

Even the small effects that are sometimes found after the pause do not necessarily indicate unconscious thinking. There may be other explanations: (1) The interval of rest may do nothing more than provide rest, so that the thinker returns to the problem in a state of "freshness," as Helmholtz suggested. (2) Another effect of the interval may be to allow the thinker to give up fruitless approaches and try new ones. Often, when we have put a lot of effort into one approach, we want that approach to succeed, and we are unwilling to give it up in favor of some alternative. (Later, we shall see a similar, and important, phenomenon in decision making, called the "sunk-cost effect.") When time passes, this attachment may weaken. (3) Finally, the interval of rest may allow extra opportunity for "suggestion from below," as in the case of Archimedes (mentioned in ch. 4).

What about Kekulé's dream of the snake chasing its tail? What about Poincaré's insight as he stepped onto the omnibus? Do not these indicate unconscious work? Again, not necessarily. Kekulé's dream might have in fact been an example of suggestion from below. The *cause* of the dream might have been nothing more than his previously seeing the undulations of the flames in his fireplace. The dream might have suggested the solution just as though someone else had shown Kekulé a picture of a snake chasing its tail for an entirely unrelated purpose. (The many possible cases in which solutions were *not* found in dreams are not recorded for posterity, and it may well be that cases such as this dream of Kekulé's are quite rare.)

Poincaré's discovery is more difficult to explain. One possibility (Perkins, 1981, p. 72) is that he did not remember it correctly. Perhaps he had actually begun to think about the problem but was unaware (or forgot) that he had done so. Woodworth and Schlosberg quote a chemist who describes how forgetful he became when he was deeply involved in thinking about a problem in chemistry: "I remember one morning I took my bath, shaved, took another bath, and in reaching out for a dry towel suddenly became aware that this was my second bath and that my mind had been deeply concentrated on a problem for half an hour" (1954, p. 839).

Another possibility is that the solution really did occur to him out of the blue but that no unconscious work occurred, other than the production of the idea itself, which may have occurred in a single step. The experience would be similar to something that happens to many of us when we try without success to recall a name, only to have it pop into our head (without any special effort) 5 minutes after we needed it, or when, while we are reading a mystery story, we suddenly realize out of the blue that the murderer must have been the butler after all. Such phenomena as these are indeed mysterious and special – as are some of our more commonplace achievements, when we think about them – but they are not peculiar to creativity, and they do not require the existence of the kind of extended unconscious trial-and-error processes of the sort Poincaré suggested.[2]

In sum, although it is possible that unconscious work contributes to creativity, the reasons for believing that it does that have been advanced so far all have other, more plausible, explanations. This by no means does away with the mysteries surrounding the creative process. Ordinary problem solving, whether it occurs in great inventors or ordinary students, still presents many mysteries to us, and much work remains to be done in understanding how it happens.

Search, goals, and self-criticism

What is crucial for success in creative tasks? The theory of actively open-minded thinking suggests three possibilities: thoroughness in searching for possibilities; thoroughness in searching for goals (or search for certain goals as opposed to others); and sufficient self-criticism and revision. Let us see what evidence about that the psychologists have found.

First, consider search for possibilities. Osborn (1953) and others have argued that a major impediment to creation is insufficient search for possibilities. If we are too self-critical during the phase of idea generation, it has been argued, we inhibit ourselves from thinking of our best ideas. We must overcome our inhibitions and "brainstorm" before we criticize and select.

Wheeler's footprint problem (1979, p. 11) seems to support this point. Here is the problem: A thief escaping from a house he has just robbed leaves footprints that appear to have been made by a pair of tennis sneakers worn down only on the inside right heel and the inside left toe. What does this tell you about the thief? *Stop reading, and think about this.* Most people get fairly quickly to the idea that the nature of the footprints must indicate participation in some sort of sport, but which one? Here, most of us are stuck. One way to get unstuck is to go through the alphabet, thinking of all of the sports that begin with each letter. In solving this problem, in other words, sheer systematic search, without self-criticism, will pay off, if we possess the critical knowledge.[3]

But how typical is this for creative problem solving? Johnson, Parrott, and Stratton (1968) asked subjects to solve various problems that require creativity, such as thinking of a title for a one-paragraph plot summary or filling in the dialogue for the last square of a four-square cartoon. Some subjects were asked to give a single answer; others were asked to think of several answers – that is, to brainstorm – and then choose the best. Judges rated the

---

[2] They are also rare. See Read and Bruce (1982).

[3] The letter F is the crucial one. The best answer is fencing.

quality of each answer (according to a list of specific criteria) that each subject produced.

A comparison between the mean (average) quality of the answers given by the single-answer group with the mean quality of the *best* answers (in the judges' opinion) in the brainstorming group revealed that the brainstorming group did better. They produced more solutions rated as "superior" by the judges. The members of this group often had not selected these answers, though, as their "best" or final during the test. Their own preferred answer was, on the average, no better (in the judges' view) than the answer produced by the single-answer group. It does not appear from this study that brainstorming before selecting one's own answer is any more effective than simply trying to think of the best answer from the outset. (We should note a possible flaw in this study. Subjects were given 7 minutes to do each problem, which may not have been enough time. Some subjects had complained, in an earlier experiment, that 5 minutes was too short a time.)

We might think that in group situations, where the combined judgment of the group is available to help people pick the "truly best" answer, brainstorming would be more useful. Studies of brainstorming in group situations, however, also have yielded mixed or inconclusive results (Stein, 1975, ch. 13): Sometimes brainstorming seems to help, but at other times it seems to hurt.

Perkins (1981, ch. 5) made a study of poets thinking aloud. He found that poets judged by experts to be very good poets do not consider any more possibilities, when they are choosing words for poems, than other poets who are not so highly regarded. Both groups usually consider only one or two alternatives to the word they choose. The more successful poets, though, are *capable* of thinking of appropriate words more quickly when asked to think of words that meet a certain condition (for example, adjectives describing the properties of an apple: "red," "round," and so forth). Instead of searching for other words that meet this sort of general requirement, Perkins found that the successful poets give themselves more complex or specific instructions about what kind of word they are looking for: for example, not just "a noun that rhymes with rain" but "a one-syllable noun that rhymes with rain and refers to something that is undesirable and lasting." They apparently used their extra fluency at thinking of appropriate words to think of *any* words that met these more demanding constraints, rather than *many* words that met simpler ones.

Of course, all of Perkins's subjects were people who took poetry seriously. If he had compared the working methods of high school students who got A's on a poetry-writing assignment to those of students who got C's, he might have found that the A students did consider more possibilities. Similarly, if Johnson, Parrot, and Stratton had designed their experiment to be done as homework rather than requiring the subjects to sit in a laboratory (where they had no amusements to distract them), the researchers might have found that when left to their own devices subjects search too little. Nonetheless, it would appear that for those who take their task seriously, insufficient search for possibilities is rarely, if ever, a big problem.

How important is the search for goals in creative work? Getzels and Csikszentmihalyi (1976) carried out a study of the creative methods used by male art students at the School of the Art Institute of Chicago. The subjects were asked to make a still-life drawing based on an arrangement of objects that the experimenters provided. The drawings were rated by expert judges. Those students whose work was more highly rated had spent more time studying and manipulating the objects before beginning their drawing. While working, the more successful artists also made more frequent rearrangements of the objects, changes of medium, and so on. Getzels and Csikszentmihalyi called the behavior of the more successful artists *problem finding* (as opposed to *problem solving*). "Problem finding" seems to be the same as what I meant earlier by "search for goals." The successful artists seemed to search more thoroughly for goals not only as they started their task but as they were carrying it out.

Perkins (1981, p. 186) puts it nicely: "Any creative activity involves narrowing down. You start with nothing, or nothing but a very general idea, and finish with a very particular product. As you proceed, more and more constraints emerge. The work so far, unless revised or abandoned, limits the possibilities of the work to come." Critical for creative achievement is, apparently, the search for constraints – ultimately a search for what one is trying to do.

Getzels and Csikszentmihalyi asked all of their subjects, after their drawings were finished, "Could any of the elements in your drawing be eliminated or altered without destroying its character?" The ones whose drawings were more successful tended to answer yes to this question. (These subjects were also rated as more successful 7 years later.) It appeared from this and other findings that successful artists regard their work as in a constant process of revision. To quote Miss Manners on social education, "A child with a living parent is never finished" - and so it is for works of art.

Put another way, it seems that successful artists are more self-critical. They seek alternative possibilities to what they have done, new goals, and evidence of flaws. When they find such evidence, they respond to it; they do not ignore it. Such a description fits many well-known artists and composers. Beethoven's manuscripts are full of crossing out and rewriting. Bruckner and Brahms revised their early work throughout their careers. J. D. Salinger is said to have reworked every sentence over and over.

What about Mozart, though, who supposedly conceived of pieces in an instant and simply wrote them down? What of the great traditions of musical improvisation such as jazz and Indian classical music? To a large extent, the creative work of the jazz musician is done long before a performance begins. The piece might not be written down like classical music, but the performer has spent hours and hours "practicing." For a jazz musician, this is not simply playing scales and exercises. It is experimenting with various kinds of chord progressions, different ways of ornamenting a chord or a melody. Here, there is a great deal of revision and trial and error. The product of all this work is not, however, a single piece of music but rather a set of more or less automatic patterns that the musician calls forth in a performance. A jazz musician's product is not a piece of music but the musician's own *skill*. The same may have been true of Bach, Mozart, and Vivaldi, composers who seemed to write quickly and revise little. It may also be true that some of these composers *did* a fair amount of revising, but in their heads, before they wrote anything down. Mozart, for one, was known to have a prodigious memory for music; he could write down long pieces after one or two hearings. Beethoven may simply have relied more on the paper and less on his memory.

In other domains, the evidence for self-criticism and the use of trial and error (not blind) is even more apparent. The great inventors, such as Edison and the Wright brothers, tried things over and over, and even after they succeeded they still looked for improvements.

It seems, then, that search for goals and the self-critical search for evidence are crucial parts of creation. The role of the search for possibilities is less clear.

Personal goals, as well as the goals of a particular thinking episode (of the sort we have been discussing), are also crucial to creativity (Perkins, 1981, ch. 9). Most people do not produce truly novel creations and inventions. I (and probably you) do not wake up in the morning with a new idea for a string quartet. That is not because either of us is lacking in some special "gift," as many of us think. (Indeed, as an adolescent, I composed music and *did* wake up with ideas for new pieces.) What is crucial is the personal goal of doing something creative. One does not write poems unless one tries to write poems. To write poems, one must walk around thinking of oneself as a poet, noticing things that one could write about, thinking of clever lines around which to build poems, and so on. Of course, once one starts writing poems (or inventing robots, or whatever), one needs to acquire a lot of specific knowledge so that one can do it better, but without the personal goal, nothing ever happens at all.

The development of creative expertise

Creative people are, we have just seen, distinguished by a desire to be creative in a particular domain. One effect of this desire is that it leads to extensive practice and learning about the domain. Such learning is ordinarily required for success.

Hayes (1985) documented the need for learning in a clever way. He counted the number of classical music recordings in Schwann's record guide for each of several major composers and plotted this number as a function of the composer's age when the music was written. As composers got older, they were more likely to write music that was "successful," in the sense of writing pieces that were frequently recorded. The interesting result was that the measure of success did not depend on the composer's age as such but rather on the number of years that had passed since the composer began writing music. Success increased steadily for 10 years, at which point composers seemed to "hit their stride," and their production leveled off. Mozart, for example, began composing when he was 4, and by the age of 14 he was producing about as much well-known music as he ever would. Other composers began later, and it still took about 10 years for them to hit their stride. (In old age, there may be some decline.) Hayes also found that other types of creative expertise, such as painting, take about a decade to develop fully, although there may be some differences from domain to domain.

Gardner (1983) suggests that creative "geniuses" often begin with early recognition of some special talent. For example, the pianist Arthur Rubinstein developed perfect pitch around the age of 3, and when the composer Igor Stravinsky was just 2 years old, he sang from memory a song he had heard only once. It is possible that special capacities affect the development of creative achievement. We do not, however, have other evidence for this possibility.

Tests of creativity

Two approaches have been used by psychologists to test creativity. The first approach was inspired by the work of Guilford (1967), who tried to classify mental abilities in much the same way that chemical elements are classified in the periodic table. One of his classifications was "divergent production," a category of tasks for which there are many "right" answers (perhaps of varying quality), so many that the tester might not know them all in advance. The question "How many uses can you think of for a brick?" is a typical divergent production item. Answers can be scored for appropriateness and quantity.

Another approach is that of Mednick (1962), who argued that a truly creative person is not merely one who produces a great variety of ideas. Rather, says Mednick, true creativity is the ability to think of an idea that is improbable, unusual, or remote, yet exactly right for the situation. Mednick devised a word-finding test called the Remote Associates Test (RAT). Here are some sample items, with appropriate answers supplied for the first two:

> Snow, down, out – fall
> Ache, sweet, burn – heart
> Off, top, tail –
> Top, pin, Panama –
> Law, case, dress –

The idea is to think of a word that is associated with all three of the words given. Each association by itself is remote; for example, "fall" is not the first or second or third word you think of when given "snow." We might say that success on this test requires both thoroughness in the search for possibilities and fair evaluation of the possibilities discovered. (The latter probably plays a small role in explaining individual differences in outcome. Some subjects are satisfied with "brief" as an answer to the last item, which is not nearly as good an answer as "suit.")

We have some evidence that such tests work. For example, Mednick (1962) found a correlation of .70 between RAT scores and the creativity of architecture students as judged by their teachers. We do not find such correlations, though, if we use measures of creativity based on performance in the world rather than performance in school. According to Wallach (1976), what *does* predict creative accomplishment is past creative accomplishment. If graduate schools want to admit students who will make creative contributions to some field, they would be wise to admit students who have already done something creative in the field.

IQ tests seem to do no better than these measures at predicting creative achievement. IQ does not predict success at all among people who have been admitted to graduate school in science, if we take as our standard the judgment of peers (Wallach, 1976). Of course, students need high IQ scores simply to get into graduate school, so people with low IQ scores generally cannot get the education needed for doing advanced work in the sciences. If, somehow, we were able to do an experiment in which we randomly admitted people to graduate school – or otherwise got people started on careers involving creativity – IQ tests might do a better job of predicting success.

Conclusion

In judging whether a creation or invention is good, we use two main criteria: novelty and success. Two different sets of circumstances seem to be needed to foster these qualities. The things that make for success in creative tasks, I have theorized, are those that make for success in any other sort of problem solving: certain mental abilities, actively open-minded thinking, and expertise in the domain, the last of which must be acquired over a long period of learning and practice.

What makes for novelty, on the other hand, is largely the desire to create. Wanting to create something that has not been done before is a strong personal goal behind creative behavior. This superordinate goal initiates a search for other goals, new goals such as designing an electronic means of storing information or a new musical form. The goal of doing something novel also sustains the long periods of effort and learning that are required to become a creative person in a particular domain.

Whether one has the ability to be creative in a given field is difficult to tell in advance. No special abilities for creative tasks, other than those involved in other tasks, appear to be needed. The main difference between the poet and the translator of poetry (aside from the latter's needing to know two languages) is the desire of the former to write poems. The best advice we can give to people who think they want to be poets is this: Read a lot of poetry, try to write poems, and see how it goes. If you are an immediate success, that is a good sign. If you are not, it may still be too soon to tell. Eventually, if success still eludes you, it would seem reasonable to try something else.

Before we turn to the theories of beliefs, decisions, and goals discussed in parts II and III, we need to look at an older theory that was long considered the ideal model of thinking. For centuries in European education, the theory of logic, invented by Aristotle, was taught as the ideal for good thinking. Even today, we hear people casually refer to "logic" as the standard for good thinking. Logic is still an important field within philosophy, but it is now no longer the only useful normative model of thinking. Logic is limited because it does not apply to many of the thinking situations that come up in daily life. The next two chapters (chs. 9 and 10) explain why logic has lost its central place as the sole normative model and describe the more limited role it plays in the modern theory of thinking.

9   Formal logic

Nothing is better than eternal happiness.
A ham sandwich is better than nothing.
Therefore, a ham sandwich is better than eternal happiness.

Nickerson (1986)

Past writers (for example, Arnauld, 1662/1964) have taken logic as a normative model of thinking. Today, people sometimes use the word "logical" as if it simply meant "reasonable" or "rational." Logic has influenced education – where it served as the basis for the teaching of thinking for centuries – and it has provided us with much of our language for talking about thinking: "premise," "assumption," "contradiction."

Today logic has lost its central place as the normative model for thinking. Why has this occurred? What are the limitations of this theory that have demoted it to a less exalted place in the modern theory of thinking? To answer that question, we must first find out what the theory of logic is.

What is logic?

Matthew Lipman has written a series of philosophical "novels" to introduce children in elementary and secondary schools to philosophical thinking (for more information on Lipman's approach, see ch. 22). In one of these, *Harry Stottlemeier's Discovery* (1974; say the name aloud and think of a famous Greek philosopher), Harry is daydreaming in class. Suddenly he hears the teacher asking him whether Halley's comet is a planet, and he struggles to come up with an answer. He reasons that all planets go around the sun; Halley's comet goes around the sun; and therefore, Halley's comet must be a planet, so he answers yes.

Later, when the immediate embarrassment has passed, Harry and his friends reflect on why he was wrong. They notice that true sentences (sentences stating a truth) beginning with "all" usually become false when they are reversed: Compare "All dogs are animals" with "All animals are dogs," or compare "All planets are things that go around the sun" with "All things that go around the sun are planets." Harry conjectures that this is true of all sentences, but a friend points out that true sentences beginning with the word

134

"some" can be switched around and remain true (and false ones can remain false): For example, "Some women are artists," "Some artists are women" (both true); "Some dogs are mice," "Some mice are dogs" (both false). Harry and his friends discover that this is also true for sentences beginning with "no": "No women are artists," "No artists are women" (both false); "No dogs are mice," "No mice are dogs" (both true).

What are Harry and his friends doing here? One answer (Popper, 1962, ch. 9) is that they are engaged in a kind of reflection (as defined in ch. 1). They are trying to formulate generalizations about the truth and falsity of expressions in language. The generalizations are expressed in terms of the *form* of the expressions. For example, one rule is that if the statement "No X are Y" is true, then the statement "No Y are X" is also true. This rule does not depend on what we plug in for X and Y. It is like many laws in mathematics, such as $A + B = B + A$, which, once again, is true regardless of the values of A and B. Of course, reflection of this sort is successful only if the search is thorough or if the thinkers are lucky in coming up with informative examples.

The *evidence* for this reflective enterprise consists of our own knowledge of the truth or falsity of various statements, plus our understanding of the words in question. It might be said that we understand the terms only because we already *know* the laws of logic, so that all we are doing is discovering what we already know; however, let us be skeptical about this claim for a while. Perhaps we understand the terms without knowing the laws of logic.

When we reflect on the truth and falsity of expressions, we try to draw conclusions that are *always* true. For example, it may *usually* be true that "when some A's are B's and some B's are C's, then some A's are C's" (for example, "Some men are scientists"; "Some scientists are New Yorkers"; "Some men are New Yorkers"), but it is not *always* true ("Some men are scientists"; "Some scientists are women"; "Some men are women" ?!). This rule, then, is not one of the laws of logic. In fact, we might conclude instead that nothing follows at all from an expression that contains two *some*'s.

Logicians study the behavior of arguments laid out in a certain form: a list of *premises* and a *conclusion* that may or may not follow from the premises. An argument laid out in this way is called a *syllogism*. When a syllogism is *valid*, the conclusion follows from the premises. That is, if the premises are assumed to be true (whether they are actually true or not), the conclusion must be true. When a syllogism is *invalid*, the conclusion can be false even if all the premises are true. The validity of syllogisms depends on their form, not on the specific terms used in them. We can use letters such as A, B, L, or M to stand for specific terms. If the syllogism is valid, no matter how we replace the letters with actual terms, it will be impossible for the conclusion to be false if the premises are true.

Consider another example:

> An L can be an M.
> An M can be an N.
> Therefore an L can be an N.

Is this a valid syllogism? Is the conclusion always true whenever the premises are true? How can you tell? Try to think of examples. "A man can be a scientist"; "A scientist can be a New Yorker"; "A man can be a New Yorker." So far, so good; but remember (from ch. 3) that good thinkers try to find evidence against a possibility as well as evidence in its favor. Try to find an example that shows the rule is *false* – that is, a *counter*example. What about substituting "men," "scientists," and "women," for L, M, and N, respectively, just as we did before? "A man can be a woman?" Aha! The syllogism is invalid; the proposed rule is false. Did you know that before? Was it part of your knowledge of the word *can*? Hmm.

Let us try another one (from P. N. Johnson-Laird, personal communication):

> A is to the right of B.
> B is to the right of C.
> Therefore A is to the right of C.

Sounds good. This must be part of what we mean by "to the right of." Or is it? Imagine three people – A, B, and C – sitting around a circular table. Indeed, A may be on B's right, and B on C's right, but A would have to be on C's left. This rule is wrong as well. We discovered that it was wrong by constructing what Johnson-Laird calls a *mental model* of a situation. The mental model served as a counterexample. This example makes it much more plausible (to me, anyway) that when we reflect on the laws of logic we are not simply discovering what we already know. Before I heard Johnson-Laird give this example, I judged that this rule was true, and I was prepared to use it to make inferences. (Luckily for me, he did not ask me to bet on it.)

As a final example, let us consider a syllogism that is one of the bugaboos of logic students:

> If A then B.
> B.
> Therefore A.

(In the shorthand form used by philosophers, here "A" means "A is true"; "B" means "B is true"; and so forth.) What happens if we substitute words for the letters?

> If it rains, Judy takes the train.
> Judy took the train today.
> Therefore it rained.

Again, this sounds good, but it is clear here that Judy might also take the train if it snows. The conclusion would not always follow, so the syllogism is invalid.

The word "if," used in these statements, actually seems to have two meanings in ordinary speech. In the *conditional* meaning, the statement "If A then B" means that B will be true if A is true and that B will be possible also if A is not true (for example, "if it snows"). In the *biconditional* meaning, the same expression means that B will be true only if A is true and not if A is false. In this case, whenever the statement "If A then B" is true, the statement "If B then A" will be true as well. The implication works both ways; hence the term "biconditional." Mathematicians often use the phrase "if and only if" to indicate a biconditional meaning.

In ordinary speech, the meaning intended is usually clear from the context. Suppose I say, "If you don't shut up, I'll scream!" You would be surprised if I screamed anyway after you shut up. Here, the natural interpretation is the biconditional, not the conditional. If the biconditional interpretation were meant, then the argument "If A then B. B. Therefore A" would be valid.

Why, then, do logicians usually insist that the word "if" be interpreted in the conditional sense? Because this is more conservative. If you do not know which sense is intended, you had better not draw the conclusion that A is true (in the bugaboo syllogism just discussed), because you might be wrong. On the other hand, suppose the statement is this: "If A then B. A." Here you *can* infer B, no matter which sense is intended.

For the same reason, logicians take the statement "Some X are Y" to be consistent with the possibility that "all X are Y," even though we would never say that some X are Y if we knew that all X are Y. The point is that we might say that some X are Y when it is true that all X are Y and we do not know it yet. (In a new city, we might notice that some taxis are yellow; it might be that all are.) Therefore, the syllogism "Some X are Y. Therefore, some X are not Y" is not valid. It is not always true.

In sum, logic is a *normative model* of inference, arrived at by *reflection* about arguments. The study of logical reasoning is a good example of the comparison of actual reasoning to normative models.

Types of logic

Logicians have developed several systems of rules. Each system concerns arguments based on certain terms.

The system of *propositional logic* is concerned with the terms "if," "and," "or," and "not." The last example about Judy and the train was in this system. Here is a more complex example of a valid argument that uses propositional logic:

> If there is an F on the paper, there is an L.
> If there is not an F, there is a V.
> Therefore, there is an F or there is a V.

The system of *categorical logic* is concerned with membership in categories. It concerns the behavior of arguments with the words "all," "some," "none," "not," and "no." This is the type of logic most intensively discussed by the Greek philosopher Aristotle, the main inventor of formal logic, and the type most studied by psychologists. Here are two examples of valid arguments of this type:

> All A's are B's.
> All B's are C's.
> Therefore all A's are C's.
>
> Some A are B.
> No B are C.
> Therefore some A are not C.

The system of *predicate logic* includes both propositional and categorical logic. It is the system now receiving the most attention from logicians and linguists, but it has not been studied much by psychologists. It includes relations among terms as well as class membership. A "predicate" is anything that is true or false of a term or set of terms. In the sentence "A man is a scientist," the word "scientist" is considered a "one-place predicate" because it says that something is true of the single term "a man." In the sentence "John likes Mary," the word "likes" is considered a "two-place predicate" because it describes a relation between two specific terms. In predicate logic, we can analyze such questions as this: "If every boy likes some girl and every girl likes some boy, does every boy like someone who likes him?"

Other systems of logic extend predicate logic in various ways. For example, *modal* logic is concerned with arguments using such terms as "necessarily" and "possibly." The idea is not simply to capture the meanings of English words as they are normally used but also, as in the "if" example described earlier, to develop formal rules for particular meanings, usually the most conservative meanings. No sharp boundary separates modern logic from "semantics," the part of modern linguistics that deals with meaning. (In the next chapter, we shall examine other extensions of logic to informal reasoning.)

The various systems of logic I have listed here constitute what I shall call "formal" logic. These systems have in common their concern with validity, that is, the drawing of conclusions that are absolutely certain from premises that are assumed to be absolutely certain. (In the next chapter, I shall discuss "informal" logic.)

If we view formal logic within the search-inference framework, we see that formal logic is concerned with the rules for drawing conclusions from evidence with certainty. That is, it is concerned only with inference, the use of evidence. It therefore says nothing about how evidence is or should be obtained. Formal logic, therefore, cannot be a complete theory of thinking. Moreover, formal logic cannot even be a complete normative theory of inference, for most inferences do not involve the sort of absolute certainty that it requires.

Nonetheless, logic may be a partial normative theory of inference. Each system of logic has its own rules that specify how to draw valid conclusions from a set of evidence, or *premises*. These rules make up the normative model.

Within logic, there are many such systems of rules, and often there are many equivalent ways of describing the same system. These rules are the subject matter of logic textbooks.

For each system of logic, we can ask whether people actually make inferences in a way that is consistent with the rules of logic. When we do think logically, we can ask how we do it. It is not necessarily by following the rules as stated in logic textbooks. When we do not, we can ask why not and whether the problem can be corrected.

For propositional logic, there is considerable evidence that people (at least adults) have learned to follow many rules that correspond directly to some of the major argument forms. For example, consider the following syllogisms (from Braine & Rumain, 1983, p. 278):

1. There is a G. There is an S. Therefore there is a G and an S.
2. There is an O and a Z. Therefore there is an O.
3. There is a D or a T. There is not a D. Therefore there is a T.
4. If there is a C or a P, there is an H. There is a C. Therefore there is an H.

These inferences are so obvious (once we understand the words) that no thinking seems to be required to evaluate their truth. Moreover, we seem to be able to draw more complex inferences by stringing these simple ones together. For example, evaluate the argument "If there is an A or a B, there is a C. There is a B or a D. There is not a D. Therefore there is a C." This argument combines the forms 3 and 4. Braine and Rumain (1983) and Rips (1983) review and report a number of studies of such reasoning. It is possible to predict the difficulty of evaluating an argument by figuring out which of the basic arguments from propositional logic must be put together in order to make it up. This approach to the study of logic has been called *natural logic*. The name reflects the idea that certain forms of argument are just as easy for most of us to use and understand as speaking. Researchers have been particularly interested in finding out how we have acquired these abilities. Studies of children suggest that some of them are slow to appear, developing only as children mature (Braine & Rumain, 1983).

Difficulties in logical reasoning

The natural-logic approach works for propositional logic, but it does not seem to work as well for categorical logic. First, categorical syllogisms seem to be much harder. Moreover, the difficulties are of a different sort. In most problems in propositional logic, we either see an answer right away, or we puzzle over the problem, sometimes solving it, sometimes not. In categorical reasoning, we almost always come up with an answer, but the answer very often turns out to be wrong. Consider this very difficult example (from Johnson-Laird & Bara, 1984): Given the syllogism

No A are B.
All B are C

what can you conclude about A and C? Most people conclude that no A are C, but this is wrong. (I will explain why later.)

Several researchers have tried to explain why categorical syllogisms are sometimes so difficult. A very early attempt was that of Woodworth and Sells (1935), who proposed that the premises of syllogisms create an "atmosphere" that affects the conclusion that is drawn. When subjects hear "Some A are B; some B are C," they naturally think, "Some A are C," even though this is wrong. The same is true of "No A are B. No B are C. Therefore no A are C." The atmosphere effect does explain a number of such errors, but not all of them (Johnson-Laird, 1983, pp. 72–76). It is also not a complete theory, because it fails to explain how anyone ever gets the right answer to these problems.

Another account of errors is that of Chapman and Chapman (1959), who pointed out that subjects often "convert" one of the premises. If the premise says that all A are B, they infer that all B are A as well. Subjects therefore reason: "All A are B. Some C are B. Therefore some C are A." This is wrong because the C's that are B's might not be A's. Some evidence in support of this account comes from a study by Ceraso and Provitera (1971). In this study, errors were reduced by restating the problem in a way that explicitly warned the subjects against conversion. They were told, for example, "All A are B, but some B might not be A."

Chapman and Chapman also theorized that subjects reason probabilistically. Instead of giving conclusions that must always be true (which is what they are asked for), subjects give conclusions that are likely to be true. Hence, when given "Some A are B. Some B are C," subjects conclude that some A are C, which is indeed likely to be true but is not always true.

The most radical account of errors in syllogistic reasoning is that of Henle (1962), who maintained that all such errors are not truly errors of logic but of understanding or interpretation. Henle points out that subjects sometimes act as though they are being asked about the truth of a conclusion, rather than whether it follows from the premises. They do not assume that the premises are not to be questioned. In other words, they *fail to accept the logical task*.

Some of the clearest examples of this phenomenon are found in studies of cultures without widespread schooling. Here is an example (from Scribner, 1977, p. 490) in which a nonliterate Kpelle (West African) rice farmer is interviewed:

> All Kpelle men are rice farmers.
> Mr. Smith is not a rice farmer.
> Is he a Kpelle man?

Subject: I don't know the man in person. I have not laid eyes on the man himself.
Experimenter: Just think about the statement.
S: If I know him in person, I can answer that question, but since I do not know him in person I cannot answer that question.

E: Try and answer from you Kpelle sense.
S: If you know a person, if a question comes up about him you are able to answer. But if you do not know the person, if a question comes up about him, it's hard for you to answer it.

What is really interesting about this case is that the farmer is *using* a syllogism much like the one he is refusing to answer (Johnson-Laird, 1985, p. 315):

> If I do not know an individual, then I cannot draw any conclusion about that individual.
> I do not know Mr. Smith.
> Therefore I cannot draw any conclusion about Mr. Smith.

The main difference between the two syllogisms (aside from the minor difference in form) is that the subject accepts the premises of the second, but he is unwilling to accept the premises of the one that he is given as a basis for reasoning. Scribner suggests that even a few grades of schooling may teach people to reason in the "genre" of formal logic, in which the premises must be accepted. This may occur even though formal logic is not ordinarily taught. Students could learn this early, Scribner suggests, from doing verbal problems in arithmetic. Even first-graders are sometimes asked to assume that "Bill has three pencils and gets two more." Students learn quickly that when they are asked how many pencils Bill has, "I don't know Bill" is not the sort of answer the teacher expects.

Young children in the United States, in one experiment, failed to accept the logical task, much as the farmer did (Osherson & Markman, 1974–5). When asked, "Is it true that this poker chip [concealed] in my hand is either red or not red?", most young children answered, "I don't know; I can't see it." The children did not seem to think of trying to answer the question on the basis of its form alone. (Other evidence indicates that they understood the meaning of the question.)

Henle (1962) points to a number of other errors, such as misinterpreting a premise (as in Chapman & Chapman's conversion), slipping in an additional premise, and omitting a premise. Although she argues that these are not "logical" errors and that reasoning proceeds correctly once these errors are made, it is not clear what she thinks a truly "logical" error would be.

Mental models

Johnson-Laird and his colleagues (Johnson-Laird & Steedman, 1978; Johnson-Laird, 1983; Johnson-Laird & Bara, 1984) proposed a different approach to logical reasoning, based on the idea of mental models. This approach applies to categorical syllogisms and perhaps to other types. In essence, the idea is that we try to form a mental model of the situation expressed in the premises and derive a tentative conclusion by examining the model. If we are sufficiently careful thinkers, we then try to find an alternative mental model, according to which the tentative conclusion we have drawn would not be true. If we fail to find such a counterexample, we assume that our conclusion is correct. This theory explains both how we succeed in obtaining correct answers and why we sometimes fail.

Let us first see how the theory works for a simple example:

> All artists are beekeepers.
> All beekeepers are chemists.

To solve such a syllogism, we imagine some sort of mental model. For example, we might imagine a few artists (indicated by A's) and a few beekeepers (B's), with some sort of tag to indicate which are the same person:

> A = B
> A = B
>   (B)

The (B) at the end indicates that there might be a beekeeper who is not an artist. (We do not have to use exactly this kind of mental model. We might, for example, imagine an A circle inside a B circle.) We then make the same kind of mental model for the beekeepers and chemists (C's). Finally, we combine the two mental models:

> A = B = C
> A = B = C
>   (B) = C
>   (C)

We can then "read off" the conclusion that all artists are beekeepers. We can fool around with this model, eliminating the (B) or the (C), and the conclusion will still hold. If we try to think of another model, we will not be able to. There is only a single model for this syllogism.

Consider now the syllogism

> Some A are B.
> Some B are C.

For this syllogism, many people come up with the following model:

> A = B = C
> (A)   (B)   (C)

That is, they imagine that some of the A's are B's and some of *these* B's are C's. If they stop here, they will conclude that some A's are C's, a common error. If they seek an alternative model, they may come up with this one:

> A = B
> (A)   B = C
>   (B)   (C)

That is, the B's that are C's need not be the same B's that are A's. Since there is no single conclusion consistent with both models, the subjects conclude correctly that nothing follows at all from these two premises.

Now let us consider the syllogism that we examined earlier:

No A are B.
All B are C.

There are three models to consider here:[1]

1.	A		2.	A		3.	A = (C)
	A			A = (C)			A = (C)
	———			———			———
	B = C			B = C			B = C
	B = C			B = C			B = C
	(C)			(C)			(C)

(Here, the horizontal line indicates separation, as in the premise "No A are B.") In model 3, all of the A's are C's. Subjects often conclude that no A are C. It is apparent that this conclusion is consistent only with the first of the three models. The only conclusion consistent with all three models is that some C are not A, and this is the correct answer.

We see that one reason for mistakes in dealing with syllogisms is that subjects sometimes draw a conclusion based on a single model, and they fail to consider alternative models, especially models that are inconsistent with their conclusion. If we think of models as "evidence" and the conclusion as a "possibility," this kind of error is an example of failure to seek evidence against a favored possibility, a basic source of poor thinking. The same can be said when subjects consider two models, but not a third model, although this error is less extreme. Johnson-Laird and Steedman (1978) and Johnson-Laird and Bara (1984) were able to predict the relative difficulty of different syllogisms, and the errors that are made, by assuming that many subjects fail to consider more than a single model. The most difficult syllogisms tend to be those that require consideration of three alternative models.

Johnson-Laird (1983) has also found that the models people form seem to be "directed." That is, the order of the terms in each premise makes a difference. Syllogisms are easiest when the first term of the conclusion is the first term in the first premise, and the second term in the conclusion is the second term in the second premise (in the order: A-B, B-C, therefore A-C). It is as though the premises had to be diagrammed in left-to-right order, with the B's of the first premise next to the B's of the second premise, before the subject could combine them. When the subject must reverse one of the premises, the task is more difficult. Because the order of the terms is called the "figure," this effect is called the "figural effect." One example of this effect is the difference in difficulty between identical problems presented with the terms in different orders. For example, given

[1] It is assumed here that there is at least one A, one B, and one C.

Some A are B.
All B are C.

almost all subjects conclude, correctly, "Some A are C." However, given

Some B are A.
All B are C.

many subjects say, "No valid conclusion," even though "Some B are A" means the same as "Some A are B." Those subjects who are correct in the second form are also more likely to state the conclusion as "Some C are A," possibly because they have switched around the "arrows" in their mental model of the second premise. The figure seems to affect both the difficulty of the problem and the way in which the conclusion is expressed.

Differences in ability to solve categorical syllogisms seem to be related both to differences in the tendency to consider alternative models and to differences in sensitivity to the figural effect. Subjects who have the greatest difficulty are often unable to put together even a single model, especially when the premises are not in the most convenient order (that is, A-B, B-C). These subjects have particular difficulty when one of the premises must be turned around. Other subjects have no difficulty when only a single model must be considered, almost regardless of the figure. The differences seem to emerge with the multiple-model problems.

Galotti, Baron, and Sabini (1986) found support for this analysis. Subjects were selected according to their scores on a test of syllogistic reasoning. Subjects were asked to give an initial answer under time pressure, and a final answer without pressure. It was thought that the initial answer might be based on a single model of both premises, and the final answer in good reasoners (high scorers) would result from consideration of alternative models, inconsistent with the initial conclusion. Good reasoners were in fact more likely to correct answers that were initially incorrect, especially on problems in which "nothing follows," which always involved more than a single model. Good reasoners also took about twice as much time as poor reasoners between initial and final answers. (The two groups were about equal in the time spent on initial answers.) Apparently, those who were good at the task were more thorough in their search, and possibly more self-critical as well. They seemed (in thinking-aloud tasks) to search for models that were inconsistent with their initial conclusion.

Logical errors in hypothesis testing

The four-card problem

Suppose you are a subject in a psychology experiment. You are given the four cards shown in Figure 9.1. You are told that each card has a letter on

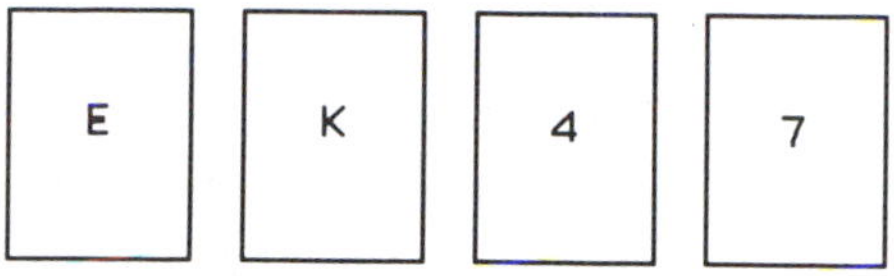

Figure 9.1. Four cards, each with a letter on one side and a number on the other.

one side and an even number on the other. Thus, the first two cards have numbers on the other side, and the last two have letters. You are given the following rule, which may or may not be true of all four cards:

If a card has a vowel on one side, then it has an even number on the other side.

Your task is "to name those cards, and only those cards, that need to be turned over in order to determine whether the rule is true or false" (Wason, 1968b). Think about this before going on.

Most subjects give as their answer E only, or E and 4. A few answer E, 4, and 7. Very few answer E and 7. Can you discover the right answer on your own? Try it before reading on. Here is a hint: One set of subgoals is to find out whether *each card* is needed. How would you determine whether each card is needed?

You might think of the following idea: Imagine each possible result you could find by turning over each of the cards, and ask yourself whether the rule could be true if the result were found. For the first two cards you would ask, "Could the rule be true if the number on the other side were even? if it were odd?" For the last two cards you would ask, "Could the rule be true if the letter on the other side were a vowel? What if it were a consonant?" If the rule could be true no matter what is on the other side, you do not need to turn over the card.

If you try this approach, you will find that you *do* need to turn over the E card, because if there is an odd number on the other side, the rule is false. You do not need to turn over the K. One surprise (for some) is that you do not need to turn over the 4. Whether the letter on the other side is a vowel or a consonant, the rule could still be true. (The rule does not say anything about what should happen when there is a consonant.) A second surprise (for some) is that you *do* need to turn over the 7. There could be a vowel on the other side, and then the rule would be false.

What has interested psychologists about this problem is that it seems easy, but it is actually hard. Subjects frequently give the wrong answer, while stating (if asked) that they are sure they are correct. Why is this problem so hard? What causes the errors? A large literature has grown up around this problem, and the results seem to illustrate some interesting facts about human thinking.

The error as poor thinking

First, some evidence suggests that the error here is in part a failure to search for evidence and subgoals – in particular (1) the subgoal of determining the relevance of each card; (2) the possibility of determining the relevance of each possible result of turning over each card; and (3) the evidence from whether these results could affect the truth of the rule. In sum, the error results from insufficient search. One piece of evidence for this is that performance improves if subjects are asked to consider only the last two cards, the 4 and 7. They are more likely to choose the 7 and less likely to choose the 4. When the task is made more manageable by cutting it down, the subjects are perhaps inclined to think more thoroughly about the two remaining cards (Johnson-Laird & Wason, 1970).

In an extension of this experiment, Johnson-Laird and Wason (1970) gave subjects the task of testing the rule "All triangles are black." Each subject was given a stack of 15 black shapes and 15 white shapes. The subject could ask to inspect a black shape or a white shape on each trial, for up to 30 trials. After each shape was selected, the experimenter told the subject whether or not it was a triangle. It is apparent here that the black shapes are not relevant, just as the 4 is not relevant in the card problem. If a black shape is selected, the rule ("All triangles are black") could be true, whether the shape is a triangle or not.

All subjects selected all of the white shapes eventually: They realized that these shapes were indeed relevant. Also, most of the subjects *stopped* selecting black shapes (which were irrelevant) even before they found a black shape that was not a triangle. (A black shape that was not a triangle would make them realize that black shapes were irrelevant.) Very likely, the repeated trials gave the subjects a chance to think about their strategy, and they realized that black shapes were irrelevant even before they were forced to this realization. No subject ended up selecting all of the black shapes.[2]

Resistance to correction

Although subjects can be helped, there is also considerable evidence of resistance to instruction. Possibly this resistance is a result of subjects' biased commitment to their initial answers. They ignore evidence against them be-

---

[2] An alternative account of the effect of cutting down the problem to two kinds of cards and of spreading it out over several trials is that these changes decrease the load on working memory. The problem as originally presented may simply be too complex to be thought about all at once. An argument against this account is that there is nothing to stop subjects from trying to overcome such memory limits by doing for themselves what the experimenters do for them, that is, thinking about cards one by one. In general, the limits imposed by working memory can be overcome by the use of more time-consuming strategies. Therefore, although performance might improve if working memory were larger, it might also improve if subjects simply thought more.

cause they want them to be correct. (A way to test this would be to give the instruction before the subject gives any answer; this has apparently not been tried.) For example, Wason (1977) reports an experiment in which subjects were faced with clear evidence that they had made an error, yet the subjects persisted in holding to their initial answer.

In the experiment, each card contained a circle or nothing in the middle, and a border or nothing around the edge. The rule to be evaluated was this: "Every card with a circle on it has a border around it." Subjects were shown the following four cards:

1. Circle in middle, edge covered up
2. No circle in middle, edge covered up
3. Border around edge, middle covered up
4. No border around edge, middle covered up

The question is to decide which cards must be uncovered in order to test the rule. The right answer here is cards 1 and 4. Card 4 must be looked at because the rule would be false if there were a circle. At a critical point in the experiment, the border of card 4 is uncovered, and the subject sees that the card has a circle in the middle. Here is an example of what one subject, an undergraduate taking advanced mathematics who had chosen cards 1 and 3, said to the experimenter about her choice:

Experimenter: Can you say anything about the truth or falsity of the rule from this card [card 4, with the cover removed, revealing a circle]?
Subject: It tells me [the rule] is false.
E: Are you still happy about the choice of cards you needed to see?
S: Yes.
E: Well, you just said this one makes it false.
S: Well, it hasn't got a . . . border on it, so it doesn't matter.

Several other subjects continued to deny that card 4 was relevant, even after they had admitted that it actually proved the rule false when it was uncovered. Apparently they were simply failing to use the very powerful evidence that was staring them in the face. If they were to use it, it would cause them to change their original selection.

Dual processes and rationalization

If these examples shows a bias in the *use* of evidence, another set of experiments suggests a related bias in the *search* for evidence. In a series of studies carried out by Evans and his collaborators (reviewed in Evans, 1982, ch. 9), it has been found that when subjects are asked to give *reasons* for their choices of cards, the reasons given often seem to be rationalizations that they thought of afterward to explain their choices rather than true determinants of the choice. Evans has made this point dramatically by arguing that reasoning

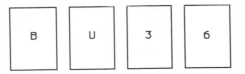

Figure 9.2. Four cards, each with a letter on one side and a number on the other.

involves "dual processes," one that actually draws conclusions and another that rationalizes the conclusions after they are drawn.[3]

The best evidence for this comes from several experiments in which the actual determinants of the choice of cards seem to have nothing to do with the reasons that subjects give. The actual choices of cards seem to be determined by an elementary process of *matching* to the elements of the rule. Subjects are given the cards shown in Figure 9.2. When subjects are asked to test the rule "If there is a B on one side, then there will be a 3 on the other side," they seem to choose the B and 3 cards simply because they are both mentioned in the rule itself.

How do we know that this is the actual determinant of the choice? One very clever way to tell is to change the rule so that it becomes "If there is a B on one side, then there will *not* be a 3 on the other." If subjects are simply matching, they will still choose the B and 3 cards. Now, however, these are the right answers. This time, the 3 card is relevant, because, if there is an A on the other side, the rule is false.

In fact, subjects tend to choose the A and 3 cards whether the rule is stated in the original, affirmative form or in the new, negative form. When they are asked to justify their answers, however, their justifications are correct only for the negative form. One subject (from Wason & Evans, 1975) who chose the 3 card justified this choice in the negative task by saying, "If there is a B on the other side, then the statement is false." This, of course, is perfectly correct. The same subject, however, immediately after doing the negative task, chose the 3 card for the affirmative task as well. Here, the justification was "If there is a B on the other side, then the statement is true." This, of course, is beside the point.

The same subject did not choose the 6 card for either rule. Again, for the negative rule, the subject gave a correct justification for not choosing the 6 card: "Any letter may be on the other side; therefore[there is] no way of knowing if the statement is true." (If only the subject had applied this argument to the 3 card!) In the affirmative condition, however, the subject justified not choosing the 6 card as follows: "If numbers are fairly random,

[3] Surely this point may be made too strongly. After all, some people do succeed in solving even the four-card problem, and many people do change their mind on the basis of reasons (evidence, goals, new possibilities). The important aspect of Evans's point is that the determinants of the conclusions we draw are, all too often, not fully rational, in terms of being sensitive to the results of a search process.

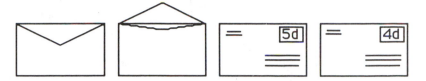

Figure 9.3. Four stamped envelopes.

then there may be any letter on the other side, thereby giving no indication unless the letter is B." Again, the subject could have chosen this card and justified it in the same way as the 3 card was justified for the negative rule.

In sum, subjects' justifications tend to be correct when they have chosen the correct cards, and incorrect when they have chosen the incorrect cards. Yet the justifications seem to play little role in determining the choice itself, for the choice remains much the same whether the rule is stated affirmatively or negatively. It would appear that the justification is indeed after the fact, that it is the result of a search for evidence *in favor* of a decision already made.

Content effects

Performance in the four-card task is affected by the content of the rules. (See Evans, 1982, ch. 9, for a review.) The clearest effects concern bureaucratic rules. Johnson-Laird, Legrenzi, and Legrenzi (1972) showed adult subjects in England a drawing of sealed and open stamped envelopes (like Figure 9.3) and asked them, "Which of the following envelopes must you examine to test the rule: If a letter is sealed, then it has a 5d stamp on it"?[4] These subjects had an easy time figuring out that one had to check the closed envelope and the 4d envelope in order to test this rule. However, when Griggs and Cox (1982) attempted to replicate this experiment using college students in the United States, there was no difference between the envelope condition and a control condition with abstract materials (like the original four-card task described earlier). The American students were helped, however, when they were asked to imagine themselves as police officers whose job it was to test the rule "If a person is drinking beer, then the person must be over 19 years of age." In this case, most students understood that the people to check are those drinking beer (to find their age) or those 19 or under (to see whether they are drinking beer).

It is clear from these results that the mere concreteness of the envelope condition did not help to make the problem easier. Rather, thinking was helped either by familiarity with the actual situation, by analogy with a similar known situation, or by a general rule for reasoning about permissions (Cheng,

---

[4] A "5d" stamp is a stamp worth 5 pence.

Holyoak, Nisbett, & Oliver, 1986). Cheng and her colleagues call such a general rule a "pragmatic inference schema." It is in between a rule of formal logic and an analogy to a specific example. We may think of it as a heuristic that leads to conformity with a formal rule in a certain kind of situation.

Another possibility is that performance is helped when subjects can *understand* the rule testing. (Here I use the word "understand" in the sense discussed in ch. 3.) When the testing of the rule has a purpose – to detect violators – subjects may understand better, and discover more easily, the arguments in favor of a certain "design" for testing the rule. One source of the difficulty of the original task may have been the subjects' lack of understanding of the task, which, in turn, resulted from the lack of a purpose, other than the arbitrary purpose provided by the experimenter.

Effects of prior belief

The examples discussed so far in this chapter have used material about which most people have no strong prior opinion. When subjects are asked to evaluate the validity of conclusions about which they do have strong prior opinions, their evaluations are affected by their opinions.

Here are two examples from an experiment that Morgan and Morton performed during World War II (1944, pp. 46–47). Subjects were given multiple-choice questions:

Usually countries that are forced into war against their will make poor soldiers. Since the Italian people were forced into this war against their will:

  1. Italian people make poor soldiers.
  2. Italian people may make poor soldiers.
  3. Italian people do not make poor soldiers.
  4. Italian people may not make poor soldiers.
  5. None of the given conclusions seems to follow logically.

Some ruthless men deserve a violent death. Since one of the most ruthless men was Heydrich, the Nazi hangman:

  1. Heydrich, the Nazi hangman, deserved a violent death.
  2. Heydrich, the Nazi hangman, may have deserved a violent death.
  3. Heydrich, the Nazi hangman, did not deserve a violent death.
  4. Heydrich, the Nazi hangman, may not have deserved a violent death.
  5. None of the given conclusions seems to follow logically.

In both cases, the effect of prevalent belief (at the time) tended to lead subjects to select answer 1, although the logically correct answer is answer 5.[5] Subjects chose the biased answer (over all problems of this sort) 36% of the time and the logical answer 20% of the time. When neutral words were used, the logical answer was chosen 33% of the time.

---

[5] Although answer 5 was counted as correct, one could argue for 2 and 4.

Evans, Barston, and Pollard (1983) asked subjects to evaluate conclusions in syllogisms like the following:

> No cigarettes are inexpensive.
> Some addictive things are inexpensive.
> Therefore, some addictive things are not cigarettes.

> No addictive things are inexpensive.
> Some cigarettes are inexpensive.
> Therefore, some cigarettes are not addictive.

Both syllogisms are valid; indeed, both are of the same form: No A are B; some C are B; therefore, some C are not A. Across a number of examples of this type, subjects accepted the syllogism 92% of the time when they agreed with the conclusion (as in the first example) and 46% of the time when they did not agree (as in the second example). Note that the syllogisms used were of this extremely difficult type. Note also that the material here is not particularly "emotional" (as in the Morgan and Morton study) but does seem to involve strong belief.

Two explanations have been offered for these effects. Henle (1962) theorizes that people "fail to accept the logical task." They make judgments about truth rather than validity. Other researchers conclude that subjects' search processes are biased, and that when subjects agree with a conclusion, they are less likely to seek a counterexample that is inconsistent with it. Evans, Barston, and Pollard (1983) found the effect of bias even when subjects were instructed very carefully that they were to judge validity rather than truth. It is therefore likely that part of the explanation is a matter of bias.

We need not conclude from these results that people are hopelessly biased. In all of the experiments, the effects of bias are relatively small, or else they occur only on extremely difficult problems. We should be wary of bias, but not so wary as to discount any argument purporting to be logical. Sometimes people make good arguments for the conclusions they believe. Sometimes they reach conclusions by good thinking (occasionally by logic, but not often). Sometimes they are right, even when we think they are not.

Conclusion

We have seen that formal logic, by its very nature, is not a complete theory of thinking. Because logic covers only inference, it cannot help us to understand errors that result from insufficient search. When we treat logic problems as examples of problems in general, however, they do serve as good illustrations of the effects of certain types of poor thinking: the failure to consider alternatives to an initial conclusion or model and the failure to seek counterevidence.

Another major limitation of formal logic as a normative model of thinking is that it deals only with conclusive arguments. Few of the rational conclusions that we draw in daily life can be made with such absolute certainty as the conclusion of a logical syllogism (even when we can be sure of the premises). For example, it does not follow logically, from the fact that smokers are much more likely to get lung cancer than nonsmokers, that smoking causes lung cancer, but one would be a fool to insist on a *logically* conclusive proof before concluding that smoking is dangerous to your health.

If logic could be made more relevant to everyday reasoning, it would be far more useful. Chapter 10 describes some efforts that have been made to extend logic to make it more applicable to ordinary thinking.

10   Logic and everyday reasoning

How can logic be made more relevant to everyday reasoning? This chapter describes two efforts to extend logic to make it more useful. One is the attempt to enumerate fallacies of reasoning in logical terms. The other is the attempt to develop normative or descriptive systems of logic in which the conclusions can vary in degree of certainty without necessarily being true or false. Both of these efforts emphasize inference (the use of evidence to draw conclusions) and the importance of standards for inference.

Logic as a standard of thinking

Theorists in the field of thinking view formal logic with mixed feelings. On the one hand, we must be grateful for the attention lavished on the idea of standards itself, on the idea that people can reflect on their own thought processes and regulate them through education and through mutual support. We must also agree that logic is sometimes useful in fields such as mathematics. As a normative standard, when it applies, it is correct.

Another argument for logic as a design is that it allows no subjectivity in the evaluation of arguments. By logic, the premises compel the conclusion in a way that does not depend on personal judgments. A mathematical proof, for example, can be judged as correct or incorrect.

We pay a price for this advantage, though. Because formal logic has no concept of "weight" of evidence or "strength" of possibilities, logic provides no way to compare two competing arguments that are both valid (or both invalid). Outside of mathematics, such competing arguments are the rule. In science, for example, most issues hinge on what scientists think is likely or unlikely, and there is always room for disagreement (however small).

Formal logic also provides no way to distinguish reasonable from unreasonable conclusions. The fact that the sun has risen every morning in the past gives us more reason to think that it will rise tomorrow morning than to think that it will not, but, logically, both conclusions are equally invalid.

More generally, there are too few cases in which we can accept premises with certainty or in which the rules of logic can lead us to conclusions that we would not have reached anyway. When formal logic does not help, we are reluctant to say that no useful standards can be found – that anything goes.

153

These difficulties have inspired various attempts to make logic more applicable to everyday reasoning. Some of these extensions are based on trying to find particular patterns of *fallacious* reasoning. Others are attempts to develop new logical systems that describe everyday, plausible reasoning. These attempts may be taken as prescriptive or normative as well as descriptive, since most of the reasoning examined is good.

Logic is concerned with inference from what is given. The standards of logic do not fault anyone for failing to think of something. Even the extensions of logic that are described in this chapter are concerned with inference, not search. Inference, as we have seen, is what logic is about. Since logic is not concerned with search, even these extensions are bound to be incomplete theories of thinking, no matter how well they serve their purpose.

Logical fallacies

Aristotle's fallacies

Aristotle pointed out the existence of certain poor forms of argument and thought, which he called "fallacies."[1] Fallacies are ways of thinking that bring about departures from the normative model, which, in this case, is the logic of syllogisms. Since the time of Aristotle, to varying degrees, educators have required their students to study the fallacies, hoping that the study of fallacies will help students avoid them.[2] Today, many colleges offer courses in logic or critical thinking that include the study of fallacies. As a result, knowledge of fallacies has spread fairly widely throughout Western culture, along with the idea that good thinking is logical thinking.

Aristotle's concern, like that of many philosophers of his time, was largely to criticize the Sophists – professors, of a sort, who traveled from city to city teaching the skills of argument to those who would pay (Russell, 1945). Partly because Greek citizens of the fifth and fourth centuries B.C. argued their own cases in court, such skills were deemed important. The Sophists were accused of being more interested in persuasion than in truth. Our idea of "sophistry" as the art of using misleading arguments comes from this source. We do not know whether the tricks of the Sophists ever persuaded anyone, but for over two thousand years teachers have been teaching about these tricks to protect their students from their pernicious influence, and students have been learning about them, both in order to be protected, and, perhaps, to use them against the un-sophist-icated.

Some fallacies involve errors in syllogisms. In the premise "If A then B," A is called the "antecedent" and B is called the "consequent." The fallacy

[1] Aristotle's discussion is largely in *De Sophisticus Elenchis*.
[2] One of the most readable discussions of fallacies and poor reasoning in general is that of Arnauld (1662/1964), part 3, chapters 19 and 20. A good recent discussion is found in R. H. Johnson & Blair (1983).

of *affirming the consequent* is to reason, "If A then B. B. Therefore A." ("If it rains, Judy takes the train. She took the train today. Therefore it rained.") The fallacy of *denying the antecedent* is to reason, "If A then B. Not A. Therefore not B." ("It didn't rain. Therefore, she didn't take the train.") If we wanted, we could make up (or find) a name for every type of error in the common syllogisms. These fallacies actually occur, for reasons we have already discussed.

Other fallacies turn on the ambiguity of language. One example of a sophistical trick from the time of the Sophists (Russell, 1945, ch. 10, p. 76) is the following:

You say that you have a dog?
Yes, a villain of a one, said Clessipus.
And he has puppies?
Yes, and they are very like himself.
And the dog is the father of them?
Yes, he said, I certainly saw him and the mother of the puppies come together.
And is he not yours?
To be sure he is.
Then he is a father, and he is yours; ergo (therefore) he is your father, and the puppies are your brothers.

Another example is the ham sandwich syllogism that begins chapter 9 of this book.

A similar but more subtle form of argument is the fallacy of *reification*. To *reify* an idea is to act as though it is real, when in fact it is only hypothetical or metaphoric. We may do this when we ask a question such as "Does the Soviet Union [or the United States] want peace?" Here, we speak as though the Soviet Union were a person with a single desire, when, in fact, it is a complex nation consisting of many people with conflicting desires. We also do this when we say something like "John is a little more intelligent than Bill." Here, we are reifying the concept of intelligence as a scale like the inches and feet we use to measure height, when in fact there may well be no such scale for intelligence. It may be that such errors depend on our way of speaking, as in the ham sandwich example. Collective terms such as "the public," "culture," or "society" may be particularly dangerous. Alternatively, our ways of speaking may merely reflect the conclusions we reach when we are misled in other ways.

Many of the other fallacies that the books warn us against fall into the general class of *non sequitur* arguments.[3] The term means "does not follow": The conclusion does not follow from the premises. Here are some specific types of non sequitur arguments:

Ad hominem. This is argument directed "at the person." For example, to argue against eugenics, we might point out that the Nazis were for eugenics.

---

[3] Knowledge of the Latin names of fallacies is helpful in understanding the literature on the subject and in impressing academics (if correctly pronounced or spelled).

From the fact that they were for it we cannot logically conclude that it is a bad idea. Scoundrels occasionally make good arguments, and we ought to evaluate arguments on their merits. Ad hominem arguments are used in politics when someone attempts to discredit an *idea* by calling its proponents bad names, such as "Communist sympathizers" or "right-wing fanatics." The purpose here seems to be to distract attention from the idea itself.

Appeal to force. The appeal to force is the same as the argument that might makes right. For example, "The United States was justified in invading Grenada because the United States is a major power." Again, whether the United States was justified or not, the conclusion does not follow from the premise. Major powers can carry out unjustifiable acts.

Argument from ignorance. "There must be flying saucers, because nobody has proved that there aren't." Or, "There must *not* be flying saucers, because nobody has proven that there *are*." Another way of stating the fallacy here is that an assumption is made about where the "burden of proof" lies, and such assumptions need to be justified. The manufacturers of chemicals that are thought to poison the atmosphere are likely to think that there must be proof of the poisoning before any action is taken. Later, we shall see that finding reasonable answers to such questions involves balancing the evidence on both sides.

Appeal to authority. "William Schockley, a Nobel laureate, has said that blacks are genetically inferior to whites in intelligence." The idea here is to use the fact that Schockley has won the Nobel Prize to strengthen the assertion. The argument would not be as impressive if the person in question were "Harry Schockley, my next-door neighbor." Sometimes, authority does lend weight to an argument. Here, it is questionable, because Schockley's Nobel Prize was in physics, not psychology or genetics. His work on the transistor gives him no special expertise on the area in question, other than his being a clever fellow.

Appeal to the multitude. "Most people smoke brand X. Therefore, it is the best brand." Likewise. People may have bad taste.

Other fallacies are based on problems with the premises, the evidence on which the conclusion is based. In some cases, a premise of an argument is questionable in its own right, as for example in the statement, "It's not worthwhile to give to international charities, because three-quarters of all contributions wind up in the hands of corrupt politicians." We cannot always ask people for the sources of their information, but some assertions (such as the dubious estimate given here) ought to arouse our suspicion. (In particular, "three-quarters" seems like an overestimate.)

In the fallacy of *straw man* arguments, someone arguing against a certain view makes up an unsympathetic description of that view, refutes the description, and concludes (perhaps incorrectly) that the view is wrong: That is, the arguer sets up a straw man and knocks him down. For example, people have argued against my own theory of actively open-minded thinking by saying, roughly, "Baron thinks we ought to consider every possibility and every piece of evidence before we decide anything. Clearly this is counter-productive." This is a straw man criticism because the theory acknowledges that search should be conducted *in moderation*, because the optimum amount of search is limited by the cost of search itself. The straw man fallacy is common in student papers that try to "take a stand" on some theoretical question. Straw man arguments are correctly perceived as rude: The makers of straw man arguments are making their opponents out to be stupid. The way to avoid this self-serving fallacy is to be charitable toward the opinions of others, to look for why they might make sense as well as why they might be in error.

Another fallacy in this category is *begging the question* (*petitio principii*, in Latin), the fallacy of assuming essentially what one seeks to show. Here is an example from Arnauld (1662/1964, p. 248):

The nature of heavy things is to tend toward the center of the universe...

Experience shows that heavy things tend toward the center of the earth...

Therefore, the center of the earth is the center of the universe.

Here, the first premise begs the question, because we would not think that this premise was true unless we already believed the conclusion. In particular, if we do *not* think that the earth is the center of the universe, we will doubt the initial premise. On the other hand, to the unwitting, the initial premise might be easier to accept than the conclusion, so begging the question may be a means of deception.

There are other fallacies not listed here. All writers on the subject have their own lists.

Fallacies and real arguments

Is there any evidence for fallacies of these sorts in actual reasoning? Perkins (1985) looked systematically for fallacies in arguments made spontaneously by high school and university students in the United States and by adults out of school – arguments about matters such as whether the military draft should exist in peacetime, whether violence on television encourages crime, whether Massachusetts should pass a law requiring a 5-cent deposit on bottles and cans, and whether a pile of bricks can be a work of art. After eliciting these arguments, Perkins asked two "critics" to criticize them in their own words. These critics did not know how their criticisms would be classified. Finally, two other researchers classified the criticisms and counted the number of criticisms that fell within each type.

Most criticisms fell into a broad group that Perkins called *sparse situation modeling*: The original reasoning did not have an elaborate enough model of the situation. These errors could also be described as failure to search for evidence against initial possibilities. They are not errors in logic as such, and they are not classical fallacies. The major subcategories (41% of all criticisms) in the sparse situation modeling group were as follows:

> *Contrary consequence.* A different line of argument leads to an opposite conclusion. For example, the reasoner would say, "The draft would increase the strength of our army; that would impress foreign powers, and so America would gain more influence over world events." The critic would say, "The draft would cause internal dissension, as it did before; the United States would be embarrassed and foreign powers would see our lack of unity."
>
> *Counterexample.* The reasoner neglects a counterexample. For example, "Art is creative. The stack of bricks is creative, so it's art." The critic might point out that science is also creative but is not art.[4]
>
> *External factor.* The reasoner neglects a reason why a generalization might not be true. For example, if the reasoner said, "More manpower would make our army stronger," the critic might say, "More manpower might have made an army stronger in the past, but nowadays it's missiles and technical expertise that count, not manpower." This is another sort of neglected counterevidence.
>
> *Neglected critical distinction.* The reasoner neglects a distinction (to be explored later) that might weaken a general statement. An example is the distinction between people's disposing of cans and bottles in parks and disposing of them at home, in the deposit case mentioned earlier.

On the other hand, some of the criticisms appeared to involve logic in the more traditional sense. In the search-inference framework, these would be called failures in the *use of evidence*, or *inference*, the part of thinking that may indeed involve logic. The major subcategories (23% of all criticisms) identified by Perkins's "critics" are as follows:

> *Disconnection.* The criticism was that the conclusion did not follow. For example, if the reasoner said, "The United States already has a lot of influence, so it can't get more," the critic would say, "Having a lot of something certainly does not imply that one can't get more of it." Note that this category corresponds to the general category of non sequitur, but most of the examples in this category do not seem to correspond to the traditional fallacies (for example, ad hominem). Moreover, as in the case of other fallacies, arguments in this form are often quite reasonable: For example, "John has won just about all the money in the poker game, so he can't win much more." Perhaps if the original statement had been stated more cautiously ("The United States *probably* can't get *much* more") the critic might not have found it objectionable at all.[5]

---

[4] Note that this example, from Perkins (p. 11), could also be described as a case of affirming the consequent, if we interpret the sentence "Art is creative" to mean "All art is creative." However, a more charitable interpretation is that it meant "Anything creative is art." With this interpretation, which the critic apparently made, the logic is sound, but the reasoner has neglected a counterexample to the premise, evidence against the generalization that anything creative is art. Whether there is a logical fallacy or not depends on how charitable we are.

[5] Criticisms are not supposed to be based on disagreement with plausible premises, in this case, the amount of power that the United States has.

Consistent quantification. A quantitative argument was stated as an objection to another argument but was actually consistent with the original argument. For example, if a reasoner said, "In my experience, most folks are not influenced by television violence," the critic would say, "You may be right about 'most people.' But television violence does not have to influence most people to increase violence – only a few." Again, the conclusion (that the argument objected to was wrong) did not follow.

Contradiction. The reasoner fails to answer an objection that the reasoner has brought up in the argument. For example, a reasoner might admit that a bottle deposit law works well in one state but then say that it will not work in Massachusetts, without saying what the difference is between Massachusetts and the other state.

Although these errors can be characterized reasonably as errors of inference, they do not represent the traditional fallacies discussed by logicians. They are not very representative, either, of the difficulties that people have in syllogistic reasoning (which, it seems, have more to do with sparse situation modeling or failure to search for counterevidence than with logic as such). We can characterize these errors as improper use of evidence; evidence that has a high weight is ignored if it goes against the reasoner's conclusion.

The importance of fallacies

When we read a list of fallacies, most of us recognize forms of arguments that we have heard. This fact could account for the perpetuation of the idea of logical fallacy over the course of history.

On the other hand, we must recall that Aristotle, who started this tradition, was particularly concerned with the Sophists, not with the difficulties that ordinary people have in thinking or decision making. Further, most of the textbooks that discuss the tradition of fallacies do not contain examples drawn from ordinary life, and, when they do, the examples turn out not to be clear ones (Finocchiaro, 1981). Those who charge others with fallacies may be guilty of the straw man fallacy themselves – in other words, of giving an unsympathetic (and therefore inaccurate) account of someone else's argument.

In my view, many of the so-called fallacies, when we notice them in people's real-life reasoning, are (at worst) cases of the *overweighing of evidence*, rather than of the use of irrelevant evidence. When a Nazi makes an argument, we cannot logically conclude that the argument is false just because the Nazi makes it, but this fact (or evidence) *does* seem to make it less *likely* to be true. (Of course, we still ought to listen.) The fact that some sightings of flying saucers have not (yet) been exposed as hoaxes does not prove that flying saucers exist, but that fact does make the existence of flying saucers more *likely* than it would be if all sightings had been exposed. If brand X is the most popular, that is at least some *evidence* that it is also the best – not decisive evidence, to be sure, but relevant evidence. Therefore, the form of the arguments themselves does not make them bad. Sometimes arguments of the same form are the best we have. The problem may be one of balance in weighing evidence.

In other cases, fallacies seem to illustrate common forms of thinking that is biased in favor of possibilities that are already strong (see chs. 3 and 15). An example of this is the straw man fallacy, in which the reasoner selectively ignores the evidence that her opponent might have a sensible point.

Most of the non sequitur fallacies point to lapses of formal logic. The conclusion does not follow logically from the premises. In daily life, however, most arguments are not matters of deductive logic, in which the truth of the conclusion is established with absolute certainty from the premises alone. An analysis of *good* arguments would surely show them to be mostly non sequiturs as well (except in mathematics and a few other fields). Instead, good arguments use relevant, but not decisive, evidence. Likewise, poor arguments are poor not because they are illogical but because they ignore some relevant possibility, goal, or piece of evidence.

For example, suppose someone is asked to think about a 5-cent deposit law. The person says, "Yes, litter will be reduced because people will return the bottles and cans for the 5 cents." We can, if we like, restate this argument as a reasonable syllogism: "A 5-cent deposit would induce potential litterers to return bottles and cans; a deposit law would require a 5-cent deposit; if potential litterers return bottles and cans, litter will be reduced; so a deposit law will reduce litter." Alternatively, we can criticize the thinker for leaving so many premises unstated. Thus, the argument can be seen as either logical or illogical, depending on how we paraphrase it, on how *charitable* we are in putting in premises that make the conclusion follow.

None of this has much to do, though, with whether the reasoning is good or bad. What does have to do with the reasoning are potential objections – in this case, in the form of counterevidence. For example, one could object, "Maybe people at home would save up their bottles and cans to return them, but the people drinking from them in parks and on picnics, who do the littering, might not bother, because it's not convenient for them." If this is a good and obvious objection, the initial reasoning is poor for not having considered it. The more obvious, the poorer. The reason this objection is relevant is that it leads to the opposite conclusion – namely, that the law will not reduce litter. It can also be seen as challenging one of the premises of the original argument, namely, "A 5-cent deposit would induce potential litterers to return bottles and cans," but this is not what is important. If the argument challenged some premise but led to the same conclusion, it would not be an objection to the conclusion.

It is possible that the teaching of logic and logical fallacies is indeed a good way to teach thinking, but not because fallacies occur often in ordinary thinking. Rather, the teaching of logic may be a good way to get students to reflect on the *form* of arguments, rather than their *content* – which we must do if

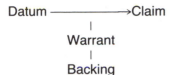

Figure 10.1. Basic structure of argument (Toulmin).

we are to make any sort of judgment of the quality of thinking – and to evaluate general rules by looking for examples and, especially, counter-examples. Moreover, many of the fallacies may represent common forms of poor thinking, and the study of fallacies may teach people heuristics for avoiding such thinking, such as "Watch out for straw man arguments."

On the other hand, there are dangers in stressing the *detection of fallacious arguments*, as opposed to the *construction of positions* that are carefully thought through. One danger is that students will become (as many already are) skeptical and even cynical, able to "shoot down" any position, to show that it is *imperfect* without asking whether it might still be *best*, despite its imperfections, and without asking how it might be improved. Moreover, the teaching of fallacies often gives students the idea that a good "critical thinker" is one who can criticize *other people's* arguments. At worst, such students can use their knowledge of fallacies as a way of defending their own beliefs and policies against any kind of challenge. We could call such students "actively closed-minded."

Extensions of logic

Another approach to making logic more relevant is to try to develop a logic of everyday arguments. By doing this, recent extensions of logical theory have made it more adequate as a descriptive and prescriptive model of everyday reasoning.

Toulmin (1958) tries to account for the structure of all arguments, not just those treated by formal logic. He suggests that arguments have a basic structure (illustrated in Figure 10.1) that includes the following elements: *datum, claim, warrant*, and *backing*. For example, consider the argument "Harry was born in Bermuda. So, presumably, Harry is a British subject." The *datum* (fact) here is that Harry was born in Bermuda. The *claim* is that he is a British subject. The *warrant* here is not explicitly stated, but if it were, it would be, "A man born in Bermuda is usually a British subject." The *warrant* is the *reason why the claim follows from the datum*. Just as the claim can be introduced with "so" or "therefore," the warrant can be introduced with "since" or "because." Harry's birth bears on his citizenship *because* people born in Bermuda are usually British subjects. Finally, the *backing* is the *justification*

Figure 10.2. Complete structure of argument (Toulmin).

for the warrant, the reason we accept it. Here, the backing consists of the various laws pertaining to British citizenship.

Notice that the word "presumably" had to be inserted in the argument. Toulmin calls this a *qualifier*. The qualifier indicates that there are conditions under which the conclusion does not follow. Qualifiers are necessary with certain kinds of warrants. In this case, there are various reasons why Harry might not be a British subject, even though he was born in Bermuda.

Toulmin adds a final element, the *rebuttal* (of the claim), which consists of the reasons why the claim might *not* hold. The rebuttal can be introduced with the word "unless." In the case of Harry, the rebuttal would be, "unless both of Harry's parents were aliens, or Harry became an American citizen, or . . ." The rebuttal gives the reasons why the qualifier is necessary. The rebuttal is like a warrant, but it argues against the claim rather than in favor of it. Just as the warrant justifies the claim, the rebuttal justifies the qualifier. Thus, the complete structure of an argument can be diagrammed as in Figure 10.2.

Warrants are of different types. Some warrants are specific to certain topics, such as law, science, mathematics, human behavior, or plumbing. In law, warrants can consist of laws and precedents set by previous cases. In science, they can be previous findings, analogies, and accepted laws.

Voss, Tyler, and Yengo (1983) applied Toulmin's scheme to actual reasoning in social sciences. They asked experts on the Soviet Union, and others, to discuss the problem of how to improve Soviet agriculture. Some of the kinds of warrants they discovered are listed in Table 10.1. For example, the psychological warrant about incentives might be used to justify a claim that certain Soviet workers would work harder with incentives, based on the datum that they are not now given incentives. That datum, in turn, might be a claim that was reached in a different argument. Of course, qualifiers such as "probably" or "presumably" would have to be inserted.

Formal syllogisms illustrate a kind of warrant. For example, consider a syllogism much like those discussed earlier in this chapter:

> Anne is one of Jack's sisters.
> All of Jack's sisters have red hair.
> So, Anne has red hair.

Table 10.1. *Some types of warrants*

Warrant type	Definition type	Example
Meta	Based on the process of problem solving	Solving a problem requires defining the constraints of the problem.
Governmental	Based on general knowledge of the way governments function.	Ministries of governments solve central problems slowly.
Logical	Based on general logical reasoning or common sense.	If an approach is unsuccessful, it should be abandoned.
Psychological	Deriving from general rules of human behavior.	People work harder when they are given incentives to work.
Analogical	Based on reasoning from what is known about a different system to conclusions about the target system	In Latin America, the peasants find extralegal ways to obtain money; this is probably true in the USSR.

Source: Adapted from J. F. Voss, S. W. Tyler, & L. A. Yengo, "Individual Differences in the Solving of Social Science Problems," in R. F. Dillon & R. R. Schmeck (Eds.), *Individual Differences in Cognition* (New York: Academic Press), Vol. 1, p. 213.

Here, the first premise ("Anne is one . . .") is the datum; the second premise ("All of Jack's sisters . . .") functions as the warrant; and the conclusion ("So . . .") is the claim. Note that no qualification is necessary here. (There are other kinds of warrants, such as those used in mathematics, that do not require qualification.) Moreover, the claim follows by virtue of the meaning of the statements. We can paraphrase the second premise as "Any sister of Jack's can be taken to have red hair." In such cases, we can replace the "So . . ." with "In other words, . . ." The claim is practically a restatement of the warrant, with the particular term ("Anne") substituted for the general term ("All of Jack's sisters"). Toulmin calls this sort of syllogism *analytic*, meaning, roughly, that the claim follows from an analysis of the premises.[6]

Note that even the syllogism just given can have different meanings, depending on the *backing* of the warrant. The backing is not stated in formal syllogisms, but it does matter. For example, the original syllogism would be valid if the backing were "Each of Jack's sisters has been checked individually and found to have red hair." Suppose, however, the backing were "All of Jack's sisters have previously been observed to have red hair." Now the syllogism is not analytic, and a qualifier is needed:

> Anne is one of Jack's sisters.
> All of Jack's sisters have red hair (a statement backed by the fact that they have previously been observed to have red hair).

---

[6] The term "analytic" is usually contrasted with "synthetic," but Toulmin prefers the term "substantive" as a contrast.

So, presumably, Anne has red hair (unless she dyed her hair, her hair turned
    white, etc).

The rebuttal, the reason for the qualifier, is the clause beginning with
"unless."

In sum, we might say that formal logic is concerned with some of the
arguments that require no qualifiers. Toulmin expands the design of logic by
admitting other kinds of warrants, suggesting a more detailed study of the
various kinds of warrants used in different fields of knowledge. He wants to
know what acceptable warrants have in common across fields and how they
differ from field to field.

Now let us see if we can restate Toulmin's design in terms of the search-
inference theory. Toulmin's *datum* clearly corresponds to a *piece of evidence*.
When possibilities are suggested by evidence, we can say that a *claim* corresponds to a *possibility*. If no qualifier is required, the evidence is sufficient
to make that possibility acceptable, and thinking can stop right there. If
qualifiers are required, other evidence and other possibilities can be considered. When possibilities are already present, evidence may strengthen them
or weaken them through the same kind of warrant.

Toulmin thus calls attention to the need for warrant in informal reasoning.
When somebody says, "The weather forecast said it will rain, so, presumably,
it will snow," the statement sounds odd because it is difficult to imagine a
warrant that connects the datum (the forecast) and the claim (snow). Likewise,
in thinking, the effect of a piece of evidence on a possibility depends on a
warrant.

The search-inference framework goes beyond Toulmin in that it describes
thinking as involving (typically) more than one possibility. Toulmin can incorporate other possibilities only as rebuttals. If we are trying to determine
Harry's citizenship, for example, evidence that he was born in Bermuda does
support the possibility that he is British. A thorough thought process would,
however, consider other possibilities, such as U.S. or Canadian citizenship,
and other evidence, such as the fact that he has a Texas accent. Rather than
making rebuttals part of the basic argument, we might think of alternative
possibilities as the general rebuttal, "unless some other possibility is better."

Moreover, the view of thinking as selecting among possibilities for certain
purposes or goals calls attention to the fact that the usefulness of warrants
depends on goals. The datum that a Cadillac is heavier than most cars does
not imply that I ought to buy one if my only goal is fuel economy, but it does
if my only goal is safety. Although Toulmin's approach is sensitive to this
role of goals, it is limited in being concerned only with inference, not with
search.

Collins and Michalski (in press) extend logic in a different way. They
propose a number of new types of syllogism to account for what they call
plausible reasoning. Plausible reasoning is equivalent to what Toulmin would
call "reasoning with qualifiers." They have examined such reasoning in the

context of dialogues in which people discuss geography, often making plausible inferences about facts of which they are unsure. Here is an example:

Q: Is the Chaco cattle country? I know the cattle country is down there (in Argentina).
R: I think it's more sheep country. It's like western Texas, so in some sense I guess it's cattle country.

Here, R brings two pieces of evidence to bear on the question. The first is that he recalls (without much confidence) that the Chaco is sheep country, and he infers from this (implicitly) that the Chaco is probably not cattle country. The second is that he recalls (confidently) that the Chaco is like western Texas, which he knows to be cattle country. This provides evidence on the other side.

The way in which the inference is made (which Toulmin would call the warrant) follows a certain pattern in each of these cases. In the first case, we can lay out the whole syllogism roughly as follows:

> Sheep are found in the Chaco (uncertain).
> Sheep and cattle are both kinds of livestock (certain, typical kinds, frequent kinds).
> Sheep are dissimilar from cattle in the kind of vegetation they are associated with (certain).
> The vegetation of a place is related to the livestock in the place (moderate dependence of livestock on vegetation, strong dependence of vegetation on livestock, certain).
> So, the livestock of the Chaco does not include cattle (weak).

Each statement takes a certain form and has certain parameters, such as its certainty, or, when the statement is about a type of something, a degree of typicality and a frequency, or, when the statement is about a dependency relationship, the strength of the dependency in both directions. The strength of the inference, which is "weak" in this case, depends on the parameters of the various statements. If, for example, R had been certain of all statements, and if the interdependence of livestock and vegetation had been strong in both directions, the conclusion would have been much stronger.

This sort of syllogism is thought to be a general form of reasoning. Here is another example of the same sort of reasoning:

Q: Can a goose quack?
BF: No, a goose – Well, it's like a duck, but it's not a duck. It can honk, but to say it can quack. No, I think its vocal cords are built differently. They have a beak and everything, but no, it can't quack.

One of the inferences here follows roughly the same pattern:[7]

> Geese honk.
> Honking and quacking are both kinds of vocalization.
> Honking is dissimilar from quacking in the kind of vocal cords with which it is associated.

---

[7] The parameters of certainty, typicality, frequency, and so on, are omitted.

The vocal cords of an animal are related to its vocalization.
So, geese don't quack.

The second argument in the Chaco example can be stated as follows:

The livestock in Texas include cattle (certain).
Texas and Chaco are places (certain, typical, low frequency).
The Chaco is similar to Texas in vegetation (moderately certain, moderate degree of similarity).
The vegetation of a place is related to the livestock in the place (moderate dependence of livestock on vegetation, strong dependence of vegetation on livestock, certain).
So, the livestock of the Chaco includes cattle (weak).

This argument differs from the first in that it is based on similarity (between the Chaco and Texas), whereas the first is based on dissimilarity (between cattle and sheep). Both arguments use one of the same premises, the one about the relationship between vegetation and livestock.

Collins and Michalski discuss other general patterns of inference that are used in plausible reasoning. One common pattern is a *lack-of-knowledge inference*, in which one makes an inference from one's own lack of knowledge: For example, "If a goose could quack, I would probably know it, so probably a goose can't quack."

In a sense, Collins and Michalski are carrying out the project that Toulmin suggested, an examination of the types of warrants used in plausible reasoning. The syllogistic patterns that they propose can also be seen as similar to the "pragmatic inference schemas" proposed by Cheng and her colleagues (1986, discussed in ch. 8). It is an open question whether these schemas or forms of inference are actually known as general rules. Alternatively, it is possible that some sort of account based on mental models can work for plausible reasoning. Johnson-Laird (as we noted in ch. 8) showed how it is possible to solve syllogisms by forming mental models, without knowing the syllogisms as patterns in their own right (the way a logician would know them). The same kind of analysis might work for plausible reasoning as well.

The development of new theories of inference in plausible reasoning (and in practical reasoning, or decision making) is an exciting area of inquiry, in which we can expect major advances in the next few years.[8] We must remember, however, that inference is only part of thinking; the other essential part is search.

Conclusion

The theories of everyday reasoning that provide the best descriptions of how people make inferences are those that are most consistent with the search-

---

[8] One question for the future is whether these new theories can help us distinguish good and poor inferences in everyday reasoning. The results discussed in chapters 11 through 14 may be relevant to this question.

inference framework. These theories allow that good inferences do not have to be certain and can admit qualification. Once the idea of uncertainty is admitted, the "goodness" of an argument depends on the relative weight of arguments for and against a possible conclusion and on the relative support that the evidence gives to this possibility as opposed to others. The theories of inference discussed later in this book all take this view.

This completes our review of basic concepts for the theory of thinking and our reevaluation of the traditional theory of logic. Part II examines normative models that we can apply to our thinking about our personal beliefs: probability theory (chs. 11 and 12), hypothesis testing (ch. 13), and judgment of correlations (ch. 14). The final chapter in part II (ch. 15) describes the general biases that cause error in choosing among beliefs and suggests some ways of avoiding them.

Part II

Probability and belief

Practically all thinking involves beliefs in some way. We make decisions on the basis of beliefs about the outcomes of each option. If I want to drive to the city, I choose my route according to my beliefs about speed and safety. When we think about the strengths of our goals, such as the relative importance of speed and safety, we do this as well on the basis of beliefs, for example, beliefs about what it would feel like to have an automobile accident. Beliefs themselves can be the objects of thought. I can think about how much the construction on the expressway is likely to slow me down, given that it is Saturday afternoon. (Is there a sports event in town?)

Part II explores three major approaches to the analysis of belief formation: probability theory, the theory of hypothesis testing, and the theory of correlation. It concludes with a chapter on biases in belief formation in general.

Probability theory (ch. 11) is a normative theory for evaluating numesically the strengths of our beliefs in various propositions. Like logic, it is a theory of inference, but unlike logic, it concerns degrees of belief rather than certainty. In chapter 12, we shall see that our belief strengths, as manifest in our judgments of probability, violate this normative model seriously. It is not just that our numbers are not exactly correct. They are often systematically out of order: We believe that one event is more likely than another when the rest of our beliefs imply the opposite. We can take steps to guard against these violations. Actively open-minded thinking can help. When probability judgments are very important, computers can help us as well.

The theory of hypothesis testing (ch. 13) concerns the selection of evidence: asking the right question to find out how much to believe some hypothesis. If we ask questions well, we can make inferences from their answers that bring our beliefs into line with the available evidence as efficiently as possible. Scientists try to do this when they design experiments, and physicians try to do it when they order tests. Again, we shall find certain biases that cause us to depart from the normative model. Some of these biases can be ameliorated by actively open-minded thinking, especially by considering other hypotheses than those we favor.

Chapter 14 deals with beliefs that concern the correlation between two variables. We tend to perceive data as showing correlations when we already believe that we will find a correlation. Chapter 15 shows that this distorting effect of prior belief occurs throughout our thinking, and the chapter also

169

explores the causes of this bias and the conditions under which it occurs. The existence of this bias is the main justification for my claim that we need to remind ourselves to be open to new beliefs and to evidence against our old ones: Our natural tendency is often the opposite.

11   Normative theory of probability

Our theory of thinking is intended to help us choose among actions and beliefs. Making such choices obviously often involves estimating the likelihood that various events will occur in the future: Will it rain tomorrow? Will I get the job I applied for? Probability theory is a well-established normative theory that deals with such estimates.

The history of the idea of probability is a long one (Hacking, 1975). It seems that the ancient Egyptians played games of chance that involved calculation of probabilities. In the seventeenth century, there was some development of the mathematical theory of probability. In part, this development was inspired by the practice of town governments raising money by selling annuities. Miscalculation of the chances of living to various ages left some towns bankrupt. One person who helped solve the problem of how to figure the price of annuities so that the seller makes a profit was Edmund Halley (also famous for discovering the comet that bears his name and for persuading his friend Isaac Newton to publish his work on planetary orbits).

Also in the seventeenth century, Blaise Pascal and others recognized that probability theory was relevant to everyday beliefs and decisions, not just to games of chance and other repeated events. Our interest in probability derives from this fact. I must point out, however, that the idea that probability is relevant to everyday beliefs is one view among others. We shall discuss these other views later in this chapter.

We shall think of probability here as a numerical measure of the strength of a belief in a certain proposition – for example, the belief that it will rain today or the belief that my sore throat is due to streptococcus. (A proposition is a statement that can be true or false. Propositions can concern future events, but they can concern present states or past events as well.) By convention, probability ranges from 0 to 1, where 0 means that the belief in question is certainly false – it will not rain – and 1 means that it is certainly true – it will rain. A probability of .5 means that it is equally likely to rain or not rain. Probability can also be expressed as a percentage, a fraction, or as an *odds* ratio – the ratio of the probability of a proposition being true to the probability of its being false. A probability of .75 is the same as 75%, or ¾, or 3 to 1 odds – because the probability of the proposition's being true (.75) is three times its probability of being false (.25).

We shall user the term *probability judgment* to indicate the assignment of a number to a belief.[1] The process of probability judgment includes evaluation of the evidence relevant to the belief in question, if any such evaluation occurs. When I judge the probability that the Democrats will win the 1988 presidential election, I engage in a process of search and inference before I assign the number. If, however, I have just gone through that process, I can assign a number to the resulting belief with no further thinking about the issue itself.

The mathematical theory of probability is a normative theory of inference. It specifies how the probability of one belief should depend on the probabilities of other beliefs that serve as evidence for or against the first belief: If the probability that it will rain is .8, then the probability that it will not rain has to be .2. If the probability of precipitation is .8 and the probability of all forms of precipitation other than rain is .3, then the probability of rain is .8 − .3, or .5. We shall see that a few simple rules determine the relation between the probability of one belief and the probabilities of other, related beliefs.

Part of our interest in the normative theory of belief stems from the role of belief in decision making. The strength of our beliefs in various consequences of our actions is and should be an important determinant of our decisions. Our belief about the probability of a certain kind of accident will determine what safety precautions we take or what kind of insurance we purchase. In chapters 16 and 17 we shall see how probabilities can be incorporated into the theory of decision making.

Although probability judgments are useful for making decisions, they concern belief only, allowing the users of such judgments to attend to the goals they have at the time. A weather forecaster tells us the probability of rain, rather than giving us direct advice about whether to carry an umbrella, because our goals may differ; some of us care more about getting wet than others. Similarly, an individual may make probability judgments at one time without knowing what goals and options will be present later, when the judgments are used.

What is the relation between this theory and everyday thinking? First, bear in mind that probability theory is a *normative* model, not necessarily a prescriptive one. That is, it is a standard by which we can evaluate the relationships among our beliefs, but it is not necessarily something we should *try* to follow.

How can we apply this standard? Our beliefs do not come with numbers assigned to them, so we cannot simply read off the numbers to determine whether they follow the theory. One way of applying the standard is to ask whether we can *assign* probabilities to beliefs in a way that follows the rules: All of our beliefs are held with various degrees of certainty. Some (such as

---

[1] Other authors sometimes use the terms "probability assessment" and "probability assignment" for the same process.

my belief that $2 + 2 = 4$) are for all practical purposes absolutely certain; others (such as my belief that every even positive integer is the sum of two primes, or my belief that the Democrats will win the 1988 election) are less than completely certain. Suppose we can compare our beliefs in degree of certainty. For any two beliefs, we can say which is more certain. If we can do this, then we could assign numerical probabilities to the beliefs. We could do this in many different ways, except that we would have to assign 1 to beliefs that were certain to be true and 0 to beliefs that were certain to be false, and we would have to make sure that we assign higher numbers to beliefs that were held with greater certainty. To determine whether a set of beliefs meet the normative standard, we could ask whether there is *any* way of assigning numbers to them so that the rules of probability theory are followed. We shall see in chapter 12 that this cannot be done in some cases.

Another way to determine whether a set of beliefs conforms to the model is to use actual numbers. We can give people numerical probabilities and ask them to make inferences from them about other numerical probabilities, as we did in the problem concerning six-children families at the beginning of chapter 2. (We assumed there that the probability of a boy was .5.) In doing experiments of this sort, we cannot always assume that people know how to assign probabilities to their beliefs in the best way. Sometimes we can set up the experiments so that our conclusions do not depend on this assumption. In other cases, we are interested in people's understanding of the normative theory itself, or in their ability to translate their beliefs into probabilities that are useful to others.

The ability to express beliefs numerically is a useful one when decisions are made by people who draw on the expertise of others. If you are trying to decide whether to undergo a surgical procedure, you might ask your surgeon how likely it is that the procedure will succeed. Likewise, military leaders can ask their intelligence officers about the likelihood of success of an attack, and political leaders can ask the same question about a peace initiative. In many such cases, information is provided verbally ("very likely"), but numerical probabilities are also used sometimes. Weather forecasters – the experts we rely on when we make our own decisions about umbrellas and outings – use numerical probabilities routinely ("30% chance of snow").

In sum, we can study numerical probabilities for three reasons. First, they can tell us about the rationality of belief – its conformity to a normative model – as long as we are careful not to assume that our subjects know how to assign numbers in a way that comes closest to the normative model. Second, we can study people's understanding of the normative model itself. Such an understanding can be useful to people who want to think carefully about the relationships among certain sets of their beliefs, such as physicians trying to diagnose a disease. Third, because probabilities are used to communicate belief strengths, we can study the accuracy of communication.

What is probability?

At the outset, one might ask whether probability judgments are really "judgments" at all. Aren't they much more objective than that? Crapshooters who know that the probability of snakeeyes is $\frac{1}{36}$ are not making a judgment; they are using the result of a mathematical calculation. Surely the weather forecaster and the surgeon are doing something like that too – or are they? How do we tell whether a probability judgment is correct? Is there an objective standard?

The question of what it means to say that a probability statement is "correct" has been the subject of competing theories, and the disagreement continues today. I would like to begin this discussion by doing some reflective thinking about the three major theories that bear on this issue (see Hacking, 1965; Savage, 1954; von Winterfeldt & Edwards, 1986).

The question of when a probability statement is correctly made has two different meanings: (1) How should we *make* or *construct* well-justified probability judgments? For example, when is a surgeon justified in saying that an operation will succeed with probability .90? (2) How should we *evaluate* such judgments after we know the truth of the matter? For example, how would we evaluate the surgeon's probability judgment if the operation succeeds, or if it fails?

These are not the same question. I may be well justified in saying that a substance is water if I have observed that the substance is odorless and colorless, with a boiling point of 212 degrees Fahrenheit and a freezing point of 32 degrees Fahrenheit. I would find that I had been wrong in hindsight, however, if the chemical formula of the substance turned out to be XYZ rather than H_2O (Putnam, 1975). In the case of water, we accept the chemical formula as the ultimate criterion of correctness, the ultimate evaluation of statements about what is water and what is not. We would still consider people to be well justified if they judged the substance to be water on the basis of its properties alone, even if our evaluation later showed that their judgment had been incorrect.

We shall discuss three theories. The first says that probability statements are about *frequencies*, the second says they are about *logical possibilities*, and the third says they are *personal judgments*. The frequency theory gives the same answer to the construction question as to the evaluation question, and so does the logical theory. The personal theory gives different answers.

The frequency theory

According to the frequency theory, probability is a measure of the relative frequency of particular events. By the simplest, most literal form of this theory, the probability of a smoker's getting lung cancer is simply the proportion of smokers who have gotten lung cancer in the past. According to this theory, unless a probability statement is based on such a proportion, it is meaningless and should not be made. If a probability statement differs from the observed relative frequency, it is unjustified and incorrect.

This theory runs into trouble right away. It would certainly make life difficult for weather forecasters. What could they possibly mean when they say that the probability of rain is 50%? They might mean "On days like today, it has rained 50% of the time in the past," but obviously they do not really mean this. Besides, if they did, they would have the problem of saying in what way the days they had considered were "like today." If these days were like today in being February 5, 1986, then there is only one such day, and the probability of rain would either be 1 or 0, and we will not know which it is until today is over or until it rains (whichever comes first). If those other days were like today in being February 5, regardless of the year, a simple record of past years would suffice for forecasting, and we could save a lot of money on satellites and weather stations. If those other days were like today in the precise configuration of air masses, then, once again, there probably were not any such days except today. The problem is thus that any event can be classified in many different ways. The relative frequency of the event, compared to other events in a certain class, depends on how it is classified.

The true frequency theorist might agree that weather forecasters are being nonsensical when they give probability judgments: But the problems of the theory do not end here. Suppose I flip a coin, and it comes up heads 7 out of 10 times – not an unusual occurrence. What is the probability of heads on the next flip? The simple frequency view would have it that the probability is .7, yet most of us would hold that the probability is .5, because there is no reason to think that the probabilities of heads and tails are different unless we have some reason to think that the coin is biased. The simple frequency view flies in the face of strong intuitions. That by itself is not reason to give it up, but it surely is reason to look seriously at some of the alternatives.

Some have attempted to save the frequency view from this last objection by modifying it. They would argue that probability is not just the observed frequency, but rather the limit that the observed frequency would approach if the event were repeated over and over. This seems to take care of the coin example. We think that the probability of heads is .5 because we believe that if we continued to flip the coin over and over, the proportion of heads would come closer and closer to .5.

Why do we believe this, though? We have not actually observed it. This approach already gives considerable ground to the view that probability is a judgment, not simply a calculation of a proportion. Moreover, this view does not deal with the weather-forecasting example. Most of us intuitively understand what the forecaster is trying to do. A theory of probability that disallows this activity is a strange theory indeed, and once again we are compelled to look for alternatives.[2]

---

[2] Another, more subtle, argument (from Hacking, 1965) against this view is that some sequences

The logical theory

The logical theory of probability is the theory usually assumed in most introductory treatments of probability, especially with respect to card games and dice. The theory is useful when we can define a set of logically equivalent, or *exchangeable* propositions: The evidence for each of these propositions is the same, and any two of them can be exchanged without affecting our beliefs in their truth, so their probabilities must be the same. Typically, we regard every card remaining in a deck as equally likely to be drawn when we make calculations in card games, because the only evidence we have for any particular card is simply that it is somewhere in the deck, and we have exactly this evidence for each of the cards.

The logical theory reached its fruition in the work of the philosopher Carnap (1950). Very roughly, his idea is that the probability of a proposition x is the proportion of exchangeable "possible worlds" in which x is true. In theory, one can list all of the possible worlds by taking every combination of the truth and falsity of all of the "atomic propositions," those propositions that can be true or false but cannot be expressed in terms of other propositions. The idea of possible worlds is used to justify the conventions of probability for exchangeable events. For example, the set of possible worlds in which I draw an ace from a deck of cards is exchangeable with the set of all possible worlds in which I draw a king.

Suppose I flip three coins. We generally think of the three flips as exchangeable, because we think that the order does not matter, and we think that the names we give to the coins do not matter either. There are eight compound events (three-flip units) that can be made up of these basic, exchangeable propositions: HHH (heads, heads, heads), THH (tails, heads, heads), HTH, HHT, TTH, THT, HTT, and TTT. In half of these compound events, the first coin comes up heads; hence, the probability of this even is ½. In ¼ of these worlds, the first two coins come up heads; hence the probability of both of these events is ¼; and so on. Of course, each of these events corresponds to an infinite set of atomic possible worlds.

Like the frequency view, the logical view holds that probability is objective – that is, it is something that can be known. When two individuals give different probability judgments, at most one can be correct. As in logic, once the premises are accepted, the conclusion follows. The assumptions here concern exchangeability.

An advantage of the logical view is that it solves the problem raised by

---

may have no limit. Consider the sequence HTTHHHTTTTT... In this sequence, H is followed by enough T's so that there are ⅔ T's, then T is followed by enough H's so that there are ⅔ H's, and so on, alternating. If you were dropped into the middle of the sequence somewhere, it would be reasonable to think that your chance of landing on a T would be .5, yet this sequence has no limit.

the coin. It explains quite well why we believe that the probability of a coin coming up heads is ½.

A disadvantage is that it is usually impossible to find exchangeable events. I cannot sensibly enumerate equally likely possibilities in order to calculate the probability of rain tomorrow, in the way that I would enumerate the possible poker hands in order to calculate the probability of a flush. Therefore, like the frequency theory, the logical theory renders many everyday uses of probability nonsensical. When I want to evaluate my physician's judgment of the probability that I have strep throat, it does not help to ask about the proportion of possible worlds in which I would have it. Likewise, the logical view is ordinarily useless as a justification for making probability judgments, except in textbook (or casino) cases of "fair" (perfectly unbiased) coins and roulette wheels.

The personal theory

The personal view of probability differs from the others in seeing probability as a personal judgment of the likelihood of a proposition or event, rather than an objective fact (Savage, 1954). By this view, a probability judgment can be based on any of one's beliefs and knowledge, including knowledge about frequencies or about the set of logical possibilities, but including other knowledge as well. Different people have different beliefs and knowledge, so two reasonable people might differ in their probability judgments. Thus, a physician may be justified in saying that a particular smoker has a .20 probability of getting lung cancer even though the relative frequency of lung cancer among smokers is .40. The patient in question might, for example, have lungs that look healthy on an X-ray film. Some other physician might be justified in saying that the probability was .30. Even if two people both had all of the relevant beliefs and knowledge for a given case, their judgments might still differ, although, as we shall see, we would not expect their judgments to differ by much.

The personal view makes the important distinction between the well-justified construction of probability judgments and their evaluation. The constructive part of the theory provides a normative theory (and in some cases a prescriptive theory) for our *thinking* about probability judgments. Probability judgments are not simply waiting in our heads to be pulled out when needed. Good thinking about probability judgments can help us both with forming beliefs consistent with our evidence and with assigning numerical probabilities to those beliefs.

The evaluation of probability judgments becomes more difficult when we accept the personal view. According to the other theories, a probability judgment can be evaluated in terms of frequencies or exchangeable events. By the personal theory, it is possible for one judge to be better than another, even if both make well-justified judgments. We need a way of assessing a judge's track record. We shall find one later in this chapter.

The main advantage of the personal view is that it applies more widely. It allows us to make probability judgments about anything, even unique events such as who will win the next United States presidential election. It therefore allows us to use our feelings that certain propositions are more likely to be true than others, even though we cannot justify these feelings in terms of relative frequencies or exchangeable events.

An apparent disadvantage of the personal view is that with this theory we have difficulty explaining why we ought to pay attention to knowledge of frequencies (for example, of the occurrence of diseases). If 40% of the last 10 million smokers have developed lung cancer, it seems wrong to believe that a particular, randomly selected smoker in this group has a 2% probability of developing lung cancer. Later, in the section on Bayes's theorem, we shall explore the reasons why the personal view does require us to attend to relative frequencies, even if we are not ruled by them.

Personalists take seriously the idea that probability judgments are always possible, even when one does not know anything about frequencies or exchangeable events. In some cases, personalists must appeal to the *principle of insufficient reason*: If there is no reason to expect one event to be more likely than another, then we should consider the two events to be equally likely. If a shuffled deck of cards is placed before us, we have no reason to believe that any particular card is more likely to be drawn than another, so we must assign a probability of $\frac{1}{52}$ to each card. This principle essentially incorporates the logical view (when it applies) into the personal view: If we have no reason to believe one proposition more than another, the events should be treated as exchangeable.

The principle of insufficient reason is controversial. The problem is that it can lead to different probability judgments, depending on how we define a "proposition" or an "event." Suppose you come into my laboratory and I show you an opaque urn full of marbles. I ask you the probability that the next marble I draw from the urn will be black. You might reason that each marble is either black or not black and that you have no reason to favor one or the other, so the probability must be $\frac{1}{2}$. Or you might reason that each marble is either black, white, gray, red, orange, yellow, green, blue, indigo, or violet, and, again, you have no reason to favor one or the other of these, so the probability of black is $\frac{1}{10}$.

The personalist can make two different replies to this problem. One is that probability, like logic, is dependent on the assumptions one makes. The two lines of reasoning just described make different assumptions about what the possible events are. Probability judgments can yield different results for different assumptions. One must choose one's assumptions carefully and then regard one's conclusions as subject to change if the assumptions change.

The second reply is that we never really need to make probability judgments from this sort of ignorance. When you come into my laboratory, you actually know a fair amount about marbles. You have seen a lot of them and you have some idea of the variety of colors. You also know something about psychologists and how likely they are to try to pull some trick on their subjects. You can put all of this knowledge together to make an informed judgment of the probability that the marble will be black. (I would guess about ¼, because I think black marbles are more common than other colors and that psychologists are far less likely to pull tricks than is commonly assumed.)

These replies do not settle the issue, which is one of great current interest. Many have felt that the real solution to the problem is to invent new theories of probability (for example, Shafer, 1976; Shafer & Tversky, 1985). The replies do allow us to proceed on the assumption that the personal view is at least a reasonable one.

In general, then, the personal view takes both relative frequency and logical analysis to be relevant to the construction of probability judgments, but it allows us to consider other factors as well, such as our understanding of how things work and our judgment of the extent to which frequency data are relevant. Because of this more liberal attitude toward the basis or justification of probability judgments, this theory offers no single, simple method for well-justified construction of probability judgments, as each of the other theories does. Many different methods can be well-justified.

The personal theory makes a clear distinction between the well-justified construction of probability judgments and their evaluation. The basis of this distinction is that complete evaluation can be done only after we know which propositions are true (or which events occurred). This after-the-fact evaluation tells us which of the many well-justified methods for constructing probability judgments work best.

Constructing personal probability judgments

According to the frequency theory and the logical theory, probability statements are reflections of objective facts in the world. According to the personal view, probability statements are judgments, and probability judgments need to be constructed by appropriate methods.

Probability as willingness to bet

What should we be trying to do when we make a probability judgment? Many theorists have argued that we should think about our personal willingness to bet that the proposition in question is true. Surely, the probability of a proposition should be one of the determinants of our willingness to act as though the proposition were true – to "bet on it" (see ch. 16). In addition, the idea that probability can be defined in terms of a tendency to take action ties the concept of probability closely to observable behavior. However, the idea that probability judgments can be constructed by thinking about our willingness to bet has drawbacks.

Ramsey (1931) argued that if we believe that the probability of an event is .5, this amounts to saying that we are equally willing to bet on the event's happening as on it not happening. To take a more complicated case, suppose I value $3 three times as much as I value $1. Suppose you ask me the probability that it will rain tomorrow, and I say that I would be willing to bet, at 3-to-1 odds, that it will. This means that I would be willing to accept $1 if it does rain, on condition that I would pay $3 if it does not. Moreover, I would be just as willing to do the opposite, to pay $1 if it rains or accept $3 if it does not. According to the betting interpretation of probability, this means that my subjective probability of rain is .75. I would regard it as three times as likely to rain (.75) as not to rain (.25).

Over a long series of making such bets, based on this same degree of belief, I would come out even, winning and losing the same amounts, if my judgments corresponded to the relative frequencies of the events. If I collect $1 every time the .75-probability event happens and pay $3 every time the .25-probability event happens, then, out of 100 events, I will collect about $75 for the more frequent event and pay out about $75 (25 times $3) for the less frequent event. This fact may help to make clear the use of the concept of betting in the measurement of probability. In sum, by this view, the way to construct personal probability judgments is to ask ourselves what odds we would consider fair. (We shall return to the connection between the personal view and relative frequencies.)

It is not clear that thinking about bets is the best way to elicit probability judgments (Shafer, 1981). We think about probabilities, and, more generally, the strengths of our beliefs, because our probability judgments help us to make decisions. We often do not know what decision to make until we think about the strengths of our beliefs about the consequences of the various options before us. We cannot consult our decisions to determine what we believe, because we need to know what we believe in order to make our decisions.[3]

Comparison with a chance setup

The idea of betting, however, can be useful in the task of explaining to judges (for example, experts) what their task is when we ask them to make probability judgments. We need not use anything as difficult to think about as betting odds. Instead, we can ask judges to compare the situation to some sort of

---

[3] One might also argue that if we could make decisions about risks directly, we would not need probability judgments to help us make them. This argument, however, can be answered. It may be useful to decompose complex decisions into simple ones, and one way to do this is by estimating probabilities of various outcomes through imagining gambles concerning just these outcomes. This subject will be discussed in more detail in chapter 16.

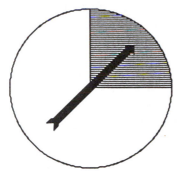

Figure 11.1. A spinner used to assess personal probability.

device with known probabilities, what Hacking (1965) calls a *chance setup*, such as an honest roulette wheel or a game "spinner" (pointer that spins). For example, suppose I want to assess my probability judgment, made as I write this chapter in 1987, that a Republican will win the U.S. presidency in 1988. Instead of thinking about what sort of odds I would be willing to take in a bet, I might simply imagine a spinner like the one shown in Figure 11.1. I might ask myself which is more likely: that a Republican will win or that the point of the spinner will land in the shaded part of the circle. I adjust the size of the shaded part until I am unable to say which is more likely. My probability judgment, when I have finished this adjustment, is the size of the shaded part (as a proportion of the whole). In practice, it would be a good idea to try this several times, sometimes starting with a small area and adjusting upward, sometimes starting with a large area and adjusting downward. Such techniques as this are used routinely in the formal analysis of decisions (ch. 16).

The chance-setup approach to probability assessment is consistent with the gambling approach. If I thought that the point of the spinner were more likely to land on the shaded part, I would be more willing to bet on that outcome; if I thought that it was less likely to land there, I would rather bet that a Republican would become president than that the point of the spinner would land on the shaded part. Although this approach helps judges understand the significance of probability judgments for action, it is important that they also understand the fact that they can construct their probability judgments by thinking about the evidence for their beliefs rather than by thinking about what choice they are inclined to make before they think about the evidence at all.

Well-justified probability judgments

Are there rules or constraints that will help in constructing probability judgments? If there are, these rules may serve as reasons we can give for our judgments, when we are asked to justify them, as well as methods for constructing them.

Surely some of these rules have to do with the use of evidence, part of the search-inference process. If you have more evidence for *x* than for *y*, you should assign a higher probability to *x*. If you get additional evidence for *x*, your probability judgment for *x* should increase. In probability theory to date, little has been said about such rules.

Other constraints on probability judgments have to do with the need for *coherence* among judgments concerning various propositions. This means that our probability judgments must obey the rules of probability *as a mathematical system*. Related judgments must "cohere" according to these rules. Three of the four basic rules that define the concept of coherence are the following:

> Two propositions, *A* and *B*, are *mutually exclusive* if they cannot both be true at the same time. If *A* and *B* are mutually exclusive, then $p(A) + p(B) = p(A \text{ or } B)$: That is, the probability of the proposition "either *A* or *B*" is the sum of the two individual probabilities. If we assume that "It will rain" and "It will snow" are mutually exclusive propositions (that is, it cannot both rain and snow), then the probability of the proposition "It will rain or it will snow" is the sum of the probability of rain and the probability of snow. This rule is called *additivity*.
>
> It is certain that any proposition will be either true or false. Hence, the probability of a proposition being true, plus the probability of its being false (called the probability of the *complement* of the proposition), must equal 1. A probability of 1 represents certainty.
>
> Two propositions are *independent* for you if you judge that learning that one proposition is true (or that it is false) will not change your judgment of the probability of the other. When two propositions, *A* and *B*, are independent, then $p(A \text{ and } B) = p(A) \cdot p(B)$. For me, whether I draw an ace from a deck of cards and whether it rains tomorrow are independent. Thus, the probability of both ace and rain equals the probability of an ace (1/13) times the probability of rain (1/2, according to the weather report), which would be 1/26.

The fourth rule of coherence will be described later when we discuss the formulas for Bayes's theorem.

Such rules put limits on the probability judgments that are justifiable. For example, it is unjustifiable to believe that the probability of rain is .2, the probability of snow is .3, and the probability of rain *or* snow is .8. If we make many different judgments at one time, or if our past judgments constrain our present judgments, these constraints can be very strong. As a rule, however, these constraints do not determine a *unique* probability for any proposition. Reasonable people with exactly the same evidence can still disagree.

One consequence of the rules is that the probability of mutually exclusive and exhaustive propositions must add up to 1.0. ("Exhaustive" means that the propositions considered are the only possible ones.) Psychological research has shown that people can easily be induced to violate this rule. Robinson and Hastie (1985) asked subjects to read mystery stories. At several points in the stories, evidence was revealed that implicated or ruled out one character or another as guilty of the crime. At each point, subjects were asked to indicate the probability that each of the characters was guilty. The probabilities assigned to the different subjects added up to about 2.0 for most subjects, unless the subjects were explicitly instructed to check the probabilities to make sure that they added up only to 1.0. When one character was ruled out, the probabilities for the others were not usually raised so as to compensate, and when a clue implicated a particular suspect, the probabilities assigned to the others were not usually lowered. (Later, we shall see many other violations of the rules.)

The rules of coherence can help us to construct probability judgments by giving us a way to check them. To return to the murder mystery, for example, if we regard the probability of the butler as .2, the neighbor as .3, and the parson as .8, we know, from the fact that the figures add up to more than 1.0, that something is wrong (unless the parson *is* the neighbor) and that we have reason to think again about the relation between these numbers and the evidence we have for the propositions in question. (Of course, coherence alone cannot tell us which numbers we ought to adjust.)

Although the coherence requirement plays an important role in the construction of probability judgments, it is still reasonable to ask how such judgments should be related to the evidence we have for them. If, in terms of the search-inference framework, we think of probability judgments as "strengths" assigned to "possibilities," we can ask how these strengths ought to be dependent on the weight of the evidence. As yet, little has been said about this, although the work of Collins and Michalski (in press, summarized in ch. 10) provides one approach.

Evaluating personal probability judgments

Let us turn now to the question of how probability judgments are to be evaluated, according to the personal theory. First, the criteria for well-justified construction, particularly coherence, can be used for evaluation as well. If a person's probability judgments are not coherent, for example, they cannot all be correct: At least one of them must be incorrect. There are two additional criteria that may be applied after the truth is known – that is, after it is known whether the event in question occurred or not: calibration and scoring rules.

Calibration

Suppose that I am a weather forecaster. On several different days, I say that there is a 75% probability of rain that day. On some of those days it does rain, and on some it does not. If my probability judgments are *well calibrated*, the proportion of these days on which it rains should be 75%, over the long run. It should also rain on 100% of the days for which I say there is a 100%

probability, 50% of the days for which I say there is a 50% probability, and so forth. If my judgments are perfectly calibrated, in the long run, these kinds of proportions will match exactly.

Note that my judgments can be coherent without being calibrated. For example, I can say that the probability of heads is .90 and the probability of tails is .10; these two are consistent with each other, but not with the facts. If my judgments are perfectly calibrated, however, they must also be coherent, for whenever I say that the probability of rain is 75%, I must also say that the probability of no rain is 25%.

Good calibration helps in making decisions. If the weather forecast is so poorly calibrated that the probability of rain is really 1.00 when the forecast says .25, I will get wet, if I regard .25 as low enough so as not to require an umbrella.

Calibration is a *criterion for evaluation* of probability judgments, not a method for making them. Calibration serves as a criterion in hindsight, after we know what happened. In principle, calibration could be assessed for judgments based on frequencies or on the logical view, but this would be superfluous. If the assumptions going into the judgments were correct, calibration would have to be perfect, and we would know what the probability judgments were without asking a judge.

It may seem that calibration is related to the frequency view of probability. In a way it is. Calibration certainly captures the idea that we want our probability judgments to correspond to something about the real world, which is perhaps the major idea behind the frequency view. By the personal view, however, a judgment can be justifiable even before the frequency data are in. For the frequency view, the judgment is meaningless unless the data are in. In addition, a personalist would argue that calibration, though always desirable, is often impossible to assess. When someone predicts the probability of a nuclear-power plant explosion, there are simply not enough data to assess her calibration.[4]

Scoring rules

We encounter certain problems in using coherence and calibration to evaluate probability judgments. Coherence does not take into account what actually happens. A judge can make completely coherent judgments and still get all of the probabilities exactly backward. (When such a judge said .80, the observed probability was .20; when the judge said 1.00, the event never happened.) Moreover, the idea of calibration does not tell us how to measure

---

[4] It is an important empirical question whether we can assess a judge's calibration *in general*, so that we could draw conclusions about her calibration in one area from her calibration in another. The answer to this question, however, has nothing to do with the question of whether judgments are in principle justifiable in the absence of frequency data.

Table 11.1. *Probability judgments made by two hypothetical weather forecasters*

A's judgment (p)	B's judgment (p)	Outcome
.90	.80	Rain
.10	.00	No rain
.50	.40	No rain
.80	.90	Rain

degree of miscalibration. A set of probability judgments is either calibrated or not; however, degrees of error surely make a difference.

More important, calibration ignores the *information* provided by a judgment. A weather forecaster's predictions would be perfectly calibrated if they stated that the probability of rain was .30 every day, provided that it does actually rain on 30% of the days. Such a forecast would also be coherent if the forecaster added that the probability of no rain was .70. These forecasts would be useless, however, because they do not distinguish days when it rains from days when it does not rain.

Is there some way of assigning a single score to a set of probability judgments, indicating everything we want to know about the accuracy of the judgments in the set? If we had such a measure, we could use it to compare the effectiveness of different judges or methods in specific situations, such as weather forecasting or medical diagnosis. As yet, nobody has discovered a uniquely best measure. Part of the field of mathematical probability, however, is concerned with the design of *scoring rules*, which are essentially formulas for evaluating the overall accuracy of a set of probability judgments (Lindley, 1982; von Winterfeldt & Edwards, 1986). These formulas use the same information that is used in judging calibration: a list of probability judgments coupled with the information about what actually happened.

Here is an example of a *quadratic scoring rule*. We look at p_i, the judgment for each of these outcomes. (The i refers to the i'th outcome; i is 1 for the first outcome, 2 for the second, and so on.) If the judge is doing a good job, p_i should be high when the event occurs and low when it does not occur. We set up the score so that a low score is good and a high score is bad (as in golf); a perfect score is zero. When the event does not happen, we look at p_i. When the event happens, we look at $1 - p_i$. The reason the rule is called "quadratic" is that we square these quantities before adding them up. Thus, the score will equal the sum of p_i^2 for outcomes that do not occur and the sum of $(1 - p_i)^2$ for outcomes that do occur.

Suppose we look at two weather forecasters' predictions of rain. Table 11.1 shows the data: probability judgments made by two judges, *A* and *B*.

By the quadratic rule, the score for judge A would be $(1-.90)^2 + .10^2 + .50^2 + (1-.80)^2$, which equals .31. The score for judge B would be $(1-.80)^2 + .00^2 + .40^2 + (1-.90)^2$, which equals .21. Because it is better to have a lower score, judge B seems to be a better forecaster. (Of course, four predictions are really too few to give a clear estimate.)

Certain scoring rules are called *proper*. This means that a judge should try to give her best estimate if she wants the highest score possible.[5] The quadratic scoring rule is proper, and it has other advantages as well.[6] Other scoring rules, however, such as the 4th power instead of the square, are also proper. In general, there is no uniquely best scoring rule. If possible, in practical applications, it is helpful to devise a scoring rule specifically for the application at hand.

Scoring rules are of considerable interest at present because of recent advances in the use of expert systems for calculating probabilities. In such systems, human experts enter basic knowledge into a computer program. For example, if the program is to provide the probability of each of several diseases for a specific patient, a physician might put into the computer probabilities of various symptoms of different diseases. The program uses various rules, such as Bayes's theorem (described shortly) to calculate the probability of each diseases from a list of the patient's symptoms. Whatever the application, it is usually possible to design several different expert systems for the same task, and it is often helpful to compare designs in terms of their results. Scoring rules are exactly what is needed to make such comparisons.

In sum, a good scoring rule serves as an overall summary of the relation between probability judgments and actual events. The rule is affected by the degree of miscalibration, and it takes information into account as well. There is no unique best scoring rule. To some extent, the way we score a probability assessor depends on why we want the probability judgments.

Bayes's theorem

An especially interesting consequence of the coherence requirement is Bayes's theorem. It is this theorem that explains how frequency information is relevant to probability judgment within the personal theory.

An example from medicine

Let us begin with a simple but very realistic example (from Eddy, 1982). Suppose that you are a physician. A woman in her thirties comes to you,

---

[5] An example of an *im*proper scoring rule is to take the absolute value instead of the square. In this case, the judge can score as high as by telling the truth, on the average, by raising judgments to 1.00 if they are over .50 and lowering them to 0 if they are under .50.

[6] If we think that there is some critical value of a probability for making a decision, and if this critical value is equally likely to occur anywhere in the interval from 0 to 1.00 inclusive, then the quadratic scoring rule estimates how often a judge will make incorrect decisions.

saying that she has discovered a small lump in her breast. She is worried that it might be cancerous. After you examine her, you think – on the basis of everything you know about breast cancer, women with her kind of medical history, and other relevant information – that the probability of cancer is .05 – that is, 1 in 20.

You recommend a mammogram, which is an X-ray study of the breast. You know that in women of this type who have cancer, the mammogram will indicate cancer 80% of the time. In women who do not have cancer, the mammogram will indicate cancer falsely 20% of the time. We can say that the *hit rate* is 80% and the *false-alarm* rate is 20%.[7] The mammogram comes out positive. What is the probability that the woman actually has cancer? Try to answer this by yourself (intuitively, without calculating) before going on.

Many people say that the probability is 80%; many others say that it is over 50%. Even some medical textbooks make this mistake (Eddy, 1982). Let us see what it would actually be, if our probability judgments are coherent. First, let us simply calculate it carefully; later, I shall explain a general formula for this sort of calculation.[8]

Suppose that there are 100 women of this type, and the numbers apply exactly to them. We know that 5 of them have cancer and 95 do not; this is from the initial judgment in the diagnosis. (We assume perfect calibration.) Of the 95 that do not have cancer, 20% will show a positive mammogram and 80% will not. Of the 5 that do have cancer, 80% will show a positive mammogram and 20% will not. Thus we have the following:

No cancer and positive mammogram	95 · .20 = 19
No cancer and negative mammogram	95 · .80 = 76
Cancer and positive mammogram	5 · .80 = 4
Cancer and negative mammogram	5 · .20 = 1

Because the patient had a positive mammogram, she must fall into one of the two groups with a positive mammogram. In the combined group consisting of these two groups, there are 23 patients. Of these 23 patients, 4 have cancer. Thus, the probability that our patient has cancer is $4/23$, or .17. It is far more likely that she was one of those who did not have cancer and who showed a positive result than that she really had cancer. Of course, a .17 chance of cancer may well be high enough to make the physician and the patient want to take the next step, probably a biopsy, but the chance is far less than .80.

Another very useful way of describing situations like this is to draw a tree diagram like the one in Figure 11.2. In this type of diagram, the number on each branch of the "tree" is the probability of taking that branch, given that

---

[7] In medicine, the term *sensitivity* is used instead of "hit rate," and *specificity* means 1 − (false-alarm rate); the "specificity" of this test is 80%. I shall stick with "hits" and "false alarms" because they are the terms generally used in psychology.

[8] In this section, I shall aim for clarity rather than mathematical rigor. I shall not show how everything done here can be derived from the rules of coherence. However, it can be. As a consequence of that fact, everything in this section is a consequence of the need for coherence.

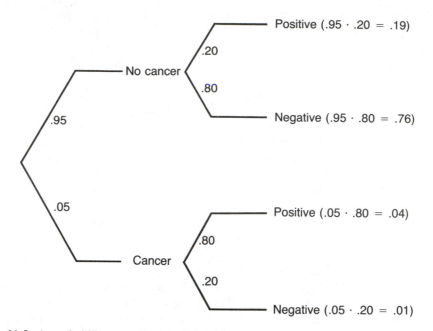

Figure 11.2. A probability tree diagram for the mammogram example.

one has gotten as far as the "root" of the branch in question (the roots are on the left). To compute the probability of getting to the end of a branch, on the right, you multiply all of the probabilities along the way. (This is illustrated in the equations at the right side of the diagram.) The advantage of this kind of diagram is that it helps you to think of all of the possibilities.

Formulas for Bayes's theorem

Let us now see how this sort of problem can be described by a general formula, derived algebraically from the rules of coherence and other assumptions.[9] First, we need to define *conditional probability*. The conditional probability of proposition A given proposition B is the probability figure that we would assign to A if we knew that B were true, that is, "conditionally" on A's being true. We write the probability of A as $p(A)$, and we write the conditional probability of A given B as $p(A/B)$. (Note that the slash here means "given," *not* "divided by.") In the medical example, if we use H to indicate the hypothesis (possibility) that the patient has cancer and D to indicate the datum

---

[9] We shall not discuss the mathematical details here. They are found in many textbooks of probability.

(fact, evidence) of a positive test result, we would have the values $p(H) = .05$; $p(D/H) = .80$; $p(D/\sim H) = .20$. The two conditional probabilities say that the probability of the datum given that the hypothesis is true is .80 and the probability of the datum given that the hypothesis is false ($\sim H$) is .20. (The symbol $\sim A$ means "not A" or "A is false," for any proposition A. $p(\sim A)$ is therefore "the probability that A is false.")

What we want to know in this case is $p(H/D)$. That is, we know that D is true, and we want to use this evidence to revise our probability judgment for the disease. Because we know that D is true, we can *conditionalize* on D. In other words, we can look at the probability of H in just those cases where D is known to be true – that is, the 23 patients.

We can calculate $p(H/D)$ from the fact that

$$p(H/D) = \frac{p(H \text{ and } D)}{p(D)} \tag{1}$$

In our example, $p(H \text{ and } D)$, the probability of the disease and the positive test result together, is .04 (4 out of 100 cases), and $p(D)$, the probability of the test result is .23 (4 cases from cases who have cancer and 19 from cases who do not, out of 100 cases. This is what we concluded before: The probability of cancer is $\frac{4}{23}$, or .17.

Why is this formula correct? Recall that the conditional probability of H given D is the probability that we would assign to H if we knew D to be true. If we think of probability as a proportion of cases, then we want to know what proportion of the cases with D also have H. This is just the number of cases with D and H divided by the number with D.

Formula 1 expresses the fourth rule of coherence, which says that our judgment of the conditional probability of A given B – our judged probability of A if we learned that B were true – should be equal to the ratio of our judgment of the probability of A and B to our judgment of the probability of B.

We can rewrite formula 1 as follows:

$$p(H/D) = \frac{p(D/H) \cdot p(H)}{p(D)} \tag{2}$$

This is because $p(D \text{ and } H) = p(D/H) \cdot p(H)$; we replace $p(H \text{ and } D)$ in formula 1. In case this is not obvious, it follows from formula 1 with H and D reversed (and from the fact that $p(D \text{ and } H)$ means the same as $p(H \text{ and } D)$):

$$p(D/H) = \frac{p(D \text{ and } H)}{p(H)}$$

Formula 2 is useful because it refers directly to the information we have. In the example, $p(D/H)$ is .80, and $p(H)$ is .05. We can make formula 2 still more useful by specifying how to calculate $p(D)$. There are two ways for D to occur; it can occur with H or without H. Thus we can conclude that[10]

$$p(D) = p(D \text{ and } H) + p(D \text{ and } \sim H)$$
$$= p(D/H) \cdot p(H) + P(D/\sim H) \cdot p(\sim H)$$

This leads (by substitution into formula 2) to formula 3:

$$p(H/D) = \frac{p(D/H) \cdot p(H)}{p(D/H) \cdot p(H) + p(D/\sim H) \cdot p(\sim H)} \tag{3}$$

Formulas 2 and 3 are called *Bayes's theorem*. They are named after Rev. Thomas Bayes (1764/1958), who first recognized their importance in a theory of personal probability. In formula 3, $p(H/D)$ is usually called the *posterior probability* of H, meaning the probability after D is known, and $p(H)$ is called the *prior probability*, meaning the probability before D is known. $p(D/H)$ is sometimes called the *likelihood* of D.

Still another version of Bayes's theorem is expressed in formula 4:

$$\frac{p(H/D)}{p(\sim H/D)} = \frac{p(D/H)}{p(D/\sim H)} \cdot \frac{p(H)}{p(\sim H)} \tag{4}$$

This form can be derived by using formula 1 to calculate $p(\sim H/D)$ and $p(H/D)$ and then dividing one by the other. Notice that the right side of the equation in formula 4 is just

$$\frac{p(D \text{ and } H),}{p(D \text{ and } \sim H)}$$

since $p(D \text{ and } H) = p(D/H) \cdot p(H)$, and $p(D \text{ and } \sim H) = p(D/\sim H) \cdot p(\sim H)$.

Formula 4 is expressed in terms of odds rather than probabilities. In our example, the odds of cancer are $^4\!/_{19}$ The term to the left of the equals sign in formula 4 is the odds of the hypothesis' being true given the datum D; this is called the *posterior odds*. To the right of the equals sign in formula 4 are two fractions. The one on the right is the *prior odds* of the hypothesis, the odds before the datum is known. In our example, this is $._{05}/._{95}$ or $^1\!/_{19}$. The other term is the *diagnostic ratio*, the probability of the datum (D), given that the hypothesis is true, divided by the probability of the datum given that the hypothesis is false. An advantage of this form of Bayes's theorem is that it is sometimes easier to assess the diagnostic ratio than to assess the two likelihoods that make it up.

This version also makes clear the two main determinants of the posterior odds: the prior odds and the diagnostic ratio. The posterior odds is simply the product of these two. Substituting the numbers from our example, we have

---

[10] The additivity rule and the rule that probabilities of mutually exclusive and exhaustive propositions add to 1 are both required for this conclusion.

$$\frac{4}{19} = \frac{.80}{.20} \cdot \frac{.05}{.95}$$

since $.80/.20$ is $4/1$ and $.05/.95$ is $1/19$. The important point is that the posterior probability should depend on two things: what the evidence says (the diagnostic ratio), and what we believed before we got the evidence (the prior odds). As we shall see, this is not always obvious.

Here is an exercise in which Bayes's theorem is used to construct a probability judgment. It is Sunday morning at 7 A.M., and I must decide whether to trek down to the bottom of my driveway to get the newspaper. On the basis of past experience, I judge that there is an 80% chance that the paper has been delivered by now. Looking out of the livingroom window, I can see exactly half of the bottom of the driveway, and the paper is not in the half that I can see. (If the paper's has been delivered, there is an equal chance that it will fall in each half of the driveway.) What is the probability that the paper has been delivered? The footnote has the answer.[11]

We should bear in mind the *purpose* of Bayes's theorem. It allows us to construct judgments of the probability of some hypothesis (the paper's having been delivered) given some data that we have observed (the absence of a view of the paper) on the basis of judgments about the probability of the data given the hypothesis and about the prior probability of the hypothesis. It is often possible to bypass the use of Bayes's theorem and judge the probability of the hypothesis given the data directly. I could have done this in the case of the newspaper. Even in such cases, however, Bayes's theorem can be used to construct a "second opinion," as a way of checking judgments constructed in other ways. We shall see in chapter 12 that the theorem can provide a particularly important kind of second opinion, because direct judgments are often insensitive to prior probabilities.

Why we should accept Bayes's theorem

Bayes's theorem is a consequence of the four rules of coherence we have stated. Why should we accept these rules? In chapter 16 we shall see that these rules are a mathematical consequence of expected-utility theory, a theory of decision making that defines how we can best achieve our goals when we make decisions under uncertainty about their outcomes, but there are other reasons, of a more abstruse (but no less important) sort.

Cox (1946, and 1979, pp. 132–142) has also shown that the four principles

[11] The prior probability is of course .80. If the paper has been delivered, there is a .50 probability that I will not see it in the half of the driveway that I can see. Thus, $p(D/H) = .50$, where D is *not* seeing the paper. If the paper has *not* been delivered ($\sim H$), $p(D/\sim H) = 1$. So, using formula 3, the probability of the paper's having been delivered is $.50 \cdot .80 \div (.50 \cdot .80 + 1 \cdot .20)$, or .67. If I want the paper badly enough, I should take the chance, even though I do not see it.

can be mathematically derived from two simpler assumptions about the relative strength of beliefs and from the laws of set theory (a form of the logic of propositions and categories discussed in ch. 9). One assumption is that once the strength of our belief in a proposition *A* is fixed, the strength of our belief in not-*A* can take only one value, for any proposition *A*. Our belief that it will not rain depends on our belief that it will rain, and vice versa. If our belief in rain increases, our belief in no rain must decrease.

The second assumption is that the strength of our belief that both *A* and *B* are true is determined once two other belief strengths are fixed: the strength of our belief in *B* and the conditional strength of our belief in *A* given *B* (that is, the strength of our belief in *A* if we were to find that *B* is true). *A* and *B* can stand for any propositions.[12] Our belief that a patient has *both* a sore throat and the flu can have only one strength once we have fixed the strength of our belief that the patient has the flu and the strength of our belief that the patient has a sore throat *if* he has the flu.

These are weak assumptions, because they do not say *what* function a belief should be of other beliefs. It is difficult to imagine how they could be wrong if we try to quantify the strengths of our beliefs. Cox shows, however, that any set of belief strength that conforms to his assumptions must also conform to the principles of coherence we have stated.[13] Cox concludes that probability is the only sensible way of representing belief strengths.

Of course, this is a normative argument. It does not imply that we should try to assign numbers to our beliefs. It does imply that if we do try to assign numbers there are severe limits on how we can do it without violating some very basic assumptions.

Why frequencies matter

Now let us return to the question of why probability judgments – and the beliefs they express – should be influenced by relative frequencies: That is, just what is wrong with believing that a randomly selected smoker's chance of getting lung cancer is .01 when 200 out of the last 1,000 smokers have gotten lung cancer? It seems that there is something wrong, but the personal view, as described so far, has trouble saying what, as long as a person's probability judgments are consistent with each other, that is, coherent. The

---

[12] Of course, *A* and *B* can be reversed, so that the belief in *A* and *B* is determined by the belief in *A* and the belief in *B* given *A*. Also, Cox does not quite state this assumption this way, because he regards all probabilities as conditional. He says that our belief in (*A* and *B*)/*C* is determined by our belief in *A*/(*B* and *C*) and our belief in *B*/*C*, where the slash indicates a conditional belief.

[13] More precisely, Cox shows that any set of belief strengths that conforms to his assumptions can be transformed into a coherent set by an exponential function. This limitation is not important for the issue at hand, however, because the exponent is fixed, and the exponential function preserves the rank ordering of probability assignments. (Heckerman (1988) extends Cox's argument, showing other advantages of probability.)

personalist's answer is that indeed it is impossible to criticize a person for any honest belief, as long as it is consistent with his other beliefs. The more information there is about relative frequency, however, in general, the closer the person's belief must come to what that information says. This is a result of the requirement of coherence itself. Specifically, Bayes's theorem implies that a probability judgment must get closer to the observed relative frequency as the number of observations gets larger.

The argument that supports this conclusion is mathematical. I shall not go through the whole argument, but here is a simple case. Suppose that there are 10 balls in an urn. Each ball is either white or black. You want to estimate the proportion of white balls. To help you do this, I draw a ball out of the urn, show it to you, and put it back. (I sample the urn "with replacement.") Then I do this again, and again. Suppose that after 100 draws, 71 of the balls have been black. What do you think the proportion of black balls is? Most people will say that 0.70 (7 out of 10) is most likely.

If we apply Bayes's theorem to this situation, we first note that there are 11 possible hypotheses about the proportion of white balls $(0, 0.10, 0.20, \ldots, 1.00)$. Each hypothesis has a *prior probability*, before any balls are drawn. The only requirement for the prior probabilities is that they all add up to 1.00. I shall also assume that none of them is zero (in cases like this, it would be unreasonable to rule out anything without evidence).

After we draw a sample of balls, the probabilities of the hypotheses – now *posterior probabilities* – change. To calculate the posterior probability of each hypothesis, we need to know the likelihood of our getting the same sample given the hypothesis; that is, we need to know $p(D/H)$. If the likelihood is high, that hypothesis will become more probable, relative to others.

Now the likelihood of a sample of 71 black balls out of 100 balls, given a hypothesis of 0.70, is fairly high. Thus, after the sample has been drawn, the probability of this hypothesis will increase, relative to others. The likelihood of finding 71 black balls in a sample of 100 balls, given, say, a hypothesis of .10, however, is extremely low, so the probability of this hypothesis will decrease after the sample has been drawn. In general, the posterior probabilities of some hypotheses will be higher than the prior probabilities of these hypotheses, and the posterior probabilities of other hypotheses will be lower. The greatest proportionate increase will occur for those hypotheses that come closest to the sample itself.

The larger the sample, the larger these effects become. The likelihood of 7 balls out of 10 being black, given a hypothesis of 0.50, is not especially low. The likelihood of 70 out of 100 is much lower, and the likelihood of 700 out of 1,000 is minuscule. (The probability of any specific number becomes smaller, in fact. The important point is that it becomes smaller faster for those hypotheses distant from the sample.) Thus, the larger the sample, the more probable the hypothesis closest to the sample proportion. When the sample is small, differences among people's prior probability judgments will excuse fairly substantial differences among their posterior probability judgments. As the sample becomes larger, it becomes more and more difficult to excuse such differences. The differences in the prior probability judgments would themselves have to be enormous. This is why the Bayesian personalist thinks that frequencies are relevant to probability judgment and belief formation.

This is not an unreasonable view. Take coin flips, for example. Our prior belief about the proportion of heads for a coin taken out of our pocket, as we noted earlier, is that proportions near .50 are very likely. Finding that 7 out of 10 flips came out heads would not change our beliefs much, because our prior probability for .50 is so much higher than our prior probability for, say, .70. If 700 out of 1,000 flips of a coin came up heads, however, we would begin to think that it was a trick coin, as improbable as we had thought that was at the outset. If 700,000 out of 1,000,000 flips came up heads, that would practically remove all doubt. We would be practically certain that we had a trick coin.

In sum, the personal view is able to account for our belief that relative frequency matters. It also explains why relative frequency sometimes does not matter very much, that is, when we have strong prior beliefs that the relative frequency is in a small range (for example, the relative frequency of heads will be close to .50). Although the personal view allows individual differences in judgment, it also asserts that the larger those differences, the less likely it is that they are the result of honest differences in prior probability judgments rather than simple errors.

We can think of the personal theory as a pair of designs, one for constructing judgments and the other for evaluating them. The main argument for the personal theory is that it allows us to assess probabilities when we need them – that is, for making decisions – using all of the information we have available.

Use of Bayes's theorem in expert systems

Bayes's theorem has been used extensively in expert systems,[14] including one that helps geologists look for mineral deposits (Duda, Hart, Barrett, Gashnig, Konolige, Reboh, & Slocum, 1976a), and many that provide probabilities for medical diagnosis (for example, Schwartz, Baron, & Clarke, 1988).[15] The basic idea is most easily explained in the case of medical diagnosis.

---

[14] This section, which is quite abstract, is included largely for the benefit of students who already have an interest in expert systems.

[15] Many systems use "certainty factors" and "belief functions" instead of probabilities. Some of the early workers who designed these systems were suspicious of probability theory for a variety of reasons (including their ignorance of its philosophical and mathematical basis). Some of these systems, particularly those using certainty factors, can lead to nonsensical conclusions. One way of fixing such systems to avoid such conclusions made them equivalent to probability theory (Heckerman, 1986). In the case of belief functions, however, the dispute

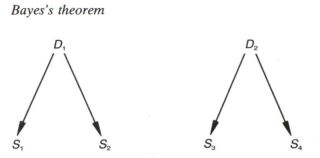

Figure 11.3. Conditional probabilities of symptoms (*S*) (given certain diseases [*D*]), when the symptoms are conditionally independent (given the same diseases).

Suppose that we are trying to determine the probability of two diseases, D_1 and D_2, and that there are four possible symptoms that a patient might have, S_1, S_2, S_3, and S_4. We ask an expert to tell us the probability of each symptom being observed, given each disease, or $p(S_j/D_i)$. From this, we know that the probability of *not* observing a symptom is $1 - p(S_j/D_i)$.[16] Now suppose we observe that some symptoms are present and others are absent. If we know the probability of the whole list of observed symptoms, given each disease, or $p(S_1, \ldots / D_i)$, this is equivalent to a likelihood in Bayes's theorem. If we know, in addition, the prior probability of each disease for a given patient, $p(D_i)$, we can apply Bayes's theorem.

The difficulty here is this: How do we calculate the probability of a whole *list* of symptoms, given each disease? One way to do this is to assume that the symptoms are *conditionally independent*. That is, *if* the patient has a given disease, the knowledge that a patient has one symptom does not affect the probability that the patient has any other symptom. The symptoms are independent *conditionally* on a patient's having the disease. If we can make this assumption, then the probability of a list of observed symptoms, given the presence of each disease, is just the product of the probabilities of the individual symptoms given the disease. Thus, $p(S_1, S_2, \ldots / D_i) = p(S_1 / D_i) \cdot p(S_2 / D_i) \cdot \ldots$ We can represent the situation with the diagrams in Figure 11.3.

In real life, however, the assumption of conditional independence for symptoms usually does not make sense. (This was one of the reasons that early workers despaired. They thought this assumption was necessary.) For example, appendicitis usually causes an inflammation of the intestines, which, in turn, causes nausea and anorexia (loss of appetite). Even if we know, from other evidence, that a patient has appendicitis, once the symptom of nausea

with probability theory seems more serious. For additional reading, see Charniak (1983); the symposium in *Statistical Science*, 1987, 2 (1); and Baron (1987).

[16] We assume here that all relevant symptoms have been asked about. If a symptom has not been asked about, the probability of knowing what we know about it – namely, that it is present or absent – is 1.

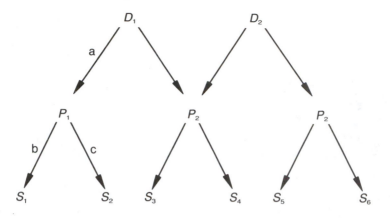

Figure 11.4. Conditional probabilities of symptoms (*S*) (given certain pathstates [*P*]) and of pathstates (given certain diseases [*D*]), when the symptoms are conditionally independent (given the same pathstates).

appears, anorexia is also more likely. Anorexia and nausea are *not* conditionally independent, given appendicitis.

The most common way to solve this problem (Charniak, 1983) is to develop a more adequate model of the situation. Instead of thinking about diseases and symptoms, we add at least one additional level, often called the level of *pathstates*. The pathstates are caused by the diseases, and the symptoms are caused by the pathstates. Pathstates are conditionally independent, given disease; and symptoms are conditionally independent, given pathstates. We get a tree like the one in Figure 11.4. Here P_1, P_2, and P_3 represent pathstates, and *a, b*, and *c* rephesent conditional probabilities of the lower state given the state immediately above.

With a tree like this, it is easy to calculate the probability of a given set of symptoms, as long as each line (branch) on the tree has been assigned a probability and as long as we know the prior probability of the disease. To get some idea of how this is done, consider only the probabilities labeled *a, b*, and *c* in the tree diagram; these are, respectively, $p(P_1 / D_1)$, $p(S_1 / P_1)$, and $p(S_2 / P_1)$. Considering only this part of the whole tree, the probability of S_1 and S_2 together, given D_1, would be $a \cdot b \cdot c$. This is because the probability of the pathstate P_1 given D_1 is *a*, and if the pathstate is present, the probabilities of the symptoms are *b* and *c*, respectively. Because the symptoms are independent, given the pathstate, we can multiply their probabilities. (For more details, see Kelly & Barclay, 1973; Duda, Hart, & Nilsson, 1976; Pearl, 1982; and Schwartz, Baron, & Clarke, 1988.)

Computers make complex calculations easy, and it may seem as though all we need to do, in order to construct an expert system, is develop the best possible normative theory and then program a computer with it. We must remember, however, that expert systems are truly *systems*. They are not only computer programs: Rather, they are computer programs, plus their justifications, plus (most important) procedures for eliciting probabilities from *people* (experts). Experts must be given the best opportunity to use their knowledge, and, if necessary, they must be helped to think about it in the most useful way. Thus, expert systems are prescriptive solutions to practical problems; they are not necessarily just realizations of a normative model. In particular, we need to do more descriptive research to find out what kinds of structures are most suited for elicitation of personal probabilities from experts and to determine the extent to which expert opinion and frequency data can each be relied upon. The design of expert systems depends as much *on the psychology of experts as on the mathematical possibilities*.

Conclusion

The theory of probability describes the ideal way of making quantitative judgments about belief. Even when we simply judge which of two beliefs is stronger, without assigning numbers to either belief, the one we judge to be stronger should be the one that is more probable according to the rules of probability (as applied to our other beliefs). Let us now turn to the psychological research in this area to find out how people ordinarily make judgments of these types. The difference between the normative theory (described in ch. 11) and the descriptive theory (ch. 12) will suggest some prescriptive improvements.

12   Descriptive theory of probability judgment

How closely do most of us follow the normative theory when we make probability judgments? Until the late 1960s, it was thought that even people with little experience did reasonably well at it intuitively. Since then, psychologists have found that we do poorly at making probability judgments – in systematic ways. It is not just that our judgments are erroneous: Our judgments are erroneous because we attend to variables that we should ignore and ignore variables to which we should attend. Misleading heuristics, naive theories, and the basic processes that cause poor thinking contribute to these errors. Luckily, research has shown that with practice and education to correct such errors, we can improve our probability judgments and become very good judges indeed.

Accuracy of probability judgments

How accurate are our probability judgments? To answer this question, let us use the normative standards we developed in chapter 11. First, we can ask whether we are sensitive to information about frequencies when such information is available. (Of course, from a personal point of view, probability judgments ought only to approximate relative frequencies, but when judges use frequency information to revise their personal probabilities, it surely helps them to perceive that information correctly.) Second, we could ask about calibration. This section is concerned with frequency judgments and calibration. A third way of assessing accuracy is to assess coherence. Several results discussed later in the chapter demonstrate systematic biases that cause incoherence (like the study made by Robinson and Hastie, 1985, mentioned in chapter 11).[1]

Frequency judgments

How good are people at assessing frequencies? A number of studies have found that when people are asked to judge frequencies of events that they have some experience with, they underestimate very high frequencies and

---

[1] A fourth method is to apply scoring rules to probability judgments, but this method has not been used much as a research tool.

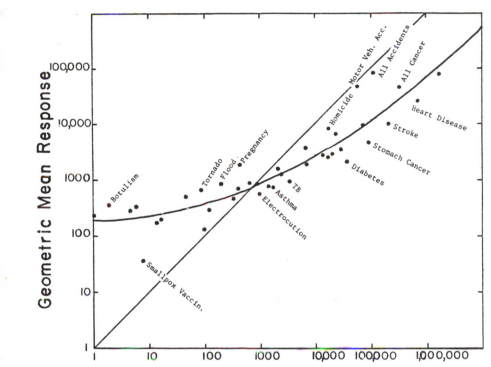

Figure 12.1. Subjects' estimates of the frequency of various causes of death as a function of actual frequency. Reprinted by permission from S. Lichtenstein, P. Slovic, B. Fischhoff, M. Layman, & B. Combs, "Judged Frequency of Lethal Events," *Journal of Experimental Psychology: Human Learning and Memory* (1978):4(6), 565, Figure 10. Copyright 1978 by the American Psychological Association. Reprinted by permission of the author.

overestimate very low ones. For example, Attneave (1953) asked subjects to estimate the relative frequency with which various letters of the alphabet occur in ordinary written English. What percentage of all of the letters in a newspaper, for example, are *a*'s, *e*'s, and so forth? Subjects tended to overestimate low probabilities (*z*'s) and underestimate relatively high ones (*e*'s). A similar effect was observed by Lichtenstein, Slovic, Fischhoff, Layman, and Combs (1978) when subjects were asked to judge the frequency with which various dangers caused deaths in the U.S. population today. The actual frequencies range from a death rate of zero for smallpox, to heart disease, with a rate of 360,000 per 100,000,000 people per year. A plot of the data from this study is shown in Figure 12.1.

These results are not really so surprising when we think about the effect of inaccuracy itself on numerical probability estimates. Errors of any sort tend to push numbers toward the middle of the probability scale. For example, an error in judging the probability of death from smallpox (0) can go only in

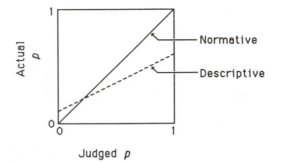

Figure 12.2. Typical pattern of results for probability of a subject's judgment being correct as a function of the subject's confidence that the judgment is correct.

one direction – up, since subjects do not give numbers less than zero as answers. There is more for us to learn from this study of Lichtenstein and her colleagues, however, and we shall return to it.

These results imply that we tend to overestimate the probability of very infrequent or unlikely events, such as accidents in nuclear-power plants or rare diseases. (Later in this chapter, however, we shall describe biases that tend to make such estimates too *low*.)

Calibration and overconfidence

How well calibrated are most people's probability judgments? Adams and Adams (1960) asked subjects to make various kinds of probability judgments – for example, subjects were asked to spell a word and then to indicate their *confidence* that they were correct as a probability figure (percentage). When subjects said that they were "100% certain" that they were correct, they were actually correct about 80% of the time. When their confidence was 80%, they were correct about 55% of the time. In general, subjects were overconfident. Although their mean confidence was 72%, their mean accuracy was 57% on the words used. Only at the very lowest probabilities, from 0% to 20%, were subjects underconfident. For example, when subjects indicated 0% confidence in a spelling (certain to be wrong), they were actually correct about 12% of the time. This pattern of results is shown in Figure 12.2.

Researchers have found this pattern of results – general overconfidence, especially when confidence is high, but underconfidence when confidence is low – in a great variety of tasks (Lichtenstein, Fischhoff, & Phillips, 1982, provide a review). Sometimes the effects were not as pronounced as in the graph in Figure 12.2. For example, subjects do not deviate from good calibration quite as much when they are asked to recognize correct spellings rather than to produce them (Adams & Adams, 1960). In other cases, though, overconfidence is extreme. Wright, Phillips, Whalley, Choo, Ng, Tan, and

Wisudha (1978; see also Wright & Phillips, 1980) gave subjects a general-knowledge questionnaire with items such as "When did the People's Republic of China join the U.N.: 1971 or 1972?" or "What is the capital of New Zealand: Auckland or Wellington?" Subjects were asked to answer the questions and to indicate their confidence as a probability. All of the items had two choices for answers, so subjects could score 50% correct by guessing; a confidence level lower than 50% was therefore never warranted. College students from Hong Kong and Malaysia were correct only about 65% of the time when they said that they were 100% certain of being correct. (The probability judgments of Indonesian students were even more poorly calibrated.) British students' answers were considerably better calibrated; they scored about 78% correct when they said that they were 100% certain. These differences are not the result of differences in knowledge about the questions: Rather, the British subjects were more cautious, using the 100% category far less often, so that they were more likely to be correct when they did use it. Wright and his colleagues suggest that cultural differences affect the way that people think about probability.

Fischhoff, Slovic, and Lichtenstein (1977) examined a number of possible explanations of the basic finding of overconfidence for high-confidence judgments. They used items like those used by Wright and his colleagues (for example, "Absinthe is: a liqueur or a precious stone?"), as well as other kinds of items – for example, items in which subjects had to indicate which cause of death was more common in the United States (for example, appendicitis, or pregnancy, abortion, and childbirth taken together).

They noted that the probability scale is limited at the top. It does not allow people to go beyond 100%, so any error may tend to make people give a spuriously large number of 100% judgments. To test this theory, they asked subjects to express their judgments as odds instead of percentages. It then became impossible to indicate 100% confidence, for that would correspond to infinite odds. This helped a little, but the basic effect was still present.

Fischhoff and his colleagues also considered as a possible explanation of overconfidence the possibility that people have little idea what probability means: "People's inability to assess appropriately a probability of .80 may be no more surprising than the difficulty they might have in estimating brightness in candles or temperature in degrees Fahrenheit. Degrees of certainty are often used in everyday speech (as are references to temperature), but they are seldom expressed numerically nor is the opportunity to validate them often available" (p. 553).

This argument does not explain all the results. Even if people do not have a good feeling for what "80% confidence" means, they do have a good idea of what 100% confidence means: It clearly means absolute certainty – no chance at all of being incorrect – yet the overconfidence phenomenon is still found with 100% judgments.

In addition to the finding of overconfidence at 100%, another finding suggests that overconfidence is not merely a result of misuse of the probability scale: People themselves are willing to act on their judgments. Fischhoff and his colleagues asked the subjects whether they would be willing to play a game. After making the confidence judgments (still using odds for their estimates), the subjects were told (p. 558),

Look at your answer sheet. Find the questions where you estimated the odds of your being correct as 50 to 1 or greater... We'll count how many times your answers to these questions were wrong. Since a wrong answer in the face of such high certainty would be surprising, we'll call these wrong answers "your surprises."

The researcher then explained:

I have a bag of poker chips in front of me. There are 100 white chips and 2 red chips in the bag. If I reach in and randomly select a chip, the odds that I will select a white chip are 100 to 2, or 50 to 1, just like the odds that your "50 to 1" answers are correct. For every "50 to 1 or greater" answer you gave, I'll draw a chip out of the bag... Since drawing a red chip is unlikely, every red chip I draw can be considered "my surprise." Every time you are surprised by a wrong answer..., you pay me $1. Every time I am surprised by a red chip, I'll pay you $1.

Of course, since the subjects' confidence was usually *greater* than 50 to 1, they stood to come out ahead if their estimates were well calibrated. Twenty-seven of 42 subjects (people who responded to an advertisement in a college newspaper) agreed to play the game. (Several other subjects agreed when the payment for a red chip was raised.) In one experiment, the game was not actually played. If the game had been played – because of the overconfidence effect – subjects would have lost an average of $3.64 per person (assuming that 1 out of every 51 chips drawn was red). Only 3 out of 36 who agreed to play would have won any money. In a second experiment, subjects were told that the game would actually be played. Thirteen out of 19 subjects agreed to play, and all 13 lost money. (Of course, the experimenter did not really take the money. Because he knew about the overconfidence phenomenon, that would have made the experiment a con game.) These results show that if the subjects did not know how to use the probability scale or the odds scale, they did not *know* that they did not know. (Now *you* know!)

The general finding of overconfidence must be qualified by an additional fact. Probability judgments are not very sensitive to the amount of knowledge that subjects have about the test items in question (Lichtenstein & Fischhoff, 1977). For example, two tests were constructed, one using difficult items and one using easy items. (All items concerned general information.) On the difficult test, the mean percentage correct was 62%, but the mean confidence rating was 74%. On the easy test, however, the mean percentage correct was 80%, although the mean confidence rating was 78%. Notice that the mean confidence ratings did not differ much for the two tests, although the mean scores did differ. As a result, although subjects were overconfident on the difficult items, they were underconfident on the easy items; they did not seem to realize how easy the items were. Even on the easy test, however, subjects were still overconfident when they gave extremely high confidence ratings: For 100% ratings, the actual percentage correct was about 93%. Thus, subjects are not *always* overconfident. Rather, it might be said that they are always overconfident *when they express extreme confidence*. More generally, it might be said that confidence ratings are not affected as much as they should be by the amount of knowledge that the subject has about the type of item or about the particular item. To put it another way, the calibration curve is not as steep as it should be.

Is it humanly possible to be well calibrated? Is the overconfidence effect the result of a bias or a limitation on our ability? We do not know the answer to this in general. We do know the answer for expert judges who make probability judgments every day as part of their work: The answer is that such people can be amazingly well calibrated.

Murphy and Winkler (1977) studied the calibration of some 25,000 weather forecasts made in the Chicago area over a 4-year period ending in 1976. Since 1965, weather forecasts have included probability information for rain, snow, and other conditions. Weather forecasters use a variety of information, including statistical tables of events of past years, but they do make their predictions on the basis of personal judgment; weather forecasts are made by people, not computers. Murphy and Winkler found that calibration was nearly perfect. When the forecasters said that there was a 100% chance of rain, it rained about 98% of the time, and so on down the line.

This does not mean that the forecasts were always very informative. Again, if you know that it rains on 1 out of every 10 days, your forecasts can be perfectly calibrated if you give .10 as the probability of rain, every day. Of course, this is not what the forecasters did.

Most important, this result shows that overconfidence can be overcome. Whatever their accuracy in predicting the weather itself, weather forecasters are extremely accurate in assessing the confidence that should be placed in their own predictions. Quite possibly, they learn this from years of feedback.

Research has demonstrated that a major cause for the phenomenon of "overconfidence when confidence is high" is a bias that I have emphasized earlier: the tendency to seek evidence in favor of an initial belief, as opposed to evidence against it. Koriat, Lichtenstein, and Fischhoff (1980) gave subjects the same sort of two-alternative questions used in the studies described earlier and asked for confidence judgments. Some subjects were asked to give reasons *for* and *against* their favored answer before assigning a confidence judgment. Other subjects gave only *for* reasons, others *against* reasons, and others none at all (as in the original studies). The overconfidence phenomenon was reduced (but not completely eliminated) in those subjects who were asked for both *for* and *against* reasons and in those subjects who were asked for *against* reasons alone. Apparently subjects were failing to think of such criticisms on their own, without the explicit instruction to do so. Subjects who were asked to give *for* reasons did not differ from the control group that gave no reasons at all. Apparently subjects think of *for* reasons on their own, without prompting.

In a related study, Hoch (1985) asked graduating business students, just beginning their search for jobs, to assign probabilities to various outcomes of their job search, such as "What is the probability that your starting salary *will* exceed _____ [dollars]?" or "What is the probability that you *will* receive more than _____ job offers by the end of the school year?" Actual data were collected on the same subjects at the end of the school year from computer records of the placement office. Subjects had generally been overconfident, although they were more overconfident when asked about high salaries as opposed to low ones, and about few offers as opposed to many. Subjects who were told to think of reasons why the event in question might not occur showed less overconfidence than subjects not told to generate reasons. (For the low-salary or few-offer events, there was little effect: subjects did *not* become *under*confident when asked to think of "against" reasons; therefore thinking of "against" reasons did not simply decrease probability estimates whether they were accurate or not.) Subjects who were told to think of reasons why the event *might occur* showed the same overconfidence as subjects not told to generate reasons. As in the study by Koriat and his colleagues, it appears that subjects generate reasons on their "favored" side without being told, but they do not tend to do as thorough a job of generating reasons on the other side. Here, the "favored" side is the optimistic one; uninstructed subjects seem to be generating reasons in favor of something they would like to be true.

In sum, one reason for inappropriately high confidence is failure to think of reasons why one might be wrong. Such inappropriate confidence could, in turn, cause a person to stop searching for alternative possibilities, leading to insufficient thinking.

Heuristics and biases in probability judgment

The rules of probability define coherence. A good way to ask whether our probability judgments are coherent is to study the *inferences* that we make from some probabilities to others. For example, in the mammogram example in chapter 11 you were asked to infer the probability that a woman patient had cancer from a few other probabilities. In the 1960s, Daniel Kahneman and Amos Tversky began to study such inferences. They were able to demonstrate consistent errors, or biases. Moreover, they suggested that these biases could be explained in terms of certain heuristics that the subjects were using to make the inferences.

The representativeness heuristic

Consider the following problem (Tversky & Kahneman, 1982, p. 156, from an earlier unpublished study):

A cab was involved in a hit and run accident at night. Two cab companies, the Green and the Blue, operate in the city. You are given the following data:

(a) 85% of the cabs in the city are Green and 15% are Blue.
(b) A witness identified the cab as Blue. The court tested the reliability of the witness under the same circumstances that existed on the night of the accident and concluded that the witness correctly identified each one of the two colors 80% of the time and failed 20% of the time.

What is the probability that the cab involved in the accident was Blue rather than Green?

Try to answer this intuitively before reading on. Did you notice that this problem is analogous to the mammogram problem? The question there was whether the patient had cancer; the issue here is whether the cab was Blue. The prior probability here is .15, because that is the proportion of Blue cabs in the city. Instead of a mammogram, we have a witness's report. The witness's "hit" rate is .80 and his "false-alarm rate" is .20. If we apply Bayes's theorem, formula 4, we get:

$$\frac{p(H/D)}{p(\sim H/D)} = \frac{p(D/H)}{p(D/\sim H)} \cdot \frac{p(H)}{p(\sim H)} = \frac{.80}{.20} \cdot \frac{.15}{.85} = \frac{12}{17}$$

Thus, $p(H/D)$ is $12 \div (12 + 17)$, or .41. Most subjects, however, say that the probability is over .50, and many say that it is .80. They think that the cab is more likely to be Blue than Green, but the correct inference from the information presented is the reverse.

Why do we make such errors? Perhaps subjects misunderstand the idea of conditional probability. They are told that the probability of the witness's reporting Blue, given a Blue cab, is .80, but when asked later what they were told, they often say they were told that the probability of a Blue cab, given that the witness reports Blue, is .80 (D. Davis, personal communication). This mistake is similar to the conversion error in logic (ch. 9), in which subjects seem to confuse the statement "All A are B" with the statement "All B are A." This mistake will account for those subjects who say that the probability of the cab's being Blue was .80, but many subjects, without going as high as .80, still give probabilities over .50.

Kahneman and Tversky (1972) proposed another mechanism for this effect, the *representativeness heuristic*. "A person who follows this heuristic evaluates the probability of an uncertain event, or a sample, by the degree to which it is: (*i*) similar in essential properties to its parent population; and (*ii*) reflects the salient feature of the process by which it was generated" (p. 431). The representativeness heuristic may be based on "the degree of correspondence between a sample and a population, an instance and a category, an act and an actor, or, more generally, between an outcome and a model" (Tversky & Kahneman, 1983, p. 295). In the taxicab problem, the data about the witness seem to be salient, or striking, for most subjects. The subjects think that the courtroom testimony is generated in a way that is like the way in which the test results with the witness were generated. (These were the results that led to the 80% figure.) The proportion of Blue cabs in the city does not appear to these subjects to be very important, although it is.

To help subjects notice this proportion, Tversky and Kahneman (1980) gave it a *causal* role in the accident. They replaced item *a* in the taxicab problem with this item: "(a') Although the two companies are roughly equal in size, 85% of all cab accidents in the city involve Green cabs and 15% involve Blue cabs." Subjects given this version were more likely to pay attention to the prior probability; this was indicated by their giving lower probability estimates. (Ajzen, 1977, found similar results.)

The bias caused by the representativeness heuristic can be illustrated in a number of other problems. Kahneman and Tversky (1973) asked one group of subjects to estimate the *proportion* of first-year graduate students in the United States in nine different fields (business administration, computer science, engineering, humanities and education, law, library science, medicine, physical and life sciences, and social science and social work). Subjects judged computer science to be the second smallest (7% of all graduate students) of the nine fields, with social science and social work the second largest (17%). (These judgments were realistic at the time the study was done, around 1970.) These proportions constitute the prior probabilities, which are often called the *base rates*, before any additional evidence about a particular graduate student is provided.

Another group of subjects was given the following personality sketch of a first-year graduate student (1973, p. 238):

Tom W. is of high intelligence, although lacking in true creativity. He has a need for order and clarity, and for neat and tidy systems in which every detail finds its appropriate place. His writing is rather dull and mechanical, occasionally enlivened by somewhat corny puns and by flashes of imagination of the sci-fi type. He has a strong drive for competence. He seems to have little feel and little sympathy for other people and does not enjoy interacting with others. Self-centered, he nonetheless has a deep moral sense.

The subjects were asked to judge how *similar* Tom W. was to the typical graduate student in each of the nine fields. The subjects considered Tom to be most similar to computer-science students and least similar to social-science and social-work students. These similarity ratings correspond to the representativeness of the sketch of each of the categories.

A third group was told that the sketch of Tom had been written by a psychologist, on the basis of projective tests, when Tom was a senior in high school. This group of subjects was asked to rank the nine different fields according to the *probabilities* of Tom's being in them. The rankings matched almost perfectly the rankings given by the similarity group. Tom was considered to be most likely to be studying computer science and least likely to be studying social science or social work. The probability ratings were not related at all to the prior probabilities. When subjects are asked to make a probability judgment, they apparently base it entirely on their beliefs about similarity, or representativeness, and not at all on their beliefs about prior probability. (It can be assumed that this group of subjects would have given the same prior probability and similarity ratings as the other groups; all groups were drawn from the same population of respondents to an advertisement in a college newspaper.) This neglect of prior probability leads to systematic errors in ranking the fields in probability, that is, in saying which of two fields was more likely. The error is therefore not just a matter of not assigning the right numbers to beliefs.

These same results were obtained even when subjects were told that the personality description was written when Tom was in the 9th grade, on the basis of an interview with a counselor, and even when the subjects were told that this sort of evidence is not very useful. These results were found again in another type of study in which subjects were actually given the prior probability information; once again, it was ignored, and probability judgments were determined by similarity. Only when subjects were given no evidence at all on which to base a similarity judgment did they make use of their beliefs about prior probability.

Psychologists themselves make this kind of mistake. Langer and Abelson (1974) showed a film of an interview to a group of psychoanalysts and a group of behavior therapists. Half of the members in each group were told that the young woman being interviewed was a student who had asked for psychotherapy. The other half were told that the student had volunteered for a psychological research project and that the interview was conducted by the researcher as part of the project. All subjects (the analysts and behavior therapists) were asked to judge whether the student interviewed was neurotic. The two subgroups of the analysts gave different judgments as a function of what they were told; they were more likely to rate the student as neurotic if they were told that she had sought psychotherapy than if they were told that she was a volunteer in an experiment. The behavior therapists gave the same rating of neuroticism, no matter what they were told.

Langer and Abelson concluded that the analysts were "biased" by what they had been told about the student and that the behavior therapists were not biased. Davis (1979) does not agree that the analysts were biased. He argues that the analysts were simply sensitive to the prior probabilities, whereas the behavior therapists were not. Surely a student who asks for psychotherapy, Davis claims, is more likely to be neurotic than the average subject in a research project. Unless one believes that the interview provides perfect information, like a diagnostic test or a witness that is always right (an impossibility), one ought to supplement the information from the interview with other information at one's disposal, such as the fact that a student had asked for psychotherapy. If anyone made an error here, Davis concludes, it was the behavior therapists, for neglecting the information about the student. Ironically, Davis points out, Langer and Abelson themselves made the same error, for they too judged the information about prior probabilities to be irrelevant.

An example that has practical meaning for college students is the use of various kinds of information on an individual's background, such as the prestige of the college a student attended or the student's social or ethnic origins, in the prediction of success in graduate school or in a job. The argument from Bayes's theorem is that such facts are often relevant. If students with a certain kind of social and cultural background are more likely to do well in graduate school or jobs than students from some other background, then that aspect of background should be used, if we seek the most accurate possible prediction. If we simply ignore group membership (when it is statistically relevant), members of disadvantaged groups can be expected, on the average, to perform less well than members of advantaged groups. Such neglect of group membership therefore constitutes a kind of special consideration for members of disadvantaged groups. There are, of course, excellent social reasons why we should try to help disadvantaged applicants by giving them special consideration, but when we do this we are pursuing other goals than picking the applicants who can be expected to perform best. The special consideration that results from simply neglecting group membership might be too much, too little, or the wrong kind of consideration, in view of these other goals. (Part III of this book discusses many aspects of decision making that are relevant to policy issues of this sort.)

Another apparent effect of the representativeness heuristic, aside from the neglect of information about prior probabilities, is the *conjunction fallacy*. Tversky and Kahneman (1983, p. 297) gave subjects the following description:

Linda is 31 years old, single, outspoken and very bright. She majored in philosophy. As a student, she was deeply concerned with issues of discrimination and social justice, and also participated in anti-nuclear demonstrations.

Subjects were then asked to rank the following items in terms of probability:

> Linda is a teacher in an elementary school.
> Linda works in a bookstore and takes Yoga classes.
> Linda is active in the feminist movement. [F]
> Linda is a psychiatric social worker.
> Linda is a member of the League of Women Voters.
> Linda is a bank teller. [T]
> Linda is an insurance salesperson.
> Linda is a bank teller and is active in the feminist movement. [T and F]

The critical items here are those that I have marked T ("teller"), F ("feminist"), and T *and* F; the other items are fillers, designed to disguise the issue. Of course, subjects rated F as very probable and T as very unlikely; however, they rated T *and* F as more probable than T alone.

Of course, the coherence requirements of probability theory make this choice impossible. The set of people who are both bank tellers and feminists cannot be larger than the set of female bank tellers; these sets would be the same only if every female bank teller were an active feminist.

What the subjects do seem to be doing, once again, is judging probability according to representativeness, or similarity. Although the description given was not judged (by other subjects) as very representative of women bank tellers, it was judged to be *more* representative of women bank tellers who are feminists. (See Tversky and Kahneman, 1983, for other examples and an interesting discussion.) This error leads to an incorrect ordering of probabilities. It therefore concerns the strengths of beliefs themselves, not just our ability to assign numbers to beliefs.

Another kind of error possibly related to the use of the representativeness heuristic is the *gambler's fallacy*, otherwise known as the *law of averages*. If you are playing roulette and the last four spins of the wheel have led to the ball's landing on black, you may think that the next ball is more likely than otherwise to land on red. This cannot be. The roulette wheel has no memory. The chance of black is just what it always is. The reason people tend to think otherwise may be that they expect the *sequence* of events to be representative of random sequences, and the typical random sequence at roulette does not have five blacks in a row.

Is use of the representativeness heuristic irrational? If so, how? In everyday reasoning, it is not necessarily irrational to use similarity in our judgments. In many cases, there is little else we can rely on as a guide to the interpretation of a piece of evidence.

When we rely exclusively on similarity, however, neglecting other reasons against our initial conclusion, such as prior probabilities, we are also failing to search for evidence. It is apparently not the case that we are unable to look for other evidence. Recall that when information about prior probabilities was given a causal role in the revised taxicab problem, which stated the companies' different accident rates, subjects attended to it. Therefore, the representativeness heuristic may, in part, reflect insufficient search and the lack of actively open-minded thinking.[2]

In situations in which very careful thinking is required, such as medical decisions potentially involving life and death, the evidence we have seen suggests that formal calculations may be worthwhile. Even the best thinking – unaided by mathematics – may give inferior results.

---

[2] In the original taxicab problem, the evidence that is ignored consists of the prior probabilities, which are given as part of the problem. The search that subjects fail to undertake may be the search for reasons why the prior probabilities are relevant.

The availability heuristic

People often judge probability by thinking of examples. Consider the following problem (Tversky & Kahneman, 1973, p. 211): Which is more likely, that a word in English starts with the letter *K* or has *K* as its third letter? The sensible way to try to answer that is to think of examples of words. This is the *availability heuristic*. Most people find it easier to think of words that start with *K* than words with *K* as their third letter, so they say that the former is more probable. Actually, the latter is more probable; we think otherwise, Tversky and Kahneman assert, because our memory of spellings tends to be organized by initial letters.

The same researchers give another example (Tversky & Kahneman, 1983, p. 295): What is the probability that a seven-letter word randomly selected from a novel would end in *-ing*? What is the probability that such a word will have *n* as its sixth letter? When different groups of subjects were asked these questions, the probability estimates were higher for *-ing* than for *n*. Of course, the former instances are included in the latter instances, so the former instances cannot be more frequent. Here, the conjunction fallacy is produced by the availability heuristic. The words ending in *-ing* are more available because the suffix *-ing* is a better retrieval cue than a single letter; subjects think of words more quickly when given this cue than when given the other.

Recall the study that Lichtenstein and her colleagues made (1978) of judgments of the frequency with which different dangers caused death in the United States. We have already noted that subjects tended to overestimate the frequency of low-probability events, and vice versa. Lichtenstein and her colleagues found, however, that there was another important determinant of errors in estimation: the frequency with which dangers were mentioned in newspapers. For example (taking into account the effect of frequency itself), tornadoes and electrocutions – which are almost always reported in the paper – are overestimated. Deaths resulting from smallpox vaccinations and many common diseases such as asthma are underestimated; these things are usually not reported.

Researchers have also demonstrated the effects of the availability heuristic in subjects' use of probability trees. When experts try to assess the probability of an event's occurring – let us say an engineer wants to predict the probability of a catastrophe in a nuclear power plant – they often use such tree diagrams as a way of trying to ensure that they have considered all of the possibilities. By breaking such a problem down in this way, we can obtain a more accurate probability assessment.

To take a more familiar example, however, consider the following list of categories of the things that can prevent a car from starting (presented in outline form rather than tree form, for readability):

Battery charge insufficient
Faulty ground connections
Terminals loose or corroded
Battery weak

Starting system defective
Switches defective
Transmission not in "park" or "neutral"
Seat belt problem (1974 cars)
Faulty starter motor
Starter drive defective

Fuel system defective
Insufficient fuel
Excess fuel (flooding)
Defective choke
Defective air filter

Ignition system defective
Coil faulty
Distributor faulty
Spark plugs defective
Defective wiring between components

Other engine problems
Oil too thick
Pistons frozen
Poor compression

Mischievous acts or vandalism
Theft or breakage of vital part (such as
    battery)
Siphoning of gas
Disruption of wiring

All other problems

Each of the sub-possibilities listed can be further subdivided. For example, "faulty ground connection" can be subdivided into "paint," "corrosion," "dirt," and "loose connections." Fischhoff, Slovic, and Lichtenstein (1978) presented this tree, with all of the sub-sub-possibilities, to a group of automobile mechanics and asked for probability estimates for the major branches. Subjects assigned a mean probability of .078 to the last category, "all other problems." A similar group of mechanics was then given the tree with two of the branches pruned, those involving the starting and ignition system. The subjects using the unpruned tree had assigned mean probabilities of .195 and .144 to these two branches, respectively. In the pruned tree, the problems that these branches represented should go under "all other problems," and the probability for that category should therefore increase from .078 to .078 + .195 + .144, or .417. The actual mean probability assigned to "all other problems" by the group with the pruned tree was .140, a slight increase but not big enough.

When something is not represented in our analysis, we tend not to think of it. This effect may weigh on the other side of the debate about nuclear power plants from the other effects we have been considering. Availability of frightening news stories, such as those about the Three-Mile Island and Chernobyl accidents, as well as overestimation of the frequency of such accidents (which very rarely occur), may tend to lead to overestimates of risk, but failure to consider what information might be omitted from the analysis may lead to underestimates. Most nonexpert estimates of accident risk are based on just this sort of analysis. People tend to underestimate the probability of "all other problems."[3]

---

[3] A well-known professor of decision theory – after lecturing on fault trees for cars not starting – went to the parking lot to find that his own car would not start. After checking all the branches of the tree that he could check without the help of a mechanic, he finally called a towing

Availability is also affected by personal experience. When we do something with another person, we may remember our own point of view more vividly than we remember the point of view of the other person – a point of view we may not even experience. Ross and Sicoly (1979) asked husbands and wives to estimate the extent to which they were responsible for a number of activities, such as cleaning the house, making breakfast, and causing arguments. Ratings of the two spouses for the same activity tended to differ. Each spouse tended to think that he or she was more responsible than the other spouse thought. As a result, the total responsibility added up to more than 100%. For example, if a husband thought that he was 60% responsible for causing arguments, and the wife thought that she was 60% responsible, that would add up to 120%. This effect held for the negative items (such as causing arguments) as well as the positive ones. In a second study, the same effect was found when basketball players were asked to estimate the extent to which the members of their own team, rather than their opponents, were responsible for "turning points" in their games.

Availability of examples can be affected by mood, and this effect, in turn, can affect probability or frequency judgments. E. J. Johnson and Tversky (1983) gave college students descriptions of various events, written like newspaper stories, to read. They then asked the students to estimate the frequencies with which 50,000 people would experience certain dangers (such as traffic accidents, fire, and leukemia) within a 1-year period. When the newspaper story concerned the violent death of a male undergraduate – for example, in a fire – estimates of *all* risks increased, whether or not they were similar or identical to the event in question. The same kinds of increases occurred when the story was simply a sad one about a young man who had just broken up with his girlfriend while undergoing other stresses from his family and his job. When the story was a happy one about a young man who experienced positive events – getting into medical school and doing well on a difficult examination – frequency estimates decreased.

The kinds of availability problems described so far cannot be called "irrational" when they occur in everyday life. It would, in most cases, take an unreasonable amount of effort to avoid the effects of memory organization or of the information we are given by others. In many cases, these effects could be avoided only with the use of systematic data analysis of the sort done by scientists. Most of the time, availability is probably as good a guide as we can expect when systematic data are not available. In extremely important decisions, however, such as those that affect many people, it is worthwhile to take every precaution we can imagine to avoid error. In such decisions, the danger of availability effects is a good reason for us to rely on

service. As the car was about to be towed away, he noticed that the car was not his. His car started with no trouble, after he remembered where he had parked it.

systematic data collection and analysis – rather than our own hunches – when numerical data are available.

Hindsight bias

Another cause of distortion that is observed in everyday reasoning can be more easily avoided. This is illustrated in the phenomenon of *hindsight bias*. Fischhoff (1975) asked subjects to read true historical accounts of incidents with which they were unfamiliar, drawn from history books as well as personal psychological case histories. One scenario concerned the battle between the British forces and the Gurkhas (from Nepal) on the northern frontier of Bengal in 1814. Subjects were asked to assign numerical probabilities to the major possible outcomes: British victory; Gurkha victory; military stalemate with no peace settlement; or military stalemate with a peace settlement. The history provided was consistent with any one of these outcomes.

Some subjects were told the outcome: The British won. These subjects were asked to rate the probability of the various outcomes as they would have if they had not been told the true outcome. The mean probability that these subjects assigned to the true outcome was .57. Other subjects were not told the outcome. They rated the probability of a British victory as only .34. Evidently, subjects who were told the outcome could not avoid what they knew in hindsight.

Similar results have been obtained from many other kinds of studies. Fischhoff (1977) give subjects two-choice questions concerning general knowledge, like those used in the studies of confidence described earlier in this chapter. Some subjects were told the answers and were asked what probabilities they would have assigned to these answers had they not been given them. Once again, these probabilities were higher than those assigned to the same items by other subjects who had not been given the answers. It appears that people tend to underestimate how much they have learned from being told something. They tend to think they knew it all along.

Slovic and Fischhoff (1977) presented subjects with descriptions of scientific experiments. For example, in one experiment, some blood from a rat that had just given birth was injected into another female rat. The question was whether the second rat would exhibit maternal behavior. Some subjects, the hindsight group, were told that the first time this experiment was done, the rat did exhibit the behavior. They were asked to estimate the probability that all of the next 10 rats would replicate this initial result. Other subjects, the foresight group, were asked how they would answer this question *if* the experiment worked on the first rat. The hindsight group gave higher proportions. For this experiment, the hindsight subjects gave a mean probability of .44, and the foresight subjects gave a mean probability of .30.

In a second study, subjects were asked to give reasons why the study worked out the way it did *and* how they would explain the result if it came out the *other* way. These instructions reduced the effect. Apparently, in this study – and very likely in the other studies concerned with hindsight bias – when subjects are given the "answer," they think of reasons why this answer must be correct. They fail to think of reasons why it might be incorrect, reasons that might occur to them if they were asked to estimate the probability of the outcome without knowing how it actually turned out.

This effect seems to be an example of one of the major biases described in chapter 3, a tendency to search for evidence in a biased way – in particular, to search for evidence that favors a possibility that is already strong. Telling people the answer is a way to make that possibility strong. Telling them to think of evidence on the other side is a way to reduce the bias.

Anchoring and adjustment

Representativeness and availability are the heuristics that have received the most study, but there are doubtless many others. The *anchoring and adjustment heuristic* affects quantitative estimates of all sorts. Tversky and Kahneman (1974) asked subjects to estimate certain proportions, such as the percentage of African countries in the United Nations. "For each quantity, a number between 0 and 100 was determined by spinning a wheel of fortune in the subject's presence. The subject was instructed to indicate first whether that number was higher or lower than the value of the quantity, and then to estimate the value of the quantity by moving upward or downward from the given number" (p. 1,128).

The number the subject started with, determined solely by the spin of a wheel, had a marked effect on the final estimate. Subjects who were given high numbers to start with gave higher estimates than those given low numbers. The adjustment was insufficient. There is nothing wrong (in principle) with forming an estimate by starting with one value and then adjusting it successively as each new piece of information comes to mind. The mistake that subjects make is not adjusting enough. This phenomenon supports the claim I made (in chapter 3) that we tend to be biased in favor of our present beliefs. We do not take sufficient account of evidence against them. (In this experiment, subjects could manifest this bias by searching their memories for evidence consistent with the initial estimate, or anchor, even though they know that this estimate is completely arbitrary.)

Underadjustment may help to explain why we tend to underestimate *confidence intervals*, an important statistical measure with numerous practical and scientific applications. A confidence interval is a numerical interval within which a certain quantity has a certain probability of falling. If we estimate some quantity (such as what the Dow Jones Industrial Average will be tomorrow) and then give an "interval" around that estimate such that the true value has, say, a 90% chance of falling within the interval, we have provided a "90% confidence interval" for that quantity. It has been found that subjects typically give confidence intervals that are too small (Alpert & Raiffa, 1982) – a kind of overconfidence effect. Perhaps people underadjust, once they have determined their initial best estimate, or anchor. They may fail to think of a sufficient number of reasons why their initial estimate could be substantially wrong.

Averaging

Birnbaum and Mellers (1983) presented subjects with a task very much like the taxicab problem. Subjects were asked to estimate the probability that particular used cars would last for 3 years. They were told the prior probability figures for cars of the same model and year, for example, 30% probability of lasting for 3 years. For most problems, subjects were also told that a judge had examined the car and had pronounced it in "good shape" (or, in other problems, in bad shape). Subjects were also given statistical information about the reliability of the judge; for example, they might be told that the judge had correctly identified 60% of the cars that would last for 3 years and 60% that would not. Each subject was given several problems of this type, so that the subject's sensitivity to prior probabilities and diagnostic evidence (what the judge said about the car) could be determined by comparing the conditions with different values of these quantities.

Subjects were generally sensitive to both prior probabilities and diagnostic evidence. (Previous studies have found that prior probabilities are not totally neglected when subjects are given several problems with different prior probabilities rather than just one problem.) The results when prior probabilities were very high (.90 probability of lasting) or very low (.10 probability) were especially interesting. Take the case in which the prior probability is .90; the judge says the car is in good shape; and the judge is correct 60% of the time for good cars, and 60% for poor cars. By Bayes's theorem, the probability that the car will last is slightly higher than .90. The odds are

$$\frac{p(H/D)}{p(\sim H/D)} = \frac{p(D/H)}{p(D/\sim H)} \cdot \frac{p(H)}{p(\sim H)} = \frac{.60}{.40} \cdot \frac{90}{.10} = \frac{27}{2}$$

Subjects typically give a value considerably *lower* than .90 under these circumstances (and a value higher than .10 when the prior probability is .10 and the judge says the car is in bad shape). When they are given the prior probability alone, they use it. They say that the probability is .90, for a prior probability of .90 (and .10, for a prior probability of .10).

What they seem to be doing is *averaging* the information they are given. (See ch. 18 for another example of averaging.) This leads them to weigh the evidence from the judge in the wrong direction. Averaging can result from a kind of anchoring-and-adjustment process in which subjects anchor on one probability (for example, the prior probability) and adjust in the direction of the other (for example, the diagnosticity of the judge's opinions). Lopes (1987a) found that subjects can be easily taught to avoid this error by thinking, first, about the direction in which each piece of evidence should change their probability judgment and, second, about how much their judgment ought to move toward a probability of 1 or 0.

Conclusion: prescriptive theory of probability

In this chapter, we have examined a number of biases in probability judgment and the heuristics that seem to cause them. How might we interpret these biases and heuristics from the point of view of *prescriptive* theory? How serious are they? Is it irrational to neglect prior probabilities when estimating posterior probabilities?

Cohen (1981) has argued that the rules of probability are not even normative, because no one has presented a good argument explaining why we ought to follow them. Violations of the rules, according to Cohen, are wrong only from the point of view of the rules themselves, as though we had violated the rules of a game. I argued in chapter 11 that the rules are not arbitrary and can be justified in terms of arguments concerning their suitability to their purpose.

The view at the opposite extreme (which perhaps no one holds) is that probability theory is both normative and prescriptive, so that any violation of it is a clear instance of irrationality. A counterexample to this extreme view is that some effects of the use of the availability heuristic are prescriptively justifiable even though they are normatively incorrect. To avoid these effects – at least in the laboratory tasks where they are found – would require much more time than it is reasonable for a person to spend. (Of course, for more important decisions, the extra time would be well spent.)

Von Winterfeldt and Edwards (1986) argue that many violations of probability theory are real and potentially serious but are not "irrational"; rather they are simply the result of ignorance – of our not having learned certain methods of mathematical calculation or estimation (like the heuristic that Lopes taught her subjects). This view could certainly account for the biases involved in averaging. The errors in averaging observed in the laboratory show only that a knowledge of probability theory does not develop on its own without instruction. The results are no more a sign of irrationality than it would be if we demonstrated that most people cannot solve problems in physics; we cannot expect them to, because they have not had a course in physics yet. People's willingness to make probability judgments despite their lack of training suggests that they are using a "naive theory" like the naive theories of physics discussed in chapter 6. Evidence of bias in averaging is evidence of a need for education – but the kind of education in question is specific to probability.

The important aspect of this view is its claim that biases are specific to calculations with numerical probabilities, as opposed to thinking or belief formation in general. It is, in my opinion, irrelevant to questions of rationality whether a bias results from mere ignorance or from something else (such as, perhaps, unwillingness to use rational methods even after learning how to use them). Rational methods are those methods of thinking that help people achieve their own goals (or the goals they ought to have). The most important of these methods are those that can be used in all thinking. If an irrational bias that affects all thinking — such as the lack of active open-mindedness — results from ignorance about rational thinking itself, the bias is still irrational, because it prevents people from achieving their goals. Therefore, the important part of Von Winterfeldt and Edwards's argument is that the biases are specific to numerical calculation.

That view holds for averaging but not for all the biases. Some of the ones that we have observed reflect two central biases that prevent good thinking in general: insufficient search, or the failure to consider alternative possibilities, goals, and additional evidence; and favoritism toward initially favored possibilities. These central biases seemed to be involved in overconfidence and in hindsight bias. They may be involved in representativeness bias as well, since information about prior probabilities could be a neglected source of evidence against initial conclusions. If people thought more thoroughly about what evidence was needed, they could take prior probabilities into account, whether or not they received special instruction in probability. Likewise, people who think critically about their own heuristics, by looking for cases in which the heuristics are misleading, can learn more useful heuristics. These central biases partly account for other, more specific, biases because they stand in the way of the learning that might correct them.

For most people, however, special instruction, as well as good thinking, is required to learn about probability theory. Probability is already taught as part of school mathematics. More systematic instruction is warranted in those parts of probability in which our naive theories seem to be particularly harmful, such as the relevance of prior probabilities and the dangers of hindsight, availability, and extreme confidence.

13 Hypothesis testing

Data! Data! Data! I cannot make bricks without clay.

Sherlock Holmes

A hypothesis is a proposition that we evaluate, or test, by gathering evidence concerning its truth or, more generally, its probability. A physician trying to explain a patient's illness forms hypotheses about the patient's disease and then tests these hypotheses by asking the patient questions and ordering various tests. A scientist trying to explain the cause of a disease also forms hypotheses and tests them by doing experiments or by gathering other sorts of evidence (such as statistics about the incidence of the disease). Chapters 9 through 11 (concerned, respectively, with logic and probability) have already discussed how inferences from such evidence are made, and chapter 14 (on correlation) will say more.

Hypothesis *testing*, the topic of this chapter, is the selection of the evidence, the asking of questions. The physician must decide what questions to ask, and the scientist must decide which data to collect. Hypothesis testing is that part of the search-inference process in which the thinker searches for evidence that can strengthen or weaken various possibilities. Each possibility is a possible answer to some question (goal) that inspired the search for hypotheses: What is wrong with the patient? What causes this disease? (Tweney, Doherty, and Mynatt, 1981, provide a good collection of articles on this topic.)

Hypothesis testing is important in everyday life and in other professions as well as in medicine and science. Fodor (1975) and others have suggested that children learn the meanings of words by testing hypotheses. When we solve a test problem from Raven's Progressive Matrices (ch. 2), we gather evidence to test some hypothesis about the rule. We try out a command on a computer in order to test some hypothesis about what the command does. Clinical psychologists test hypotheses in the same way physicians do, and, of course, detectives test hypotheses all the time.

Hypothesis testing is an essential part of actively open-minded thinking because it involves putting our beliefs to the test of evidence. The very act of testing a favorite hypothesis requires that we be open to the possibility that it is incorrect (if we are willing to make the correct inference from counterevidence) and that we challenge our hypotheses actively rather than

218

waiting passively for counterevidence to come along (Horton, 1967; Popper, 1962).

Before we can test hypotheses, we must have them in mind. Hypothesis formulation is the search for possibilities to test. A good hypothesis answers the original question, can be tested by gathering additional evidence, and is consistent with the evidence at hand. A scientist must try to think, simultaneously, of good hypotheses and good experiments to test them. Sometimes we collect evidence in the hope that it will suggest a hypothesis – as Sherlock Holmes did so well – rather than to test a hypothesis that we have in mind.

This chapter is concerned with the normative, descriptive, and prescriptive theory of hypothesis testing. The theory of probability – coupled with a simple theory of decision making–turns out to provide a good normative model. Departures from this model suggest certain prescriptive heuristics: considering alternative hypotheses, and looking ahead by asking what we will do with the information we seek when we get it.

Hypotheses in science

An example from medicine

A classic case of hypothesis testing in science, which illustrates how vital hypothesis testing can be, was the work of Ignaz Philipp Semmelweis on the causes of childbed fever, or puerperal fever (Hempel, 1966), a disease that is now known to bear large responsibility for the high mortality rate for new mothers that was a fact of life, in Europe and the United States, until the late nineteenth century. Semmelweis's work was done in the 1840s, before the acceptance of what we now call the "germ theory" of disease and the use of antisepsis. The Vienna General Hospital had experienced a very high rate of deaths from puerperal fever for several years (over 10% in some years) among women who had just given birth in the First Maternity Division. The prevalence of the disease in the Second Maternity Division was much lower (around 2%).

Semmelweis, a physician in the First Division, set out to discover the cause. He first put aside a number of hypotheses on the basis of evidence already at hand. For example, he reasoned that the epidemic could not be the result of overcrowding, because the First Division was less crowded than the Second. (Women tried to avoid it.) Most other possible factors, such as diet and general care, were identical in the two divisions. One difference was that in the First Division, deliveries were done with the mothers on their backs during delivery, and in the Second, on their sides. Semmelweis could not imagine how this could matter, but he ordered that all deliveries be done with mothers on their sides – to no avail. Another hypothesis was that the disease was psychologically transmitted by the priest, when he passed through the wards of the First Division (with a distinctive bell to indicate his presence) in order to administer the last rites to a dying patient. The hypothesis was that this demoralized the other patients, already weakened by childbirth, and caused their deaths. Semmelweis induced the priest to enter the wing by a roundabout route without his bell, so that he would not be noticed. Again, there was no change: New mothers still died.

A colleague of Semmelweis died of an infection received from a scalpel that had been used to perform an autopsy. Semmelweis noticed that the colleague's symptoms resembled those of puerperal fever. It occurred to him that deliveries in the First Division were done by medical students and physicians who often had just performed autopsies, whereas deliveries in the Second Division were done by midwives. He hypothesized that "cadaverous matter" – material from the corpses that stuck to the students' hands – might be the casue of the disease. To test this hypothesis, he induced the students and physicians to wash their hands in a solution of chlorinated lime, which he thought would remove the cadaverous matter, before delivering babies. This succeeded: The incidence of puerperal fever was sharply reduced, to the level of the Second Division.

Following this great success, on one occasion Semmelweis and his colleagues examined a woman in labor who suffered from a festering cervical cancer and then proceeded to examine 12 other women without washing their hands, confident that they could do no harm, since the first woman was alive. Eleven of the 12 others died of puerperal fever. This tragedy convinced Semmelweis to broaden his hypothesis to include "putrid living matter" as well as cadaverous matter. (Semmelweis himself was later to die accidentally in a similar way.)

Of course, Semmelweis was still not quite right. As we know today (after the laborious testing of many other hypotheses by many scientists), bacteria were the problem. Students and interns transferred the bacteria from the corpses of women who had died of the puerperal fever to women who were not yet infected. Other women still got the disease, because there were other paths by which the bacteria could be transmitted. Of course, Semmelweis's work was by no means in vain. It led others, such as Pasteur, more directly to the germ theory, and it saved many lives along the way. Incorrect hypotheses may still be of considerable value both in practical terms and in narrowing the search for further hypotheses.

Semmelweis's work illustrates nicely how hypothesis testing often works. To use the terms of the search-inference framework, a hypothesis is a *possibility*. The hypothesis usually concerns a possible *cause* of some event. Roughly, a "cause" is an event or state whose presence or absence would make the event in question occur or not occur, if the hypothesized cause could be manipulated.[1]

---

[1] Often, causes cannot be manipulated. When we say that the shape of the moon's orbit is "caused," or determined, by the earth's gravity, we cannot test this by removing the gravity and seeing what happens. Still, to say that the orbit is determined by gravity is to make a claim

In the simplest sort of hypothesis testing, we imagine some result that would definitely be obtained if the hypothesis were true, and we look for that result. For example, Semmelweis's hypothesis that the position of delivery was important implied that changing the position would reduce the incidence of the disease. This result was not found, so that hypothesis was eliminated. His hypothesis that cadaverous matter caused the disease implied that hand washing would help. Because it did help, the hypothesis was accepted.

This simple method has its dangers. When a predicted result is found, we must still be wary of the possibility that there are *alternative explanations*. An alternative explanation is another hypothesis – aside from the one we are testing – that is also consistent with a result. In fact, Semmelweis discovered an alternative and better explanation of the cadaverous-matter hypothesis, and we have now accepted a still-better alternative: The cause was micro-organisms specific to the disease in question. Alternative explanations are one of the bugaboos of science.

Despite the existence of alternatives to the cadaverous-matter hypothesis, Semmelweis still succeeded in his original goal of reducing the incidence of the disease. We test hypotheses because of some goal, and when that goal is achieved, the presence of alternative explanations can become a matter of curiosity rather than substance. For Semmelweis, the main goal was to find a cure for the disease. (Of course, the pursuit of alternative explanations in this case was not a matter of mere curiosity. Although hundreds of lives were saved, even more were saved with each new step in medical knowledge.)

In science, the worst situation – which happens all too often – is to do an experiment to test some hypothesis, have the experiment succeed, and then discover that we have overlooked a plausible and important alternative hypothesis that could have been eliminated if only a different experiment had been run. For example, if Semmelweis had tested his delivery-position hypothesis by asking the midwives to do all of the deliveries (rather than by asking the students to use the position that the midwives used), he would not have known whether the delivery position or something else was at fault. If he had then changed the students' methods, expecting an immediate cure, he would have been surprised to find no improvement. In general, the way to avoid such surprises is to anticipate alternative explanations in advance, before doing an experiment – especially when the experiment is expensive or time-consuming.

A second danger is that a hypothesis will be falsely rejected because of a bad experiment. Suppose Semmelweis had tested his hypothesis by asking the students to examine their hands to make sure they were clean, and if not, rinse them off in a basin of water instead of chlorinated lime. This experiment would very likely have failed, and Semmelweis might have falsely concluded

about what *would* happen if we could remove the gravity. Note also that the term "cause," as used here, includes partial causes, or influences.

that transmission of material on people's hands had nothing to do with the disease. The same situation would have come about if chlorinated lime did not turn out to kill bacteria.

Any experiment involves additional assumptions other than the hypothesis itself: for example, the assumption that the chlorinated lime (or water) would remove the offending substance. If the experiment fails, the hypothesis is not necessarily disproved, for some other assumption may be at fault. The best experiments are those in which the key assumptions are very likely to be true. For example, we have a great deal of evidence that high temperatures kill bacteria. If we boil an object that we suspect is contaminated for an hour and find that it is still capable of transmitting disease, we conclude that the disease is not bacterial, yet the bacterium in question may turn out to be an oddity, a type that can withstand high temperature.

In the early stages of scientific investigation, scientists must stumble around in the dark, using methods that are still untested in order to establish facts, which, if they are established, validate the methods themselves.

Testing scientific hypotheses

Much of the literature in the philosophy of science is concerned with the normative and prescriptive theory of hypothesis formulation and testing. In science, hypotheses are often derived from *theories*, which are coherent explanations of several different phenomena. Newton's theory of gravitation, for example, explains the motions of the moon and the planets, and the trajectories and acceleration of bodies in free fall near the earth. A new hypothesis derived from this theory is that gravitational force is reduced at the tops of mountains.

The work of Karl Popper has had an especially important influence on our thinking about theories and how they are tested (see Popper, 1962, especially ch. 1). Popper wanted to carry out a "rational reconstruction" of scientific practice: That is, he wanted to look at the actual practice of scientists and describe it in the most "charitable" way. He assumed that scientists were often rational, and he tried to use this assumption to discover the nature of rationality in science.

Popper was particularly interested in trying to distinguish the method of formulating theories in the more successful sciences, such as modern physics (especially Einstein's theory of relativity), from the method used in what he considered questionable sciences, including the psychoanalytic theories of Adler (for whom Popper had worked for a time) and Freud and the political theory of Marx. Popper criticized these latter theories for their apparent capacity to explain any result or observation. When some Freudians or Marxists were given counterexamples to their favored theories, he said, they always had some explanation of why the counterexample was not a good one. At worst, they would accuse their critic of bias, terming it "resistance" or "false consciousness."

In contrast, Popper noted, Einstein's theory of relativity made a strong prediction about the exact angle at which a beam of starlight would be bent as it passed by the sun. If the angle had been anything other than predicted, Einstein would have had to admit that his theory was incorrect, but the prediction was accurate. Einstein's theory, in contrast to Freud's or Marx's, was therefore *falsifiable* – that is, capable of being proved false by an experiment or observation. Moreover, Einstein's theory was a great advance, because the prediction was *risky*: In terms of the other theories accepted at that time, the angle that Einstein's theory predicted was considered extremely unlikely.

Popper therefore concluded that sciences advance successfully by making theoretical statements that are "bold conjectures" and then trying to refute them through experiment or observation. Those conjectures that survive the attempts to refute them become accepted theories, such as the theory of relativity, but they are never finally "proved," since they can always be refuted in the future (just as Newton's theory was partly refuted by the success of Einstein's).

Popper's theory set the agenda for reflection about the prescriptive theory of science. Subsequent philosophical writers have criticized Popper's argument, qualifying it in important ways. "Bold conjectures," they point out, are often wrong, especially if the theory that predicts certain observations is unlikely to be true. Popper's theory does better as an account of successful theory formulation in hindsight than as a prescription for scientific practice. The procedure he advises is not very practical: It is a little like telling a scientist, "Take a wild guess, *and be right*!"

John Platt (1964) suggested that scientists should attempt to play the game "20 questions"[2] with nature using a more conservative strategy, which he called "strong inference." Rather than making a bold (unlikely) conjecture, the scientist should divide the possible hypotheses about some phenomenon roughly in half and then try to rule out one of the halves. When we play 20 questions, we usually begin with some question like "Is it alive?" If the answer is positive, we then ask, "Is it animate?" Each question divides the possibilities roughly in half. Likewise, in real science, we might ask whether a disease is transmitted by an organism. If the answer is yes, we might ask whether the organism is bacterial, and so on. Platt argues that this is a more efficient strategy than asking "boldly" whether the disease is caused by a spirochete (when there is no reason to think that it is).

Another difficulty with Popper's theory is that it assumes that hypotheses

[2] In this game, one person thinks of something (a person, object, or animal, for example), and the other tries to discover what it is by asking no more than 20 questions, to which the answers given are only yes or no. The "scientist" may guess the word at any time, but if she is wrong, she must give up for that word.

can be falsified. Platt's theory has this assumption as well, for it assumes that one half of the hypotheses or the other will be eliminated by a good question. We have already seen that this assumption may be too idealistic to serve as a prescriptive theory for scientific practice. It is rarely, if ever, true that a scientific theory can be refuted by any one observation or experiment. Usually it is possible – with more or less plausibility–to find some reason why the experiment was not a good test of the hypothesis. In some cases, like the case of rinsing the hands in a basin of water, the experiment may truly be a poor one.

Imre Lakatos (1978) attempts to answer this criticism by arguing that most scientific theories have a "core" of crucial claims, along with a "periphery" of claims that can be changed as needed. A particular hypothesis involves both core and peripheral claims. If the hypothesis is rejected by an experiment, we can reject the peripheral claim and keep the core. For example, he says, the core of the Ptolemaic theory of astronomy was the claim that the sun and the planets revolve around the earth. Over the years, many peripheral claims (about "epicycles," or orbits within orbits) had been added, subtracted, and modified, in order to explain the fact that the planets seemed at times to reverse direction relative to the stars. The core of the Ptolemaic theory was protected by these modifications. When Copernicus showed how the planetary motions could be explained more simply by assuming that the earth and the planets revolved around the sun, no crucial experiment or potential observation was known that could be used to demonstrate which of the two theories was superior. The Copernican theory won out, according to Lakatos, because this theory was more *progressive* as a program for research; one could ask and answer more questions within it than within the Ptolemaic theory. When Kepler assumed the Copernican theory was true, for example, he was able to show that planets moved in elliptical orbits, and Newton, in turn, showed how these ellipses could be explained by the inverse-square law of gravity.

For Lakatos, then, a theory is useful if it generates valuable research. Lakatos's view implies that theories cannot be compared directly with one another, to determine their closeness to truth or their probability. We can compare theories only in hindsight, after we have seen what research they generated. Again, this view is not useful advice to practicing scientists, unless they can foresee the future.

We could, however, use probability theory (as we do with other hypotheses) to evaluate the effect of experimental results on hypotheses. By asking about the effect of various results on our hypotheses before we do an experiment, we can determine the value of the experiment before we do it. To find how the probability of a sicentific hypotheses changes when we obtain an experimental result, we would assign a prior probability to each hypothesis, $p(H)$. Observations and experimental results would constitute the data, the D's. After assigning a likelihood to each datum given each hypothesis,

$p(D/H)$, we could then use Bayes's theorem to calculate the posterior probability of the hypothesis, $p(H/D)$. The data cannot, in science, be expected to raise the probability of a hypothesis precisely to 1 or lower it precisely to zero. Other things being equal, however, a good scientific experiment would be one with potential outcomes that have a high probability, given some hypothesis, and a low probability, given others. If we obtain such a result, our probabilities for the various hypotheses would change greatly, and we would therefore have learned a lot.

Probability theory would constitute part of the *normative* theory of science. The other part of the normative theory would be the theory of decision making, which is explored in part III. (This view – that the normative theory of science consists of probability theory and decision theory – is advocated by Horwich, 1982, especially pp. 1–15, 51–63, and 100–136. I expressed my own support for it earlier in *Rationality and Intelligence*, 1985b, ch. 4.) The theory is normative but not necessarily prescriptive: Although scientists can, and sometimes do, calculate probabilities as specified by this theory, they can probably do nearly as well by following certain prescriptive rules of thumb, which we shall discuss shortly.

This normative theory can help us to understand why the prescriptive advice of Popper and Platt, on how to formulate and test scientific hypotheses, is good advice when it is possible to follow. For Popper, a good result (D, datum) is one that has a probability of 1, given the hypothesis being tested (H), and a very low probability given any other hypothesis ($\sim H$). If the critical result is found, the probability of H increases considerably, because the diagnostic ratio is so high.[3]

For Platt, a good *experiment* is one that seeks a result with a probability of 1, given one set of hypotheses, H_1, and a probability of 0, given some other set H_2; H_2 is the same as $\sim H_1$ (everything not in H_1). If the result is found, we know that the truth is in H_1; if not, we know that the truth is in H_2. Moreover, Platt specifies that the sets should be chosen so that $p(H_2)$ and $p(H_1)$ are about .5. By this choice of hypotheses to test, it is possible to ask the fewest questions to determine exactly where the truth lies – that is, in which sub-hypothesis of H_1 or H_2.

More generally, however, we should look for results in which the conditional probabilities for results, given the important hypotheses, differ greatly. Whether we seek results with probabilities of 1 or 0 will depend to some extent on why we need to know and how sure we need to be. We do not always need absolute certainty in order to take some practical action or in order to accept some scientific theory as very likely true, for the purposes of

---

[3] Popper would disagree with this account, because he regards probability as a poor criterion of the value of a theory. He argues that the "most probable" theory is always the least interesting, citing, as an example, a noncommittal statement such as this: "The light will be bent some amount, or possibly not at all." He does not, however, consider *change* in probability of a hypothesis as a criterion of the value of a *result*, which is what is argued here.

planning our next experiment. A good heuristic to keep us on the trail of such results is this: "Be sure to consider alternative hypotheses." If our planned experiment or observation cannot distinguish the hypothesis of interest from the alternatives, it is not a good experiment. If no experiment can do so, our hypothesis is untestable, and we ought to reexamine our goal in formulating it.

The psychology of hypothesis testing

Concept formation

A traditional theory in psychology (Bruner, Goodnow, & Austin, 1956), now largely discredited, holds that knowing a *concept* amounts to knowing how to classify some instance as a member of a certain category. It was argued, moreover, that we classify instances on the basis of *cues* (ch. 5). For example, in card games, knowing the concept "spade" amounts to knowing how to classify cards as spades or nonspades. In this case, there is a single relevant cue, the shape of the little symbol in the upper left-hand corner of each card. The concept "seven," in cards, is based on a different cue – the number printed in the corner (or seven symbols in the middle of the card). Cues are also called *attributes* or *features* of things.

In some cases, the theory holds, a concept is characterized by a *conjunction* of cues or features: that is, by all of them together, an "and" relationship. The concept "seven of spades" is characterized by both the shape of the symbol *and* the number. A "bachelor" is characterized by the features "unmarried, male, adult." In other cases, a concept is characterized by a *disjunction* of features: that is, one of several features, an "or" relationship. A "face card" (in some card games) is either "a card with a picture" or "an ace." "Earned income" consists of "wages, salaries, tips, commissions, etc."

According to the traditional view in psychology (which is by no means well accepted today), we ordinarily learn concepts by testing hypotheses about the cues or features. Consistent with this view is the finding that young children, while they are first learning the meanings of words such as "dog," often make mistakes that appear to be based on incorrect hypotheses that they have not yet eliminated by critical tests or evidence. A young child might first suppose that the word "dog" refers to any four-legged animal. Only by trying the word out on cows and being corrected does the child discover that this hypothesis is incorrect. Similarly, one child used "ba-ba" to refer not only to herself but to other people, and the cat as well (Ingram, 1971); her concept was defined by the single feature of animacy. At some point she observed that adults used the word "baby" to refer only to creatures that were small and human as well as animate. When testing a hypothesis about the meaning of a word, a child often has to wait for evidence provided by other people: Adults do not always provide feedback when a child uses a word incorrectly, so, the theory claims, it is difficult for children to carry out experiments to actively test their hypotheses. Bruner and his colleagues also distinguished between deterministic and probabilistic cues, as we discussed in chapter 5.

Given this view of concepts, psychologists hoped to improve their understanding of how we learn concepts by asking subjects to learn artificial concepts in the laboratory. Bruner, Goodnow, and Austin performed a classic set of experiments using this design (1956). In most of their experiments, the stimuli were cards (special ones, not an ordinary deck) that varied along four dimensions: number of forms printed on them (1, 2, or 3); number of borders (1, 2, or 3); type of form (cross, square, or circle); and color (green, red, or black). Some subjects were asked to discover a deterministic concept that described a particular category, a subset of the 81 cards. For example, a category might be "black crosses" or simply "black." Subjects could do this by pointing to one of the cards and asking the experimenter whether or not the card was in the category. This was called a *selection* experiment, because the subjects selected the cards. In *reception* experiments – which we discussed in chapter 5 – the experimenter chose the cards (randomly). The subject guessed whether each card was in the category or not and received feedback from the experimenter.

Bruner and his colleagues discovered a number of *strategies* that subjects used in these two kinds of experiments. One strategy (used by some subjects in both selection and reception experiments) was *simultaneous scanning*. The subject would take all of the features of the first positive instance (or case in which the experimenter said, "Yes, this card belongs to the category") as an initial hypothesis. For example, if this card had "1 red cross with 2 borders," the subject would take the conjunction of these features as the initial hypothesis. With each new positive instance, the subject would eliminate any of these features not present. For example, if the next positive instance were "2 red crosses with 3 borders," the subject would conclude that the number of forms and the number of borders were irrelevant, so that the new hypothesis would be simply "red cross." This strategy is conservative; it never leads to an error in which the subject says that something is in the category when it is not – unless the category is disjunctive, in which case the subject will have a very hard time discovering the category at all.

A second strategy is *successive scanning*, in which the subject tests one hypothesis at a time. For example, the subject might hypothesize that the concept is "red" and go on to select (in the selection task) red cards that differed on other attributes. The subject would continue, until the hypothesis was shown to be wrong, and would then change the hypothesis in a way consistent with the card that proved it wrong. For example, if a red square turned out not to be a member of the category, the new hypothesis might be "cross." An advantage of this strategy is that it makes few demands on the subject's memory. A disadvantage is that it is inefficient. Unlike the simultaneous-scanning strategy, which effectively evaluates a number of hypotheses simultaneously, the successive-scanning strategy cannot make any use of the information provided by past trials (unless the cards are kept in view).

In the selection task, the subject can vary one feature at a time, after finding a single positive instance. For example, if "2 red crosses with 3 borders" is a positive instance, the subject might try "2 red crosses with 1 border." If the answer is yes, the subject will have good reason to think that the number of borders does not matter. If the answer is no, the subject will have good reason to think that "3 borders" is part of the concept. This strategy was called *conservative focusing*. It is somewhat like Platt's method of strong inference, because each card eliminates one set of hypotheses.

In another strategy, the subject varies all attributes but one. For example, after the same first positive instance, the subject may try "1 red square with 1 border." If the answer is yes, the subject will have good reason to think that the category is "red." This strategy was called *focus gambling*, because the subject was unlikely to get a yes answer; if the answer *is* yes, however, the subject can be pretty confident that the hypothesis is correct. This strategy is analogous to Popper's method of bold conjecture and risky experiment.

Bruner and his colleagues explained the choice of strategy in terms of cognitive load, or cognitive capacity – especially the memory requirements of keeping track of a number of hypotheses at once. They suggested that the less demanding strategies, particularly successive scanning, were used when demands on memory were greatest. In formulating this view of concept learning, the researchers were implicitly making a distinction between normative (ideal – no memory limits) and prescriptive views of how the task ought to be done, and they suggested (again, implicitly) that people generally follow the prescriptive model.

The view of concept learning that lay behind this work has since been largely discredited. Putnam (1975) has pointed out that the concept of "water" has little to do with the *features* that we usually associate with water, such as being liquid, transparent, freezing at 32 degrees Fahrenheit, and boiling at 212 degrees Fahrenheit, having a density of 1, and so on. As noted earlier, if a substance were found that had all of these properties but had the chemical formula XYZ rather than H_2O, we would say that it was not water, because we take the chemical formula as definitive, not the observable properties. Similarly, if a fruit looked and tasted like an orange but came from a tree that was grown from an apple seed, we would say that the fruit was an (unusual) apple, not really an orange. Concepts about *natural kinds* (categories that exist in nature) *are shaped by scientific theories*.

Similarly, Wittgenstein (1958) has pointed out that many other concepts that we have seem to lack defining (deterministic) features altogether. Take, for example, the concept of a game. There is essentially nothing that is true of all games – no defining features. (For every feature you can think of, such as being done for fun, there are games that do not have it, such as jousting.) Games are not united by any features, but rather by what Wittgenstein called a *family resemblance*. Each game shares some features with some other games. Of course, *within* games, many concepts do have simple definitions: for example, a strike, in baseball, has a disjunction of features: Either the batter swings and misses, the batter fouls (except after two strikes), or the ball goes through the strike zone.

In sum, the idea that concepts have defining features applies only to man-made categories such as "forward pass," "resident alien," and perhaps "past participle." The work of Bruner and his colleagues on strategies for discovering such concepts, therefore, seems to tell us little about the learning of concepts in general. It still may say something, however, about the testing of hypotheses in other situations, such as science and diagnosis.

Confirmation bias

Although Bruner, Goodnow, and Austin did not set out to look for flaws in human reasoning, they did make one observation that inspired others to look for such flaws (p. 86):

Human subjects – and the same may be true of other species as well – prefer a direct test of any hypothesis they may be working on. [Suppose that] a subject is faced with deciding whether a white door or a black door is the correct entrance to a reward chamber and adopts the hypothesis that the white door is correct. There are two ways of testing this hypothesis. The *direct way* is to try the white door. The *indirect way* is to try the black door.

Similarly, when subjects use the successive scanning strategy, they choose examples consistent with their current hypothesis, rather than those that are inconsistent.

Inspired by this finding, Wason (1960, 1968a) told subjects that the sequence 2 4 6 followed a rule, which they were to discover by providing additional three-number sequences as tests. The experimenter would tell the subject whether each of these sequences followed the rule or not. One difference between this procedure and that of Bruner and his colleagues is that both the number of possible hypotheses and the number of possible sequences that could be used to test them were infinite. This fact makes the situation more like those typically faced by scientists.

Typically, a subject would hypothesize that the rule was "numbers ascending by 2" and give sequences such as 3 5 7, 1.5 3.5 5.5, 100 102 104, and −6 −4 −2 as a series of tests. If the subject followed this strategy – basically the successive-scanning strategy with direct tests – the experimenter would keep saying yes in response to each test. Subjects always got the yes answer they expected, and they never questioned their favored hypothesis. Many subjects, after several trials like this, concluded that their hypothesis must be correct, and they announced that they had discovered the rule. The experi-

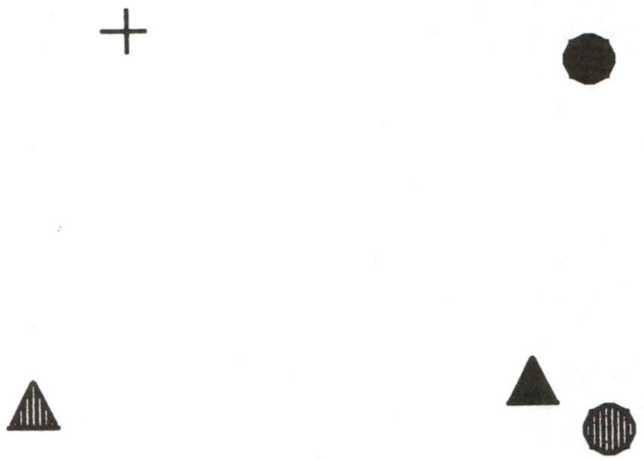

Figure 13.1. Display like that used by Mynatt, Doherty, and Tweney (1977), adapted from C. R. Mynatt, M. E. Doherty, & R. D. Tweney, "Confirmation Bias in a Simulated Research Environment: An Experimental Study of Scientific Inference," in *Quarterly Journal of Experimental Psychology* (1977):*29*, 89.

menter then told them that they were incorrect and that they could continue. At this point, some subjects attempted to make changes in the wording of the rule without changing its meaning: For instance, "The first number is 2 less than the middle number, and the third number is 2 more." Other subjects finally attempted an indirect test, such as 2 3 5, got a yes answer once again, and then went on to produce a complex hypothesis such as this: "The first two numbers are random, and the third is the second plus 2." The "correct" rule (the rule that the experimenter followed in giving feedback) was simply "ascending numbers." Many subjects did discover this rule. To do so, however, they had to use an indirect test of their original hypothesis.

Wason's point was not just that subjects had difficulty discovering his rule (which, because of its simplicity, might be considered a kind of trick). Instead, he suggested that many subjects failed to consider alternative hypotheses, such as "numbers ascending by a constant" or even "ascending numbers." Wason's result, however, is not entirely clear. Like Luchins, whose work was described in chapter 4, Wason may have been mistaken in concluding that subjects were violating a normative or prescriptive model. Subjects may have been trying to test alternative hypotheses for which the answer would be no (for example, ascending even numbers; numbers ascending by 2 but less than 100; positive numbers ascending by 2; and so forth), but they may have failed to mention these hypotheses. Nonetheless, Wason's experiments inspired a host of similar efforts.

Mynatt, Doherty, and Tweney (1977) examined subjects' behavior in a simulated research environment involving figures displayed on a computer screen (see Figure 13.1). The subject was to try to account for the motion of a particle, which was fired from the position marked by the plus (+). The rule was that the particle stopped moving when it was near any gray figure (until fired again). Subjects were presented with an initial display consisting of a gray triangle and, on a separate area of the screen, a black triangle next to a gray (shaded) circle. Subjects were then given a series of choices in which they had to choose one display, out of two, in order to test their hypothesis about what caused the particle to stop moving. Subjects whose initial hypothesis was "triangle" consistently chose displays that showed gray triangles rather than displays showing other gray figures. It appeared that they did not consider the alternative hypothesis, "gray figures," and they therefore did not choose tests that would distinguish this alternative from their favored hypothesis.[4]

Mynatt and his colleagues (following Wason) suggested that the subjects were trying to "confirm" their hypothesis rather than test it or falsify it. As I shall point out later, it is not clear what this suggestion means. The term "confirmation bias," introduced by these researchers, has, however, come to be used to describe the phenomenon of employing direct tests that fail to test alternative hypotheses, and the term has stuck. We might think of this bias as resulting from a *confirmation heuristic*: "To test a hypothesis, think of a result that would be found if the hypothesis were true and then look for that result (and do not worry about other hypotheses that might yield the same result)."

Mynatt, Doherty, and Tweney (1978) examined extended thinking-aloud protocols of subjects working on a similar test problem. The subjects worked on their own (without choices). Many tests that the subjects made yielded positive results when the favored hypothesis was true. Mynatt and his coauthors suggest that such results should be interpreted as confirmation bias only if the subject did the test for the purpose of getting a positive result. They point out, however (p. 400), that "it was often difficult to determine unambiguously what type of evidence subjects were *seeking* (as opposed to what they got)." Although subjects were classified as sometimes seeking confirmation rather than disconfirmation, it is plausible that they simply *expected* confirmation, which would be reasonable if they thought their hypothesis was true.

Snyder and Swann (1978) asked each subject to interview another "target" subject, supposedly to determine whether the target subject was an "extrovert" (or, for other subjects, an "introvert"). The subjects tended to ask questions for which a yes answer would support the hypothesis that they were asked to test ("Do you like to go to parties?") or questions that assumed that the hypothesis was true ("What would you do to make a party more lively?").

In another test of confirmation bias, Shaklee and Fischhoff (1982) gave

---

[4] These subjects might, however, have considered and rejected the hypothesis "gray" on the basis of the initial display, because they might have attributed the cessation of motion to the black triangle rather than the nearby gray disk. In order to correct this mistake later, subjects might have had to recall the display itself. Thus, their difficulties might have resulted from memory problems or misperceptions.

subjects an event such as "Diane rode her bike to work." They also gave them some possible causes for the event, such as "Diane's car wouldn't start" and "There were no parking places on campus"; a fact implicating one of the causes, such as "Even in bad weather, she rode her bike"; and some questions that might be asked, such as "Had Diane's car been giving her trouble lately?" and "Did Diane ride her bike for convenience?" Subjects were asked which question they "would most like to have answered in trying to explain" the initial event. Subjects strongly tended to choose the question most likely to yield a yes answer if the implicated cause were true. This by itself might not be a bias, for the chosen question might still have been the best one. In another experiment, however, the researchers labeled one cause as already known (and omitted the implicating fact). Subjects were told that the alternative causes were not mutually exclusive. Subjects still tended to ask the question corresponding to the known cause. This is such an extreme form of confirmation bias that one wonders whether the subjects understood the instructions.

Baron, Beattie, and Hershey (in press) extended the Shaklee and Fischhoff experiment in a variety of ways, finding that subjects did indeed seem to use a "confirmation heuristic" in which they favored tests or questions that gave a yes answer if their favored hypothesis were true. Here is one of their test questions:

A patient has a .8 probability of having Chamber-of-Commerce disease and a .2 probability of Elk's disease. (He surely has one or the other.) A tetherscopic examination yields a positive result in 90% of patients with Chamber-of-Commerce disease and in 20% of patients without it (including those with some other disease). An intraocular smear yields a positive result in 90% of patients with Elk's disease and in 10% of patients without it. If you could do only one of these tests, which would it be? Why?

The "tetherscopic" examination yields a yes answer if the favored hypothesis ("Chamber-of-Commerce disease") is true. Many subjects chose the tetherscopic examination for this reason, even though the "intraocular smear" is a better test in this case. (To see why it is better, note that one could interpret a negative result on the intraocular smear as a positive indication of Chamber-of-Commerce disease; looking at it this way, the test has a 10% false-positive rate, instead of the 20% rate for the tetherscopic examination.)

In another procedure, subjects were given problems much like those of Shaklee and Fischhoff, except that the hypotheses were most easily seen as mutually exclusive (only one being true) rather than compatible. Here is an example:

> You are at your friend's house. Their young son is sent off to run his bath. Later you notice that water is dripping through the kitchen ceiling. You suspect that the child let the water overflow.
> Question 1. "Was the bathtub over the kitchen?"
> Question 2. "Was it raining?"
> Question 3. "Was the drip present before the child went upstairs?"

Subjects were asked to imagine themselves in the situation, knowing nothing more about it than they were told here, but in possession of their general knowledge. They were asked to evaluate each question (with a numerical rating) as a test of their hypothesis. They were later asked to give their own probability judgments for the hypothesis (the child had let the water overflow) and for a yes answer to each question, first assuming the hypothesis to be true, and then assuming it to be false. In this case, which was typical, subjects gave the highest rating to question 1, which yielded a yes answer if the hypothesis were true. The probabilities that the subjects provided, however, indicated that question 3 would have been the most informative, because it had such a *low* probability of providing a yes answer if the hypothesis was true; a positive answer would essentially rule out the hypothesis. (Skov & Sherman, 1986, obtained similar results.)

In sum, it does appear that subjects asked questions designed to yield yes answers if their favored hypothesis was true, even when these were not the best questions. (Sometimes, or perhaps most of the time, these were the best questions.)

Another experiment that seems to show the use of a confirmation heuristic is one that Jane Beattie and I designed (1988). Every subject was given an envelope with four cards inside it. Each card had a letter (*A, B,* or *C*) and a number (*1, 2,* or *3*) printed on it. The task was to determine whether a certain rule was true of all four cards in the envelope. The rule, for example, might be "If there is a B, then there is a 2." The subject could ask to know whether certain cards were in the envelope, naming the card by *both* letter and number (B1, B2, B3, and so forth). For the hypothesis just given, the correct answer would include B1 and B3; however, many subjects asked only for B2. Of course, if the rule was true, B2 would be in the envelope, but if the rule was false, B1 or B3 would be present, and B2 could still be present. The subjects' choice of card was made apparently without thinking about what card would be found if the rule was false.[5]

Two heuristics can be used to avoid the negative effects of the confirmation heuristic. In the first, we ask, "*How likely is a yes answer, if I assume that my hypothesis is false?*" A good test is one that has a high probability of some answer if the hypothesis is true and a low probability if it is false. We need not have a specific alternative hypothesis in mind; rather, we can estimate the latter probability on the basis of general background knowledge. For example, in the case just given, we might be able to estimate the probability of a yes answer to question 3 if the hypothesis is false without actually thinking of all the other possible hypotheses. Or, in medical diagnosis, we would choose a test that would be unlikely to be positive unless that patient had the disease

---

[5] In chapter 9, we examined a similar task in which the subject named only the letter. In that task, almost all subjects choose the B card, so they always can get a result that could potentially disprove their hypothesis. In our task, the subjects who choose only the B2 card could not possibly get such a result.

that we suspect; if the patient has appendicitis, for example, the white blood cell count ought to be high.

The second heuristic advises, "*Always try to think of alternative hypotheses; then choose a test most likely to distinguish them – to make some less probable and others more probable.*" For example, in medical diagnosis, before thinking about what test to do, we would think about what diseases ought to be considered. We would not just consider the most likely or the most dangerous but would look for alternatives as well. The advantage of this heuristic over the first is this: If we fail to consider alternatives, we may end up asking a question or doing a test that would have the same answer for several different hypotheses. For example, the white blood cell count may be high for other infections besides appendicitis, so this test may not distinguish appendicitis from some of the major alternative hypotheses. By thinking of *specific* alternative hypotheses, we may get a better idea of the probability of a result if the favored hypothesis is false. It may even be useful when we do not have a favored hypothesis. These heuristics are both candidates for prescriptive models for any situation in which one is evaluating hypotheses.[6]

What are the causes of confirmation bias, when it occurs? I have discussed some of them elsewhere (Baron, 1985b, ch. 4). They are not mutually exclusive; several causes may be at work. One cause involves conflict of goals. Subjects who are asked to test hypotheses may be trying to achieve a different goal as well: They behave as though their goal was to get positive results – to hear the answer "yes" – rather than useful information. Tschirgi (1980) gave subjects problems like the following:

John decided to make a cake. But he ran out of some ingredients. So:

> he used margarine instead of butter for the shortening
> he used honey instead of sugar for the sweetening
> he used brown wholewheat flour instead of regular white flour.

The cake turned out great; it was so moist.

John thought the reason the cake was so great was the honey. He thought that the type of shortening (butter or margarine) or the type of flour really didn't matter.

What should he do to prove this point? (p. 4)

The subjects were given three choices: Use sugar instead of honey; keep the honey, but change everything else; or change everything. Most subjects who were given this version of the problem chose to keep the honey. In another version, subjects were told, "The cake turned out just terrible. It was so runny." In this case, when subjects were asked what test they would carry out, most said that they would use sugar instead of honey.[7]

---

[6] They are modeled loosely on the prescriptions of Popper and Platt, respectively. Popper and Platt, however, would both want some results to rule out some hypotheses with certainty, and this is not always possible.

[7] Note that these two strategies correspond, respectively, to conservative focusing and focus gambling.

Both of these tests are equally informative and equally valuable (Baron, 1985b, p. 143). If we keep the honey and change everything else, the cake will most likely turn out as it did the first time (whatever way that was), if our hypothesis is true, and the cake will turn out differently if our hypothesis is false. If we change only the honey, the cake will turn out differently if our hypothesis is true, and the cake will turn out as it did the first time if our hypothesis is false. The situations are completely the same except for the reversal of "as it did before" and "differently."

The reason the subjects choose different tests in the two cases is that they quite legitimately are pursuing two goals: information and a *good cake* at the end of their experiment. The effect of their desire for a good cake on their choice of how they will test their hypothesis is harmless, in this case; either choice is a good one. In other situations, the conflict of goals may not be so harmless. This is particularly true when there is no real value in a "positive" result. For example, in the 2 4 6 task, the desire to obtain yes answers may inhibit subjects from thinking of tests that would yield no answers if their favored hypothesis is true, which would in this case be more informative. Subjects may like to hear the word "yes," and physicians may like to hear that a test result was "positive," but these words have no value in themselves. If we seek to hear them at the expense of obtaining real information, we are very likely subverting the achievement of our goals.

Schwartz (1982) demonstrated the detrimental effects of seeking reward in a different way by asking one group of subjects to try to earn rewards (nickels) by pressing two buttons (*L* and *R*, for *Left* and *Right*) in a certain pattern. Pressing the button moved a light through a five-by-five matrix of squares, starting in the upper left corner; pressing L moved the light down one square, and pressing R moved it one square to the right. A second group of subjects was asked to discover the *rule* that leads to reward (although they were not given monetary rewards for correct sequences of button presses). The rule itself was based simply on the relative number of L's and R's; any sequence of four L's and four R's could produce it (probabilistically). Such a sequence moved the light from upper left to lower right without running off the edge.

Subjects in the reward group usually developed "stereotyped" sequences, such as LLLLRRRR. At the end of the experiment, when they were asked to give the rule, these subjects stated exactly the pattern they had been using, and they often felt that this pattern was necessary, the only one that would work. The discovery group usually did discover the rule. When the reward group took part in a second experiment with the same instructions as the discovery group, they were less likely to discover the rule than the discovery group was. Apparently their ability to discover the rule was inhibited by their tendency to work for reward rather than information. The reduction of the motivation to discover rules seems to have carried over to a new task.

In a later experiment, Schwartz (in press) examined the finding that stereotypy led to the confusion of sufficiency with necessity. After pretraining in either the "reward" or "rule" condition, subjects were asked to solve problems analogous to the four-card problem discussed in chapter 9 but using the same apparatus that Schwartz had used earlier (the matrix and buttons). Subjects were asked to test rules concerning either the necessity or the sufficiency of some condition, in order to get a "point" toward their total score. For example, a rule about necessity was "I get a point only if the light goes through the shaded square." Here, if the rule were true, going through the shaded square would be *necessary* in order to get a point. A rule about sufficiency was, "If the light goes through the shaded square, I get a point." Here, going through the square is *sufficient*, but there may be some other way to get a point. Subjects in the rule condition did well at testing both kinds of rules. Subjects in the reward condition, however, did well at testing the rule about sufficiency but poorly at testing the rule about necessity. Statements about necessity require tests with sequences that do *not* move the light through the shaded square (to see whether there is any other way of getting the reward). Subjects in the rule condition made far fewer such tests than those in the reward condition, as though they were still interested in getting the reward.

These experiments probably are analogous to real situations – for example, in classrooms – in which people are induced to work for extrinsic rewards such as grades. The reward may be effective in encouraging the work in question, but it may reduce the commitment to other valuable goals – such as satisfying one's curiosity – that could otherwise motivate the same behavior (see ch. 6). Once students find a way of getting the reward of grades, they may be less inclined to try other ways of thinking that might teach them something about the real world that would ultimately enable them to obtain rewards much more important to them than good grades.

Information bias and the value of information

At several points, in earlier chapters, I have suggested that the value of information can be calculated. In essence, what we want to calculate is the extent to which specific information that we have or can get will help us to decide correctly among actions, such as which disease to treat or which scientific hypothesis to accept as a basis for further experimentation. Let me suggest how this might be done, in the context of some examples from medical diagnosis. Medical diagnosis is useful for this purpose because probability is obviously involved: Only rarely can a physician diagnose a disease with absolute certainty. Scientific reasoning, I have argued, is also probabilistic, but it is more difficult to analyze many scientific situations in this way, because it is more difficult to determine what the possible hypotheses are.

Consider the following diagnostic problems (Baron, Beattie, & Hershey, in press) for a group of fictional diseases:

1. A patient's presenting symptoms and history suggest a diagnosis of globoma, with about .8 probability. If it isn't globoma, it's either popitis or flapemia. Each disease has its own treatment, which is ineffective against the other two diseases. A test called the ET scan would certainly yield a positive result if the patient had popitis, and a negative result if she has flapemia. If the patient has globoma, a positive and negative result are equally likely. If the ET scan were the only test you could do, should you do it? Why or why not?
2. A [different] patient has a .8 probability of umphitis. A positive Z-ray result would confirm the diagnosis, but a negative result would be inconclusive; if the result is negative, the probability would drop to .6. The treatment for umphitis is unpleasant, and you feel it is just as bad to give the treatment to a patient without the disease as to let a patient with the disease go untreated. If the Z-ray were the only test you could do, should you do it? Why or why not?

In their answers to both problems, many subjects said that it would be worthwhile to perform the test in question, even if it was somewhat costly, and even though they understood that this test was the only one that could be done before a decision about treatment was made. (In the first problem, they also assumed that the three diseases were equally serious, and equally treatable, so that we would treat only the most likely disease.) In neither case, however, can the test affect the action to be taken. In the first problem, because the probability for globoma is so high (.8), we will treat globoma no matter what the test says; globoma will be the most likely disease before and after treatment. Likewise, in the second problem, we will treat the umphitis, no matter what the test says. The tests, which would give inconclusive results, are worthless for the purpose of deciding what to do. They cannot affect our decision.

Sometimes we want information because we are simply curious. In treating patients, however, we clearly should not spend money or take risks simply to satisfy our own curiosity: Our goal is to help the patient get well. Subjects who feel that the tests are worth doing may be pursuing an inappropriate goal (satisfying their curiosity or seeking information for its own sake), which, on reflection, they would not pursue. In fact, when we interviewed and presented this argument to them, all of them admitted that the tests were worthless.[8]

We can think about these problems more formally in terms of the concept of "expected utility" (described in detail in ch. 16). *Utility* is, in essence, *subjective value* – how much something matters to us. In these problems we have been considering, we can assume that there is some utility in treating

---

[8] Anecdotes suggest that physicians make the same error. In one case, a physician wanted to do a CAT scan (an expensive test) for a woman with acute lower-back pain. An X-ray had already been done and had ruled out essentially all of the likely conditions that would require any treatment other than bed rest. When the woman asked the physician why he wanted to do the CAT scan, he said that he wanted to "confirm a diagnostic impression." When the woman asked whether any test result could possibly affect treatment, the physician could not think of any way in which it might. The test was not done, and the woman recovered.

Table 13.1. *ET scan results and incidence of three diseases in 100 patients*

	Globoma	Popitis	Flapemia
Positive ET scan	40	10	0
Negative ET scan	40	0	10
All patients	80	10	10

the right disease (in problem 1) or making the correct decision (in problem 2), and no utility in treating the wrong disease or making the wrong decision. The units for measuring utility are arbitrary, so we can say (to allow us to calculate) that the utility of a correct decision is 1, and the utility of an incorrect decision is 0.

Expected utility applies to a choice with probabilistic (uncertain) outcomes. It is the average utility we would obtain if we made the same choice repeatedly and the outcomes occurred with their respective probabilities. It is therefore the utility we can *expect* on the average. In these problems, there are two choices: test or no test. (There are also essentially two outcomes, correct treatment or incorrect treatment.) To calculate expected utility, we consider all of the outcomes of a given choice, such as not testing. We multiply the probability of each outcome (given the choice) by its utility, and we add up these numbers across the outcomes. For example, in problem 1, for no test the probability of a correct treatment is .8 (assuming we treat globoma), and the probability of an incorrect treatment is .2. The utility of a correct treatment is (we have assumed) 1, and the utility of an incorrect treatment is 0. The expected utility of this choice (no test) is thus $.8 \cdot 1 + .2 \cdot 0$, or .8. Because we have defined the utility of a good outcome as 1 and the utility of a bad outcome as 0, the expected utility is equal to the probability of a good outcome.

Note that the utility of the other choice, testing, is the same. The probability of correct treatment is still .8, with or without doing the test. This is because doing the test cannot change the overall probability that the patient has globoma. Table 13.1 may make this clear. The top two rows of Table 13.1 shows ET scan test results for 100 patients, indicating how many patients with each disease had each test result. The bottom row, the sum of the other two rows, shows the overall prevalence of the three diseases. If no test is done, the figures in the row for "all patients" allow us to calculate the probability of the three diseases: .8 for globoma, and .1 for each of the others. If the test is done and is positive, the top row indicates that the probability of globoma is still .8. The same is found for a negative result. Therefore the test outcome cannot affect our judgment of the probability of globoma, the most likely disease, and we should treat globoma with or without knowledge of the test result.

Table 13.2. *Z-ray test results and incidence of umphitis in 100 patients*

	Umphitis	No umphitis
Positive Z-ray	50	0
Negatve Z-ray	30	20
All patients	80	20

Table 13.3. *Z-ray test results and incidence of umphitis in 100 patients*

	Umphitis	No umphitis
Positive Z-ray	50	0
Negatve Z-ray	20	30
All patients	70	30

Table 13.2 gives similar information for problem 2. In this case, the test can affect the probability of the most likely disease, but it again cannot affect our decision about treatment. If we do not do the test, we will have an 80% chance of giving the correct treatment, so the expected utility of this choice would be $.8 \cdot 1 + .2 \cdot 0$, or .8. If we do the test and it is positive, the expected utility would be higher; likewise, if the test is negative, the expected utility would be lower: But we must decide whether or not to do the test *before we know what the outcome will be*. Therefore, we must think of what we will do for each outcome of the test. We realize that, for either outcome, we will treat umphitis. Regardless of the outcome of the test, we will treat the same 80 patients correctly that we would have treated otherwise.

The test would have some value if the situation were as shown in Table 13.3. Here, if we do the test and it is positive, we would treat umphitis and be correct every time. If we do the test and it is negative, this time we would *not* treat umphitis, and we would be correct 60% of the time (30 out of 50 patients). Overall, if we do the test, we would treat 80 out of 100 patients correctly. If we do not do the test, however, we would treat umphitis, and we would be correct only 70% of the time; we would treat correctly only 70 out of 100 patients: Therefore, in a group of 100 patients, we would treat 70 correctly if we do not do the test, and we would treat 80 correctly if we do the test. This is because the test result makes a difference; it affects the action we would take. Overall, the expected utility of the *test* is $.8 - .7$, or .1. This corresponds to the 10 extra patients out of 100 who would be treated correctly only if the test is done.

In sum, a test has some expected utility only if it can affect the action we would take. Subjects in experiments, however, show a bias in which they seek

Table 13.4. *Test results and incidence of two diseases for 100 patients*

Test results	Disease A	Disease B
Positive	64	8
Negative	16	12

information even when it cannot affect action. This *information bias* can occur elsewhere: in medical practice, in organizations, and in daily life. What is not worth knowing is not worth knowing.

Utility and alternative hypotheses

We can use this approach to understand the value of considering alternative hypotheses, as discussed earlier in this chapter. Suppose that we think that the probability that a patient has disease A is .8. We know of a test that yields a positive result in 80% of the patients with disease A. Is the test worth doing?

Many would say yes. I suggest that we would need to know more before we decide. A good heuristic is to ask what other disease the patient may have if she does not have disease A. Suppose the answer is disease B. Then we would want to know what the probability of a positive result from that same test would be if the patient had disease B. Suppose the probability is .4. Then, for 100 imaginary patients, we would have a table like Table 13.4. Even if the test is negative, disease A will be our best guess. Therefore, the test has zero utility. The problem is that the test has too high a "false-positive" rate (8 out of 20 patients, or .4). Perhaps we could find a more useful test, with a much lower false-positive rate than .4, even if it also has a lower hit rate than .8. We will not think of looking for such a test, however, if we do not ask how likely we are to observe the same results if the alternative hypothesis is true.

The same need to consider whether a result is consistent with alternative hypotheses – before looking for the result – occurs in science. As we can see from the present example, this heuristic can be justified by a normative theory based on the idea of expected utility, a theory we shall explore in chapter 16.

Conclusion

Actively open-minded thinking can avoid one of the main biases in hypothesis testing, the failure to consider alternative hypotheses (possibilities). In addition, more careful search for goals can avoid the confusion of the goal of seeking information that is useful in decision making with the goal of seeking information in general, or the goal of obtaining positive results or having our predictions confirmed. These applications of the prescriptive theory of actively open-minded thinking can bring us closer to the normative theory of hypothesis testing as specified by probability and expected-utility theory.

There is more to science than hypothesis testing, however. In formulating hypotheses to test, the scientist must not only consider whether they are testable but also whether they are likely to be true. To meet the latter requirement, we must think well about what we already know (and the better we know it, the better we can think about it). We must make sure that our hypotheses are consistent with the evidence already available before we bother to collect new data.

The rigorous standards of science are often put in opposition to the idea of "learning from experience." In the next chapter, we ask just how good we are at learning from experience about the relation between one variable and another.

14   Judgment of correlation and contingency

Many of our beliefs concern the relation between one quantity and another. We may ask whether the speed at which galaxies move away from us is related to their distance from the earth or whether IQ is related to income. Often we are concerned with such relationships because we want to decide whether to manipulate one thing in order to affect another. What is the relationship between the amount of studying we do and the grades we get? between our appearance and the way other people respond to us? between the amount of sleep we get and our ability to pay attention? Over the long term, how do the foods we eat affect our health? How does the way in which children are disciplined affect their behavior as adults?

This chapter is concerned with the inferences that people make concerning such relations. The normative theory is provided by statistical definitions of correlation. Like probability theory, the statistical theory of correlation is widely used in science and is valued for its mathematical clarity. (Unlike probability theory, however, the assumptions behind it are not assumed to apply to every situation. It is therefore normative only when certain assumptions are true.) Descriptively, we shall see that many people systematically violate the normative theory. Prescriptively, we may be able to come closer to the normative model by considering all of the relevant evidence, including the evidence against what we already believe.

Correlation, cause, and contingency

Typically, such inferences are made from data (evidence) in which the two quantities in question have both been observed for a number of items. Thus, for a group of children, we might have the data concerning height and weight given in Table 14.1. In this instance, the two columns of figures are obviously *correlated*. The greater the child's height, the greater the weight. When we say that height is *positively correlated* with weight among people, we mean that taller people tend to weigh more than shorter people: As one figure goes up, so does the other, and vice versa.

We can measure the association between two different quantities on a scale of 1 to -1 by a *correlation coefficient*, abbreviated r. (The formula for r is found in most statistics texts.) The coefficient r measures the extent to which one variable can be predicted as a linear function of the other. A correlation

242

Table 14.1. *Height and weight for five children*

Child	Height (in.)	Weight (lb.)
A	48	45
B	43	35
C	51	55
D	46	44
E	45	40

coefficient of 1 indicates that one measure is a perfect linear function of another, or has a *perfect* positive correlation with it. An example is the relationship between degrees Fahrenheit (F) and degrees Celsius (C): if we know one of these, we can calculate the other exactly by a simple linear formula, $F = 1.8 \cdot C + 32$. A correlation of 0 indicates no linear relationship at all. In a long sequence of dice rolls, for example, there ought to be no correlation between the number thrown on one roll of the dice and the number thrown on the next roll. A correlation of -1 indicates a *perfect negative correlation*; for example, there is a perfect negative correlation between a person's height and the distance of the person's head from the ceiling of the room I am now in. The correlation coefficient for the height column and the weight column in Table 14.1 is 0.98, very close to 1.00. (Again, consult a statistics book for the formula for r.)

The correlation coefficient is only one among many reasonable measures of correlation. It has certain convenient mathematical properties, and it can be shown to be the best measure for achieving certain goals. These issue are discussed in statistics books. For our purposes, the most important property of the correlation coefficient is that it treats all observations equally. For example, it does not weigh more heavily those pairs of numbers that are consistent with the existence of a positive correlation, as opposed to a negative or zero correlation.

We can investigate correlations, or associations, when each variable concerns membership in a category. (Such variables are called *dichotomous* because membership and nonmembership constitute a dichotomy.) We may ask, for example, whether "presence of blue eyes" (membership in the category of blue-eyed people) is correlated with "presence of blond hair" in a population of people. To calculate the correlation, we can assign a 1 to "presence" of each variable (blue eyes or blond hair) and a 0 to "absence" of each variable for each person and then calculate the correlation by using the resulting numbers. (This yields a "phi coefficient.") Another reasonable way to measure the association between two dichotomous variables is to subtract conditional probabilities. For example, we can subtract the conditional probability of blue eyes given blond hair from the conditional probability of blue eyes given nonblond hair. If the first conditional probability is higher than the other, then knowing that a person has blond hair makes it more probable than otherwise that the person has blue eyes. If the two conditional probabilities are equal, then whether a person has blond hair tells us nothing about whether the person has blue eyes, and it makes sense to say that the two variables are unrelated. (We shall discuss more examples of this measure later in this chapter.)

Correlations are sometimes confused, in scientific analysis and everyday reasoning, with *causal* relationships. It is important to realize that they are not the same: Establishing a correlation does not establish causation, though it often provides *evidence* about causation, because causation is one reason that correlations can exist. (To establish causation, other reasons must be ruled out.) For example, the use of marijuana and the use of heroin may be *correlated*, but it is not necessarily true that one *causes* the other. There may be some third factor, such as exposure to drug dealers or rebellious attitudes, that is a more likely cause of both. If this third factor explained the correlation, then stopping the use of marijuana would not necessarily reduce the use of heroin. When we ask whether use of marijuana *causes* use of heroin, we are asking what *would* happen to heroin use if marijuana use were changed. A correlation between marijuana use and heroin use provides evidence for some causal relationship, but it does not establish one with certainty. Often, a more conclusive way to find out about causal relationships is to do an experiment. For example, correlations between diets with high amounts of saturated fat and heart disease provide evidence that the former caused the latter. Experiments in which some people have been induced to eat less fat can show that the relationship is indeed a causal one, if heart attacks become less frequent in these people (and not in others).

When we speak of correlations in a situation in which causal relationships are assumed, we can use the term *contingency*. A contingent relationship exists of one variable causally affects another. If smoking causes cancer, then cancer is, to some extent, *contingent* upon smoking. Our perception of contingency is an important determinant of our success at achieving our goals. Does the Soviet Union respond favorably when the United States threatens it? If I drink three cups of coffee after dinner, will I be able to get to sleep tonight? If I try listening to people more, will they like me better? Of course, getting the answers to these kinds of questions does not always involve trial and error; there are ways of understanding such things that allow us to make reasonable guesses without any experimenting at all. We do not experiment, for example, in order to find out whether strong acids are really dangerous to drink. (Those who do, at any rate, are probably not around to argue with me.) Some of our learning, however, does involve observation.

Accuracy of judgment

How good are people at intuitively judging correlations, and where do we tend to go wrong? Jennings, Amabile, and Ross (1982) asked this question

Table 14.2. *Incidence of symptom and disease for 100 people*

		Disease (D)	
		Present	Absent
Symptom (S)	Present	37	33
	Absent	17	13

in the most straightforward way. Subjects (who had not studied statistics) were asked to study lists of number pairs. For each list, the subjects estimated the strength of relationship on a scale of 100 to -100. The true correlation coefficients of the numbers in each list differed from list to list; the range was from 0 to 1. Subjects gave ratings near 100 for correlations of 1, and ratings near 0 for correlations of 0. For correlations of .5, subjects gave ratings of about 20. These results tell us that the naive idea of "degree of relationship," although it resembles correlation, is not quite the same as the relationship measured by the correlation coefficient r. This deviation from mathematical correlation is not an error, for r is only one of many possible measures of association, and there is no reason subjects should use this particular measure. (Their judgments were closer to r^2, and closer still to $1 - (1 - r^2)^{.5}$; both of these measures are perfectly reasonable measures of the correlation, because they treat all observations equally just as r does.) The data also suggest that people have greater difficulty seeing the difference between a correlation of 0 and one of .5 than they do seeing the difference between .5 and 1. Again, this is not an error; it is simply something that might be useful for us to know.

Attentional bias

Attentional bias in judging correlation

More interesting results were found by Smedslund (1963) in a situation involving dichotomous variables. In one study a group of nurses was asked to look through 100 cards supposedly representing "excerpts from the files of 100 patients." The nurses were asked to find out "whether there was a relationship (connection)" between a particular symptom and a particular disease. Each card indicated whether the symptom was present or absent and whether the disease was ultimately found to be present or absent in each case. Table 14.2 shows the number of cases of each of the four types: symptom present and disease present; symptom present and disease absent; symptom absent and disease present; and symptom absent and disease absent.

From such a table, it is possible to determine whether a correlation exists between the symptom and the disease. In this case, the symptom is not correlated at all with the disease. Out of 70 patients who have the symptom,

37 have the disease, a little more than half. Out of 30 patients who do not have the symptom, 17 have the disease, again a little more than half. A given patient has a little more than a 50% chance of having the disease, whether this patient has the symptom or not. The symptom is useless in determining who has the disease and who does not, in this group of patients.

Nonetheless, 85% of the nurses said that there was a relationship between the symptom and the disease. Smedslund presented the subjects with other kinds of relationships. For example, by switching the 17 and the 13, a real (if weak) relationship between symptom and disease was created; here, the nurses were no more likely to think there was a relationship than they were in the original case. Smedslund found that the best predictor of the subjects' judgment of relationship was the proportion of the total number of cases in the upper left-hand cell. If the symptom and disease were both frequently "present" as indicated by high figures in that cell, subjects tended to think that there was a relationship. Subjects seem to attend largely to this cell, when they should (normatively) have been attending to the whole table.

As Nisbett and Ross point out (1980, p. 92), the reasoning exhibited by these subjects is much like that of many laypeople when they discuss a proposition such as "Does God answer prayers?"

"Yes," such a person may say, "because many times I've asked God for something, and He's given it to me." Such a person is accepting the data from the present/present cell as conclusive evidence for the covariation proposition. A more sophisticated layperson may counter this logic by asking for the data from the present/absent cell (i.e., prayers present, positive outcome absent): "Have you ever asked God for something and not gotten it?"

In fact (Nisbett and Ross point out), even these two cells are not enough. If positive outcomes are just as likely to occur when we do *not* pray for them as when we do, there is still no relationship. We need to know the absent/present and absent/absent cells, the ones at the bottom of the table, as well as the two others.

Many other experiments have supported Smedslund's general conclusion that subjects tend to ignore part of the table. In asking whether a symptom predicts a disease, subjects attend most consistently to the present/present cell (see, for example, Shaklee & Tucker, 1980; Schustack & Sternberg, 1981; Shaklee & Mims, 1982; Arkes & Harkness, 1983). Many subjects, however, behave like the "more sophisticated laypeople" described by Nisbett and Ross, paying attention to the present/absent cell (that is, symptom present and disease absent) as well as the present/present cell. In essence, when these subjects want to know whether the symptom (S) predicts the disease (D), they pay attention most often to the probability of D given S, that is, $p(D/S)$, but they neglect $p(D/{\sim}S)$. Other subjects compare the present/present cell to the absent/present cell. In essence, these subjects attend to $p(S/D)$ and neglect $p(S/{\sim}D)$, the probability that subjects would have the symptom even without the disease.

A consequence of the lack of attention to the "symptom absent" or to the "disease absent" part of the table is that people who have the chance do not *inquire* about the half of the table they would not attend to. For example, Beyth-Marom and Fischhoff (1983, following Doherty, Mynatt, Tweney, & Schiavo, 1979) asked subjects to determine whether "Mr. Maxwell," a fictitious person whom, they were to imagine, they had just met at a party, was a professor. The subjects were told that Mr. Maxwell was either a professor or an executive and that he was a member of the Bear's Club. The subjects were asked which of several additional pieces of information they would want to have in order to determine his profession. They were asked, for example, whether they would rather know, "what percentage of the professors at the party are members of the Bear's Club" or "what percentage of the executives at the party are members of the Bear's Club." Although 89% of the subjects thought the first item was relevant (because it came from the "disease present" part of the table – the "disease" in question being "professor"), only 54% thought that the second item was (because it came from the "disease absent" part of the table). In fact, both pieces are relevant (as is the percentage of professors at the party).

In a similar study, Doherty and Falgout (1986) gave subjects an opportunity to keep or throw away various pieces of data in making an inference about whether cloud seeding causes rain. Although subjects varied greatly in their choice of data, the dominant pattern was to keep data only from the present/present and present/absent cells, that is, those cells in which cloud seeding was done (and rain occurred or did not occur).

Kuhn, Phelps, and Walters (1985) asked children and adults to judge whether a fictional product called EngineHelp makes cars run well. The experimenter told the subjects, "Six people I talked to said they use EngineHelp and they all said their cars run well." A majority of the children, and one-third of the adults, concluded from this single cell that EngineHelp did help. Most of the others said, correctly, that there was not enough information. Then subjects were told, "Two other people I talked to said that they use EngineHelp and that their cars run poorly." The responses were about the same as after the first cell, even though subjects still knew nothing about the absent/absent and absent/present cells.

Attentional bias can be understood as failure to look for evidence against an initial possibility, or a failure to consider alternative possibilities. If there are many observations in the present/present cell (or – as we shall see shortly – if we already think a correlation is present), we may just stop there. If you think that God answers your prayers, it stands to reason that some piece of good fortune is a result of prayer. Further thinking might involve looking for alternative possibilities (such as the possibility that the good fortune would have occurred anyway) and looking for evidence that might distinguish these possibilities from our favored possibility (what happens when you do not pray). Attentional bias can therefore be correctable by actively open-minded thinking.

Attentional bias in judging contingency

The underweighing of the "absent" cells has its parallel in the judgment of contingency. An especially important contingency judgment for decision making is a situation in which we try to judge whether certain outcomes are contingent upon some action of our own: that is, whether we can "control" such outcomes, in the sense of making them occur or not, according to our goals. Jenkins and Ward (1965) asked subjects to push one of two buttons on each trial of a learning experiment. After each response, the subject saw either "Score" or "No Score" light up on a panel. The experiment was set up so that the subjects received the Score light with a certain probability P after one button was pushed and another probability Q after the other button was pushed. (Expressed as conditional probabilities, $P = p$(Score/one button) and $Q = p$(Score/the other button).) After 60 trials, the subjects were asked how much control they had over the outcome.

Jenkins and Ward argued that the subjects' actual degree of control – the normative model for this judgment – was the difference between the probability (P) of scoring with one button and the probability (Q) of scoring with the other. That is, control would be $|P-Q|$, the absolute value of the difference. If pushing the first button led to the score with a probability of .7 and the second led to the score with a probability of .2, then the degree of control would be $|.7-.2|$, or $.5$.[1]

Subjects judged their degree of control almost entirely in terms of the frequency with which the Score light appeared. Subjects thought they had the greatest control in a condition in which they "scored" with probability .8 no matter which button they pushed. In general, subjects thought they had about as much control in this condition as in a condition in which they scored with probability .8 with one button and with probability .2 with the other. (Although Jenkins and Ward suggested that subjects were attending to the probability of scoring with *either* button, the results are not exact enough to rule out another interpretation: Subjects might have been attending to the probability of scoring with the *one* button most likely to produce the score light. If this interpretation is true, the results would agree completely with the findings about attentional bias, in which subjects typically attend to the probability of the outcome given the "present" cue only.) The fact that subjects think they have some control over the outcome even when they have no control at all has come to be called the *illusion of control*.

These results were obtained despite the fact that subjects were explicitly instructed that "*control* means the ability to produce the 'no score' light as well as to produce the 'score' light." Subjects were also explicitly warned that

---

[1] Other reasonable measures of association, such as the phi coefficient described earlier, give very similar results, which are quite different from the subjects' judgments.

Table 14.3. *Incidence of response and outcome for 120 trials*

		Outcome	
		Score	No score
Response	A	48	12
	B	48	12

there might be no relation at all between their responses and the outcomes. The same results were obtained in the judgments of subjects who merely watched other subjects do the experiment. Therefore, we cannot explain the results in terms of some effect of the choice itself; the "spectator" subjects made no choices. The results were also obtained when subjects were explicitly asked to try to "control" the outcome rather than to "score"; these "control" subjects had to say aloud in advance which light they were trying to produce.

In a questionnaire given after the experiment, subjects were shown tables of outcomes similar to Table 14.3. The figures in this table reveal that the Score light came on with a probability of .8 regardless of the response. Once again, even with the tables before them the subjects judged their degree of control in terms of the probability of success rather than in terms of the difference in results produced by the two buttons.

Part of the subjects' difficulty seems to result from the fact that they must press one button on each trial. When they are asked how much "control" they had over the outcome, they tend to assume that they have a fair amount, because, they reason, if they did not push any button, there would be no outcome. Allan and Jenkins (1980) tried the procedure with a single button. The subjects could press or not press on each trial, and after 100 trials the subjects were asked to estimate the degree of influence they had, or the degree of connection between pressing the button and the outcome. In this procedure, subjects still showed the illusion of control: They still said they had some control (influence or connection) over the outcome even when they actually had none. The illusion was smaller with one button than with two, however: Subjects tended to give lower ratings of their degree of control. In this study, subjects' ratings were affected by the actual amount of control; subjects estimated that they had more control in a .9 − .1 condition (outcome appears with probability .9 when they press, .1 when they do not press) than in a .9 − .5 condition. With either one button or two, however, they thought they had more control in a .9 − .7 condition than in a .3 − .1 condition; the degree of control in these conditions is the same, but the Score outcome is much more frequent in the former.

Effect of goals on illusion of control

Alloy and Abramson (1979) gained more insight into the control illusion by designing a variation on this experiment. They tried the experiment using (relatively) depressed and nondepressed college-student subjects. Depression was measured by the Beck Depression Inventory, a self-rating questionnaire that asks subjects about feelings of sadness, hopelessness, and other negative feelings. Many college students show scores on this measure that are as high as those of patients who seek psychotherapy for their feelings of depression. The very interesting result of this experiment was the discovery that whereas students who were not depressed showed the illusion of control when they received a reward of 25¢ that was not contingent on their pressing a button, depressives did not show the illusion of control in this situation. The depressive students tended to say that they had no control in this case. When the reward *was* contingent on their pressing a button, however, the depressed subjects rated their control just as high as did the nondepressed subjects. (This shows that the difference between the groups was not just a tendency to say "No control," regardless of the facts.) Even nondepressives showed no illusion of control when the outcome in question was a loss of 25¢ rather than a gain of 25¢. This narrows the illusion of control down to a specific circumstance: The illusion of control was found only in nondepressed subjects working for a *gain* rather than a *loss*.

What was the difference between the depressives and nondepressives? Alloy and Tabachnik (1984) speculated that the nondepressives *expect* to have control over outcomes and that this expectation biases their perception of the correlation between their responses and the outcomes. Nondepressives are more inclined to believe that they have discovered a way of controlling the outcome, even when they have very little evidence for such control. For example, they may think that if they follow the rule "Press the button if the desired outcome occurred on the trial before last or did not occur one trial before that," that outcome would occur. Using such rules becomes an increasingly difficult task over the course of 40 trials. The subject cannot recall the entire sequence of presses and outcomes in order to test new rules. The typical nondepressed subjects may have been forever trying new rules, and forever optimistic that *this* new rule would be the right one. The depressed subjects, on the other hand, may have engaged in this sort of behavior less often.

Schwartz (in press) has questioned this explanation. Schwartz looked for an illusion of control in a task similar to that used by Allan and Jenkins and by Alloy and Abramson. The subjects were not selected for depression, but they were divided into two groups that received different training for the experiment. Both groups first performed Schwartz's confirmation bias experiment (described in ch. 13), in which they learned how to get a reward by pressing a button to make a light perform a sequence of movements through a matrix. One group of subjects was given the "reward" condition, in which they were told that the task was to obtain a reward. The other was given the "rule" condition, in which the task was to discover the rule relating the sequence to the reward. You will recall that the reward condition made subjects less successful at discovering rules in a subsequent task of the same type, presumably because they were less inclined to look for rules.

After the training, Schwartz had both groups of subjects do a button-pushing experiment similar to the ones done by Allan and Jenkins and by Alloy and Abramson. The subjects in the rule group did *better* at learning that there was no contingency than had the subjects in the reward group. The illusion of control was found in the reward group, but not in the rule group. It would seem that those who do not fall for the illusion are those who look for rules. It is possible that depressed subjects did look for rules in the Alloy and Abramson experiment, perhaps because they were not interested in reward.[2]

Effects of prior belief

Illusory correlation

A second bias in the judgment of correlation concerns the effect of prior belief about what the correlation ought to be. People tend to find in the data what they think (before they look) will be there.

The most dramatic example is a series of studies done by Chapman and Chapman (1967, 1969). They wondered why clinical psychologists continued to use certain projective tests in psychological diagnosis, particularly the Draw-a-Person Test, even though these tests had been shown to be useless. In the Draw-a-Person Test, patients are asked simply to draw a human figure on a blank sheet of paper. It was thought that patients "project" various aspects of their personalities into their drawings. For example, suspiciousness of others was thought to be associated with atypical eyes, and concerns about manliness were thought to be associated with broad shoulders.

Many studies have shown that these ideas are simply wrong. When drawings made by paranoid patients (who are suspicious) are compared with drawings by people who are psychologically normal, no differences are found in the eyes. What puzzled Chapman and Chapman was the fact that clinical psychologists continued to use the test although they knew about the findings. Informally, many of them said that they simply did not believe the negative results. One commented, typically, "I know that paranoids don't seem to draw big eyes in the research labs, but they sure do in my office" (Chapman & Chapman, 1971, pp. 18–19).

---

[2] It is also possible, though, that the rule pretraining made subjects better able to *discover* rules and that there is more than one reason for not falling for the illusion: either thinking very well or not thinking at all.

To find out whether people were really capable of detecting such correlations, the Chapmans collected a number of these drawings and labeled each drawing with a psychological characteristic, such as "suspicious of other people" or "has had problems of sexual impotence." The labels for each picture were carefully chosen to ensure that there was absolutely no correlation, within the set of pictures, between each label and the features of the human figure thought to be associated with it. For example, human figures with elaborated sexual features were as likely to occur when the label did not indicate sexual concerns as when it did. These drawings, with the labels, were shown to college-student subjects who had never heard of the Draw-a-Person Test. When they were asked to *discover* what features of the drawing tended to go with what labels, the students "discovered" exactly the correlations that most clinicians believed to be present – for instance, suspiciousness and abnormal eyes – even though there was no statistical correlation. Note that the subjects were asked to describe what characteristics of the drawings went with what labels for the drawings they were shown; they were not asked what they thought was true in general.

The same kind of results were found for the Rorschach ink-blot test, in which patients describe the images they see in a series of ink blots. When students were given a number of blots together with the responses made to them by patients with various diagnoses (which the students were also given) and asked to discover what features of Rorschach responses correlated with homosexuality, they once again "discovered" the correlations that most clinical psychologists believed to be present (for example, homosexuals were thought to be more likely to see a woman's laced corset in one of the blots). Once again, these features were not actually correlated with homosexuality. Research had shown, in fact, that other features tended to be correlated with homosexuality (for example, interpreting a certain blot as a giant with shrunken arms). Subjects did not discover the real correlations, however, even though they were actually present in the information given to them. In sum, subjects' expectations about what ought to correlate with homosexuality led them to perceive the correlations that they expected, but they failed to perceive the correlations that were present.

Personality traits

Prior belief can also distort our perception of correlations among personality traits. It has been well known for a long time that people who fill out questionnaires about other people's personalities are subject to a "halo effect." If, for example, a teacher thinks that a child is intelligent, she will also tend to rate this student as well behaved, even if the child is no better behaved than average. This is presumably the result of the teacher's belief that intelligent children also tend to be well behaved. Because the teacher expects such a correlation, she tends to perceive it in children's behavior. The correlations that people expect to see, however, are not always the ones that are present.

This was demonstrated in a study done by Shweder (1977; further discussed and reanalyzed by Shweder & D'Andrade, 1979). Shweder reanalyzed the data from a much earlier study of introversion and extraversion in children in a summer camp (Newcomb, 1929). The counselors at the camp provided daily ratings of the behavior of each child, on such items as "speaks with confidence of his own abilities," "takes the initiative in organizing games," and "spends more than an hour a day alone." Because the daily ratings were made as soon as possible after the occurrence of the relevant behavior, the ratings were presumably as accurate as possible. From these data, it was possible to measure the correlation of every type of behavior with every other type of behavior over the entire summer. For example, the correlation between "gives loud and spontaneous expressions of delight or disapproval" and "talks more than his share of the time at the table" was .08, indicating a very weak relationship between these two behaviors; children who tend to exhibit the first behavior are not much more likely to exhibit the second behavior than children who do not exhibit the first. Shweder made a list of all of these correlations, one correlation for each pair of behaviors.

At the end of the summer, when the details of day-to-day happenings had been forgotten, the counselors filled out ratings of the same children on the same items. This situation is more like the questionnaires used in personality measurement, where ratings are based on long-term memory rather than specific day-to-day events. Once again, a list of correlations was made, one correlation for each pair of behaviors. Shweder then looked at the correlation of the two lists. If the correlation of the two lists was high, those behavior pairs that had high correlations in one list would have high correlations in the other, and likewise for low correlations. For the two items described earlier, the correlation based on memory was .92 (rather than .08); thus, in this case, a high correlation in one list went with a *low* correlation in the other. Although the degree of difference observed for these two items was extreme, the two lists of correlations were, in general, not themselves correlated: The correlation between the daily-rating correlations and the memory-based correlations was about .25,[3] which is low.

Why is there such a weak relationship between the correlations of daily ratings and the correlations of the memory ratings? Perhaps because of a sort of halo effect. People think that certain traits ought to go together, so when they give a high rating on one, they tend to give a high rating on the other as well, and vice versa.

To get a better idea of what people *think* ought to go with what, in personality, Shweder asked a number of University of Chicago undergraduates

---

[3] This was the average over several studies of this type; see Shweder and D'Andrade (1979, p. 1081).

to rate all of the pairs of behavioral descriptions from the summer-camp research for "conceptual similarity," thereby creating a third list. These conceptual-similarity ratings correlated strongly (about .75) with the memory-based correlations, but not very strongly (about .26) with the daily-rating correlations. In short, the conceptual similarity of a pair of behaviors was strongly related to the correlation between the two traits in the memory ratings, but neither conceptual-similarity nor memory-rating correlations were strongly related to the actual daily-rating correlations. When people make inferences based on memory, they tend to remember what they think they ought to remember; they do not remember accurately what actually happened.

Prior belief and attentional bias

Kuhn, Amsel, and O'Loughlin (1988) found a type of illusory correlation – another effect of prior beliefs – in the evaluation of hypotheses about dichotomous variables like those used in the study of attentional bias. Their results suggest that attentional bias can be increased by prior belief. Specifically, when prior belief is present, we tend to focus on the evidence that supports our belief and ignore the evidence against it. This mechanism could explain some of the results of experiments concerning biased attention. For example, if subjects in the contingency experiments had a prior belief that they could control the outcome, they would tend to ignore evidence against this belief.

Although Kuhn and her colleagues used both children and adults as subjects, the results were much the same for both, except for a group of graduate students in philosophy (who did not show illusory correlation).

Subjects were told about some experiments in which children in a boarding school were deliberately given different combinations of foods (at each table in the dining room) by researchers, in order to determine whether the foods affected the probability of the children's getting a cold. Each subject stated her own hypotheses first. Then subjects were shown the data (table by table) and were asked to describe what the data showed. When subjects were asked whether the data showed that the food made a difference, they interpreted the evidence in a way that was colored by their hypotheses. For example, one subject thought that the type of water (tap or bottled) would make a difference but that the type of breakfast roll would not. The evidence presented was identical for both variables, since tap water was always given with one type of roll and bottled water with another, yet the subject interpreted the evidence as showing that water made a difference and rolls did not. When another subject believed that mustard caused colds, she looked selectively for cases in which mustard had been eaten and colds had occurred, and she ignored cases in which mustard had been eaten and colds had not occurred.

Note that subjects in this experiment and in the Chapmans' experiment were asked to describe the evidence, not to *use* the evidence to draw a conclusion (as in the other experiments discussed in this section). Kuhn and her colleagues actually asked subjects both to say what they thought *was true*, after seeing the evidence, and to say what they thought *the evidence indicated by itself*. Many of the subjects failed to distinguish these two questions. They gave the same answer to them, and they seemed surprised if the experimenter asked the second after the subjects had answered the first. The researchers suggest that a basic problem may be the difficulty of putting aside one's prior belief in order to evaluate the evidence on its own. The problem certainly seems to be analogous to that discussed in the chapters on logic, in which we saw that people cannot always put aside their doubts about the truth of premises in order to decide whether a conclusion would follow *if* the premises *were* true.

Conclusion

Illusory correlation and attentional bias distort our perception of the evidence available to us. We think evidence weighs more heavily on the side of beliefs we already hold than it actually does. Because of this distortion, our beliefs are likely to be less sensitive to counterevidence than they ought to be. In the next chapter, we shall take a broader look at the resistance of beliefs to counterevidence.

15 Biases and beliefs

The human understanding when it has once adopted an opinion draws all things else to support and agree with it. And though there be a greater number and weight of instances to be found on the other side, yet these it either neglects and despises, or else by some distinction sets aside and rejects, in order that by this great and pernicious predetermination the authority of its former conclusion may remain inviolate.

Francis Bacon

Irrational belief persistence is the tendency to search for evidence, and to use evidence, in a way that supports beliefs that are already strong for us (prior beliefs) or beliefs that we want to be true. This kind of bias, we saw, seems to cause a number of errors we have encountered in part II, such as illusory correlation and overconfidence in extreme probability judgments, and I shall argue that it is the major bias in thinking about beliefs of all types.

This chapter considers beliefs in general, including the strongly held personal beliefs that shape a person's moral, social, and political attitudes. Discovering a useful normative model for beliefs of these types is difficult. We saw in chapter 11 that beliefs should, ideally, conform to probability, in the sense that the strength of belief should be determined by probability and should increase as probability increases. This model is difficult to apply, however, to complex beliefs that are formed over a long period. Beliefs about whether capital punishment is justified, for example, are based on a large and interrelated set of other beliefs concerning morality and human behavior. An analysis in terms of probability would take a long time.

Another reason that probability theory does not help with such beliefs is that we often lack a simple criterion of "true" or "false" (although we may be able to say that one belief is better supported by evidence than another). The proposition that "free enterprise is the best economic system" cannot be assigned a probability unless we can say what it means for such a proposition to be true or false. (Recall that probability has been defined only for propositions that can have such truth values.) What if the truth is that free enterprise is best for certain goods and services under certain conditions? Probability theory does not apply to propositions that are partially true.

Because of these difficulties, psychologists have developed other criteria of rationality that are easier to apply than probability theory. We shall find

256

that people often violate these constraints because of the tenacity with which they hold on to their favored beliefs.

Many of the things that we call "beliefs" are really personal goals. A person who says that she believes strongly that abortion is wrong (or not wrong) may be willing to spend some time every day campaigning for her views. Someone else could assign the same probability to the same proposition (that abortion is wrong, or not wrong) but may regard the issue as unimportant compared to other issues. The difference is that they have made different decisions about their goals, about the strength of their desires to act on their beliefs. We cannot analyze such differences in goals in terms of probability theory, because goals – unlike beliefs in the narrow sense – are not propositions that can be classified as true or false. We can, however, apply the more general criteria of rationality to the formation of personal goals.

When we speak of the formation of beliefs, in this chapter, we are talking to some extent about the formation of goals. We shall put aside the distinction between beliefs and goals here. Both beliefs and goals are bases for action. Most research has not distinguished them, and I shall not discuss them separately in the rest of this chapter at any length. It is worthwhile to bear in mind, though, that people think about their goals in much the same way in which they think about their beliefs.[1]

Irrational persistence of belief

The nature of irrational persistence

The irrational persistence of belief is one of the major sources of human folly, as many have noted (Bacon, 1620/1960; Janis & Mann, 1977; Nisbett & Ross, 1980; Kruglanski & Ajzen, 1983). We tend to hold to our beliefs without sufficient regard to the evidence against them or the lack of evidence in their favor.

Irrational belief persistence affects our lives in many forms in addition to those already discussed concerning judgment of probability and correlation. Good students, for example (like good scholars), must remain open to counterevidence and criticism, willing to be persuaded of alternative views and willing to criticize their own efforts so as to improve them; poor students often seem to be rigid in defending their mistaken beliefs about what they are learning in school (Baron, Badgio, & Gaskins, 1985).

Certain forms of psychopathology, such as delusions, are essentially defined

---

[1] One might think that goals are somewhat special, because arguments about goals usually refer to other goals: For example, arguments that people should become more politically concerned often refer to general moral or religious goals that people already have. Arguments about beliefs, however, also make reference to other beliefs. If there is a difference between beliefs and goals, it may be only that belief strength is limited – one can be no more certain than 100% – but the strength of goals has no natural limit.

by irrational persistence of belief. A delusional patient is not just someone who believes (wrongly) that her sneezing and coughing mean that she is dying of an incurable disease; she is someone who continues to believe this even after five reputable physicians tell her that her symptoms are caused by a simple allergy to ragweed. Depressives, Beck has argued, maintain their depression by ignoring evidence that could cheer them up and by taking seriously only the evidence consistent with their gloomy outlook (Beck, 1976). Beck's cognitive therapy of depression tries to teach the patient to treat the relevant evidence more impartially.

Irrational belief persistence has also been implicated in faulty decision making by individuals and governments alike. In any war in which one side clearly loses, the loss is apparent before it occurs, but both the government and people of the losing side continue to believe that they can see victory just around the corner. Moral beliefs that underlie political controversies, such as those concerning abortion, sex, or racial inequality, also seem particularly resistant to arguments or evidence.

Irrational belief persistence can cause serious difficulties in personal matters such as relationships and business ventures, too. In romance and in business, confidence is usually a good thing, because it inspires us to undertake difficult ventures, to initiate relationships, to pursue lofty goals, but when the evidence tells us that a particular endeavor – whether a love affair or a new company– is not getting off the ground after several attempts, we need, for our own sakes, to be responsive to the evidence, and sometimes we are not.

Irrational belief persistence involves two types of biases that we have frequently encountered earlier in this book:

1. The *overweighing* of evidence consistent with a favored belief or the *underweighing* of evidence against it: for example, a general's attending to reports of enemy casualties and ignoring reports of their troop strength.
2. The *failure to search impartially* for evidence: for example, when supporters of United States intervention in Nicaragua search for historical analogies, they are likely to discover the Munich agreement with Hitler, and opponents, when they search for analogies, are likely to discover United States support of Batista in Cuba or the unsuccessful Bay of Pigs invasion.

Some belief persistence is not irrational. Often the evidence against a belief is not strong enough to make a convincing case for giving it up. Michael Faraday persisted in believing that electrical currents could be induced with magnets despite several failures to produce such currents experimentally and finally, of course, succeeded (Tweney, 1985). If we all gave up beliefs as soon as there was evidence against them, we would hold very few beliefs with any certainty, and we would give up many beliefs that were true.

The amount of belief persistence that is *rational* is whatever best serves the goals of the thinker; in most cases, the goal is to adopt beliefs that provide the best basis for decisions that achieve those goals. We cannot judge the rationality of persisting in a belief by knowing the truth in hindsight: Although rationally formed beliefs are, on the whole, more likely to be true than irrationally formed beliefs, we cannot assume that false beliefs are always irrationally formed. For example, many efforts have been made to show that it was irrational of President Roosevelt and his advisers not to suspect that the Japanese would attack Pearl Harbor. Such critics claim that the president and his policymakers possessed much evidence that favored such an attack but explained it away or ignored it. Some evidence must always be "explained away" or considered less important, however, even when beliefs are true: Evidence is not always consistent. The question is how much explaining away is *too* much? For every failure to predict something that actually happened, Jervis asserts, "we could look at an event that did not take place, and, acting as though it had occurred, find a large number of clues indicating the event's probable occurrence which the officials had ignored or explained away" (1976, p. 175).

If we want to find out if, when, and why irrational persistence of belief occurs, we need some normative standards for belief persistence itself.

The order principle, the primacy effect, and total discrediting

How can we tell whether people are weighing evidence in a way that is normatively correct? We have discussed the difficulties in using probability theory as our normative standard. A good alternative might be to focus on the process of weighing evidence itself and to look for general normative principles that a *rational response to evidence* would have to obey. Once we find such constraints, we can ask whether people violate them.

One such principle is the *order principle*: *When the order in which we encounter two pieces of evidence is not itself informative, the order of the two pieces of evidence should have no effect on our final strength of belief*. Or, put more crudely, "When the order doesn't matter, the order shouldn't matter." Suppose I want to find out which of two political candidates is better, and I start out with no opinion at all. I run into a trusted friend, who tells me that candidate X is better. Later, another equally trusted friend tells me that candidate Y is better, but by this time I have already formed an inclination to vote for X, so I question the second friend very carefully. It was simply chance that made me run into X first, so the order of the evidence does not matter, yet I might end up favoring X because that evidence came first.

Such an effect is called a *primacy effect*, because the first piece of evidence is weighed more heavily than it should be. One explanation of the primacy effect is that the initial evidence leads to an opinion, which then biases the search for subsequent evidence, as well as the interpretation of that evidence when it is found. This would be *normatively* irrational. If this kind of response to evidence can easily be avoided, we can say that it is *prescriptively* irrational as well.

Many psychological studies have reported primacy effects in judgment (see, for example, Hovland, 1957; Anderson, 1981, ch. 3), as well as *recency effects*, which might be taken to indicate the opposite bias of oversensitivity to evidence. Many of these studies have used a method devised by Asch (1946) in which the subjects were given a list of adjectives describing a person, such as "intelligent, industrious, impulsive, critical, stubborn, envious" or "envious, stubborn, critical, impulsive, industrious, intelligent." The impressions of the person were more favorable given the first list than the second, even though one list is simply the reverse of the other. The term "intelligent," in the first list, seemed (to Asch) to color the interpretation of the later terms; of course, "envious" would have the opposite effect.

Although Asch and others found primacy effects in this type of experiment, others, such as Stewart (1965), found recency effects. Recency effects do not necessarily imply that subjects were too open-minded. Another explanation is that subjects did not follow the instructions to consider all of the evidence equally. In Stewart's experiment, the data from many subjects had to be excluded because the subjects responded only to the most recent item rather than to all the items. Even subjects who tried to respond to all the items could have had difficulty suppressing the tendency to respond to the most recent item alone. This tendency can make primacy effects difficult to discover.

Most studies that show primacy effects are not relevant to the question of rationality in belief persistence. There are two general reasons why not. First, often a great deal of evidence is presented, and later (or earlier) evidence is differentially forgotten at the time a judgment is made. Although violation of the order principle would be normatively irrational for someone with perfect memory, it would not be irrational when we take memory into account, as we must for our prescriptive perspective, since (as stressed in ch. 2), such a perspective must reflect what is *humanly possible*. Second, the subjects in most experiments might have had reason to believe that earlier (or later) evidence was actually more informative. In most natural situations, the most important evidence is presented first (or last, depending on the situation), and it would take at least a little effort to convince subjects that this was not true in the laboratory as well.

Peterson and DuCharme (1967) designed an experiment that minimizes both problems. Subjects were told that a sequence of poker chips would be drawn at random from one of two urns, urn C or urn D. The subject's task was to estimate the probability that the chips were drawn from urn C (or from urn D). Urn C contained 3 red, 2 blue, 2 yellow, 1 green, and 2 white chips. Urn D contained 2 red, 3 blue, 1 yellow, 2 green, and 2 white chips. After each chip was drawn, subjects provided a probability judgment about which urn was more likely. The most recent chips are surely freshest in the subject's mind, so a primacy effect cannot be explained in terms of forgetting the most recent evidence. The experimenter arranged in advance the exact order in which the chips would be drawn. The color frequencies of the first

30 chips favored urn C. The next 30 were the mirror image of the first 30, with red and blue switched, and yellow and green switched. At the end of 60 trials, then, the subject should have thought the two urns to be equally likely. In fact, it took about 20 more chips favoring urn D before subjects reached this point. They seem to have become committed to their initial favoritism toward urn C. Because they still favored urn C after 60 trials, when the evidence was equal for both urns, they showed a primacy effect.

There is some reason to think that irrational primacy effects, and irrational persistence in general, are found only when subjects make some *commitment* to the belief suggested by the earliest evidence they receive. If they simply note the evidence and its implications, without forming a desire that its implications be true, they may remain open-minded until all of the evidence is in; they will effectively be using all the evidence simultaneously, and irrational persistence will not occur. For example, Dailey (1952) found that subjects were less sensitive to new evidence when they answered inferential questions after receiving early evidence in an impression-formation task (with information presented in paragraphs rather than as adjectives) than when they did not need to make any inferences.

Another experiment that suggests a similar phenomenon is that of Bruner and Potter (1964). Each subject was shown a series of pictures on slides. Each slide was present several times. The first presentation was very much out of focus, but focus became gradually clearer over the series. After each presentation, subjects were asked to state their best hypothesis about what the picture was. Subjects began stating hypotheses early in the series. They tended to stick to these hypotheses even after the slide came into focus. Their early hypotheses seemed to inhibit their recognition of what was actually on the slide. This was demonstrated by giving the same slides to other subjects but beginning only slightly out of focus. These subjects had little difficulty recognizing the pictures, even though the original subjects, given this degree of focus, could not recognize the pictures – presumably because they were committed to their original hypotheses, and these hypotheses guided their search for and use of evidence from the slide.

A different type of experimental design, called *total discrediting*, has been used to demonstrate irrational belief persistence (Anderson, Lepper, & Ross, 1980). The idea is to present some evidence that induces a particular belief. For example, subjects are given questionnaire responses of two different firefighters, one rated as better than the other at the job. Some subjects are given evidence indicating that risk taking is positively associated with firefighting performance, other subjects are given the reverse. The evidence is then discredited by telling the subject that the evidence was totally fabricated, and the belief is then assessed. The direction of the initial belief manipulation continues to influence the belief, even after discrediting. Those who were initially led to believe that risk taking is associated with success continue to believe it. This is technically a violation of the order principle, but it is a special case, since the second piece of evidence is meaningless without the first. (In addition, Wegner Coulton, & Wenzlaff, 1985, point out that part of this effect is due simply to the difficulty of "wiping out" any information from one's memory; some measures of the effect are affected by evidence even when the subject is warned in *advance* that the evidence is false.)

This phenomenon seems to be the result of the subject searching memory for other evidence consistent with the original belief at the time when the initial belief is created. After the discrediting, the additional evidence remains and continues to affect belief. If there is irrationality here, it may be in the initial effort to bolster the belief by searching memory for evidence in favor of the belief but not for evidence against it.

Does this phenomenon show true irrationality from a prescriptive point of view? At the time when the initial evidence is presented, I suggest, the bolstering may occur by *automatic* elicitation of consistent memories rather than by intentional search for supportive evidence. This effect might be very difficult to avoid. At the time when the final belief is tested, the subjects may simply be unable to distinguish which evidence for their current belief was elicited by the original manipulation and which they would have thought of in any case. If they were to be more cautious, they might end up dismissing everything that they could think of as potentially biased. Prescriptively, then, this effect might not be irrational, because it might not be avoidable without unreasonable effort. This issue seems to have been largely settled by C. A. Anderson (1982), however, who found that asking subjects to use a heuristic designed to avoid bias – considering whether one could argue for the other side – substantially reduced the basic effect. Therefore, the original bias is one that can be overcome, if only we think in a way that is fairer to alternative possibilities.

In sum, beliefs created in an experiment seem to affect the search for and use of subsequent evidence in a way that maintains the beliefs. This is the basic mechanism that leads to violations of the order principle.

The neutral-evidence principle

A second normative principle is the *neutral-evidence principle*: *Neutral evidence should not strengthen belief.* By "neutral evidence" I mean evidence that is, on the whole, equally consistent with a belief and its converse. Neutral evidence might consist of mixed evidence, that is, some evidence in favor of a belief and equal evidence against it.

The neutral-evidence principle would be violated if we tended to interpret ambiguous evidence as supporting a favored belief. For example, each side of an international conflict often believes that the other side is up to no good. An offer of concessions may be interpreted as a sign of weakness or trickery rather than as evidence against the favored belief. Likewise, if the evidence is mixed, one side may attend only to the evidence that supports its initial belief, so that the belief is strengthened by this part of the evidence but *not* weakened by unfavorable evidence.

The neutral-evidence principle was clearly violated by subjects in experiments that Pitz and his colleagues (Pitz, Downing, & Reinhold, 1967; Pitz, 1969) carried out, using Bayesian probability theory as a normative standard. Subjects observed a series of balls drawn from one of two bingo baskets – devices for the random selection of balls. The baskets differed in the proportion of balls of different colors that they contained. For example, one basket had 60% red balls (and 40% black), and the other 40% red. After each draw, the ball drawn was returned to the basket, so that the proportion of red balls in the basket stayed the same for all draws. The subjects could not see the balls in each basket. After each ball, the subject made a judgment of the probability that the balls were all drawn from one of the baskets. When two successive balls were of different colors, the normative model (Bayes's theorem) specifies that no overall change in probability of the subject's hypothesis should occur, yet subjects usually *increased* the probability assigned to their more likely hypothesis after seeing two balls of different colors. If they thought the balls were from the first basket, for example, they counted a red ball as evidence in favor of this hypothesis, but they failed to count a black ball as equally strong evidence against it.

This "inertia effect" was present only when subjects made judgments after each draw; when the judgment was delayed until the series was over, confidence was a function of the difference between the number of red and black balls drawn, just as Bayes's theorem says it should be. (When an inertia effect was present, confidence increased with the number of draws even when the difference was constant.) Pitz (1969) suggests that subjects need to commit themselves to a judgment in order to display resistance to evidence against that judgment.

Lord, Ross, and Lepper (1979) showed an apparent violation of the neutral-evidence principle in a situation where such errors in daily life have deadly serious consequences. They selected subjects who had indicated that they favored, or opposed, capital punishment in responses to a questionnaire. Each subject was then presented with mixed evidence on the effectiveness of capital punishment in deterring crime. Each subject read two reports, one purporting to show effectiveness and the other purporting to show ineffectiveness. (Although the reports appeared to be actual journal articles, they had been fabricated by the experimenters.) One report compared murder rates in various states in the country before and after adoption of capital punishment. The other compared murder rates in states with and without capital punishment. The results were manipulated so that only the first report showed deterrence for half the subjects and only the second report showed deterrence for the other half.

The effect of each report on the subject's belief was stronger when the report agreed with the belief than when it did not. Subjects rated the report that agreed with their opinion as "more convincing," and they found flaws more easily in the reports that went against their belief. (Of course, neither kind of report is conclusive evidence, but both kinds are better than no evidence at all.) In the end, subjects *polarized*: that is, they became stronger in their initial belief, regardless of its direction. If anything, mixed evidence should have made subjects less sure of their belief.

This study is disturbing, because it suggests that evidence is useless in settling controversial social questions. Of course the results may be limited to certain types of cases. People do not always have a chance to find flaws in evidence, and the result could be dependent on the greater effort to find flaws in arguments on the other side. Also, attitudes toward capital punishment may be as much a function of basic moral beliefs as of beliefs about its effectiveness as a deterrent. Opponents of capital punishment tend to feel that "two wrongs do not make a right" (even if the second wrong *does* prevent other wrongs), and proponents tend to feel that "the punishment should fit the crime" (even if it *does not* prevent other crimes). Counterevidence is therefore easily resisted, in this case, by simply attending to the moral reasons for or against capital punishment, but such an attention shift is unnecessary when the evidence on deterrence is favorable to the choice consistent with one's moral belief.

It is important to note that this "polarization effect" can be detected only when the bias against counterevidence is extreme. Normatively, we might expect that beliefs would move toward the middle of the range when people are presented with mixed evidence. If people have stronger (or more) evidence for the side they favor, then mixed evidence, which is equally strong on both sides, would add proportionately more strength to the other side. If we could apply a precise normative model to belief revision, it might specify some exact amount of movement toward neutrality. When beliefs do not move toward neutrality at all, they may move *less than they should* according to such a model. When we cannot apply such a model – as we cannot in the case of the capital-punishment experiment – we cannot detect such resistance to evidence unless it leads to polarization.

Note that the illusory correlation effect (described in ch. 14) could lead to violation of the neutral-evidence principle. If people interpret zero correlation as consistent with their belief in a positive correlation, they will maintain that belief more tenaciously than they should. The experiments on illusory correlation, together with the experiment by Lord and his colleagues in which subjects tended to find flaws only in the evidence that went against them, suggest that a major mechanism of irrational persistence involves distortion of one's perception of what the evidence would mean to an unbiased observer.

An extreme example of the violation of the neutral-evidence principle was found by Batson (1975). In his study, the evidence presented was not even neutral, but was entirely against the belief in question, for the relevant subjects. Fifty female high school students who attended a church-sponsored youth program were given a questionnaire that included items concerning the divinity of Jesus: For example, "Jesus actually performed miracles," and "Jesus was only human." The students were then divided into two groups, according to their answer to the question "Do you believe Jesus is the Son of God?" (Forty-two answered yes; 8 answered no.) Subjects in the two groups were then asked to read, discuss, and evaluate some material purportedly "written anonymously and denied publication in the *New York Times* at the request of the World Council of Churches because of the obvious crushing effect it would have on the entire Christian world" (p. 180). The writings claimed to show, on the basis of newly discovered scrolls, that the New Testament was fraudulent. Eleven of the 42 believers accepted the veracity of the article. This group became even more convinced of the divinity of Jesus than they had been before reading the article. (The believers who did not accept the veracity of the article did not change their belief, and the nonbelievers also strengthened their disbelief in the divinity of Jesus, even though most of them did not accept the article either.) The believers who accepted the article had the greatest need to strengthen their belief in the divinity of Jesus, and they did so despite being given nothing but negative evidence.

Determinants of belief persistence

Let us now consider some possible determinants of irrational belief persistence. General beliefs about thinking itself can play a role. As we noted in chapter 3, people have their own standards for thinking, some of which encourage poor thinking. Certain goals can also be factors: We may persevere in our beliefs because we desire to hold those beliefs or because we desire to believe that we are good thinkers, good decision makers, and morally good people. Other factors, such as external demands to account for one's decisions, or stress, can increase or decrease irrational persistence.

Beliefs about thinking

The heuristics that we use to form our beliefs are maintained by certain explicit beliefs about how thinking should be conducted–beliefs transmitted through the culture (Perkins, Allen, & Hafner, 1983; Baron, in press a). People differ in their beliefs about how one should draw conclusions. Some think that changing one's mind is a sign of weakness and that a good thinker is one who is determined, committed, and steadfast. Such people, if they followed their own standards, would be more likely to persist in beliefs irrationally. Others believe that good thinkers are open-minded, willing to listen to the other side, and flexible. Most of us probably subscribe somewhat to both of these beliefs. Whatever our beliefs, most of us desire to be good thinkers, so we try to follow our own standards.

The reflective judgment interview. Kitchener and King (1981) and their colleagues (King, Kitchener, Davison, Parker, & Wood, 1983) theorized that our ideas about how beliefs ought to be formed and how beliefs are actually formed change, as we mature, in a well-defined developmental sequence. In their experiments, subjects were given a Reflective Judgment Interview in which they were presented with belief dilemmas. For example, they might have been told (Kitchener & King, 1981, p. 104):

There have been frequent reports about the relationship between chemicals that are added to food and the safety of those foods. Some studies indicate that such chemicals can cause cancer, making these foods unsafe to eat. Other studies, however, show that chemical additives are not harmful, and actually make the foods containing them more safe to eat.

Each dilemma was followed by a standard series of probe questions designed to elicit the subject's assumptions about reality, knowledge, and justification. The researchers identified seven developmental stages that people move through as they get older, very likely in part as a result of education. (The most sophisticated subjects tested were graduate students.)

In stage 1, the researchers find, people hold that there is simply no question about what is true. The truth is known either through direct experience or through authorities. For example (Kitchener & King, 1981, p. 93):

Subject: Somebody had to start this world, so I have to believe in my religion that there's a God.
Interviewer: Have you ever doubted that?
S: No, I'm not a religious freak or nothing. I just go to church and think it's common knowledge. Somebody had to start it.

This stage contains the seeds of its own demise, as authorities often disagree with each other, and what is "common knowledge" to one person is blatant falsehood to another.

In stage 2, the researchers assert, people solve this problem by holding that there is an objective, knowable reality but it is not known to everyone; it is known only to legitimate authorities. True disagreements between authorities are therefore impossible. For example, a subject explains how two scientists can go through the same procedures and come up with different results (p. 94):

S: It's like the commercials, like big companies such as Bayer or Excedrin . . . I just saw a commercial on it. Their scientists study this and they are being paid to say it's okay!
I: What if neutral experts disagree?
S: If they both did it the same way, if they use the same chemicals and everything, I don't think it could have come out differently. If they did, then somebody probably did something wrong, like adding something extra.

Subjects like this one are unwilling to acknowledge differences in interpretation.

In stage 3, Kitchener and her colleagues theorize, people hold that objective reality is there but may not be known, even to legitimate authorities. Therefore it is possible for scientists not to know an answer to some question in their field. While people are waiting to find out the truth, they are free to believe what they choose to believe, but there is no basis other than "what feels right" for these beliefs. Alternative points of view among experts are understood as areas of uncertainty, where any point of view is as good as any other.

In stage 4, according to the theory, people dispense with the idea of objective truth. One person's belief about anything is as good as another's. "I can't really say on this issue [creation versus evolution]. It depends on your belief, since there is no way of proving either one." No evaluation is possible, even for the individual.

In stage 5, people hold a similar view, but allow that methods of justification exist *within* specific domains. At this stage, a person might argue that from the point of view of a nuclear physicist the risks of nuclear-power plants are acceptable but from the point of view of an environmentalist, they are not. Each belief is justified within the particular framework, and no comparison is possible.

In stage 6, people continue to hold that truth is ultimately subjective: "There's no such thing as objective, unbiased reporting" (p. 99). There is, however, a belief that some justifications are better, "more compelling," than others, and the principles of good justifications hold across different domains. One should try to bring one's beliefs into line with the best justifications.

In stage 7, the highest stage, the researchers conclude, people believe that there is an objective reality, which is known imperfectly through our own perceptions and interpretations. Nonetheless, it is possible to determine, through critical inquiry, that some judgments are more correct than others. Knowledge is the result of a process of critical inquiry and must always be open to criticism and improvement. Beliefs are justified by passing through this gauntlet of inquiry. Specific criteria for evaluation may vary from domain to domain (for example, science, religion), but there are always ways of judging which of two ideas is a better approximation to reality. For example (p. 100):

S: It's my belief that you have to be very skeptical about what you read for popular consumption . . . even for professional consumption.
I: How do you know what to believe?
S: I read widely . . . of many points of view. Partly (it's) reliance on people you think you can rely on, who seem to be reputable journalists, who make measured judgments, then reading widely and estimating where the reputable people line up or where the weight of the evidence lies.

Same person reflecting about another issue:

S: It's (the view that the Egyptians built the pyramids) very far along the continuum of what is probable.
I: Can you say one (point of view) is right and one is wrong?

S: Right and wrong are not comfortable categories to assign to this kind of item . . . [I prefer to say] more or less likely or reasonable . . . more or less in keeping with what the facts seem to be.

To summarize, the first four stages involve a gradual break with the idea that truth is absolute and known to all. The breakdown of this idea is what leads to subjectivism or relativism. The last (higher) four stages involve a gradual recognition of the possibility of general standards of justification. They are a way of growing out of the complete subjectivism of stage 4.

The research done so far does not determine whether the developmental sequence observed is inevitable or whether (for example) it is a result of going through a certain kind of educational system that encourages these beliefs in roughly the order indicated. There is little reason to think that stages cannot be skipped. It is also possible that general standards can be acquired earlier, so that the middle stage of relativism can be avoided.

What is clear is that the higher stages encourage actively open-minded thinking, and the lower stages discourage it. The higher stages imply that thinking is worthwhile, that progress can be made. The lowest stages imply that thinking is futile because only authority or direct experience can lead to truth, and the middle stages imply that thinking is futile because no answer is better than any other. In addition, the highest stages imply that beliefs can always be improved; this encourages openness to alternatives and to counterevidence.

Evaluation of thinking. To examine the relation between beliefs about thinking and thinking itself, I began by measuring subjects' beliefs about good thinking, in two different ways (in press a). First, subjects were asked how they thought people ought to respond to challenges to their beliefs. How, for example, should college students respond when they meet new ideas about religion or politics? Subjects were classified according to whether or not they thought people ought to think further, with a view to revising their beliefs if it is warranted. Second, subjects were asked to give grades (A through F) to hypothetical thinking protocols for the quality of thinking. Some protocols considered arguments on only one side of an issue (for example, on the question of whether automobile insurance rates should be higher for city dwellers than for suburbanites, "My first thought is that each group of people should pay for its own accidents. City dwellers surely have more accidents, and their cars get broken into and stolen a lot more"). Other arguments presented evidence on the other side as well (for example, "On the other hand, it doesn't seem fair to make people pay for things they can't help, and a lot of people can't help where they live").

Subjects' thinking itself was also measured by looking at whether they themselves produced two-sided or one-sided arguments when asked to consider some question, such as the question about ocean-floor minerals described in chapter 3. Those thinkers who gave higher grades to two-sided protocols, and who thought that we should be open-minded when our beliefs are challenged, were more likely than other subjects to produce two-sided thinking themselves. It appears that people's beliefs about thinking affect the way they themselves think.

Why do some fail to realize that two-sided thinking is better than one-sided thinking? It is possible that belief in one-sided thinking is the result of the evolution of institutions, such as organized religions and nations. To keep its adherents from one generation to the next, each of these institutions must convince them that its views are correct, even though many outsiders will argue otherwise. Those institutions that inculcate an ideology in which defense of one's belief is a virtue and questioning is a vice are the ones most likely to overcome challenges from outside.

Another possibility is that people are confused about two different standards concerning thinking, which we might call the "good thinker" (active open-mindedness) and the "expert." Because experts *know* the answer to most questions, they usually do not have to consider alternatives or counterevidence. If we admire experts, then we may come to admire people who are "decisive" in the sense of being rigid. When a news commentator criticizes a political candidate for waffling and being unsure (as might befit a good thinker faced with many of the issues that politicians must face), the implication is that the candidate is not expert enough to have figured out the right answer yet. Similarly, a person who adopts a know-it-all tone – speaking without qualification or doubt – is giving a sign of expertise. Some parents (perhaps because they *are* experts about the matter under discussion) talk this way to their children, who come to think of it as a "grown-up" way to talk.

This confusion of expertise with good thinking may reinforce the institutional pressures. Those who are considered wise and respected members of the institution or group may talk like experts, encouraging their followers to "know" rather than to think. And how are the followers supposed to "know"? By listening to the experts, of course.

A third possibility is that people confuse the standards of the thinker with those of an *advocate*. A good lawyer is an advocate for her client. She tries to defend her own side, and she considers the other side of the case only for the purpose of rebutting it. It is inconceivable that she would change her mind, at least in court. She deliberately takes sides, knowing that there is another lawyer on the other side, and a judge to ensure that the opponent is treated fairly. Similarly, in democratic groups, public-spirited people often advocate a point of view they do not necessarily accept but feel is neglected, knowing that the other side of the issue will be well defended. Thus the individual can approach an issue in a one-sided way with the comfort of knowing that the group as a whole will "think well," in the sense of considering alternatives and counterevidence. There is room for one-sided advocacy as part of a larger process of two-sided (or many-sided) group thinking. Even in groups, however, respect and tolerance for the other side is required if the group is to function well. The danger is that people's standards for thinking may be confused with standards for skill as an advocate. That is why debating teams do not necessarily encourage good thinking.

Distortion of beliefs by desires

We now consider the ways in which beliefs are affected by desires (long-term personal goals or temporary goals). These effects may help to explain irrational belief persistence, and they are also of interest in their own right. They have long been known to psychotherapists as types of bias that can seriously interfere with personal functioning, but they are probably just as insidious in the realm of politics.

Self-deception. Persistence in an irrational belief can be a kind of self-deception in which we make ourselves believe something through the use of heuristics or methods of thinking that we would know (on reflection) are incorrect. By this view, if we were aware that our thinking was biased when we did it, we would not accept its results. This account assumes that irrational persistence occurs even in people who can recognize good thinking in general when they see it.

The best evidence for self-deception as a phenomenon in its own right comes from a study that has nothing to do with belief persistence. Quattrone and Tversky (1984) first asked each subject to take a cold pressor pain test, in which the subject's arm was submerged in cold water until the subject could no longer tolerate the pain. After that, the subject was told that recent medical studies had discovered two types of hearts, one type being associated with longer life and fewer heart attacks than the other. The two types could be distinguished by the effect of exercise on the cold pressor test. Some subjects were told that exercise would increase tolerance in the good type of heart; others were told that it would decrease tolerance in the good type. Subjects then repeated the cold pressor test, after riding an exercycle for 1 minute.

In general, subjects' tolerance changed in the direction that they were told was associated with a good heart; if they were told that exercise increased tolerance in people with good hearts, they managed to tolerate the cold water a bit longer, and vice versa. Only 9 of the 38 subjects indicated (in an anonymous questionnaire) that they had purposely tried to change in the direction associated with a good heart. The remaining 29 showed just as large a change in tolerance (in the good direction) as the 9 who admitted that they tried to change. In general, the 9 who admitted trying to control their results did *not* believe that they really had a good heart, but the 29 who did not admit to "cheating" did believe it. The 9 admitters therefore failed in their attempt to deceive themselves, because they were caught in the act (by themselves, of course), and therefore they could not accept the results of the deception. The 29 others were successful in keeping from themselves what they had done to create their beliefs.

This experiment illustrates the essential features of all self-deception (see Elster, 1979, 1983): the presence of a desire to have a certain belief; an action or inaction designed to create or strengthen that belief; and an unawareness of the relation between the ultimate belief and the motivated action that gave rise to it. If you neglect to mention disturbing symptoms to your doctor, you must forget that you have done this if you want to be cheered up when she pronounces you to be in excellent health.

Wishful thinking. Psychologists have found other examples of beliefs distorted in the direction of desires. Svenson (1981) found, for example, that most drivers believe that they are safer and more skillful than average, and Weinstein (1980) found that most people believe they are more likely than average to live past 80.

McGuire (1960) gave subjects questionnaires containing a number of propositions, such as the following:

> Any form of recreation that constitutes a serious health menace will be outlawed by the City Health Authority.
> The increasing water pollution in this area has made swimming at the local beaches a serious health menace.
> Swimming at the local beaches will be outlawed by the City Health Authority.

Notice that the third proposition is a conclusion that follows from the first two, the premises. Each proposition (premises and conclusions) was to be rated for *probability* on a scale of 0 to 100. After this, the same items were rated for *desirability* on a five-point scale, from "very desirable" to "very undesirable." There was a correlation between the mean probabilities and mean desirability ratings across the propositions; that is, the propositions rated as more probable were also rated as more desirable, on the average. This suggests a wishful-thinking effect, but it could be explained in other ways. (For example, probabilities may affect desires, or desirable events could really be more likely than undesirable ones.)

Other results are more difficult to explain away. In most cases, the rated probability of the conclusion could be predicted from the rated probabilities of the premises: It was approximately the product. For example, if the first premise in the list just given were assigned a probability of .5 and the second a probability of .6, the third would be assigned a probability of .3 (since $.5 \cdot .6 = .3$). When the conclusion was rated as undesirable (and the premises were not undesirable), however, this product rule did not work. The conclusion might be given a probability rating of .2 rather than .3. It seems that people are unwilling to draw conclusions from their other beliefs (with the usual strength) when they wish those conclusions to be false.

McGuire also had subjects come back a week later and fill out the same questionnaires. Probability ratings of the first premise and the conclusion tended to change, increasing the relationship between belief and desirability. In the example, the probability assigned to the first premise tended to decrease, and the probability assigned to the conclusion tended to increase.[2] Wishful thinking seems to affect the change in beliefs that occur over time.

Some wishful thinking is not irrational, however, as we noted in chapter 3, for certain unpleasant beliefs may themselves make us unhappy or unable to carry out our other plans. The prescriptive difficulty is to set policies for ourselves that will permit wishful thinking and self-deception only when they are harmless or useful.

Dissonance resolution: eliminating conflict among beliefs. A related phenomenon occurs when we make a difficult decision. Often there are reasons favoring the path not taken. After the decision, we seem to give these reasons less weight than we gave them before the decision. Festinger (1962) asked adolescent girls to rate a number of popular records for attractiveness. The experimenter then asked each girl to choose among one of two records that she had rated as moderately attractive. When the records were rated again, the record chosen was given a higher rating than before, and the record rejected was given a lower rating than before. Presumably the subjects were more convinced, the second time, that they had good reasons for their original decisions.

In a similar experiment (Festinger, 1962), subjects were paid to write an essay advocating a position (in politics, for example) with which they disagreed. Those paid only a little to do this tended to change their opinion in the direction of the essay they wrote. Those paid a lot did not change. Those paid only a little desired to believe that they had written the essay for a good reason. Because they did not do it for the money, they thought, they must have done it because they really agreed with the position more than they initially thought.

In another classic study, Festinger and Carlsmith (1959) induced subjects to participate in a psychology experiment that they deliberately made boring and tedious. After the experiment, each subject was asked to convince the next subject (actually a confederate) that the experiment was interesting and fun. Half of the subjects were paid $1 for their participation in the experiment; the other half were paid $20. After this, the subjects were interviewed about their true opinion of the experiment. The group paid $1 had a more favorable opinion of the experiment.

Festinger (1962) explains these results as a process of "reduction in cognitive dissonance." When the choice is difficult, the reasons for one decision are "dissonant" with the reasons for the other, and the dissonance can be

---

[2] The probability assigned to the second premise did not change. This does not negate the conclusion that the probability assignments to members of the same group became more consistent as time passed.

reduced by playing down the reasons for the choice not made or inventing reasons for the choice made (for example, that the dull experiment was really interesting).

Surely we try to eliminate conflict among our beliefs. Most of our attempts to do this, however, are completely rational. When we find evidence against a belief that we favor, for example, we often reduce the strength of the belief so as to "reduce the dissonance." These experiments, however, seem to show some sort of *irrationality*. What is irrational here? The idea of "dissonance reduction" does not by itself seem to capture it.

The reason for this sort of postdecisional change could be that people like to believe that they are "good" decision makers – both morally good and intelligent. They change their beliefs about their reasons for *having made* a decision so that their beliefs fit their desire that they be good in these ways. When they write an essay opposing their real view for only a small amount of pay, it is easiest to justify that decision (a bad financial deal) by thinking that they really have some sympathy for that position. Likewise, they may justify doing a boring task for a small amount of pay by thinking that they actually liked the task. Similarly, when they make a difficult decision between two choices, they may later have doubts about whether they made the best decision unless, in retrospect, they see the decision as not so difficult at all; they therefore play down the value of the rejected choice. These experiments seem to illustrate a form of wishful thinking, where the "wish" is the desire to be a good decision maker, and the beliefs that are affected are those about our reasons for having made a decision.

A number of experiments support this view. Cooper (1971), for example, found that the effect of past decisions on beliefs was larger when the outcome of the decision could be foreseen than when it could not. The decision in question involved agreeing to work with another subject (a confederate) in a task in which the amount of payment depended on the performance of both subjects. In order to receive high payment, both subjects had to solve aptitude test problems and, after each problem, indicate accurately whether they had answered it correctly or not. The subject was told that her partner was either "too timid to publicly state that she had [the problem] correct" or else was "a little too sure of herself." In fact, the partner did (always) lower the score for both subjects by being either too timid or too overconfident, but half of the time the source of the difficulty was the opposite of what the subject expected. The interesting result was that the subject liked the partner more (thus justifying her own decision to take part in the experiment) when the difficulty had been foreseen than when it had not. When the difficulty was the opposite of what was expected, the subject could not have foreseen it and therefore had less reason to convince herself that her decision had been a good one.

Another study (Aronson, Chase, Helmreich, & Ruhnke, 1974) showed that subjects can even feel responsible for *unforeseen* (but potentially foreseeable) outcomes and that this responsibility can lead them to justify their decision in hindsight. Subjects were asked to make a video tape recording in which they made arguments (from an outline the experimenter gave them) advocating government regulation of family size – a position with which they disagreed – ostensibly for use in another experiment. In one condition, subjects were told, *before* they agreed to make the tape, that those who would watch the tape would be either highly persuadable (other students who were unsure of their opinion) or not at all persuadable (students who were strongly against government regulation). Subjects who thought that their audience was persuadable changed their opinion more in the direction of favoring government regulation than the other subjects. Presumably, this is because the subjects who thought that they might persuade their audience thought that they would be doing a bad thing to convince someone else of a totally erroneous view, so they convinced themselves that the view was acceptable, and thereby also maintained the belief that they themselves were good people.

In another condition, the subjects were told nothing about the audience until after they had made the tape. The same effect was found, although it was smaller: That is, subjects changed their own attitude more in the direction of favoring regulation when they were told, after making the videotape, that the audience was persuadable, even though they had known nothing about the persuadability of the audience when they agreed to make the tape. Apparently these subjects blamed themselves for being duped. The effect was not found when the subjects were told initially that the tape would not be shown to anyone and were later told that it would be. In this condition, subjects were able to let themselves "off the hook" because the experimenter's lie had been so blatant.

In general, then, people do not like to think of themselves as liars or bad decision makers, and they manipulate their own beliefs so as to convince themselves that they are not. This appears to be a type of wishful thinking, possibly also involving self-deception.

Beliefs as a cause of desires. In many of the experiments just discussed, subjects wanted to think of themselves as good decision makers. This desire brought about (or strengthened) a belief that they had made a good decision. This sort of belief can itself affect *other* desires: The goals we try to achieve can be shaped by what we think it is good to try to achieve. Our beliefs about what it is good to do, in turn, can be shaped by our past behavior – even if we did not play as great a role in choosing that behavior as we think we did.

Axsom and Cooper (1981) asked some moderately overweight women who wanted to lose weight to go through a "therapy" procedure consisting of performing some annoying cognitive tasks, such as reading nursery rhymes into a "delayed auditory feedback" machine, which played back their voices into headphones after a fraction of a second. In fact, there was no reason to think that this procedure would cause weight loss, except that the subjects believed that it might. A "high-effort" group of subjects did such tasks for five hourly sessions. A "low-effort" group did the same tasks, but only for a few minutes each session, sitting in a waiting room the rest of the time. The high-effort group lost more weight, and kept it off. One year later, they weighed an average of 6.7 pounds less than when they had started, whereas the low-effort group weighed only 0.3 pounds less.

The women who went through the difficult program would have made a foolish decision (in agreeing to participate) unless they had really wanted to lose weight. This fact probably caused them to believe that they wanted to lose weight, and this belief, in turn, made them continue to want to. More generally, whenever we make a sacrifice for some goal, our motivation to achieve that goal is strengthened: Otherwise the sacrifice would have been in vain. Another general lesson from these experiments is that our goals are what we *think* they are. If you infer from your behavior that you really want to lose weight, then you really *will* want to lose weight.

Beliefs can also produce a "sour grapes" effect. When something seems impossible or difficult for us to attain, we *want* it less. Sometimes this is rational: If we can adjust our desires to reality, we will be happier. Changing our belief is irrational, though, when we are too easily persuaded to give up a goal that we could achieve (Elster, 1983).

Whether this effect is rational or not, it seems to occur. Harris (1969) asked subjects to rate the desirability of a number of phonograph records, one of which they would be given at the end of the experiment. Then subjects were told that a certain record would not be given away, and the ratings were done again. The excluded record was given lower ratings than it had been given when it was a possible goal.

Perhaps the simplest demonstration of the effect of beliefs on desires was carried out by McGuire (1960) as part of the study (described earlier in this chapter) in which subjects were asked to rate the probability and desirability of various propositions. When McGuire gave the subjects arguments designed to change their *probability judgments* for the propositions, the desirability ratings for those propositions changed as well. A message to the effect that pollution made swimming dangerous, for instance, made this fact both more probable and less undesirable. We might call this the "Pangloss effect," after Dr. Pangloss, the "sage" in Voltaire's *Candide*, who, after each tragic episode in the story, explains at great length why it was "all for the best."

Selective exposure. People maintain their beliefs by exposing themselves to information that they know beforehand is likely to support what they already want to believe. Liberals tend to read liberal newspapers, and conservatives tend to read conservative newspapers. Those who voted for George McGovern for U.S. President in 1972 watched eagerly as the winner, Richard Nixon, was raked over the coals in the Watergate affair of 1973, while those who had supported Nixon were relatively uninterested (Sweeney & Gruber, 1984).

In an experiment conducted during the 1964 election campaign, subjects were given an opportunity to order free brochures either supporting the candidate they favored or supporting his opponent (Lowin, 1967). Subjects received samples of the contents of each brochure. When the arguments in the sample were strong and difficult to refute, subjects ordered more brochures supporting their own side than brochures supporting the other side. When the arguments in the sample were weak and easy to refute, however, subjects tended to order more brochures on the other side. People can strengthen their own belief by convincing themselves that the arguments on the other side are weak or that their opponents are foolish, as well as by listening to their own side. Many other studies have found this sort of bias toward information that can strengthen desired beliefs (Frey, 1986).[3]

Selective exposure can lead to self-deception. Imagine that you want to believe that some course of action is correct, so you ask a friend to tell you all the reasons why it is good. If you then say to yourself, "This must be a great plan, because it has only good points and no bad points," you are neglecting the fact that you have not asked for the bad points. People who select biased information and then believe it as though it were unbiased are manipulating their own beliefs.

Desires and irrational persistence. What is the relation between the effects we have been discussing and the general phenomenon of the irrational persistence of belief? For one thing, the "dissonance" experiments are a type of irrational persistence in their own right. What seems to persist is each person's belief that he is a good decision maker, moral and intelligent. This belief is maintained, however, in a peculiar way. When a person runs into evidence against the belief, evidence suggesting that a bad decision may have been made, the person changes his beliefs about his own desires ("I must really have wanted it, or I wouldn't have done it for so little money," or "put in so much effort," and so forth). These beliefs about desires, in turn, may influence the desires themselves, as we have just seen.

Just as we want to think of ourselves as good decision makers, we want to think of ourselves as good belief formers. When a belief is challenged, our first impulse is often to bolster it (Janis & Mann, 1977), in order to maintain our belief in our earlier intelligence. We want *to have been right all along* – whereas it would be more reasonable to want to be right in the present (even if that means admitting error). This is what makes us into lawyers, hired by

---

[3] Early studies of selective exposure (reviewed by Freedman and Sears, 1965) failed to find an overall preference for information on the subject's side, but the arguments on the other side in these studies were often easy to refute, so subjects who chose information on the other might have done so in order to refute it.

our own earlier views to defend them against all accusations, rather than detectives seeking the truth itself.

Other factors

We have been discussing the major causes of irrational belief persistence. Several other factors have been shown to increase or decrease the amount of this bias that subjects show – or the extent to which thinking is actively open-minded – although none of these factors could provide a sufficient account of the existence of the bias.

Value conflict and integrative complexity. One measure of what I call actively open-minded thinking is the scoring of arguments for "integrative complexity," a method developed by Schroder, Driver, and Streufert (1967), Suedfeld and Rank (1976), and Suedfeld and Tetlock (1977). Using this method, Tetlock measured the integrative complexity of speeches of U.S. senators (1983a) and personal interviews given by members of the British House of Commons (1984). Examination of differences among ideological groups led Tetlock to an interesting hypothesis about why people sometimes consider counterevidence and sometimes do not.

Integrative complexity is scored on a 1 to 7 scale. A score of 1 is given to statements that express only a one-sided view, neglecting obvious arguments on the other side; for example (Tetlock, 1983a, p. 121):

Abortion is a basic right that should be available to all women. To limit a woman's access to an abortion is an intolerable infringement on her civil liberties. Such an infringement must not be tolerated. To do so would be to threaten the separation of Church and State so fundamental to the American way of life.

Scores of 3 are given when the statement is "differentiated" – that is, when it includes arguments (evidence or goals) for both sides; for example (p. 121):

Many see abortion as a basic civil liberty that should be available to any woman who chooses to exercise this right. Others, however, see abortion as infanticide.

Scores of 5 or higher are given when the person making the argument succeeded in "integrating" opposing arguments, presenting a reflective statement about the criteria by which arguments should be evaluated; for example (p. 121):

Some view abortion as a civil liberties issue – that of the woman's right to choose; others view abortion as no more justifiable than murder. Which perspective one takes depends on when one views the organism developing within the mother as a human being.

From the perspective of the search-inference framework, differentiation involves consideration of counterevidence to an initial possibility, so it displays actively open-minded thinking. Integration sometimes involves search for goals, criteria by which the evidence will be weighed, but in other cases it seems to represent the use of evidence to draw a conclusion. Integration is therefore not necessarily good in itself except in showing that the subject completes his thinking about the topic within the allotted time. However, all the results I shall describe using the integrative complexity measure depend largely on distinctions among levels 1 through 3, which do not involve integration. We may therefore regard the level of integrative complexity as a measure of the tendency to consider arguments on both sides of an issue (differentiation).

In the United States, Tetlock (1983a) found, integrative complexity was highest on the political "left" ("liberal Democrats") and lowest on the "right." It would appear that left-wingers tend to be better thinkers. In the British interviews (Tetlock, 1984), however, the highest scores were obtained by the "moderate socialists," who corresponded in their beliefs roughly to those on the left in the United States. The "extreme socialists," those on the extreme left of respectable British politics, were lower in complexity than those closer to the middle of the political spectrum.

Tetlock did not draw the most obvious conclusion – that moderate leftists are the best thinkers. He suggested that integrative complexity is affected by what people think about and its relation to their "values" – or what I would call their personal goals. Thinking is differentiated (and hence more integratively complex, in these studies) when personal goals conflict. Moderate liberals typically have conflicting goals for many of the questions they face, in particular the goals of equality and economic efficiency, which conflict in such questions as whether the rich should be taxed to help the poor (thus reducing economic incentive but increasing equality). By this "value pluralism" model, conservatives would show complex thinking when *their* goals conflicted – for example, when concern for individual freedom clashed with concern for national security over the question of compulsory military service. In terms of the search-inference framework, counterevidence is most likely to be discovered when it supports a goal, and additional goals are most likely to be discovered when they are already personal goals of the thinker. (Of course, even if Tetlock is correct, there can *also* be differences among people holding different political views in the kind of thinking that led to those views.)

Tetlock (1985) tested the value pluralism model directly by asking college students to write down their thoughts about questions that involved conflicting values, such as "Should the [Central Intelligence Agency] have the authority to open the mail of American citizens as part of its efforts against foreign spies?", a question that pits national security against individual freedom. Each subject was asked to rank all the values that were pitted against each other by the various questions. The differentiation of subjects' thinking was higher when the values underlying the question were ranked close together (and when they were both highly ranked). Subjects thus tended to give a differentiated answer to the question about opening mail if they valued *both* national security and individual freedom. Subjects who ranked only one of these values highly found the question easy to answer and were less prone to consider evidence on both sides. There were also individual differences in differentiation that were consistent across the various questions: Some people just showed more differentiated thinking than others. The effect of value conflict, however, was found even within individuals. A single subject could show more differentiated thinking on one question than on another question when the first question involved values that were conflicting for that subject and the second question did not.

In sum, people are more open to counterevidence when the counterevidence invokes a personal goal. Irrational belief persistence is therefore most likely to occur when personal goals are strong and one-sided. The sources of irreconcilable conflict among people often lie in people's single-mindedness, that is, in their tendency to adopt some personal goals and not others. In principle, then, such conflict can be reduced if people think more openly *about their personal goals*. In practice, however, such reflection about personal goals is a slow process at best.

Accountability. When we express their beliefs to others, we usually have the goal of being liked by those people. We therefore tend to accommodate our statements to the beliefs of our audience. When we must justify our views to an unknown audience, we are inclined to imagine various possible audiences, so that we try to accommodate our statements to many different points of view. In this way, *accountability* for one's judgments increases active open-mindedness.

Tetlock (1983b) found that accountability reduced the primacy effect in a judgment task. Subjects read evidence concerning the guilt or innocence of a defendant in a criminal case. When subjects did not need to justify their judgments, they showed a strong primacy effect: They judged the defendant as more likely to be guilty when the evidence pointing toward guilt came first than when it came second. (Subjects had no reason to think that the order of the evidence mattered, so this experimental condition demonstrates a clear violation of the order principle, described earlier in this chapter.) When subjects were told (before reading the evidence) that they would have to justify their judgments to an associate of the experimenter, they showed no primacy effect at all.

In a similar study, Tetlock and Kim (1987) gave each subject another person's answers to some items of a personality questionnaire and asked the subject to predict the person's answers to other items and to give confidence ratings. When the experimenter told the subjects that they would have to justify their judgments in a tape-recorded interview after the experiment, their judgments were more accurate, their overconfidence was reduced, and their thinking was more "integratively complex." These beneficial effects of accountability on the quality of thinking imply that thinking will be best (and irrational belief persistence minimized) in situations that require such accountability – such as a judge, writing a legal opinion – and worst in situations that do not require it – such as a citizen, voting by secret ballot.

Stress. Janis and Mann (1977) proposed that the quality of decision making is affected by "stress," which occurs when it is difficult for the decision maker to see how to avoid extremely negative outcomes. Excessive stress leads to a state of "hypervigilance," in which the decision maker considers one option after another, with little search for evidence. When the decision maker does seek evidence, the search is unsystematic, and the most useful evidence is often overlooked. On the other hand, a small amount of stress – enough to make the decision maker aware of the importance of the decision but not so much as to cause hypervigilance – can lead to more purely "vigilant" decision making, in which the decision maker searches thoroughly for alternatives and evidence. (Janis and Mann do not specifically mention search for goals, but presumably they would think that it is more thorough too.)

In some cases, the effect of stress results from time pressure alone. When time is short, decision makers are forced to restrict their search. Kruglanski and Freund (1983) have found that several biases, including the primacy effect, are increased by time pressure.

Keinan (1987) found that stress can impair thinking even when time pressure is absent. Subjects were asked to solve analogy problems, such as "Butter is to margarine as sugar is to . . . beets, saccharin, honey, lemon, candy, chocolate" (p. 640). The problems appeared on a computer display. The subjects had to examine each of the six alternative answers, one at a time, by pressing the corresponding number on the computer keyboard. The computer recorded the number of alternatives that were examined and the order in which they were examined for each problem.

When subjects were told to expect painful electric shocks during the experiment, they often responded before examining all of the alternatives (on the average, on about 5 of the 15 problems). Other subjects, who expected no shocks, rarely did this (on the average, only once out of 15 problems). Subjects who expected shock were less likely to scan the alternatives in a systematic order (for example, 1, 2, 3, 4, 5, 6), and they were less likely to answer correctly (36% correct versus 59% for the group that did not expect shocks). (In fact, no subject received any shocks.) These negative effects of stress occurred even when subjects thought they would receive shocks only if they answered incorrectly too often, so that the threat of shock provided an incentive to answer correctly. Keinan suggests that stress – in the form of fear – can distract our attention and cause us to search less thoroughly.

Groupthink

Biases such as irrational belief persistence are found when thinking is done by groups as well as by individuals. Since much important thinking is done by groups, this field is important. As we noted in chapter 1, the thinking of groups has analogies with the thinking of individuals. Possibilities and goals are suggested; evidence (arguments) is brought forward; and conclusions are drawn. If, when the group first starts its work, everyone already has a fixed belief, it will be hard to give a fair hearing to other possibilities. There are "hanging juries" as well as "hanging judges."

To a certain extent, the factors that operate in group thinking are the same as those that operate in individual thinking. After all, a group is simply a collection of individuals, and if the individuals making up a group tend to show a certain bias, then the group tends to show it as well.

In other ways, group thinking differs significantly from individual thinking. Groups have an opportunity to overcome some of the biases shown by individuals, because it is possible to choose the members of the group so as to represent a variety of points of view. On the other hand, the individual members may be too willing to assume that this has been done when it has not been done. A group consensus sometimes seems much more obviously "right" than the same conclusion reached by an individual, even though the members of the group are all alike in sharing the characteristics that lead to the consensus. Would it be any surprise if a group of automobile workers in the United States "agreed" that importing of Japanese cars should be stopped, or if a group of Toyota dealers agreed that importing should not be stopped?

Janis (1982) studied the rationality of group decision making and the biases that distort group decisions by reviewing the history of major foreign-policy decisions made by the president of the United States and his advisers. Some of these decisions displayed poor thinking, and others displayed good thinking. As it turned out, the former led to poor outcomes and the latter led to good outcomes. It is to be expected that better thinking will lead to better outcomes on the average, but Janis is aware that the correlation is not perfect. He tried to select his cases according to the kind of thinking that went into them rather than according to the outcome. The examples include what he regarded as the poorly made decision of President Kennedy and his advisers to attempt the Bay of Pigs invasion in Cuba in 1961; the well-made decisions of practically the same group during the Cuban missile crisis in 1962; the poorly made decisions of President Johnson and his advisers to escalate the Vietnam War over several years; and the poorly made decisions of President Nixon and his advisers to withhold information concerning White House involvement in the Watergate break-in from 1972 to 1974.

Janis's selection of cases was supported by Tetlock's study (1979) analyzing the "integrative complexity" of public statements by prominent decision-making groups. Tetlock found that the poorly made decisions were associated with statements at or near the lowest level, but the well-made decisions were associated with well-differentiated statements.

Janis identifies three major causes of poor group thinking, presented here in outline form:

Type I. Overestimation of the group

   1. *Illusion of invulnerability.* This is often fostered by past successes (for example, a landslide or surprising victory in an election). For example, in the Bay of Pigs invasion, it was clear to the group that many risks were involved, yet little serious consideration was given to the question of what would happen if the worst outcomes materialized (as they did, in practically every case).

   2. *Belief in the inherent morality of the group.* This encourages mistakes of a form in which immoral means are used to obtain supposedly moral ends, as seems to have occurred in all of the poorly made foreign-policy decisions listed earlier. Janis does not assume that the ends *never* justify the means – only that sometimes they do not and that a bias toward belief in the morality of the ends prevents group members from asking whether the means are in fact justified in the case at hand.

Type II. Closed-mindedness

   3. *Collective rationalization.* Group members convince themselves that they do not have to consider outside information or alternatives. For example, in the Bay of Pigs fiasco, the Cuba experts of the State Department were not consulted because, it was argued, secrecy needed to be preserved. This was in fact a thin rationalization, since the press was already full of rumors of an impending invasion. During the Vietnam War escalation, members of the planning group deceived each other by withholding negative evidence.

   4. *Stereotypes of out-groups.* Just as the groups are overconfident in their own powers and morality, they tend to believe that their opponents are weak, foolish, and immoral. They therefore underestimate their opponents, both domestic and foreign. Kennedy underestimated Castro in the Bay of Pigs invasion. Johnson underestimated both his military enemies and domestic opponents.

Type III. Pressures toward uniformity

   5. *Self-censorship.* Members of the group hold back from mentioning their doubts about the policy under discussion. They often feel that they will lose their "effectiveness" by expressing disagreement and that their job is to be "team players." Many participants in decisions characterized by "groupthink" (to borrow George Orwell's term) have severe guilt and regret after a bad outcome for failing to voice their own doubts and questions while the decision was being made.

   6. *Illusion of unanimity.* Self-censorship and other devices create an illusion of unanimity. For example, during the planning of the Bay of Pigs invasion, an opponent of the plan (Chester Bowles) was invited to a meeting but not given a chance to speak. His silence was interpreted as tacit agreement. At another point, Senator William Fulbright, another opponent, was invited to present his case to the group, but after the presentation Kennedy moved on to other business right away, so that group members were prevented from expressing agreement or raising questions.

7. Direct pressure on dissenters. Usually this is not necessary, but sometimes dissent does surface. After John Dean, the White House counsel, told President Nixon that the policy of trying to suppress information was failing, Dean was told by several others to stop "talking surrender" (p. 231).

8. Self-appointed mind-guards. Some members of the group take it upon themselves to keep others in line with the supposed consensus. For example, during the planning of the Bay of Pigs invasion, Robert Kennedy "took [Arthur] Schlesinger aside and asked him why he was opposed. The President's brother listened coldly [as Schlesinger answered] and then said, 'You may be right or wrong, but the President has made his mind up. Don't push it any further. Now is the time for everyone to help him all they can' " (Janis, 1982, p. 40). (Robert Kennedy was later to play exactly the opposite role during the Cuban missile crisis.)

By contrast, when good thinking occurs in groups, there is a commitment of the group to a friendly (and sometimes not so friendly) interchange of arguments pro and con, not to a decision already tentatively made. Loyalty to the group is defined in terms of loyalty to the process of making the best decision, not loyalty to a decision already made. Visitors to President Kennedy's inner circle during the Cuban missile crisis were often surprised at the freedom that members had to bring up seemingly irrelevant ideas and suggestions. (Kennedy apparently had learned something about group decision making from the Bay of Pigs.) Information was sought out from a variety of sources, especially people expected to disagree with the group, and these people were questioned thoroughly. (Janis suggests that assigning one member of the group to be devil's advocate can help to prevent groupthink.)

Janis does not deny that there were other causes of poor decision making in his examples. For example, he noted an excessive concern not to appear "soft on communism," for domestic political reasons. Had presidents Kennedy and Johnson considered the possible outcomes of their poor decisions motivated in this way, Janis argues, they would have realized that they were ultimately undercutting even this goal. One of the advantages of Janis's analysis is that it can explain poor decision making while allowing that very good decision making could occur in similar circumstances. Decision makers are not simply the victims of their political biases, and the purported existence of these biases does not provide a full explanation of poor decisions. In good decision making, questioning is always possible.

Conclusion

This chapter has provided the main evidence for my claim that we tend to be biased in favor of our initial ideas. I showed this by comparing our responses to evidence with normative principles such as the order principle and the neutral-evidence principle. The prescriptive policy to avoid these biases is actively open-minded thinking. We have explored some of the factors that facilitate and inhibit such thinking.

Many of the biases discussed in this chapter are prevalent in conflict situations between two groups: for example, the United States and the Soviet Union, the Israelis and their Arab opponents, each nation and its trading partners (or would-be partners), and the advocates and opponents of abortion, free trade, and many other public policies.[4] If people learned to think more rationally – to consider counterevidence and to form their ideologies with more sympathy for the variety of goals that people pursue – such conflicts could be reduced. We often suppose that only the other side thinks poorly, that they, not us, are the ones in need of education. Even if this is true, no harm is done by making sure that our own house is in order. Careful attention to the quality of our own arguments can even uplift – by example – the reasoning of our opponents.

[4] For those interested in further reading on biases and conflict, Jervis (1976) provides an excellent discussion.

Part III

Decisions and plans

Part II was concerned with thinking about beliefs. Part III is about decision making, the thinking we do when we choose an action, including both the decisions that affect only the decision maker and the decisions that affect others, that is, decisions that raise moral questions. We shall also examine long-term planning, with special emphasis on the choice of personal goals. Part III is concerned mostly with inference rather than search, in particular, with how we infer a course of action from our goals and from evidence concerning the consequences of our options for achieving them.

Chapter 16 describes the fundamental normative model of decision making, the idea that utility – or desirability of outcomes – should be maximized. This model serves as a theoretical ideal that we can use to justify prescriptive models, and it is also the basis of decision analysis, a set of formal yet practical methods used by decision makers in business, government, and medicine. Chapter 17 reviews some descriptive models of decision making. These models are considerably more elaborate than any descriptive models we have encountered so far, and some of them raise questions about how we should interpret the idea of utility maximization itself. Should we, for example, take into account our feeling of regret that results from our having made a decision that happened to result in a bad outcome (aside from our feelings about the outcome itself)? Chapter 18 examines further our ability to make consistent quantitative judgments without the aid of formal theories. Chapters 19 and 20 extend the analysis to moral aspects of decision making. I argue that the fundamental normative basis of decision making does not change when these considerations are brought in: We still should try to maximize the utility of outcomes, but we must consider outcomes for others as well as for ourselves. Chapter 21 discusses planning and the potential conflict between goals for future outcomes and goals for immediate outcomes. These conflicts are roughly analogous to those between self and others: We can think of our future selves as somewhat different people from our present selves.

16 Normative theory of utility and choice

This chapter concerns the normative theory of decision making: that is, the theory of how we should choose among possible actions under ideal conditions. The best decision, I argue, is the one that best helps us to achieve our goals. This idea follows directly from the definition of rationality introduced in chapter 3.

The application of this criterion, however, is not always so clear. Decisions often involve conflict. There may be conflict between the desirability of an outcome and its probability: The job at Harvard appeals to Ellen more, but the chances of obtaining tenure are better at Yale. The conflict may be between goals: The Yale job is better for her career, but the Boston area is a nicer place to live than New Haven. The goals involved can be those of different people: The Harvard job is better for Ellen, but her husband will have a better chance of finding a job in New Haven. How do we resolve such conflicts?

The best normative answer is that we measure the extent to which each consequence of each option (for example, Harvard or Yale) achieves each goal for each person. This measure of goal achievement is called *utility*. Our goals, of course, are what we want to achieve. The normative model states that we should try to maximize total utility, that is, choose the option that will yield the greatest total utility. When outcomes are uncertain, we take this uncertainty into account by multiplying the utility of each outcome by its probability. (We shall discuss the arguments for multiplication later.) This theory of how we should measure and maximize utility is called *utility theory*.

Utility is also called "subjective value" or "desirability." It is not the same as "pleasure." The concept of utility respects the variety of human goals. It represents *whatever* people want to achieve. Some people do not want "pleasure" as much as they want other things (such as virtue, productive work, enlightenment, respect, or love – even when these are painful things to have). The utility of an outcome is also different from the amount of money we would pay to achieve it. Money is not a universal means to achieve our goals. As the Beatles said, "Money can't buy me love," and there are many other things that money cannot buy. Utility is also not quite the same thing as "happiness," for we are happy, in a sense, if we expect to achieve our goals even if we are not now achieving them (Davis, 1981).[1] Finally, utility is not the same as "satisfaction," which is the feeling that comes from achieving our goals. We do not experience the achievement of many of our goals, but that makes them no less important in our decision making. Many composers of music, for example, strongly desire that their music be played and enjoyed long after they are dead. Those who have achieved this important goal have not had the satisfaction of achieving it.

We shall consider utility theory in three parts: The first part, called *expected-utility theory*, is concerned with making a "tradeoff" between the probability of an outcome and its utility. Should you spend time applying for a graduate-school fellowship that you well may not receive? At issue are both how likely you are to receive the fellowship and how desirable it would be if you did. To decide what to do, we analyze choices into outcomes that can occur in different states of the world. To compute the utility of each choice, we multiply the utility of the outcome by the probability of the state that leads to it, and we add across the states.

The second part of utility theory, called *multiattribute utility theory (MAUT)* is concerned with making tradeoffs among different goals. Should you spend more time on your studies or take a part-time job to earn extra money? At issue are the relative importance to you of your studies and your need for money. In MAUT, we calculate the utility of an option by breaking each consequence into attributes (each attribute corresponding to a goal), measuring the utility of each attribute of each option, and adding across the attributes. We can use MAUT to determine the utility of outcomes in an expected-utility analysis.

The third part of utility theory discusses decisions that involve conflict among the goals of different people. When we make such decisions by maximizing utility, we are following *utilitarianism*, a moral philosophy first developed by Jeremy Bentham (1789) and John Stuart Mill (1863) and defended recently (in a modified form) by Richard M. Hare (1981). Modern utilitarianism is basically the claim that *the best action*, from a moral point of view, *is one that maximizes expected utility over all relevant people*. We may think of this statement as a *normative model for moral decisions*. I shall have little to say about the special problems of this part of the theory until chapters 19 and 20. Until then, however, let us bear in mind that many of our personal goals concern other people, and some of our decisions – particularly those that concern the policies of governments or other institutions – have consequences mainly for other people. The desires of other people can therefore be treated as if they were our own goals.

Utility theory is concerned with inference, not search. We assume that we

---

[1] Happiness in this sense – the *expectation* of achieving our goals – can be, but need not be, a personal goal. We can want to achieve our goals yet not care whether or not we *expect* to achieve them. If we try to pursue this kind of happiness as a goal, we can achieve it all too easily by *deceiving* ourselves into believing that our other goals will be achieved.

have already before us our possible choices, our goals, and all the evidence we need; we do not need to search for these. If the decision involves buying a car, for example, we already have a list of possible cars and the strengths and weaknesses of each. If the decision concerns whether to undergo (or perform) surgery, we know as much as we can about the possible consequences, and we assume that their probabilities have already been estimated. Utility theory therefore provides at best only part of a normative standard of decision making. The rest of the standard has to do with thorough search for alternative actions, goals, and evidence about consequences and their probabilities. The theory of probability (ch. 11) provides an additional normative theory, which tells us how probabilities of consequences should be calculated.

Utility theory began in the seventeenth century. Its development since that time was largely associated with economic theory, where it became part of the descriptive theory of the behavior of buyers and sellers in markets. Psychologists became interested in utility theory in the early 1950s, soon after the publication of von Neumann and Morgenstern's (1947) *Theory of Games and Economic Behavior.*[2] In 1953, the economist Maurice Allais argued that expected-utility theory fails as a descriptive model of decision making. Allais – and many others to follow – also questioned the normative status of the theory. Many scholars (especially economists, but also some psychologists and philosophers) have been reluctant to admit that people are sometimes irrational, so they have tried to develop criteria of rationality that are consistent with our behavior.

The years since 1953 have seen constant tension between the attackers and defenders of expected-utility theory as normative. Both camps have engaged in efforts to develop better descriptive models of decision making. The attackers, who assume that people are always rational, argue that better descriptive models will lead to better normative models. The defenders, who acknowledge the existence of irrational decision making, argue that the descriptive models will tell us where we deviate from the normative model and will allow us to ask what, if anything, we can do about it. I take the view that our decisions are often irrational, and I shall defend utility theory as a normative model. I shall also point out, however, that there is room for various interpretations of utility theory as a normative model. The best interpretation of utility theory is still an open question even for those who believe, as I do, that the theory is essentially correct and that the descriptive violations of it are real examples of irrationality.

The normative theory of decision making is closely related to an applied field called *decision analysis*, which has been thoroughly discussed in several excellent works (for example, Raiffa, 1968; Brown, Kahr, & Peterson, 1974; Keeney & Raiffa, 1976; Behn & Vaupel, 1982; von Winterfeldt & Edwards,

---

[2] Edwards and Tversky (1967) reprint some important papers from this period.

1986; Watson & Buede, 1987). Decision analysis has been applied to such questions as where in the vicinity of Mexico City to put the airport; where to locate a national radioactive-waste disposal site in the United States; which school desegregation plan the city of Los Angeles should accept; and hundreds of other problems in business and government. Decision analysis is roughly the attempt to apply normative theory directly. Making accurate estimates of the quantities that go into the normative model – probabilities and utilities – is, however, a problem of applied psychology in its own right. (I discussed the technology of probability estimation briefly at the end of ch. 11.) Decision analysis also includes many practical (prescriptive) techniques for searching for options (possibilities), evidence, and goals.

Expected-utility theory

We have seen that some of the tradeoffs we must make involve conflicts between utility and probability. Simple examples are choices such as whether to live with a disturbing health problem or risk surgery that will probably help but that could make the condition worse; or whether to put money into a safe investment or into a risky investment that will probably yield more money but could result in a big loss. A decision of this sort is a *gamble*, of the sort we discussed briefly in chapter 11. Expected-utility theory deals with decisions that can be analyzed as gambles. The problem with gambles is that we cannot know the future, so we must base our decisions on probabilities.

Expected value and expected utility

When a simple gamble involves money, the *expected value* of the gamble can easily be computed mathematically by multiplying the probability of winning by the monetary value of the payoff. For example, suppose I offer to draw a card from a shuffled deck of playing cards and pay you $4 if it is a heart. The probability of drawing a heart is .25 (because there are four equally likely suits), so the expected value of this offer is .25 · $4, or $1. If we played this game many many times (shuffling the cards each time), you would, on the average, win $1 per play. You can therefore "expect" to win $1 on any given play, and, on the average, your expectation will be correct. To calculate the expected value of a more complex gamble, with many possible outcomes, simply multiply the probability of each outcome by the value of that outcome, and then sum across all the outcomes. For example, if I offer you $4 for a heart, $2 for a diamond, and $1 for anything else, the expected value is .25 · $4 + .25 · $2 + .50 · $1, or $2. This is the average amount you would win over many plays of this game. Formally,

$$EV = \sum_i p(i) \cdot v(i) \tag{1}$$

where EV stands for expected value; i stands for all of the different outcomes; $p(i)$ is the probability of the "i-th" outcome; $v(i)$ is the value of the i-th

Table 16.1. *Decision table for Pascal's Wager*

	State of the world	
Act	God exists	God does not exist
Live Christian life	Saved (very good)	Small inconvenience
Live otherwise	Damned (very bad)	Normal life

outcome; $p(i) \cdot v(i)$ is therefore the product of the probability and value of the i-th outcome; and Σ_i is the total of all of these products.

The use of expected value as a way of deciding about money gambles seems reasonable. If you want to choose between two gambles, it would make sense to take the one with the higher expected value, especially if the gamble you choose will be played over and over, so that your average winning will come close to the expected value itself. This rule has been known by gamblers for centuries. (Later, we shall see why this might not really be such a good rule to follow.)

The same method can be used for computing expected *utility* rather than expected monetary *value*. The philosopher and mathematician Blaise Pascal (1623–62) made what many regard as the first decision analysis as part of an argument for living the Christian life (Pascal, 1670/1941, sec. 233). His famous argument is known as Pascal's Wager (Hacking, 1975). The question of whether God exists is an ancient one in philosophy. Pascal asked whether, in view of the difficulty of proving the existence of God by philosophical argument, it was worthwhile for people to live a Christian life – as though they were believers – in the hope of attaining eternal life (and of becoming a believer in the process of living this life). In answering this question Pascal argued, in essence, that the Christian God either does exist or does not. If God exists, and if you live the Christian life, you will be saved – which has nearly infinite utility to you. If God exists, and if you do not live the Christian life, you will be damned – an event whose negative utility is also large. If God does not exist, and if you live the Christian life, you lose at most a little worldly pleasure compared to what you would get otherwise. The basic argument was that the expectation of living the Christian life was higher than that of living otherwise, almost without regard to the probability of God's existence. Not to live the Christian life is to take a risk of an eternity in hell, in exchange for a little extra worldly pleasure. The expected utility of this choice is low.

We can express this situation in table form (Table 16.1). If we wanted to assign numerical values to the various utilities expressed in Table 16.1, we could assign them using an appropriate scale. For this table we could assume, for example, that the utility of a "normal life" is 0; the utility of a small inconvenience is a small negative number; the utility of being damned is a large negative number; and the utility of being saved is a large positive number.

Zero utility can be assigned to any one of the outcomes (it does not matter which); this then becomes our reference point. For example, in the table, we could assign a utility of 0 to "normal life" and a small negative number to "small inconvenience," or we could assign 0 to "small inconvenience" and a positive number to "normal life." Likewise, the units of utility are arbitrary, but once we choose a unit, we must stick with it. We could take the difference between "normal life" and "small inconvenience" as our unit, or we could, just as reasonably, call that 10 units. In these ways the measurement of utility resembles the way in which temperature was measured before people knew about absolute zero: The two common scales that we use (Celsius and Fahrenheit) have different zero points and different units. (An interval of one degree on the Celsius scale represents a greater difference in temperature than does a difference of one degree on the Fahrenheit scale.) The measurement of utility is unlike the measurement of length or weight, where there is only one natural zero point (although the units are still arbitrary).

The concepts and relationships displayed in tables of this sort lie at the heart of most utility analyses of decisions that must be made under uncertainty. Naturally, given our limited ability to predict the future, this includes most decisions. The outcome depends not only on which option we choose (live the Christian life or not) but also on which of various propositions – called unknown "states" – are true (the Christian God exists or not). Such tables have three elements: *states, options*, and *outcomes*. The *states* represented in the table are arranged so that they are mutually exclusive: Only one *can* be true. They are also exhaustive: One of them *must* be true. When we assign probabilities, it is to these states. In the gambling example used earlier, the relevant unknown "state" of the world is whether the card will be a heart or not. The states correspond to the column headings ("God exists," "God does not exist").

Options are the possible courses of action we are considering. In the table, they correspond to the row headings ("Live Christian life," "Live otherwise"). They must all be feasible. For example, one could argue that "Live Christian life" is not a feasible option; rather, the proper expression of this choice would be "*Try* to live Christian life." In this case, success or failure at living a Christian life would distinguish the uncertain future states. We would then expand the list of states to include "God exists, and I succeed," "God exists, and I fail," and so forth.

The entries in the middle portion of the table are the *outcomes*. Outcomes are simply the descriptions of whatever would occur if an option is taken and a certain state comes about. Outcomes can themselves include other options, other states, and so on. For example, "normal life" surely includes many other choices, some of which might involve more inconvenience than the Christian life. We could, if we like, expand the whole analysis to include these, or we could treat the outcome as a whole, using some sort of expectation as a substitute for all of the other choices and their consequences. There is no single right answer to the question of how much detail to include in an expected-utility analysis.

Each outcome has a utility assigned to it, which represents the extent to which it achieves the decision maker's goals. If this utility is expressed as a number, and if each state is assigned a numerical probability, we can calculate the *expected utility* of each *option* by multiplying the probability of each outcome by its utility and by summing across the outcomes in the row. The mathematical formula for calculating expected utility is as follows:

$$EU = \sum_i p(i)u(i) \tag{2}$$

Here, *EU* stands for *expected utility*, and $u(i)$ stands for the utility of the *i*-th outcome. In the next section, we shall explain why formula 2 is normative, why it ought to serve as a standard for good decision making.

To rephrase Pascal's argument in the language of modern utility theory, Pascal argued that the expected utility of living the Christian life was higher than that of not living it. For example, suppose that the probability of God existing is .50. In this case, it is fairly obvious that EU(Live a Christian life) is greater than EU(Live otherwise), since $.50 \cdot u$(being saved) $+ .50 \cdot u$(the small inconvenience of living a Christian life if God does not exist) is greater than $.50 \cdot u$(being damned) $+ .50 \cdot u$(a normal life). Even if the probability of God's existence is very small, say .01, the differences in utility are still sufficiently great that $.01 \cdot u$(being saved) $+ .99 \cdot u$(the small inconvenience of living a Christian life if God does not exist) is greater than $.01 \cdot u$(being damned) $+ .99 \cdot u$(a normal life).

Another way of looking at this is to say that the *utility difference* between being saved and being damned is so great that it is worthwhile to live the Christian life, even if the probability of God's existence is very small. We can use the difference between outcomes to determine expected utility. When we compare two options, we can compare them within each column in a utility table; we then multiply the difference between the two utilities by the probability of the state. If the expected utility of option A is

$$EU_A = \sum_i p(i)u_A(i)$$

and the utility of option B is

$$EU_B = \sum_i p(i)u_B(i)$$

then the difference between the two utilities is

$$EU_A - EU_B = \sum_i p(i)[u_A(i) - u_B(i)] \tag{3}$$

You can see here why it does not matter which outcome is selected as the zero point. The decision between two options depends only on *differences* between utilities in each state *i*, not the absolute values of the utilities. Naively, we tend to think of some outcomes as being favorable and others as unfavorable *in themselves*; however, the fact of the matter is that outcomes are all relative. No one has yet succeeded in giving a sensible interpretation to the idea of a natural zero point for utility.

The units do not matter either, because changing the units would simply change the size of the difference between EU_A and EU_B. All that matters for the decision between option A and option B is whether this difference is positive (higher utility for A) or negative (higher utility for B), not its size.

Pascal advocated this sort of analysis as what we would call a normative theory of decision making in general. Implicit in his approach is the decomposition of decisions into states, options, and outcomes (or consequences). To each state, we can assign a number expressing our personal probability judgment, and to each outcome we can assign a number representing its utility. Once we have made these assignments, we can calculate the expected utility of each option (or compare the expected utilities of two options, as in formula 3) by a method completely analogous to the calculation of the expected value of gambles.

A numerical utility estimate, as used in this kind of analysis, is not something that exists in the head, to be read off as if from a thermometer. It is, rather, a *judgment* of the desirability of an outcome, made like any other judgment. Utility judgments are useful for making important decisions. We must remember, however, that expected-utility theory is a normative model, not a prescriptive one. If tried to calculate expected utilities for every decision we make, we would spend our whole lives making calculations. Instead of doing this, we adopt prescriptive rules of various sorts, including rules of personal behavior and rules of morality. If these rules are good ones, they will usually prescribe the same decisions that we would make if we had time to carry out a full analysis.

Why utility theory is normative

Why should we follow expected-utility theory, even if we had time to do so? Why should we take it as an ideal standard of a rational decision? Why, in particular, should we *multiply* utilities of outcomes by their probabilities? One "argument" for this "design" concerns the long-run effects of following expected-utility theory. This rule for decision making is the one that helps us achieve our goals to a greater extent, in the long run, than any other rule.

To see this, consider the analogy between expected *value* (formula 1), and expected *utility* (formula 2). In both cases, we are trying to maximize something. In one case it is wealth, in another, it is utility. In both cases, we will do better *in the long run* by making all of our decisions in agreement with the formula than by any other method at our disposal. (Remember, we cannot see into the future.)

If, for example, I have a choice between $4.00 if a heart is drawn and

$1.00 if any red card (heart or diamond) is drawn, the expected value of the first option ($1.00) is higher than that of the second ($0.50). In the long run – if I am offered this choice over and over – I am bound to do better by taking the first option every time than by any other policy. I will win on 25% of the times on which I choose the first option, so I will average $1.00 each time I choose it. I will win on 50% of the times on which I choose the second option, but my average winning will be only $0.50. Any way of playing that tells me to choose the second option on some plays of the game will lead to a lower total payoff on those plays. In a sufficiently large number of plays, I will do best to choose the first option every time.

The same reasoning can be applied if I am faced with many different *kinds* of decisions. Even if the amount to be won and the probability of winning change from decision to decision, my total wealth will be highest at the end if I choose the larger expected value every time.

Similarly, if utility measures the extent to which I achieve my *goals*, I can add up utilities from different decisions just as I can add up my monetary winnings from gambling. The greater the total utility, the more my goals have been achieved. If I maximize expected utility for every decision I make, then, over the long run, I will achieve my goals more fully than I could by following any other policy.

The same reasoning applies when we consider decisions made by many people. If a great many people make decisions in a way that maximizes the expected utility of each decision, then all these people together will achieve their goals more fully than they will with any other policy. This extension of the argument becomes relevant when we reflect on the fact that sometimes the "long run" is not so long for an individual. Decisions like that described in Pascal's Wager are not repeated many times in a lifetime. Even for once-in-a-lifetime decisions, the expected-utility model maximizes everyone's achievement of his goals, to the extent to which everyone follows the model. Moreover, if we give advice to many people (as I am implicitly doing as I write this), the best advice is to maximize expected utility, because that advice will lead to the best outcomes for the group of advice recipients as a whole.

The idea that we can add together utilities from the outcomes of different decisions in the same way that we add together monetary winnings from different monetary gambles requires some comment. Two points need to be made. First, this idea requires that we accept a loss in utility at one time – or for one person – for the sake of a greater gain at another time – or for another person. If I am offered the game I have described, in which I have a .25 chance of winning $4.00, I ought to be willing to pay some money to play it. If I have to pay $0.50 each time I play, I will still come out ahead, even though I will lose the $0.50 on three out of every four plays.

Similarly, if many people choose to have a surgical operation that they know has a .0001 probability of causing death, in order to achieve some great medical benefit, some of these people will die, but, if the utility of the medical benefit is high enough, the extent to which all the people together achieve their goals will still be greater than if none of them chooses the operation. When we add utilities across different people, we are saying that the loss to some (a few, in this case) is more than compensated by the gain to others (a great many, in this case). We shall examine this assumption at greater length in chapters 19 and 20.

The second comment about adding utilities is that sometimes it does not make sense to do so, because the utility of one outcome depends on the outcomes of other decisions. To take a simple example, suppose I enter two lotteries, one with a prize of a vacation in the Caribbean next month and the other with a prize of a vacation in the Caribbean two months hence. The utility of the second vacation would be lower if I won the first lottery as well. I would have had enough vacation for a while. To avoid this problem of utilities not being constant as a function of the outcomes of decisions, I can redescribe my decisions. Rather than thinking of this as two separate decisions – whether to enter one lottery and whether to enter the other – I can think of it as one decision. For this decision, there are four options – enter neither, enter both, enter the first only, and enter the second only – and four possible outcomes – win neither, win both, win the first only, and win the second only. The long-run argument applied only to decisions that have been described in a way that makes the utilities of outcomes independent of other outcomes. Because the long-run argument applies across people, as we have seen, this can always be done.

In addition to the long-run argument for expected-utility theory, mathematicians have shown that expected-utility theory is implied by certain principles, or "axioms," that are closely related to the idea of rational decision making as whatever helps us achieve our goals. These axioms create an internal consistency among the choices we would make at a given time – something like the idea of coherence discussed in chapter 11. This rather amazing fact was discovered by Ramsey (1931),[3] and the theory was developed more formally by von Neumann and Morganstern (1947), Savage (1954), and Krantz, Luce, Suppes, and Tversky (1971). The two main axioms are called *weak ordering* and *independence*.

The idea of *weak ordering* has two parts. Weak ordering means, first, that our choices must be *connected*: For any two choices, we must either prefer one to the other, or we must be indifferent between them; "not deciding" is not allowed. Second, our choices must be *transitive*, a mathematical term that means, roughly, capable of being placed in order. More precisely, if we prefer X to Y and Y to Z, then we must prefer X to Z. I cannot simultaneously prefer apples to bananas, bananas to carrots, and carrots to apples. Weak ordering is clearly required if we are to assign utilities to our choices. The

---

[3] Frank Plimpton Ramsey was a philosopher and mathematician who died at the age of 26, while he was still a graduate student at Cambridge University, after making major contributions to scholarship.

Table 16.2. *The independence principle*

		State	
		Win	Lose
Option	Lottery 1	Europe	V
	Lottery	Caribbean	V

Note: The nature of V should not affect the choice between 1 and 2.

rule we adopt is that we should choose the option with the highest expected utility, so we must assign a number to every option representing its expected utility. (Numbers are connected and transitive.)

Connectedness and transitivity are consequences of the idea that expected utility measures the extent to which an option achieves our goals. Any two options either achieve our goals to the same extent, or else one option achieves our goals better than the other; and if X achieves our goals better than Y, and Y achieves them better than Z, then it must be true that X achieves them better than Z.[4]

The principle of *independence* says that if there is some state of the world that leads to the same outcome no matter what choice you make, then your choice should not depend on that outcome. For example, suppose you are planning a trip, and there are two lotteries you can choose, 1 and 2. Lottery 1 will give you a trip to Europe if your birthday number is drawn from a hat, and lottery 2 will give you a trip to the Caribbean if your birthday number is drawn (in the same drawing). If you lose, you will take some local vacation, V. The choice is shown in Table 16.2. The point is that it does not matter what V is; V is irrelevant. If you prefer lottery 1 to lottery 2, you should have the same preference about what you would most like to win regardless of whether the alternative is a drive in the country near your home or a less expensive trip to Europe.

This principle is, once again, a consequence of the basic idea of a rational decision as one that best achieves our goals. The extent to which an *outcome* achieves our goals does not depend on other outcomes that *do not occur*. In

---

[4] Another way to understand the value of transitivity is to think about what happens if one has fixed *intransitive* choices over an extended period. Suppose X, Y, and Z are three objects, and you prefer owning X to owning Y, Y to Z, and Z to X. Each preference is strong enough so that you would pay a little money, at least 1¢, to indulge it. If you start with Z (that is, you own Z), I could sell you Y for 1¢ plus Z. (That is, you pay me 1¢: Then I give you Y, and you give me Z.) Then I could sell you X for 1¢ plus Y; but then, because you prefer Z to X, I could sell you Z for 1¢ plus X. If your preferences stayed the same, we could do this forever, and you will have become a *money pump*. Following the rule of transitivity for stable preferences avoids being a money pump. This money-pump argument, of course, applies only to cases that involve money or something like it.

either lottery, you do not experience winning and losing at the same time. These outcomes occur in "different worlds," so to speak. In the example, your preference for Europe or the Caribbean should not depend on the nature of V. This fact has implications for your decision among options as well. If two options have different outcomes only in certain states (in the example, the state in which you win the lottery), then your preference between the *options* should depend on your preference for the *outcomes* in those states only. If you do not follow this rule, you will fail to achieve your goals best whenever these states occur.[5]

The principle of independence is also a consequence of the expected-utility formula, so it must apply to our decisions if we make them in agreement with this formula. By the formula, the utility of lottery 1 in the example is $p(\text{Win}) \cdot u(\text{Europe}) + p(\text{Lose}) \cdot u(V)$, and the utility of lottery 2 is $p(\text{Win}) \cdot u(\text{Caribbean}) + p(\text{Lose}) \cdot u(V)$. The choice depends on which utility is larger. For comparing the two utilities, we can ignore the common term $p(\text{Lose}) \cdot u(V)$.

If weak ordering and independence – plus some other axioms of lesser importance – have been adhered to in a person's choices, it can be proved that this person will follow expected-utility theory. That is, it is possible to assign a utility to each outcome (or option) and a probability to each state, such that the choice that is made will maximize expected utility. Mathematicians use many different proofs for this (see Krantz, Luce, Suppes, & Tversky, 1971, ch. 8), so that a proposition that appears as an "axiom" in one proof may be presented in another proof as a "theorem" that follows from some other axioms. In all of these proofs, some form of independence and weak ordering are regarded as the most essential of the axioms. Other axioms that mathematicians have identified are less essential for our purposes. For example, one is, roughly, that if you are indifferent between the two outcomes, you can replace one outcome with the other in a more complex decision, and you will not change the decision.

Note that following expected-utility theory means following probability theory as well. The probabilities we assign to the states must be additive and must add up to 1 (because the states are assumed to be mutually exclusive and exhaustive). The arguments for expected-utility theory therefore provide additional support for probability as a normative model of belief.

---

[5] This argument for the independence principle assumes that our goals are fixed. If our goals change as a function of what outcomes can occur, the principle can be violated even though we still choose what best achieves our goals in each case. For example, if my goals change so that my *desire* to go to Europe exceeds my desire to go to the Caribbean only when the "lose" state of both lotteries leads to a vacation in Mexico, I will violate the independence principle. This fact does not undercut the argument for the independence principle, however, because we have assumed all along that utility theory is a model of inference, taking our goals and beliefs as given and therefore fixed. We must, however, be aware of possible changes in desires or goals when we ask whether the independence principle is descriptively true of our decisions.

The utility of money

Let us apply expected-utility theory to gambles that involve money. In analyzing money gambles, we may think that we ought to choose on the basis
of expected (monetary) value, for we may assume that the utility of money
is the *same* as its monetary value. This, as we shall see, is not true, since it
neglects an important factor; but let us assume, for the moment, that the
expected utility of a gamble is simply its expected value.

If I offer you a chance to win $4 if a coin comes up heads on two out of
two tosses, the expected value of this gamble is $1 (since there is a .25
probability that both tosses will be heads, and .25 · $4 is $1). Therefore, you
ought to have no preference between $1 and this gamble. Taking this argument
one step farther, you even ought to be willing to *pay* me any amount less
than $1 for a chance to play the gamble. If you have a ticket allowing you to
play the gamble, you ought to be willing to *sell* it for any amount over $1.

Most people would not pay anything close to $1 to play this game, and
many would sell it for less than $1, given the chance. It does not seem to be
the case that we evaluate gambles by their expected value.

Daniel Bernoulli, in 1738, reported (Bernoulli, 1738/1954) a more dramatic
demonstration of this point (a demonstration that he attributes to his cousin,
Nicholas Bernoulli). Because his paper was published in a journal whose title
translates roughly as *Papers of the Imperial Academy of Sciences in Petersburg*,
this demonstration has come to be called the *St. Petersburg paradox*. It is as
follows:

Peter tosses a coin and continues to do so until it should land "heads" when it comes
to the ground. He agrees to give Paul one ducat if he gets "heads" on the very first
throw, two ducats if he does it on the second, four if on the third, eight if on the
fourth, and so on, so that with each additional throw the number of ducats he must
pay is doubled. Suppose we seek to determine the value of Paul's expectation. (1954,
p. 31)

The *expected value* of this gamble is infinite. To see this, note that there
are infinitely many possible outcomes: heads on the first throw, heads on the
second, and so on. The higher the number of tosses required, the less likely
the outcome, but the higher its value. The probability of the first outcome is
½ and its value is 1 ducat, so it contributes and expectation of ½ ducat. The
probability of the second outcome is ¼, and its value is 2 ducats, so it contributes (¼) · 2, or ½ ducat again. The contribution of the third outcome
(heads on the third throw) is likewise ⅛ · 4 or ½ ducat again. Using the
formula for expected value (formula 1),

$$EV = \tfrac{1}{2} \cdot 1 + \tfrac{1}{4} \cdot 2 + \tfrac{1}{8} \cdot 4 + \tfrac{1}{16} \cdot 8 + \ldots$$
$$= \tfrac{1}{2} + \tfrac{1}{2} + \tfrac{1}{2} + \tfrac{1}{2} + \ldots = \infty$$

Bernoulli concludes, however (p. 31), "Although the standard calculation
shows that the value of Paul's expectation is infinitely great, it has . . . to be

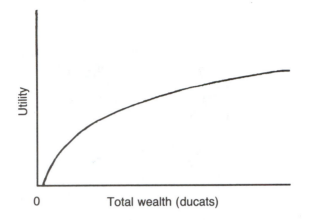

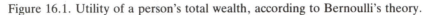

Figure 16.1. Utility of a person's total wealth, according to Bernoulli's theory.

admitted that any fairly reasonable man would sell his chance, with great pleasure, for twenty ducats." If we present the problem in dollars rather than ducats, most people whom I have asked will pay no more than $3 or $4 to play and will sell their chance to play for not much more.

To explain this reluctance, Bernoulli suggested that the utility (in Latin, *emolumentum*) of wealth is not simply its money value. Rather, the value of an *additional* ducat to Susan decreases as Susan's wealth (or income) increases. An extra dollar meant a lot to her when she was making $10,000 a year, but now that she earns $60,000 a year an extra dollar does not seem so important. As our wealth increases, it becomes more difficult to achieve our personal goals by spending money, because we are already spending it on the most important things. (The utility of goods other than money is even more sharply dependent on the amount we have. If you love oranges, you will achieve your goal of eating oranges much better with 1 orange per day than with none, and better with 2 than with 1, but if someone is already giving you 5 oranges per day, an additional orange would probably make no difference at all − unless you treated the orange like money and tried to trade it for something else. Money is less like this than most goods, because it is so versatile.)

Bernoulli suggested that the utility of wealth, for most people, is roughly proportionate to its logarithm.[6] If this were true, the difference in utility between a total wealth of 1,000 ducats and a total wealth of 10,000 ducats would be about the same as the difference between 10,000 and 100,000. The graph in Figure 16.1 shows the relationship between utility and wealth in Bernoulli's theory. As shown in the graph, the value of each additional ducat

---

[6] Specifically, Bernoulli argued that "it is *highly probable that any increase in wealth, no matter how insignificant, will always result in an increase in utility which is inversely proportionate to the quantity of goods already possessed.*" This assumption yields a logarithmic function. Bernoulli gave no other justification for this function.

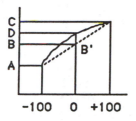

Figure 16.2. Graph illustrating the fact that the expected utility of a fair bet is less than the utility of not betting when the utility curve is concave.

declines as total wealth increases. Economists call this the *marginal utility* of wealth, that is, the utility of wealth at the "margin" of growth in wealth. The idea of declining marginal utility (with the logarithmic function) does explain the reluctance of people to spend very much to play the St. Petersburg game. The extra utility of the high winnings from the very improbable outcomes (for example, heads on the 10th toss) is no longer high enough to compensate for their low probability.

The idea of declining marginal utility would explain why people are reluctant to gamble on even bets. Very few people will accept a bet with "fair" odds, such as winning $100 if a coin comes up heads and losing $100 if it comes up tails. In Figure 16.2, point *B* is the expected utility of a fair gamble between −$100 (point *A*) and $100 (point *C*). Because there is an even chance of winning and losing, *B* corresponds to the midpoint, *B'*, of the dashed line. Point *D* shows the utility of $0, that is, the utility of refusing the gamble. Point *B* is lower than point *D* because the slope of the curve is decreasing (because of the declining marginal utility of the gambles). In other words, the curve is *concave* (as seen from the bottom; convex curves bow in the other direction). Such concavity of the utility curve explains why, in general, people are averse to taking risks. This desire to avoid risks is called *risk aversion*. Although we shall see in chapter 17 that there are other causes of risk aversion aside from the concavity of the utility curve, some concavity is present.

When individuals make decisions concerning amounts of money that are very small relative to their total lifetime income, they will do best in the long run if they essentially ignore their risk aversion and think about expected *value*. For example, suppose you have a choice of two automobile insurance policies. One policy costs $100 more per year than the other, but the less expensive policy requires that you pay the first $200 of any claim. If your probability of making a claim in a given year is .4, your choice each year is between a sure loss of $100 and a .4 probability of a $200 loss, an expected loss of .4 · $200, or $80. Over many years, you will save an average of $20 per year by purchasing the less expensive policy, even though it involves a greater risk. (The same reasoning applies to maintenance contracts.) Because your savings account will have $20 more in it each year (or you will owe your creditors $20 less), your savings will add together over time. The declining marginal utility of money is more relevant when we are considering large amounts of money accumulated over a lifetime.

The fact that the marginal utility of money is generally declining for large amounts of money has implications for the distribution of income and wealth in society. If $1,000 means more to *me* when I have only $2,000 in my bank account than when I have $200,000, then it seems reasonable to assume that, in general, $1,000 would mean more to poor people *in general* than to rich people in general. Accordingly, in designing a system of taxation, it makes sense to require the rich to pay more. Such an uneven distribution of the *monetary* burden makes the distribution of the *utility* burden more even. It also allows the government to impose the smallest total utility burden across all taxpayers in return for the money it gets. In fact, most systems of taxation operate on some version of this principle. Similar arguments have been made for directly redistributing wealth or income from rich to poor. We must, however, consider the effects of any scheme of redistribution or unequal taxation on *incentive to work*. In principle, it is possible to find the amount of redistribution that will strike the ideal compromise: In this state, any increase in redistribution would reduce total utility by reducing incentive, and any decrease in redistribution would reduce total utility by taking more utility from the poor than it gives to the rich in return.

Decision analysis

Decision analysis, as we shall discuss it, is the attempt to assess utilities and probabilities of outcomes, in order to calculate the expected utility of decision options. Such an analysis can be used as a way of making a decision, or as a "second opinion" about what the decision should be. We have already discussed *probability* judgment in chapter 11. Before we discuss the practical problems of measuring utility, let us be clear about what we are doing.

One thing we are *not* doing is reducing everything to money, as would be done in the simplest form of *cost-benefit analysis*, a technique used by business organizations and government agencies for the same purposes as decision analysis. How would it work to apply cost-benefit analysis to a question of life or death? Suppose a very wealthy patient is trying to decide whether or not to have a coronary bypass operation. The operation promises to relieve his pain and weakness and perhaps reduce the risk of death from a heart attack some years hence, but the operation is itself dangerous and may cause immediate death with some probability, P. We could analyze this decision by asking how much money the patient would pay to avoid immediate death (L). The risk of the operation would then be the loss of L. We also ask how much he would pay for the beneficial effects of the operation (if these could be assured) ($*B*). We could then suppose that the patient is presented with a gamble and should make the decision on the basis of the *expected value* of the gamble. By this weird reasoning, the expected value of the operation would be $(1 - P) \cdot \$B - P \cdot \$L$, since $(1 - P)$ is the probability of actually getting the benefit $\$B$, and the equivalent of $\$L$ would be lost with probability P. If the expected value is greater than the cost of the operation, the patient should have the operation.

What is wrong with this method? We cannot assume, in this situation, that the utility of money is a linear function of the amount. Our patient would probably be willing to part with his entire fortune in order to avoid immediate death. Therefore, even if P were quite small, this calculation would tell him to avoid the operation, when in fact the risk of death may truly be worth taking to improve the quality of his remaining life. Because of the declining marginal utility of money, the utility of avoiding death has been overestimated by this method. (Another problem with cost-benefit analysis is that, when we try to convert everything to money values, there is a danger that we will confuse the market value of something with its subjective value to those affected, as pointed out by Schwartz, 1986, and by Baron, in press b.)

What we *are* doing in decision analysis is reducing everything to a common coin of expected utility. We are assuming that once we have measured the utility of some outcome (or of some attribute of an outcome), we know everything that we need to know about it, for the purpose of making the decision. Outcomes can be fully represented by their utilities – by *how much they help us achieve our goals*.

A decision analyst may use her own utilities, or she may try to estimate the utility for other people by putting herself in their position, or she may ask them for their own utilities. Asking the people involved is not always best. Because medical patients, for example, often lack experience with the consequences that they must consider, a physician or nurse may do a better job of deciding on their behalf than the patients themselves.

We can think of decision analysis as a "design" (see ch. 6). The structure is that of utility theory (including both expected-utility theory and multi-attribute utility theory, which we shall discuss later in this chapter), plus a number of prescriptive techniques for thinking of options, consequences, and goals. The *purpose* of decision analysis is to make decisions. The *arguments* for decision analysis consist of the reason why the theory is normative, which we just discussed, and the fact that we depart systematically from the normative model when we make decisions without analyzing them, a fact that we shall discuss in the next chapter.

Because decision analysis is a standard for rational decision making, it is also be used to evaluate decisions after they are made. For example, it has been used as a standard in medical malpractice cases – specifically, to explain why decisions were reasonable risks to take even when they turned out badly

(Forst, 1974; Bursztajn, Hamm, Gutheil, & Brodsky, 1984). Of course, it would be best in such cases to carry out the analysis *before* the decision is made and to pay attention to its results. Decision analysis can also be used to understand and resolve conflict among different decision makers. If the disagreement is about the probability of outcomes, more information might be sought; if it is about utilities, some sort of average might be appropriate, or the parties might discuss their images of the outcomes to find out why their utilities differ. More generally, decision analysis can be used in the early stages of thinking about a decision, before all the possibilities and evidence are available, as a way of finding out what sort of possibilities or evidence are needed or of discovering what our goals are. We must remember that utility theory itself is only a method of inference. If it is to be useful, it must be coupled with sufficiently thorough search for possibilities, evidence, and goals.

We noted earlier, in connection with Pascal's Wager, that the amount of detail used in a decision analysis is arbitrary. The least amount of detail is none at all. One could simply assign a utility to a whole option (for example, living the Christian life), just as we assigned a utility to "normal life" in the Pascal's Wager example. This is essentially what is done when decisions are made "holistically," or without analysis. In the light of this fact, what should we do when a decision analysis disagrees with what we would do without it? Suppose you are deciding whether to accept a certain job. You want to accept it, but you carry out a decision analysis (concerning the probability of receiving an offer of a better job), and the analysis says that you should wait. What should you do? Should you always follow the analysis?

My answer is – not necessarily. If you know that you have carried out the analysis perfectly, you ought to do what it says – but you can never be sure. In fact, you do not have one analysis, but two, one being your original intuition, which is essentially an assignment of utility directly to your two choices (Brown & Lindley, 1985). You should try to understand why the two analyses differ (some of the problems we shall discuss in the next chapter may be at fault). It may be that the analysis has left out some important factor, such as your admiration for the people with whom you would be working. In the end, you have to ask yourself how good each analysis is, how well it serves its purposes. Perhaps the best way to think of a decision analysis is as a *second opinion*. As in the case of medical decisions, it can be reasonable to ignore a second opinion, but in some cases the second opinion calls your attention to some important factors that you had ignored before.

The measurement of utility

With this in mind, let us proceed to the problem of measuring utility. This problem has both a theoretical and a practical aspect. The theoretical problem is to state the conditions under which utility can be measured using each of the methods that have been devised. The practical problem, which we shall not discuss in detail here, is to state the conditions under which each method should be used.

Direct scaling

The simplest way to estimate utility is to assign numbers to the various outcomes. For example, suppose you must decide whether to accept a job or to refuse it and hope for a better offer, which you expect with a probability of .5. There are three possible outcomes: the job you have been offered (B); the better offer (A); and the job you would have to take if the better offer does not come through (C). To assess your expected utility, you might assign a value of 100 to job A, and a value of 0 to job C, and ask yourself where job B falls on this scale. Clearly, if the value of job B is greater than 50, the expected utility of accepting job B is higher than that of waiting.

There is much to be said for the simplicity of this approach, but it has a couple of defects. First, you (the judge of your utilities) have not been told much about what the numbers you assign are supposed to mean. The only requirement that is obvious to you is that higher numbers should correspond to higher utilities. You are free to assign ratings that express the square of the utility (or some other function) rather than the true utility. If this were true, a rating of 36 for job B would correspond to a true utility of 6, and the rating of 100 would correspond to a utility of 10. Although the analysis would say that you should decline job B (because 36 is less than 50, which is half the assessed utility of A), the true utilities would say that you should take job B (because 6 is greater than 5, which is half the true utility of job A).

Another problem with direct scaling (and perhaps with other methods) is that psychological experiments suggest the relative ratings chosen depend on the set of stimuli used. For example, if subjects are asked to rate the length of rods, the actual lengths of which are 1, 3, 5, 7, 8, 9, and 10 inches, they tend to rate the longer rods as more different in length and the shorter rods as closer in length than they really are. If, on the other hand, subjects are given rods with lengths 1, 2, 3, 4, 6, 8, and 10 inches, the reverse is found (Poulton, 1979). The same may be true for rating utilities.

Difference measurement

The first problem can be solved by giving the rater a clear conception of what it means to rate utility, rather than some function of utility such as the square. Perhaps the most important requirement of an accurate utility scale is that it should reflect *differences* between utilities as well as the utilities themselves. The idea of difference measurement is to ask the rater to compare differences between outcomes, rather than outcomes themselves. If you say that the utility *difference* between A and B is equal to the difference between B and C, then we can safely assign a utility to B that is halfway between the utility of A and C. If A is 100 and C is 0, then B would be 50.

Suppose I want to measure my own utility for various levels of total wealth. I might begin by picking a lower and an upper limit on the range that I shall consider, say $0 and $1,000,000. I then ask myself to cut this interval in half subjectively. I seek an amount of wealth (x), such that the subjective difference between $0 and x is the same as the subjective difference between x and $1,000,000. If I cannot do this right away, I might pick some value arbitrarily, such as $500,000, and ask whether it is too high or too low.[7] If the value is too high (as it is), I might adjust it downward by half the difference, to $250,000, and so on, going up and down by half of the difference each time, until I come close to the value I seek. For me, this would be about $150,000. That is, the subjective difference in utility between $0 and $150,000 is about the same as the subjective difference between $150,000 and $1,000,000.

If I have trouble thinking about differences in utility directly, I might ask myself which *change* would be subjectively greater: the change from $0 to x or the change from x to $1,000,000. Again, I might ask which would be a more pleasant surprise, expecting $0 and finding that the truth was actually x, or expecting x and finding that the truth was actually $1,000,000.

I could continue in this manner, dividing the utility interval in half each time. If I assigned a utility of 0 to $0 and a utility of 8 to $1,000,000, I would assign a utility of 4 (halfway between 0 and 8) to x, once I discovered what x was. I could then divide the interval between $0 and x in half in the same way, and assign this wealth a utility of 2, and so on. In my case, I might assign a utility of 2 to $50,000, since this would be subjectively halfway between $0 and $150,000.

Notice that the bottom and top value of the scale could be chosen arbitrarily. To use utilities in decision analysis, we need only *relative* values. For example, suppose that I have $50,000 in savings and I want to know whether I ought to invest it in a real-estate deal that has a .5 probability of netting me $1,000,000 and a .5 probability of losing everything. The expected utility of the deal is $.5 \cdot u(\$1,000,000) + .5 \cdot u(\$0)$. The way I have scaled utility, this would be $.5 \cdot 8 + .5 \cdot 0$, or 4. This is higher than the utility of my current wealth, which is 2, so I ought to go for it.

Suppose I had used a different scale, though, so that I had assigned a utility of 100 to $0 and a utility of 200 to $1,000,000. When I cut this interval in half, I would have discovered that the utility of $150,000 is 150, halfway between 100 and 200, and the utility of $50,000 is 125. In this case, the

---

[7] This method exposes me to the risk of an anchoring-and-adjustment bias, however (see ch. 12).

expected utility of the real-estate deal is 150, and the utility of my current wealth would be 125, still less than 150, and by the same proportion of the total range as before.

In order for difference measurement to be used, the utilities of outcomes must be related by a condition called *monotonicity*. Consider the following outcomes, laid out in order of desirability. The letters A through F might stand for different amounts of money, or different jobs.

A B C D E F

Suppose that the difference between A and B is subjectively equal to the difference between D and E, and the difference between B and C is subjectively equal to the difference between E and F. It must be the case, then, that the difference between A and C is also equal to the difference between D and F (Krantz, Luce, Suppes, & Tversky, 1971, ch. 4). If this monotonicity condition is not met, inconsistencies will arise in the scale. To see how this might happen, imagine that F is directly *above* E, rather than to the right of it. Then the distance between E and F could still be the same as that between B and C, yet the distance between A and C would be greater than that between D and F. The outcomes would not lie along the same line.

Note that the difference method can be used directly, as in the examples just given, or it can be used as a check on the direct-rating method. If the rater understands that the differences between ratings are supposed to be meaningful, this may be enough to correct distortion of the scale. Either way, the monotonicity condition can serve as a check. As yet, no one has asked experimentally whether monotonicity applies either to direct ratings or to difference measurement. (Perhaps this question has not been asked because no one has thought of a reason why the monotonicity condition would ever be violated systematically.)

One problem with the difference method is that it requires a large number of possible outcomes (as is the case when we are rating some continuous quantity like wealth), so that it is possible to find outcomes halfway between other outcomes. If it is to be used for a decision analysis with a few outcomes, we can add hypothetical outcomes to the set being rated.

Standard gambles

Suppose we accept Bernoulli's idea that we choose gambles according to the principle of expected utility. If we do, then this leads to yet another method for measuring utility. We can decide how we would gamble and then *work backward* from our choice of gambles to determine our utilities.

For example, suppose I want to discover my utility for wealth, in the range between $0 and $1,000,000. I could ask myself this: At what amount $x would I be indifferent between $x and a gamble in which I have a .5 chance of gaining $1,000,000 and a .5 chance of losing everything? If I judge gambles as Bernoulli says I do (and as expected-utility theory says I ought to), I would say that $x is $150,000, the same point yielded by the difference method. (In fact, very few people give the same results with the two methods. Most people are more averse to risks than the theory says they ought to be. We shall consider the reasons for this in ch. 17.) In a similar manner, we could use 50–50 gambles of this sort to bisect utility intervals, exactly as we did with the method of differences; in this way, I could discover $y such that I would be indifferent between $y and a gamble in which there was a .5 chance of $x and a .5 chance of $0, and so on.

We might ask how this method could possibly be valuable, since the usual reason for wanting to discover utilities in the first place is to make decisions about gambles (for example, the job choice described earlier). Decisions are sometimes complex, however, and we can use this method to break them down. Another advantage of this method is that we can use it even with only a few outcomes.

Consider, for instance, the decision that many couples face about whether a woman who is expecting a baby should have amniocentesis. That is a test that determines whether a fetus has Down's syndrome, a condition that usually means that the child will be severely mentally retarded and have other serious medical problems. Parents who have the test done should be willing for the mother to have an abortion if the test is positive: The test itself can cause a miscarriage, so there is no reason to do it unless one is prepared to act on the results. Amniocentesis is usually done in women over 35, because the probability of Down's syndrome increases with the mother's age; however, this is an arbitrary cutoff point. From a decision-analytic point of view, the choice of whether or not to do the test depends on the parents' relative utilities for the four possible outcomes: normal birth, Down's syndrome, miscarriage, and abortion.[8]

The situation can be represented in a tree diagram (see Figure 16.3). Here, the plus (+) and minus (−) branches represent the outcome of the test. The probabilities are chosen for illustrative purposes only. We have assigned a *dis*utility of 100 to a Down's syndrome birth and a utility of 0 to a normal birth. To make the decision, we must know the two missing utilities, $u(M)$, the utility of a miscarriage, and $u(A)$, the utility of an abortion, on this 0 to 100 scale.

To assess $u(M)$, the couple can imagine a simpler decision in which they must choose between a miscarriage for sure and a gamble between a Down's syndrome child with probability p and a normal child with probability $1 - p$. The question is, at what value of p will the couple be indifferent between the miscarriage and the gamble? Suppose it is .02. Then we know – again making

---

[8]   In the present discussion, based on Hill, Bedau, Chechile, Crochetiere, Kellerman, Ounjian, Pauker, Pauker, and Rubin (1978, ch. 10), we ignore complications other than miscarriage, and we ignore the possibility that the test is fallacious. Both of these factors must be considered in a full analysis.

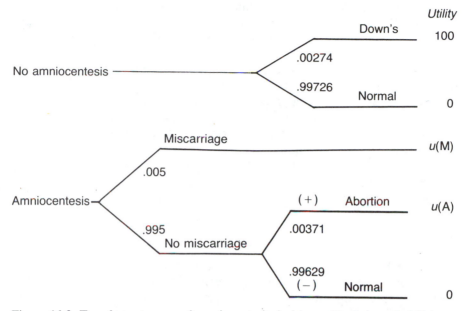

Figure 16.3. Tree for outcomes of amniocentesis decision, with their probabilities.

the usual assumption that the couple chooses as Bernoulli says they will – that the expected disutility of the gamble is the utility of the miscarriage. The expected disutility of the gamble is .02 · 100 + .98 · 0, or 2. Hence, $u(M)$ = 2. In the same manner, we can assess the utility for an abortion. For example, if p for an abortion is .03, then $u(A)$ is 3. We can then replace $u(M)$ and $u(A)$ with their estimated values to calculate the *overall* expected utility of the choice of amniocentesis, and we can compare this to the expected utility of not having amniocentesis, which, in this case, is .274. In this case, the expected disutility of the test is .005 · 2 + (.995 · .00371) · 3 + (.995 · .99629) · 0, or about .011. In this case, the expected disutility of the test is less than that of not having the test, so the couple should have it.

This example shows how the method of gambles allows us to break down a complex decision into a set of simpler ones. Of course, each of the "simple" ones could also be analyzed into more outcomes, each with its own probability. Down's syndrome, for example, has many manifestations, and miscarriages may be harmful to the mother or less harmful, and have fewer or more numerous implications for future births. In this example, we have treated such outcomes as miscarriage and abortion as holistic entities, not to be analyzed further. We could have treated amniocentesis itself as a holistic outcome and made the decision without analysis at all. (This is what most people do.)

Of course the gambles method of measuring utility is valid only if Bernoulli's assumption that people choose gambles according to their expected utility is correct. In fact, as we shall find in examining the descriptive theory in chapter 17, we do not always choose in this way. For example, people may prefer a gamble (such as a Down's syndrome child with probability p and a normal child with probability $1-p$) to a quite certain outcome (such as a miscarriage with probability 1), even though the gamble would have the same "true" expected utility (see ch. 17). The knowledge that a particular bad outcome is certain to occur apparently interferes with making decisions consistent with expected-utility theory; the hope of avoiding any bad outcome seems to take control. The difference method of measuring utility, when it can be used, is probably more accurate. In particular, people frequently violate the axioms assumed to hold for the method of gambles (transitivity and independence), but there is as yet no reason to suspect that people violate the axiom required for the method of differences (monotonicity).

Conjoint measurement

Another technique for measuring utility is useful when outcomes can be described in terms of two or more attributes.[9] For example, it might make sense to think of your utility for a computer as the sum of your utility for memory size and your utility for price. (The lower the price, the higher the utility. We are assuming all other attributes to be the same, in this example.) The amazing thing about the technique of conjoint measurement is that we can discover *both* utility functions simply by asking you about your preferences among suitably chosen examples of computers. The method assumes that your utility for computers is indeed the sum of the utilities on the two dimensions (price and memory), but this assumption itself can be checked.

The basic idea of conjoint measurement is the use of one dimension to define a *quantitative unit*, which we then use to discover equal-utility intervals along the other dimension. Suppose that the range of memory size was from 64K to 640K, and the range in price was from \$2,500 to \$500. You can discover the utility of the money by defining a unit on the memory dimension, as shown in Figure 16.4.

Suppose you take the unit of utility as the difference between 64K and 128K. Let us call this 1 *utile*. What price is 1 utile more than \$2,500? (Utility increases as price decreases.) To answer this, ask yourself at what price \$x you would be indifferent between 128K for \$2,500 and 64K for \$x. You can determine x by starting with a value that is clearly too high and lowering it until you are indifferent, and then starting with a value that is clearly too low and raising it. If you encounter a range of indifference, you can choose the middle of the range as your best guess. If you are indifferent between 128K for \$2,500 and 64K for \$x, then it would make sense to assume that $u(\$2,500) + u(128K) = u(\$x) + u(64K)$, or $u(\$x) - u(\$2,500) = u(128K) - u(64K)$.

---

[9] An "attribute," in this case, is a value on a dimension. The price of a given computer, for example, is an attribute on the "price" dimension.

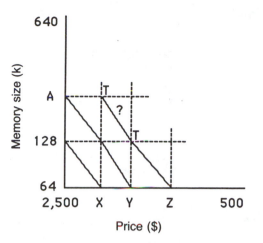

Figure 16.4. The principle of conjoint measurement of the utility of two attributes of a computer: price and memory size. (The lines connect points judged to have equal utility. The question mark indicates an equality that was inferred from the other judgments.)

Hence, if $u(128K) - u(64K)$ is 1 utile, then $u(\$x) - u(\$2,500)$ must be 1 utile as well.

We could then mark off another utile on the price dimension by asking at what price $\$y$ you would be indifferent between 128K for $\$x$ and 64K for $\$y$. For the next utile, we could ask at what price $\$z$ you would be indifferent between 128K for $\$y$ and 64K for $\$z$, and so on.

Once we have defined 1 utile on the price dimension, we can then use *this* unit to mark off steps on the memory dimension in the same way. For example, we can ask at what memory size A you would be indifferent between A at $2,500 and 128K at $\$x$. (To improve accuracy, we can use more than one interval on each dimension as the unit.) In theory, the method of conjoint measurement is like the method of differences, except that the differences compared are on different attributes instead of a single attribute.[10]

Once we have gone this far, we ought to be able to check what we have done by asking about the two points labeled T in the figure. We ought to be indifferent between these two points: A for $\$x$ and 128K for $\$y$. This condition is called the *Thomsen condition* (Krantz, Luce, Suppes, & Tversky, 1971, ch. 6). It must be satisfied for all sets of points of this form in order for this scaling method to work. The Thomsen condition serves as a check on this method, just as monotonicity does on the difference method.

When there are three or more dimensions, we can replace the Thomsen

---

[10] In practice, the method of conjoint measurement can be applied to data in which judges simply express a large number of preferences among pairs of options spread throughout the space in Figure 16.4: The analyst then *infers* the equivalent intervals from these preferences (Tversky, 1967; Keeney & Raiffa, 1976).

Table 16.3. *Value of three attributes for each of four*
computers

Model	Memory	Disk size	Price
AT	64K (0)	10M (0)	$500 (100)
BT	640K (100)	20M (50)	1,500 (50)
CT	64K (0)	30M (100)	2,500 (0)
DT	640K (100)	20M (50)	2,500 (0)

Note: Utilities on each dimension are in parentheses. (*K* indicates
kilobytes of memory; *M* indicates megabytes of disk storage space.)

condition with a simpler condition called *independence*[11] – a term that does
not mean quite the same thing here as it did in our earlier discussion of
expected-utility theory.[12] This means that the tradeoff between any two dimensions does not depend on the level of a third. For example, if you are
indifferent between 128K for $2,500 and 64K for $2,000 when the computer
has a 10-megabyte hard disk, you will still be indifferent between 128K for
$2,500 and 64K for $2,000 when you have a 30-megabyte hard disk. The
tradeoff between money and memory is not affected by the size of the hard
disk. This condition ensures that the contribution of each dimension to overall
utility will be the same, regardless of the levels of other dimensions.

Multiattribute utility theory (MAUT)

MAUT as a type of decision analysis

Conjoint measurement is one of the more amazing "rabbit out of the hat"
tricks that mathematicians have been able to show us in utility theory. It
provides the theoretical basis for a widely used method of decision analysis
known as *multiattribute utility theory* (MAUT). Like other forms of decision
analysis, MAUT is based on the idea expressed in the motto "Divide and
conquer." In this case, the division is into *psychologically independent attributes*: that is, attributes that the decision maker views as being separate and
independent. If the dimensions are indeed independent, proper application
of MAUT ensures that the decision made will maximize the achievement of
our goals: The attribute on each dimension determines the extent to which
we achieve the goal corresponding to that dimension, so we can measure the
utility of each option on each dimension and add up the utilities on the various
dimensions in order to determine the total utility of the option.

[11] Independence implies the Thomsen condition (Keeney & Raiffa, 1976, sec. 3.5.3). The term
"independence" has been used for a variety of conditions, each of which may imply different
types of measurement (von Winterfeldt & Edwards, 1986, chs. 8 and 9).

[12] Note, however, that the two senses of "independence" are actually related once we look at
states as dimensions of choices. The probability of a state corresponds exactly to the weight
of the dimension in MAUT.

If the attributes in the particular decision do not seem to be psychologically independent from the outset, MAUT, in its basic form, has no normative status and should not be attempted. For example, suppose you were using MAUT to decide which computer to buy, and the three dimensions were price, memory size, and hard-disk size. You could use a MAUT analysis if you regarded these three dimensions as independent. You might think that a large memory makes disk size less important, however, so that you would be willing to pay less extra money for a large disk if the computer had a large memory than if it had a small memory. In this case, the size of the memory would affect the tradeoff between price and disk size: If you tried to use disk size to measure the utility units for price, you would get different results for different memory sizes. You need not go through the whole MAUT analysis to determine whether this is the case; you can just ask yourself directly whether this would occur.

It is also important to make sure that the dimensions really refer to different things. For example, it would not be helpful to add a fourth dimension, "ease of use," to your analysis, because ease of use is affected by memory and disk size. If you did this, you would be counting the effects of memory and disk size more than once. A suitable new dimension would be "keyboard layout."

Although conjoint measurement provides the theoretical basis for MAUT, you do not have to use conjoint measurement to estimate the utilities for a MAUT analysis. Once you have established that the dimensions are independent, you can use any of the measurement techniques described in the last section: difference measurement, direct rating, or any other method, on one attribute at a time.

After doing this, you must decide how to weigh the attributes relative to one another. For example, suppose you have found that the three dimensions of the computer really are independent for you. You assign a utility of 100 to the most desirable end of each dimension, and 0 to the least desirable end. Suppose that you gather data on four different models, organized as in Table 16.3, with the utilities *on each dimension* shown in parentheses. You cannot simply add up the utilities for each model and compare them to decide among them. If you do, model BT will win, but perhaps you do not care very much about memory size. If price is more important to you, you will want model AT; if disk size is more important, you will want model CT. To use MAUT, you need to determine the *relative* importance of the dimensions.

There are many ways to make this determination (von Winterfeldt & Edwards, 1986). Conjoint measurement is only one of them. Another, simpler way is to determine your scale for each attribute and to estimate the utility of the extreme of the scale for one attribute on the scale for another attribute. For example, suppose that price is more important than disk size. You could ask yourself, "How much more than $500 would I pay in order to replace a 10-megabyte disk with a 30-megabyte disk?" Suppose the answer is "$1,000 more," so that the total cost is $1,500. You have now found that the scale for disk size should be weighed half as much as the money scale, for the difference between the two ends of it equals only the difference between $500 and $1,500, a utility difference of 50 on the price scale.

Suppose you find, on the other hand, that the memory scale is equal to the disk-size scale, so that you are indifferent between a 640K memory with 10-megabyte hard disk and 64K memory with a 30-megabyte disk. Then the memory scale would also get half as much weight as the price scale. To compute the total utility of each model, you would multiply the memory and disk-size utilities by .5 before adding them. (Equivalently, you could multiply the price utility by 2. This would just change the units.) This would yield utilities of 100, 125, 50, and 75 for the four models, respectively. Your analysis would tell you to choose model BT after all.

Notice that when you determine the weight of the scales, you need to know what the ends of the scales are. Unless you know the ends, you cannot ask yourself whether the range in memory size is more important than the range in price, or vice versa, and this is the question that you must answer. If the price range is only from $1,500 to $1,600, for example, price would not be very important.

As an exercise, you might try applying MAUT to a personal decision, such as which apartment to rent, or to a public policy question. A good example of a policy question is the optimal speed limit for motor vehicles. The speed limit affects a number of different dimensions, such as property damage from accidents, injury and death from accidents, gasoline use, pollution, speed of transportation for goods, and speed of transportation for individuals. You do not need to look up the data to see how such an analysis would work. You might try a holistic estimate first, in which you simply give your opinion. Then use your own best guesses for the effect of different speed limits on the various dimensions, and give your own utilities for the dimensions.

MAUT can be modified considerably for the analysis of real decisions. For example, suppose you have one usable eye, and it has a cataract that your doctor must eventually remove. You must decide whether to have the cataract removed now or wait a month. Your vision is getting slowly worse. A successful operation will restore your vision fully, but a failure will leave you blind. The probability of failure is something your doctor can tell you. What you need is an estimate of the relative utility – for the next month – of the three possible outcomes: restored vision, blindness, and your present vision (assuming that it does not change over the course of the month). How can you think about this? One way is to think of the various activities that you can do in some outcome but not another. The activities should be separate and independent: For example, you cannot count "reading" and "doing your job" if your job involves reading. (You can count "reading for pleasure.") You can assign utilities to these activities by finding groups of them that are equivalent.

Suppose that there are 10 activities, all with the same utility. You can do

9 of them now but you will not be able to do them if you are blind, but there is one you cannot do now but would be able to do if your vision were restored. If we assign a utility of 100 to restored vision and 0 to blindness, the utility of your present condition is 90. You should have the operation now if the probability of success is greater than .90, since its expected utility would then be at least .90 · 100 + .10 · 0, or 90. Of course, after doing an analysis like this, you could decide that the activities were not independent after all, because the loss of the ability to engage in one of them would be much worse if it were the only one left than if there were other alternatives. Nonetheless, an analysis of this sort could help you to think about your decision in a new way. If you repeated this process month after month, eventually you would reach a point at which the activities you would gain back from success would be worth the risk of failure.

Rules and tradeoffs

When it comes to matters of public policy or major personal decisions, some people regard MAUT with a certain suspicion (Schwartz, 1986). MAUT seems to require that people make tradeoffs they think should not be made. For example, some people think that it is wrong to "trade off" human life for anything. They claim to want to follow this rule: Human life comes before anything else – before any other dimension or any other consideration.

Taken literally, they are saying that the weight of the human-life dimension is infinite relative to all other dimensions, so that any two policies (for example, about the speed limit) must be evaluated first on that dimension and then on other dimensions only if they are equal on that one. Such rules are called *lexical rules*, because they give a list of the *order* in which different considerations are considered (a "lexicon" is a dictionary, an ordered list). A lexical rule for buying cars might say that reliability comes first and that only when two cars are equally reliable should style be considered. A couple might decide that the wife's job takes priority. Some people try to follow lexical moral rules: "Never kill anyone, except in war or self-defense"; "Never lie"; "Never break the law"; "Never eat pork (unless you are starving)." Notice that exceptions are allowed, but they are spelled out in advance, as part of the rule. When the exception is absent, the rule takes priority over everything else.

Alternatively, when we make *tradeoffs*, we take into account the magnitude of each competing consideration in the case at hand. We may consider a car's reliability to be more important than its style, but if we think the Fiat is *almost* as reliable as the Toyota but *much* more attractive, we will take the Fiat. If Yale is almost as good for the wife as Princeton and is also much better than Princeton for the husband, Yale will probably be chosen. A person who tells "white lies" to save the feelings of others (for example) might have to weigh the possible damage caused by telling the truth against the magnitude of the lie or the possible damage that results from telling it.

Many of the most controversial and difficult issues that we face as individuals and as a society involve the conflict between tradeoffs and rules. We know, for example, that air pollution kills people (through disease) but that curbing air pollution costs money. How much money should be spent, to save how many lives? If we follow a rule that life is more important than anything else, we could end up spending enormous amounts of money. To take another example, we believe in basic human rights, but in some countries governments have argued that certain rights must be denied to preserve the stability of the state. Again, many of us believe that in personal relationships love ought to "conquer all," yet we are often faced with choices that put romance in jeopardy for the sake of one person's job or education.

People who think they want to follow lexical rules no matter what may, after reflecting, find that in fact they simply have a very high *subjective weight* for one dimension as opposed to another; they do not really think that one dimension has absolute priority. Consider the claim that life should come before everything else. Suppose that a health insurance company (in determining what treatments its policies will cover) has a choice of saving the life of Mr. Smith by paying for a heroic operation that will cost millions of dollars or else paying for treatment to cure arthritis in 1 million policyholders. (I pick arthritis because it is painful but not usually life threatening.) If we wanted to put life ahead of everything else, we might still balk and decide to pay for Mr. Smith's operation. Now let us suppose, however, that the success of the operation is not a certainty but rather a probability (P). Suppose that P were .001. Would we still prefer the operation? What if P were .000001? It seems that there must be a value of P sufficiently small so that our preference would switch. If such a value of p exists (above 0), then we are, in fact, willing to trade off the two attributes at issue – life and pain. That is, we are willing to say that some finite interval on the pain scale is equivalent to a nonzero interval on the life scale. The nonzero interval on the life attribute is just the interval between no change at all and a p probability of saving a life. This interval is equivalent to (or less than) the interval between the status quo and the arthritis cure, on the pain scale.

Some of our resistance to the idea of making tradeoffs is caused by our attachment to certain *prescriptive* rules of decision making. Lexical rules may prevent us from sliding down *slippery slopes*, in which one decision, justified in its own right, sets a precedent for similar decisions that are not well justified. A decision analysis might tell an official, for example, that the gain from taking a small bribe is greater than the harm that this single act would cause. The slippery-slope rule would tell the official, however, that accepting one bribe might be like trying cocaine "once"; it might become a habit, and then the harm would be much greater. Similarly, people argue that if we allow life to be sacrificed for one reason (mercy killing, for example), we might be more willing to allow it to be taken for other reasons (lack of enforcement of safety regulations, for example).

Instead of invoking the slippery-slope rule, I would argue that the decision analysis that led to taking the bribe was seriously incomplete, because it ignored a major consequence of the choice in question, namely, its effect on later decisions about bribes. Therefore, we do not need the "slippery-slope" argument, if we do a thorough analysis. Also, when we decide to favor one dimension (goal), such as life, we are always ignoring some other dimension, such as pain, and that bias could lead us down a slippery slope as well: If we insist on taking small chances to save lives when we could be curing pain instead, we might become callous to pain. Slippery slopes can work both ways. To neglect this fact is to fail to be sensitive to evidence on both sides of the question.

Nonetheless, lexical rules can be useful prescriptive devices for self-control. As a rule of thumb, it may be helpful to us to think that certain things always "come before" others – but it is difficult to justify such rules as normative in decision making (Baron, 1986, in press b). We shall return to these issues in chapter 19.

Conclusion

Utility theory as a *normative* model tells us what it means for a decision to be best for achieving our goals. The theory has been widely applied as the basis of decision analysis. It plays another important role, however, in justifying the *prescriptive* model of actively open-minded thinking described in chapter 3. Actively open-minded thinking about decisions helps us to achieve our goals because it helps us to maximize utility. The expected utility of a neglected possibility (option) could be higher than that of any option that was considered, so we do well to search thoroughly for options. Likewise, neglecting a possible piece of evidence (possible consequence) or goal (attribute), or weighing the evidence in a biased way, could lead us to choose an option with less utility than the best option we could choose. Parallel arguments can be made for the importance of actively open-minded thinking in belief formation. Beliefs formed after a thorough search for evidence and an unbiased evaluation of that evidence are the most useful for decision making. They reflect the evidence available most accurately and correspond to better-calibrated probability judgments, so they help us to maximize utility in the long run.

Utility theory also justifies my claim that thorough search is a virtue to be practiced in *moderation*. The utility of search is negative, and the compensating expected benefits decline as search continues: There is a point of diminishing returns in the expected utility of thinking itself.

In the next chapter we shall look at the descriptive theory of decision making. Departures from utility theory, we shall discover, provide further reasons not to trust decisions made without adequate thought or formal analysis.

17 Descriptive theory of utility and choice

> Don't gamble. Take all your savings and buy some good stock and hold it
> till it goes up. If it don't go up, don't buy it.
>
> Will Rogers

Although the normative principles of choice appear reasonable enough to most people, psychological research has shown that we violate these principles systematically when we make decisions: That is, the violations are not just a consequence of the random variation to be found in any difficult judgment; rather, they are usually in a particular direction.

On the face of it, the descriptive models presented in this chapter differ considerably from the normative models presented in the last chapter. This raises a familiar question: Is the normative model really normative? I shall argue that it is still normative but that some of the descriptive findings raise interesting and complex questions about how the model should be interpreted in certain situations, particularly those in which decision makers have, or expect to have, emotional responses to the decision itself (as distinct from the consequences of the option chosen). We shall also explore the reasons why people deviate from the normative model, and I shall suggest that the deviations are caused by misleading heuristics.

Much of our discussion will concern the way in which we respond to *risk*, that is, uncertainties that could have a large effect on the outcome of an option. Risky options are those that could lead to outcomes much better or much worse than the outcomes of less risky options. Examples of risky options are speculative investments, decisions to have dangerous surgery, and bluffs in a high-stakes poker game or in a military confrontation. We tend to be averse to risks when the alternative is a gain that is certain (a gain with a probability of 1), even when the expected utility of the risky option is high. Bernoulli thought that such risk aversion for gains was rational – given our declining marginal utility for gains – but psychological research has found determinants of risk aversion that cannot be explained this way. We are therefore biased in making decisions when outcomes are uncertain, just as we are biased in the various ways we discussed in part II.

Biases are also found in decisions made without risk, the kinds of decisions that could be analyzed by MAUT, with no reference to probability. Many of

319

Table 17.1. *Ratings of five applicants on three dimensions*

Applicant	I	E	S
a	69	84	75
b	72	78	65
c	75	72	55
d	78	66	45
e	81	60	35

these biases can be described in terms of incomplete search for goals. In the extreme form of this bias, the decision maker makes a decision by considering the extent to which the options achieve a single goal: the "bottom line," the defeat of communism, the downfall of capitalism, the protection of abstract "rights," and so on. Such single-mindedness – in its extreme and less extreme forms – is often brought about by situational factors that encourage attention to a certain goal, but regardless of its cause it can be cured by actively open-minded thinking.

Before we discuss the making of decisions under risk (when outcomes are uncertain), let us first look at this somewhat simpler case of decisions under certainty.

Bias in decisions under certainty

For decisions under certainty, the combined probability of all outcomes is assumed to be 1.[1] Because of this, the independence condition for gambles is not relevant. Weak ordering is still relevant, though, and we can ask whether people's choices obey this condition.

Intransitivity of preferences

Tversky (1969) decided to test the idea that the axiom of transitivity is violated because of overweighing and underweighing of differences in utility. In one experiment, he asked subjects to choose which of two applicants for college to accept. The applicants were described in terms of three numerical ratings, one for intelligence (I), one for emotional stability (E), and one for social facility (S). The numbers were carefully chosen to reflect the subjective weights that individual subjects placed on each of these attributes. One subject was given the set of profiles shown in Table 17.1, which presented ratings for five applicants, *a* through *e*. The applicants were presented to the subject in all possible pairs (along with other pairs), and the subject was asked to judge,

---

[1] This may be quite a simplification, since practically any outcome can be analyzed further as a gamble. You may get what you want, but there is some probability that you will not enjoy it as much as you expected, and some probability that you will enjoy it more.

on the basis of the ratings, which applicant was better qualified. For the pairs a–b, b–c, c–d, and d–e, the typical subject favored applicants higher in the list, a over b, b over c, and so forth. The difference within each pair in *I*, for intelligence, seemed too small to matter. For the a–e comparison, however, subjects typically favored e over a. For these extreme pairs, the difference in the ratings for intelligence was great enough to outweigh the differences in the other two dimensions. (Subjects were instructed to consider intelligence as the most important attribute.)

The result was a violation of transitivity. Applicant a was preferred to b, b to c, c to d, d to e, but then e was preferred to a. It was impossible to assign numbers to the five applicants so that the applicant with a higher number would be consistently chosen over an applicant with a lower number. Tversky (1969, p. 45) suggests that similar violations occur outside the laboratory:

Consider . . . a person who is about to purchase a compact car of a given make. His initial tendency is to buy the simplest model for $2089.[2] Nevertheless, when the salesman presents the optional accessories, [the purchaser] first decides to add power steering, which brings the price to $2167, feeling that the price difference is relatively negligible. Then, following the same reasoning, he is willing to add $47 for a good car radio, and then an additional $64 for power brakes. By repeating this process several times, our consumer ends up with a $2593 car, equipped with all the available accessories. At this point, however, he may prefer the simplest car over the fancy one, realizing that he is not willing to spend $504 for all the added features, although each one of them alone seemed worth purchasing.

A general principle of decision making seems to be at work in this example. People tend to underweigh or ignore small differences, such as those between applicants a and b in intelligence, as opposed to large differences. Of course people *should* weigh small differences less than large ones, but they overdo it. Therefore, relatively large differences, such as those between applicants a and b in emotional stability and social facility, or between applicants a and e in intelligence, play a larger role than they ought to. It is as though we simplified our decisions by ignoring small differences altogether.

Elimination by aspects

Tversky (1972) developed a descriptive theory to explain why some decisions are apparently more difficult to make than others. When decisions are difficult, Tversky says, we shift back and forth, favoring now one option and now another, as we think about the decision, until we make our choice. If we are asked what we favor at a given time, then, it is fairly probable that at various times we will mention each of the options as our preference. This process could produce violations of utility theory, under certain conditions.

Suppose you are indifferent between a trip to Paris and a trip to Rome.

[2] The $2,089 is not a misprint; Tversky was writing in 1969.

Since you are attracted to both cities, this is a difficult choice. Now you discover that the airline that would fly you to Rome offers a free bottle of wine on the flight. Would this tip the balance? Surely not, for most people: You would still find it difficult to choose. If you were asked where you were going, on various occasions, you would probably say "Paris" half the time and "Rome" half the time, and the bottle of wine would not matter.

The bottle of wine probably *would* matter, though, if there were two airlines with flights to Rome that were *identical*, except that one offered the wine and the other did not. This would induce a consistent preference for the flight with the wine; you would (assuming that you have any interest in wine at all) then be likely to prefer this airline 100% of the time.

As Tversky puts it (p. 284), "Choice probabilities . . . reflect not only the utilities of the alternatives in question, but also the difficulty of comparing them." Rome and Paris differ in a great many attributes or "aspects." A single bottle of wine is one attribute in favor of Rome, but so many others must be weighed that this one gets lost. The bottle of wine makes a big difference, however, when everything else is the same.

In another example, suppose that you are indifferent between receiving a record of a Beethoven symphony and a record of some piano pieces by Debussy. You might even slightly prefer the Beethoven. Your probability of favoring the Debussy at any given time would then be about .50, or a little less. Now suppose you are given a choice among three records: the Debussy, the Beethoven symphony, and a different, but equally attractive, recording of the same Beethoven symphony. What would be your probability of choosing the Debussy now? Most people think it would still be about .50 – maybe a little less but still a lot more than .33, which is what your choice probability would be if you were considering three equally attractive but very different choices. Tversky suggested, however, that the probability of choosing each Beethoven would be much lower, about .25. It is as though we had first made a decision between Beethoven and Debussy, and then, if we had decided on Beethoven, we decide which Beethoven we prefer.

Tversky provides a general descriptive model that accounts for these examples, as well as the data from several experiments. He suggests that we make complex decisions by looking for favorable aspects (attributes), one aspect at a time, across all of the choice alternatives. For example, in comparing Paris with Rome, you would search your memory for attractive aspects of each city: For example, you might think about the Louvre in Paris, or St. Peter's in Rome, or the fact that you do not speak Italian.[3] Whatever attribute you find, you *eliminate* all of the options in the choice set that lack this single attribute. If you think of the Louvre first, you eliminate Rome, and the decision is made. You might, of course, think of some aspect of these cities that does not distinguish them for you, such as "good food." In this case,

---

[3] In this analysis, an "attractive aspect" could be identical to the *absence* of an unattractive aspect.

you simply continue the search for aspects. When there are more than two options, you may find an aspect that allows you to eliminate one of them but leaves others for you to consider. Tversky also assumes that you tend to think of the more important aspects first, but the order of thinking of aspects is not fixed. Because the order is not fixed, the choice you would make is somewhat unpredictable, especially when two options each have many different but attractive aspects.

In the Rome–Paris example, we can think of many different attributes that distinguish Rome and Paris. Your chance of finding one of these before hitting on the bottle of wine as the decisive attribute is quite high – so high that the wine is unlikely to affect your choice. (For it to do so, you would have to hit on it before any other distinguishing attributes.) When the choice is between Rome with wine and Rome without, however, there are no other distinguishing attributes. You would go through all the attributes and find them identical for the two choices before you hit on the wine, so you would choose the trip with wine with probability 1.

In the record example, many people are likely to think of attributes that make us favor Debussy or Beethoven in general. If we think of an attribute that favors Beethoven, this will probably eliminate the Debussy. If there are two Beethoven records to choose from, however, we will then have to continue the search for more attributes to distinguish them. We are unlikely to discover an attribute that allows us to eliminate *one* of the Beethoven records *and* the Debussy all at once. This is why we appear to make the decision in two steps, first between Beethoven and Debussy, then, if we decide on Beethoven, between the two Beethoven recordings.

This elimination-by-aspects model need not be used all the time in order for it to have its effect. We might think of it as a *heuristic* for making decisions, a heuristic that is used some of the time. (It has actually been observed in thinking-aloud protocols of decision making on such things as choices of apartments; see Payne, Braunstein, & Carroll, 1978; Svenson, 1979.)

Tversky points out that this heuristic is encouraged by advertisers who try to induce people to focus on certain attributes of the products they are promoting. Producers of products with a low share of the market – let us say a particular soap – want people to see their soap as quite distinctive and not easily compared to others, so that the consumers' attention is focused on the attributes that are favorable to their product. On the other hand, the makers of inexpensive aspirin try to induce people to see all of the competing pain killers as practically identical to each other as medicines (equally effective, and so forth), so that the only relevant attribute becomes the price: "All aspirins are the same. Why pay more?" (Tversky, 1972).

Tversky gives another example from a television commercial for a computer-programming school (1972, p. 287):

"There are more than two dozen companies in the San Francisco area which offer training in computer programming." The announcer puts some two-dozen eggs and one walnut on the table to represent the alternatives, and continues: "Let us examine

Table 17.2. *Value of two options in two dimensions, with one value to be filled in*

Options	Cash	Coupon book value
Gift package A	$10	
Gift package B	$20	$18

the facts. How many of these schools have on-line computer facilities for training?" The announcer removes several eggs. "How many of these schools have placement services that would help you find a job?" The announcer removes some more eggs. "How many of these schools are approved for veterans benefits?" The announcer continues until only the walnut remains. The announcer cracks the nutshell, which reveals the name of the company, and concludes: "This is all you need to know in a nutshell."

Use of the "elimination-by-aspects" heuristic is a way to avoid searching for goals (attributes). The decision maker simply searches for *any* goals that will eliminate options. This heuristic can therefore lead to less than optimal decisions. When we make a decision on the basis of a single outstanding attribute, we may ignore a host of smaller differences in other dimensions that would, taken together, favor some other option. For example, in deciding whom to vote for as our U.S. senator, we might base our decision on a single issue that we care greatly about or on the candidate's party. If we were to consider all of the issues and qualifications of all of the candidates, we would often want to vote differently.

Although this heuristic leads to departures from the normative model of decision making, it may be prescriptively sensible, especially for the simpler decisions of daily life, where little is at stake. When we attend to single attributes for more important decisions, however, we may make more serious mistakes.

Avoidance of tradeoffs

People tend to make holistic decisions in terms of a single dominant dimension (type of attribute). They are apparently unwilling to make tradeoffs – or less willing than they ought to be.

Slovic (1975) asked subjects to equate differences on two dimensions. For example, in one pair of dimensions, subjects were asked to consider gift packages varying in the amount of cash included and in the value of a coupon book offering products and services with some stated monetary values. Subjects were then asked to fill in the missing value in a table like Table 17.2 in such a way as to make the two choices equally attractive. Suppose subjects placed $50 in the blank space, thereby indicating that a change from $18 to $50 on the coupon dimension would exactly compensate a change from $20 to $10 on the cash dimension. Later, after filling out several more of these tables, subjects were asked to make hypothetical choices between alternatives that their own individual ratings indicated to be equally attractive. For example, subjects would be asked to choose between $20 in cash plus an $18 coupon book and $10 in cash plus a $50 coupon book. Subjects consistently made these choices in terms of the more important of the two dimensions – in this case, the amount of cash. The first option was chosen, even though subjects' earlier judgments indicated that the judgments ought to be equally attractive. The earlier judgments forced subjects to consider the tradeoff between the two dimensions, but when subjects were asked to make the holistic choice, they were free to ignore the less important dimension.

Montgomery (1984) suggested that we generally try to avoid making tradeoffs. When faced with a clear conflict between dimensions, he asserts, we try to think of reasons why one dimension can be completely ignored in decision making. Often, these single-minded arguments involve social roles: A good soldier must obey his commander (even if his commander tells him to kill innocent people); a good scholar must seek and publish the truth (even if someone will use it to promote racist doctrine); a good politician must defend the interests of her constituents (even if she must trample on the interests of others); a lawyer's duty is to his client (even if he must help his client commit perjury). This is not to say that a good soldier should *not* obey his commander, and so forth: It is just to say that in doing so he ought to be aware of what goals he may be sacrificing. Soldiers, scholars, politicians, and lawyers are people, and they have goals other than those associated with their roles. On some occasions, these other goals may outweigh the main one stemming from the work role. Such single-minded arguments reflect insufficient search for goals.

An interesting practical example of the effect of single-mindedness comes from a study by Gardiner and Edwards (1975). In California, proposals for "developing" the Pacific coastline (housing developments, for example) are controversial. Some Californians favor them, focusing on the economic advantages of increased employment and the like. Others oppose them, focusing on the environmental disadvantages of increased demands on resources and physical unattractiveness. The California Coastal Commission, which had the task of approving or disapproving such proposals, was often completely polarized, with members who held these opposite views constantly at each other's throats. Gardiner and Edwards were aware that each proposal could be ranked as better or worse on the two dimensions. Some proposals had relatively great economic advantages combined with relatively little environmental disadvantages, and these proposals, they felt, clearly ought to be given priority.

Gardiner and Edwards asked 12 knowledgeable subjects, including two members of the Coastal Commission, to rank order several proposals like the ones the commission normally considered. The subjects, like the commission, fell into two groups – prodevelopment and proenvironment. These holistic ratings showed very little agreement between the two groups of subjects. Members of each group were paying attention only to the dimension that was most important to them. Then the researchers asked subjects to carry out a MAUT analysis, in which subjects individually rated each proposal on each of the major dimensions and then assigned a weight to each dimension. Of course, the prodevelopment subjects gave greater importance to the economic dimensions, and the proenvironment subjects gave greater importance to the environmental dimensions. Nonetheless, each group now gave *some* weight to the *other* group's favored dimension. When new rankings were calculated from these analyses, there was now very good agreement between the two groups. Some proposals apparently were fairly satisfying to both groups. This became readily apparent only when the decision procedure forced attention to dimensions that each group had considered unimportant, as well as those that it initially considered important.

We conclude that attention to a single, dominant dimension can lead both to unnecessary disagreement between groups and to violation of each individual's true preferences. Making tradeoffs helps – when we have the time to do it.

Bias in decisions under uncertainty

A number of findings indicate that we systematically violate expected-utility theory when making decisions under uncertainty. Many of these demonstrations are in the form of hypothetical decisions. Sometimes, researchers gave these hypothetical decisions to subjects, but in other cases the author of a paper simply presents the examples to the reader, hoping that the reader will at least understand how people are inclined to respond in a certain way. I shall do the same here. If you are not inclined to make the choice that others make, try to understand why they might make it. In all the cases I shall discuss, subjects do yield the choice patterns of interest, even when investigators have used small amounts of real money in place of hypothetical outcomes.

Preference reversals and contingent weighting

Lichtenstein and Slovic (1971, 1973) discovered a very basic violation of expected-utility theory. They asked subjects to choose between two gambles: one gamble (called the P Bet) featured a high probability of winning a modest sum of money; the other gamble (called the $ Bet) featured a low probability of winning a relatively large sum of money. Here is an example (from Tversky, Sattath, & Slovic, 1988):

> P Bet   29/36 probability to win $2
> $ Bet   7/36 probability to win $9

Most subjects preferred the P Bet. Subjects were also asked how much money each bet was worth to them. (For example, subjects were asked the lowest amount for which they would sell the opportunity to play one of the bets, or, in other experiments, they were simply asked what amount of money was just as valuable to them as the bet. The method used did not affect the main findings.) Most subjects gave higher monetary values to the $ Bet, thus "reversing their preference." For example, a subject says that the P Bet was worth $1.25 and the $ Bet was worth $2.10. This pattern of responses violates the transitivity axiom of expected-utility theory. A subject prefers the P Bet to the $ Bet, presumably prefers the $ bet to $2 (since she said that the $ Bet was equivalent to $2.10), prefers $2 to $1.50, and presumably prefers $1.50 to the P Bet (since she stated that the P Bet was equivalent to $1.25); she has gone full circle. This result has been replicated in a variety of situations, many of which involved real money rather than hypothetical gambles (for example, Grether & Plott, 1979; Tversky, Sattath, & Slovic, in press).

Tversky, Sattath, and Slovic (in press) explain such "preference reversals" (and other results) in terms of the idea of *contingent weighting*. According to this idea, we can think of each gamble as a two-attribute outcome, the two attributes being probability and dollar amount. The probability of winning is more important to most subjects, so they attend to this probability when they choose between the two gambles, just as subjects attend to the cash amount (rather than the value of the coupons) in the Slovic experiment on choice between equally valued options (described in the last section). When the experimenter asks the subjects to state a dollar amount, however, this question calls their attention to the amount to be won, so they weigh this dimension more heavily. The weighting of a dimension is said to be "contingent" on the way in which preferences are elicited. This phenomenon could also be an example of the more general difficulty that we have in searching thoroughly for goals. When we choose gambles, we think about two goals: being likely to win; and winning as much as possible if we do win. We tend not to consider both of these goals, and we are easily induced to make our choice in terms of one or the other.

The Allais paradox

Allais (1953) proposed the following hypothetical decision: Suppose you were offered the choices (between different amounts of money) given in Table 17.3. You are to make one choice in situation X and one in situation Y. Notice that the table also gives the probability of each outcome.

Most people are inclined to choose option 1 in situation X and option 4 in situation Y. In situation X, they are not willing to give up the *certainty* of winning $1,000 in option 1 for the chance of winning $5,000 in option 2: This extra possible gain would expose them to the *risk* of winning nothing at all. (If you do not happen to feel this way, try replacing the $5,000 with a lower

Table 17.3. *The Allais paradox*

Situation X		
Option 1	$1,000,	1.00
Option 2	$1,000,	.89
	$5,000,	.10
	$0,	.01
Situation Y		
Option 3	$1,000,	.10
	$0,	.90
Option 4	$5,000,	.11
	$0,	.89

Note: The figures given after the dollar amounts are probabilities.

Table 17.4. *The Allais paradox as a lottery*

	Ball numbers		
	1	2–11	12–100
Situation X			
Option 1	$1,000	$1,000	$1,000
Option 2	0	5,000	1,000
Situation Y			
Option 3	$1,000	$1,000	$ 0
Option 4	0	5,000	0

figure, until you do. Then use that figure in choice 4 as well.) In situation Y, they reason that the difference between the two probabilities of winning is small, so they are willing to try for the larger amount.

Now suppose (as suggested by Savage, 1954) that the outcomes for these same choices are to be determined by a lottery. Balls numbered from 1 to 100 are put into an urn, which is shaken well before any ball is drawn. Then a ball will be taken out, and the number on the ball will, together with your choice, determine the outcome, as shown in Table 17.4. The dollar entries in the table represent the outcome for different balls that might be drawn. For example, in option 2, you would get nothing if ball 1 is drawn, $5,000 if ball 2, 3, 4, . . . or 11 is drawn, and so forth. This situation yields the same probabilities of each outcome, for each choice, as the original gambles presented in Table 17.3. For example, in option 1, the probability of $1,000 is .01 + .10 + .89, which is 1.00.

It is apparent from Table 17.4 that options 1 and 2 are identical to options 3 and 4, except for the outcome for balls 12 through 100. Moreover, the

Table 17.5. *Expected utilities of options in the Allais paradox*

Situation X			
Option 1	$.01 \cdot u$ ($1,000)	$+ .10 \cdot u$ ($1,000)	$+ .89 \cdot u$ ($1,000)
Option 2	$.01 \cdot u$ ($0)	$+ .10 \cdot u$ ($5,000)	$+ .89 \cdot u$ ($1,000)
Situation Y			
Option 3	$.01 \cdot u$ ($1,000)	$+ .10 \cdot u$ ($1,000)	$+ .89 \cdot u$ ($0)
Option 4	$.01 \cdot u$ ($0)	$+ .10 \cdot u$ ($5,000)	$+ .89 \cdot u$ ($0)

outcome in the column farthest to the right does not depend on the choice made in each situation. In situation X, whether you choose option 1 or option 2, you would get $1,000 if the ball drawn is between 12 and 100. Situation Y is the same, except that the common outcome for the two choices is $0.

By the "independence axiom," described in chapter 16, we should ignore these common outcomes in making such a decision. We should choose options 1 and 3, or options 2 and 4. When choices are presented in this tabular form, it becomes easier for us to see what is at issue. Many subjects do in fact change their choices to make them consistent with the expected-utility axioms when they are shown in the table (Keller, 1985). Other subjects stick to their choices of options 1 and 4 even after being shown the table (Slovic & Tversky, 1974). As the economist Paul Samuelson put it (1950, pp. 169–170), they "satisfy their preferences and let the axioms satisfy themselves."

Because the choice of options 1 and 4 violates the independence axiom, we cannot account for these choices in terms of expected-utility theory. The expected utility of each choice (using data from Table 17.3) is calculated in Table 17.5. If we prefer option 1 to option 2 and if we *did* follow expected-utility theory, then the expected utility of option 1 must be higher than that of option 2, so, from Table 17.5,

$$.01 \cdot u(\$1,000) + .10 \cdot u(\$1,000) > .01 \cdot u(\$0) + .10 \cdot u(\$5,000)$$

since the term $.89 \cdot u(\$1,000)$ may be dropped from each side. Exactly the opposite inequality,

$$.01 \cdot u(\$1,000) + .10 \cdot u(\$1,000) < .01 \cdot u(\$0) + .10 \cdot u(\$5,000),$$

is true if we prefer option 4 over option 3 (because $u(\$0)$ is dropped). There is therefore no way of assigning numbers to $u(\$0)$, $u(\$1,000)$, and $u(\$5,000)$ so that both inequalities will be true. Prospect theory will enlighten us about the nature of this paradox.

Lopes (1987b) and Shafer (1986) have suggested that the *context of possible outcomes* affects our utilities, so that when the chance of winning something is high, the utility difference between $1,000 and $0 seems larger to us than when the chance of winning something is low. As we shall see, however, the choices that we make in the Allais paradox are consistent with a more general descriptive theory – prospect theory.

Prospect theory

In 1979, psychologists Daniel Kahneman and Amos Tversky proposed a *descriptive* theory, which they called prospect theory, that accounted for almost all of the available data concerning decisions under risk. It has inspired many other similar attempts. (Because research in this field is extremely active, only a brief summary of these recent developments can be offered, later in this chapter.) It is important to remember that prospect theory is descriptive, not normative. It explains how and why our choices *deviate* from the normative model of expected-utility theory. Kahneman and Tversky's guiding idea, however, was to take expected-utility theory as their basic theory and then to modify it as little as possible in order to make it account for the observed violations of expected-utility theory, such as those observed in the Allais paradox. The theory applies directly to situations – like the Allais paradox – in which we choose among options that are described to us in terms of their possible outcomes and the numerical probabilities of these outcomes.

Prospect theory, as a modification of expected-utility theory, has two main parts, one concerning probabilities and one concerning utilities. The theory retains the basic idea that we make decisions as though we multiplied something like a subjective probability by something like a utility: The more probable a consequence is, the more heavily we weigh its utility in our decision. According to the theory, however, we distort probabilities, and we think about utilities as changes from a reference point. The reference point is easily affected by irrelevant factors, and this fact leads us to make different decisions for the same problem, depending on how it is presented to us. Let us look at the probability part first.

Probability: the pi function

Pi and the certainty effect. In essence, prospect theory begins with the premise that we do not treat the probabilities as they are stated; instead, we distort them, according to a particular mathematical function that Kahneman and Tversky named the "pi function," using the Greek letter π instead of the usual p for probability. Instead of multiplying our utilities by p, the researchers proposed, people multiply by $\pi(p)$.[4] The function is shown in Figure 17.1. For example, in a gamble some people prefer ($30) to ($45, .80), but they prefer ($45, .20) to ($30, .25). Here ($30) means $30 for sure; ($45, .80) means $45 with probability .80 and $0 with probability .20, and so forth. If

---

[4] In chapter 12, we discussed distortions of probability judgments. These distortions can operate when we judge the probabilities of the outcomes ourselves, but in the situations described by prospect theory, the probabilities of the outcomes are given to us. We distort the probabilities when we use them to make decisions. If the probabilities are not given to us, both kinds of biases – those discussed here and those discussed in chapter 12 – can occur.

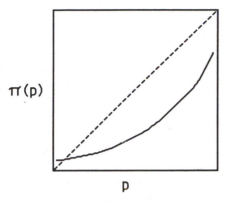

$\pi(p)$

p

Figure 17.1. π, the weight applied to the utility of each outcome, as a function of p, the probability of the outcome, according to prospect theory.

you prefer ($30) to ($45, .80), this would imply – using the expected-utility formula – that

$$u(\$30) > .80 \cdot u(\$45)$$

If you prefer ($45, .20) to ($30, .25), this implies that

$$.25 \cdot u(\$30) < .20 \cdot u(\$45)$$

Both inequalities cannot be true. Each side of the second inequality can be derived from the corresponding side of the first by multiplying by .25. This pattern of choices is called the *certainty effect*, because subjects appear to be attracted by the absolute certainty of the $30.

The π function explains the certainty effect, because of the fact that $\pi(1.00)$ is much higher than it ought to be relative to $\pi(p)$ for other values of p (except for very low values, which are not used in this problem). Certainty is over-weighed. Put another way, it appears that other values of p are *under*weighed relative to $p = 1.00$.[5]

An interesting consequence of the π function is shown in the following problem (based on Tversky & Kahneman, 1981, p. 455):

Consider the following two-stage game. In the first stage, there is a .75 probability of ending the game without winning anything, and a .25 chance to move into the second stage. If you reach the second stage, you have a choice between ($30) and ($45, .80). However, you must make this choice before either stage of the game is played.

Most subjects think about this problem in the same way as they thought about the choice of ($30) versus ($45, .80). They therefore choose ($30). These are

[5] It is not simply that certainty is *desired* for its own sake or that uncertainty is avoided. The certainty effect is also found in the domain of losses. People seek to *take* risks to *avoid* a certain loss, just as they seek to avoid risks to *obtain* a certain gain.

the same subjects who chose ($45, .20) over ($30, .25), however. Think about the two-stage gambles for a moment, though. If you calculate the overall probability of $30, assuming that that option is chosen, it is .25, the probability of getting to the second stage. Likewise, the probability of $45, if that option is chosen, is .25 · .80 (the probability of getting to the second stage multiplied by the probability of winning if you get there), or .20. Therefore, the probabilities of the outcomes in the two-stage gambles are identical to the probabilities of the outcomes in the gambles ($30, .25) and ($45, .20), yet the common pattern of choices is reversed.

Subjects who show this kind of reversal (as many do) are violating what Kahneman and Tversky (1984) call the *principle of invariance*. The invariance principle asserts that *one's choices ought to depend on the situation itself, not on the way it is described.* In other words, when we can recognize two descriptions of a situation as equivalent, we ought to make the same choices for both descriptions. Subjects seem to violate this principle.[6] The invariance principle would seem to be a principle of rational choice that is at least as fundamental as other principles we have assumed as part of utility theory, such as transitivity and independence. Violations of the invariance principle are also called *framing effects*, because the choice made is dependent on how the situation is presented or "framed."

Note that $\pi(p)$, unlike p itself, is not additive. In general, $\pi(p) + \pi(1-p) < 1$. Therefore, we cannot assume that the 1.00 probability of $1,000 in the Allais paradox can be psychologically decomposed (as in Table 17.4) into .01 + .10 + .89. At least part of the bias shown in the Allais paradox is caused by the certainty effect operating on option 1.[7]

Is the certainty effect rational? Why should we not weigh certain (sure) outcomes more than uncertain ones? One reason why not is that it leads us to more inconsistent decisions, decisions that differ as a function of the way things are described to us (or the way we describe things to ourselves). Second, our feeling of "certainty" about an outcome is often, if not always, an illusion, or, to put it more precisely, another sort of artifact of the way things are described (as we noted in ch. 16). For example, you may think of ($30) as a certain outcome: you get $30. Unless having money is your only goal in life, though, the $30 is really just a means to other ends. You might spend it on tickets to a football game, for example, and the game might be close, and so exciting that you tell your grandchildren about it – or it might be a terrible game, with the rain pouring down, and you, without an umbrella, having to

---

[6] The different patterns of choices in the Allais paradox, depending on whether the situation is presented in a table or not, are another example of violation of the invariance principle.

[7] Quiggin (1982), Segal (1984), and Yaari (1985) have shown that the major results ascribed to the π function, including the certainty effect, can be accounted for by other transformations of p that preserve additivity. The trick is to rank the outcomes in order of preference and calculate, for each outcome, Q, the probability of doing at least as well as that outcome. These Q's can be transformed freely, preserving additivity of p, as long as Q is 1 for the worse outcome. Reviews of other recent developments of this sort are found in Fishburn (1986), Sugden (1986), and Machina (1987).

watch your team get slaughtered. You might use the money to buy a book that enlightens you more than a year of college – or a book that turns out to be a lot of trash. In short, most, if not all, "certain" outcomes can be analyzed further, and in doing so one finds, on close examination, that the outcomes are themselves gambles. The *description* of an outcome as certain is *not* certainty itself.

An important consequence of the certainty effect (McCord & de Neufville, 1985) is the conclusion that people do not conform to the assumptions underlying the method of gambles when this method is used to measure utility. When people say that they are "indifferent" between ($5) and ($20, .5), we cannot assume that their utility for $5 is literally halfway between that of $0 and that of $20. They underweigh the .5 probability of winning $20 relative to the 1.0 probability of winning $5. Most likely, the true halfway point is higher than $5.[8]

Overweighing and underweighing probabilities. Another property of the π function is the *over*weighing of very low probabilities. This may also contribute to the Allais paradox. The .01 probability of winning nothing looms larger in our minds than it ought to. The fact is that the .01, in option 2, is the same as the *difference* between the probability of winning nothing in option 3 and option 4. In option 2, the .01 seems quite significant, but in options 3 and 4, it seems like a small difference. Normatively, of course, a difference of .01 is the same, whether it is between 0 and .01 or between .89 and .90.

Likewise, part of the effect in the Allais paradox may be that we overweigh the .01 probability of winning nothing in option 2. This effect may remain even when the problem is presented to us in the form of a table.

Our tendency to overweigh very low probabilities may explain why some of us buy both insurance (such as life insurance for an airline flight) and lottery tickets, even though these are *opposites* in terms of assumption of risk. When we buy insurance, we are paying someone *else* to accept risk; when we buy a lottery ticket, we are paying someone to let *us* take the risk. Both choices are reasonable, if the low-probability event is overweighed. We probably focus too much on the very low chance of winning the lottery or of being killed in a plane crash.[9]

Elstein, Holaman, Ravitch, Metheny, Holmes, Hoppe, Rothert, and Rovner (1985) found a case in which this effect apparently distorted common medical practice. The use of the hormone estrogen as therapy for menopausal

---

[8] There is no simple solution to this problem except to use other methods for measuring utility, such as difference measurement. The shape of the curve of the π function makes it very difficult to choose gambles that mean what they seem to mean in terms of utilities.

[9] Bernoulli, of course, can explain why people buy insurance. The disutility to the purchaser of very large losses (damage to property and so forth) is very great because of the shape of the utility curve for wealth. Bernoulli cannot, however, easily explain playing the lottery, except through a convex utility curve, which would predict that people would not buy insurance.

women has been shown by several studies to be quite effective in reducing the risk of osteoporosis, a degenerative bone condition that often leads to fractures and death (from complications of the fractures) in older women. Estrogen seems to reduce the incidence of death (and other serious effects) from osteoporosis by several percentage points, but it also has been shown to increase the risk of endometrial cancer from practically zero to a small fraction of 1%. A decision analysis (using utility estimates provided by physicians) indicates that this small risk is worth it for most patients. Many more lives would be saved by the prevention of complications from fractures, for example, if estrogen replacement were more widely used, yet the researchers found most physicians were reluctant to prescribe estrogen for anyone. This reluctance, they theorized, is the result of overweighing the low probability of endometrial cancer.

In the laboratory (and the real world), the overweighing of low probabilities is again shown in people's willingness to buy tickets in a "fair" lottery (one in which the seller of the tickets pays out in prizes an amount equal to the receipts from ticket sales). Many people are willing to spend a dollar for a .001 probability of winning $1,000. The same people, however, avoid fair gambles with larger probabilities of winning. People in general appear to be risk-averse, yet they take risks that offer very low probability of gain.

When probabilities of some outcome are sufficiently small, we tend to disregard that outcome completely in our decisions. We behave as though we had a *threshold* below which probabilities are essentially zero. Schwalm and Slovic (1982), for example, found that only 10% of their subjects said they would wear seatbelts when they were told that the probability of being killed in an automobile accident was about .00000025 per trip, but 39% said they would wear seatbelts when they were told that the probability of being killed was about .01 over a lifetime of driving. The second probability is derived from the first using the average number of trips per lifetime. People treat a probability of .00000025 as essentially zero, so it does not matter to them how many trips they take when the probability is so low.

A similar "threshold effect" for money can provide another explanation of people's willingness to buy lottery tickets. People may perceive the $1 spent for the lottery ticket as trivial compared to the prize, and therefore essentially not worth considering at all. (Such people do not apparently think about the low probability of winning.) Of course, for those who play the lottery every week over a period of years, the dollars add up.

Utility: the value function and framing effects

Let us now look at the part of prospect theory that concerns utility. According to prospect theory, individuals evaluate outcomes as *changes from a reference point*, which is usually their current state. Because we take different conditions as the reference point, depending on how a decision is described to us, we

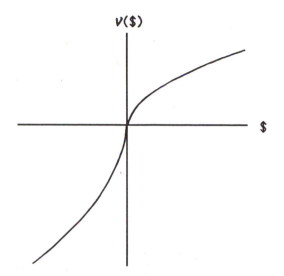

Figure 17.2. The value, v, of a monetary gain or loss as a function of the amount of gain or loss, according to prospect theory.

can make different, inconsistent decisions for the same situation depending on how it is described.

The value function. As noted in chapter 16, Bernoulli viewed the utility of financial gains or losses to an individual as a function of the person's *total wealth after the gain or loss occurred*. Therefore, if one already has $10,000, the added utility of winning $30 would simply be $u(\$10,030) - u(\$10,000)$. Kahneman and Tversky, by contrast, suppose that we evaluate the utility of the $30 gain by itself, as $u(\$30)$, essentially without regard to our total wealth. They propose that we make decisions as if we had a *value function* for gains and losses, with the curve depicted in Figure 17.2. The horizontal axis is not wealth, but rather the monetary gain (to the right), or loss (to the left), compared with one's reference point (the middle). The vertical axis is essentially utility, but they use the letter $v(.)$, for value, instead of $u(.)$ to indicate the difference between their theory and standard utility theory. (Do not confuse this v with the v used to represent monetary value in chapter 16, even though the two v's look alike.) They acknowledge that this value function might change as a person's total wealth changes, but they suggest that such effects of total wealth are small.

The value function shows that we treat losses as more serious than equivalent gains. We consider the loss in value from losing $10 is greater than the gain in value from gaining $10. That is why most of us will not accept a bet in which we have an even chance of winning and losing $10, even though the expected value of that bet is $0.

A second property of the value function is that it is convex for losses (increasing slope as we move to the right, as shown in the lower left of Figure 17.2) and concave for gains (decreasing slope, as shown in the upper right). This means that subjects avoid risks in the domain of gains and seek risks in the domain of losses, when gains and losses are defined in terms of expected monetary change from their reference point. Because of the concavity in the domain of gains, people usually decline to pay $10 in return for a chance to win $20 with a probability of .5. They prefer the safer option here because the value of $10 is higher than the expected value of $20 with a probability of .5, which is .5 · $v(\$20)$.[10] In other words, $v(\$10)$ is more than half of $v(\$20)$: A $10 bird in the hand is worth two $10 birds in the bush. In the domain of losses, however, the same people might prefer a loss of $20 with a probability of .5 to a loss of $10. They prefer the riskier option here because the expected value of a loss of $20 with a probability of .5 is higher (less negative) than twice the value of $-\$10$.[11] Here, $v(-\$10)$ is "less negative" than half of $v(-\$20)$, and "less negative" would be preferred.

The differently curved value functions for gains and losses result in what is called the *reflection effect*. As we have just seen, the choice reverses when the signs of the outcomes are changed. If we choose the risky option for losses, we tend to choose the safe option for gains, and vice versa.

Framing effects for values. Using the value function in decision making is not necessarily irrational. If people's goals are to avoid losses and to seek gains, well, that is reasonable enough. It is a little more difficult to understand how people can care proportionately more about small financial losses than about large ones, but there is no accounting for taste. The function *can* lead to irrationality, however, when we are able to lead people into adopting different reference points by describing the situation differently.

As Thaler points out, for example (1980), a "cash discount" on a purchase and a "credit card surcharge" are different ways of describing the fact that there are two prices, one for cash and one for credit. Purchasers, however, perceive a "cash discount" as a gain, compared to the credit card price, and they perceive the "credit card surcharge" as a loss, compared to the cash price. Because, in the value function, the slope of the loss function is steeper than the slope of the gain function, consumers are more willing to use their credit card when they perceive it as giving up a "cash discount" (foregoing a small gain in value) than when they perceive it as accepting a "credit card surcharge" (accepting a larger loss). If merchants profit more from the higher of the two prices, they will do well to call the difference a "discount."

Tversky and Kahneman (1981, p. 251) gave the following problem to a group of subjects:

---

[10] Let us put aside, for this example, the π function, which would make people behave as though the probability was lower than .5.

[11] We again ignore the π function.

Imagine that the U.S. is preparing for the outbreak of an unusual Asian disease, which is expected to kill 600 people. Two alternative programs to combat the disease have been proposed. Assume that the exact scientific estimate of the consequences of the programs are as follows: Program A: (200 saved)
Program B: (600 saved, .33)

Most subjects chose program A, presumably because they did not want to take the substantial risk (probability .67) that nobody would be saved at all. Other subjects, however, were presented with the same problem, except that the choices were as follows:

Program A: (400 die)
Program B: (600 die, .67)

When the problem was presented this way, most subjects chose program B, presumably because 400 deaths seemed almost as bad as 600 and because it seemed worthwhile taking a chance that nobody would die at all.

Note that the two versions of the problem are identical. The situation is merely described differently, the first emphasizing the saving of life (a gain) and the second, death (a loss). In the first version, the reference point is the expected future if nothing is done: 600 dead. Subjects see the outcomes as gains (people saved), compared to this "worst case." Subjects chose program A because they are risk-averse in the domain of gains. Because the curve of the value function is concave, $v(200$ lives) is higher than the expected value $.33 \cdot v(600$ lives).

In the second version the reference point is shifted to the present state, in which nobody has died; the outcomes are described as losses (deaths). The curve is convex, and subjects are risk-seeking: $.67 \cdot v(-600$ lives$) > v(-400$ lives).[12] We have here an excellent example of a framing effect, a violation of the invariance principle. Subjects give different judgments, depending on whether outcomes are *described* as gains or losses.

To summarize this description, prospect theory predicts two major kinds of deviations from expected-utility theory. One type concerns distortion of stated probability. At the very least, subjects do not deal with stated probabilities as they ought to.[13] The second type of distortion concerns the value function. There is nothing necessarily wrong with the function itself, but once we start thinking of outcomes by comparing them to some imagined reference point, it becomes relatively easy for our perception of that point to be ma-

---

[12] One may well wonder whether it makes sense to have anything other than a linear utility function for lives saved or lost. If the function is curved, the 600th person to die is "worth less" than the first person. This seems highly unfair to the 600th person. If we accept the view (advanced in chapter 19) that everyone's utilities are equally important, we are inconsistent if we do not worry as much about each individual death, when many people die at once, as we worry about individual deaths, when people die one at a time.

[13] As yet, these demonstrations have not been extended to cases in which probabilities are known to the subject but never stated as numbers.

nipulated. We end up making different decisions depending on how the reference point is described to us or how we describe it to ourselves.[14] We could, as an antidote to this sort of error, try hard to use a constant imagined state for all decisions. As yet, no research has been done to determine whether such corrective heuristics work.

Mental accounting: framing effects with multiple certain outcomes

In the early 1980s, many automobile manufacturers in the United States started to offer rebates to customers who purchased their cars. Why rebates? Why not just reduce the price of the car by the "rebate" amount? It seems like a dubious sales technique, since there is an obvious economic disadvantage to it for purchasers: If the state has a sales tax, they have to pay sales tax on the full price of the car.

Thaler (1985) argues that the rebate program seemed more attractive to consumers than a simple price reduction because consumers keep separate *mental accounts* for the price of the car and the rebate. If the price of the car was simply reduced from $8,000 to $7,500, the buyer would, according to Kahneman and Tversky's value function, gain a subjective value of $v(-\$7,500) - v(-\$8,000)$. This is a small gain, because the curve of the function for losses is convex and has a low slope in this range. If, on the other hand, the buyer codes the $500 separately, the gain would be $v(\$500)$, a large gain, because the value function is steeper near zero.

Thaler suggests that we either *integrate* or *segregate* multiple outcomes (gains or losses) of a single option. If we integrate outcomes, we add them together before we apply the value function; they are considered as part of the same mental account. If we segregate different outcomes from each other, we apply the value function to each gain or loss and then mentally add or subtract the derived values to find the total gain or loss. In general, segregation appears to be irrational, but integration can be difficult when the goods in question are not monetary; indeed, MAUT, as we saw, assumes that we do not integrate dimensions that are expressed in different units (for example, the salary of a job and its consistency with our personal goals).

Despite the rationality of integration in most circumstances, by segregating outcomes at appropriate times we can deceive each other – and even deceive ourselves – into thinking that we are getting more for our money. One simple principle here for a seller (including the person who wants to sell something to himself) is the motto *Segregate the gains, integrate the losses*. The late-night television advertisements for kitchen utensils offer a long list of (segregated) gains from buying the product, as does the car dealer who wants to add many options (for only a small additional fee). In the latter case, each

---

[14] Unlike the part of prospect theory dealing with probabilities, to which several alternatives have been proposed (as we noted earlier), the part dealing with the role of the reference point has not been seriously challenged.

option alone may not be worth it if considered separately, but if its price is integrated with the loss already taken in deciding to purchase the car, the additional decrease in value is slight (because the value curve is not steep at this point). The options themselves are mentally segregated because they are different sorts of things: they cannot simply be added. The subjective value of each option does not change as new options are added, but the subjective value of the *price* of each option does decrease because it is integrated with the price of everything else.

We sell things to ourselves as well. Some of us would not pay $5 for a dessert or $15 for a $5 bottle of wine if we bought them in a bakery or liquor store but are quite willing to pay that much if they are added on to a restaurant bill that is already over $50. The dessert or the wine is segregated, but the loss of the $5 or the $15 is integrated with the total price of the dinner. As an addition to the bill, the extra price does not seem so much. In general, integration of losses reduces their effect on our decision; segregation of gains increases their effect. This combination, therefore, encourages any *transaction* in which someone suffers a loss to obtain a gain – for example, pays money to obtain a combination of goods or services.

Mental accounts affect the effort we make to save money when we buy things. The degree of effort seems to depend on the subjective value of the money saved, not the amount of the money. Many of us are willing to spend as much effort to save $1 on a $10 purchase as we would to save $100 on a $1,000 purchase. Here is a good example (Tversky & Kahneman, 1981, p. 457):

Imagine that you are about to purchase a jacket for $125, and a calculator for $15. The calculator salesman informs you that the calculator you wish to buy is on sale for $10 at the other branch of the store, located 20 minutes drive away. Would you make the trip to the other store?

Most subjects asked were willing to make the trip to save the $5. Very few subjects were willing to make the trip to save $5 on the jacket, though, in an otherwise identical problem. In both cases, the "real" question is whether you would be willing to drive 20 minutes for $5. If the savings is part of your mental account for the calculator, the savings is subjectively greater than it is if it is part of your account for the jacket, because of the convexity of the curve of the value function for losses.

More generally, whenever we spend money in order to buy something or in order to make an investment, we are in effect "mixing" gains and losses: We lose whatever money we pay and we gain the purchase or investment. If we mentally segregate these gains and losses from each other, the losses will appear to be greater than if we integrate them, because of the curves of the value function for losses and gains.

As a result, monetary losses appear more acceptable if they are integrated with gains. For example, most employees are not as upset by the deduction of taxes, insurance, investments, charity contributions, and union dues from their paychecks as they would be if they had to pay each of these things separately. Deduction practically ensures mental integration, because many employees do not bother to think about what their take-home pay would be without the deductions. Separate payment would permit the employees to mentally segregate the accounts. It is not necessarily wrong to think about a paycheck in this integrated way; in fact, one can argue that this is the right way to think about things, if we want to approach expected-utility theory. The deductions might be worthwhile when seen as a reduction in our total income. The problem arises when we do *not* integrate gains and losses for other purchases, such as books or common stocks, which we are therefore less likely to purchase than we would be if they, too, were deducted from our paychecks.

Reference point effects: the reference price

We have already seen that subjects tend to evaluate outcomes by comparing the outcomes to their reference point. A number of other reference points seem to be involved in decision making. (Still others are discussed in ch. 21.) In purchasing behavior, one common reference point is the idea of a fair price, or market price, or what Thaler (1985) calls a *reference price*. Consider the following scenario (from Thaler, 1985, p. 206):

> You are lying on the beach on a hot day. All you have to drink is ice water. For the last hour you have been thinking about how much you would enjoy a nice cold bottle of your favorite brand of beer. A companion gets up to go make a phone call and offers to bring back a beer from the only nearby place where beer is sold, a small run-down grocery store. He says that the beer might be expensive and so he asks you how much you are willing to pay for the beer.

Your friend will buy the beer only if it is less than the price you state. $1.50 was the median price that subjects given this description were willing to pay. When "fancy resort hotel" was substituted for "run-down grocery store," though, the median price went up to $2.65.

Thaler argues that subjects took into account the idea of a fair price for the beer, given the type of establishment that was selling it. (Note that the consumer of the beer would not consume any of the "atmosphere" of the fancy hotel – presumably the factor that permits the hotel to charge more.) In addition to considering the value of the money lost and the beer gained, we seem to take into account an additional value having to do with the extent to which the price is above or below the reference price.

This hypothesis explains a number of otherwise curious phenomena of the marketplace, such as "discount prices" advertised as being below the "suggested retail price." When certain rather expensive goods are purchased once every few years, at most, many consumers do not know what the price "ought" to be, so it is possible to make them think that they are getting a 50% discount on a new camera, stereo system, or set of silver flatware by mentioning a "suggested retail price" of twice the asking price.

Another common device is to change the goods in some way so that the reference price is unknown. Have you noticed that movie theaters sell unusually large candy bars? This is handy for pricing, since we cannot recall what the price would be elsewhere.

Alternatives to prospect theory

Prospect theory modified expected-utility theory by proposing that we distort probabilities and that our utilities are dependent on an unstable reference point. Another kind of modification of expected-utility theory proposes that the utility of each outcome depends not only on the outcome itself but also on other outcomes that would occur in different parts of the utility table – that is, in different "states of the world" (within the same option) or in different options (within the same state). We think about outcomes by comparing them to other possible outcomes. In particular, we think about the emotions that we will experience when we compare the outcome that does occur to other outcomes that could have occurred.

Regret and rejoicing

One of these modifications, called regret theory, was proposed independently by Bell and by Loomes and Sugden in 1982. According to this theory, we *regret* our decision if we learn that the outcome would have been better if we had chosen differently, for example, if we decide to carry an umbrella and find that it does not rain or if we decide not to carry an umbrella and find that it does rain. We *rejoice* in our decision if we learn that the outcome would have been worse if we had chosen differently, for example, if we carry an umbrella and it rains or if we do not carry an umbrella and it does not rain. When we make a decision, we anticipate these feelings and take them into account.

This anticipation in itself does not necessarily lead to any departures from expected-utility theory. (We noted in connection with Table 16.1 that we can compare options column by column in the utility table.) According to regret theory, however, we overweigh these anticipated feelings of regret and rejoicing when the difference between outcomes is large.[15] For the umbrella decision, the large differences between outcomes probably occur if it rains: In this "state of nature," we rejoice greatly if we have an umbrella but regret our decision if we do not. If it does not rain, the difference between outcomes is relatively small (carrying an umbrella needlessly or not), so here we do not

---

[15] Note the similarity to Tversky's finding concerning intransitivity of preferences. The common factor is the neglect of relatively small differences when large ones are present.

Table 17.6. *Analysis of "inconsistent" choices according to regret theory*

Outcome probability			Outcome probability				
First pair	.80	.20	*Second pair*	.05	.20	.15	.60
Option 1	$30	$30	Option 3	$30	$30	$0	$0
Option 2	$45	$0	Option 4	$45	$0	$45	$0

take our feelings into account. In this case, our anticipation of regret and rejoicing would make us more inclined to take the umbrella than would an analysis of expected utility that ignored these feelings.

Both regret and rejoicing apply to our decision making itself. It is as though we pride ourselves on a well-made decision, if the outcome is good, and blame ourselves for a poorly made decision if the outcome is poor. Perhaps we anticipate our own confusion between the quality of our decision making and the quality of its outcome (Baron & Hershey, 1988).

Regret theory can explain the phenomena that are explained by the π function in prospect theory. Consider the inconsistency observed by Kahneman and Tversky between the choice of $30 as opposed to $45 with a probability of .80 and the choice of $30 with a probability of .25 as opposed to $45 with a probability of .20. Many people choose the first option in the first pair but the second option in the second pair. According to regret theory, we can represent these two pairs as in Table 17.6. The table for the first pair of options (1 and 2) represents outcomes of these options in two states of the world (with probabilities .80 and .20, respectively). We think about this decision by comparing $v(\$45)$ to $v(\$30)$ in the first column and by comparing $v(\$30)$ to $v(\$0)$ in the second column. The latter difference is larger, and we tend to overweigh it. Specifically, we think about our regret if we chose option 2 and receive $0 (knowing that we would have received $30 if we had chosen option 1), or our rejoicing if we chose option 1 and received $30 (knowing that we would have received $0 from option 2). The difference between $v(\$45)$ and $v(\$30)$ is not so great, so the feelings of regret and rejoicing in this state of nature play little role in our decision.

For the second pair of options (3 and 4), the situation is more complicated. We can think of each gamble as being played (or "resolved"), whether we choose it or not. We see that there are four possible states of the world, corresponding, respectively, to the four columns: win if either gamble is played; win with option 3 but lose with option 4; win with option 4 but lose with option 3; and lose with either. The table is constructed on the assumption that the two gambles are independent; therefore, the probability of winning with option 3 is the same whether or not option 4 wins.

Here, we have two main sources of regret, corresponding to the second and third columns. If we take option 3 we might experience regret because

Table 17.7. *How regret theory can explain risk seeking*

	Competitor advertises (p = .50)	Competitor does not advertise (p = .50)
Take no action	$ 5 million	$15 million
Lower price	$11 million	$11 million
Advertise	$ 6 million	$16 million

we could lose that gamble but would have won if we had taken option 4. Exactly the opposite could happen if we take option 4. Further, the potential regret, in both cases, is about equally strong. (The smaller difference, between $30 and $0 in the second column, is a little more likely, so the two effects are about equal, if we take probability into account.) The small difference in the first column (between $30 and $45) does not induce much anticipated regret, because regret depends more heavily on large differences. In this pair of choices, anticipated regret does not lead strongly to either choice. Because of this, the potentially greater winning in the first column is likely to determine the choice made. Subjects will therefore be likely to choose option 1 in the first pair but option 4 in the second, the pattern we previously noted to be inconsistent (in the section on the π function of prospect theory).

Anticipated regret can lead to risk seeking even when people are otherwise risk-averse, as in the following example (modified from Bell, 1985b): A division manager for a company knows that there is a 50% chance that a competitor will begin an advertising campaign for a comparable product. The possible profits from three different options (take no action, lower the price of the product, advertise) are listed in Table 17.7. (The total market is affected by advertising.) Notice that the expected value is the same for lowering the price and for advertising. Moreover, the risk is lower for lowering the price, so if the national company is at all risk-averse (for example, because of its declining marginal utility for money), the best decision would be to lower prices. Others, however, (and the manager herself) are more likely to think that advertising is better, because it makes $1 million more profit than "no action," no matter what the competitor does. Compared to "no action," there will be no cause for regret.

In regret theory the manner in which the choices are paired up is crucial. Loomes (1987, in press) gave subjects in Great Britain choices like the ones shown in Table 17.8. Subjects were told that a ticket had been drawn randomly from a set of 24 tickets, labeled 1 through 24. The subjects could win a money prize, in English pounds (£), depending on which of the two options they chose (A versus B, and C versus D) and which ticket number had been drawn. (Each subject made several hypothetical decisions, but a game for one of these decisions was chosen at random and played for real money at the end

Table 17.8. *Two pairs of options with identical probabilities and outcomes but different pairings of outcomes and states*

Option	Ticket number			Option	Ticket number		
	1–9	10–21	22–24		1–9	10–12	13–24
A	£24	£ 0	£0	C	£24	£ 0	£0
B	0	16	0	D	16	16	0

of the session.) Notice that option A is identical to option C in terms of outcomes and their probabilities. In both cases, there is a 9/24 chance of winning 24 (tickets 1 through 9). Similarly, option B is the same as option D in these terms: There is a 12/24 chance of winning £16 (tickets 10 through 21 in option B, 1 through 12 in option D). Thus, by expected-utility theory (or prospect theory), options A and C should be equally popular.

In fact, A was chosen a little more often than B, but D was chosen much more often than C. Presumably this was because the relatively small difference between £24 and £16 was less striking than the difference between £16 and £0, when subjects compared choices C and D. What subjects appeared to be most worried about, when faced with a choice of C and D, was that ticket 10, 11, or 12 would be drawn if they chose C. For choices A and B, these kinds of worries were about equally strong for either choice.

Anticipated regret may also be involved in medical choices. In deciding whether to have treatments and operations, we may think in terms of avoiding the worst possible outcome (death), at the expense of avoiding other serious, and much more likely, outcomes. This may underlie the reluctance of physicians to prescribe estrogen for menopausal women.

Regret theory can explain most of the findings that are accounted for by the π function of prospect theory (Bell, 1982; Loomes & Sugden, 1982). It cannot, however, explain framing effects: These are not in dispute.

Disappointment and elation

Recall from chapter 16 that most people are risk-averse. They avoid a 50–50 gamble, if given a choice of a certain (sure) outcome with equal *expected utility* (not just equal monetary value). For example, *if* your utility for money can be expressed as a linear function in the range from $0 to $10, you will prefer $5 for sure to a .5 chance to win $10. Regret theory cannot explain this effect: As shown in Table 17.9, regret theory would concern itself with the differences in the columns, and the utility difference between $10 and $5 is the same (we have assumed) as that between $5 and $0. Therefore, the potential regret would be the same with either option.

Another explanation of risk aversion is that we make comparisons within

Table 17.9. *Representation of a fair bet*

	.5	.5
Option 1	$ 5	$5
Option 2	10	0

the rows as well as within the columns. If you take option 2 in Table 17.9, for example, you will experience *disappointment* if you win $0, comparing it with the $10 you might have won, and you will experience *elation* if you win $10, compared with the $0 you might have won. In general, if the anticipated disappointment effect is larger for you than the anticipated elation effect, you will tend to avoid risks. Any risk involves the possibility of losing, and if you focus on how you will feel if you lose – more than on how you will feel if you win – you will avoid the risk.

The following example (based on Quinn & Bell, 1983) illustrates the disappointment phenomenon: Person A goes to the movies and turns out to be the theater's 1,000th customer. She is given a check for $100. Person B goes to a different theater and turns out to be the 1,000,000th customer. He is given a chance to spin a spinner. He has an 80% chance of winning $50,000, and a 20% chance of winning $100. As luck would have it, he wins the $100. Which person do you think is happier with the $100? Most people say that A is happier; B is disappointed that he did not win the $50,000.

Disappointment and elation (Bell, 1985a) are the counterparts of rejoicing and regret. Disappointment and elation involve comparisons of different outcomes caused by different states within a single choice. Regret and rejoicing involve comparisons caused by different choices within a single state.

Rationality of regret and disappointment in decision making

Is it rational to be sensitive to such factors as disappointment and regret when making decisions? The question is not as easy to answer as it seems. We could argue, on the one hand, that by being sensitive to these feelings, we fail to maximize our expected utility, because we act in ways that are contrary to those specified by expected-utility theory. This is true, if we assume that feelings such as disappointment and regret have no utility for us. We could argue, however, that these feelings do have utility, because they reflect our personal goals, and that they should therefore be included as part of our analysis of any decision. If we consider them as consequences of the decision, then it is obviously rational to take them into account.

In my view, this last argument, though correct, is somewhat too simple an answer (1985b, ch. 2). These feelings, although real, arise specifically from our attitudes (*beliefs and goals*) concerning decision making and risk themselves. If we could change these underlying attitudes, we might be able to achieve our other goals more effectively, since we would not have to limit our choices by trying to avoid regret and disappointment. The first argument would apply, of course, if we *can* change our attitudes, and the second argument would apply if we *cannot*. (Some intermediate position is required if we are not sure about what our feelings will be.)

Suppose, for example, that you are considering purchasing a particular stock. On the basis of everything you know about this stock, a simple calculation of expected utility leads you to the conclusion that it is, overall, a better bet than some safer investment (such as a Treasury bond) might be. Still, you are held back by your fear that the price of the stock will go down and that you will blame yourself for a bad decision (feel regret) or will be disappointed that the price did not go up. If you are sure that you will experience these feelings *in addition* to the simple loss of utility from losing money (which you have already included in your calculations), you would be rational not to buy the stock. If you think you could put these feelings aside, however, you ought to go ahead and buy the stock. To put these feelings aside is to take a "philosophical" attitude toward the outcomes of decisions. You must be able to tell yourself, if you end up losing, that you knew that this could happen, and you made the best decision you could; you lost anyway, but there is nobody to blame, and it is no use crying over what might have been. Anyone who is used to taking risks (for example, surgeons and stock portfolio managers) probably is able to handle feelings of regret in this way. You learn to put your losses behind you and move on.

The ambiguity effect

Ambiguity and "unknown probability"

Another phenomenon concerning decisions under uncertainty was discovered by Daniel Ellsberg (of "Pentagon Papers" fame) in 1960. Ellsberg found that subjects violate the axioms of expected-utility theory by seeking to avoid risks associated with situations in which the probability is (or appears to be) "unknown." Suppose there is an urn containing 90 balls. Thirty of them are red, and 60 of them are either black or yellow – we do not know which. A ball is to be drawn from the urn, and we can win some money, depending on which ball is drawn and which option we take. Table 17.10 lists the options and the possible winnings. Most subjects lean toward option X. They "know" that they have a ⅓ chance of winning in this case (30 out of 90 balls). They do not like option Y because they feel that they do not even know what the "real probability" of winning is. It appears to them that it could be as high as ⅔ or as low as 0. Note, however, that if the principle of insufficient reason (see ch. 11, "the personal theory") is adopted, we can assume that the prob-

Table 17.10. *Demonstration of the effect of ambiguity*

| | 30 red balls | 60 balls[a] | |
		Black	Yellow
Option X	$100	$ 0	$0
Option Y	0	100	0

[a] The relative number of black and yellow balls is unknown.

Table 17.11. *A different set of outcomes with the same urn as in Table 17.10*

| | 30 Red | 60 balls[a] | |
		Black	Yellow
Option V	$100	$ 0	$100
Option W	0	100	100

[a] The relative number of black and yellow balls is unknown.

ability of winning is ⅓, given either option, and we conclude that we ought to be indifferent between the two options.

Now consider the options listed in Table 17.11. In this example, most subjects prefer option W, because they "know" that their chance of winning is ⅔, whereas their chance of winning with option V could be as low as ⅓ or as high as 1. (Again, the principle of insufficient reason would dictate indifference.)

Together, this pattern of choices violates the independence principle, since subjects reversed their choice merely because the "yellow" column was changed. By the independence principle, this column should be ignored, because it is identical for the two options in each pair.

Many of us, nonetheless, feel a strong temptation to make the choices as Ellsberg's subjects (mostly economists) did, choosing X and W. Becker and Brownson (1964) have even found that subjects will pay money to avoid making choices in which the probabilities seem to be "unknown." Ellsberg used the term *ambiguity* for this kind of unknown risk. A situation in which the "probability is unknown" is called *ambiguous*.[16]

Effects of ambiguity can influence our responses to real risks in the world (Slovic, Lichtenstein, & Fischhoff, 1984). Some risks, such as those of nuclear power and DNA technology ("genetic engineering"), are perceived as ambiguous, and others, such as the risk of accidents in coal mining (which is

[16] Ellsberg cites a distinction that economists (such as Knight, 1921) made between "risk" and "uncertainty," the latter term covering what Ellsberg meant by "ambiguity."

very high), are perceived as known. If ambiguity affects our social choices, we will opt for the known risks over the unknown ones – perhaps wrongly.

Another real-life example concerns the risk calculations used to set the rates for insurance premiums. Insurance companies base these premiums on statistics – for example, for automobile insurance, statistics about the frequency and cost of car accidents among various groups of drivers. Insurance companies are always reluctant to cover unknown risks, such as the risk of military attack for the tanker ships that were bringing oil out of Iran during the early days of the Iran–Iraq war (without insurance, the tankers would not attempt the voyage). When policies to cover unusual risks like that are provided (often by the famous Lloyds of London consortium, which pools capital from several sources), subjective probability estimates are used instead of observed frequencies. These subjective estimates are felt to be ambiguous, and Lloyds charges higher premiums than they would if the same probabilities were based on frequency data. (This principle may also be involved in the high cost of medical malpractice insurance in the United States, reflecting the insurance industry's feeling that there is "ambiguity" about national trends in the size and fairness of damage awards.) Hogarth and Kunreuther (in press) have shown how such factors can lead to the total breakdown of markets for insurance.

Rationality of the ambiguity effect

As argued already, ambiguity effects violate the independence principle. In chapter 16, I argued that this principle is normative, since outcomes that do not depend on our choice and that do not occur (such as the outcome determined by "yellow," if the ball is not yellow) should not affect our utilities for outcomes that do occur (such as the outcomes determined by red or black balls).

The personal theory of probability (ch. 11) implies that the idea of "unknown" probabilities makes little sense. Because probabilities are properties of the person, not the world, the only way in which a probability could be "unknown" is for a person not to have reflected enough about the situation. To say that a probability is "unknown" is to assume that probabilities can be known only if relative frequencies have been observed or if the possibilities can be analyzed logically into exchangeable alternatives.

Let us reexamine the ambiguity effect described in the Ellsberg experiment. Looking more carefully, we can see that any argument for option X (or W) can be matched by a comparable argument for option Y (or V). Yes, it *could* be the case (in deciding between option X and option Y) that the urn has 60 yellow balls, and this is an argument for option X, but it could also turn out that the urn contains 60 black balls, and this is an equally strong argument for option X. We conclude that there is no good reason to prefer option X over Y. If we are not indifferent, we seem to be contradicting a very fundamental principle of decision making: When there are equally strong reasons in favor of two choices, then there is no overall reason to prefer one option or the other. (Likewise, if we must pay extra in order to make option X, we would be irrational to choose option X, because there is one reason to favor option Y that is not matched by an equivalent reason for option X – namely, the need to pay.)

Ultimately, I would argue, the ambiguity effect is another kind of framing effect, dependent on the way a problem is described. If we were given a great many choices like X and Y, but with *different urns*, we could assume that red and black would be drawn equally often over the whole sequence of choices. (If we do not assume this, then we must have some reason to think that one color is more likely than the other, and we would always bet on that color – choosing X and V, or Y and W, consistently and therefore not violating the independence axiom.) Therefore, a choice between X and Y is just a choice between one member of a sequence in which the red and black are equally likely. It would not do any injustice to describe the situation that way. If the situation were described this way, there would be no difference between the Ellsberg situation and one in which the probabilities were "known."

On the other hand, consider an apparently unambiguous case, in which an urn has 50 red balls and 50 white ones. It would seem that the probability of a red ball is .5, but think about the top layer of balls, from which the ball will actually be drawn. We have no idea what the proportion of red balls is in that layer; it could be anywhere from 100% to 0%, just like the proportion of black to yellow balls in the original example. By thinking about the situation in this way, we have turned an unambiguous situation into an ambiguous one.

In sum, ambiguity may be a result of our perception that important information is missing from the description of the decision. In the last example, we brought out the missing information by focusing attention on the top layer of balls. Information is always missing in any situation of uncertainty, though, and so we can make any situation ambiguous by attending to the missing information. Conversely, we can make any ambiguous situation into an unambiguous one by imagining it as one of a sequence of repeated trials.

Why, if the ambiguity effect conflicts with normative models, is it so compelling to some people? Slovic and Tversky (1974) found that many subjects stuck to their (nonnormative) choices of X and W even after they read an explanation of the independence axiom. One explanation hinges on our feeling that there is something we would very much like to know before we make the decision.[17] Of course, in any risky decision, we would like to know what the outcome will be, but in the "ambiguous" cases, there are more specific things we would like to know, such as the proportion of black balls in the urn, the intentions of the Iraqis, or the intentions of legislators concerning tort reform.

---

[17] See Frisch and Baron (in press) for other explanations of ambiguity effects.

Perhaps, then, we avoid ambiguous options because we really want to exercise another option: that of obtaining more information. When this other option *is* available – as it often is – it is perfectly rational to choose it, providing that the information is worth obtaining (see the discussion of the value of information in ch. 13). When the information is not available, however, or not worth the cost, we would do better to put aside our desire to obtain it and go ahead on the best evidence we have, even if it is "ambiguous" and even if we must use the principle of insufficient reason. More generally, we can think of our tendency to avoid ambiguous decisions as a useful heuristic that points us toward the option of obtaining more information. From a *prescriptive* point of view, we probably do well to follow a rule of thumb that tells us to avoid irreversible commitments when information is missing. If we can learn to put this rule aside when the missing information is truly unavailable, however, we shall achieve our goals more fully in the long run.

Conclusion

We have seen in this chapter that several factors – not all fully understood – lead us to violate expected-utility theory in its simple form. Some apparent violations, such as those caused by regret or disappointment, are not necessarily violations at all. In these cases, an overly simple analysis could have neglected real emotional consequences of decisions. (It is also possible, however, that we sometimes fail to consider the option of trying to control our emotional responses in order to achieve other goals.)

Other violations of the theory, such as ambiguity effects, might result from our using generally useful heuristics in situations in which they are harmful rather than helpful in achieving our goals. Prescriptively, we would do well to learn to distinguish the different kinds of cases. (In the case of ambiguity, I argued that what matters is whether it is worthwhile to wait until we can obtain the information we see as missing.) If we thought more about the heuristics that govern our decisions, we might be able to learn when these heuristics are helpful shortcuts and when they are self-made blinders that prevent us from achieving our goals.

Certain violations concern neglect of goals, when several attributes are relevant to a choice. These illustrate a kind of single-mindedness that can result from insufficient search for goals. In other violations, we seem to attend largely to the most important difference, as in regret effects. A failure to search for evidence may be involved here.

These last violations of the theory, as well as the framing effects and probability distortions we discussed, provide additional arguments for the use of decision analysis as a tool for making important decisions. All of the violations in question occur in holistic judgments, but they can be avoided if utility theory is used to provide a "second opinion" for holistic decision making. The same violations, however, make it more difficult to use decision analysis: The method of gambles, in particular, can yield invalid measurements of utility, because it is distorted by the certainty effect.

The violations of utility theory discussed in this chapter indicate clearly that the options we choose are often not the ones that best achieve our goals in the long run. In view of these findings, we can no longer assume – as many economists do – that we always know what is best for us and express this knowledge in our choices. The question of how we should deal with these violations is not fully solved. I have suggested that actively open-minded thinking and the judicious use of decision analysis are parts of the answer to this question, but we may also need to learn new heuristics specifically for making decisions.

18   Quantitative judgment

Quantitative judgment is the evaluation of cases on the basis of a set of evidence and with respect to a set of criteria. Some judgments involve assigning numbers: for example, assigning grades to students' essays, salaries to employees, or sales quotas to sales people. Quantitative judgments can involve ranking people or things: ranking entrants in a beauty contest, applicants for graduate school (to be accepted in order of rank as places become available), or applicants for a job. In some cases, the judgment is basically a matter of determining whether a person or thing is above or below some cutoff point: For example, is this patient sufficiently depressed so as to require hospitalization? Quantitative judgment, then, consists of *rating*, assigning numbers or grades; *ranking*, putting things in order on some dimension; and *classifying*, which in this chapter will mean assigning something to one of two groups.

When we judge livestock, paintings, or automobiles with a view to purchasing, we are really making a decision about whether to purchase or how much to offer. We can think of judgments as those parts of decisions that involve inference. In most experiments on judgment, a subject is presented with the evidence and with the goal and is asked to use the evidence. For example, a subject might be given a student's test scores, grades, and disposable income and asked to judge the student's worthiness for a scholarship on a 100-point scale, or a subject might be given a list of adjectives describing a person and asked to judge the person's generosity.

The study of judgment is closely related to Multiattribute Utility Theory (MAUT) (discussed in ch. 16). In most judgment tasks that have been studied, the cases to be judged can be described in terms of a set of attributes, just as if MAUT were going to be applied.

A major question in the study of judgment concerns the relative efficacy of unaided holistic judgment – in which the judge simply assigns a number to each case – and judgment aided by the use of calculations like those done in MAUT. The answers to this question have strong implications for decision making in government, business, and the professions, and in any situation where important decisions are made about a number of cases described on the same dimensions.

Table 18.1. *Measures used in regression example*

Abbreviation	Definition
GPA	High school grade point average on a scale from 0 to 4.0.
SAT	Total Scholastic Aptitude Test Score on a scale up to 1600.
REC	A rating summarizing the letters of recommendation on a scale from 1 to 5. This rating is assigned by an admissions officer who reads the letters of recommendation and assigns the number.[a]
ESS	A rating of the student's own essay on a 1 to 5 scale.

[a] Notice that here a judgment is used as input for another judgment.

Multiple linear regression

Most of the literature on judgment has looked at situations in which each of a number of possibilities, such as applicants for college, is characterized by several numbers. Each number represents a value on some dimension, or *cue*, such as grades or quality of recommendations. The judge's task is to evaluate each possibility with respect to some goal or goals, such as college grades as a criterion of success in college. Each dimension or cue has a high and low end with respect to the goal; for example, high test scores are assumed to be better than low test scores. In these situations a certain kind of normative model is assumed to apply, specifically, a statistical model called *multiple linear regression* (or just *regression*, for short). Let me illustrate in the following example.

Suppose that we are admissions officers at a college, and our task is to rate several applicants. For each applicant, we have the ratings, scores and other information given in Table 18.1. Suppose also that we have a computer, and we want to discover a formula for predicting the applicant's *college* grade-point average, which we call COL.

We have data on a number of students who are now at the college. For each student, we know the four variables given in the table (SAT, the aptitude test score; REC, a rating of the letters of recommendation; ESS, a rating of the essay; and GPA, high school grades), and we know COL. What we want is a predictive index, PRE, a measure that comes as close as possible to predicting COL for the new applicants from the four other variables. Table 18.2 shows, for 10 of the college students, the four variables, the college grades (COL), and the predictive index (PRE). The last column is the error in each prediction, the difference between PRE and COL. PRE was calculated using a computer program for multiple linear regression (a technique described in detail in most modern statistics texts). The numbers in the first five columns were typed into the computer. The regression program was told to assume that COL is a linear function of the four other variables – that is, to assume that the following equation is true:

Table 18.2. *Data and prediction* (PRE) *for regression example*

Student	COL	Predictors SAT	REC	ESS	GPA	PRE	Error
1	3.8	1500	4.0	4.0	4.0	3.910	0.110
2	3.6	1310	4.0	3.0	3.6	2.902	− 0.698
3	3.5	1300	5.0	3.0	3.9	3.560	0.060
4	3.2	1280	3.0	5.0	3.7	3.428	0.228
5	3.0	1260	4.0	4.0	3.5	2.921	− 0.079
6	2.8	1210	3.0	4.0	3.4	2.631	− 0.169
7	2.5	1320	5.0	3.0	3.5	2.807	0.307
8	2.2	1220	4.0	3.0	3.2	2.129	− 0.071
9	2.0	1200	2.0	5.0	3.0	1.997	− 0.003
10	1.5	1170	3.0	2.0	3.2	1.811	0.311

$$COL = a \cdot SAT + b \cdot REC + c \cdot ESS + d \cdot GPA + e + error$$

The error is a different number for each student, but each of the other coefficients – a, b, c, d, and e – is the same for all students. The coefficients a through d may be seen as weights; they indicate how much each of the variables (SAT, and so forth) affects COL. The coefficient e is a constant that is added or subtracted so that the mean predicted COL comes out right. The computer figures out the values of a, b, c, d, and e so as to make the error as small as possible. (Usually the computer does this by minimizing the mean of the squares of the error values.) Once we know the values of the coefficients, PRE is found by using the same equation but without the error:

$$PRE = a \cdot SAT + b \cdot REC + c \cdot ESS + d \cdot GPA + e$$

PRE would be as close as we can come to predicting COL with this kind of formula, if all we knew were the other four variables. Using the data given in Table 18.2, the values of a through e, respectively, are 0.000175 (for SAT); 0.092 (for REC); 0.217 (for ESS); 1.893 (for GPA); and − 5.161 (the constant e added at the end). Therefore, the equation for PRE is as follows:

$$PRE = 0.000175 \cdot SAT + 0.092 \cdot REC + 0.217 \cdot ESS + 1.893 \cdot GPA - 5.161$$

Notice that the constant (− 5.161) would not be needed if all we wanted to do were to compare students with one another. What we are trying to do, though, is to compare the four variables with each other, to determine their relative importance. The four values a through d represent the relative importance of each of the four variables.[1]

---

[1] A better measure of importance would take into account the amount of variation on each variable. In this case, SATs would be more important, because they vary by hundreds of points instead of just a few.

Notice that SAT is unimportant in the formula. Notice also, however, that SAT *does* correlate with COL: The student with the highest COL got the highest SAT, and the two students with the lowest COL got the two lowest SATs. How could this happen? The answer is that SAT correlates with GPA in high school, and GPA in high school *also* correlates with COL. The reason that SAT correlates with COL appears to be that it correlates with GPA. Here, SAT seems to measure something like the ability to get good grades, but it does not measure this as well as the grades themselves. If we did not know high school GPA, then the SAT *would* be a useful predictor of COL in this example.

This example is, of course, overly simple in many ways. In deciding whom to admit to college, there are other predictors to consider aside from these four factors, and there are other things to predict besides college grades. Many of these variables can be expressed as numbers, but when we apply a numerical formula of this sort we may always run across unusual cases that require us either to make exceptions or add a variable to the formula for the benefit of a single case. Would it make sense to include a measure of every applicant's criminal record, when probably only a few applicants have any record at all?

Moreover, the idea of a formula might be too simple. The basic idea of the model – that everything is multiplied by a weight representing its importance and all of the values are then added together – might be wrong. One way in which the model could be wrong is that there might be an *interaction* between two variables; this means that the *importance* (or weight) of one variable depends on the *value* of the other. For example, perhaps we should weigh REC more when a student does poorly on the Scholastic Aptitude Test; this would amount to accepting students who did well either on that test or in REC (or both), no matter how badly they might have done on one of the measures. Thus, when one of these two measures was high, the other would not matter.

Another way in which the model could be wrong is that some variables might not have a simply linear effect: The importance of a variable might be different for different parts of its range. For example, the difference between an SAT of 1100 and one of 1200 might be much more important than the difference between an SAT of 1300 and one of 1400. The effect of the SAT would then be *curvilinear* rather than linear. (We might want to use for our calculations something such as the square root of SAT rather than SAT itself.) We shall return to this question.

The lens model

Suppose we asked an admissions official to predict COL (college grades) without the benefit of the formula. We could then obtain a list of judgments that we could place beside the true values for comparison, as shown in Table

Table 18.3. *Data for regression example, with judgments* (JUD)

Student	COL	Predictors SAT	REC	ESS	GPA	PRE	JUD
1	3.8	1500	4.0	4.0	4.0	3.910	4.0
2	3.6	1310	4.0	3.0	3.6	2.902	3.1
3	3.5	1300	5.0	3.0	3.9	3.560	3.8
4	3.2	1280	3.0	5.0	3.7	3.428	3.4
5	3.0	1260	4.0	4.0	3.5	2.921	3.0
6	2.8	1210	3.0	4.0	3.4	2.631	2.7
7	2.5	1320	5.0	3.0	3.5	2.807	3.0
8	2.2	1220	4.0	3.0	3.2	2.129	2.3
9	2.0	1200	2.0	5.0	3.0	1.997	1.9
10	1.5	1170	3.0	2.0	3.2	1.811	2.1

18.3. We could then ask several questions about these judgments. For example, we could ask how close they come to the true values, or whether the judgments themselves could be predicted from the four main variables, and so on.

One useful way to think about this kind of situation is the *lens model*, based on the work of Brunswik (1952), Hammond (1955), and others. This term results from the sort of diagram shown in Figure 18.1, which is supposed to look something like light rays being focused by a lens. Each line in the diagram represents a relationship, usually a correlation. (Some possible lines of correlation are left out of my diagram.) Each variable has a particular role. COL is the *criterion*, the thing to be predicted. JUD is the *judgment* provided by the judge. PRE is the value of COL predicted from the regression formula.

The new idea in the diagram is MUD (the Model of the jUDge). This is what we get if we try to predict JUD from the four main variables, just as we originally tried to predict COL from these variables. MUD is a *model of the judge*, just as PRE is a model of the criterion. In this example, MUD is based on the following equation:

$$MUD = 0 \cdot SAT + 0.1 \cdot REC + 0.1 \cdot ESS + 2.0 \cdot GPA - 4.8$$

Compared to PRE, the judge depends a little too much on GPA (2.0 for the judge versus 1.893 for PRE) and not enough on ESS (0.1 versus 0.217). This leads the judge, for example, to predict too high for student 10, whose ESS rating was very low. On the whole, however, the judge does well, almost as well as the formula for PRE. (Because that formula was chosen to minimize error, the judge cannot possibly do as well on evaluating these students' potential, unless the judge uses the same formula.)

Notice that the correlation between MUD and JUD is perfect (1.00) in this case. MUD is identical to JUD. This is not the usual case. It seems that

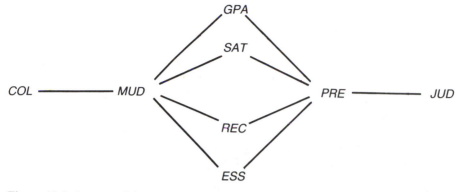

Figure 18.1. Lens model.

our judge was calculating rather than making an intuitive judgment, but the judge was not using quite the best formula for the calculations.

We can use the lens model to answer a great variety of questions about judgment in particular situations. Most of these judgment situations are quite similar to the one in the example just given. A judge is asked to predict some numerical criterion, such as stock prices, success in school or work, livestock quality, or *COL*, from a set of numerical predictors. The predictors (or the criterion) themselves sometimes represent summaries of other judgments. There is reason to think that each of the predictors might be related to the criterion in a simple way – that is, by either a positive or a negative correlation. Let us consider some of the questions about such judgments, and their answers.

Which does better, the judge or the best-fitting model of the data (PRE)? In practically every study in which this question has been asked, the answer is that the model does better over a set of judgments. When possible, it is always better to use a formula than an individual human judgment (Meehl, 1954; Goldberg, 1970; Dawes, 1971, 1979; Dawes & Corrigan, 1974; Camerer, 1981). This has been found in studies of the judgment of psychoticism (from personality-test profiles), graduate student success, success of people in various jobs, and future stock prices.

Which does better, the judge (JUD) *or the model of the judge* (MUD)? Again, in practically every study, the answer is that the model of the judge does better than the judge. Suppose we have a judgment task such as predicting college grades, and we have a judge who claims to be able to do it. Consider two ways we could proceed. The first is to have the judge make judgments of every case. The second is to have the judge make judgments of a number of cases, enough so that we can find a formula that predicts *the judge's judgments*. Then we would tell the judge to go home, and we would use the formula for all the cases, including those the judge already judged. The fact is that the second method is better than the first, even for the cases that the judge already judged. (Note that we are using the formula for predicting the *judgments*, not the formula for predicting what the judge is trying to predict. The latter formula, when we can find it, works even better at predicting the criterion.)

This is a rather surprising result. Why does it happen? Basically, it happens because the judge cannot be consistent with his own policy (unless, like our judge in the example, he calculates on his own). He is unreliable, in that he is likely to judge the same case differently on different occasions (unless he recognizes the case the second time). As Goldberg (1970, p. 423) puts it,

> The clinician is not a machine. While he possesses his full share of human learning and hypothesis-generating skills, he lacks the machine's reliability. He "has his days": Boredom, fatigue, illness, situational and interpersonal distractions all plague him, with the result that his repeated judgments of the exact same stimulus configurations are not identical. He is subject to all those human frailties which lower the reliability of his judgments below unity. And if the judge's reliability is less than unity, there must be error in his judgments – error which can serve no other purpose but to attenuate his accuracy. If we could remove some of this human unreliability by eliminating the random error in his judgments, we should thereby increase the validity of the resulting predictions.

We can, however, think of reasons why the judge might still be better than the model of himself. In particular, there might be interactions or curvilinear relations (nonlinearities) that are not represented in the linear models we have been considering. It might really be true that SATs are more important in the middle range than the higher range, for example. If this were true, the judge would be able to take it into account, and the linear model of the judge would not.

The judge might also have additional information not included in the linear model, such as observations made during a personal interview with the applicant. This gives the judge an unfair advantage over the model, however, since it is possible for the judge to assign numerical ratings to that information and include it in the model.

The fact is that in the great variety of situations examined so far, interactions and nonlinearities have never been as important as the error to which Goldberg refers. There are sometimes nonlinearities and interactions in the true situation, and there are sometimes nonlinearities and interactions in the judge's judgments, but the nonlinearities and interactions expressed in his actual judgments have little to do with the nonlinearities and interactions actually present (Camerer, 1981).[2]

In general, then, it is better to use the formula than the judge, because the formula eliminates the error. This method is called *bootstrapping*. We pull ourselves up by our bootstraps: We improve our judgment by modeling ourselves. A good example of the successful use of bootstrapping methods is

---

[2] We have already seen, however, an exception to this generalization in the study of concept learning discussed in chapter 5, where it was found that subjects could make use of interactions between pairs of features in deciding whether a stimulus was a member of a category.

a formula devised by Gustafson, Tianen, and Greist (1981), which predicts suicide attempts in psychiatric patients on the basis of variables that can be assessed in clinical interviews (such as extent of suicide plans and degree of isolation from other people). The predictions are more accurate than those made holistically by the judges.

When we use bootstrapping to make decisions, we estimate weights from holistic decisions, rather than from systematic considerations of tradeoffs; we calculate the weights so as to best explain a person's holistic ratings.[3] Although bootstrapping does better than holistic judgments, it is still derived from such judgments. We noted in chapter 17 that less important dimensions will be underweighed in holistic judgments. Bootstrapping does solve the problem of random error, but it does not remove the effects of this underweighing. Studies have found that in a bootstrapping procedure the dimensions considered less important in fact receive less weight, relative to other dimensions, than in a MAUT procedure (von Winterfeldt & Edwards, sec. 10.4). In addition, bootstrapping led to greater disagreement among judges than MAUT.

Another way to reduce judgment error is to average the judgment of several different judges. When this is done, the errors of different judges tend to cancel each other out. Such *composite* judgments are indeed more accurate than judgments made by individuals. If enough judges are used, they may do as well as a formula based on the composites themselves. Goldberg (1970) examined the ability of 29 clinical psychologists to predict the diagnosis of mental patients ("psychotic" versus "neurotic") from test profiles. The best prediction was accomplished by the composite of the 29 judges. A model of the composite did a little worse, but not significantly so. Next best was a model of the average *individual judge*, and worst of all was the average individual judge alone. Although use of many judges for prediction may help, it is much more time-consuming than use of a single judge. The model of the group may be best of all, taking efficiency into account.

Formulas may do better than judges even when there is no objective way at all to measure the criterion. For example, suppose we wanted to judge desirability of prospective graduate students, on the basis of GREs (Graduate Record Examination scores), college GPAs, and ratings of letters and essays, for the purpose of admitting candidates to graduate school. We do not know, in this case, what "desirability" means. It is not the same as grades in graduate school, for nebulous things such as quality of scholarship are important as well. What we do is to take a judge, or a committee of judges, and ask them to rate a number of prospective students. We then find a formula (MUD) that accounts for *their judgments* (JUD). We tell the judges to go home, and we use the formula.

Because of the findings that MUD is better than JUD at predicting an

---

[3] We also assume that the utility scales are linear.

objective criterion, we can assume with some confidence that here, too, *MUD* would do better, *if there were an objective criterion*. The fact that there is not can hardly be expected to affect the superiority of *MUD* over *JUD*. We can be confident that we are doing better with the formula than with the formula derived from the judge's judgments, even when we cannot measure how much better we are doing. Another advantage of a method like this is that it may prevent complex judgments from being reduced to single numbers, such as use of grades alone as a measure of academic success or (in war) body counts of enemy soldiers as a measure of military success.

Do we need the judge at all? Dawes (1979) points out that in most situations of interest the variables we use to make predictions tend to be correlated with each other. For example, grades, *SAT*s, and recommendations tend to be correlated; a student who does well on one measure tends to do well on others. In such cases, the precise weight we give to each variable does not make much difference. If we overweigh one variable and underweigh another, and if the two are correlated, our judgments (in relative terms) will not be very different. In our example, the judge did almost as well as the ideal model even though he weighed things somewhat differently.

What this implies is that we can often do quite well if we simply know *which* variables to use (and in which direction). For example, in our case concerning graduate students, an expert might tell us that grades, recommendations, and essays were all important, but *SAT*s were not. (It would not have produced such different results if we had used *SAT*s.) Often, consulting an expert is not really necessary. Of course, there are cases, such as medical diagnosis, in which a nonexpert has no idea what is relevant. Would you know which measures to look at in order to determine whether someone has diabetes? In such cases, an expert can go a long way simply by knowing what is relevant, whether she weighs it correctly or not.

When we use the method of weighing all predictors equally, we must make sure that they are all expressed in the same sort of units. In our *COL* example, *REC*, *ESS*, and *GPA* have about the same range, but *SAT* has a much larger range. If we simply added up the predictors, *SAT* alone would determine the ranking, so the predictors would not be weighed "equally" at all. The way this problem is usually handled is to divide each predictor by the *standard deviation* of that predictor. The standard deviation is – like the range between the highest and lowest scores – a measure of the extent to which that predictor varies across all the cases (here students).[4] In our *COL* example, the standard deviations of the predictors are: *SAT*, 89; *REC*, 0.90; *ESS*, 0.92; and *GPA*, 0.30.

Dawes (1979) describes a number of cases in which such an equal-weighting method has been used with apparent success. In those cases in which the

---

[4] The standard deviation is essentially the square root of the average difference between each score and the average score.

question can be asked, the equal-weighting model did better than the judge by himself. So great is the judge's unreliability that we can do better than the judge (in most cases) by knowing only which variables are relevant.

Why are people so resistant to the making of decisions by formula? Universities and colleges typically pay an admissions staff substantial amounts to read each application and weigh all of the variables. Faculty members do the same for applicants to graduate school and applicants for jobs. Business managers devote great time and effort to such matters as the setting of sales and production quotas. In all of these cases, there is a need for human judgment, to be sure; somebody has to read the letters of recommendation and (at least) assign numbers to them, but there is no apparent need for the human judge when it comes to combining all of the various pieces into a single overall judgment. This is done better by formula.

Many people say that they are reluctant to use formulas because they want to be free to use a special policy for special cases: Among graduate-school applicants, for example, the foreigner whose poor command of English keeps *SAT* scores down or the handicapped person who has overcome enormous odds just to meet minimal admission standards, and so on. This is not a good reason to reject formulas altogether. These cases do not have to be ignored when we use the formula. We can include a "special factors" variable in our formula, or omit tainted data (such as a verbal *SAT* score for foreigners), or we can simply scan through the pile of applicants looking for such exceptions and judge just these individually.

Another explanation of the reluctance to use formulas is that the judgment procedure often has other goals besides simply making the best judgment. For example, when my own department admits graduate students, the admissions committee asks faculty members who are likely to get these students in their laboratories to make an overall evaluation of each such applicant. The admissions committee does this not because it believes, for example, that a physiological psychologist is a better judge of physiological applicants than the committee is; rather, it wants to alert faculty members who are not on the committee to the fact that certain students may end up working in their laboratories. (A memorandum to this effect would technically serve the purpose, but it is well known that many of us do not read memos.)

Another objection to formulas is the argument that individuals cannot be (or should not be) reduced to a single number. This is essentially the objection I made to the idea of IQ as a single measure of intelligence in chapter 7. When we put individuals in rank order for some purpose, however, we are already reducing them to a single scale. The only issue is whether we do it well or badly given all the goals we ought to have.

Many of the people who object to the use of formulas are unaware of a hidden cause for their belief – *overconfidence* in their own powers of judgment. Psychologists have found this overconfidence factor elsewhere, in probability judgments (see ch. 12) and in such other phenomena as the overuse of interviews for evaluating applicants. Hiring and admissions personnel often feel that they need a personal interview with each of many applicants, as though the 15- or 30-minute sample of behavior will stack up against the 4 years of data represented in a student's transcript and recommendations or the 10 years in a resumé. Evidence suggests that interviews ordinarily add nothing to the validity of prediction based on all other data that are usually available (Schmitt, 1976). If you were choosing members of an Olympic team, would you set up a 30-minute tryout or look at each person's track record (literally) over the last few years? An interview, of course, is like a 30-minute tryout.[5]

Overconfidence in judgment has been found in an experiment by Arkes, Dawes, and Christensen (1986), who asked college-student subjects to choose which of three baseball players had won the "Most Valuable Player Award" of the National League in each of the years from 1940 to 1961 (excluding those years in which pitchers won the award). Subjects were given the batting average, the number of home runs hit, the number of runs batted in, and the position of the player's team, for each of the three players listed for each year. Subjects were told – correctly – that the position of the player's team was an extremely useful cue, which would lead to 14 correct choices out of 19 if it was the sole basis for the judgment. Subjects who knew more about baseball (as determined from their answers to a baseball quiz) were more confident in their ability to "beat" the simple rule they had been given concerning team position. As a result of this confidence, they used the position rule less often and were actually less accurate in choosing the award winner (9.4 correct out of 19) than were other subjects with more modest knowledge of baseball (11.4 correct). Neither group of subjects did as well as they could have done by taking the experimenter's advice and attending only to team position. Overconfidence can be exacerbated by expertise.

We are not always, or usually, good judges of our own ability as judges. As a result, we waste a great deal of effort making judgments that could be made more accurately by formula. The use of a formula guarantees that errors will be made. With human judgment, there is at least a vain hope that judgments will be perfect. As Einhorn (1986) puts it, we need to "accept error to make less error."

When we, as applicants, are rejected for a job or a school by a formula, we feel that an error is likely; the formula could not possibly have seen our special attributes (even though the teachers who gave us the grades and wrote the letters of recommendation, whose ratings go into the formula, had every opportunity to do so). When we are rejected by a person, we are more likely to feel that the rejection was based on real knowledge, yet, as we have seen, people make more errors than formulas (if we use people's judgments of specific dimensions as inputs).

[5] On the other hand, an interview, even by telephone, may provide important information not usually included in a resumé, such as how serious the candidate's interest in the position in question is.

A warning is in order lest anyone get carried away with the idea of replacing human judges with computers, or even hand calculators. Although many of the objections to formulas are (arguably) mere mystical rhetoric, one is worth heeding. This is that the use of formulas may encourage us to use only the predictors that are easily quantified. For example, in admitting students to graduate school, we might tend to rely too heavily on test scores and grades and not enough on recommendations or research papers. If admissions committees do this, then students will overemphasize tests and grades too, as they prepare themselves for graduate school. The solution to this problem is to turn recommendations and research papers into numbers so that they can be included in a formula. Indeed, in most of the examples given so far in this chapter, the *input* to the judgment process has consisted of other judgments, for which human judges are necessary. In many of the situations in which formulas are useful, the numbers are already available; for example, college admissions offices make ratings on applicants' essays, and even on their overall "sparkle," although these numbers are not included in a formula.

The research that I have been discussing does not suggest that formulas should replace people altogether. It suggests, rather, that formulas should replace people *at the single task of combining a set of piecemeal judgments into an overall summary score.* That is all: and, for most judgments, that is not a very big part of the total effort.

The mechanism of judgment

Do judges really weigh cues numerically? The question is particularly acute when the task involves classifying stimuli into two categories (such as "neurotic" and "psychotic") on the basis of numerical predictors. A reasonable alternative strategy, it might seem, is to set cutoff points on each predictor. In order to be classified as psychotic, for example, a patient would have to exceed the cutoff point on a certain number of predictors (perhaps one, perhaps all). Although such a strategy would probably not be optimal, since it throws away information about how far from the cutoff point each patient is, we might use it anyway because it is easy. (A patient who is far above the cutoff point on one predictor and just below it on another is probably more likely to be psychotic than one who is just above the cutoff on both, yet the use of a strategy requiring both cutoff points to be exceeded would classify the former patient as neurotic and the latter as psychotic.)

Thinking-aloud protocols have been used to study judgment tasks (as well as other thinking tasks), and these results suggest that individual judges often use some sort of cutoff strategy (Payne, 1976; Einhorn, Kleinmuntz, & Kleinmuntz, 1979). Here are some fictional protocols (from Einhorn and his colleagues, p. 473) of a typical judge deciding whether a patient is psychologically "adjusted" or "maladjusted," on the basis of three numerical cues, x_1, x_2, and x_3, which represent scores on various psychological tests:

Case 1. I'll look at x_1 first – it's pretty high ... the x_2 score is also high. This is a maladjusted profile.

Case 2. Let's see, x_1 is high but ... x_2 is low, better check x_3 – it's low, too. I would say this is adjusted.

Case 3. This person's x_1 score is low. Better check both x_2 and x_3 then – both pretty high. Ummm ... likely to be maladjusted.

Case 4. x_1 is fairly low here ... x_2 is quite high ... this is an interesting case ... x_3 is very low ... I'd say adjusted.

Case 5. x_1 is extremely high – this is maladjusted.

Case 6. x_1 is an iffy score ... let's see x_2 and x_3. Both are mildly indicative of pathology – I guess, that taking all three are pointing in the same direction, call this maladjusted.

Einhorn and his colleagues point out that these protocols can be described in terms of various rules involving cutoffs. For case 1, it looks as though the judge is applying some sort of cutoff point to the x_1 and x_2 scores. If these are high enough, she does not look at x_3. In case 2, it looks as though there is a rule instructing her to look at x_3 when the other cues conflict. Case 4 is "interesting," because two cues that are usually correlated conflict. In case 5, it looks as though the judge is applying another cutoff point to x_1; if x_1 is sufficiently high, she does not look at the other cues at all.

Einhorn and his colleagues point out that these protocols are also consistent with the use of a "compensatory" strategy more in line with the linear model itself. For example, suppose that the scores were all on a 1 to 10 scale, and the judge's linear model was the following formula:

$$y = .6 \cdot x_1 + .2 \cdot x_2 + .2 \cdot x_3.$$

The patient is called maladjusted if the score y is 5 or greater. The six cases could then be represented like this:

1. $y = .6 \cdot 7 + .2 \cdot 6 = 5.4$ (maladjusted)
2. $y = .6 \cdot 7 + .2 \cdot 1 + .2 \cdot 2 = 4.8$ (adjusted)
3. $y = .6 \cdot 3 + .2 \cdot 8 + .2 \cdot 8 = 5.0$ (maladjusted)
4. $y = .6 \cdot 4 + .2 \cdot 9 + .2 \cdot 1 = 4.4$ (adjusted)
5. $y = .6 \cdot 10 = 6$ (maladjusted)
6. $y = .6 \cdot 5 + .2 \cdot 6 + .2 \cdot 6 = 4.4$ (adjusted)

The reason for not looking at x_3 in case 1, then, is that the first two cues are sufficient to put the case above the cutoff point. Likewise, x_1 alone does this in case 5. The judge could be using a compensatory rule, based on a weighted combination of all three attributes, and yet could still appear to be using something like cutoff points applied to individual attributes.

In sum, the use of protocols here may be misleading if it leads us to think that judges are not using some sort of subjective weighing scheme much like the linear model itself. Thus the linear model may be a good description of what judges actually do, even though evidence from protocols appears initially to suggest that it is not. Of course, judges are not entirely consistent in the way they weigh various cues, and they may not be consistent in their protocols either. It is this inconsistency that makes the use of a formula attractive.

Impression formation

Linear models can be applied even when the stimuli to be judged are not presented in the form of numbers. The *impression-formation* task invented by Asch (1946) is a good example. Asch was interested in the basic processes by which we form impressions of other people's personalities. His experimental procedure involved a very simple situation in which some of these processes could be studied. The subject was given a list of adjectives describing a particular person and was instructed to make some judgment about the person on the basis of these adjectives. For example, Asch told subjects in one group that a certain person was "intelligent, skillful, industrious, warm, determined, practical, cautious." Subjects were asked to make judgments about this person on other dimensions, such as those defined by the adjectives "generous versus ungenerous." (Try it.) Another group of subjects was given the description "intelligent, skillful, industrious, cold, determined, practical, cautious" and asked to make the same judgment. Notice that the two descriptions are identical except for the words "warm" and "cold."

Asch (a Gestalt psychologist) found that the first group tended to make many more positive judgments than the second group. He suggested that the subjects formed impressions of a person as a whole. The parts worked together to create an overall impression, which, in turn, affected the meaning of the various parts. For example, when he asked subjects to give a synonym of the word "intelligent" in the two descriptions, subjects given the second description tended to give synonyms such as "calculating," whereas those in the first group gave synonyms such as "clever." The terms "warm" and "cold" seemed to be *central* to the whole description. They appeared to affect the meanings of the other terms (which Asch called *peripheral*).

Asch's account makes sense intuitively, but it has been questioned by many investigators (see Anderson, 1981, for a review). An alternative explanation (to Asch's) of the findings concerning synonyms (of words such as "intelligent," for example) is that the subjects found it difficult to follow the instructions to give a synonym only of the word they were told to attend to. The word "calculating," for instance, is in fact an associate of the word "cold." Subjects might have associated to the word "cold" itself, or perhaps to both "cold" and "intelligent" in combination – but without the meaning of "intelligent" changing under the influence of the word "cold" (Anderson, 1981, p. 216).

The rest of Asch's results can be explained by a simple algebraic model, a variant of the linear regression model. Each adjective has a certain weight on each scale. For example, "warm" has a very high weight on the scale from "generous" to "ungenerous," and "cold" has a very low weight. (This is because we generally think that warm people are generous. The reason we think this is not relevant to the controversy at hand.) Anderson (1981) points out that a good account of all the results can be obtained by assuming that the subject *averages* the weights of the separate adjectives on the scale in question. If "generous" has a value of $+10$ and "ungenerous" has a value of -10, "warm" by itself might have a value of $+6$ and "cold" a value of -6. "Intelligent" might have a value of $+1$ by itself. A person described as warm and intelligent would have an average of $(6+1) \div 2$ or 3.5, which would come close to the subject's rating.

The averaging model applies to a great many judgments of the sort we have been discussing, judgments whose stimuli can be decomposed into separate attributes or features. For example, in one study (Anderson & Butzin, 1978), children were asked to play Santa Claus. Their task was to give a "fair share" of toys to other children, each of whom was described in terms of need (how many toys they already had) and their achievement (how many dishes they had washed for their mothers). The subjects were sensitive to both variables, and the number of toys allotted to each child was a linear combination of the two variables (each given a certain weight).

The averaging model is completely consistent with the linear regression model. Of course, "averaging" implies dividing by the number of cues or dimensions. As long as the number of cues is held constant, however, we do not know whether a subject is adding their weights or averaging them. The results obtained in connection with the averaging model therefore provide additional support for the regression model as a description of behavior, and vice versa.

Averaging, adding, and the number of cues

As noted, the term "averaging" implies that subjects add up the impression from each cue and then divide by the number of cues.[6] In the experiments described so far, the number of cues is held constant, so, for all we know, subjects might simply be *adding* the impressions from the separate cues. They might then divide (or multiply) by some number that would be the same regardless of the number of cues, merely in order to produce responses that fell within a reasonable range. To find out whether subjects are adding or averaging, we need to vary the number of cues.

The simplest way to do this is to compare the effect of one cue and two cues. When this is done, presentation of two equally positive cues usually leads to a higher rating than either term alone but less than the sum of the two ratings. It would seem that subjects do something in between adding and

---

[6] Actually, each *scale* (for example, friendliness, intelligence) is assumed to have a different *weight* for a given judgment. These weights correspond to the coefficients a through e in the regression example. The weight depends on the relevance of the scale (for example, friendliness) to the judgment being made (for example, generosity). The value of each cue (for example, the word "friendly") on its own scale (for example, friendliness) is thus multiplied by this weight before being added. Then this sum is divided by the sum of the weights themselves, rather than just by the number of cues.

averaging. For example, if the personality rating (on a scale of "generosity" in which 0 represents neutrality) for "happy" alone were 3 and the rating for "friendly" alone were 3, the rating from the two together might be 4, which is higher than the average of 3 and 3 (that is, 3) but less than their sum (that is, 6).

To explain such findings (and others) Anderson assumes that subjects have some sort of starting point or initial impression (just from knowing that it was a *person* being described, perhaps) that had to be averaged in. Suppose that "happy" and "friendly" each has a weight of 6, and the initial impression has a value of 0. Given one of the terms, the average would be $(0 + 6) \div 2$ or 3. Given two of the terms, the average would be $(0 + 6 + 6) \div 3$, or 4.

Another kind of explanation of subjects' behavior holds that they often "fill in" missing values, which they then use to make their final judgment. A subject told that a subject is "happy" might fill in the "neutral" value of friendliness, or predict the value of friendliness from the value of happiness (by assuming that happy people are friendly, for example) – or do neither. Following this filling in (if it occurs) subjects might either add or average the values at hand.[7] For example, the hypothetical result just described could be explained if the adding model were true and if subjects took a happiness value of 3 to imply a friendliness value of 1 (and vice versa), since $3+1=4$. If this kind of explanation can be given, adding and averaging models may be difficult to distinguish.

Subjects might differ from one another in their choice among these strategies, and they might change what they do from trial to trial or from situation to situation. Although there is evidence that some subjects do infer missing values in some situations (Yamagishi & Hill, 1981; Levin, Johnson, & Farone, 1984), the full range of possibilities remains to be investigated.

In certain situations, an adding model seems to be normatively correct, and in these situations departures from that model lead to fallacious judgments. The clearest cases are those in which two cues are independent, which means that the value of one cannot be predicted at all from the value of the other. Although the cues are independent of each other, they are both relevant to prediction of a criterion. For example, suppose that in a certain pool of applicants for graduate school (let us say a pool from which applicants who clearly will be rejected have already been removed, perhaps by self-selection), amount of research experience and *GRE* scores are independent. Within this pool, *GRE* score and research experience are unrelated. Now suppose that the *GRE* score is missing for one applicant, and we make a judgment of acceptability on the basis of research experience alone. Since the applicant's research experience is near the top of our scale, we give the applicant a very high rating, compared to others in the pool. Then the applicant takes the

---

[7] Adding and averaging would be indistinguishable, if subjects *always* filled in missing values.

Graduate Record Examination, and the scores turn out to be a little better than the average of those in the pool. Should we raise our rating for this person or lower it?

Most people would lower it (Lichtenstein, Earle, & Slovic, 1975), but they should raise it. The lowering of the rating is just another example of subjects behaving roughly as though they were averaging the two cues; the second cue lowers the subjective average of the two. (Any account that explains departures from the adding model can explain this.)

Why should the rating be raised? Before we find out the applicant's *GRE*, our best guess is that it is at the average of the group. This is what we would guess if we knew nothing at all, and since the applicant's research experience is unrelated to *GRE*, we should still guess that the *GRE* is average after we knew about research experience. Therefore, when we find out that the student's *GRE* is a little better than average, we ought to think that this student is even *better* than we would have predicted when we did not know her *GRE*. (This argument depends on the cues being independent. If the cues are highly correlated, a moderate level of one should make us suspect the validity of a very high value on another.)

Representativeness in numerical prediction

The representativeness heuristic (discussed in chapter 12) seems to cause biases in quantitative judgment just as it causes biases in probability judgment. In the example I just gave, we expect the *GRE* to be above average because that kind of *GRE* score is more similar to (more representative of) the applicant's research experience than an average *GRE* score would be. We seem to have made a prediction based on similarity rather than on the normative model, which holds that we ought to ignore research experience – which is useless information because it is unrelated to *GRE* score – and to guess the average *GRE* score.

As another example, suppose you are told that a certain student ranked in the 90th percentile in terms of grade point average (*GPA*) in his first year of college. What is your best guess of the student's *GPA*? Suppose you say 3.5 (between *B* and *A*), because you think that this is the 90th percentile for *GPA*. (So far you have done nothing unreasonable.) Now what *GPA* would you predict for another student, who scored in the 90th percentile on a test of mental concentration? or for another student who scored in the 90th percentile on a test of sense of humor? Many subjects give the same prediction of 3.5 (Kahneman & Tversky, 1973, pp. 245–247). This may be because a *GPA* of 3.5 is most *similar* to the 90th percentile on the other measures.

In fact – as I shall explain shortly – your prediction should *regress* toward the mean (the average grade for the class, which was judged to be about 2.5 by Kahneman & Tversky's subjects), the worse the predictor is. In the extreme, if the subject were in the 90th percentile on shoe size, that would probably have no relation at all to grades, and your best guess would be that the student would have a *GPA* at the class mean of 2.5. Sense of humor is probably as useless as shoe size in its power to predict college *GPA*, so your best guess might be a little over 50% (or a little under, if you think that humor gets in the way of good grades). Mental concentration is probably a better predictor than sense of humor but not as good a predictor as the percentile rank in *GPA* itself, so the best prediction should be somewhere between 2.5 and 3.5.

To see why we should regress toward the mean, let us suppose a student scores at the 90th percentile on the mental concentration test, and let us ask whether we would expect the student to obtain a *GPA* of 3.5 (which, let us assume, is the 90th percentile for *GPA*), or higher, or lower. Mental concentration is not a perfect predictor of grades, so some of the students who score in the 90th percentile on the mental concentration test will do better than a *GPA* of 3.5, and some will do worse. More students will do worse than will do better, however, because there are more students with a *GPA* below 3.5 than there are with a *GPA* above it. There are, for example, more students with a *GPA* of 3.4 than with a *GPA* of 3.6, because 3.4 is closer to the mean *GPA*. It is therefore more likely that a randomly selected student will have a *GPA* of 3.4 and a mental concentration score at the 90th percentile than a *GPA* of 3.6 and a mental concentration score at the 90th percentile. The same argument applies to *GPA*s of 3.3 and 3.7, 3.2 and 3.8, and so on. If we predict that students in the 90th percentile in mental concentration will have a *GPA* of 3.5, we are, in effect, ignoring the prior probability of their *GPA*'s being above or below 3.5 (as discussed in ch. 12). We can think of the mental concentration score as a datum, from which we must infer the probability of various hypotheses about the student's *GPA*. The hypotheses below 3.5 are more likely at the outset, so they remain more likely after the datum is obtained.

In sum, the representativeness heuristic seems to cause us to neglect the effects of unpredictability. This results in many misinterpretations in daily life. For example, when a person is learning a difficult skill such as flying an airplane, performance on a given maneuver varies unpredictably from trial to trial. If we look at those trials in which performance is exceptionally good, then it is very likely that performance will be worse on the next trial. If we look at trials on which people do poorly, then people are likely to do better on the next trial. Now suppose that we adopt a policy of rewarding student pilots when they do well and punishing them when they do badly. Further, suppose that the reward and punishment have only small effects, compared to the variation in performance from trial to trial. It will *appear* that the reward makes the pilots do worse on the next trial and that the punishment makes them do better (Kahneman & Tversky, 1983).

In ordinary life, we are always asking questions that show that our expectations are based on the representativeness heuristic. Why is it that brilliant women (men) marry men (women) who are not quite as brilliant? Why is it that the food in restaurants tends to be better the first time you go than the second? The answers to these questions have to do with unpredictable variation. Brilliant women (men) marry men (women) who are not quite as brilliant because equally brilliant partners are hard to find, and it just might be that we look for other things in a mate besides equivalent brilliance. Why is the food in restaurants better on the first visit than the second? Because you go back a second time only when the food is very good the first time. Very likely you have gone to that restaurant on a good day (for that restaurant). When you go on a bad day, you are disappointed, and you do not go back.

Classification

Suppose we change the task slightly. Instead of looking at a policy already formed over years of experience (as our personal method of assessing personality is), we require the subject to learn to make judgments during the experiment. On each trial, subjects make a prediction and are then given feedback about the actual value of the criterion they were trying to predict. The cue and criterion variables can now be entirely artificial, with labels such as x and y instead of GPA and SAT. When this procedure is used, subjects still make their judgments in terms of linear rules (Klayman, 1984). In general, if the system in question obeys linear rules, subjects will learn them about as well (or as badly) as they do in real life.

Suppose we make one more change. Instead of the variables being continuous quantities, with each variable taking several possible values, we use variables with only two possible values each. For example, let us assume that from such variables as a person's hair color (light or dark), shirt color (light or dark), hair length (short or long), and smile (open or closed) we are supposed to guess whether the person's name is Asch or not (Medin, Dewey, & Murphy, 1983). (Clearly, this is a very artificial task.) Once again, the results do not seem to change much (Smith & Medin, 1981). Subjects' judgments can be predicted fairly well on the basis of a linear combination of features.

In this kind of task, though, certain experiments suggest that something else is going on. The results from these experiments may have implications for judgment research as a whole. The fictional medical case-study findings given in Table 18.4 were used in an experiment by Medin, Altom, Edelson, and Freko (1981, p. 39). Subjects were presented with these cases as examples, one by one, and were told that the initials represented patients with "burlosis," a fictitious disease. In the table, *1* represents the presence of a symptom, and *0* represents its absence. Notice that the last two symptoms, discolored gums and nosebleed, are perfectly correlated. Otherwise, all symp-

Table 18.4. *Case-study data for judgment experiment*

Case study	Swollen eyelids	Splotches on ears	Discolored gums	Nosebleed
R. C.	1	1	1	1
R. M.	1	1	1	1
J. J.	0	1	0	0
L. F.	1	1	1	1
A. M.	1	0	1	1
J. S.	1	1	0	0
S. T.	0	1	1	1
S. E.	1	0	0	0
E. M.	0	0	1	1

Note: 1 = symptom present
       0 = symptom absent

Source: D. Medin, M. W. Altom, S. M. Edelson, and D. Freko, "Correlated Symptoms and Simulated Medical Classification," *Journal of Experimental Psychology: Learning, Memory, and Cognition* (1982), *8*, 000.

toms are equally useful: The same number of patients has each of the four symptoms.

After studying these cases, subjects were asked to classify new cases. In this particular experiment, the subjects were asked to say which of two matched cases was more likely to have burlosis. For example, the subject might be given the cases 1101 and 0111. (The order of the ones and zeros corresponds to the order of the four symptoms in the table; thus the first case has the first two symptoms and the fourth, but no discolored gums.) In these two cases, the second case preserves the correlation between the third and fourth symptoms, and subjects generally said that this person was more likely to have the disease. (This case matched one of the original cases, a person with initials S. T. A subsequent experiment showed that subjects are sensitive to correlated symptoms even without such matching.)

Putting this result in the context of this chapter, it appears that these subjects were sensitive to an interaction between two variables. When discolored gums are present, the cue value of nosebleed is positive; patients with nosebleed are more likely to have the disease than those without it. When discolored gums are absent, the opposite is true; patients with nosebleed are *less* likely to have the disease than those without it. This is an interaction. Moreover, the results indicate that subjects are sensitive to the interaction. This is an exception to the more usual finding that judges are not sensitive to interactions actually present.

One explanation of this finding is that subjects classified the new cases on the basis of their similarity to the cases they had seen. Recall that classification on the basis of similarity to examples is one of the mechanisms by which people learn to classify instances (ch. 5). Read (1983) found that social judgments were often made on the basis of similar cases, especially when no general rule had been formulated by the person making the judgment. Read asked subjects to predict whether a member of an unfamiliar primitive tribe engaged in a certain behavior, such as drawing symbols on a piece of bark with one's own blood, after giving the subjects information about other members of the tribe who either engaged in the behavior or did not. When the subjects did not understand the rule governing the behavior in the tribe, they based their predictions on the similarity between each new case they were given and individuals they had been informed about who had also engaged in the behavior.

The same mechanism seems to operate in real judgment tasks. Faculty members whom I have worked with on a graduate admissions committee frequently evaluate applicants by comparing them to students already admitted into the program. Similarly, political leaders often make analogies to particular cases, such as the Munich agreement with Hitler.

The use of similarity to old examples as a basis for categorization of new instances has both advantages and disadvantages. An advantage is that it sensitizes judges to interactions, if they are present. Notice that in the disease experiment, the case with the correlated symptoms is more similar to many of the examples given than is the case without them. (It is identical to one example, S. T., as noted, but this is not necessary for the result.)

The disadvantage of this mechanism of learning is that it "sensitizes" us as well to interactions that are not really there. For example, suppose a particular woman has done very well at a graduate school. This woman had as an applicant (contrary to the usual pattern for women who take the Graduate Record Examinations) a high quantitative *GRE* score and a low verbal *GRE* score. A judge admitting new graduate students to that school might tend to think very highly of applicants with the identical pattern, even to the point of favoring such applicants over other applicants with high scores on *both* parts of the *GRE*. It is extremely unlikely that such a preference would be valid. Most likely, those who do well on everything are more likely to succeed than those who do well on only some things. The problem here may be in using a single, salient exemplar rather than a great many exemplars.

Conclusion

The main lesson of the research on quantitative judgment is that people are overconfident in their holistic judgments. Increased awareness of our limitations as judges and decision makers ought to improve our mutual tolerance of one another, and it can also lead to increased acceptance of new methods for decision making.

In matters of public policy, as well as in our personal lives, we often disagree when moral questions – matters of right and wrong – are involved. Improved methods of decision making will therefore not remove all of our disagreements unless we can agree on these moral issues as well. In the next two chapters, we discuss these questions. Chapter 19 provides an overview of the nature of moral reasoning; chapter 20 discusses decisions that involve conflict between individuals and groups.

19 Moral thinking

Moral thinking is important for decision making as a whole, since most real decisions involve moral issues. We often are not aware that moral issues are involved in our everyday decisions, but wherever our choices affect the utilities of others, a moral decision must be made. The choice of one's work, for example, is often considered to be a purely personal decision, but we can do various amounts of good or harm to others by choosing different paths through our working lives. The saintly aid worker who helps the poor in return for poverty-level wages and the Mafia leader who bleeds the rich and poor alike are only the extremes of a continuum on which each of us has a place. Likewise, personal relationships are not really so "personal" when they involve promises that are kept and broken, expectations of loyalty that are set up and violated, and responsibilities that are fulfilled or neglected. Of course, certain issues much more obviously involve moral questions: abortion, property rights, capital punishment, aid for the poor, and almost all other issues that arouse political passions are among these.

The most basic moral judgments are statements about what *decision* someone in a certain situation, or a certain kind of situation, should make. Should Susan have an abortion? Should legislators or judges change the law concerning abortions? Should Henry join a political demonstration concerning this issue? Unlike other judgments about what someone should decide to do, moral judgments have a special character: They are universal. They are meant to ignore the identity of the relevant people, so that they apply to anyone in the same situation. If it is wrong for me to steal a book from the library, then it is wrong for you too, if you are in the same situation.

Moral rules are taught to us as children, and they become some of our most strongly held beliefs. Sometimes these *moral intuitions* come into direct conflict with the beliefs of others. In these cases, and in others in which thinking about moral issues is needed, it is difficult for us to think well, because in this area our prior beliefs are strong, and we tend to be biased in their favor. We do not see moral issues as an area in which actively open-minded thinking is appropriate. The traditional beliefs we are taught may represent the conclusions of good moral thinking that was done by others in the past, but when they are passed on to us in the form of beliefs that we cannot question, we do not learn the details of the normative theories that stand behind them.

374

The general philosophy that underlies utility theory – utilitarianism – is one such normative theory that has been used to justify moral decisions and prescriptive moral rules. It is not possible, within the scope of the following chapter, to present a defense of the entire position of utilitarianism; my aim has to be more modest. I shall simply argue that utilitarianism provides a way to understand and analyze moral issues in terms of the consequences of decisions. It also provides a way for us to think critically and constructively about our basic moral intuitions, the beliefs we acquired as children. When we think in this way, we find that many of our intuitions are good ones, but some – like other heuristics that we use for judgments and decisions – are misleading or are applied in inappropriate situations.

The first part of the chapter examines the nature of moral judgments, with special attention to the reasons why they must be universal. In the next section, I argue that utilitarianism (as opposed, for example, to "rights" theories) is the most useful normative theory for thinking about moral decisions. Next, we consider R. M. Hare's distinction between "intuitive" and "critical" moral thinking, and some applications of this distinction. By "critical," Hare means roughly what I mean by "normative," and his term "intuitive" includes both "prescriptive" and "descriptive" aspects. Hare argues that we should usually follow our moral intuitions – for example, that it is wrong to commit adultery – rather than attempting to calculate the costs and benefits of adultery for all concerned on a case-by-case basis. We should also, however, be able to think critically about our intuitions themselves and about decisions in particularly important cases.

The psychological research of Lawrence Kohlberg suggests that Hare's distinction corresponds to different "levels" of moral thinking that subjects display in responses to hypothetical moral dilemmas. We can interpret Kohlberg's findings as showing that may people are not capable of critical-level thinking about many issues. These people do not understand the justification for their intuitions, their feelings that certain things are right or wrong. Kohlberg's work has inspired other efforts that have substantially revised the details of his theory.

Morality and utility

Does being moral conflict with maximizing expected utility? Some have argued that the idea of personal utility, by its very nature, implies seeking one's own "pleasure" or "satisfaction," so that the use of the maximization of utility as a normative criterion tends to make us selfish (B. Schwartz, 1986). Surely many economists think of people as pure "self-interest maximizers," and certainly such cynical views tend to become self-fulfilling: If theorists tell you that your fellows *are* self-interest maximizers, and you believe it, you may argue, "Why should I care about them when they do not care about me?"

As we noted in chapter 16, however, there is nothing inherent in the idea of utility that has to lead to this conclusion. Utility is a judgment of desirability, and we often desire that the desires (goals) of *others* be satisfied; in this way, our utilities are linked with theirs. People are altruistic, then, *in the sense that they often have desires that others' desires be satisfied.* I, and most other people, would rather see *you* get what you want than not, other things being equal: My desire, therefore, depends on your desire. If I act on this desire and do something for you, you may say that I am just indulging my *own* desire for your welfare, so I am being selfish after all; but this is a generous kind of "selfishness" that should not bother us much. More serious is the kind of selfishness that leads people to neglect, or even frustrate, the desires of others.

A deeper question is whether people can be altruistic even *beyond or against their own desires, on behalf of others*. Can people act against their own desires for the sake of morality – or would we just say that they *desire* to act morally, in addition to their other desires? We shall return to this question later.

The logic and illogic of moral judgments

Prescriptiveness and the naturalistic fallacy

The philosopher Richard M. Hare (1952, 1963, 1981) points out that a moral statement is like an imperative statement. Logically, the statement "You should not steal" resembles, in usage, the statement "Do not steal." Hare calls both moral and imperative statements *prescriptive*. They prescribe or recommend an action (or inaction): They tell us to do (or not do) something. It would be inconsistent to say, "You should be kind to animals – but don't be."

Prescriptive conclusions do not follow without qualification, as an inference, from a set of premises unless at least one of the premises is also prescriptive (Hare, 1952). For example, the argument "It would be helpful to me if you opened the door; therefore, open the door" is not valid without the added premise "Do whatever would be helpful to me."[1] Moral statements such as "You should keep promises" are also prescriptive, and they cannot be inferred from nonprescriptive statements alone.

This has an interesting consequence. We cannot draw moral conclusions (logically) from facts alone. From the fact that Harry's father says that Harry should not marry a gentile, it does not follow that Harry should not marry a gentile, unless we also believe that he ought to do what his father says. From the fact that the Bible says to keep the sabbath, we cannot conclude that we ought to keep the sabbath, unless we also believe that we ought to do what the Bible says. From the purported fact that males evolved to spread their

---

[1] If we adopt Toulmin's theory for extended logic, described in chapter 10, we might say that this inference is valid, but the warrant or backing must involve a prescriptive statement such as "Do whatever would be helpful to me."

seed widely whereas females evolved to seek the protection of a single male, we cannot conclude that infidelity in marriage is more excusable for males than for females, unless we also believe that people should do what they (purportedly) evolved to do. From the purported fact that people were not made to reproduce by artificial means, we cannot conclude that artificial insemination is immoral, unless we also believe that people ought to do only what is "natural."

All of these mistaken inferences are examples of the *naturalistic fallacy* – perhaps one fallacy of logic that does occur in daily life. To commit the naturalistic fallacy is to *draw a conclusion about what ought to be true solely from what is true*. It reflects a kind of confusion about the origin of moral rules themselves.

In many cases, people who commit the naturalistic fallacy would be quite willing to accept the premise they need – for example, that one should do what the Bible says or that one should not do what is unnatural – but simply have not given the matter much thought: Their acceptance of such principles is unreflective. A person who says that artificial insemination is wrong because it is "unnatural," for example, may have no objection at all to our using telephones, automobiles, and railroads, and may not notice that these things also violate the principle that whatever is unnatural is wrong. Similarly, the belief that one ought to do what the Bible says is sometimes maintained by neglecting alternative possibilities or counterarguments. (Of course, there are also people who believe in the Bible who *have* considered alternative possibilities and counterevidence.) In short, the naturalistic fallacy is often caused by poor thinking.

Universality and the fallacy of relativism

Moral statements are more than just prescriptive. As Hare (1963) points out, the difference between the statement "Tell the truth!" and the statement "Open the door!" is that the former is universal or impersonal: That is, it is meant to apply to anyone who is in certain circumstances. A universal rule need not be very general, for the "circumstances" may be very precisely defined, as, for example, in this moral statement: "Dormitory residents should turn off their record players on weekdays during exam period, when people nearby are trying to study and are disturbed by the music." Although precisely these circumstances do not arise very often (considering mankind as a whole, at any rate), this moral prescription applies to *anyone* in these circumstances. To apply "universally" is to apply to all people in exactly those circumstances. The rule, whatever it is, should apply equally well to John Jones and to Susan Smith. That would not be the case for the statement "Open the door!" It would make perfect sense to give such a command to one person – on a whim, say – even though you would not give it to someone else in the same circumstances.

The requirement of universality comes from one of the reasons we want moral rules in the first place. If we think of moral rules as a design (in the sense defined in ch. 6), then a major purpose of this design is to *regulate conduct concerning issues that concern us all*. A moral rule or judgment is, therefore, a type of premise to which anyone can appeal.

Failure to understand the universality of moral rules results in the fallacy of *relativism*. To the relativist, moral questions are simply questions of taste. What is right (or wrong) for one person, the relativist says, may not be right (or wrong) for another person in exactly the same situation: It depends on the person's own moral beliefs. I may think smoking marijuana is wrong, but if you think smoking it is moral, then it is not wrong for you to smoke marijuana. By this view, we can "agree to differ" about morality, just as we agree to differ about whether we like the taste of chili pepper. If moral judgments are universal, however, such relativistic judgments are not truly moral judgments at all, for it is in the very nature of moral judgments that they apply to everyone in the circumstances specified by the rule. If Judy and Jane are both pregnant, for example, and if their circumstances are the same in other important respects, one cannot think that abortion is wrong for Jane, but right for Judy, just because it is Jane's opinion that abortion is wrong and Judy's opinion that abortion is right. If one truly thinks this, then one has no real moral opinion about abortion at all: One thinks that abortion is a matter of taste. It also follows that if one thinks that all moral questions are matters of opinion, then one has, in effect, no real moral beliefs at all.

To say that relativism is a fallacy is not, of course, to say that everyone already agrees about moral questions such as premarital sex, euthanasia, or world government: On the contrary, we obviously disagree about such matters very strongly, but the reason our moral disagreements are so vehement is precisely because moral rules are supposed to be universal: Each side believes that its opinion applies to everyone, and that people ought not to differ about moral questions – even though we know that in fact they do.

If moral judgments are not matters of taste, then it follows that some answers to moral questions (like some answers to virtually any question) are better than others. People often reject this idea, claiming that "we all have a right to our own opinions" about moral matters. Notice, though, that the question of whether people have a right to hold their opinions is different from the question of whether some opinions are better than others.

In addition, we can believe that our opinions are best and still believe that it is morally wrong to try to force people to agree with us (for example, by prohibiting the publication of opposing arguments). Aside from the harm done to people in forcing them to do anything, we cannot be sure that we ourselves have unique access to the better answers. (In this way, morality is no different from science, we can argue: No scientist can be sure of believing the best theory either, although some theories are better than others.)

Granting that we should not exterminate our moral opponents or prevent them from speaking freely, it seems inconsistent not to try to make other people behave in ways we think right. If we are willing to act on our moral beliefs ourselves, universality requires that we be willing to try to make others act on them as well, within the limits set by our beliefs about tolerance, freedom of expression, and following the law. People who think that abortion is morally wrong ought to try to stop it, using whatever means are allowed by their other principles (which could include their respect for others and their understanding that they might be wrong). Of course, those who feel that abortion should be permitted ought to act in the opposite way. Again, this requirement stems from the premise that true moral judgments are universal and set standards of behavior for everyone.

Utilitarianism as the normative theory

Maximizing expected utility for everyone

These two properties – prescriptiveness and universality – suggest a way of thinking about moral issues in which people have conflicting desires. To think about the best thing to do in such situations, we can try to put ourselves in the position of all parties simultaneously. It is easiest to think about such decisions when we ourselves have little or no stake in the outcome. For example, suppose you are in charge of a college dormitory and you must decide when to allow John to play his record player in the dormitory (and at what volume) and when he should not. To do this, you would put yourself in the position of John (who wants to hear his records) and also of the person he might be bothering (Judy, who lives in the room below). You would ask whose desire is greater: John's, to hear his music, or Judy's, to get her work done. Because moral judgments are universal, it does not matter what particular individuals are involved; the answer should be the same even if John and Judy switched places. (When they switch places, they must switch their desires too.) Notice that when we do this, we are basically trying to maximize their combined utility, as if we were applying MAUT (ch. 16), with each person providing one dimension of a decision involving two independent dimensions.

A more difficult case is one in which the decision maker's desires are affected. What if John himself must decide on an appropriate policy? From a purely moral point of view, the best decision here is the same as if it were made by a disinterested third person.[2] When we think morally about such conflicts, we should try to put ourselves in the other person's place as well as our own, no matter whose skin we inhabit. Because of its resemblance to the biblical rule "And as ye would that men should do unto you, do ye also

---

[2] We shall return to the question of how we should resolve such conflicts between morality and self-interest.

to them likewise" (Luke 6:31, also Matthew 7:12), Hare (1963, chs. 6 and 7) calls this sort of thinking a "Golden Rule argument."

Many moral issues involve consequences of acts for the satisfaction of people's desires (the achievement of their goals). If we take this view of what morality is basically about, and if we then try to apply expected-utility theory to our decisions, we are led to adopt various forms of *utilitarianism* as our approach to moral questions (Hare, 1981). The basic idea of modern utilitarianism is that we treat each moral decision as a choice among competing acts. Each act has certain consequences, with different probabilities, for certain people. To decide which act is morally best, we simply add up the utilities of the consequences for all of the people. The best acts are those with the highest expected utility, across all of the people.

This is essentially what is done when we apply decision analysis to social questions such as medical treatment policies. We assume that the utilities of different outcomes of medical treatment for different people can be measured and added (and, therefore, traded off). For example, if the utility of death from a certain heart operation is -100 (relative to the patients' current painful life), the utility of improvement is 20 (on the same scale), and the probability of death from the operation is .05, then the expected utility from the operation (relative to the current state) is $.05 \cdot (-100) + .95 \cdot (20)$, or 14 per person. For 1,000 people to whom these figures apply, the expected total gain in utility, if all have the operation, is 14,000. On the basis of this analysis, we would decide to advise all 1,000 patients to have the operation, yet 50 of these people will probably die (if all patients accept our advice), so total utility would increase for everyone at the expense of a great loss in utility for a few.

Utilitarianism, like decision analysis, attends only to future effects of choices. It ignores the past. Utilitarians seek to punish bad behavior only because punishment deters future bad behavior, not because of any belief in the inherent necessity of retribution or punishment. They go out of their way to keep promises, for example, only to support the institution of promise making (because of its future value to all), not because of any binding force inherent in promises themselves.

Older forms of utilitarianism spoke of maximizing total pleasure or happiness, but (for reasons given at the beginning of ch. 16) more recent versions have tended to emphasize maximizing the achievement of personal goals, just as modern utility theory itself does. Many writers speak of utility as the satisfaction of preferences. The term "preference" suggests a decision, however, and we have found that our decisions are not always the ones that best achieve our goals. It does not do anyone any good to give them something they "prefer" now but that actually prevents them from achieving their goals. Our personal goals, together with our beliefs about the effects of our choices, are the *reasons* for our preferences, as expressed in our decisions, not our preferences themselves.[3] Other writers speak of utility as the satisfaction of desires. The term "satisfaction," however, suggests an emotion that we experience only after our goal is achieved, and, as I pointed out in chapter 16, for many of our important goals we cannot have this experience (for example, our goal that our children have a long and happy life after we die). I shall therefore continue to assume that our main concern is with the achievement of our personal goals.

When we use utilitarian concepts in our everyday reasoning, however, we do not need to be so precise in our expression. We often speak of "paying attention to other people's feelings" when we are trying to emphasize the basic message of utilitarianism, that what matters in our decision making is the consequences of what we do for people (not just the people near to us but those distant in time and space as well).

Utilitarianism assumes that all people are weighed equally. If we are concerned with maximizing the achievement of goals, then it should not matter whose goals are at issue. We can treat everyone's goals as though they all belonged to the same person.

Utilitarianism is not the view that the right answer to moral questions should be decided by adding up people's moral opinions; in fact, we might even want to exclude such opinions from a utilitarian analysis on the ground that prior belief often does not reflect our best thinking (Baron, 1986). In the nineteenth century, for example, many people favored the institution of slavery so much that they desired that slavery continue to exist, as a moral goal, just the way some of us today desire that other people be prohibited from having (or that they be allowed to have) abortions. If such desires had been considered in a utilitarian analysis of slavery, they might have been strong enough to tip the balance in its favor. Because utilitarian analysis, like decision analysis, is a way of determining what our action should be, both kinds of analysis should exclude prior desires concerning the action itself (as opposed to its consequences). If they include such desires, they are useless for their purpose; they are no longer a "second opinion" but an echo of the first opinion.

Rights theories

Utilitarianism conflicts with many of our intuitions, the basic moral beliefs we have acquired from our culture. Does the state, for example, have a right to protect us from ourselves by passing laws requiring motorcycle riders to wear helmets, or should citizens be considered autonomous, capable of run-

---

[3] Some forms of utilitarianism consider effects of choices on the satisfaction of *rational* preferences only, those preferences that people would have on reflection. But the form of reflection is not usually specified. An implication of the view I have presented here is that the relevant sort of reflection is about how to achieve our personal goals and about what those goals should be.

ning (or ruining) their own lives as they see fit? A utilitarian would have no choice but to argue that the state should protect us from ourselves, if the harm avoided is, on balance, greater than the harm from the interference. Utilitarians have been called, with some justice, "moral busybodies." A utilitarian saint is a "Jewish mother" to the world.

Other moral theories take autonomy to be more fundamental, so that any violation of autonomy requires special justification. A very popular moral theory of this sort in the United States is based on the theory of moral rights. The "unalienable rights" that Jefferson refers to in the *Declaration of Independence*, for example, reflects a long tradition of political "rights" theory. The laws of the United States itself are not themselves a moral system, but many have argued that they are based on such a system and that the system that they are based on recognizes the idea of individual rights. (Parts of the law – particularly the laws pertaining to environmental regulation – also recognize utilitarianism.) It is commonplace for political movements in the United States today to base their demands on the idea of rights: the "right" to life (of fetuses, usually); the "right" to control one's own body (that is, have abortions); the "right" to medical care of a certain quality; the "right" to profit from one's good luck. The most sophisticated rights theory formulated in recent years is probably that of the American philosopher John Rawls (1971), which proposes a fundamental right (the right to equal liberty) from which all other legitimate rights are derived.[4]

For rights theories in general, a "right" can be seen as a consequence of a moral rule about what to do – or (most typically) not do – in a given situation: For example, "Do not murder"; "Do not interfere forcibly with a person's control over her body"; "Do not prevent a person from having his say." Each of these rules generates both a right and a duty: for example, a right not to be murdered (a right to life) and a duty not to murder. Many rights involve some sort of autonomy, in the case of the first rule, a right to noninterference and a duty not to interfere in certain ways.

Many rights theories, including Rawls's, justify the idea of autonomy by thinking of morality as a kind of contract or agreement, usually a hypothetical one. By this argument, our moral obligations result from our participation in a society. We take certain benefits from this participation, and, in return, we have agreed to give up to the society certain *limited* parts of our own autonomy. In return for other people honoring and protecting our autonomy (for example, our right to life and property), we agree to honor and protect (through government) the autonomy and rights of others. Beyond the de-

---

[4] I do not mean to suggest that rights theories are uniquely parochial and limited to one national tradition. Jefferson was strongly influenced by the British philosopher John Locke, and, conversely, utilitarianism has been described to me by one American philosopher (Samuel Freeman) as a "British national treasure."

mands of such agreements, however, there are no moral obligations (in the simplest form of these theories), and we can be as selfish as we like.

Rights theorists generally believe that people behave morally if they follow all of the rules concerning the rights of others, but usually that is impossible to do, because in many cases the rules conflict. For example, in deciding whether to allow abortion, the right of the fetus to live conflicts with the right of the mother to make decisions that affect her own health. Rights theories have various ways of resolving such conflicts. One is to conclude that it is impossible to be moral. Another is to set up a lexical order of rules (see ch. 16), so that certain rules are always given priority (for example, right to life over right to make medical decisions for oneself). Still another is to pare down the list of rights to one or two basic ones (as Rawls did).

As an example of the conflict between rights theories and utilitarianism, consider the case of John, a member of a fraternity, who likes to play his record player very loudly on warm spring days, with his window open. He may think he has a "right" to do this. (There is no rule against it, he thinks.) Jon, who walks through the campus, finds John's taste in music (hard rock) offensive; it bothers him not just to hear it, but to have it going through his head for several hours afterward. (He rushes home after work to wash it out with a dose of Debussy.) Jon may think he has a "right" not to be assaulted in this way. (He would like there to be a rule against it, to protect his right.) A utilitarian would have to weigh Jon's displeasure against John's pleasure. A utilitarian would also have to consider the number of people who are bothered by John's music, and the effect of John's music as a precedent for others and for John himself at other times, which leads to effects on still more people. A rights theorist might ignore the number affected, arguing that violating the rights of even one person is as bad as violating the rights of a million people.

As another example of the conflict of theories, let us consider the question of the amount of income tax (if any) that people with different income levels should pay. A utilitarian analysis usually focuses on two facts: First, the "marginal utility" of income is declining (ch. 16), which means that total utility increases if we tax those with high incomes and use part of the taxes to subsidize those with low incomes (either by reducing their taxes or by supplementing their incomes). Second, some differences in income are needed to provide incentives for people to work and thereby provide the goods and services that give money its value. Declining marginal utility by itself would lead to equality of income, but the need for incentive, it is argued, justifies economic inequality. By utility theory, the question of the best compromise on the taxation issue becomes a mathematically and empirically difficult, but morally simple, calculation. The solution is simply whatever form of taxation maximizes total utility, all things considered. (Notice that "total utility" here is not measured by such indices as the Gross National Product, for such indices count the monetary value of expensive luxury goods just as much as the value of "necessities." The utility of $3,565 worth of medical care, however, is probably much greater than the combined utility of an $815 wristwatch and a $2,750 fountain pen.)

Rights theorists, on the other hand, take varying positions on this issue, depending on which rights they consider primary. *Libertarian* rights theorists (often found on the political right wing), such as Nozick (1974), argue that people have a basic right to keep what they earn, even if all would benefit if the more prosperous were forced to give up some of their income. (Where this right came from is left unanswered.) *Liberal* rights theorists (often found on the political left wing) such as Rawls (1971) argue that the poor have a right to first consideration (lexical priority), so that the sole consideration should be to maximize the benefit of the poor. (This might still allow differences in income, because of the same incentive principle that the utilitarian acknowledges.) The utilitarian solution is roughly in between these two: unlike the "libertarian" solution, it permits taxing the rich to help the poor, but, unlike the "liberal" solution, it does not give the poor absolute priority over everyone else.

Sometimes rights theories are defended by the argument that the utilities of different people cannot be compared. This argument is not convincing. Although interpersonal comparisons are often difficult to make, just as it is often difficult to compare one's own utilities for very different kinds of outcomes (health, wealth, or wisdom, for example), it is certainly not impossible to compare utilities for different people – and sometimes it is easy. If I could effect a cure of one case of malaria by contributing $5 to a charity, for example, the gain to the person cured would surely be greater than the loss to me. We must remember that we do not need to compare the overall levels of happiness or life satisfaction for two individuals (which might be more difficult) but merely the difference between *outcomes*: my having $5 more or less, and the other person having (or not having) malaria.[5]

Critical and intuitive moral thinking

Some philosophers have resolved the conflict between utilitarianism and rights theories by arguing that utilitarianism does not apply to specific acts (as we

---

[5] Hare (1981, p. 123) suggests that interpersonal comparisons can be used to measure utility. The basic idea is, in effect, to use each person's outcomes as an independent dimension in a MAUT analysis. The measure of utility obtained in this way is theoretically the best measure to use for utilitarian calculation when different people are involved. This point becomes important when this measure conflicts with measures derived for each individual by other methods. For example, by the method of interpersonal comparison, one square meal, to a poor and hungry person, could have more utility than an $815 watch has to a rich person, but a utility analysis within each person could reveal that the watch had more utility.

would assume using utility theory), but rather to the moral *rules* that we adopt and try to live by. This approach is called *rule utilitarianism*, as distinct from *act utilitarianism*, which we have just been discussing. According to rule utilitarianism, the question is not whether John should play his record player in a given case, but rather whether utility is maximized if people are, in general, free to play their record players or not. Rule utilitarians try to show how the moral rules and rights we attempt to live by generally maximize utility. If it turns out that some rules do not, then they are suspect.

Rule utilitarians are faced with a problem: If we apply utilitarianism to rules, why not apply it to acts as well? If we do not, we are sure to end up failing to maximize utility in a given case. For example, if we insisted upon a blanket rule against playing record players on campus, it would prohibit playing them even when everyone is absolutely sure that all the rock-music haters have cleared out. The solution to this problem is to have separate normative and prescriptive theories of moral decision making.

Recall that a prescriptive theory is a set of rules designed to specify what people should do (or how they should decide what to do) in certain real situations. Most moral codes, and many prudential rules (such as "Honesty is the best policy"), are intended to serve this purpose. When people behave at variance with prescriptive rules that we have accepted, we can criticize their behavior (constructively) by pointing to the discrepancy.

A normative theory, you recall, is what we would like, on reflection, to have our behavior conform to if we could. For example, the normative theory of decisions, discussed in chapter 16, might specify that we want to maximize utility within the individual decision maker, and the normative theory of morality might specify that we want to maximize total utility across individuals. A normative theory is a set of standards, not ordinarily a guide to action.

Normative moral theories can be used to justify prescriptive moral theories. For example, if we wanted to argue that "honesty is the best policy," we could try to show that our following this rule would result in greater utility for all than would our trying to calculate the best option in each individual case. If we tried to calculate utilities, we would make so many mistakes – both through well-intentioned error and through self-serving biases – that we would do better to follow the simple rule, according to the standard of the normative theory itself, utility. In some cases, when time for decision making and calculation is not at issue because of the importance of the decision, the normative model may become the prescriptive model, as when utility theory is used in decision analyses. By this account, one task of normative theorists is to reflect about the rules themselves on behalf of everyone.

Asserting the distinction between normative and prescriptive theories is a way of dividing up the task of reflecting about the kind of theory we want. We first reflect on what we would want if we were not constrained by certain limitations, and then we use the theory developed in this way, plus the descriptive facts about actual constraints, to design the final, prescriptive, theory. The prescriptive theory is our basis for advice and criticism. The constraints themselves may excuse failure to conform to the normative theory.

Hare (1981) makes a distinction between critical thinking and intuitive thinking in making moral decisions. By "critical" thinking, Hare means the kind of thinking we do when we try to apply the normative model directly to our decisions. For Hare – whose normative model is utilitarian – this does not necessarily mean that we carry out a decision analysis with numbers. Another way to apply the utilitarian normative model is to try to put ourselves simultaneously in the positions of all the people who are affected by a decision (with their goals, not ours) and to make whatever decision best achieves the whole set of goals. Because, descriptively, this is not only difficult but prone to systematic biases (such as attributing our own goals to others), we do better not to try to think this way very often. That is, we achieve greater utility, in the long run, if we do not try to maximize utility all the time but, instead, try to follow certain prescriptive rules, such as "Life is more important than property" or "Do not commit adultery."

Hare thinks that many of these rules correspond closely to the moral intuitions that most people have, but he also thinks that intuitions can be unjustifiable from a critical perspective, if only because they become out-moded in the course of human history. We can therefore distinguish between the intuitions that we have – which we would learn about from a descriptive study of moral thinking – and the intuitions we could have that would bring us closer to the results that the normative model itself would dictate. The latter intuitions, of course, would constitute what I have called a prescriptive account.

In Hare's theory, the Prole, a hypothetical creature whose methods we all may use, makes moral decisions intuitively by following simple rules. (Hare borrows the name from the brainwashed proletarians in George Orwell's novel *1984*.) Such intuitive rules, Hare points out, are taught to us throughout our childhoods, and we become attached to them, feeling guilty when we violate them, even if we think we ought to do so. The Archangel (another hypothetical creature whose methods we all may use) makes moral decisions by critical thinking. These decisions are ordinarily about specific actions, which are described in as much detail as possible. In other cases, the critical Archangel might reflect not about specific actions but about intuitive rules to be followed by the intuitive Prole. Some of these rules would tell us when critical reasoning itself was appropriate (for example, not when time is short or when self-interest is likely to lead to strong biases). This use of critical thinking is an example of the use of normative models to justify prescriptive ones. *Critical moral thinking*, as Hare defines it, *corresponds to act utilitarianism, and intuitive moral thinking corresponds to rule utilitarianism*.

The distinction between critical and intuitive moral thinking helps us understand why utilitarianism so often seems to conflict with moral intuitions.

For example, utilitarians justify punishment only as deterrence, not as retribution. They argue that if the harm done to criminals by executing them is balanced by a reduction in murders, capital punishment is justified, but punishment is not justified by the idea of retribution alone (insofar as the desire for retribution is the expression of a moral opinion or intuition). Such an analysis conflicts with various intuitions: that killing is wrong under any circumstances; that "two wrongs don't make a right"; that retribution is part of punishment; and that the punishment should "fit the crime."

Hare would argue that most of these intuitions are useful ones; in general, they lead to actions that maximize utility. Moreover, it is often best to follow these intuitions rather than to attempt critical moral thinking. Critical thinking is difficult because the effects of any choice may be hard to determine; for one thing, moral choices have consequences extending far into the future as precedents for later moral choices.[6] When we try to think critically, we are also subject to self-serving biases. For example, political terrorists often conclude that the harm they do is justified by the greater good, but the history of political terrorism suggests that this sort of reasoning is usually incorrect. On the other hand, our intuitions can be wrong. They are, after all, the product of our early training, not of careful reflection. We should not rely on our intuitions alone for objections to utilitarianism (or to any other view).

The critical-intuitive distinction provides an argument against rights theories. Most of these theories are justified by our intuitions about the rights that people should have. We were taught about these rights throughout our schooling, and we feel strongly about them. Moreover, most rights are easy to justify as prescriptive rules that, in the long run, maximize utility. For example, the right of free speech ensures that we will be exposed to the information we need to elect our government wisely. Other rights, such as the right to worship (or not worship) as we choose, allow us to pursue the personal goals that are important to us, without the threat of interference from busybodies who think they know what everyone else's goals ought to be.

Most important, the general rights of autonomy are justified by the fact that each individual generally knows more than anyone else about the nature of his or her personal goals and how to achieve them. (We take away the rights of autonomy in exactly those cases in which this is probably not true: young children and mental patients.) In many cases, by this argument, the assumption that people know what is good for them is not true, but it is true more often than not, and since it is impossible to ascertain (for adults outside of institutions) just when it is true, we maximize utility by assuming that it is generally true of everyone. This argument implies that autonomy is not a fundamental moral principle but rather a generally well-justified intuition,

[6] To see how difficult utilitarian thinking is, try to think through the abortion question from this point of view. Then you may want to read Hare's article "Abortion and the Golden Rule" (1975).

suitable as a guide to daily life but not as the fundamental basis of a moral theory.

The critical-intuitive distinction also helps us understand the importance of moral motives and goals. Take the classic dilemma in which a cruel dictator offers you the following choice: Either you shoot one of his political prisoners for him, or he will shoot 10 others, as well as the one. There is no way out, and the choice you make will not be known to anyone else. Clearly, the (critical) utilitarian solution here is to shoot one prisoner. Losing one life is not as bad as losing 11; but many would balk. They would stand on (intuitive) principle and refuse to take part. More important, we might admire them for this stand.

Hare argues that both sides are right, in different senses. If we used critical thinking, we would conclude that it is right to shoot but that it is also right to develop an intuitive rule against participation in wanton killing. (If more people adhered to such a rule, dictators like the one in question would not so easily come to power.) We admire the person who refuses to shoot for sticking to what is basically a good rule, even though the right *act* goes against the rule in this case. Moral motives are important, even when they go against right acts. In the long run, things work best if people have good motives, even if their acts occasionally go astray (from the critical point of view) as a result.[7]

Hare's theory helps us understand a great variety of intuitions, including, as we have seen, those intuitions about rights and about lexical rules (against killing) that underlie theories that compete with utilitarianism. Intuitions need not conflict with utilitarianism, however. The following quotation, from a subject interviewed by Gilligan (1982, p. 67) as part of a study of moral reasoning, illustrates a set of moral intuitions that seem to represent a pre-scriptive, or intuitive, form of utilitarianism itself:

[What makes an issue moral is] some sense of trying to uncover a right path in which to live, and always in my mind is that the world is full of real and recognizable trouble, and it is heading for some sort of doom, and is it right to bring children into this world when we currently have an overpopulation problem, and is it right to spend money on a pair of shoes when I have a pair of shoes and other people are shoeless? It is in part a self-critical view, part of saying, "How am I spending my time and in what sense am I working?" I think I have a real drive, a real maternal drive, to take care of someone – to take care of my mother, to take care of children, to take care of other people's children, to take care of my own children, to take care of the world. When I am dealing with moral issues, I am sort of saying to myself constantly, "Are you taking care of all the things that you think are important, and in what ways are you wasting yourself and wasting those issues?"

---

[7] One could also argue that the refusal to shoot is a kind of self-indulgence, a selfish concern with one's own guilt feelings at the expense of 10 lives. Although from Hare's point of view this is true, it is beside the point, which is that the guilt feelings would result from failing to follow a good rule.

Simple moral systems and the omission–commission issue

A common type of moral system, to which most of us subscribe to some degree, consists of a manageable list of moral rules, usually of the form "Thou shalt not . . ." The rules have absolute priority, but as long as we follow the rules we are free to ignore moral considerations completely, if we so choose. No tradeoff is allowed between violation of the rules (or even, in the extreme, mere risk of violation of the rules) and moral considerations outside the rules (for example, effects of our actions on other people's goals). Let us call these systems *simple moral systems* (Baron, 1986). The term "simple" indicates only that this morality is defined by lexical rules rather than tradeoffs (which require judgment).

This basic theme has numerous variants. Many rights-based moral theories are rule systems built on lexical rules. These rules state that a certain type of right (for example, the right to life, the right to control one's body) should never be violated. Each such right is assumed to be lexically prior to some other right. Prominent counterexamples to the rule are handled by adding conditions: "Free speech is an inalienable right, except that you may not yell 'fire' in a crowded theater or sell pornography to minors." These systems explicitly reject the idea that rights, or duties, once stated, can be traded off with *any* sort of consideration, under any conditions.

Simple moral systems often stress a distinction between acts of omission and acts of commission. By this reasoning, it is more blameworthy to cheat (a commission) than to fail to prevent someone else's cheating (an omission). Similarly, we might favor a tax deduction for charitable gifts but oppose an equivalent government subsidy to charities, and we might agree that patients who are in irreversible comas can be allowed to die of starvation (which involves no "act" on anyone's part) but disapprove of their being killed with a lethal injection.

This distinction between omission and commission, however, may be the result of a cognitive illusion – specifically, a framing effect (Kahneman & Tversky, 1984). When we think of a certain outcome as normal, expected, or part of the status quo (for example, death from starvation, in countries where famines are common), then we see our failure to prevent that outcome as an act of omission. If an outcome is not expected (starvation in the United States), then we see causing it as an act of commission. We tend to feel that the evil done by tearing up one's check to Oxfam (a charity that aids famine victims) on the way to the post office – a commission – is greater than the evil done by not writing the check – an omission – and we institutionalize feelings of this sort into our prescriptive moral codes.

These distinctions are normatively irrelevant because they amount to *variant descriptions of the same situation*. Why should the consequences we choose be affected by what we are told will happen if we "refuse to make a choice"? Instead of refusing to make a choice, of course, we actually have made a choice in favor of whatever outcome will occur if we do not stop it. We can avoid the framing effect by focusing on the difference between the consequences of two *actions* we might take. If you are told that you are to help a person in need, does it matter whether the way to help the person is by pushing button x, not pushing button x, or pushing button y (which is another way of saying "not pushing x")? If you fail to help, is the degree of immorality any different in these three cases? (See Singer, 1979, chs. 7 and 8, and Bennett, 1981, for further defense of this position.)

The omission-commission distinction may strengthen our intuition that autonomy is a fundamental right. Interfering with someone else's autonomy, even to help them, is a commission, and if we harm them inadvertently, we think, we are to blame for the results. If, on the other hand, they come to harm because of their own actions, the fact that we did not intervene to stop them seems morally irrelevant, even if we could have easily done so. For example, we think that taking from the rich to help the poor is morally unnecessary: It invades the autonomy of the rich and hurts them, and if we do nothing for the poor, then we are still not responsible for their poverty. (If the status quo was that the rich were already taxed to help the poor, however, perhaps we would regard this as better than removing the tax, thus taking from the poor to help the rich.)

In this section, I have presented a descriptive theory – the idea of simple moral systems – that explains many of the intuitions that we hold. If this theory is correct, it suggests, prescriptively, that some of our intuitions hold us back from doing things that could help others. These intuitions help us to maintain the belief that we are completely moral, because they define immorality only in terms of the harm we do through our actions and they neglect the good we fail to do through our inactions. If, like the person quoted at the beginning of this chapter, we adopt intuitions more in line with utilitarianism, we will come to believe that we are morally imperfect, for few of us do all that we can do to help others. Some of us would be demoralized by such a belief. On the other hand, the goal of being morally perfect might be, on reflection, one that we can give up. We might do more good in the long run by accepting our imperfection, while making the effort to do what we can, than by accepting a system that tells us that perfection is within our reach.

The development of moral thinking

Let us say that we accept Hare's distinction between critical and intuitive moral thinking. How will we know when each kind of thinking is appropriate? When should we follow our basic moral intuitions, and when should we try to think critically about consequences? A convenient answer is that since only certain favored people are capable of critical thinking, the rest of us should respect the moral views of these experts and follow them without question.

Although this theory sounds outrageous to those brought up to believe in democracy, it has been around in one form or another for most of human history and still survives today. It is approximately the view held by many Roman Catholics and by some adherents of other faiths. If it is true that only a few are capable of critical thinking, this theory would still be the best prescriptive solution. My argument in this chapter, however, is that "critical" moral thinking, like other kinds of good thinking, can be learned.

The psychologist Lawrence Kohlberg (for example, 1963, 1970), building on the work of Jean Piaget (1932/1948) and others, proposed a developmental theory of moral judgment. Kohlberg asserts, in essence, that the capacity for critical thinking takes time to develop. Children, then, must be assumed to be Proles: The best we can hope for is that they will acquire basic moral intuitions to go by until they can learn to think critically. Some people may never move beyond the level of moral intuitions. Others, however, perhaps almost everyone, can learn to think critically about moral issues, if they have the kinds of experiences that promote such development.

Kohlberg's theory is based on interview studies in which he asked both children and adult subjects to decide how they would solve certain moral dilemmas. One dilemma, for example, concerns a man, Heinz, whose wife is dying of an illness and who cannot raise the money to pay for a drug that might cure her. The main question is whether he should steal the drug from the druggist who has it, in order to save his wife. The dilemma is presented in an interview situation, to make sure that the subject accepts the assumptions made. (Subjects try to deny that such a situation could exist; the interviewer insists that they have to imagine it.) After giving an answer, the subject is asked for thorough justification, and the interviewer probes farther by asking things like "Would it make any difference if Heinz didn't love his wife?" and (if the subject says that Heinz should steal the drug) "Should Heinz be punished? Why or why not?" The structure of the interview therefore permitted Kohlberg to probe subjects' underlying beliefs about such issues as the law and the basis of interpersonal obligations (duty versus ties of affection). (Kohlberg was interested in these underlying beliefs, not in whether the subject answered yes or no to the original question.) Subjects are classified by scoring their responses for the kinds of justifications they use.

Kohlberg (as he expected, on the basis of Piaget's work) found that the answers children gave for dilemmas like this one changed systematically as the children grew older. He was able to classify the responses into what he called six stages of the development of moral judgment, which he grouped into three levels: the *preconventional level* (stages 1 and 2); the *conventional level* (stages 3 and 4); and the *postconventional level* (stages 5 and 6). Although children go through these stages in order, he theorized, the stages are not closely tied to age. Stage 1 predominates below the age of 10, but there are numerous exceptions, and many adults in the United States never advance beyond stage 3 or 4. In countries where education was not as widespread as in the United States, such as Mexico and Turkey, even fewer adults reached stage 5.

Loosely summarized, Kohlberg's theory is that "preconventional" thinkers have not yet acquired moral intuitions; "conventional" thinkers have acquired moral intuitions; but only "postconventional" thinkers are capable of critical thinking. (This summary is "loose" because Kohlberg also emphasizes the use of both rights arguments and utilitarian arguments at the postconventional level.)

At the *preconventional level*, Kohlberg concluded, subjects confuse morality with the self-interest of the individual: For example, they argue that Heinz should not steal the drug because he would be punished or that he should steal it because he needed his wife to cook for him. Note that Kohlberg is not claiming that the subjects were selfish – rather, that the subjects judge the morality of others' actions in terms of whether the action is in the actor's (here, Heinz's) self-interest.

At the *conventional level*, Kohlberg concluded, subjects confused morality with convention. They make moral judgments according to whether conventional role expectations were being fulfilled or whether the law was being followed. The roles, or the law, were not themselves questioned. Ties of affection were also used as the basis of judgment. Subjects said, for example, that Heinz should steal the drug because he would feel guilty if he did not, or because he loved his wife, or because it is the law of God that life should be saved. "Conventional" moral judgments included those judgments referring to virtues and vices: greed, sloth, respect, honesty, and so forth. These are, of course, very widespread moral intuitions.

At the *postconventional level*, the subjects made judgments in terms of what we might call a moral philosophy, some idea that could apply across cultures and that could be used to justify or criticize law or convention. Both utilitarianism and rights theories would fit here. For example, a subject who thought at this level might argue that the wife's right to life was more important than the druggist's right to get paid (as a moral right, not a legal right), or that stealing the drug would maximize utility.

These six stages, in Kohlberg's view, had a theoretical justification, as well as an empirical one. Higher stages were more adequate than lower ones, from a normative point of view: Higher stages could resolve conflicts that lower stages could not resolve; for example, postconventional stages could resolve conflicts between competing laws or conventions. Higher stages made distinctions that lower stages did not make, such as the distinctions between morality and self-interest, and between convention and morality. Higher stages were also capable of being applied in a wider set of circumstances: Postconventional reasoning, for example, could apply cross-culturally.

There is, therefore, a clear analogy to be made between Kohlberg's contrast between conventional and postconventional levels and Hare's contrast between intuitive thinking and critical thinking. Postconventional thinking provides the same sort of justification for conventional thinking that Hare's critical thinking provides for the intuitive moral rules that we live by most of the time. Similarly, Kohlberg argues that we use conventional reasoning most of the time, unless we are compelled to use the postconventional level. Finally, Hare's suggestion that the intuitive level is appropriate for the moral education of children, who are incapable of critical thinking, fits well with Kohlberg's finding that conventional thinking is developmentally earlier.

Kohlberg suggests that reasoning develops toward more adequate principles because the principles are more adequate: The new principles and distinctions, once learned, are found useful. Kohlberg and his colleagues demonstrated, in several experiments, that development could be accelerated by encouraging children to think about and discuss moral conflicts. Teachers did not need to provide "answers" in order to promote this moral development: Children and adolescents simply needed to be encouraged to reflect and argue in an open atmosphere.

Kohlberg's dilemmas were deliberately chosen to be difficult for as many stages as possible. In other, less unusual moral situations, however, a person's "stage" might have a larger influence on the content of moral belief. For example, a person at stage 4 would say that civil disobedience is almost always wrong, and a person at stage 5 would say that civil disobedience could often be right. People at stages 3 and 4 would be able to justify blind obedience to authority (even when the authority ordered, say, mass killing), whereas people at stages 5 and 6 would not. These issues are directly related to the difference between conventional and postconventional thinking: Civil disobedience flouts convention and law for the sake of a higher morality, and blind obedience can be justified only by belief in conventional relationships of authority.

The content of belief, in turn, does seem to have some effect on behavior. Haan, Smith, and Block (1969), using Kohlberg's stages, found that participants in the Berkeley "Free-speech Movement" of 1964 (the beginning of the college protest movement of the 1960s) tended to be either postconventional or preconventional in their moral thinking. The postconventional students participated out of high moral purpose – to bring about the "new society" or the "revolution"–and the preconventional students participated because "they were tired of being treated like numbers." The conventional students thought the whole protest movement was morally wrong.[8]

---

[8] A recent reanalysis of these data by Candee and Kohlberg (1987), using a completely revised version of Kohlberg's system for scoring responses to dilemmas, failed to find any subjects who were truly preconventional, but the reanalysis still found that subjects with some postconventional reasoning were the most likely to sit in. Candee and Kohlberg do not attempt to explain the original finding that those who were classified as preconventional gave different justifications for sitting in than those classified as postconventional. It is not clear to me that

Of course, the level of moral thinking does not completely determine one's moral beliefs – since people may have different understandings of relevant factual matters – and the content of belief does not fully determine action: People do not always act on what they think is right. Nonetheless, moral judgment is clearly not irrelevant to moral action.

Kohlberg's theory has been criticized. Gilligan (1982) has argued that Kohlberg's definition of good moral reasoning is biased toward abstract principles of justice, particularly rules and rights (expressed in the form of prohibitions against violation of rights, rather than injunctions to help), and away from consideration of the particulars of situations and of the opportunity to do positive good. Gilligan regards the latter orientation of caring and responsibility as more characteristic of women, with men preferring rights and rules. The available evidence does not support this claim about gender differences (Ford & Lowery, 1986), but Giligan's argument that Kohlberg's scheme is unfair to those with a "care and responsibility" approach to morality – regardless of their gender – can still be correct.[9] Gilligan suggests that there is a developmental sequence *within* each approach. She cites the subject quoted earlier in this chapter (the one who wanted to "take care of the world") as an example of the highest form of reasoning within the "care and responsibility" orientation.

Another criticism concerns Kohlberg's interview method. People are able to use and recognize principles that they cannot express verbally because of (for example) vocabulary limitations. A more sensitive measure of whether a child understands a certain principle is to devise a situation in which that principle is revealed in a single judgment. The research we have described on decision making (ch. 17), for example, uses situations in which the principle that a subject uses is revealed in a pattern of choices.

Turiel (1983) questioned whether children really fail to understand the distinction between morality and convention. The children were given simple stories that tested the issue directly. The point about conventions is that they could change, if everyone agreed to change them, whereas moral rules could not. Turiel and his collaborators asked the children whether it would be OK to call one's teacher by her first name if everyone thought it was OK, or to bow instead of shaking hands. They also asked whether it would be OK for a bully to push another kid off the top of a slide if everyone thought it was OK. Even 2nd-graders (surely at Kohlberg's "conventional" level) said it would be OK to change the conventions but not the moral rules: It would still be wrong to push someone off of a slide, even if everyone thought it was not wrong.

the revised scoring system is truly better than the old version, which was more closely related to the theory as I have described it.

[9] Shweder, Mahapatra, and Miller (1988) also argue that Kohlberg ignored the diversity of sophisticated moral views. Kohlberg's scoring system, they argue, is biased in favor of the contractual theory of rights that Kohlberg favored.

Turiel went on to propose a separate developmental sequence for thinking about conventions. At the highest level of this sequence, subjects understand that conventions have a functional value. The best example is the convention about driving on the right (or left) side of the road. It does not matter which side we choose, but we all benefit from choosing one side. Turiel suggested that many real dilemmas (and some of Kohlberg's dilemmas, although not the Heinz dilemma) involve conflicts between morality and convention, which can be resolved in a variety of ways. Turiel studied the resolution of such conflicts by making up new dilemmas, such as one about whether people should be allowed to sunbathe in the nude when other people were offended simply by knowing about the existence of nude sunbathing. Subjects differed in whether they considered the offense to be a morally relevant consequence and therefore a reason not to sunbathe in the nude.[10]

Shweder, Mahapatra, and Miller (1988) questioned Turiel's conclusions about the distinction between morality and convention by pointing out that these conclusions were based on data from cultural groups (in the United States) that have a long tradition of distinguishing morality and convention. Shweder and his colleagues presented descriptions of various transgressions to Hindu residents of a village in India and to "Judeo-Christian" residents of Chicago. They found that the two groups differed, at all ages, in their evaluations of the transgressions. For example, Hindus thought that the son who, the day after his father's death, had a haircut and ate chicken (in violation of Hindu laws) committed a far worse offense than the hotel proprietor who made a rule that invalids and disfigured persons were not allowed in the dining hall. Americans thought the reverse.

Very few Hindu subjects of any age took the transgressions to be violations of convention, by Turiel's criteria: The Hindus said that the transgressions would be wrong even if people all thought they were not wrong and that the transgressions were wrong in other cultures. Only adults and older children in the United States distinguished morality and convention with substantial frequency. In this study, unlike Turiel's, young children in the United States– like the Hindu subjects of all ages – failed to distinguish between morality and convention; they said, for example, that eating a dog for dinner would be wrong even if everyone thought it was not wrong (although, unlike the Hindus, they did not object to eating beef). Shweder and his colleagues concluded that the distinction between morality and convention is not culturally universal and is learned during childhood in cultures that make such a distinction. Shweder therefore agrees with Kohlberg that children do not distinguish between morality and convention.

[10] A utilitarian analysis of this problem would, I think, take the feeling of being offended as a real consequence, and therefore a reason not to sunbathe, but such an analysis would also consider two additional factors: the possibility of helping people to change their beliefs so that they are not offended, and the precedent-setting effect of giving in to people who claim that they are offended as a way of controlling others. The problem is not a simple one.

This controversy is still unresolved. On the one hand, Turiel went out of his way to pick transgressions that were easy to think of as conventional, and Shweder did not. This fact may account for the discrepancy in the results found for American children. On the other hand, Hindus could have treated transgressions as moral because they took very seriously the moral consequences of violating conventions (like those in the nude sunbathing example): They might have thought, for example, that the spirit of the dead father would be deeply hurt by the son's getting a haircut the day after the father's death. With such a belief, they would find it easy to see this violation of "convention" as a violation of morality as well. The findings of Shweder and his colleagues at least suggest that there could be an important germ of truth in Kohlberg's claim that children often fail to distinguish between morality and convention.

Smetana (1982) went on to suggest a third domain, that of *personal* decisions. She interviewed women who were considering whether to have an abortion and found that many of her subjects rejected the relevance of moral considerations to their decision. For example, one subject said, "If[the mother does not] want the child, then there's no reason to bring it into the world. . . . She should think about herself first. It's because it's her right as a person, to be able to do what she thinks is right for herself" (p. 45). Some responses of this sort could result from a failure to search for goals. In general, failure to consider consequences for others (such as the person who would be born) as a goal of one's decision making can cause behavior that harms others. Failure to consider such consequences can be the result of a self-deceptive maneuver designed to avoid guilt feelings, which other subjects experienced when they found themselves unable to put these consequences out of their minds, even when they concluded that having an abortion was best, all things considered. On the other hand, subjects who treat abortion as a purely personal decision could simply be inarticulate: They may have considered the moral arguments against abortion and rejected them (as many philosophers have done, such as Singer, 1979).

Smetana argues that the so-called preconventional reasoning found by Kohlberg could result from subjects treating Kohlberg's dilemmas as personal rather than moral problems. Many of her subjects treated both real and hypothetical abortion dilemmas as personal, even though some of these same subjects used advanced moral reasoning in Kohlberg's dilemmas. If she is correct, preconventional moral reasoning is not moral reasoning at all, but rather a failure to understand the question as it is intended by the researcher.

Emler, Renwick, and Malone (1983) have criticized Kohlberg's claim that stages are limited by cognitive development, that postconventional reasoning is beyond the thinking of those who reason conventionally (because they have not yet understood the relevant concepts and distinctions), and that once these latter are understood they will be seen as superior and will be adopted. This claim is crucial for the argument that children are incapable of critical thinking. Emler and his colleagues argued that the distinction between conventional and postconventional reasoning – as Kohlberg scored it – often reflects a distinction between two political ideologies rather than two levels of development. The "postconventional" answers often sounded more left-wing.

Emler and his colleagues found that subjects who initially reasoned at the conventional level could easily be induced to reason at the postconventional level if they were told to "answer as if you were an extreme radical." The researchers used a multiple-choice test of moral reasoning in which subjects were asked to say which of several issues was important (Rest, 1975). The results of this test correlated highly with the results of Kohlberg's interviews, but this multiple-choice test was not so obviously dependent on the subjects' ability to express their views verbally. The results suggested that people often choose to reason at a lower stage even after they understand a higher one. This does not mean that there is no such thing as development of moral reasoning. It could be that such development consists of a change in *standards* for what is good reasoning and what is not (rather than a change in *ability* to reason in various ways), or it could be that some people do find certain forms of reasoning difficult, but these difficulties do not account for differences among adults in responses to Kohlberg's test.

As yet there have been no attempts to teach children directly to do moral thinking at the critical level. It is possible that Kohlberg's theory may be unduly pessimistic about their ability to do this. Of course, this does not mean that a child can be a sophisticated social thinker; it may take a great deal of *knowledge* of other people and of specialized subjects (such as economics or anthropology) to think well about complex social issues. It is possible, however, that the "basic" form of critical thinking – thinking about the consequences of one's choices for the feelings of others – is truly basic and is therefore not that difficult to apply to the situations that children are called upon to deal with.

Conclusion

Much more work remains to be done on the subject of moral reasoning. A search for biases, of the sort that we have found in other decision making, would be a worthwhile approach. The normative model could be some form of utilitarianism. Once departures are discovered, we could go on to ask whether the normative model is wrong and, if not, whether there are some prescriptive heuristics that could bring people's reasoning closer to it than the heuristics they use. Kohlberg more or less attempted to do this, in that his conventional and preconventional levels can be seen as departures from the normative (or prescriptive) model expressed by his idea of postconventional reasoning. Future investigation should focus on whether Kohlberg was wrong about the difficulty of understanding and using sophisticated forms of moral reasoning.

In sum, the role of psychology here is an important one: to discover and understand biases in moral thinking and to study ways of correcting these biases, possibly earlier in childhood than Kohlberg thought possible. Of course, some of the biases in moral thinking are exactly the biases that occur in all thinking: failure to consider goals (in this case, moral goals), biased search for evidence and biased inference – particularly those biases that favor our belief that we are morally good people and do not need to improve – and failure to examine critically our own intuitive rules.

In the present chapter, we have considered moral questions largely from the perspective of a disinterested observer who is equally concerned about everyone involved. This is not a useless perspective, since many of our moral decisions – such as those concerning political action or inaction – have little effect on ourselves as individuals. We have, however, dealt only briefly with the issue of conflict between self and others. In the next chapter, we tackle this issue directly.

The best chance for gains comes through cooperation.
                                    Fortune cookie message

This chapter focuses on a specific type of moral decision problem: decisions involving situations in which the narrow self-interest of the individual conflicts with the interest of the group as a whole. Retired people who have medical insurance that covers all expenses stand to gain (from extra medical attention and reassurance) if they visit their doctor weekly, sick or not, but if everyone in their group did this, their insurance premiums would skyrocket. People who watch viewer-supported television can save their money by not contributing to support the station they watch, but if everyone did this the station would be off the air, and all who like to watch it would suffer. Each farmer stands to gain from letting the family cows graze on the commons, the common pasture for the town, but if everyone did this the pasture would disappear (Hardin, 1968).

Such situations are called *social dilemmas*, or *commons dilemmas* (by analogy with the common-pasture example). In a simple social dilemma, each person is better off doing one sort of thing (given what others do), but all are better off if all do something else. The action that is best for all is called *cooperation*; the action best for the self is called *defection*.[1] It is best for all (cooperative) not to overgraze the common pasture but best for each to do so.

Because so many situations can be analyzed as social dilemmas, much of the philosophy and psychology of morality is contained in this problem. The following or breaking of many moral rules can be seen as cooperation or defection, respectively. If everybody lies, we will not be able to depend on each other for information, and we will all lose. Likewise, if nobody keeps promises, it will be impossible to make agreements unless they are consummated immediately. Cheating on one's taxes (making the government spend

---

[1] The basic theory of cooperation and defection comes from the mathematical theory of games, which was developed largely by the mathematician John von Neumann as early as the 1920s. This theory first attracted the attention of social scientists and philosophers in the early 1950s, after the publication of von Neumann and Morganstern's *Theory of Games and Economic Behavior* (1947), the same book that called attention to utility theory.

399

more money on enforcement), building up arms stocks in the context of an arms race, accepting bribes, polluting the environment, and having too many children are all examples of defection.

Social dilemmas also lie at the foundation of all economic systems. If people are sufficiently selfish, each person benefits most by consuming the fruits of others' labor and laboring himself as little as possible – but if everyone behaved this way, there would be no fruits to enjoy. All economic systems can be seen as ways of inducing people to do their share of the labor and moderate their consumption – in comparison to this dreaded state of anarchy. An effective way to induce people to do these things is to require monetary payment in return for consumption and to require labor in return for money. (Both capitalist and communist systems rely largely on this principle.) As we shall see, however, this is not the only solution people have thought of. Other solutions to social dilemmas try to reduce selfishness itself, to encourage motives that promote cooperation (such as the motive to do useful work), or to induce cooperation with other sorts of sanctions.

Research from social psychology reveals that we often fail to recognize that we are behaving selfishly (or inappropriately deciding to defect) because of motives such as envy or greed. Another cause of defection, which has not been much researched, is simply failure to think about the needs of other people (especially people far removed from us by geography or by time – people of foreign lands or the people of the future who have not yet been born). To avoid such biases and make good decisions about social dilemmas, individuals need a way of deciding whether to cooperate or defect in a given situation. Continuing the utilitarian approach introduced in chapter 19, I propose a theory of *weighted utilitarianism* as a normative decision theory for social dilemmas. Prescriptively, we can approximate this theory by drawing on traditional modes of cooperative behavior that have developed and by using certain heuristics that counteract the most common causes of defection and insufficient thought.

Laboratory versions

Psychologists have invented a variety of laboratory games for studying co-operation and defection. The games are used to study the circumstances in which subjects cooperate with fellow subjects or defect and to establish the motives for these behaviors.

Prisoner's dilemma

The *prisoner's dilemma* is a laboratory task that has been extensively used, in a number of versions, to study cooperation and defection. The name comes from the following story, on which "prisoner's dilemma" tasks are modeled: Two people, Art and Bob, suspected of having committed a certain crime,

Table 20.1. *Effects of cooperation* (C) *or defection* (D) *on prisoners' jail terms (years)*

	Bob Chooses C		Bob chooses D	
	Art's term	Bob's term	Art's term	Bob's term
Art chooses C	2	2	8	0
Art chooses D	0	8	6	6

Table 20.2. *Effects of cooperation* (C) *or defection* (D) *on subjects' pay*

	Bob chooses C		Bob chooses D	
	Art's pay	Bob's pay	Art's pay	Bob's pay
Art chooses C	$ 8	$8	$2	$10
Art chooses D	$10	$2	$4	$ 4

are taken into custody by the police. The district attorney is convinced that they are guilty of the crime but does not have enough evidence to convince a jury. The district attorney separates the suspects and offers each a choice between two actions: The suspect can confess and provide evidence concerning the involvement of both suspects (act *D* – for Defect) or not confess (act *C* – for Cooperate – with each other, of course, not with the police). The outcomes for both players depend on what they both do, as shown in Table 20.1. If both choose *D* (confess), they will both be sent to jail for 6 years. If both choose *C* (not confess), they will be sent to jail for 2 years on a lesser charge. If only one confesses, however, that one will be set free, and the other will have the book thrown at him and receive the maximum sentence of 8 years.

Putting aside the morality of trying to get away with a crime, *C* is the *cooperative* act. If both suspects choose *C*, they will both be better off than if both choose *D*, yet no matter what Bob decides to do, Art will get 2 years less by choosing *D* than by choosing *C*, and the same reasoning applies to Bob's choice. Both suspects appear to be better off by choosing *D*, given what the other does, but together they would be better off choosing *C*. This is because the choice of *D*, while gaining 2 years for the suspect who makes it, forces the other suspect to *lose* 6 years.

In laboratory experiments modeled after this case, the outcomes for subjects are usually designed to be positive rather than negative. Table 20.2 shows a case in which each subject (Art or Bob again) gains $2 by defecting, no matter what the other subject does, but both subjects are $6 better off if they both cooperate than it they both defect. In other words, by choosing *D*

Table 20.3. *Effects of the number of cooperators (those choosing* (C) *on the payoffs for cooperators and defectors (those choosing* D)

	Number of players who choose *C*			
	0	1	2	3
Option *D*	$6	$10	$14	—
Option *C*	—	$ 4	$ 8	$12

rather than *C*, each player gains $2 for himself and causes the other player to lose $6.

Effects of repetition

In the typical prisoner's dilemma laboratory task (and in some real-world analogs of it, such as arms races) the game is played repeatedly by the same two subjects. This leads to various attempts on the part of each player to make the other player cooperate. Players adopt various strategies to induce cooperation: A *strategy* is a rule that determines which choice a player makes on each play. Axelrod (1984) argues that one of the most effective strategies, both in theory and in fact, is the "tit for tat" approach. You begin by co-operating, but after that you imitate the other player's choice on each successive play, thereby "punishing" uncooperative behavior.

If such a strategy is effective in getting the other player to cooperate, the game is not really a social dilemma at all, for the strategy itself becomes an action that is best for both players. When games are repeated, it is helpful to think not of individual plays but rather of strategies as the choices at issue. When we study performance in laboratory games, then, we must be aware of the fact that repeated games may not actually involve social dilemmas at all. The laboratory studies I shall review, however, use nonrepeated games and are therefore true social dilemmas.

N-person prisoner's dilemma

The basic prisoner's dilemma can be extended to several people. (*N* stands for the number of people.) In one form of this game, each choice of option *C* – as opposed to option *D* – leads to a small loss for the player who makes the choice and a large gain for everyone else overall. Table 20.3 displays the options in a three-person game being played for money. Choosing option *C* moves a player down and to the right: One more player has chosen *C*. Therefore, each choice of *C* loses $2 for the person who makes it but increases the payoff for each of the other players by $4, resulting in a total increase of $12. In some versions of the game, the benefit to everyone is gained only if every-

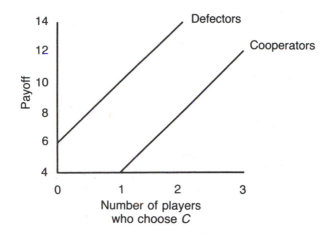

Figure 20.1. Effects of the number of cooperators (those choosing *C*) on the payoffs of cooperators and defectors (those choosing *D*), based on data in Table 20.3.

one cooperates or if some minimal number cooperate. Such a version requires mutual trust. Each player must believe – or be willing to take the risk – that the others will cooperate.

We can illustrate the situation with the graph in Figure 20.1. The graph represents the payoff for cooperators and defectors as a function of the number of cooperators. The slope of the lines represents the benefits that accrue to *others* from each person's decision whether to cooperate or defect; each person's decision to cooperate (rather than defect) moves everyone else one step to the right on their respective line. A decision to cooperate, however, moves the person who makes it from one line to the other, as well as one step to the right. The "dilemma" arises from the fact that the vertical distance between the lines is greater than the amount of increase resulting from one step to the right.

In general, these laboratory situations present people with a choice of two actions: cooperate (*C*) and defect (*D*). Such games are analogous to many situations in daily life in which the interests of individuals conflict with the interests of "society" or, more generally, other individuals. In many of these real-world situations, people do not have a chance to try to make others cooperate. They cannot develop a "strategy," and their behavior does not influence others. It is as though the game was played only once.

Normative and prescriptive theory of social dilemmas

The problems caused by the existence of social dilemmas are among the most important that human beings have to solve. If we could learn always to cooperate, wars would disappear and prosperity would prevail. Even without achieving such a utopia, more cooperation would solve many other human problems, from conflicts among roommates and family members to problems of protecting the world environment. These are problems for a prescriptive theory, a theory that takes into account ordinary human behavior. It has been my approach throughout this book, however, to stand back from the immediate problem and try to develop a set of standards that we can apply to evaluate possible prescriptive solutions, that is, a normative theory. Especially in a domain that is so full of prescriptive panaceas as this one – from Marxist revolution to laissez-faire capitalism (at the national level of the problem) – we need to know what makes a prescriptive theory good before we argue about which one is best. We also need a descriptive account of human motives and behavior in social dilemmas. We need to know where the problem is before we try to fix it.

The problem of normative theory is made especially difficult because of a clear conflict between two different ways of applying utility theory. First, utility theory is a normative theory of satisfying personal goals. Some of these goals are altruistic (as we have noted throughout), but there are, for most of us, other goals that are purely selfish and that sometimes conflict with the goals of others. Second, utility theory, in the form of utilitarianism, has been applied as a normative theory of what is best for everyone, a moral theory that treats all individual goals as equally important, no matter whose goals they are. Because some goals are selfish, these two applications of utility theory cannot give the same answer to every question about what we should do.

To call attention to this conflict, which lies at the heart of the problem of normative theory for social dilemmas, I shall, as an expositional device in this section, discuss only selfish goals. Clearly, if people are sufficiently altruistic, social dilemmas will disappear, since there is no conflict between self and others, but we are not always so altruistic, and that is when the problems arise.

We shall consider the three normative theories that are the obvious candidates for the normative theory of social dilemmas. At the one extreme of altruism, we have what I shall call the *cooperative theory*. Very close to this theory stands *utilitarianism* itself. At the extreme of self-concern, we have what I shall call the *self-interest theory*. Finally, in the middle, we have a special form of utilitarianism that I shall call the *theory of weighted utilitarianism*. This theory, I shall claim, best meets the needs of both individuals and groups and therefore also has the best claim to be our normative theory of decision making for social dilemmas and the standard by which we evaluate our prescriptive theory.

Let us consider these views in the context of a classic example: walking across the lawn instead of on the sidewalk, in a public place. Suppose that everyone prefers to have a nice lawn in front of the college library, but each of us can benefit (save time) by taking a shortcut across the lawn. In this situation, "cooperation" can be defined as staying on the sidewalk (avoiding the shortcut), so that the grass does not get trampled to death. A few people

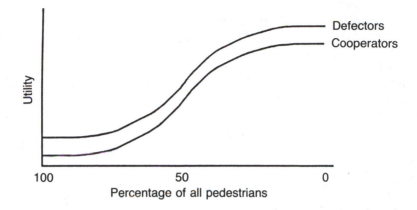

Figure 20.2. Total utility for cooperators (those who do not walk on the grass) and defectors in the grass-walking example as a function of the number of cooperators. Utility is derived both from the appearance of the grass and from taking the shortcut. (*Note:* The utility scale has no units.)

could walk on the grass without killing it, however; it takes a fair amount of traffic to kill the grass. If a lot of people have already walked on the grass, though, one more will not make any difference, because it will be too late to save the lawn.

We can diagram the situation as in Figure 20.2. The upper curve is for defectors, because there is always some personal benefit to taking the shortcut. Notice that the slope – the benefit to others from cooperation – changes as a function of the number of cooperators. In the middle region, around 50%, the slope is highest, because at that point an additional defector ruins a little more grass, and so the benefit to all decreases.

The *cooperative theory* states that one should choose whatever would be best for everyone if everyone made the same choice. In all of the examples given so far, it would be better if everyone cooperated, so everyone should cooperate. Indeed, Dawes (1980) defines "social dilemmas" as situations in which defection increases personal benefit (holding constant the actions of others) but the benefit of each is maximized if *all* choose cooperation. In the grass-walking example, nobody should take the shortcut, *no matter how many others did likewise*. The cooperative theory is a natural extension of the contractual view of morality discussed in chapter 19. It holds that the right question to ask is "If we were all going to agree to do one thing or the other, what would we agree to do?" Of course, given the choice between all co-operating and all defecting, we are all better off if we cooperate, so that is what we would agree to do. Then, by imagining that a hypothetical contract has already been made, it holds that cooperation is what each of us *should* do. If we do not cooperate, we violate the contract.

The problem with the cooperative theory is that it often conflicts with the maximization of utility (Regan, 1980). If everyone has already trampled the grass to death, why should I be the only one to obey the "Keep Off the Grass" sign? I would only decrease net benefit by hurting myself. (Let us put aside such arguments as the fact that by being seen to walk around the grass I might encourage others to do likewise. We have not counted such precedent setting as an outcome in our analysis, and if we did count it, Figure 20.2 would look different.)

Schelling (1978, p. 236) gives another example of the conflict between the cooperative theory and utility maximization: In summer, it is best for everyone if everyone is on daylight saving time. By the cooperative theory, each of us ought to live according to daylight saving time, *even if everyone else around us is on standard time*. This example shows, again, that the effect of what we do depends on what others do. In this case, it is best to conform.

The *self-interest theory* says that I should always do what is best for me and ignore everyone else. Therefore I should always walk on the grass. Two different forms of this theory are often confused. One form says that we should not care about other people. Hardly anyone seriously holds this theory. (We shall return to it, however, in ch. 21.) The second form says that it is best for everyone if individuals look out for their own interest. This theory is, in fact, taken seriously by many as a *moral* theory, because it *is* concerned with what is best for everyone. This theory seems to be the underlying justification for various defenses of free enterprise, for example; it is often argued that the best society for everyone is a society in which all individuals pursue their own self-interest.

The problem with this theory is that it essentially denies the existence of social dilemmas. We may define such dilemmas as cases in which pursuit of narrow self-interest is *not* best for everyone. (We shall make this definition more precise later, but it accounts for all the cases we have encountered so far, and it is consistent both with the definition we shall give and with Dawes's definition.) If there are any such cases – and there sure are many – this theory simply ignores the problem that they create; it gives up on the problem we are trying to solve. As a normative theory, it amounts to saying that morality makes no claims on individual behavior. (It might be more defensible as a prescriptive theory, but later I shall argue against that too.)

If we apply *utilitarianism* (which we examined at length in ch. 19) to the grass-walking problem, it says that I should cooperate as long as the benefit to others from doing so is greater than the cost to me. Therefore, I should cooperate when the number of other cooperators is about 50%, but not at either end of the percentage range. At the high end, I may not know exactly how many cooperators there are; it would be difficult to determine whether I will be the critical person who starts the decline of the grass. It seems sensible here to compute *expected utility*, given my personal probabilities for the different numbers of cooperators.

The problem with utilitarianism, as a normative standard, is that it is too demanding. Taken seriously, it would require us to give away money whenever someone else has a stronger need for it than our own.[2] Singer argues that it would reduce us all to a standard of material living far below what many of us are used to (1979, ch. 8). A similar problem exists with the cooperative theory, but the problem is even worse, because we must sacrifice our own interest even when nobody else benefits.[3] It is asking too much to expect people to behave in this way.

If saintliness is too much to expect, however, pure selfishness is too little. A better solution, as I suggested in "Tradeoffs among Reasons for Action" (1986) is a kind of *weighted utilitarianism*, in which the normative standard is based on a utilitarian analysis, with our own interest weighted more than the interest of others.[4] This is a compromise between the utilitarian and self-interest theories, but it aims to be a *consistent* compromise. The point of consistency is to provide the greatest benefit to others in return for the least sacrifice to ourselves. If we all weighed the interests of others around the world one-tenth as much as our own individual interests (a level that might still swell the coffers of Oxfam), for example, we might end up doing more good, for the same amount of self-sacrifice, than if we behave inconsistently, sometimes making enormous sacrifices but achieving little good and at other times omitting the small sacrifices that might do a lot of good.

Within this consistency constraint, we should (normatively) consider the goals of others to some optimal extent: not so much that we could not pursue the personal goals that make life worthwhile for us, but not so little that – if everyone cared so little about others – we would all suffer from our mutual lack of concern. By this view, defection is a normatively permissible response if the self-sacrifice required to cooperate is too great or the benefits to others too small. As for walking on the grass, this theory says that it could be all right to do so, depending on how strongly you want to do it. On the other hand, if you can do a lot of good with a small self-sacrifice, you are obliged to do that as well. In particular, you should *want* to make a self-sacrifice if the good you can do is sufficiently large compared to the sacrifice required. Weighted utilitarianism should be seen as a theory of moral motivation rather than of decisions about individual cases.

If we provisionally accept this theory, then we will also want to replace

---

[2] It would also make us rather dull people (Wolf, 1982). We would be totally wrapped up in helping each other, but what goals would we help each other achieve? Would there be anyone left to be a comedian or a concert pianist? Who would laugh or listen to music, when they could be helping someone else instead?

[3] If our capacity for self-sacrifice were limited, we would do less good for people by trying to follow the cooperative theory than by trying to follow utilitarianism, because, by the cooperative theory, we would use up our capacity for nothing.

[4] Singer (1979, p. 181), Bennett (1981, p. 78), and Hare (1981, ch. 11) proposed theories very similar to mine, but they took their theories to be prescriptive (in my sense) rather than normative.

Dawes's definition of social dilemmas with one (based on Pruitt, 1967) in which we define social dilemmas as *situations in which one option (cooperation) maximizes net expected benefit over all players but another option (defection) maximizes expected benefit to the self.*

Defined in this way, the idea of social dilemmas seems to capture many of the kinds of conflicts that we call "moral," particularly those cases in which self-interest conflicts with the interests of others and in which many people face the same choice. An appropriate normative theory for social dilemmas would seem to require, first, cooperation – but only when cooperation can accomplish some net good – and, second, *consistent tradeoffs* (across situations) between self-interest and the expected benefits of cooperation. Prescriptively, we could attempt to approximate this normative ideal.

Motives in social dilemmas

With this analysis in mind, let us examine some of the descriptive theory concerning the motives for behavior in social dilemmas that has been developed through psychological research. (Such motives, we shall note later, are not the only cause of defection: Simple thoughtlessness about the needs of others can play a role.) Let us begin with the motives or goals that operate in such situations. These motives can be treated as "dimensions" of utility in a MAUT analysis. If you imagine yourself in a social dilemma (either a real one or a laboratory simulation), it will be apparent that some familiar motives are involved: self-interest, or greed; empathy and altruism; envy of others; the desire for fairness or equity. Let us reexamine these well-known "virtues" and "vices" from the point of view of psychological research.

Altruism

Adam Smith, the author of *The Wealth of Nations* (1776), is famed as the theorist of unbridled capitalism, or (supposedly) the self-interested pursuit of profit. How interesting to discover that his first book (1759/1976) was entitled *The Theory of the Moral Sentiments*. In it, he says, "How selfish soever man may be supposed, there are evidently some principles in his nature, which interest him in the fortune of others, and render their happiness necessary to him, though he derives nothing from it except the pleasure of seeing it. . . . That we often derive sorrow from the sorrow of others, is a matter of fact too obvious to require any instance to prove it" (p. 7). Even today, people contribute to charity and advocate the cause of those less fortunate, and they take pleasure in the good fortune of others. More generally, we can solve social dilemmas by increasing the level of altruism: If our utilities depended heavily enough on each other's gains and losses, no conflict would exist between maximizing the utility of the individual and maximizing the utility of the group.[5]

As Smith suggested, emotional *empathy*, the tendency for people to experience emotions that they observe others experiencing, is a source of altruism. This could be the reason why pictures or films of famine victims inspire an outpouring of contributions in the United States and Europe. To measure such empathy in the laboratory, Krebs (1975) asked one subject to watch another subject (actually a confederate) performing a task. In some conditions, the confederate either won money or appeared to receive an electrical shock, as a result of the spin of a roulette wheel. Krebs had convinced the observers that they were either similar (or dissimilar) to the confederate by showing them, in advance, a questionnaire that the confederate had supposedly filled out, which agreed (or disagreed) with the subjects' opinions on various issues. When the confederate was perceived as similar, the observers demonstrated more physiological response (increased heart rate and the like) as a function of the outcome experienced by the confederate. Also, when the confederate was perceived as similar, subjects were more likely to sacrifice some of their own reward for the confederate, when given an opportunity to do so. Krebs concluded that the feelings of empathy made the subjects behave more altruistically.

Another source of altruism is the desire to participate in a *communal* relationship, that is, one in which it is assumed that all involved in the relationship care about each other (Clark & Mills, 1979). We find communal relationships in families, in romantic relationships, among friends, and among coworkers. Some theorists have treated communal relationships as though they involved a kind of *exchange* – "You scratch my back, and I'll scratch yours." Although exchange relationships surely exist, they are not the same as communal relationships. In communal relationships, people act because of the desires of others, not to return favors. When someone in a communal relationship returns a favor in kind – for example, John brings a bottle of wine as a gift when Mary invites him to dinner, and then Mary brings exactly the same wine when John invites *her* to dinner – the communal relationship is undermined because it appears to be based on exchange. In communal relationships, the participants keep track of each other's "needs," not of what they have done for each other in the past (Clark, Mills, & Powell, 1986).

Clark and Mills (1979) demonstrated this distinction in an experiment in which they manipulated the desire of unmarried male subjects to form a communal relationship with an attractive female "subject" (in fact a confederate) in the same task. When the woman was described as unmarried, most

---

[5] In Table 20.3, where cooperation provides a total of $12 for others at the expense of $2 for oneself, subjects who followed weighted utilitarianism would cooperate if they weighed others more than ⅙ as much as they weighed themselves (assuming utility is proportionate to dollars). If we describe this as a change in the utilities of each subject, then the task is no longer a social dilemma when this weight is exceeded.

male subjects did want to begin a communal relationship with her. The experiment was designed so that the men could (and always did) help the woman by giving her some of their extra "points" that they earned for doing their task quickly. If she returned their favor in kind by later giving each of them some of *her* points, they tended to like her less as a result. If she simply thanked them, they tended to like her more. When the men were told that the woman was married, most of them did not want to form a communal relationship, and they liked the woman *better* when she returned their favor in kind than when she just thanked them.

Clark, Ouellette, Powell, and Milberg (1987) found that subjects were more willing to help another "subject" by blowing up balloons (for a "creativity experiment" that involved using the balloons) when the other "subject" was described as unmarried and interested in meeting new people than when the other subject was portrayed as married. (This time, Clark and her colleagues used both male and female subjects, and they showed the real subjects a picture of the other "subject," who was, in all conditions, an attractive member of the opposite sex.) This effect of the expectation of a communal relationship was larger when the subjects were led to believe that the other subject was sad, having "just got[ten] some bad news from home."

Clark and her colleagues also asked whether people differ in the desire to form communal relationships and whether these individual differences affect "helping" behavior. To measure individual differences in this desire, Clark and her colleagues developed a questionnaire in which each subject rated a series of descriptions on a scale from "extremely characteristic [of me]" to "extremely uncharacteristic." The items on the questionnaire concerned both willingness to help others (for example, "When making a decision, I take other people's needs and feelings into account" or "I believe it's best not to get involved taking care of other people's personal needs" – the latter item was counted negatively) and the desire to be helped by others (for example, "It bothers me when other people neglect my needs"). Subjects who scored high on this desire for communal relationships were more helpful to the experimenter when she asked them to help her alphabetize reference cards "for her thesis," especially when the subjects had been told that the experimenter "was looking pretty down" (p. 97).

It would seem that empathy and the desire to form and maintain communal relationships are helpful for altruistic behavior (behavior that helps another at one's own expense), but they may not be necessary. Some people apparently act out of a more abstract knowledge that their action is morally right. People who act out of religious convictions often have this sort of motivation, but purely moral behavior is also found in people with no religious belief at all but strong moral beliefs. Nagel (1970) has suggested that the argument "How would you feel if someone did that to you?" appeals to us as an argument that is relevant to our own decisions for very fundamental reasons. This appeal is not based on our having been taught the Golden Rule, nor is it based on our expectation that someone *will* do to us whatever we do to them. Nagel's explanation of the appeal of this argument is obscure and difficult to summarize, so I shall not attempt to give the details. I bring it up just to raise the possibility that there is something like a "pure" motive for concern with others, a motive not tied to empathy, or to the desire for communal relationships, or to anything else we shall discuss. I know of no research on this sort of motivation, but my experience with toddlers suggests that even they can understand this kind of argument. Because very young children have not had time to learn much about morality from their culture, they might be good subjects for the study of such motivation.

Envy, fear, and greed

We have examined some of the dispositions that cause us to cooperate. (Later, we shall examine more of these.) Other sorts of dispositions cause us to defect. The simplest of these is *greed*, which may be seen as placing an excessively high weight on one's own desires compared with those of others. *Envy* arises out of the desire to do at least as well as – or (preferably) better than – others who are similar to us. It is a motive that is satisfied by hurting others, so, like greed, it opposes altruism directly. Finally, the *fear* that others will not cooperate causes us to defect when we believe that the benefits of cooperation require that most people cooperate or when we feel that it is unfair for a few people to cooperate while many others take advantage of their self-sacrifice without doing their share. This motive opposes altruism only when we think that others are not altruistic.

Most people apparently adhere to an ideal of fairness, equity, or equality. They compare their own treatment and outcomes with those of others, and, if they feel that they are not being treated fairly, they justify selfish behavior by seeing it as a remedy for injustice.[6] The city teenager who blasts everyone on the street with the sound of his "boom box" may not just do it because he likes the sound: He may feel he is getting even with those who have cars (with stereo radios and tape decks) that he cannot afford. In other words, we seem to be as concerned about our position *relative* to others as we are about our position itself. Messick (1985, p. 93) illustrates one form of this concern:

I did an informal experiment with my sons to illustrate this point . . . In isolation from each other, I gave them a choice between a dish containing two peanuts and one containing three. With no hesitation, they both chose the three peanuts. The next step was to put one peanut next to the dish containing two[,] and four peanuts next

[6] A fair amount of literature concerns itself with the standards by which people judge what is fair (for example, Walster, Walster, & Berscheid, 1978). At issue is whether, or when, people favor standards such as equality of outcomes over other principles such as "to each according to his contribution" or "to each according to his need." A review of this literature would take us too far afield.

to the dish containing three. I then asked the boys again to tell me which dish they preferred, with the additional stipulation that the peanuts beside the dish that they chose would be given to their brother: if they chose three, the brother got four; if they chose two, the brother got one.

Needless to say, making their outcomes interdependent changed the choice situation dramatically. The younger boy chose the dish with two peanuts and explained that he did not want his brother to get four when he would only get three. The older boy still chose the dish with three but explained that he did not mind giving his brother four peanuts because he was sure that he would . . . be able to get some back for himself. He too was not indifferent to relative position.

The motive of *envy*, Sabini and Silver claim (1981, ch. 2), amounts to an attempt to hurt another person because you feel that you are hurt by that person's gain. Messick (1985) found that envy operates in laboratory games as well as in the real world. Subjects in his experiments chose the "defection" response in order to avoid falling behind another player, even when they knew that they themselves would ultimately get fewer points (and less money) as a result. People seem to have a conception of fairness that provides a standard for relative outcomes. They are hurt when they feel that they are getting less than they deserve according to this standard. They are strongly motivated to avoid letting the outcome for themselves be less than what they think is fair from this point of view.[7]

The motive to avoid falling behind, or being treated unfairly, has also been called *fear* (meaning not physical fear, but fear of being a "sucker"). Fear contrasts with another primary motive for defection, *greed*. Greed, as we use the term here, is simple selfishness (when it conflicts with moral behavior) – that is, an unusually high weight given to one's own desires as opposed to those of others. Greed is essentially the desire to be a "free rider," to ride for free while everyone else is paying.

Dawes, Orbell, Simmons, and van de Kragt (1986) performed an experiment designed to distinguish the roles of fear and greed in causing defection. There were three conditions (see Table 20.4): a standard condition; a condition that eliminated fear; and a condition that eliminated greed. If subjects cooperate more in the condition that eliminates fear than in the standard condition, then we can conclude that fear prevented cooperation, and if subjects cooperate more in the condition that eliminates greed, then we can conclude that greed prevented cooperation. For all three conditions, each of seven subjects was given a note that could be exchanged for $5 at the end of the experiment. Each subject could either keep the note or contribute it to a pool. Subjects were told that if a certain number of subjects contributed to the pool (three out of the seven in one experiment, five out of seven in another), the whole group would receive a $70 bonus – that is, $10 for each

---

[7] A similar motive is *competition*. In competition, I have argued (1985a), one's basic goal is, in itself, to do better than someone else, by as much as possible. Competition does not necessarily seek to remedy some hurt or unfairness. Competition is an appropriate motive in games and sports in which it is the true goal of the game. Elsewhere, competitive motives are inappropriate.

Table 20.4. *Experimental conditions used by Dawes and his colleagues to distinguish between fear and greed*

	Standard condition		Money-back guarantee		Enforced contribution	
	Bonus	No bonus	Bonus	No bonus	Bonus	No bonus
Contributors	$10	$0	$10	$5	$10	$0
Noncontributors	$15	$5	$15	$5	$10	$5

person. The subjects all decided individually, at the same time, whether or not to contribute, without knowing what other subjects had decided and without being able to influence anyone. Subjects also knew in advance that they would not see each other as they left the experiment with their winnings, and the game was played only once. This situation is much like the grass-walking example, because in order for the benefits of cooperation to be available, a critical number of cooperators is required. If you know that everyone else is cooperating or that nobody is, you do no harm by defecting (keeping the $5).

In the "money-back guarantee" condition, subjects were told that contributors would get their $5 back if there were too few contributors to produce the $70 bonus. Therefore, subjects had no reason to *fear* that there would not be enough contributors. If defections are caused by fear, we would expect to have fewer defectors – and more contributors – in this condition than in the standard condition.

In the "enforced-contribution" condition, subjects were told that *non*contributors would have to *pay* $5 if there *were* enough contributors to produce the bonus. Greed could therefore play no role in causing defections. Nobody could be tempted to try to get a "free ride" on the contributions of others.

The proportion of cooperators (averaging across two experiments) was about 58% in the standard condition, 63% in the money-back guarantee condition, and 90% in the enforced-contribution condition. Defections were therefore substantially reduced when greed – the temptation to take a free ride – was eliminated, but reduction of fear had no significant effect.

Although the failure of the money-back guarantee to increase cooperation could imply that fear was not a motivation, Dawes and his fellow researchers provide another explanation. If subjects *believed* that this condition would affect *other* subjects, they would think it more likely that they could get away with defecting without hurting anyone, because enough others would contribute so that the bonus would be provided anyway. This effect would cancel out the effect of reduction of fear itself. On the other hand, if subjects believed that the enforced-contribution condition would encourage others to contribute, they would have no less reason to contribute themselves, since they would probably have to contribute anyway. The experiment therefore provides evidence for greed, but leaves the status of fear in doubt.

It is worth noting, before we leave this experiment, that more than half of the subjects cooperated, even in the standard condition. This behavior is difficult to justify in terms of self-interest, for it is unlikely that the choice made by any given subject would be critical in determining whether the bonus was provided or not.

An experiment by Yamagishi and Sato (1986), carried out in Japan, provides evidence for both motives (fear and greed). On every trial, each of five subjects was given a number of points (worth money), some of which the subject could contribute to a common pool. All subjects received bonus points that depended on these contributions.

There were two conditions of interest, which differed in terms of the system used for determining the number of bonus points. In the *minimum* condition, the number of bonus points was determined by the size of the contribution of the subject who had contributed the *least*; if only one subject contributed nothing, there would be no bonus at all. This is analogous to preserving the reputation of a group: One "bad apple," it is said, can spoil things for everyone. Here, fear would be the major cause of defections: If you think that someone else is going to be a fink and give very little, there is no advantage to anyone from your not "finking out" yourself by giving nothing or very little. Greed would play only a small role here, because too much of it would penalize you as well as everyone else.

In the *maximum* condition, the bonus depended on the amount given by the highest contributor. This is like volunteering for a dangerous mission on behalf of a group, when only a few volunteers are required. Here, one is little affected by a few defectors, so fear of someone else's defecting plays little role. One need not fear that one's own cooperative action will be useless to the group, either. Greed, however, may play a larger role, for one's own contribution also matters little, except in the unlikely event that one is the highest contributor.[8]

We can diagram the two conditions roughly as shown in Figure 20.3 (if we think of cooperating as making a large contribution and defecting as making a small one). Note that the curve for the minimum condition resembles the curve for the left half of the grass-walking graph (Figure 20.2) and that the maximum condition resembles the curve in the right half.

Yamagishi and Sato found that friends cooperated more than strangers in the minimum condition but not in the maximum condition. Presumably friends were less afraid that they would cheat on each other by giving less money, but friendship had no effect on personal greed. Subjects were also given a questionnaire about their attitudes toward public questions, with items de-

[8] Yamagishi and Sato called the two conditions "conjunctive" and "disjunctive," respectively.

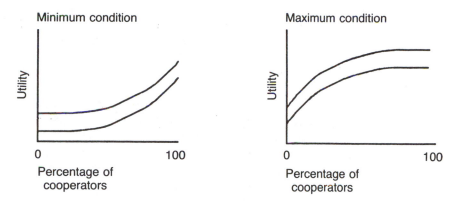

Figure 20.3. Utility for cooperators and defectors as a function of the number of cooperators for situations resembling Yamagishi and Sato's minimum and maximum conditions. Upper curves are for defectors; lower curves are for cooperators.

signed to assess both fear and greed as general motives in the subjects. Here are some "fear" items (pp. 69–70):

> Help to developing nations should be limited to the minimum, because it is only exploited by a small group of people.
> During the oil shock, people rushed to stores to buy a stock of toilet paper because people are concerned only with their own interest and not with the benefit of society.
> There will be more people who will not work if the social security system is developed further.

Here are some greed items (p. 70):

> In order to be a successful person in this society, it is important to make use of every opportunity.
> It is not morally bad to think first of one's own benefit and not of other people's.

The score on the fear scale correlated with defection in the minimum condition but not in the maximum condition. In the minimum condition, where only one "fink" could prevent everyone from getting a bonus, subjects who expressed fear and distrust in the questionnaire were more likely than other subjects to defect. The score on the greed scale correlated with defection in the maximum condition, but not in the minimum condition. In the maximum condition, subjects who were greedy according to the questionnaire were the ones more likely to defect. These results not only indicate the existence of individual differences in the motives in question, but they also suggest that the motives are quite general, affecting attitudes toward public issues as well as behavior in laboratory experiments.

In the minimum condition, subjects' *expectations* about what others would do correlated highly with their own behavior; this was less true in the maximum condition. In the maximum condition, subjects compared their own behavior with the behavior they expected from others. Note that this effect is pretty much in line with the utilitarian model: If others do not cooperate in the minimum condition, then one's contribution will not do much good. The important point here, though, is that subjects differ in their expectations.

The danger of this sort of social comparison is that the standard of fairness is often ambiguous (Messick, Bloom, Boldizar, & Samuelson, 1985). In a complex society, it is practically always possible to find someone who is treated better than you are *in some way*, no matter how lucky you are. If each of us focuses on aspects of comparisons that make us feel treated unfairly, each will feel justified in demanding (or taking) more at someone else's expense. One professor will feel that she deserves more pay because she is such a good teacher; a second will feel that she deserves more because her research is so important; a third, because she feels that she is an intellectual leader among her colleagues. The residents of a poor country focus on the sheer inequality between them and the residents of prosperous countries; the residents of the latter feel that they "deserve" their prosperity because of their hard work, their superior government, and their other virtues.

These processes are illustrated in an experiment done by van Avermaet (1974; reported in Messick, 1985). Subjects were instructed to fill out questionnaires until told to stop. They expected to be paid, but they did not know how much. Each subject was given either three or six questionnaires (depending on the experimental condition) and was told to stop after either 45 or 90 minutes. When the subject finished, she was told that there had been another subject who had had to leave before he could be told that he was supposed to be paid. The experimenter, who also said he had to leave, gave the original subject $7 (in dollar bills and coins) and asked her to send the other subject his money (in the stamped, addressed envelope provided). The subject was told that the other subject had put in either more, the same, or less time and had completed more, the same, or fewer questionnaires.

At issue was how much money the original subject would send to the "other" subject (actually, of course, a confederate). Subjects who *either* worked longer *or* completed more questionnaires than the "other" gave the other *less* than $3.50. Subjects apparently seized on any excuse to see themselves as deserving more. When the original subjects were equal to the other on *both* dimensions, they sent almost exactly $3.50 on the average. Only when subjects did worse on *both* dimensions (time and number of questionnaires) was there a tendency to send more than $3.50 to the other (however, the increase was not statistically significant). It appears that subjects seize on any excuse to send the others less than themselves; they divide the money equally only when there is no excuse to give more to themselves. This phenomenon may be related to the sort of irrational persistence of belief discussed in chapter

15; here, subjects seem to use evidence so as to maintain the belief that they deserve more.

What is of special interest about this experiment is that it shows how a fallacy in reasoning can lead to departure from a normative model (in this case, MAUT). Normatively, the subjects ought to weigh the two dimensions (time and number of questionnaires) equally, or at least *consistently*; however, subjects weigh one dimension more when it suits them, whichever dimension it is.[9] What appears to happen in this experiment, and very likely in many real-life analogs, is that people seek a distinction between themselves and others in order to justify selfish behavior.

We have reviewed several causes of defection. Which of these are the result of poor thinking? Greed is not necessarily a result of poor thinking. People who are sufficiently selfish will achieve their own goals best by being greedy (provided it doesn't hurt them in the long run by giving them bad reputations). Perhaps they have not thought well about their goals, but we cannot be sure. Poor thinking is more directly implicated when people who are concerned about others forget to bring this concern to bear on their decisions (as we discuss later).

Envy and fear can also result from poor thinking. The idea that we should defect in order to "get even" often involves a biased choice of a reference group. If I want to justify slacking off in my work, I can think of myself as underpaid by comparing myself to my college classmates who are now wealthy corporate attorneys and successful businessmen, but if I think of reasons against this conclusion, I can think of a larger group of people around the world (including psychology professors in other countries, for example) whose standard of living is, on average, far below my own. People who conclude that they are being treated unfairly, or who fear that they will be so treated, are often using an imagined reference group that was cooked to order, just as van Avermaet's subjects picked the dimension of comparison to favor themselves.

Fairness as a positive motivation

The other side of the coin in the van Avermaet experiment is that only 2 of 92 subjects apparently failed to send any money at all to the other. When there was no relevant distinction between the subjects, the money was split. The demands of fairness are sufficiently strong that people will sacrifice their own money for the sake of fairness, even to people they do not know (and

---

[9] Even if subjects simply weigh their own interest more, the normative model would have them do this consistently; therefore, they should give themselves as much money, on the average, when they and the other subject were unequal in opposite directions on the two dimensions as they did when they and the other subject were equal on both.

with whom they therefore have no chance of establishing a communal relationship).

Kahneman, Knetsch, and Thaler (1986) found additional evidence for such a motive. Suppose you are told that you and a student in a different class have a chance to divide up $10. You will offer the other student some part of the $10. If the other student accepts the offer, he will get the amount you offered, and you will get the rest. If the other student rejects the offer, you will each get nothing. How much would you offer? Most of the subjects asked by Kahneman and his co-workers offered $5, even though they probably could have gotten away with less. When they were asked what was the minimum they would accept if the other subject made the offer, most required more than $1.50; if the other subject offered less than that, they would prefer to see both subjects get nothing rather than tolerate such unfairness. (This is the negative side of fairness motivation, the desire to hurt others, even at one's own expense, in order to restore equality.)

In a second experiment, each student in a class was told to divide $20 with an anonymous other student in the same class. There were only two options, an equal division of $10 each and an unequal division of $18 for the decision maker and $2 for the other. The other student could not reject the offer. The subjects knew that after they made their decisions only some of them would be chosen at random for actual payment. Out of the whole group of subjects, 76% divided the money equally.

In a second part of the experiment, each subject who was not selected to be paid was told that she would make a second decision about sharing some money among herself and two other students. One other student, called E (for even), had decided on an even division of the $20 in the first part of the experiment, and the third student, called U (for uneven) had decided on an unequal division. The subject had two options: She could allocate $5 to herself, $5 to E, and nothing to U, or she could allocate $6 to herself, nothing to E, and $6 to U. The question here was whether the subject would sacrifice $1 of her own money in order to punish another subject who had been unfair and reward another subject who had been fair. Out of the whole group of subjects, 74% chose to make this sacrifice (81% of those who had themselves chosen equality in the first part, but only 31% of those who chose inequality). In sum, subjects are, once again, willing to sacrifice their self-interest for the sake of fairness. Walster and her colleagues (1978, ch. 3) review a number of studies that make the same point.

Although the motive to be fair is a source of altruism, the principle of fairness can be difficult to apply consistently. Harris and Joyce (1980) told subjects about various situations in which a group of partners had opened a business (e.g., selling plants at a flea market). The partners took turns operating the business, so different amounts of income were generated while each partner was in control, and different costs were incurred. (Costs for one partner were extremely high because of an accident.) When subjects were asked how the *profits* should be divided among the partners, many subjects favored equal division. When subjects were asked how they would divide up the *expenses*, they tended to divide these equally, even though they understood that the resulting division of profits would be unequal (because each partner would keep what was earned during her turn, after paying her share of the expenses). Judgments of fairness seem to exhibit framing effects like those we encountered in chapter 17.

We have considered four different kinds of goals or motives in social dilemmas: altruism always favors cooperation; greed or self-interest always opposes it; fairness opposes cooperation when we believe that we have been treated unfairly and favors cooperation when we believe that someone else has been treated unfairly; and "fear" – the desire to cooperate only when we believe that others will – favors cooperation if we believe that others will cooperate but opposes cooperation if we believe that others will not. Weighted utilitarianism holds that we should balance our own selfish desires against those of others in a consistent way. Clearly, an appropriate balance of greed and altruism will help us do this. Prescriptively, however, fairness motivation probably also helps make us conform to the normative model, since it makes us particularly attentive to the desires of the unfortunate, who can benefit more than others from our attention. Fear could be related to fairness, in that we do not want to be "suckers": We think it is unfair if we cooperate when others defect. It is not clear that this motive is one that we need.

We often depart from the normative model (weighted utilitarianism) by focusing on whatever goal is consistent with our self-interest. We thus use the goal of fairness – in the form of envy – to motivate defection, but we are somewhat less inclined to use this goal when it dictates self-sacrifice (although we *do* use it sometimes). We use fear – in the form of distrust – to justify defection as well. This is why we consider envy and distrust to be vices. It is not that they are never appropriate; it is, rather, that we are inclined to overuse them to justify selfishness, so we must fight them. The prescriptive implication of the findings we have discussed, then, is that we should give others the "benefit of the doubt," for (as van Avermaet showed) we are inclined to give ourselves that benefit when doubt exists. Actively openminded thinking will help us in carrying out this prescription by making us aware of reasons that go against our initial selfish tendencies.

The voter's illusion

So far we have examined those factors that increase or decrease cooperation, and we have seen that poor thinking – particularly distortion of our beliefs – is one factor that works against cooperation. There are other kinds of poor thinking that *promote* cooperation. These are easily seen in the case of voting in political elections. Voting is a simple act of self-sacrifice for the benefit of others. It takes a little effort, but, if enough people put in that effort (including the effort of informing themselves), we are all better off, because, as a society, we will tend to choose the candidates who will be most likely to help us achieve our goals.

One error in people's thinking about voting is the conclusion that self-interest alone makes it worthwhile to vote. (This error has never been formally documented in an experiment, but we can observe it informally by discussing the issue with people who vote.) It is extremely unlikely that one vote is critical in any election, and even if it is the difference one vote would make to the voter who casts it is probably small – too small, given the low probability, to justify voting at all in terms of self-interest alone (Riker & Ordeshook, 1968).

It is possible that people vote out of some feeling of moral obligation. From a utilitarian point of view, voting is probably worthwhile: If 50 million voters can, together, make a small improvement in the lives of each of 50 million people (perhaps the voters themselves – but to a utilitarian it does not matter), voting is worthwhile if the benefit (utility gain) to each person is worth the trouble (utility loss) of casting one vote.

It is also possible that people vote because they misunderstand the situation. For one thing, they may believe that they vote out of self-interest; they do not make the calculations required to see that their self-interest is hardly affected. There is a danger in this belief, in that it could inhibit people from voting on the basis of what is best for everyone. They may think that they should vote their own narrow self-interest. If enough people did this, the needs of those who cannot wield power through voting, such as children, minorities, people in the future, or people in other countries, would be neglected. It might be better for everyone if people who voted out of self-interest just decided that voting was not worthwhile – although the rest of us would then have to look out for them.

There is, however, another incorrect reason for voting, which is less insidious. People may think that their own choice affects others' choices. Of course, this is true, in that a vote sets a precedent through example, but the belief in question may go beyond that. Voters may reason, "If people on my side vote, I'll probably vote too. My voting will thus be linked with theirs. Hence, I'd better vote, because if I don't, they won't either." The same reasoning could apply to any social dilemma, of course. The essential confusion here is between *diagnostic* and *causal* relationships. Their own voting is *diagnostic* of the overall turnout on their side, but it does not affect the turnout, except for their own vote. (The same reasoning is involved in the Quattrone and Tversky experiment on self-deception described in ch. 15.)

Quattrone and Tversky (1984) told subjects about a hypothetical election in a country with 4 million supporters of party A, 4 million supporters of party B, and 4 million nonaligned voters. Subjects were told that they were supporters of party A. Some subjects were told that the election depended on whether more of the supporters of party A or the supporters of party B turned out to vote. These subjects said that their side (party A) was substantially more likely to win if they voted than if they did not vote. They were also quite willing to vote. Other subjects were told that the election depended on whether more of the nonaligned voters voted for party A or for party B. These subjects thought that the probability of their side's winning was not much different whether they voted or not. They were less willing to vote than the subjects who were told that the election depended on the turnout of party supporters. Of course, one vote is one vote; in fact, these latter subjects would have just as much influence on the election whether it was "determined" by the party supporters or by the nonaligned voters. In short, people may think that their vote affects other people, when in fact they are only themselves *affected* by the same factors that affect other people.

Thoughtlessness

Another possible cause of defection in social dilemmas is simple *thoughtlessness*. The person who plays his radio loudly while walking along the sidewalk, rather than expressing social envy, may simply not be *thinking* about whether anyone else is being bothered. Likewise, the woman who buys her 27th pair of new shoes in the last 2 years does not *think* about whether someone in Africa might put the $79.95 (plus tax) to better use.

This possibility has not been studied, to my knowledge, but it seems worth studying. Religions try to teach people to be thoughtful of others. Do they succeed? Can children be taught thoughtfulness in school? It seems likely that part of such instruction would involve instruction in good thinking: If we search thoroughly, we are more likely to discover the needs of others than if we do not.

Solutions to social dilemmas

Experimental approaches

Let us turn now to the prescriptive question of how we can bring about cooperation. The experiments of Kahneman and his colleagues suggest that the utility of fairness to others sometimes outweighs the individual's self-interest. This fact may provide a way out of the typical social dilemma in which all individuals suffer collectively because many (or all) pursue their self-interest. "Contract" theories of social decision making suggest that one way to achieve fairness, with relatively little self-sacrifice, is for people involved in a social dilemma to make an *agreement* to enforce cooperation. Essentially, they agree to assess a penalty of some sort against anyone who defects, a penalty large enough to make defection unprofitable. This can be done through the election of a government, or the delegation of the enforcement power to an existing authority such as a chief, boss, parent, ruler, or mediator. People will be inclined to accept such a situation to the extent to which they are sure that fairness will increase as a result of the change.

Messick and his colleagues (for example, Samuelson, Messick, Rutte, & Wilke, 1984) have studied the effects of departures from fairness in a laboratory game designed to resemble the classic "commons" dilemma. Six subjects sat at six different computer terminals and watched displays showing the changing levels of a common resource pool. At the outset the pool contained 300 units. On each trial, each player could take up to 30 units for himself. After all players had taken what they wanted, a variable number of units (about 30) was added to the pool. (The units were worth real money.) Each subject saw on the display the amounts that the other players took and the new level of the pool after all players had consumed what they wanted. Subjects knew that if the pool ran out, the experiment was over. Subjects were told both to try to get as many points as possible and to make the resource pool last as long as possible.

In fact, the display was manipulated by the experimenter so that each subject "saw" the other subjects behave in different ways. In some conditions, the other subjects appeared to behave more or less the same way, leading to the appearance of fairness. In other conditions, the subjects' behavior differed drastically: some behaved like absolute pigs, and others were quite modest in their demands. The average change in the size of the pool was also manipulated so as to make the pool appear to increase, decrease, or stay about the same in size.

Subjects were more likely to take more for themselves when there appeared to be no danger of the pool's running out; when there was danger, subjects moderated their demands, even if their demands had been minimal throughout. Subjects were also asked whether they would like to elect a leader to apportion the resources for the next play of the game. Subjects were more likely to say yes when the pool had run out quickly because units were taken out faster than they could be replenished.

Of greater interest here is the response to the perceived variability among the other players. The researchers ran the experiment in both the United States (Santa Barbara) and the Netherlands (Groningen), and they found that subjects' behavior apparently was affected by their nationality. When the amounts taken by other subjects differed by large amounts, American subjects tended to take more for themselves. It seemed that they did not want to be "suckers." "If some pig is going to lead the whole gang to ruin, well, I might as well share in the spoils," they seemed to reason. Dutch subjects responded differently. In the same situations, they were not more likely to increase their own harvests. When asked if they wanted to elect a leader to apportion the pool on the next play of the game, American subjects were equally likely to want a leader, regardless of whether they saw the other subjects as highly variable in their demands or not. Dutch subjects were considerably more likely to want a leader when the other subjects' demands were variable than when they were all about the same.

In short, Americans tended to respond to unfairness by joining in, by avoiding being "suckers." Dutch subjects responded to unfairness by trying to eliminate it through electing a leader. This study reminds us that the way in which people weigh moral and social considerations is very often a function of the way in which they are brought up and educated and of the culture in which they live. The Dutch subjects may have tended to regard large differences among the other subjects as morally outrageous. The Americans seemed to regard such differences as a sign that self-indulgence was acceptable.

The election of a leader is not the only way to solve a social dilemma, and it is possible that Americans may have seen this idea as unnecessarily authoritarian. The parties can simply make an agreement among themselves to abide by certain rules. In a laboratory task, this often occurs when the participants talk among themselves about the situation. Dawes, McTavish, and Shaklee (1977) found that simply giving the subjects a chance to talk about a laboratory dilemma – in which each subject could choose to cooperate or defect – increased cooperation from about 30% to about 70% of responses. (Mere social contact had no effect: When the subjects spent the time discussing another issue, cooperation did not increase.) In such discussion, there is an implicit threat; subjects made it very clear to one another that they would each be very angry with anyone who defected (possibly to the point of retaliating outside of the experiment). It is doubtful that this solution could be used in large-scale social dilemmas, because they involve too many people to sit down and talk, but television publicity campaigns for various causes sometimes use a related method. Respected (or ordinary) citizens appear on television and proclaim their intention to perform some socially beneficial action – contribute to the local public television station, clean up their own litter, restrict their fertility (in China). This may have the effect of making people think that an implicit agreement is in force – a thought that can become self-fulfilling.

In a subsequent experiment, Orbell, van de Kragt, and Dawes (in press) found that the beneficial effects of discussion made subjects more willing to cooperate, even with other people who had not been involved in the discussion. In each session, 14 subjects were randomly divided into two groups of 7. Each subject had a note worth $6, which she could either keep or give away (anonymously). Every $6 given away was augmented by $12 from the experimenter. The subject's contribution, plus the bonus, went into a pool that was to be divided up (in one condition) among the other 6 members of the subject's own group or (in the other condition) among members of the other group of 7. Half of the groups in each condition participated in a discussion, and half of the groups did not. Finally, just before the final choices were made, half the groups in each of these subconditions were told that the benefits of their contributions would be switched: Subjects who had been told before the discussion that contributions would go to their own group were then told that the benefits would go to the other group, and vice versa.

When there was no discussion, about 33% cooperated, even when benefits went to the other group – an interesting fact in itself. No beneficial effect of discussion was found when subjects thought that the benefits would go to the other group during the discussion. Therefore, the discussion did not promote general altruistic or cooperative motives. Discussion had a beneficial effect, however, when the subjects thought that the benefits would go to their own group; 79% cooperated. In this case, the discussion aroused feelings of general obligation, possibly of a communal sort. The most interesting finding was that when the subjects thought, during the discussion, that the benefits would go to their own group but were then told that the benefits would go to the other group, the discussion still had a beneficial effect: 59% cooperated. It was as though, once the subjects understood the importance of cooperation, they realized that it did not matter much whether others had been involved in the discussion or not. This result is encouraging, if we are interested in promoting cooperation among strangers. It suggests that promoting cooperation among people who know each other can be used to teach the benefits of cooperation in general.

Modes of cooperation

Alan Fiske (in press) suggests that we can classify solutions to social dilemmas into four different modes of cooperation. Each mode has associated with it certain "virtues" and "vices," and an enforcement mechanism that operates when these internalized traits of character are not enough. Fiske calls these the *communal mode*, the *authority mode*, the *equity mode*, and the *market mode* of social organization.

The *communal mode* (essentially the same as that described by Clark, which we examined in the section on altruism) is often used for family dinners. All help themselves, trying at the same time to be concerned about the needs of others. In communal production, everyone pitches in, but nobody keeps track of how much each person is doing. Although in Western culture this mode characterizes family units, in some African societies and elsewhere it governs the life of villages, and even strangers (such as anthropologists) are welcomed quickly into the ongoing communal relationship among villagers. One advantage of the communal mode is its capacity to adjust to differences among people in desires and abilities. In laboratory social dilemmas, such as the experiment by Dawes and his colleagues described earlier, this mode may come into effect as a result of communication among the subjects.

The communal mode relies on altruism and empathy. The "vices" of this mode are greed and sloth (laziness). Enforcement is often carried out by gossip or, in extreme cases, by expulsion from the group. This mode depends heavily on the education of participants in the virtues of the communal mode itself, as opposed to institutional rules and structures. It requires certain "virtues" in the participants but no explicit structure or *agreement* to maintain cooperation, as long as these virtues are displayed.

Fiske's *authority mode* involves an explicit social ranking. In some societies men are served dinner before women, and women before children. This is not really a solution to the social dilemma, because it essentially allows some to defect (for example, the men, who can take for themselves at the expense of the women and children).

The authority mode, however, is related to one real solution of the social dilemma, in which an authority is set up to enforce cooperation. (This was the solution that some groups adopted in the cooperation experiment described earlier.) To carry out this task, the authority usually demands some sort of priority, a kind of payment. For example, the director of a business or the head of a department is allowed to choose the best office, and military officers are given special privileges according to their rank. The virtues of the authority mode are thus the responsibilities of the leader and the loyalty of the follower. The military leader is responsible for the safety of those under his command, and when he fails in this task he is guilty of a serious offense. Those under the leader must follow the leader loyally, without always asking for explanations, for the sake of efficiency. The vices are abuse of authority and disloyalty. Enforcement is done by the authority, with the help of loyal followers.

The *equity mode* involves equal or fair division, according to a formal rule agreed on by all. This is the rule used for allocating party favors at children's birthday parties: All of the children get exactly the same favor (whether they want it or not). In many African societies, this mode is used for organization of labor: All workers get together to till a field, with a drum beating to make sure that everyone does exactly the same number of strokes. More elaborate versions of the equity mode involve some sort of "fine tuning" of the rules to adjust for circumstances, as in the case of most taxation systems, which take into account the ability to pay. The equity mode is sometimes used when subjects in laboratory dilemmas have a chance to discuss: Subjects agree on a certain equal division of gains or a certain rule. The virtue required by this mode is simply that of playing by the rules. The vice is cheating. Enforcement is usually part of the rule itself: There are specified penalties for infractions.

The *market mode* involves buying and selling through a market, usually with a system of prices. Markets depend on agreements between pairs of people – buyers and sellers. A market is a partial solution to a social dilemma, because two people can agree to cooperate. "I'll do my part of the work, if you'll pay me [that is, give me my share of the consumption]." Markets are somewhat limited, though, in that there is often no way to collect payment. For example, a private market in national defense (in which each citizen contracts with the army for defense) will not work, because, to avoid being conquered, the army would have to defend those who do not pay as well as those who do. The same holds for curbing pollution and paying for scientific research.

A market transaction does not occur unless both parties agree, so it is a safe bet that both will benefit and neither will suffer. If nobody else is hurt by a transaction, markets lead toward *Pareto optimality* (optimality in the sense defined by Pareto, 1909/1971): Any transaction must make someone better off and no one worse off, until the (optimal) point is reached at which any change must make someone worse off. The market mode is the only one in which there is no provision for asking one person to sacrifice so that someone else receives a greater benefit – for example, to take from the rich in order to help the poor (on the grounds that the same amount of money means more to the poor).

Although we often think of the "free market" as not really a social organization at all but something more like a "state of nature" or anarchy, Fiske points out that this is not the case. Real markets require at least two virtues if they are to work: accurate representation of what one is selling, and promise keeping. Few market transactions would be made if the buyer had to insist on absolute proof of every claim that was made by the seller and if the exchange had to be made simultaneously, without any sort of credit or trust. Therefore, the market is actually a highly organized social system, regulated by moral standards, and, for cases in which these fail, explicit laws. Its virtues are truthfulness about what one has to sell and honor in keeping one's word. The vices are deception and promise breaking. Enforcement can be built into market agreements, but it usually requires some other mode (such as an authority that protects the market).

Many social errors involve attempts to use the wrong mode. For example, you do not pay your mother for cooking your dinner, although you may thank her. Offering her money would be an insult, because the relation between mother and children is usually communal. We also frown on the use of the market mode for assigning grades to students (although we know of cases in which grades have indeed been sold). Grades are supposed to be determined by equity or authority. Prostitution, in both its literal and its more general meaning, involves an inappropriate extension of the market mode.

Of course, these modes are rarely used in their pure forms. Most social organization is a mixture of two or more modes. For example, the use of the copying machine in my department of the university is governed by a mixture of all four modes. Each faculty member and graduate student gets equal allotments for certain purposes (equity – but faculty get more, so this is also ranked authority). Additional use can be paid for (market). Some members also give their access to others in times of need, as when a student is told, "You can sign my name in the book" (communal). Without some sort of social organization, however, the department would soon use up its budget on photocopying alone, to the detriment of all.

The point of this analysis is to suggest that there are many different ways of solving social dilemmas. Each has advantages and disadvantages in certain situations. Much of the real stuff of political argument concerns just what these are.

Conclusion

Defection in social dilemmas can be seen as a paradigm of a great deal of immoral behavior, because defection involves indulging one's narrow self-interest at a great expense to others. In general, we have noted three types of poor thinking that cause such immorality. The first is that people hold incorrect theories – accepted without adequate critical scrutiny – about what behavior is right: For example, some people believe that selfishness is a virtue. Second, people fall prey to the temptation to weigh their self-interest more than it ought to be weighed. They sometimes do this by self-deception (ch. 15), convincing themselves that they are not really being selfish or that their behavior is justified. Third, people do not think enough about the effects of their choices on others, possibly because they believe that morality is nothing more than honoring certain prohibitions (ch. 19).

We can oppose the first cause by presenting people with the arguments in favor of weighted utilitarianism, specifically, that following this theory will help us achieve our goal of helping others with minimal sacrifice of our other goals. We can oppose the last two causes by teaching certain prescriptive heuristics. The tendency to overweigh self-interest through rationalization can be opposed by the heuristic "Give the other guy the benefit of the doubt." The tendency to ignore the effects of choices on others can be opposed by the simpler heuristic – which we try to drum into children's heads almost daily – "Think about other people's feelings." In the complex world in which we live, these guidelines may need to be supplemented by other heuristics specifically directing our attention to the effects of our choices – for example, our political choices – on people in distant lands, as well as people not yet born. This kind of thinking requires active open-mindedness, because such arguments often are not obvious, and even when they are presented clearly we tend to resist them.

21   Decisions about the future

> But you must bind me hard and fast, so that I cannot stir from the spot where you will stand me, . . . and if I beg you to release me, you must tighten and add to my bonds.
>
> Homer, *The Odyssey*

In the last chapters, we examined conflicts between self and others. In this chapter, we look at a different kind of conflict, that between the present and the future. Many of our decisions require us to choose between satisfying our goals for the immediate present and our goals for our futures: Should I do the crossword puzzle or work on this book? (I will enjoy doing the puzzle now, but if I miss the deadline for this manuscript, I will be unhappy later.) Should a student go to a movie or get started on a paper? If she goes to the movie, she may regret it later, when she has to finish the paper at the last minute. Should Bill take a job he likes now, or should he go to graduate school and get a job he likes even better later? Should I learn the violin, putting up with the scratching and sawing in order to play Bach later? We can think of these kinds of conflicts as analogous to social dilemmas: Instead of a conflict between self and other, the conflict is between a "present self" and a "future self."

A basic problem we have in such conflicts is that we are biased in favor of our present self. Our future self, like "others" in social dilemmas, is distant and has less claim on our attention. We begin to be aware of this problem in childhood, and we develop methods of *self-control*. Like Ulysses, who had himself bound to the mast of his ship so that he could hear the song of the Sirens without giving in to the temptation to visit them (see the quotation that begins this chapter), we learn to "bind" ourselves by making decisions before the temptation occurs, so that we will not succumb to it.

We can think of decisions about the future as *plans* or *policies*. A *plan* is a decision to do something at a future time. When we cook a meal, we usually have some plan in mind. We do certain things at one time and put off other things for the future. The crucial step here is that we decide now to do something at a later time. There would be no point in planning if we were unable to hold ourselves to this decision. The study of planning, therefore, is intimately tied up with the study of self-control. A *policy* is a plan that binds us to perform a certain action regularly or under certain conditions. We might establish a policy of practicing the violin for half an hour every day, for example, or a policy of never picking up hitchhikers. A plan is not a policy when it involves only a single, isolated decision, such as planning to go to the movies on a certain day. A policy applies to a whole class of behavior that recur regularly in our lives.

Some policies are made all at once, but policies also result from individual decisions made without any idea that these decisions will affect the future. Without realizing that we are doing so, we set *precedents* for ourselves (Hare, 1952, ch. 4). Suppose a friend who has missed a class you take together asks to borrow your notes. If you decide to lend them, it will be difficult for you to make a different decision if she asks again. Even if a different friend, who does not even know the first one, asks you for the same favor, you will tend to be bound by your initial precedent.

The same mechanism of precedents applies to the most minute details of our lives, such details as what we eat, when we go to bed, and the way we deal with other people. Practically every decision we make sets a precedent for the same decision in similar cases in the future. In this way, we form policies for the various domains of our lives. At times, of course, we think about these policies and change them. At any given time, however, we can be said to be following certain policies whether we have thought about them or not.

Plans and policies *create new personal goals*, or they change the strength of old ones. If I make a decision to take up the violin, that gives me a new set of goals right away: finding a good teacher, finding time to practice, obtaining a good instrument. I will also not be surprised if this decision creates or strengthens other goals over time: I will come to like violin music more than I do now, and I will develop certain musical standards. If I start early enough, I could even acquire the goal of being a professional musician. When we make plans and set policies, then, we are making decisions about our own personal goals.

Up until this point, in part III, we have been concerned to discover the best ways of making decisions that will enable us to achieve our personal goals. We have, on the whole, regarded these goals as "givens." We are now ready to consider how these goals themselves are chosen. These personal goals that we create for ourselves are the most important determinants of our identities as individuals. They are what we stand for, what makes our lives worth living. They are, as noted, chosen through a variety of decisions. Some decisions are apparently trivial: A choice to work on a philosophy term paper instead of one in psychology sets a precedent for similar decisions, which could eventually make the decision in favor of a career in philosophy rather than psychology. Other decisions are made after great agonizing: Should I sacrifice the income I could earn in computer science for a career as a philosophy professor? Is my desire to help others strong enough to make me want to live in a poor country for several years, possibly at the cost of not finding a spouse? Should I retire from working, and what should I do in my retirement?

Most of us, then, are fairly well aware that if we are to have a life plan for the future that will be likely to work for us, we need to search for our major goals and choose among them. Some kinds of decisions, such as those about religious commitments, can be made at any time. We are encouraged to consider other kinds of issues especially seriously at certain times in our lives, particularly at the transition from adolescence to adulthood (with respect to work and marriage), during the childbearing years (with respect to the single decision of bearing children), and at the time of retirement from work. People at these transition points are often encouraged to consider various goals in an actively open-minded manner, seeking evidence from many sources (personal experience, the lives of others, newspapers, works of scholarship, and literature) before making major commitments. Students, at least, tend to be aware of the danger of treating such choices as if they had already been made, without seeking alternatives and counterevidence.

This chapter concerns the theory of plans and policies. The main issue is the extent to which we consider our future interests as we make decisions. Our main problem is a tendency to weigh these future interests too little (compared to what a normative theory would specify), just as we often underweigh the interests of other people. Psychological research has much to tell us about why we have this problem and what we can do about it. Let us begin, however, with a discussion of the normative theory for choosing personal goals.

The choice of personal goals

How should we choose our personal goals? We can either think about decisions that could affect our goals, or we can think about our goals directly. When we think about decisions that could affect our goals, we should be aware of such consequences. For example, psychological researchers who accept military contracts sometimes change their personal goals for their research (ever so slightly) toward the goals of those who support them, and those who study handicapped populations, such as the deaf, sometimes become advocates on behalf of their subjects. Neither of these effects is, by itself, sufficient reason to turn down military funding or to refrain from studying the deaf, for the researchers could have no particular objection to such a change in goals, or they may feel that the risk of such change is worth taking. Anyone who thinks carefully about such decisions, however, must admit that the possibility of such consequences should be considered, along with other consequences. To decide whether we want such consequences, we must ask the next question: How should we think about goals themselves?

When we think about our goals, we must rely on our present goals concerning our future goals. One of these present goals is that we prefer achievable goals to unachievable ones (other things being equal), as suggested by Rawls (1971, ch. VII). This principle argues against choosing such goals as making certain beliefs true ("defending the faith"), for if the beliefs in question are false, the goal is futile. The same principle tells us that it can be rational to give up a goal that is constantly frustrated and has no chance of being achieved.

On the other side, as Rawls points out, most of us want to develop our talents and to strive for difficult achievements. This too is a rational goal, because developing our talents makes us more effective in doing things for other people, and this is usually one of our goals. Without talent, the musician cannot bring us pleasure, the scientist and scholar cannot enlighten us, our leaders cannot govern us well, teachers cannot teach us well, doctors and nurses cannot care for our illnesses, manufacturers cannot give us affordable goods of high quality, and parents cannot give us the kind of upbringing we should have. Because talents are so important to others, societies develop (to varying degrees) ways of encouraging people to develop their talents, such as rewarding them with respect and money when they have succeeded, so the development of our talents helps us achieve these goals as well. The development of talent, however, is often a risky enterprise. We must strike a balance between the risks of striving for high achievement and the principle that our goals should be achievable.

Another consideration in thinking about personal goals is the relative ease or difficulty of changing our own goals. I heard a story of a music professor who did not like modern atonal music. He tried to "develop a taste" for such music by listening to the complete works of Anton Webern (four long-playing records) daily for several months, but at the end he liked Webern's music as little as he had at the outset. Others, however, claim to have had more success in shaping their own goals: People who have forced themselves to give up smoking often report that (over a period of months) they lose their desire to smoke; those who try to reduce their consumption of saturated fat report learning to like fish; and those who have undergone religious conversions report losing their desire to live in ways they have come to see as sinful. The simplest way of trying to shape our goals is to behave as if we already had them, according to the proverb "Where the hand leads, the heart follows."

More generally, the choice of goals is a decision problem in which we evaluate the consequences of our decisions just as we would evaluate the consequences of any other decisions, except that the goals we apply to this decision include our goals for our future goals. We must evaluate the total consequence of having a new goal and being able to achieve it to whatever degree we expect. When we think about having a child, we should not ask how much we now care about the welfare of this future child but rather how much we desire to have the child and care about its welfare in the future, as parents tend to. Similarly, when we make career choices, the relevant question is not how much we now want to do the work of a scientist or teacher but rather how much we will want to do it once we have started down the path that leads to that career. Of course, we could conclude that starting down one path or another will have little effect on our goals. We may find that we do not want ourselves to have certain goals in the future, and we can even try to bind ourselves so that we do not develop them, like those scientists who refuse support from the military partly because they fear that their political goals will change as a result of accepting it. If, however, we become open to changes in our goals, we could realize that many more options are open to us than we previously thought.

The creation of life plans and personal goals is often taken to be a kind of discovery, as though the answer was there all along and our task is only to find it, but what does it mean to say that the answer was "there all along"? As I have argued elsewhere (1985b, ch. 2), the decision to get married, to have a child, to get involved in politics, to learn to play tennis, is usually more like taking on a new set of goals than it is like pursuing goals already present. It is as though we permit another person – the "spouse" in us, the "parent," the "activist" – to share our life. We cannot find our goals simply by asking what they have been or what other people would like them to be, for the goals we would choose in these ways could differ from the goals we would want to have for our own futures.

Many popular ideas about good personal goals are simply attempts to hold up certain ways of living – the fashionable life, competitive success, peace of mind, piety – as better than others. They are not very helpful for planning our personal lives, because they do not provide *reasons* or evidence for choosing these personal goals instead of many other possibilities we could choose.

Good reasons for sticking to plans

Once we have begun a plan or course of action, it is difficult to change. Some of the reasons for this are good, and some are poor. A good reason to stick to our plans is that they usually involve other people, who have, in turn, planned their own lives partly in terms of ours. A music student moves to a new city to study under a great master, who promises to work with the student for 2 years, but after 6 months the master decides to have nothing further to do with students. It is good to be a "dependable person," one who can be counted on to carry out plans once they are made.

Another good reason to stick with a plan is that plans very often build their own momentum. If you spend years building up a clientele for your dress shop, you cannot expect to be as successful if you suddenly move it to another town. The same goes for skills and knowledge you have developed. If you spend a long time learning the ins and outs of a certain method of production, you will be valued for your knowledge, but you cannot expect others to value you as much, for quite a while, if you suddenly switch to another line of work. Of course, plans can go bad, and then this kind of reason does not apply. Also, this sort of reason to stick with a plan tends to vary with age. The younger one is, the more one has to gain from thinking about the future rather than the past.

A final reason for keeping a plan is that if we do not, we lose some of our faith in our own ability to make plans and keep them. This reason may not apply when we otherwise have good reason to break a plan. We can make a distinction between trusting ourselves to keep foolish plans and trusting ourselves to keep worthwhile plans. If you give up a foolish plan, you may not lose any faith at all in your own ability to stick to a worthwhile one.

Beyond these four reasons – the interlocking of one's personal plans with others' plans, the value of dependability, the increased chances for success as plans are carried out, and the value of trust in ourselves – there may be no good reasons for sticking to plans. All of these reasons concern future costs and benefits. They may all be overwhelmed by other reasons concerning the future. If a plan is not succeeding, it may be rational to change it, even if the losses just listed are incurred.

Bad reasons for sticking to plans: biases

Change is difficult. Clinical psychologists are often faced with people who would be happier if they changed their goals or their policies for achieving them. Some of these people know this and still cannot bring themselves to make crucial choices: to decide to quit smoking, to break up with a boyfriend, to go back to school, to retire, to stop bullying other people, or to resist being bullied. Certain types of biases or errors in the way that people think about plans can exacerbate the difficulty of changing them. These biases are usually studied in minor decisions, but they seem to operate in large decisions as well. Of course, we must keep in mind that there are also good reasons to *stick* to plans. Still, some awareness of what makes us stick to them when we should not may help us to decide just *when* to stick to them.

The sunk-cost effect

Sometimes people act as though the very commitment they have made requires them to keep going. This is like "throwing good money after bad." Another name for it is the *sunk-cost effect*: Once funds have been "sunk" into a plan, the only way not to waste them, it seems, is to sink still more. We see this sort of rationale operating in public policy making as well as in our personal lives. It figured, many now think, in such possible misadventures as the Vietnam War and the Tennessee-Tombigbee Waterway project. A senator expressed sunk-cost thinking when he said, about the latter project, "To terminate a project in which $1.1 billion has been invested represents an unconscionable mishandling of taxpayers' dollars" (Senator Jeremiah Denton, November, 1981, quoted by Arkes & Blumer, 1985).

Such a position is irrational; it subverts one's own (or society's) goals. Once you have determined that the best course of action for the future is to change plans – having weighed the effect on others and all of the relevant factors – the time, effort, and money you have spent in the past does not matter one bit. Sticking to a futile plan will not make your earlier decision the right one, if it was really wrong. When we concern ourselves with sunk costs, we are basing a decision on the past, not on its consequences.

This effect was demonstrated experimentally by Arkes and Blumer (1985). If you had been a subject in one experiment of theirs (p. 126), you would have been told to imagine that you had paid $100 for a ski trip to Michigan and $50 for another ski trip to Wisconsin. Money considerations aside, you would prefer the trip to Wisconsin. If you then discover that the trips are on the same weekend and that you cannot sell either ticket, which trip would you choose? Most subjects picked the less preferred trip to Michigan.

This result shows a kind of framing effect, a result of segregating the mental accounts for the two ski trips. Subjects felt that they would "waste less money" by taking the $100 trip. If they had integrated the two accounts, they would have realized that $150 had been irretrievably spent and that the choice was between the more preferred and the less preferred trip.

Another of Arkes and Blumer's experiments (pp. 132–133) shows this clearly:

On your way home you buy a tv dinner on sale for $3 at the local grocery store . . . Then you get an idea. You call up your friend to ask if he would like to come over for a quick tv dinner and then watch a good movie on tv. Your friend says "Sure." So you go out to buy a second tv dinner. However, all the on-sale tv dinners are gone. You therefore have to spend $5 (the regular price) for a tv dinner identical to the one you just bought for $3. You go home and put both dinners in the oven. When the two dinners are fully cooked, you get a phone call. Your friend is ill and cannot come. You are not hungry enough to eat both dinners. You can not freeze one. You must eat one and discard the other. Which one do you eat?

Although most subjects said it did not matter, over 20% said that the $5 dinner should be eaten. If these subjects integrated the costs, they would have seen that $8 was already lost, and that the dinners were identical.

In another experiment, subjects were told,

As the president of an airline company, you have invested $10 million of the company's money into a research project. The purpose was to build a plane that would not be detected by conventional radar . . . When the project is 90% completed, another firm begins marketing a plane that cannot be detected by radar. Also, it is apparent that their plane is much faster and far more economical than the plane your company is building. The question is: should you invest the last 10% of the research funds to finish the radar-blank plane? (p. 129)

In this condition, 41 out of 48 subjects said they should. In another condition, in which the $9 million had not been invested and the only issue was whether to invest $1 million, only 10 out of 60 said they should. This effect was not changed much by changing the story so that the subject was in the role of an outside observer rather than president of the company. Personal involvement does not seem to be crucial.

Thaler (1980, pp. 47–50) explained the sunk-cost effect in terms of prospect theory's value function for gains and losses combined with his idea of integration (ch. 17). When $9 million has already been invested, the additional $1 million is perceived as a small *additional* loss of value, because the value function for losses has a low slope at this point. The extra $1 million is *integrated*, in subjects' thinking, with the $9 million already spent. The additional "benefit" – a nearly worthless plane – seems to outweigh the small *additional* loss. In other words, the value of the plane appears greater than the difference between the value of losing $9 million and the value of losing $10 million:

$$v(\text{plane}) > v(\$9 \text{ million}) - v(\$10 \text{ million})$$

When the $9 million has not been spent, the value of $1 million is much greater than when it is added to $9 million already spent, because the value function is steep near zero. Hence,

$$v(\text{plane}) < -v(-\$1 \text{ million}).$$

The sunk-cost effect could also be explained in terms of regret, in the sense of self-blame (Arkes & Blumer, 1985, p. 137). If we spent the $9 million "for nothing," we might regret it more than if we "at least got something."

Escalation of commitment

The sunk-cost effect may be exaggerated when the decision maker is responsible for the original decision. People want to believe that they are good decision makers, so they persist in believing that an initial decision was a good one, even when it appears not to be. Arkes and Blumer found that the sunk-cost effect was somewhat reduced (in one experiment) when subjects were told that the original decision to develop an airplane had been made by someone else; however, the effect was still present.

Staw (1976) found other evidence for a role of commitment to one's own decision. He gave business students a written case study of the recent history of a business firm. Some students were told that, as financial vice president of the firm, they had $10 million to invest and were asked to decide which of two divisions of the business they would invest it in for research and development. Half of these students were told that the division they had chosen did well after the investment; half were told it did badly. They were then asked to divide an additional $20 million between the two divisions. When the chosen division had performed badly, the allocation to that division the second time around averaged about $13 million (out of $20 million), but when the division had done well the allocation averaged only about $9 million.

Other subjects were not asked to make the original decision on the investment of the $10 million; they were told that it had been made by someone else. These subjects allocated about $8 million to the division that had received the $10 million when they were told that the division had done well, and they allocated about the same amount of money when they were told it had done badly. In short, subjects allocated extra money to the division that had previously received $10 million only when *they* had decided to allocate the original $10 million and when the division in question did badly. Presumably this was caused by a desire to believe that their original decision had been a good one, leading to a belief that the original decision had been a good one, leading to additional investment in a cause that seemed likely to succeed (see ch. 15).

The same results are found when the decision involves hiring people who perform either well or badly (Bazerman, Beekun, & Schoorman, 1982) and when the decisions are made by groups instead of individuals (Bazerman, Giuliano, & Appleman, 1984).

The endowment effect

Another, very similar, source of resistance to change is the *endowment effect*, an unwillingness to give up what one has (one's endowment) for what one would otherwise prefer to it, as shown in the following examples, from Thaler (1980, pp. 43–44):

1. Mr. R. bought a case of good wine in the late 1950s for about $5 a bottle. A few years later, his wine merchant agreed to buy the wine back for $100 a bottle. He refused, although he has never paid more than $35 for a bottle of wine.
2. Two survey questions: (a) Assume you had been exposed to a disease which if contracted leads to a quick and painless death within a week. The probability you have the disease is .001. What is the maximum you would be willing to pay for a cure? (b) Suppose volunteers were needed for research on the above disease. All that would be required is that you expose yourself to a .001 chance of contracting the disease. What is the minimum payment you would require to volunteer for this program? (You would not be allowed to purchase the cure.)

In example 1, Mr. R. will not accept $100 for a bottle of wine, although he would not pay more than $35 for (presumably) the same bottle. In both cases, however, the choice is between wine and money. It might help to think of the true value of the wine as the amount that would have the same desirability as the wine, *if Mr. R. had to choose between a gift of money and a gift of wine* (having neither at the outset). Most likely, this value would be between $35 and $100, because the endowment effect induces an unwillingness to part with money, when one has the money, and with wine, when one has the wine.

In example 2, the value of not having to risk getting the disease, measured against the price for getting rid of it (a), is far lower (for most people) than the same value measured by the payment required to take it on. In general, it appears that there is some value to keeping what we already have. If it is good (as in example 1), we require more payment to give it up than we would spend to acquire it. If it is bad (example 2), we would pay less to give it up than we would require to take it on. (Thaler's examples are hypothetical, but Knetsch and Sinden, 1984, demonstrated the endowment effect in laboratory experiments with small amounts of real money.)

This effect can also be explained in terms of prospect theory (Thaler, 1980) – in particular, in terms of the assumption that the subjective value of a loss is greater (in absolute terms) than the subjective value of the equivalent gain. Any of these situations involves a transaction, giving up one thing in exchange for something else. If we suppose that the thing given up (for example, the bottle of wine) and the thing gotten in return (the $100) would have the *same* value if they were both received, we can see why Mr. R. would not want to make the trade. The thing given up (the wine) would then have a larger (absolute) value when it is perceived as a loss, because losses are valued more than gains. Therefore Mr. R. would require even more money in order to trade. On the other hand, when asked how much he would pay for the wine, the value of the money is increased because the money is now seen as a loss. Therefore he would not be willing to pay as much. The negative value of $35 would be greater than the value of the wine, because the $35 is now seen as a loss.

Put mathematically, $v(\$100) < -v(-\text{wine})$, but $v(\text{wine}) < -v(-\$35)$. The absolute value of the loss is greater than the value of the gain.

The endowment effect seems to operate in planning as well as in ordinary transactions. When we change a plan or policy, we sometimes give up the expected benefits of continuing to follow that plan in return for the benefits of some other plan. (Of course, other factors may be involved, some rational, some irrational.) When the endowment effect operates on policies, we might call it an *inertia* effect, a kind of resistance to changing our course.

More generally, the sunk-cost effect, the commitment effect, and the endowment effect can cause us to stick to our plans even when the rational reasons listed in the preceding section are not sufficient to keep us from switching, given the greater expected future benefits of a new course. We may stick to our old course because we feel that we have sunk too much into it to give it up – even though putting more into it will only increase the waste. Likewise, by analogy with the endowment effect, we may feel that the loss of the advantages of our current course outweighs the gain from switching to a new course, although we would choose the new course if we looked at the whole situation afresh.

Sometimes we stick to plans irrationally because of our basic aversion to risks, resulting from the certainty effect (ch. 17). Our present course seems to us to have consequences known with certainty; however (as argued in ch.

17), this may be an illusion resulting from our failure to consider the true variability of the consequences that might result from our present course.

Finally, a major change of plans, especially when it involves a change of goals, may seem to a person to involve a loss of self, a partial death in which some of the self is replaced with a different person. A change of this sort creates a sense of personal loss that may not be easily compensated for by the creation of a new person inside one's skin. The fear of such a loss, too, is irrational if the new person is otherwise to be preferred (see Parfit, 1984). People who are interested in changing themselves and others must recognize that such changes are far more emotionally involving than a mere calculation of "gains and losses" suggests.

Discounting

Which would you prefer: to get $100 today or $110 a month from now? Many people prefer the immediate reward. Hungry pigeons do too: Faced with a choice between pecking a key that gives them immediate access to food for 2 seconds and a key that gives them access to food for 6 seconds – 10 seconds later – they repeatedly choose to peck the former, even though the next opportunity to peck will come at a fixed time after their choice is made. Mischel (1984) found that young children, faced with a choice between getting an attractive toy (that they could keep) in 5 minutes and a less attractive toy immediately, chose the latter. We can, it seems, be unfair to our own futures: we become *temporally myopic* (nearsighted).

The preference for immediate over larger but delayed rewards is one of the most familiar behaviors of the animal kingdom. Human beings are perhaps not as bad as most other species in this regard, but we do seem to have problems. In psychology, the phenomenon is often called *impulsiveness*,[1] and the attempt to control it is called *impulse control* (Ainslie, 1975). Economists call it *discounting* the future, because future gains or losses are discounted, or underweighed, relative to immediate ones.

Economic theory of discounting

The simplest economic theory of discounting is that people behave as though any gain provides an opportunity to earn interest (or, equivalently, to pay off some debt and avoid paying interest), as though it were a monetary gain. The reason you prefer $100 immediately to $110 later, the theory goes, is that you behave as though you would begin earning interest on the money as soon as you got it. Therefore, if your subjective rate of interest, your personal *discount rate*, is high enough, the $100 would be worth more than

---

[1] In chapter 7, a different meaning of "impulsiveness" was discussed: fast and inaccurate responding as a disposition or cognitive style. The two concepts may be related, because people may respond quickly to gain the reward of removing themselves from the task.

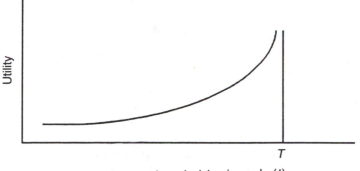

Times when decision is made (*t*)

Figure 21.1. Utility of a reward as a function of the time at which a decision is made. (The utility scale has no units. The reward is available at time *T*.)

$100 to you a month from now. If you were indifferent between $100 now and $150 a year from now, your discount rate would be about 50% per year.[2] Note that this is an "as if" theory, meant to explain all behavior of this type: Pigeons do not usually earn interest on their food, and people may behave *as if* their personal discount rates were much higher than the actual interest rate available in the market.

This economic theory suggests that we could think of discounting in terms of a function relating the utility of a reward to the time at which the reward is available. In psychology, it is customary to plot this function by thinking of the reward as being available at a fixed point in time, *T*, and by thinking of the *opportunity to choose* that reward (versus some other) as being available at different times, *t*, where *t*<*T* (see the graph in Figure 21.1). The closer *t* (the time when the choice is made) is to *T* (the time when the reward will be received if it is chosen), the greater the utility of the reward.

Note that the standard economic theory predicts that rewards lose their utility at a constant (percentage) rate over time, becoming less valuable the farther off in the future they are. If the utility of $100 to you a year from now will be 50% of the utility of $100 if you get it today, then 2 years from now the utility of $100 to you will be 25% of what it is today, and 3 years from now it will be 12.5%.[3]

Normative theory of discounting

There are good economic reasons to think that this form of the decay curve – of utility as a function of delay – is normative, as long as there is no known

---

[2] It could be less, if the subjective interest was compounded.
[3] Mathematically, this amounts to exponential decay.

reason why the utility of the reward will change.[4] One is the idea of interest rate, already noted. If you have $100 now, you can invest it and end up with somewhat more a year from now, say $110. Therefore, you might be indifferent between getting $100 now and getting $110 a year from now, for this reason alone. Similarly, if you need $100 now, the value of $100 now might be equivalent to $120 a year from now, if you would otherwise have to borrow the $100 at a rate of 20%.

Another reason why discounting makes sense is that unforeseen events can affect the utility of money (or any outcome) to an individual. For example, in the interval between now and when you collect the $100, the economy could be hit by an enormous wave of inflation that makes the money worthless; you could die; or, to end on a more pleasant note, you could become a millionaire and have no need for such a piddling amount. If we make the assumption that each of these events is as likely to happen at one time as at any other, the same curve results. If you think that there is a 1% chance of such an event's occurring in the next year, the expected utility of $100 a year from now would be 1% less than it would be otherwise, because there is a 1% chance that its utility would be zero. The longer you wait, the more likely it is that one of these things will happen, so the lower the utility of the $100.

So far, we have assumed that you care just as much about your utility in the future as you do about your immediate utility, but we do not even need to assume that in order to derive a curve of this form as the normative model. What we do need to assume is that your relative preference for two future outcomes at different times depends only on what the outcomes are and on the time *difference* between them. For example, if you are asked to choose between $100 now and $110 in a year, your choice will depend only on the amounts of money and the fact that the time difference is 1 year; it will not matter (barring special circumstances such as immediate needs that will pass) whether both outcomes are put back a year. Your preference is therefore *independent* of the delay, until the first reward is available. Note that if you violate this *delay-independence* assumption, your preference for the outcomes changes simply as a result of the passage of time. Unless you learn something that makes a difference during that time – and we have assumed that you do not – such changes are unwarranted.[5] Note also that this assumption of delay independence says nothing about valuing the future as much as the present. It does imply, however, that *if* you value the future less than the present, you do it in a consistent way. Such consistency can be shown to imply (barring special events) that in each unit of time (into the future) the value of a reward

---

[4] For example, the utility of a car increases when the owner can obtain a driver's license. Here, we put such predictable changes aside.

[5] Of course, you are free to change your mind, but there is no reason why you should change it in any particular direction – for example, from the later, larger outcome to the smaller, earlier one. This is the important point.

will fall off by a constant percentage of its value at the beginning of the interval (Strotz, 1955; Lancaster, 1963).[6]

For the time being, however, let us assume that one ought to be impartial toward all times of one's life. If we think of people at different times as though they were different people, this amounts to the assumption made by utilitarianism that everyone should be treated equally. (Note that when we apply utilitarianism to decisions about others, we ought to consider their future preferences as equal in importance to their present preferences. This often gives us a strong moral reason to go against what people *say* they want when *they* do not think enough about their own future.) This assumption of impartiality still implies (except when there are special circumstances) a discount function like that shown earlier, in which the rate of loss with increasing delay is constant as a percentage.

Descriptive data on discounting

Attempts to estimate the personal discount rate have given varying results. Some economists (for example, Modigliani, 1986) have suggested that the discount rate for money corresponds roughly to the actual rate of interest and that most people try to spread out their income over their lives so as to achieve a constant income (adjusted for inflation). The fact that many people put their money in pension funds and other methods of saving is surely consistent with this view. Pension funds ensure a relatively constant income after retirement; failure to save for retirement is surely an example of underweighing the future, unless one knows that one will never retire. By this view, people care as much about their future as about their present.

Thaler and Shefrin (1981) have argued, however, that such saving is not spontaneous. It is, rather, the result of conscious efforts at self-control. When such efforts are absent – when people do not think about the idea of saving, for example – Thaler and Shefrin found that consumers had an extremely high discount rate – much higher than the current rate of interest. When subjects in an income maintenance experiment were asked, "What size bonus would you demand today rather than collect a bonus of $100 in one year?", answers indicated subjective discount rates of between 36% and 122%, far higher than the highest interest rate charged at this time.

The high subjective discount rate (and resulting neglect of the future) is illustrated in the effect of mandatory pension plans (provided by employers) on voluntary saving. If people really looked out for their future, in this case, then those without mandatory pension plans would start their own voluntarily. Other things being equal, people without mandatory pension plans should save more (on their own) than those that have them, yet (before the intro-

---

[6] That is, it will decay exponentially.

duction of government incentives in the form of tax breaks), this was not the case.

Another study reviewed by Thaler and Shefrin examined purchases of home air conditioners. Air conditioners differ, of course, in initial cost and operating expense (including the cost of electricity). The researchers found that people paid most attention to the initial cost. If one calculates the subjective discount rate from such purchase decisions, it is over 25%, well over any interest rate available at the time. (If one wanted to maximize income, one ought to buy the more expensive but more economical model – if necessary, borrowing money to buy it.)[7]

The rationality of discounting

What should the discount rate be? We have been assuming that people should be utterly impartial toward all parts of their future lives. They should be just as concerned about themselves a year from now as they are about themselves this minute. Is this right?

We have already noted that temporal impartiality is consistent with some discounting, because of interest rates and unforeseen events. We might also wish to take into account the fact that some goods last so long that time to enjoy them may be shorter if we get them later, because life is finite. Beyond these reasons, there are no additional general reasons to favor the immediate future over the distant future. In many cases, such as those studied by Thaler and Shefrin, it can be assumed that only the interest rate is relevant, to a first approximation. It is therefore fair of Thaler and Shefrin to conclude that we are probably temporally myopic – that is, more concerned about the immediate future than we ought to be if we were impartial toward all parts of our future lives.

What if someone says, "I just don't care about my future. I care only about the present, and I dare you to call me irrational for doing so"? Aren't people free to say this and to ruin their own future lives if they feel like it? Surely they may live to regret this attitude, but just because we regret something does not mean that it is irrational. (We could, for example, regret the rational behavior of others that works to our disadvantage.)

This issue is not settled. Parfit (1984) has argued that rationality does not in fact require impartiality toward all parts of one's future life. He does point out that we have some reasons for being concerned with our future. Interestingly, some of these reasons are the same as those that we have for being concerned with other people. Parfit argues that, in a sense, the "you" that exists 10 years from now is not the same person as "you" today – closely

---

[7] The conclusions of Thaler and Shefrin have been questioned by Modigliani (1986), who has found that many economic data can be accounted for by assuming that people treat all periods of their lives equally. Few of these data, however, directly concern the temporal myopia that Thaler and Shefrin have suggested.

related, perhaps, but not the same. Therefore, your concern about yourself in 10 years might be the same as your concern with someone very close to you, which might, in turn, not be quite as great as your concern with yourself at the moment. Even if we accept Parfit's view, however, delay independence would still be a basic requirement of consistency in achieving our goals over time.

In the long-run argument for utility theory (ch. 16), we assumed that we have some concern for our futures: If our futures did not matter to us, the long run would be irrelevant. The arguments for why we should care about our future are therefore important in justifying utility theory as a theory of rational choice (although there is also another approach to justifying utility theory in terms of basic principles that do not concern the long run). If Parfit is correct, the long-run justification for utility theory is fundamentally moral. It concerns consideration of ourselves at different times, just as the rest of morality concerns consideration of different people.

Despite Parfit's reservations, many of us feel a strong pull toward an attitude of impartiality toward all parts of our future lives. There is certainly nothing *ir*rational about such an attitude in its own right. If we think of our lives as a whole, we may be able to form a better plan for each part than if we merely live for the immediate future, through a kind of cooperation among the different parts for the ultimate benefit of all parts (Elster, 1985). Of course, such planning requires self-control.

Self-control

Why we need self-control

People are aware of the difficulty of self-control and of their tendency to neglect the future. When they see a situation as one that requires self-control, they often take steps to *bind themselves* to a course of behavior, even if they must pay money in order to do so. So, for example, people join Christmas Clubs in banks – which guarantee them money to spend on Christmas presents, at the expense of receiving only an extremely low rate of interest on these savings.

One mechanism of self-control is the use of more or less categorical rules that people make up for themselves, for example (Thaler, 1985, p. 199):

1. Mr. and Mrs. J. have saved $15,000 toward their dream vacation home. They hope to buy the home in five years. The money earns 10% in a money-market account. They just bought a new car for $11,000, which they financed with a three-year car loan at 15%.
2. Mr. S. admires a $125 cashmere sweater at the department store. He declines to buy it, feeling that it is too extravagant. Later that month he receives the same sweater from his wife for a birthday present. He is very happy. Mr. and Mrs. S. have only joint bank accounts.

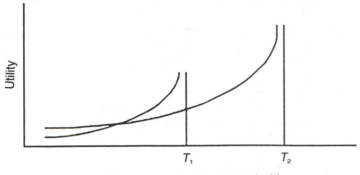

Times when decision is made (*t*)

Figure 21.2. Utility of two different rewards as a function of the time at which a decision is made. (The utility scale has no units. Rewards are available at times T_1, and T_2, respectively.)

In the first case, the J.'s would clearly do better to break into their savings; the effective interest rate would be 10%, not 15%. To do so, however, would be to violate their self-imposed rule. Like the Christmas Club contributor, they pay for their self-control. Similarly, Mr. S. does not allow himself to buy "extravagant" items, even though his pleasure in receiving the sweater indicates that the items are worth the money to him. Because of the joint bank accounts, he ends up paying anyway. A "gift" is often an excuse to break a rule of self-control. Marketers of expensive goods often suggest other kinds of "exceptions" to the rules of self-control: "Here's to good friends. Tonight is something special."

It is clear from the examples just given that we take active steps to control ourselves. In a way, the idea of self-control is a paradox. We either want the fourth bottle of beer, or we do not. What could it possibly mean to want it but keep ourselves from having it because four would be too much? If we keep from having it, isn't that because we do not really want it?

A familiar way of looking at this is to say that there are actually two people within each of us, locked in a perpetual struggle for control of our behavior: the id and the superego, the child and the adult, the foolish and the wise. Self-control occurs when the superego (adult, wise) wins. Indulgence occurs when it loses.

Whatever sense such an idea may make, we do not need it to explain the phenomenon of self-control. Ainslie (1975, 1982, 1986) has proposed an account of self-control that concerns the effect of time. Consider again the function relating the utility of a reward to time, but now let us consider two rewards (Figure 21.2). The first reward, which would be received at T_1, is smaller than the second, which would be received at T_2. Imagine that you must choose between the two. The first represents the temptation, such as having the fourth beer of the evening; the second represents some greater reward that would be received farther in the future, such as not having a hangover the next morning. Now if you make the choice at breakfast that morning (to the far left of the graph), notice that the utility of the second, greater reward (not having a hangover) is higher. As you approach the time at which the first reward (drunkenness) is available (the evening), however, its temptation increases, enough so that its utility surpasses that of the later reward. Therefore, if you make your choice in the morning, well before the temptation, you will choose (relative) sobriety, but if you make it when the temptation is at hand, you will (very likely) give in. Put another way, instead of two people, we can think of one person's preferences at different times. In the morning, the person will decide against the beer; in the evening, the person will decide in favor.

Knowing this, the "morning person" will try to *bind* the "evening person." Of course, they are the same person, so what is really happening is that people try to bind themselves, to control their own future behavior. The paradigm case is Ulysses.

Note that for this theory to work, the curve on the graph has to have a certain shape. It has to be very steep just as you approach the time of the reward. Ainslie's theory suggests that the economists' idea of a constant discount rate is incorrect. That idea implies that the utility of a reward increases by a constant percentage for every unit of time; that is, the utility at the end of the time unit is some multiple (greater than 1.00) of the utility at the beginning of the unit. If this were true, any reward with a higher utility at the beginning of each time unit would be higher at the end as well, and there would be no crossover of the sort shown on the graph. Therefore, Ainslie's theory requires a particular shape for the curve relating utility to time.[8]

This theory predicts that preferences will reverse as a function of the time at which they are made (relative to the time the rewards are available). Therefore, delay-independence will be violated. Ainslie and Haendel (1983) tested this prediction by asking subjects to choose between two prizes to be paid by a reliable company. The larger prize always had a greater delay. For example, the choice could be between $50 immediately and $100 in 6 months, or between $50 in 3 months and $100 in 9 months, or between $50 in 12 months and $100 in 18 months. Notice that in this example there is always a 6-month difference between the two prizes. A constant discount rate would imply that either the smaller or the larger prize would be chosen in all three cases. The smaller prize would be chosen if the discount rate was high enough to double the value of the money in 6 months. In fact, most subjects chose

---

[8] Ainslie recommends replacing the usual exponential function with a hyperbola. The hyperbola is consistent with a number of experiments discussed under the category of the "matching law" (see Rachlin, Logue, Gibbon, and Frankel, 1986, who also provide an interesting account of the certainty effect by interpreting probability as delay). However, other functions would work.

the smaller reward, in the first case (0 versus 6 months), and the larger reward in the last case (12 months versus 18 months). Subjects could not wait for the larger reward when the smaller one was available immediately, in clear violation of delay-independence.

Solnick, Kannenberg, Eckerman, and Waller (1980) tested the same prediction by asking subjects to work on mathematical problems while hearing "white noise" ("hiss") in the background. When a "choice window" was illuminated on a panel, the subject could press one of two buttons to turn off the noise. One button turned off the noise immediately for 90 seconds, and the other turned it off for 120 seconds, starting 60 seconds after the button was pressed. (The time interval between successive illuminations of the choice window was constant.) Subjects preferred the immediate, smaller reward. If, however, a 15-second delay was added, so that the delays were 15 versus 75 seconds rather than 0 versus 60 seconds, subjects chose the larger, delayed reward.

These experiments show violations of delay-independence, a violation that is non-normative even if we do not accept temporal impartiality as normative. Our reasons for being temporally myopic (neglecting the future) seem to go beyond a mere consistent underweighing of our future utility (just as we might underweigh the utility of others). They may instead result from a basic impulsiveness that we should – for our own future good – learn to control.

Methods of self-control

Ainslie (1982, 1986) suggests four general ways in which we solve the problem of binding ourselves.

Extrapsychic devices. One way is to remove the choice. We can throw away the bottle of scotch, or throw away the ice cream we are trying to avoid (so that when we want it late at night, it will not be there, and it will be too late to buy any). Christmas Clubs fall into this category; this and other mechanisms of forced saving help people avoid the temptation to spend money. Even some pigeons learn to peck a key to remove temptation: Given a choice between a small immediate reward and a large delayed reward, they choose the former, but if they were given a key that would simply *eliminate* the tempting smaller reward (earlier, before the choice was made), they often peck it (Ainslie, 1975, pp. 472–473).

We can also make contracts with other people. We can agree, for example, to pay a friend $100 if she catches us smoking, thus raising the cost. Some people rely on the sunk-cost effect as a means of self-control, paying large amounts of money for a "cure" of some bad habit (a smoking or alcohol clinic, a "fat farm," a psychotherapist), so that they are then motivated to maintain their new self-control in order to make sure that "all the money does not go to waste." (The additional cost of the self-denial may be integrated with the money already spent, as described earlier.)

Control of attention. One can try to manipulate one's attention so that one is not reminded of the availability of a temptation. A person at a party who is also on a diet may become deeply engrossed in conversation when the hors d'oeuvre tray is passed around. A person who does not want to be sexually tempted may focus on other things, avoiding the issue.[9] Attention control can be revoked at any time, so it may require continued effort (unlike extrapsychic devices, which operate on their own once they are put into effect).

Mischel and his colleagues have examined the use of attention-control strategies in children (Mischel, 1974, 1984; Mischel & Mischel, 1983). In a typical experiment, a child is told that she can receive two marshmallows when the experimenter returns, or she can request and receive one marshmallow at any time before that. At issue is how long the child waits before requesting the single marshmallow. Waiting is easier when the marshmallow is covered up than when it is in view, and when the child thinks about such things as the fluffiness of the marshmallow rather than about the taste. Older children (and children with higher IQs) know these things and make use of these attention-control strategies to help themselves wait. Preschool children choose to keep the marshmallow in view and to think about its taste, almost guaranteeing their failure. (These results are analogous to those on the learning of memorization strategies discussed in chapter 5.)

Control of emotion. People can cultivate emotions incompatible with the emotion associated with giving in to the temptation. A person who is afraid of getting angry may cultivate friendliness. (If he is a poor actor, he will be perceived as "sickly sweet.") A woman afraid of being seduced may start a quarrel. Or a person may simply refuse to let an emotion develop.[10]

Personal rules. The most interesting mechanism is to make up rules for ourselves: no more than three beers per evening; no more than one scoop of ice cream per day, and so forth. The effect of these rules is to redefine the situation. Instead of seeing a conflict between a fourth beer tonight and a clear head tomorrow morning, we see a conflict between these two choices repeated over and over for the indefinite future. By defining the situation this way, we ensure that our behavior tonight will set a *precedent* for future behavior in situations that we have defined as the same, as members of the

---

[9] Such efforts at attention control correspond to various "defense mechanisms" postulated by psychoanalytic theory, such as repression, suppression, and denial. These defense mechanisms can be understood as attempts at self-control. Indeed, Freudians would see them in similar terms, as the superego's ways of mediating the battle between ego and id.

[10] These mechanisms correspond to the Freudian defenses of reaction-formation and isolation of affect.

same class. Therefore, if we give in to temptation tonight, we can expect to give in on every other similar night. If we remember this rule when we are offered the fourth beer, we will see it not as a single choice but as a choice for a long string of similar occasions. Because all of the future occasions are far away in time, the utility of not having the beer (on these future occasions) considerably outweighs the utility of having it. This difference in favor of moderation may be large enough to outweigh the difference in favor of indulgence that would otherwise be present.[11]

To some extent, this mechanism can operate even without the conscious formulation of rules. As we noted earlier, each decision we make sets a precedent for making the same decision in similar situations in the future. When we decide to have the fourth beer (the first time we have the opportunity), we are likely to have four beers on similar occasions in the future. If we simply recognize this fact the first time that the decision is presented to us, we may make the decision differently, with more awareness of distant consequences, than if we see the decision as applying to a single case. It is possible that many bad habits, such as smoking, begin in this way, with an apparently isolated decision that sets a precedent. If I try a cigarette that someone offers me at a party, I am likely to make the same decision (to accept one) again later, and soon I will be hooked. What is critical, then, in order for this mechanism to work, is the recognition that single decisions establish patterns over the indefinite future.

We respond to our own violation of our personal rules in two ways. We can rationalize the violations by making up exceptions. The alcoholic trying to reform suddenly discovers an old buddy whom he has not seen for years – a situation that requires a drink – or else it is his half-birthday, or his second-cousin's wedding anniversary. If this mechanism is relied upon too much, the rule itself is weakened, but it may never be totally destroyed in the person's mind, even though an external observer would surely think it was. Rationalization of this sort is an example of wishful thinking (ch. 15).

If we do not rationalize the violation but feel guilty, we may try to compensate for the violations by inventing some sort of self-punishment – in essence, the piling up of rules (concerning penalties) on rules (concerning behavior). The bulemic woman may force herself to fast totally after a day of overeating, leading to the cycles of fasting and overeating that characterize this disorder. This mechanism is often used when the initial rules are too strict.

If personal rules are violated and one of these mechanisms is not used, the person may suffer defeat: A temporary or more permanent inability to exercise self-control (in some area, or in general) may result. In view of the need for self-control, for the sake of both personal welfare (for example,

---

[11] This mechanism corresponds to the defenses used by compulsives.

smoking) and making contributions to society (for example, doing one's job responsibly), these topics are of great importance for future research.

Emotions and time

Ainslie explains violations of delay-independence in terms of the steepness of the discounting curve when a reward is available soon. This is a purely mathematical account, like the economic theories it opposes. Loewenstein (in press) has suggested that several emotional factors play a role in our decisions concerning time, particularly the emotions we feel when we wait for some outcome to occur. Some of these emotions can explain the steepness of the discounting curve, but Loewenstein's theory makes other predictions as well.

When we look forward to pleasant outcomes, we experience what Loewenstein calls "savoring." This emotion is positive, like the experience of the outcome itself. The corresponding emotion for bad outcomes is "dread." Other emotions are derived from the contrast between our current state and a future outcome. When we are unhappy because an expected improvement has not occurred yet, we experience "impatience." When we are impatient, we want to get our current deprived state over with as quickly as possible. (There is a corresponding emotion of being happy because an expected bad outcome has not yet occurred, but it has no common name, perhaps because it is rare compared to the emotion of dread.) Impatience causes impulsiveness, but sometimes, Loewenstein suggests, we avoid impulsiveness through the positive emotion of savoring rather than through self-control. We put off a pleasant outcome, such as a vacation, so that we can gain the pleasure of looking forward to it in addition to the pleasure of experiencing the outcome itself. Conversely, when subjects are given a choice of a painful electric shock immediately or the same shock some time later (minutes, or days), most subjects choose the immediate shock (Loewenstein, in press). According to Loewenstein, this is because they want to avoid the dread of the shock, in addition to avoiding the shock itself.

In short, some of our emotions are caused by our expectations about outcomes, and we have goals concerning these emotions as well as concerning the outcomes themselves. By Loewenstein's account, these emotions would be absent in decisions we made for other people *who would not know what outcomes would occur until the outcomes did occur*. The situation is similar to that concerning the emotions of regret and disappointment (discussed in ch. 17): These emotions are real consequences of our choices, but sometimes we would do well to try to suppress them (or even to make them stronger, as when we use savoring as a means of self-control).

Emotions also come about from our looking back on good or bad outcomes after they occur, and still other emotions are connected with uncertain future outcomes, as well as certain ones ("fear" for negative outcomes, "hope" for positive ones). Loewenstein and Linville (1986) proposed that some of these emotions provide incentives for us to deceive ourselves about the probability of an uncertain future outcome, such as whether we will get a good grade on an examination or whether our application for a job will be accepted. Two desires are in conflict: our desire to avoid disappointment if our expectations are too high and the good outcome does not occur, and our desire to savor the outcome before it occurs, which we can do only if our expectations are high enough. When a good future outcome is far away in time, we are better off if we believe that it is likely to occur, because we can savor it for a long time, but when the outcome is imminent we have little time to savor it, and our main concern is to avoid disappointment, so we are better off if we believe it is not likely to occur – if we "don't get our hopes up."

Loewenstein and Linville tested this account by giving subjects a test that the subjects thought was related to intelligence. Half of the subjects were told that they would receive their scores immediately after the session, and the other half were told that they would receive their scores in 2 weeks. As the researchers predicted, the first group of subjects had lower expectations about their scores than the second group, and, as the end of the session approached, the expectations of subjects in the first group fell even more. (The experimenters did not ask the subjects in the second group about their expectations after the session.) In sum, this experiment suggests that we have desires concerning our hopes and disappointments and that we manipulate our expectations (deceive ourselves) to maximize the utility we derive from them.

Although this experiment does not concern decision making, it does show that we have emotions concerning future outcomes and that we are concerned with these emotions as well as with the outcomes themselves. Some of these emotions, particularly the impatience that results from the contrast between our present state and a better state that we could choose to have very soon, could cause us to neglect our futures irrationally.

Plans and identity

In the sixties, college students often told their friends (usually as an excuse for a period of avoiding all their classes and assignments) that they were having an identity crisis, that they were trying to discover "who they were." At first, one was tempted to tell such people, "Don't be silly. You are Charles J. Smith. You come from some town in South Dakota, and you want to be a doctor. You have a girl friend back home whom you promised to marry in the local church when you graduate." This sort of comment, of course, elicited nothing but a groan of despair.

Erikson's theory of identity

The idea of an identity crisis comes from Erik Erikson (1950, 1968). Identity, in Erikson's approach, is two things: (1) your plan for the future and (2) a theory, a set of beliefs that explains your past and justifies your plan. It tells you whom you stand with and whom you stand against. It specifies your goals, explains why those goals are good ones for you, and tells you how to achieve them. It has to do with every aspect of your life: your schoolwork, your career, your relationships with other people, your politics, your moral beliefs, and your tastes. The establishment of one's identity is a major task of adolescents and young adults in Western cultures, but various aspects of this task occupy us throughout our lives, from infancy to old age.

Although each individual's identity is unique, it consists, in part, of identification with groups. A good example of both the uniqueness and the identification is Freud's identity as a Jew, which he described in an address to the Society of B'nai B'rith, in Vienna, in 1926 (from Erikson, 1968, pp. 20–21):

What bound me to Jewry was (I am ashamed to admit) neither faith nor national pride, for I have always been an unbeliever and was brought up without any religion though not without a respect for what are called the "ethical" standards of human civilization. Whenever I felt an inclination to national enthusiasm I strove to suppress it as being harmful and wrong, alarmed by the warning examples of the peoples among whom we Jews live. But plenty of other things remained over to make the attraction of Jewry and Jews irresistible – many obscure emotional forces, which were the more powerful the less they could be expressed in words, as well as a clear consciousness of inner identity, the safe privacy of a common mental construction. And beyond this there was a perception that it was to my Jewish nature alone that I owed two characteristics that had become indispensable to me in the difficult course of my life. Because I was a Jew I found myself free from many prejudices which restricted others in the use of their intellect; and as a Jew I was prepared to join the Opposition, and to do without agreement with the "compact majority."

The process of identity formation is often difficult in a culture with conflicting values and goals. Marcia (1966), following Erikson, described three general types of problems in identity formation: *foreclosure, fortification*, and *confusion*. In *foreclosure*, people miss the chance to form their own identity freely. They essentially let their parents and others tell them who they are going to be and what they are going to stand for, without question. When asked why they chose their course of study or their religion, the answer is usually something like "That's what we've always assumed" or "That's how I was brought up." They do not consider alternative possibilities for their basic goals. Of course, in traditional societies there effectively *are* no alternatives, and it may not make sense to speak of foreclosure as a deficiency.

In *fortification*, identity appears to be too strong. The line between "us" and "them" is too sharply drawn. The person loses (or never acquires) the ability to see things from other people's point of view. This might be seen as an example of irrational persistence (ch. 15): Counterevidence is not sought, and when found it is ignored. Fortification can coexist with foreclosure. Fortification is characteristic of fanatics – and also of some saints and great achievers. The latter, however, should be seen as lucky rather than wise in their choice of identity; from the inside, life for them may be no different from the life of a destructive fanatic.

Confusion is a loss of identity. It is usually temporary, and it corresponds to what Erikson referred to as the identity crisis. It is often part of a change – for example, in religious commitment, career, or sexual identity. It frequently results from good thinking about goals, but of course the thinking is not good if it does not eventually decide among the goals at issue.

Dank (1971) describes the typical pattern of the resolution of a particularly difficult form of identity confusion: that of those male homosexuals who gradually come to admit to themselves that their identity as heterosexual persons cannot stand up. Dank found that there was (at the time he did his study) ordinarily a 6-year interval between the time that such a person became aware of his sexual feelings toward people of the same sex and the time at which he *decided* to be a homosexual: that is, chose this as a goal. In the meantime, Dank found, most homosexuals continued to believe what they had been taught: that homosexuals are sick, that they cannot possibly be happy. While believing this, they nevertheless formed homosexual relationships, which they first saw as aberrations or exceptions. Guilt was often intense. Eventually, Dank found, many homosexuals "came out," or admitted to themselves and other homosexuals that they were indeed homosexual.

In the words of one subject, "I had this feeling of relief; there was no more tension ... I guess the fact that I had accepted myself as being homosexual has taken a lot of tension off me." Coming out, in essence, often signifies to the subject the end of a search for identity. (Dank, 1971, p. 190)

This is a dramatic and painful change of identity for many homosexuals, who must fight against traditional moral values that tell them that what they are doing is deeply wrong. The same thing happens to other people, however, when they change their religious beliefs or their commitment to a career choice that had previously been their goal. The period of painful identity confusion may involve intense conflict between the old and the new. Of course, the new need not always win, and often it is best to consider changing and then not change.

Is identity really a choice? Aren't homosexuals born the way they are? Isn't it more a matter of *discovering* that one is homosexual, rather than *deciding*? We must distinguish here between homosexual desires – which may be difficult to control – and what one chooses to do about them. Desires are one kind of fact that a person must contend with in making a choice, but they are not the only fact. Often, on balance, it is better to live with some desire unsatisfied; often, it is not. Moreover, one's desires may be shaped by one's choices. The same goes for careers and religion.

Stages of identity formation

Perry (1971), studying college students, found that many of them went through three main stages of identity development while they were at college, resembling the stages of moral development proposed by Kohlberg (ch. 19) and by Kitchener and King (ch. 15). Perry interviewed a number of Harvard students each year, over a period of several years, about all aspects of their work and their lives. He found that the students moved predictably through stages in the way they thought about truth, morality, religion, and their careers. In rough outline, the main stages look like this:

Absolutism	Truth is defined by authority. The job of the professor is to convey the truth to students. If professors present two points of view, this is because they want the students to discover which is correct.
	Religion, morals, and career plans are largely defined for one by others, such as one's parents. Any rejection of these ideas is rebellion, pure and simple.
Relativism	There is no truth. One can argue for any view on any subject. Professors show us how to do this when they argue for different points of view.
	Religion, morals, and career are arbitrary. There is no basis for choosing one philosophy over any other. One can argue for any position, and none is really better than any other. Career choice is also arbitrary.
Commitment	Even though one may argue for any position, one must ultimately choose a philosophy of life as one's own. In classes as well, one must defend a point of view, even while recognizing other views.
	A career or way of life must also be chosen. Once a choice has been made, a personal commitment must follow. The same goes for personal relationships.

According to this scheme, a typical student enters college with an absolutist commitment to a religion, a career plan, and, more generally, a way of life. For example, the student may think of herself as a believer in Judaism, and she may plan to go to medical school and become a physician. At some point, she begins to question all of these aspects of her earlier identity. Her values concerning personal relationships are also challenged and shaken. In the end, however, she realizes that she cannot go on without some sort of commitment. As a senior, she becomes an atheist and decides to get an M.B.A. – or else, she returns to some or all of her original plans, which will be stronger for having survived this period of questioning.

These, Perry holds, are the main stages, but there are also transitional stages between them. A student need not move through from one stage to another all at once; the student may be an absolutist about religion and a relativist about politics, or vice versa. Students do not always go through all of the stages while they are in college. Some may enter college as relativists and leave committed – or unchanged. Others do not reach the stage of commitment until after college.

The stages that Perry identified are parallel, I think, with Marcia's and Erikson's views about identity. Absolutists, I suggest, are in a state of "fore-closure," relativists in a state of "confusion," and committed students in a state of mature identity formation.

Perry argues that the thinking and learning done in college has a lot to do with the movement from stage to stage. In particular, he claims, the transition out of absolutism is accelerated by professors' demands, at Harvard, that students consider alternative points of view, especially in subjects such as history, literature, and philosophy, where the students were well-informed enough to understand the controversies among scholars. (In the sciences, these controversies exist as well, but it often takes students several years of learning the basics before they can understand what the arguments are about.) Perry reports that students who wrote papers expressing only a single point of view, no matter how elegantly or thoroughly, were surprised to find that their grade was C, whereas students who learned how to present all sides fairly found that their grades improved.

What is so good about deciding for oneself? Does choosing one's own life plan really make life better than it would be if we just "took the path of least resistance" or "did what is expected of us"? Let us begin with the absolutist approach, in which major decisions in one's life are made by others. We could argue that, for some situations, others do know best. For example, a young man's parents might tell him not to marry outside of his religion or ethnic group because such marriages are likely to fail. When he falls in love with a young woman who is an outsider, they strongly advise him not to marry her. Obviously, a young couple, caught up in romantic love, may not be thinking rationally enough to make an impartial judgment about this.

Advice may be helpful. Suppose, though, that the young lover takes his parents' advice without question, breaks up with the young woman (or man) who seems to be his true love, and goes ahead with his life. Perhaps he will find another woman he wants to marry – but if he does, will he trust the strength of his feelings, knowing that their object can so easily be replaced? Perhaps he will never find another woman whom he will feel as strongly about. Although he may try to be a good husband to someone else – and even succeed – he may regret his decision, for it was *his* decision to take his parents' advice. He may wonder what life would have been like had he followed his own wishes. He may even read a convincing article in the paper reporting a study showing that marriages of the sort he wanted to make work out as well as any.

Suppose, on the other hand, that he listens to what his parents have to say but insists that they also give reasons so that he can think about the matter. Yes, they have known many marriages between P's and Q's that have failed – but haven't they also known many marriages between P's and P's that have failed as well? Have competent researchers studied this question? Can one really pit one's own meager experience against a statistical sample of hundreds? And even if group compatibility is one factor in marriages, what are the chances of finding another woman who would be as suitable for me on other relevant dimensions? If the parents can answer these questions, or give better arguments, their advice carries greater weight.

After this kind of questioning, our young lover may still wind up unhappy, whatever he decides, but if so, he will regard his misfortune as a matter of bad luck rather than an occasion for self-blame. He will have uncovered all of the reasons that he could, on both sides of the question. This must be better than making his decision on the basis of one or two reasons alone – either his own feelings or his parents', for example. In short, a reflective commitment, made with full knowledge of other possibilities and the reasons for them, is more likely to achieve one's goals than an unreflective one, and, even if it does not achieve our goals, it is less likely to lead to self-blame. What goes for decisions like this goes for all the others, such as choices about morals and careers.

But what about relativism? When it comes to making decisions, relativism just does not work, for the belief that all possibilities are equally good leads to "no decision," that is, a decision to take as little action as possible. This is, of course, a kind of decision, and not necessarily the best one: A young woman who cannot decide whether to marry the man she loves will sooner or later have the matter decided for her.

Relativism is also inconsistent. A relativist, we saw, thinks that no point of view is right, that any point of view is as good as any other – but he cannot mean precisely this, for it would imply that relativism itself (being one point of view) is no better than any other. "If any point of view is as good as any other, then why isn't *the point of view that relativism is false* as good as any other?" (Alan Garfinkel, quoted in Putnam, 1981, p. 119).

The advantage of *reflective commitment* over the earlier stages, then, is the advantage of good thinking in general. By considering all of the realistic possibilities, searching openly for evidence on all sides, and weighing the evidence fairly, we are most likely to achieve our goals, and most likely to choose the goals that are best for us.

Morality, prudence, and personal plans

Choosing the basic goals for our lives may be the most important moral choice we make. Why should we consider the interests of others in choosing these goals? First (as we saw in considering the idea of personal utility), it is in our own interest to have moral goals among our goals. The essence of morality is not self-sacrifice but benefiting others, and there are many ways in which it is possible for individuals to "do well by doing good."

Second, moral goals are part of life. To live without a moral ideology and without trying somehow to serve others is, in a way, like living without love, or music. It is missing something good that life has to offer. Moral goals, in general, reinforce other goals rather than conflict with them.

Third, there are reasons for being moral that are more purely logical (Gewirth, 1978; Nagel, 1970). If I care about consistency of belief, then I will find it difficult to argue that I ought to want to satisfy my desires, not yours. Some of the properties of "me" that make me want to satisfy my desires (for example, "personhood") are also properties of you, and therefore I ought to want to satisfy yours as well. Such arguments from consistency (admittedly only sketched here) give us a reason to satisfy each other's desires. Such reasons may not be overriding – there may be other reasons for me to want certain things just for myself – but they *are* reasons.

Most of us have the goal of not hurting people. If we combine this goal with the argument (ch. 19) that the distinction between omission and commission is normatively irrelevant to decision making, then we must conclude that we ought to desire to help people as well. The reasons for not hurting people and the reasons for helping them are the same: We care about the achievement of their goals.

Parfit (1984) offers another argument from consistency. Most of us, he points out, care about our own future. Does it make sense, Parfit asks, to care about your own future – the future "you" who is a different person from the present "you" – but not about someone else's present? Is there a relevant difference? In either case, our concern goes beyond our own immediate welfare. Let us look at an example.

Consider three people: Jill-1, Jill-2, and Jack. Now it just so happens that Jill-2 is Jill-1 as she will be in the future, say 10 years from now. Why should Jill-1 care more about Jill-2 than about Bill? Is it because Jill-2 will share memories with Jill-1? Probably not. Imagine that Jill-2 is amnesic (forgot her past), or that Jill-1 could transfer all of her memories to Bill. Would this change Jill-1's reasons for caring about Jill-2?

What about the fact that Jill-1 makes plans for Jill-2? Would this justify her caring about Jill-2? Again, this does not seem relevant. Jill-2 could change the plans that Jill-1 makes, or Jill-1 might neglect to make any, and it would not seem to matter. In fact, Parfit argues, it is difficult to think of *any* reason why anyone ought to care about herself in the distant future that does not also apply to caring about someone else in the present (or future), at least to some degree.

The question "Why be moral?" occurs to many people, but the question "Why care about one's own future?" occurs to few. By showing the similarity of these questions, Parfit helps us to realize that it may not be any more difficult to care about other people than it is to care about our future selves.

The virtues connected with caring about one's own future are often called *prudence*, and *prudential* judgments are those concerned with one's long-term interest (just as certain moral judgments are those involving the interests of others). Both prudence and morality require that we put aside immediate temptation for the sake of some distant good – our own future, or the interests of others. Therefore, self-control is a virtue required for both morality and prudence.

Moreover, prudent behavior and moral behavior usually reinforce one another (as most of our parents told us). If we are good to other people, if we respect their concerns and interests, if we keep our commitments to them, then we, in turn, will benefit in the future, for others will be obliged (usually) to treat us the same way. Similarly, concern for one's own long-term future is likely to motivate certain behavior that turns out to benefit others. For example, the hard work required to become a physician pays off not only in terms of the respect and tangible rewards that physicians earn but also in terms of the good works that physicians accomplish on behalf of others: curing their illnesses.

Conclusion

Decisions that determine the course of our future lives are frightening, for each of us can choose only one of the paths open to us, but we all make these decisions, with or without thinking. Here, as elsewhere, actively open-minded consideration of the options before us can help us achieve our goals. Thinking, however, does not guarantee a good life. Luck, good and bad, is ever-present.

Part IV

Teaching

So far, this book has discussed a number of biases in which people depart from normative models for making judgments and decisions. We have also considered ways in which people depart from the prescriptive model of active open-mindedness. The problem now is this: What can be done?

We saw earlier that using computers has great promise, but thorough discussion of that solution here would take us too far afield. The concern of this chapter is with another solution, education. The question of using prescriptive rules for our thinking and decision making hinges on what is feasible, and that, in turn, hinges on what can be taught.

Every man is born with a live computer of limitless possibilities, but without the instruction manual.
The most important job of science today is to draw up that manual.
Machado (1980)

The idea that education ought to teach people to think well goes back to Socrates, and our understanding of how to do this has deepened over the centuries with advances in philosophy and psychology. A major proponent of that view in the early twentieth, John Dewey, argued that one of the key functions of education is to teach students to think reflectively and critically (see Dewey, 1933). His ideas, and those of others, led to a movement known as "progressive education," which emphasized understanding rather than rote learning, critical thinking rather than blind acceptance, and realistic rather than abstract experience. Eventually, during the 1920s, this movement began to lose sight of its original goals and methods, culminating in educational experiments such as the Summerhill School (Neill, 1964), in which students were essentially given complete freedom to control their own course of learning. The idea of progressive education became identified in many people's minds with the idea of license and lack of discipline. When the bathwater was thrown out, the baby went with it. Dewey's ideas about the importance of thinking failed to take hold in public education, where it has been replaced by an emphasis on factorylike efficiency in covering tiny pieces of knowledge and skill. (In some private schools, however, and in the hands of a few public-school teachers, Dewey's ideas have survived.)

Meanwhile, in the 1930s, during the depression and the rise of fascism, a concern with people's susceptibility to political propaganda led to a renewed emphasis on "critical thinking," much of which amounted to training in the detection of fallacious arguments (ch. 10). Other educators who came later (for example, de Bono, 1976) wanted to improve creativity in schools as Osborne and Gordon had done (or claimed to do) in organizations (see ch. 8) through instruction in brainstorming. Soon this tradition merged with a more serious stream of inquiry beginning with Bloom and Broder (1950), who examined the thinking processes of college students by asking them to think aloud. Whereas de Bono emphasized freedom from constraints, brain-

461

storming, and the like, Whimbey and Whimbey (1975), in a revival of Dewey's original ideas, emphasized reflectiveness and active open-mindedness. The Whimbeys also argued that intelligence could truly be increased through the sort of training they recommended.

More recently, educational philosophers such as Paul (1984), bothered by what they regarded as the shallowness of Americans' political opinions (especially during the Vietnam War), suggested ways of teaching people to be more critical of political dogma. Others (for example, the National Commission on Excellence in Education, 1983) have recently been concerned with the decline of scores on tests of "higher-level reasoning" in the United States. Another important recent influence is Luis Alberto Machado (1980), a Venezuelan who was appointed (at his own request) minister of state for the development of human intelligence in his country during the Campins administration (1979–84). He initiated several programs, including an experimental course, designed to increase intelligence, which has been evaluated formally (Adams, 1986; Herrnstein, Nickerson, de Sánchez, & Swets, 1986). All of this has led to increasing interest in the teaching of thinking in recent years (Nickerson, Perkins, & Smith, 1985; Nickerson, in press). It might be said that we are witnessing the rebirth of Dewey's original idea of progressive education, which is not the same as the license it came to be in the "progressive" schools.

This chapter examines some of the influential ideas in this movement, using the concept of good thinking that we have been examining throughout this book. I shall argue that successful educational programs succeed because they encourage active open-mindedness: that is, they teach people to search more thoroughly for possibilities, evidence, and goals and to be more open in the search for and use of evidence. Let us begin, however, with some discussion of what we might hope to teach when we teach thinking.

What can be taught

Certain important limits on what we can teach have already been described in this book. We noted in chapter 7 that we cannot expect to improve people's capacities, the biological determinants of mental performance, through instruction. We also noted, in chapter 5, that we cannot teach *general skills* through repetitive practice or drill. Drill improves performance with familiar material but not with new material. Practice is useful for teaching recognition of letters and words (since the letters and words stay pretty much the same after the student leaves school) but probably does not help to teach a person to think well about material never before encountered.

In addition, the teaching of specific skills and facts – such as the multiplication table, foreign-language vocabulary, or the names and dates of history – is not the same as the teaching of thinking. This is not to say that such teaching is unimportant – only that we are not talking about that here.

Heuristics

Earlier in this book we specifically identified many habits or methods of thinking that we know can be taught – heuristics, for example. Perhaps you recall (from ch. 13, on hypothesis testing) the useful heuristic of thinking of alternative hypotheses before gathering data, a way to avoid collecting useless data that do not distinguish the hypothesis of interest from its alternatives. In the chapter on social dilemmas, we noted that the heuristic of "giving the other guy the benefit of the doubt" can help us to avoid bias in making moral judgments. Can you think of heuristics to avoid other effects such as the endowment effect (ch. 17), the sunk-cost effect (ch. 21), the certainty effect (ch. 17), and the effects of framing and mental accounting (ch. 17)?[1] Perhaps the most general heuristics of all are those connected with active open-mindedness: "Consider alternative possibilities"; "When making choices, think about relevant goals that you might be ignoring"; and "Look for evidence against the first idea you think of before plunging in."

Teaching students to use heuristics as if they were a "skill" like long division is not enough. We must also make sure that students want to think well, so that they will use the methods they learn after they are out of school. "Wanting to think well" has two parts: Students must know what "thinking well" is, and they must desire to follow these standards. Just as a person can believe in God and still desire to side with Satan, mere knowledge of the standards is not enough. In addition to wanting to think well, students must believe that they are capable of thinking effectively.

Standards and beliefs

Standards of thinking and beliefs about thinking can be taught as though they were facts (and are surely often taught this way), but such teaching is a kind of deception.[2] A more effective way to teach standards is to give arguments for them and rebut arguments against them, as I have done in this book. The teacher can also model this approach, demonstrating by personal example that one can conform to the standards and be satisfied as a result.

Beliefs, as we have seen, affect our thinking. Certain beliefs about the nature of good thinking, and about the effectiveness of thinking, make for good thinking in general; other beliefs tend to prevent it. Among the helpful

---

[1] Here are some suggested answers: For the endowment effect, imagine a choice between the good in question and the money, assuming you had neither. For the sunk-cost effect, make decisions by thinking only about present and future consequences, not past history. For the certainty effect, think about *un*certainties lying behind apparent certainties. For the effects of framing, compare everything to the status quo. For mental accounting, integrate everything possible.

[2] Deception in education can be justified, if the good it does outweighs the harm, but the harm is considerable, for it undermines the trust that teachers need.

ones are the belief that thinking often leads to better results and that difficulties can frequently be overcome through thinking (rather than, say, through
luck); that good thinkers are open to new possibilities and to evidence against
possibilities that they favor; and that there is nothing wrong (per se) with
being undecided or uncertain for a while.

Among the unhelpful beliefs is the belief that changing one's mind is a
sign of weakness; that being open to alternatives leads to confusion and
despair; that quick decision making is a sign of strength or wisdom; that truth
is determined by authority; that we cannot influence what happens to us by
trying to understand things and weigh them; and that use of intuition alone
is the best way to make decisions. If people do not believe that their thinking
about something is useful, they will not think about it. This is perhaps the
major argument one hears against thinking about things such as nuclear war,
religion, or morality: "These matters are beyond me. They are best left to
experts who are capable of thinking about them–if anyone."

The helpful beliefs act to oppose the natural biases of insufficient search
and favoritism toward strong possibilities; the unhelpful beliefs (though they
may contain a germ of truth) act to support these biases.

An important property of the standards and beliefs of good thinking is
that they can be taught in full generality, and – in contrast to the teaching of
habits or methods – we have no reason to suppose that they are any less
effective when taught as general standards (using specific examples) than when
taught as standards for specific domains of thinking such as science.

An example from research on children's responses to failure in thinking
tasks illustrates the role of beliefs about thinking in determining thinking.
The amount of effort that children put into their schoolwork is probably in
large part a function of how much good they think effort will do. This belief,
in turn, is influenced by past successes and failures. When student subjects
are made to fail on one task (for example, an insoluble problem), they are
more likely than other subjects to fail on similar tasks in the future. Diener
and Dweck (1978) asked children to do a series of arithmetic problems, with
every fifth problem being beyond the child's level and therefore insoluble.
Some children tended to fail on the problems they did just after the insoluble
ones, even though they were able to solve similar problems when they had
not just experienced failure. Other children did better, if anything, on subsequent problems. Subjects were asked to talk aloud as they worked. The
first, "helpless" group tended to blame their failures on such factors as stupidity, a trait that would persist into subsequent problems and therefore
provide a reason (if true) for lower expectations. ("Helplessness," in this
case, is defined as a detrimental effect in which failure on a problem impairs
performance on the next problem.) Members of the second, "mastery-ori-
ented" group did not spontaneously explain their failures at all but tended
to remark that they would have to try harder on the next problem, implicitly

attributing their failure to lack of effort. This explanation gave them no reason to lower their expectations about the value of thinking.

Dweck (1975) found that such helplessness can be remedied, at least in a specific context. In this study, the experimenter sat next to the child as the child worked through a series of problems, some of which were designed to be too difficult to solve correctly in the time allowed. After each such programmed failure, the trainer said, "You needed _____ [to reach the criterion of success] and you only got _____. That means you should have tried harder" (p. 679). As a result, subjects began to attribute their failures to lack of effort, rather than to such factors as stupidity, and their tendency to become helpless as a result of failure was reduced. Because the helplessness effect was reduced, overall performance improved as well, as a result of the training. This technique probably works by increasing the children's *belief* in the effectiveness of their own thinking.

Goals

Standards and beliefs are useless unless a student has the *goal* of *discovering the truth and making good decisions*. Surely just about everyone has these goals to some extent, but the real issue is the strength of these goals relative to others. For example, good thinkers frequently find themselves reaching conclusions that they or their peers do not like; a strong commitment to "intellectual honesty" is required if standards of thinking are to be maintained.

The goals of thinking well can be taught by showing students that these goal will help them achieve the goals that they already have. This can be demonstrated in many ways: by argument, by example, or by inducing the students to adopt the new goal (or to increase its weight) as an experiment. It should not be hard to teach the goals associated with good thinking by this method, for good thinking is supposed to help people achieve other rational goals, regardless of what those goals might be. Goals can also be taught by modeling. Students may come to want something because someone they like or admire wants it. Goals cannot be taught directly by imperative statements: We can tell a person to *do* something, but it does not make sense to tell anybody to *want* something. (Nor can goals be taught as though they were facts, even with deception – in contrast to beliefs.)

Goals that work against actively open-minded thinking – intolerance of doubt (Dewey, 1933), of ambiguity (Rokeach, 1960), or of inconclusiveness or lack of "closure" (Wollman, Eylon, & Lawson, 1979) – have been cited as sources of poor thinking. (The specific instruments used to measure these closely related properties are beside the point here.) Since doubt (unlike effort) is a ubiquitous property of thinking, intolerance of doubt can function as a general goal of *not thinking*.

We sometimes avoid thinking because we are afraid of failing in a thinking task that is important to us. If we do not try to do the task, we cannot properly be said to fail, and we can maintain a belief in our ability to have succeeded. In this way we satisfy our fear of failure, because we do not really fail.[3]

Another goal that works against thinking is a desire not to reconsider a decision already made (Janis & Mann, 1977) or a belief already formed (as dealt with in the literature on cognitive consistency, for example, Abelson, Arsonson, McGuire, Newcomb, Rosenberg, & Tannenbaum, 1968). This goal causes us to avoid, in particular, thinking that might lead to conclusions inconsistent with those already drawn. Of course, this goal is rational up to a point, for it is rational not to think too much in general. The same reasons that make us avoid thinking in general, however, can make us avoid – more than we ought to – situations that would cause doubt and therefore give us reason to think. Further, it might be best to learn to live with certain conflicts unresolved, so that we are not inhibited from thinking in general by the fear that we will be compelled to resolve every doubt we encounter. Again, intolerance of doubt may play a role.

Among the positive goals that encourage good thinking are curiosity (a positive value attached to the search for evidence in particular) and the desire for competence (White, 1959). Also, for at least some people, thinking is fun. These goals are surely natural ones, but they are also affected by culture and upbringing, McClelland found (1960). These goals work against the common biases that cause too little thinking.

Moral goals can assist us too. A person who has the goal of being a good citizen would probably want to think well as a way of satisfying that goal. This motivation is not a trivial reason for wanting to think rationally. It is in the domain of public debate that charges of irrationality are most frequently made, and so the desire to avoid such charges can be a powerful goal in those who participate at all. Those on each side of a controversial issue, such as the abortion controversy or the Arab–Israeli conflict, go to great lengths to portray themselves as "reasonable" while they portray those on the other side as fanatics. Often, our best hope for the solution of such conflicts is that both sides will take seriously their claims to be reasonable.

All of the goals I have listed are affected by culture, and certain ones are very likely due entirely to cultural beliefs about how people ought to run their intellectual lives. Cultures that encourage rational thinking are those that value questioning, inquiry, the satisfaction of curiosity, and intellectual chal-

---

[3] Aside from its effect on thinking, this sort of goal seems irrational, in two ways. First, pure fear of failure (as distinct from desire for success) serves no purpose in achieving our other goals; for this purpose, the only problem with trying and failing is the lost time taken away from plans more likely to succeed, not the failure itself. Second, people who behave in this way may be basing their self-esteem on an image of what they might have done, rather than one of what they habitually do. Once again, this serves no general purpose of achieving other goals, especially in children – although it may be an appropriate feeling for adult victims of injustice or bad luck.

lenge. Cultures that oppose such thinking are those that value authority, quick decision making, correctness (even achieved by guessing) rather than good thinking, and constancy of opinion to the point of rejecting new evidence. Of course, most cultures are not purely positive or negative from this point of view; rather, they teach conflicting beliefs, which lead to conflicting goals.

In short, the teaching of thinking *may* involve the teaching of methods and habits, but it *must* involve the inculcation of beliefs, standards, and goals. This requirement implies that the teaching of thinking cannot be divorced from an ideological commitment to good thinking among all those who influence the young.

Transfer

Transfer of learning (ch. 5) is the effect of learning in one situation on learning or behavior in a very different situation. If we are teaching *thinking*, transfer is essential. Because thinking (as defined in this book) is what we do *when we do not know what to choose, desire, or believe,* thinking will be most essential in situations that we have not encountered before. Can teaching of thinking transfer? A number of studies suggest that it can.

Some studies have examined the effects of certain courses on reasoning about judgments and decisions. Schoemaker (1979) found that students who had taken a statistics course gave more consistent answers to questions involving choices of gambles. Students who had not taken the course were also more likely to bid more than the maximum amount that could be won in order to play a gamble with positive expected value, and more likely to require more money than the maximum loss in order to play a gamble with negative expected value.

Fong, Krantz, and Nisbett (1986, experiment 4) found that statistical training transfers to solving everyday problems involving statistical reasoning. Half of the men enrolled in a college statistics course were interviewed by telephone at the beginning of the course, and the other half were interviewed at the end. The interview (conducted by a woman experimenter) ostensibly concerned sports and began with questions concerning sports controversies (such as what colleges should do about recruiting violations) in order to hide the fact that the basic concern was with statistics. Then subjects were given questions concerning such matters as why the winner of the Rookie of the Year award in baseball usually does not do as well in his second year as in his first. A nonstatistical response might be "because he's resting on his laurels; he's not trying as hard in his second year." A statistical response that reflects understanding of the principle of regression to the mean in numerical prediction (ch. 18) would be "A player's performance varies from year to year. Sometimes you have good years and sometimes you have bad years. The player who won the Rookie of the Year award had an exceptional year. He'll probably do better than average his second year, but not as well as he did when he was a rookie." Students gave more good statistical answers of this sort at the end of the course than at the beginning. Therefore, these students did transfer what they had learned to cases where it is relevant.

Nisbett, Fong, Lehman, and Cheng (1987) carried out other studies in which they examined the effects of various kinds of university instruction on statistical, logical, and methodological reasoning. The researchers measured statistical reasoning by asking subjects to suggest explanations of certain facts, such as that the Rookie of the Year typically does not do as well in his second year or that "a traveling saleswoman is typically disappointed on repeat visits to a restaurant where she experienced a truly outstanding meal on her first visit" (p. 629). Each fact could be explained either in terms of nonstatistical factors ("Her expectations were so high that the food couldn't live up to them") or statistical ones ("Very few restaurants have only excellent means, odds are she was just lucky the first time"). Subjects were given credit here for mentioning the statistical explanations as possibilities (which they were, whether the other explanations were also true or not).

To measure logical reasoning, the researchers gave subjects problems involving conditional reasoning, including versions of the four-card problem described in chapter 8. To measure methodological reasoning, the researchers asked subjects to comment on flawed arguments. One item (from a newspaper editorial) argued for the learning of Latin and Greek on the grounds that students who had studied these languages in high school received much higher than average scores on the Verbal Scholastic Aptitude Test.[4] Another item concerned a claim that the mayor of Indianapolis should fire his police chief because crime had increased since the chief began his tenure in office.[5]

Nisbett and his colleagues found that logical reasoning, as measured by their test, did not improve from the beginning to the end of two introductory college courses in logic (one emphasizing formal logic, the other emphasizing informal fallacies). It did not improve as a result of two years of graduate school in chemistry, either. Logical reasoning did improve, however, as a result of two years of graduate school in law, medicine, or psychology. The researchers suggest that these three fields emphasize logical reasoning to some extent. This improvement was found in two different kinds of studies, one in which students just beginning graduate school were compared to students who had just completed their second year, and the other in which the same students were tested at the beginning and the end of their first two years of graduate training.

Statistical and methodological reasoning showed a somewhat different pattern. The largest improvement by far occurred among psychology students,

---

[4] Subjects were scored as giving correct responses if they pointed out that students who studied Latin and Greek in high school were unusually competent and would probably do well on the test even without studying these languages.

[5] Subjects were scored as correct if they pointed out the potential relevance of crime-rate increases in other cities over the same period.

probably because training in such things as the use of control groups is an important part of graduate work in psychology. Methodological reasoning also improved with medical training, which places some emphasis on the conduct and interpretation of medical research, but there was essentially no improvement from training in either law or chemistry. These studies provide further evidence that appropriate education, in which certain methods of reasoning are explicitly emphasized, can have general effects on the tendency to use these methods in everyday problems unrelated to the areas in which the methods were taught. They also suggest that some of these effects can be specific to certain methods. In particular, legal training affected logic but not statistics.

The tests used by Nisbett and his colleagues did not measure actively open-minded thinking, which I have argued is the most general method of all. (The improvements found in medical and psychology students could have resulted from increases in such thinking, however. For example, a more thorough search for possibilities could unearth the ones that the researchers were looking for.) Can actively open-minded thinking itself be improved by instruction? Again, the answer is positive.

In an important paper, Otto Selz (1935) described a few relevant studies.[6] In one, an experimental and a control group of students, aged 11 to 13, were given an intelligence test consisting of completion problems (stories with words left out); word-ordering problems (arranging words into a sentence); verbal-analogy problems; and number-series completions. The experimental group was given training on only the completion problems for 1 hour on each of two successive days. The training was designed to make students take into account the requirements of the task, checking each possible answer to see if these requirements were met. Subjects were taught both to explain why answers did not meet the requirements and to justify answers when they seemed to fit. The training was done in the form of what seemed to be a lively competitive exercise in which students were called upon to defend their answers at the blackboard, while other students in the group chimed in with criticisms and explanations. After the training, a second intelligence test was given.

The experimental group showed substantial improvement not only on the completion test, on which they were trained, but also on all of the others, to roughly the same extent. For example, on one of the completion tests the "experimentals" improved their scores from 60% to 78% correct, whereas the "controls" improved only from 60% to 63%, and on the analogy test the experimentals went from 28% to 69%, whereas the controls went from 33% to 41%. Of great interest is the finding that the experimental group was more

[6] Selz, a Jew living in Nazi Germany, eventually lost his life, turning down a chance to leave Germany because he underestimated the danger. This paper, one of his last, was published despite objections to the publication of a paper by a Jew. The editor of the journal was himself persecuted as a result.

than twice as likely than the control group to scratch out an answer and correct it in the posttest (244 instances, versus 103), although the experimentals had been less likely to do this in the pretest (22 instances, versus 41). Again, this finding held to a roughly equal extent over all tasks. Apparently the students learned to be more critical of initial possibilities, seeking evidence against them as well as alternative possibilities. Although these results were from a short-term study with an immediate posttest, there is no reason to think that they would change qualitatively with more extensive training and a more delayed posttest.

In a more recent attempt, Irene Gaskins and I conducted an 8-month training study in her school for reading-disabled children, the Benchmark School (Baron, Badgio, & Gaskins, 1985). The teachers in the school (including Gaskins) identified three cognitive styles that they felt were holding many children back from academic success, even when their initial reading problems had been largely corrected. We called these styles *impulsiveness, rigidity*, and *nonpersistence. Impulsiveness* consisted of failing to think sufficiently on an individual problem or when answering a question. *Rigidity* consisted of an unwillingness to consider alternatives to an initial possibility concerning how something should be done or about the truth of some issue. *Nonpersistence* was the failure to complete extended activities, such as seatwork assignments; it can be taken as a sign of lack of motivation. Our training program was designed to overcome these biases by emphasizing three slogans: "Take time to think"; "Consider alternatives"; and "Keep at it." The value of these new styles was explained in terms of hypothetical examples, practice exercises were done, and individual children were also given feedback about their classroom behavior.

The program was a success, according to teacher ratings of the styles we tried to train; the experimental group improved considerably and the control group hardly at all. The training also affected ratings of academic performance given by teachers of children who had graduated from the Benchmark School and gone to other schools. In addition, children did slow down and take more time to think in a few different laboratory measures using tasks other than those used in training, including syllogisms and arithmetic word problems. Those children who had been rated as particularly impulsive also improved in their overall accuracy on these tasks.

Perkins, Bushey, and Faraday (1986) taught high school students to think in an actively open-minded way through a 16-session course that emphasized searching thoroughly for arguments on both sides of an issue. Students were taught that the arguments they consider when thinking about a controversial issue should be *true* (to the best of the thinker's knowledge), *relevant* to the issue, and *complete* – that is, all important relevant arguments should be considered. Controversial issues were discussed in class, and students were encouraged to generate and evaluate (for truth and relevance) arguments on both sides, especially the other side.

Before and after the course, students were tested by asking them to write down their thoughts on issues that were "genuinely vexed and timely" and that could be discussed on the basis of knowledge that most people have. Four issues were used: "Would providing more money for public schools significantly improve the quality of teaching and learning?" "Would a nuclear freeze agreement between the U.S. and the U.S.S.R. significantly reduce the possibility of world war?" "Should all 10 year olds be required to fulfill a one year social service obligation?" and "Would a ban on selling and owning handguns significantly reduce violent crime?" Two of the issues were used at the beginning of the course, and the other two were used at the end. To ensure that the issues themselves did not account for the change, each issue was used for some students at the beginning and for an equal number of students at the end.

The course nearly doubled the number of arguments that students gave on the *other* side from their own. The rated quality (truth and relevance) of these arguments increased as well. These gains were not simply the result of greater thoroughness in general: The course did not increase the number or quality of arguments on the student's own side. The effect was truly a matter of increased open-mindedness. Perkins and his colleagues also examined the effects of other courses that involve thinking in some way: a first-year law-school class, a high school debate class, a first-year college class that taught "critical thinking," and a graduate course on thinking. None of these courses affected otherside arguments significantly, although the law-school class and the critical-thinking class increased the number and quality of arguments on each student's *own* side. In sum, we can successfully teach actively open-minded thinking by encouraging it directly, but not by simply requiring students to think.

Current efforts could fail, even when they encourage good thinking in the classroom, because they do not explain the relevance of good thinking to issues outside of the classroom in sufficiently general terms. Transfer is more likely when instruction is given in general terms. Schleser, Meyers, and Cohen (1981) trained children to be more careful in doing the Matching Familiar Figures Test (MFFT), the perceptual matching test that measures the tendency to search for evidence extensively, even when time is required (see ch. 7). Children were instructed (through modeling, then through prompting, then without prompting) to talk out loud to themselves while doing the task. In the "specific" experimental condition, the talk concerned only the task itself: for example, "I have to pick one of these pictures which is just the same as the one here. I have to look real close at each part of the picture. I have to go slow, I have to compare each part." In the "general" condition, the talk was of the sort that could apply to many different tasks: for example, "I'm going to answer a question: I have to stop and think about what the question is asking." Both groups showed considerable improvement at the MFFT; however, only the group given the "general" training improved on a second task, in which the subject had to choose which of several pictures of a scene corresponded to the viewpoint of the experimenter (who viewed the scene from an angle 90 degrees away from the subject's).

Another possible reason for failure of some efforts to teach thinking is overreliance on extrinsic reward. Recall (from ch. 6) that extrinsic reward reduces the transfer of intrinsically motivated activities to situations in which the reward is unavailable. Good thinking is, for most people, intrinsically motivated, once people accept the standards of active open-mindedness.

Most of the studies just reviewed have measured transfer with tests of the sort used in school or in the psychology laboratory. (The sole exception is the study done by Fong and his colleagues on statistical thinking, which used a telephone interview about sports as the measure.) Further research is needed on transfer to thinking in less artificial settings. The lack of such research, however, is no excuse for supporting the status quo in education. The decision to institute new educational programs must inevitably be made under uncertainty. We must make a probabilistic prediction of the outcome on the basis of the evidence at hand. Study after study in the educational literature has found that students are influenced by what they are taught in school. There is no reason to think that the teaching of thinking will be the first major exception to this principle. When I combine this argument (as a "prior probability") with the evidence I have just reviewed, my personal probability for the success of well-designed programs to teach good thinking is very high. Moreover, as I shall point out, the risk is very low, given that such programs can be integrated with the content ordinarily taught in school.

The design of teaching methods

Methods for teaching thinking (or anything else) are inventions or designs (in Perkins's sense; see ch. 6). The theory of actively open-minded thinking provides a set of purposes and arguments that we can use to understand and improve such designs. This section illustrates the relevance of this theory to two of the many methods that have been and that might be used for teaching good thinking in general or in specific areas: the tutorial method and thinking assignments.

Tutorial method

The goal of the tutorial method is to make the student internalize the values and some of the rules of good thinking. The method, in its basic form, requires one-to-one interaction between a tutor and a student. The tutor must be an expert in the domain being discussed, in the goals of instruction, and in the methods of teaching.

The most fully worked out example of the tutorial method is the technique presented by Blank (1973) for teaching preschool children, particularly those whose background makes it likely that they will have academic trouble in the higher grades. The teaching is integrated into a preschool program, with a low ratio of children to teachers, so that the teacher can spend a few periods a day with each child. The method is therefore expensive, but the data available suggest that it is well worth the cost. Blank reports gains of 14 IQ points, relative to control groups with no special training or with an equal amount of one-to-one interaction not of a tutorial character (these two control groups not differing from each other). Blank correctly points out, though, that the IQ test is probably less sensitive than other measures to the quality of the child's thinking, because (as I argued in ch. 7) the IQ test is not designed to be sensitive to the subject's quality of thinking, so these results may well underestimate the effects of the program.[7]

In Blank's method, the tutor gives the child instructions to follow or questions to answer. The tutor looks for a level of difficulty of questions and instructions that is great enough to produce occasional errors yet not so great as to induce total frustration. The idea is to give the child the experience of successful search for possibilities, evidence, and goals. If the task is too easy, search will not be needed; if it is too hard, search will fail.

The heart of the method is the tutor's response to errors. As Blank puts it (pp. 88–89):

The confrontation of error has value which goes beyond helping the child recognize why a particular response is incorrect. The need to examine the "wrong" response not only solidifies the "right" response, but it also leads the child to gradually internalize the "rules" used by the teacher to demonstrate the appropriate response. As a result, even when the adult is not present, the child has techniques by which to evaluate his thinking (for example, if he has an appropriate idea, he may try it out to see if it works because this is the pattern that has been set by the teacher).

Here are some of the techniques the tutor uses to respond to the child's errors:

Delay. This should be used when the "child is capable of performing the response demanded although he has not done so before because of his impulsivity" (p. 90). For example, if the student starts to follow a command before the teacher has finished giving it, the teacher says, "Wait a minute, listen to . . ." This may induce the child to *search for possibilities, evidence, or goals* before responding, thereby working against impulsiveness.

Introduce a cue to restructure the situation. Blank gives the following example (p. 93): "Teacher – 'Why do you think we couldn't get this sponge into the (small) cup and we could fit the marble?' Child – 'Because it's a

---

[7] Lazar, Darlington, Murray, Royce, and Snipper (1982), reviewing the results of a number of preschool programs (not including Blank's), find that effects on IQ are generally small, if present at all, yet effects on school success, defined as not dropping out, not being put in a special class, and not staying back a year, are substantial. Since Blank's program does seem to affect IQ, even though it is no more directed at this goal than are any other programs, we might expect even greater effects on school performance.

sponge.' Teacher – 'Okay, *I'll cut this sponge in two*. Now it's still a sponge. Why does it go into the cup now?' " It seems to me that this is actually the presentation of counterevidence to a principle (possibility) implied by the child's explanation, namely, the principle that sponges do not fit into cups. Therefore, the point of this technique is to teach the child to seek counter-evidence (or potential counterevidence) when testing a general proposition.

Relate the unknown to the known. For example, a child who fails to answer a question about how the spaghetti will "feel" after it is cooked is asked if he can recall how the potatoes felt after *they* were cooked. This seems to encourage the child to make the generation of a possibility into a subepisode of thinking in which the goal is to recall a similar case. Of course, here the teacher does the work for the child, but this can serve as an example. As I have commented elsewhere, this could be a very useful general heuristic for generating possibilities (see Baron, 1978, pp. 429–434).

Other techniques take the form of hints, which are essentially ways of simplifying the problem to bring it within a suitable range of difficulty, without eliminating the need for the child to think. A good way to do this is to isolate components of the task. For example, "The teacher presents a group of blocks in a pattern and then says, 'Now you make this pattern over here with these blocks.' " If the child does nothing, the teacher says, "Show me the block at the bottom. Get one like it" (Blank, 1973, pp. 92–93). Another simplification technique is to make the question asked more specific ("How did the stove feel?" instead of "Why did you remove your hand from the stove?"). Such techniques do not include the common ploy of simply giving the answer in the form of a question ("Was it because the stove was hot?"), which might encourage an unthinking yes from the child. In contrast, Blank's simplification techniques (and she has many) apparently encourage thinking and discourage stopping too soon. These effects result from the child's increased expectation that thinking will help. If the child cannot answer the question asked or if a teacher makes the question so easy that the child need not think, the child instead learns that thinking is not a very effective way to deal with questions and instructions. Blank's techniques encourage search for possibilities and evidence by increasing confidence that thinking helps to achieve the child's goals. At the same time, Blank never recommends simply "encouraging" the child by saying "Very good!" no matter what the child has answered. If the answer is inadequate, the question should always be simplified, so that the child figures out the answer on her own. The avoidance of blind encouragement prevents the child from developing overconfidence (in the thinking done so far), a false kind of "self-confidence" that probably increases the bias to cut off search prematurely.

In a second study of the tutorial method, Collins (1977) analyzed the Socratic method of teaching, in which the tutor teaches by asking questions, at the high school and college levels. He proposes no new techniques, because he assumes (correctly, I think) that the method has been in more or less continuous use since the time of Socrates himself. (Blank, as it happens, cites her own experience with the method when she was a graduate student at Cambridge University as one of the major influences on her own work.) Rather, Collins tries to state a theory of tutorial dialogue at this level. The theory takes the form of a set of rules thought to be used by good Socratic tutors. Collins worked on the theory by examining a set of actual (and imagined) tutorial dialogues; his own work is an example of reflective thinking.

Collins's main example concerns a geography student's discovery, using his own knowledge, of a general rule for the conditions required for the growing of rice. Using illustrations from this example, Collins lists certain rules that tutors use. I shall quote a few of them here. Note that each rule specifies the conditions for its use (Collins, 1977, pp. 342–350):

Rule 1: Ask about a known case. If (1) it is the start of a dialogue, or (2) there is no other strategy to invoke, then (3) pick a well-known case and ask what the value of the dependent variable is for that case, or (4) ask the student if he knows a case with a particular value of the dependent variable. Example: Ask the student "Do they grow rice in China?" or "Do you know any place where rice is grown?" . . .

Rule 5: Form a general rule for an insufficient factor. If (1) the student gives as an explanation one or more factors that are not sufficient, then (2) formulate a general rule asserting that the factor given is sufficient and ask the student if the rule is true. Example: If the student gives water as the reason they grow rice in China, ask him "Do you think any place with enough water can grow rice?"

Rule 6: Pick a counterexample for an insufficient factor. If (1) the student gives as an explanation one or more factors that are not sufficient, or (2) agrees to the general rule in Rule 5, then (3) pick a counterexample that has the right value of the factor(s) given, but the wrong value of the dependent variable, and (4) ask what the value of the dependent variable is for that case, or (5) ask why the causal dependence does not hold for that case. Example: If a student gives water as the reason they grow rice in China or agrees that any place with enough water can grow rice, pick a place like Ireland where there is enough water and ask "Do they grow rice in Ireland?" or "Why don't they grow rice in Ireland?" . . .

Rule 15: Request a test of the hypothesis about a factor. If (1) the student has formulated a hypothesis about how the dependent variable is related to a particular factor, then (2) ask him how it could be tested . . .

Rule 24: Trace the consequences of a general rule. If (1) a student agrees to a general rule such as Rule 5 or Rule 7, then (2) ask if he agrees with the consequences of that rule in a particular case. Example: If the student states that it is necessary to have flat terrain to grow rice, then point out that since they do not have flat terrain in Japan, they must not grow much rice and so must import most of the rice they eat.

The theory of actively open-minded thinking suggests reasons why these techniques (and others not presented) are effective in teaching thinking. Rule 1 is a way of suggesting a possibility, when the goal is to come up with necessary and sufficient factors for some dependent variable, such as growing rice. This rule therefore acts as a heuristic for generating possibilities; it is a way to encourage the initiation of a subepisode of thinking, with a possible factor as its goal. If this technique – and each of the others – is to be effective in teaching good thinking, students must learn to ask themselves the same kind of question in the tutor's absence. These tutorial devices come to function as heuristics to overcome biases, if the student internalizes the tutor's role. Specifically, the student's anticipation of what the tutor might say serves as a goad to carry out the request that the tutor might make, even in the absence of the request itself.

Rule 5 asks the student to state a general principle. The goal of the entire process here is a principle, so that an explanation of a single case is not a real possibility. For an explanation of a single case to become a possibility, it must be stated in the correct form, which in this case is the form of a general principle. Only when the possibility is represented in this way can the appropriate kinds of evidence, examples, and counterexamples be brought to bear. Rule 5 might simply encourage the student to form a representation of a possibility, so that evidence relevant to it can be sought, particularly counterevidence.

Rules 6, 15, and 24 encourage the choice of relevant evidence from memory or imagination. In particular, they encourage the search for counterexamples as evidence against general principles. This overcomes any bias in favor of confirming rather than disconfirming evidence in reflective thinking (presumably the most important bias in this sort of thinking). Other rules proposed by Collins probably have the same effect I suggested for Blank's simplification rules. They essentially simplify the problem, in order to keep the student thinking about it. They also provide ways for students to do this for themselves, just as rule 1 does. (These ways may tend to be more specific to the content used.) They therefore probably have the effect (among other effects) of increasing the student's appreciation of the value of thinking.

The effectiveness of the tutorial technique at any level probably depends on the willingness of students to internalize, to take over for themselves, the role of the tutor. The technique itself promotes the goals of good thinking through a process of personal identification, and it promotes as well the belief in the effectiveness of good thinking, through demonstration. To use the method most effectively, then, the tutor must be aware of the several "levels" of message being conveyed to the tutee – both the instruction in heuristics and habits, and the inculcation of beliefs and goals.

Thinking assignments

Designing thinking assignments. Thinking and decision making may also be done with the use of assignments and exercises that involve thinking, such as those often used as part of the "case method" of instruction in law schools and business schools. The theory that good thinking is actively open-minded implies certain general properties that these assignments ought to have:

1. Assignments should involve a complete thinking task, if at all possible. The components of thinking lose their purpose, and therefore their nature,

when extracted from the whole task. It is doubtful that practice at the separate components of thinking – search for possibilities, search for evidence, search for goals, and use of evidence – will transfer very much to thinking tasks in general. Further, there is no reason to think that the separate components are any easier to learn by themselves than they are to learn in the context of real thinking. Everyone carries out real thinking all the time; it may in fact be more difficult to break it into pieces than to leave it whole.

It is sometimes useful, though, to separate the task into its parts for purposes of explication. For example, students working as a group on a practical dilemma might first be urged to think about the problem individually. Then students can offer suggestions about possibilities (What *could* you do here?) before they give the arguments for and against each one.

2. If possible, the structure of the task must be made explicit, in terms of search for possibilities, evidence, and goals, and use of evidence.

3. The task should be designed to teach some lesson about thinking, for example:

> Often one's first impulse changes if other points of view or other arguments are considered.
> You need to make a special effort to think of reasons why your original idea might be wrong.
> Overconfidence in an initial idea makes people less inclined to consider alternatives or counterarguments.
> People try to simplify decisions by ignoring relevant goals.
> Very often you cannot be sure, and you must go with a best guess.
> You cannot make an idea be right if it is wrong. To choose the goal of defending a belief (rather than seeking the truth) is to risk futility. Nobody is obliged to defend a belief.
> We cannot judge good thinking from its outcome, although, in general, good thinking does tend to lead to better outcomes.
> There is no point in trying to have been right all along. It is better to try to be right in the end.
> When making decisions, it pays to think about decisions in terms of precedents, outcomes, and probabilities of outcomes.
> We need to make a special effort to think of consequences that are distant in time or in our relationship to the people affected.

4. The teacher should be willing to discuss issues in the philosophy of thinking as they come up. Many students raise questions about the role of authority, intuition, and power ("Might makes right"). The teacher must be prepared to defend the ideal of reflective thinking, while acknowledging its limitations (and without bending over backward to do so).

5. If possible, thinking tasks should be real: for example, writing a letter to a real member of Congress or to a newspaper. We must be on the lookout for real tasks that can be used for educational purposes.

6. If possible, thinking tasks should be fun, so as to teach the lessons that thinking *can* be fun and that criticism can be helpful rather than threatening. At the very least, the tasks should be fun for the teacher, so that students

can see someone having fun while thinking well. Moreover, tasks should be of interest for their own sake or for the sake of the goal to be achieved. If one cares about being right in the end and not about having been right all along, one can accept criticism of ideas without embarrassment. The only embarrassment comes with criticism of one's methods of thinking. Even here, students can be taught that they are *on their way* to becoming good thinkers and that thinking can always improve, so that criticism here can still be helpful rather than threatening.

An example: Gabriel's choice. Paul Adorno and I developed a lesson for a 10th-grade "college-bound" English class in an inner-city Philadelphia school. The lesson illustrates some of the points just made. It was based on James Baldwin's novel *Go Tell It on the Mountain*. The story is about a boy growing up in Harlem in the 1930s and the history of his family, especially his father Gabriel.

Gabriel grew up in the South, rebellious and sinful, but he "got religion" around the time his mother died. After his conversion, he became a preacher, and the respect he earned for this outstripped his tender age. He married Deborah, a devout and somewhat older woman who had been raped as a child and who was considered something of a martyr. Gabriel worked for a white family, and an attractive younger woman, Esther, also worked for this family. Gabriel befriended Esther, out of what he thought was a desire to reform her and convert her. As their friendship grew, it became physical, and, after Gabriel and Esther made love (according to one student in the class) exactly nine times, Esther told Gabriel that she was pregnant. Gabriel felt responsible, but he wanted neither to hurt Esther nor give up his work as a preacher, as he feared he would have to if there was a scandal. He had a chance to earn small amounts of extra money by going "into the field."

We asked the class the following question: At this point in the story, what could Gabriel do? (What are the possibilities?) What are the reasons for and against each possibility? What should he do? (Which possibility is best?) The students had to answer these questions as homework, and their answers served as the basis for a 40-minute class discussion.

Here are the two main possibilities. The arguments for and against each possibility are indicated with plus ($+$) and minus ($-$), respectively.

1. Send Esther to Chicago with Deborah's savings: ($+$) avoids embarrassment; ($+$) Gabriel could continue preaching; ($+$) avoids hurting Deborah; ($-$) abandons child; ($-$) risk of blackmail. (This is what actually happened in the story; and some of the class had read ahead.)
2. Tell Deborah and let her decide: ($+$) Deborah might want child; ($+$) clean conscience; ($-$) Esther might want to keep child; ($-$) Gabriel might have to stop preaching.

Many other possibilities were suggested but not discussed in detail: Leave with Esther; commit suicide; leave by himself; kill Esther; kill Deborah; arrange adoption.

In discussing the pro and the con arguments with the class, we pointed out that different arguments were related to different goals. Gabriel's major goals were to be a holy man; to avoid hurting Deborah; to avoid hurting Esther; to have a son (possibly by Deborah) who would carry on his religious work; and to continue preaching. We realized that the choice between answers 1 and 2 (or something like this choice) depended in large part on the relative importance of these goals. Some students felt (perhaps rightly) that Gabriel would absolutely forfeit his goal of being a holy man if he did anything less than confess his sin to Deborah.

We also discussed the fact that many of the arguments involved unknown outcomes – decisions under risk, as it were. We discussed whether a decision made under risk could turn out badly (relative to some other choice) and still be the best decision, given what was known at the time.

Finally, we tried to emphasize the general point that important decisions such as this one require thorough and fair consideration of all possibilities, evidence, and goals. (We would like to have discussed which of these, if any, Gabriel ignored, but, unfortunately, we did not have time.)

Teaching decision making

Decision making has been taught routinely to business and medical students and to military officers for several years. The training is sometimes included as part of courses in thinking (see Wheeler, 1979). Although few formal evaluations of the effectiveness of decision-making courses have been made, word-of-mouth reports suggest that students of expected-utility theory or MAUT seldom use these methods later in their decision making, unless they become professionals in the field. The study of formal methods, however, may help these students to avoid many of the errors that characterize informal decision making in others. It may also help them understand formal analyses carried out by others, even when these are only reported in the press.

We have evidence that it is possible to teach decision making to children and adolescents. For example, Kourilsky and Murray (1981) reported on a program designed to teach "economic reasoning" to 5th- and 6th-grade children, in part in the classroom and in part through a seminar for parents. Economic reasoning essentially involves making tradeoffs among potential outcomes, considering what one might do with the money other than spend it impulsively. The program increased the use of economic reasoning by parents and children, and they were reported to be satisfied with the actual economic decisions that they made.

Feehrer and Adams (1986) wrote a curriculum for a unit in decision making as part of an 8th-grade program designed to increase intelligence (in the sense of ch. 7, not just IQ tests). The curriculum, designed for one of many experiments sponsored by the Venezuelan government in the early 1980s (Nickerson, Perkins, & Smith, 1985), deals with the analysis of decisions into possible choices and their probable consequences, consequences that differ in likelihood. Students are encouraged to trade off probability and utility informally; are taught to gather information that will improve probability estimates; and are urged to evaluate information for relevance and credibility. The curriculum also addresses tradeoffs among attributes, in the form of "preference tables." All of the examples are based on detective stories.

A promising approach is to give additional emphasis to the types of errors that people make in the absence of decision analysis, such as temporal myopia; single-mindedness (neglect of relevant goals); impulsiveness (failure to consider alternatives and evidence); neglect of probability; and framing effects. This emphasis both explains why formal analysis is sometimes useful and warns the students against the errors themselves. Particular emphasis might be given to instruction in heuristics designed to avoid these errors. Heuristics are useful both in informal thinking about decisions and in the construction of a formal analysis. Examples are "Think about the precedent-setting effect of a choice, as well as the direct effect"; "Ask whether there are future effects"; "Consider alternatives." A useful instructional technique is to discuss a decision and then, as impulsive solutions are suggested (for example, in "Gabriel's choice," killing Esther or Deborah) ask the class what might be wrong with the idea. It usually turns out to be one of the errors in question (for example, failing to consider alternatives or relevant goals).

Teaching moral thinking

The two main approaches to education in moral thinking in the past have been indoctrination into a particular moral code and free discussion of moral dilemmas (Kohlberg, 1970). Indoctrination discourages actively open-minded thinking because it discourages discussion of alternatives or arguments. Unless the student is lucky in being taught by those who truly know the right answers, indoctrination is also likely to lead to moral beliefs that are difficult to defend. Discussion of dilemmas encourages thinking. A discussion leader can impose standards of good thinking on such a discussion without at the same time imposing particular answers to the dilemmas or particular moral views (Hare, 1978). Of course, such a teaching strategy takes some skill and some self-awareness in the teacher – but then so do many other teaching strategies.

An approach to moral education that I have defended (Baron, Brown, & Frisch, 1987), which to my knowledge has not been tried, is to regard moral thinking as an extension of decision making. The errors that people commit in moral thinking are much like those that they commit in other decision making (see chs. 19 and 20). The outstanding errors in moral thinking include failure to recognize the precedent-setting effects of choices; neglect of consequences of a choice for the feelings of others; neglect of consequences for those far away or those in the future; failure to recognize the conflict between self-interest and the interests of others (thoughtlessness); and the omission–

commission framing effect. Discussion of such errors need not imply acceptance or rejection of any particular moral code. All moral codes recognize the relevance of the effect of our choices on others. People who support these codes may feel that morality is not limited to such effects, but they can hardly object to more systematic instruction in thinking about them.

Of course, this approach is compatible with the discussion approach. The main difference is in the selection of examples for discussion and the emphasis on general properties of solutions that seem poorly thought out, as in the discussion of decisions.

Education in moral thinking may not reduce the crime rate, for some crimes result from simple overweighing of self-interest; people would still want to do these things even if they were aware of the effects of their actions on others' feelings. It is possible, however, that some blatantly immoral behavior *is* the result of failure to think through the effect of one's choices on others and would be prevented by moral education. Bad effects can also result from good intentions; some of this is just bad moral luck. At other times the intentions result from poor thinking about what the right course of action is. When this occurs in the decisions of government leaders or in the decisions of those who choose them, many people feel the bad effects. Moral education might do some good after all, if it helped to prevent this.

Teaching thinking versus teaching content

An argument frequently used to oppose the teaching of thinking in schools is that it will detract from the teaching of content. This argument makes sense if we are talking about the addition of new programs in thinking itself; however, none of the methods I have discussed require this. All can be incorporated into the teaching of material that is valuable in its own right. Even the study of decision making and moral thinking can be incorporated into health classes or history classes; history lessons based on the analysis of classic decisions (such as President Truman's decision to drop the atomic bomb) are already popular. In some subjects, such as mathematics and history, it seems impossible to truly learn the content without thinking well.

How can the teaching of thinking best be combined with the teaching of content? In order to teach any subject in this way, we have to consider how the knowledge taught will eventually be used as part of a process of thinking. In this thinking, what will be the *possibilities*? What sort of *evidence* will be relevant? How will the evidence be *weighed*? How will the *goals* of thinking be defined? What kinds of *heuristics* will eliminate *biases* in thinking in this domain?

The answers to these questions will, of course, vary from subject to subject. Many subjects are already taught in a way that focuses on the thought process characteristic of the domain: examples are the case method, in law and business schools; the research seminar, in graduate schools; the course in studio art, in art schools; and literature and history courses that encourage scholarly analysis rather than regurgitation of facts.

A desire to teach good thinking in a content domain ought to affect the standards by which students are evaluated, as well as the organization and content of the teaching itself. The present theory argues against the use of "speed" examinations – that is, examinations in which the speed of working, rather than the effectiveness of thinking, has a strong influence on the grade. If examinations can be used to encourage good thinking, failure to use them this second way is a missed opportunity. Use of speed tests gives some students the idea that the ability to think well does not matter much and that they need not try to cultivate it.

When possible, examinations and other assignments ought to require actual thinking rather than "rote recall." In grading essay examinations and papers, the highest grades should be reserved for work showing active openness to possibilities other than the one being defended. Students should learn to do more than simply back up a one-sided view, as though they were lawyers charged with defending it.

In certain science courses, it is also possible to require students to develop hypotheses of their own about a given phenomenon and to develop tests of these hypotheses, that is, to do what amounts to writing a grant proposal. This sounds like an ambitious goal, but it will not sound so ambitious if teachers teach students how to do this, first of all, by giving examples of doing it themselves. The task can be made easier by choosing easily understood phenomena. Computer simulations might also help, by allowing students to carry out the experiments they have designed with relative ease. Teachers can also review the course of scientific history with students, so that the students see that science is more a matter of stumbling from error to less error than of intuitively perceiving truth.

Will the emphasis on thinking and the use of course content in making arguments and other exercises in thinking detract from the amount of content taught? In some courses – for example, those in gross anatomy for medical students – this is a serious problem. In other courses, teachers probably overvalue the content itself, underestimating the amount of it that will never be used, that will be quickly forgotten, or that will be rendered useless or trivial by new advances in the discipline or by new ideas that the student encounters later. Overvaluation of the content of a course allows a teacher to continue to use the more "objective" methods of examination – which turn out to require less work to grade.

Is the use of thinking assignments for student evaluation less fair than the use of "objective" examinations? Not necessarily. This criticism may really mean that we tend to overvalue evaluation itself.

The teaching of good thinking *along with content* can begin at any age. It has been argued that preadolescents are not ready for truly reflective thinking. One argument to the contrary is the experience of Lipman (1985), who has designed a curricular program called "Philosophy for Children," which strives to do what its title says, teach philosophical, reflective thinking to children from kindergarten up. Lipman has written several novels that the children read and discuss, using a tutorial method adapted to a larger group (see ch. 9 for an example). The program has been successful in arousing students' interest in thinking, and its graduates seem to do better in school as a result.

Conclusion

Schools are a focal point for the transmission of intellectual standards, and they are therefore absolutely essential to any effort to maintain or improve the quality of our thinking. Schools and teachers are limited, however, in what they can do. Teaching, we have recognized, cannot improve the biological capacities that are the determinants of mental performance. Cultural influences, however, are greater problems. Schools exist only as part of a larger society, which conveys its values about thinking in many ways.

The family is surely of major importance in this regard. Discussions around the dinner table can just be arguments, a matter of fighting for power and control, but they can also be real discussions that offer opportunities for thinking. (This does not exclude argument, but it requires a type of argument in which the children are allowed to have their say.)

Other institutions of society are relevant as well. Business managers can encourage (or discourage) good thinking in their subordinates. Clinical psychologists and other counselors of individuals have an opportunity to encourage or discourage good thinking. Journalists and politicians have immense power over the quality of our thinking about public issues: If they treat their audiences as though they were incapable of thinking, their expectations will become self-fulfilling. Last but not least, individuals can affect the quality of thinking through the judgments we make about each other: Do we prefer to have friends who are open-minded and intellectually playful, or do we tolerate friends who are stubborn know-it-alls? If we are to have a society of intelligent thinkers, we cannot rely on teachers to bring it about on their own.

The encouragement of active open-mindedness throughout society will not make us all geniuses, but it may make the world a more reasonable place in which to live.

References

Abelson, R. P., Aronson, E., McGuire, W. J., Newcomb, T. M., Rosenberg, M. J., & Tannenbaum, P. H. (Eds.), (1968). *Theories of cognitive consistency: A sourcebook*. Chicago: Rand McNally.

Adams, M. J. (Coordinator), (1986). *Odyssey: A curriculum for thinking*. Watertown, MA: Mastery Education Corporation.

Adams, P. A., & Adams, J. K. (1960). Confidence in the recognition and reproduction of words difficult to spell. *American Journal of Psychology, 73*, 544–552.

Ainslie, G. (1975). Specious reward: A behavioral theory of impulsiveness and impulse control. *Psychological Bulletin, 82*, 463–496.

Ainslie, G. (1982). A behavioral economic approach to the defense mechanisms: Freud's energy theory revisited. *Social Science Information, 21*, 735–779.

Ainslie G. (1986). Beyond microeconomics: Conflict among interests in a multiple self as a determinant of value. In J. Elster (Ed.), *The multiple self* (pp. 133–175). Cambridge University Press.

Ainslie, G., & Haendel, V. (1983). The motives of the will. In E. Gottheil, K. A. Druley, T. E. Skoloda, & H. M. Waxman (Eds.), *Etiologic aspects of alcohol and drug abuse*. Springfield, IL: Thomas.

Ajzen, I. (1977). Intuitive theories of events and the effects of base-rate information on prediction. *Journal of Personality and Social Psychology, 35*, 303–314.

Akerlof, G., & Dickens, W. T. (1982). The economic consequences of cognitive dissonance. *American Economic Review, 72*, 307–319.

Allais, M. (1953). Le comportement de l'homme rationnel devant le risque: Critique des postulates et axioms de l'école américaine. *Econometrica, 21*, 503–546.

Allan, L. G., & Jenkins, H. M. (1980). The judgment of contingency and the nature of the response alternatives. *Canadian Journal of Psychology, 34*, 1–11.

Alloy, L. B., & Abramson, L. Y. (1979). Judgment of contingency in depressed and nondepressed students: Sadder but wiser? *Journal of Experimental Psychology: General, 108*, 441–485.

Alloy, L. B., & Tabachnik, N. (1984). Assessment of covariation by humans and animals: The joint influence of prior expectations and current situational information. *Psychological Review, 91*, 112–149.

Alpert, W., & Raiffa, H. (1982). A progress report on the training of probability assessors. In D. Kahneman, P. Slovic, & A. Tversky (Eds.), *Judgment under uncertainty: Heuristics and biases* (pp. 294–305). Cambridge University Press.

Anderson, C. A. (1982). Inoculation and counterexplanation: Debiasing techniques in the perseverance of social theories. *Social Cognition, 1*, 126–139.

Anderson, C. A., Lepper, M. R., & Ross, L. (1980). Perseverance of social theories: The role of explanation in the persistence of discredited information. *Journal of Personality and Social Psychology, 39*, 1037–1049.

Anderson, J. R. (1976). *Memory, language, and thought*. Hillsdale, NJ: Erlbaum.

Anderson, N. H. (1981). *Foundations of information integration theory*. New York: Academic Press.

485

Anderson, N. H., & Butzin, C. A. (1978). Integration theory applied to children's judgments of equity. *Developmental Psychology, 14*, 593–606.

Arkes, H. R., & Blumer, C. (1985). The psychology of sunk cost. *Organizational Behavior and Human Decision Processes, 35*, 124–140.

Arkes, H. R., Dawes, R. M., & Christensen, C. (1986). Factors influencing the use of a decision rule in a probabilistic task. *Organizational Behavior and Human Decision Processes, 37*, 93–110.

Arkes, H. R., & Hammond, K. R. (1986). *Judgment and decision making: An interdisciplinary reader*. Cambridge University Press.

Arkes, H. R., & Harkness, A. R. (1983). Estimates of contingency between two dichotomous variables. *Journal of Experimental Psychology: General, 112*, 117–135.

Arnauld, A. (1964). *The art of thinking (Port Royal Logic)* (J. Dickoff & P. James, Trans.). Indianapolis: Bobbs-Merrill. (Original work published 1662)

Aronson, E., Chase, T., Helmreich, R., & Ruhnke, R. (1974). Feeling stupid and feeling guilty – two aspects of the self-concept which mediate dissonance arousal in a communication situation. *International Journal of Communication Research, 3*, 340–352.

Asch, S. E. (1946). Forming impressions of personality. *Journal of Abnormal and Social Psychology, 41*, 258–290.

Asch, S. E. (1969). A reformulation of the problem of associations. *American Psychologist, 24*, 92–102.

Asch, S. E., Ceraso, J., & Heimer, W. (1960). Perceptual conditions of association. *Psychological Monographs, 74* (3, Whole No. 490).

Asch, S. E., & Ebenholz, S. M. (1962). The principle of associative symmetry. *Proceedings of the American Philosophical Society, 106*, 135–163.

Attneave, F. (1953). Psychological probability as a function of experienced frequency. *Journal of Experimental Psychology, 46*, 81–86.

Ausubel, D. P. (1963). *The psychology of meaningful verbal learning*. New York: Grune & Stratton.

Axelrod, R. (1984). *The evolution of cooperation*. New York: Basic Books.

Axsom, D., & Cooper, J. (1981). Reducing weight by reducing dissonance: The role of effort justification in inducing weight loss. In E. Aronson (Ed.), *Readings about the social animal* (3rd ed.). San Francisco: Freeman.

Bacon, F. (1960). *The new organon and related writings*. New York: Liberal Arts Press. (Original work published 1620)

Baddeley, A. D. (1976). *The psychology of memory*. New York: Basic Books, 1976.

Baddeley, A. D. (1983). Working memory. *Philosophical Transactions of the Royal Society, London, B302*, 311–324.

Ball, W. W. R. (1939). *Mathematical recreations and essays* (11th ed.). New York: Macmillan.

Baron, J. (1973). Semantic components and conceptual development. *Cognition, 2*, 189–207.

Baron, J. (1977). What we might know about orthographic rules. In S. Dornic (Ed.), *Attention and performance VI*. Hillsdale, NJ: Erlbaum.

Baron, J. (1978). Intelligence and general strategies. In G. Underwood (Ed.), *Strategies in information processing* (pp. 403–450). New York: Academic Press.

Baron, J. (1985a). Rational plans, achievement, and education. In M. Frese & J. Sabini (Eds.), *Goal directed behavior: The concept of action in psychology*. Hillsdale, NJ: Erlbaum.

Baron, J. (1985b). *Rationality and intelligence*. Cambridge University Press.

Baron, J. (1985c). What kinds of intelligence components are fundamental? In S. F. Chipman, J. W. Segal, & R. Glaser (Eds.), *Thinking and learning skills. Vol. 2: Research and open questions* (pp. 365–390). Hillsdale, NJ: Erlbaum.

Baron, J. (1986). Tradeoffs among reasons for action. *Journal for the Theory of Social Behavior, 16*, 173–195.

Baron, J. (1987). Second-order uncertainty and belief functions. *Theory and decision, 23*, 25–36.

Baron, J. (in press a). Beliefs about thinking. In J. F. Voss, D. N. Perkins, & J. W. Segal (Eds.), *Informal reasoning and education*. Hillsdale, NJ: Erlbaum.

Baron, J. (in press b). Utility, exchange, and commensurability. *Journal of Thought*.

Baron, J., Badgio, P., & Gaskins, I. W. (1986). Cognitive style and its improvement: A normative approach. In R. J. Sternberg (Ed.), *Advances in the psychology of human intelligence* (Vol. 3, pp. 173–220). Hillsdale, NJ: Erlbaum.

Baron, J., Beattie, J., & Hershey, J. C. (in press). Heuristics and biases in diagnostic reasoning: II. Congruence, information, and certainty. *Organizational Behavior and Human Decision Processes*.

Baron, J., Brown, R. V., & Frisch, D. (1987). *Toward improved instruction in decision making*. Unpublished manuscript, Psychology Department, University of Pennsylvania, Philadelphia.

Baron, J., & Hershey, J. C. (1988). Outcome bias in decision evaluation. *Journal of Personality and Social Psychology, 54*, 569-579.

Baron, J., & Treiman, R. (1980). Some problems in the study of differences in cognitive processes. *Memory and Cognition, 8*, 313–321.

Bartlett, F. C. (1958). *Thinking*. London: Allen & Unwin.

Batson, C. D. (1975). Rational processing or rationalization? The effect of disconfirming evidence on a stated religious belief. *Journal of Personality and Social Psychology, 32*, 176–184.

Bayes, T. (1958). An essay towards solving a problem in the doctrine of chances. *Biometrika, 45*, 293–315. (Original work published 1764)

Bazerman, M. H., Beekun, R. I., & Schoorman, F. D. (1982). Performance evaluation in dynamic context: The impact of a prior commitment to the ratee. *Journal of Applied Psychology, 67*, 873–876.

Bazerman, M. H., Giuliano, T., & Appelman, A. (1984). Escalation of commitment in individual and group decision making. *Organizational Behavior and Human Performance, 33*, 141–152.

Beattie, J., & Baron, J. (1988). Confirmation and matching bias in hypothesis testing. *Quarterly Journal of Experimental Psychology, 40A*, 269–297.

Beck, A. T. (1976). *Cognitive therapy and the emotional disorders*. New York: International Universities Press.

Becker, J. W., & Brownson, F. O. (1964). What price ambiguity? Or the role of ambiguity in decision making. *Journal of Political Economics, 72*, 62–73.

Behn, R. D., & Vaupel, J. W. (1982). *Quick analysis for busy decision makers*. New York: Basic Books.

Bell, D. E. (1982). Regret in decision making under uncertainty. *Operations Research, 30*, 961–981.

Bell, D. E. (1985a). Disappointment in decision making under uncertainty. *Operations Research, 33*, 1–27.

Bell, D. E. (1985b). Putting a premium on regret. *Management Science, 31*, 117–120.

Bennett, J. (1981). Morality and consequences. In S. M. McMurrin (Ed.), *The Tanner Lectures on human values* (vol. 2, pp. 45–116). Salt Lake City: University of Utah Press.

Bentham, J. (1948). *An introduction to the principles of morals and legislation*. Oxford: Blackwell Publisher. (Original work published 1843)

Bernoulli, D. (1954). Exposition of a new theory of the measurement of risk (L. Sommer, trans.). *Econometrica, 22*, 23–26. (Original work published 1738)

Beyth-Marom, R., & Fischhoff, B. (1983). Diagnosticity and Pseudodiagnosticity. *Journal of Personality and Social Psychology, 45*, 1185–1195.

Binet, A., & Simon, T. (1905). Methodes nouvelles pour le diagnostic du niveau intellectuel des anormaux. *L'Année Psychologique, 11*, 191–244.

Birch, H. G., & Rabinowitz, H. S. (1951). The negative effect of previous experience on productive thinking. *Journal of Experimental Psychology, 41*, 121–125.

Birnbaum, M. H., & Mellers, B. A. (1983). Bayesian inference: Combining base rates with opinions of sources who vary in credibility. *Journal of Personality and Social Psychology, 45*, 792–804.

Blank, M. (1973). *Teaching learning in the preschool*. Columbus, OH: Merrill.

Block, N. J., & Dworkin, G. (1976). *The IQ controversy: Critical readings*. New York: Pantheon.

Bloom, B., & Broder, L. (1950). *Problem-solving processes of college students*. Chicago: University of Chicago Press.

Braine, M. D. S., & Rumain, B. (1983). Logical reasoning. In J. Flavell & E. Markman (Eds.), *Handbook of child psychology: Vol. 3. Cognitive development* (4th ed.). New York: Wiley.

Bregman, A. S. (1977). Perception and behavior as compositions of ideals. *Cognitive Psychology, 9*, 150–292.

Brehmer, B. (1980). In one word: Not from experience. *Acta Psychologica, 45*, 223–241.

Brickman, P., Coates, D., & Janoff-Bulman, R. (1978). Lottery winners and accident victims: Is happiness relative? *Journal of Personality and Social Psychology, 36*, 917–927.

Brooks, L. R. (1978). Nonanalytic concept formation and memory for instances. In E. Rosch & B. B. Lloyd (Eds.), *Cognition and categorization*. Hillsdale, NJ: Erlbaum.

Brown, A. L. (1974). The role of strategic behavior in retardate memory. In N. R. Ellis (Ed.), *International review of research in mental retardation* (Vol. 7, pp. 55–111). New York: Academic Press.

Brown, A. L. (1975). The development of memory: Knowing, knowing about knowing, and knowing how to know. In H. W. Reese (Ed.), *Advances in child development and behavior* (Vol. 10, pp. 103–152). New York: Academic Press.

Brown, A. L., Campione, J. C., & Barclay, C. R. (1979). Training self-checking routines for estimating test readiness: Generalization from list learning to prose recall. *Child Development, 50*, 501–512.

Brown, R. V., Kahr, A. S., & Peterson, C. R. (1974). *Decision analysis for the manager*. New York: Holt, Rinehart, & Winston.

Brown, R. V., & Lindley, D. V. (1986). Plural analysis: Multiple approaches to quantitative research. *Theory and Decision, 20*, 133–154.

Bruner, J. S., Goodnow, J. J., & Austin, G. A. (1956). *A study of thinking*. New York: Wiley.

Bruner, J. S., & Potter, M. C. (1964). Interference in visual recognition. *Science, 144*, 424–425.

Brunswick, E. (1952). *The conceptual framework of psychology*. Chicago: University of Chicago Press.

Bryan, W. L., & Harter, N. (1899). Studies on the telegraphic language. *Psychological Review, 6*, 345–375.

Bursztajn, H., Hamm, R. M., Gutheil, T. G., & Brodsky, A. (1984). The decision-analytic approach to medical malpractice law. *Medical Decision Making, 4*, 401–414.

Camerer, C. (1981). General conditions for the success of bootstrapping models. *Organizational Behavior and Human Performance, 27*, 411–422.

Campione, J. C., Brown, A. L., & Ferrara, R. A. (1982). Mental retardation and intelligence. In R. J. Sternberg (Ed.), *Handbook of human intelligence* (pp. 392–490). Cambridge University Press.

Candee, D., & Kohlberg, L. (1987). Moral judgment and moral action: A reanalysis of Haan, Smith, and Block's (1968) Free Speech Movement data. *Journal of Personality and Social Psychology, 52*, 554–564.

Carey, S. (1985). Are children fundamentally different kinds of thinkers and learners than adults? In S. F. Chipman, J. W. Segal, & R. Glaser (Eds.), *Thinking and learning skills: Vol 2. Research and open questions* (pp. 485–517). Hillsdale, NJ: Erlbaum.

Carnap, R. (1950). *Logical foundations of probability*. Chicago: University of Chicago Press.

Carpenter, W. B. (1876). *Principles of mental physiology*. New York: Appleton.

Carroll, J. B. (1982). The measurement of intelligence. In R. J. Sternberg (Ed.), *Handbook of human intelligence* (pp. 29–120). Cambridge University Press.

Cattell, R. B. (1963). Theory of fluid and crystallized intelligence: A critical experiment. *Journal of Educational Psychology, 54*, 1–22.

Ceci, S. J., & Liker, J. K. (1986). A day at the races: A study of IQ, expertise, and cognitive complexity. *Journal of Experimental Psychology: General, 115*, 255–266.

Ceraso, J., & Provitera, A. (1971). Sources of error in syllogistic reasoning. *Cognitive Psychology, 2*, 400–410.

Chapman, L. J., & Chapman, J. P. (1959). Atmosphere effect reexamined. *Journal of Experimental Psychology, 58*, 220–226.

Chapman, L. J., & Chapman, J. P. (1967). Genesis of popular but erroneous psychodiagnostic observations. *Journal of Abnormal Psychology, 72*, 193–204.

Chapman, L. J., & Chapman, J. P. (1969). Illusory correlation as an obstacle to the use of valid psychodiagnostic signs. *Journal of Abnormal Psychology, 74*, 271–280.

Chapman, L. J., & Chapman, J. P. (1971). Test results are what you think they are. *Psychology Today*, November, pp. 18–22.

Charniak, E. (1983). The Bayesian basis of common sense medical diagnosis. *Proceedings of the National Conference on Artificial Intelligence, 3*, 70–73.

Cheng, P. W., Holyoak, K. J., Nisbett, R. E., & Oliver, L. M. (1986). Pragmatic versus syntactic approaches to training deductive reasoning. *Cognitive Psychology, 18*, 293–328.

Chi, M. T. H. (1985). Interactive roles of knowledge and strategies in the development of organized sorting and recall. In S. F. Chipman, J. W. Segal, & R. Glaser (Eds.), *Thinking and learning skills: Vol. 2. Research and open questions* (pp. 457–483). Hillsdale, NJ: Erlbaum.

Chi, M. T. H., Feltovich, P. J., & Glaser, R. (1981). Categorization and representation of physics knowledge by experts and novices. *Cognitive Science, 5*, 121–152.

Clark, E. O., Glanzer, M., & Turndorf, H. (1979). The pattern of memory loss resulting from intravenously administered diazepam. *Archives of Neurology, 36*, 296–300.

Clark, M. S., & Mills, J. (1979). Interpersonal attraction in exchange and communal relationships. *Journal of Personality and Social Psychology, 37*, 12–24.

Clark, M. S., Mills, J., & Powell, M. C. (1986). Keeping track of needs in communal and exchange relationships. *Journal of Personality and Social Psychology, 51*, 333–338.

Clark, M. S., Ouellette, R., Powell, M. C., & Milberg, S. (1987). Recipient's mood, relationship type, and helping. *Journal of Personality and Social Psychology, 53*, 94–103.

Clement, J. (1983). A conceptual model discussed by Galileo and used intuitively by physics students. In D. Gentner & A. L. Stevens (Eds.), *Mental models* (pp. 325–340). Hillsdale, NJ: Erlbaum.

Cohen, L. J. (1981). Can human irrationality be experimentally demonstrated? *Behavioral and Brain Sciences, 4*, 317–331.

Cohen, N. J., & Squire, L. R. (1980). Preserved learning and retention of pattern-analyzing skill in amnesia: Dissociation of knowing how and knowing that. *Science, 210*, 207–210.

Collins, A. (1977). Processes in acquiring knowledge. In R. C. Anderson, R. J. Spiro, & W. E. Montague (Eds.), *Schooling and the acquisition of knowledge*. Hillsdale, NJ: Erlbaum.

Collins, A., & Gentner, D. (1986). *How people construct mental models*. Cambridge, MA: Bolt, Beranek, & Newman.

Collins, A., & Michalski, R. (in press). The logic of plausible reasoning. *Cognitive Science*.

Coombs, C. H., Dawes, R. M., & Tversky, A. (1970). *Mathematical psychology: An elementary introduction*. Englewood Cliffs, NJ: Prentice-Hall.

Cooper, J. (1971). Personal responsibility and dissonance: The role of foreseen consequences. *Journal of Personality and Social Psychology, 18*, 354–363.

Cox, R. T. (1946). Probability, frequency, and reasonable expectation. *American Journal of Physics, 14*, 1–13.

Cox, R. T. (1979). Of inference and inquiry – an essay in inductive logic. In R. D. Levine & M. Tribus (Eds.), *The maximum entropy formalism*. Cambridge, MA: M.I.T. Press.

Craik, F. I. M., & Tulving, E. (1975). Depth of processing and the retention of words in episodic memory. *Journal of Experimental Psychology: General, 104*, 268–294.

Cronbach, L. J., & Snow, R.E. (1977). *Aptitudes and instructional methods: A handbook for research on interactions*. New York: Irvington.

Dailey, C. A. (1952). The effects of premature conclusions upon the acquisition of understanding of a person. *Journal of Psychology, 33*, 133–152.

Dank, B. M. (1971). Coming out in the gay world. *Psychiatry, 34*, 180–197.

Davis, D. A. (1979). What's in a name? A Bayesian rethinking of attributional biases in clinical judgment. *Journal of Consulting and Clinical Psychology, 47*, 1109–1114.

Davis, W. A. (1981). A theory of happiness. *American Philosophical Quarterly, 18*, 111–120.

Dawes, R. M. (1971). A case study of graduate admissions: Application of three principles of human decision making. *American Psychologist, 26*, 180–188.

Dawes, R. M. (1976). Shallow psychology. In J. S. Carroll & J. Payne (Eds.), *Cognition and social behavior*. Hillsdale, NJ: Erlbaum.

Dawes, R. M. (1979). The robust beauty of improper linear models. *American Psychologist, 34*, 571–582.

Dawes, R. M. (1980). Social dilemmas. *Annual Review of Psychology, 31*, 169–193.

Dawes, R. M., & Corrigan, B. (1974). Linear models in decision making. *Psychological Bulletin, 81*, 97–106.

Dawes, R. M., McTavish, J., & Shaklee, H. (1977). Behavior, communication, and assumptions about other people's behavior in a commons dilemma situation. *Journal of Personality and Social Psychology, 35*, 1–11.

Dawes, R. M., Orbell, J. M., Simmons, R. T., & van de Kragt, A. J. C. (1986). Organizing groups for collective action. *American Political Science Review, 80*, 1171–1185.

de Bono, E. (1976). *Teaching thinking*. London: Penguin.

de Charms, R. (1976). *Enhancing motivation in the classroom*. New York: Irvington.

Deci, E. L., & Ryan, R. M. (1987). The support of autonomy and the control of behavior. *Journal of Personality and Social Psychology, 53*, 1024–1037.

Dewey, J. (1933). *How we think: A restatement of the relation of reflective thinking to the educative process*. Boston: Heath.

Diener, C. I., & Dweck, C. S. (1978). An analysis of learned helplessness: Continuous changes in performance, strategy, and achievement cognitions following failure. *Journal of Personality and Social Psychology, 36*, 451–462.

Doherty, M. E., & Falgout, K. (1986). *Subjects' data selection strategies for assessing event covariation*. Unpublished manuscript, Department of Psychology, Bowling Green State University, Bowling Green, OH.

Doherty, M. E., Mynatt, C. R., Tweney, R. D., & Schiavo, M. D. (1979). Pseudodiagnosticity. *Acta Psychologica, 43*, 111–121.

Dörner, D., & Kreutzig, H. (1983). Problemlosefahigkeit und Intelligenz. *Psychologische Rundhaus, 34*, 185–192.

Duda, R. O., Hart, P. E., Barrett, P., Gashnig, J., Konolige, K., Reboh, R., & Slocum, J. (1976a). *Development of the Prospector Consultation System for Mineral Exploration*. AI Center, SRI International, Menlo Park, CA.

Duda, R. O., Hart, P. E., & Nilsson, N. J. (1976b). Subjective Bayesian methods for rule-based inference systems. In *Proceedings of the 1976 National Computer Conference*, (pp. 1075–1082). AFIPS, Vol. 45.

Duncker, K. (1945). On problem solving. *Psychological Monographs, 58*, Whole No. 270.

Dweck, C. S. (1975). The role of expectations and attributions in the alleviation of learned helplessness. *Journal of Personality and Social Psychology, 31*, 674–685.

Dweck, C. S., & Elliott, E. S. (1983). Achievement motivation. In P. H. Mussen, (Ed.), *Carmichael's manual of child psychology*, Vol. 2. New York: Wiley.

Eddy, D. M. (1982). Probabilistic reasoning in clinical medicine: Problems and opportunities.

In D. Kahneman, P. Slovic, & A. Tversky (Eds.), *Judgment under uncertainty: Heuristics and biases* (pp. 249–267). Cambridge University Press.

Edwards, W., & Tversky, A. (Eds.) (1967). *Decision making*. Harmondsworth: Penguin.

Einhorn, H. J. (1986). Accepting error to make less error. *Journal of Personality Assessment, 50*, 387–395.

Einhorn, H. J., Kleinmuntz, D. N., & Kleinmuntz, B. (1979). Linear regression *and* process tracing models of judgment. *Psychological Review, 86*, 465–485.

Ellis, A. (1987). The impossibility of achieving consistently good mental health. *American Psychologist, 42*, 364–375.

Ellsberg, D. (1961). Risk, ambiguity, and the Savage axioms. *Quarterly Journal of Economics, 75*, 643–699.

Elstein, A. S., Holzman, G. B., Ravitch, M. M., Metheny, W. A., Holmes, M. M., Hoppe, R. B., Rothert, M. L., & Rovner, D. R. (1986). Comparison of physicians' decisions regarding estrogen replacement therapy for menopausal women and decisions derived from a decision analytic model. *American Journal of Medicine, 80*, 246–258.

Elster, J. (1979). *Ulysses and the sirens: Studies in rationality and irrationality*. Cambridge University Press.

Elster, J. (1983). *Sour grapes: Studies of the subversion of rationality*. Cambridge University Press.

Elster J. (1985). Weakness of will and the free-rider problem. *Economics and Philosophy, 1*, 231–265.

Emler, N., Renwick, S., & Malone, B. (1983). The relationship between moral reasoning and political orientation. *Journal of Personality and Social Psychology, 45*, 1073–1080.

Ericsson, K. A., Chase, W. G., & Faloon, S. (1980). Acquisition of a memory skill. *Science, 208*, 1181–1182.

Ericsson, K. A., & Simon, H. A. (1980). Verbal reports as data. *Psychological Review, 87*, 215–251.

Erikson, E. H. (1950). *Childhood and society*. New York: Norton.

Erikson, E. H. (1968). *Identity youth and crisis*. New York: Norton.

Ernst, G. W., & Newell, A. (1979). *GPS: A case study in generality and problem solving*. New York: Academic Press.

Evans, J. St. B. T. (1982). *The psychology of deductive reasoning*. London: Routledge & Kegan Paul.

Evans, J. St. B. T., Barston, J. L., & Pollard, P. (1983). On the conflict between logic and belief in syllogistic reasoning. *Memory and Cognition, 11*, 295–306.

Fancher, R. E. (1985). *The intelligence men: Makers of the IQ controversy*. New York: Norton.

Feehrer, C. E., & Adams, M. J. (1986). *Odyssey: A curriculum for thinking. Decision making*. Watertown, MA: Mastery Education Association.

Festinger, L. (1962). Cognitive dissonance. *Scientific American, 107* (4).

Festinger, L., & Carlsmith, J. M. (1959). Cognitive consequences of forced compliance. *Journal of Abnormal and Social Psychology, 58*, 203–210.

Feuerstein, R. (1980). *Instrumental enrichment*. Baltimore: University Park Press.

Finocchiaro, M. (1981). Fallacies and the evaluation of reasoning. *American Philosophical Quarterly, 18*, 13–22.

Fischhoff, B. (1975). Hindsight≠foresight: The effect of outcome knowledge on judgment under uncertainty. *Journal of Experimental Psychology: Human Perception and Performance, 1*, 288–299.

Fischhoff, B. (1977). Perceived informativeness of facts. *Journal of Experimental Psychology: Human Perception and Performance, 3*, 349–358.

Fischhoff, B., Lichtenstein, S., Slovic, P., Derby, S. L., & Keeney, R. L. (1981). *Acceptable risk*. Cambridge University Press.

Fischhoff, B., Slovic, P., & Lichtenstein, S. (1977). Knowing with certainty: The appropriateness of extreme confidence. *Journal of Experimental Psychology: Human Perception and Performance, 3*, 552–564.

Fischhoff, B., Slovic, P., & Lichtenstein, S. (1978). Fault trees: Sensitivity of estimated failure probabilities to problem representation. *Journal of Experimental Psychology: Human Perception and Performance, 4*, 330–334.

Fishburn, P. C. (1986). Reconsiderations in the foundations of decisions under uncertainty (Working paper). Murray Hill, NJ: Bell Laboratories.

Fiske, A. P. (in press). Moral relativism within Moose culture: Four modes of social relationships. *Ethos*.

Flavell, J. H. (1970). Developmental studies of mediated memory. In H. W. Reese & L. P. Lipset (Eds.), *Advances in child development and behavior* (Vol. 5, pp. 181–211). New York: Academic Press.

Flavell, J. H. (1971). Stage-related properties of cognitive development. *Cognitive Psychology, 2*, 421–453.

Flavell, J. H. (1977). *Cognitive development*. Englewood Cliffs, NJ: Prentice-Hall.

Fodor, J. A. (1975). *The language of thought*. New York: Crowell.

Fong, G. T., Krantz, D. H., & Nisbett, R. E. (1986). The effects of statistical training on thinking about everyday problems. *Cognitive Psychology, 18*, 253–292.

Ford, M. R., & Lowery, C. R. (1986). Gender differences in moral reasoning: A comparison of the use of justice and care orientations. *Journal of Personality and Social Psychology, 50*, 777–783.

Forst, B. E. (1974). Decision analysis and medical malpractice. *Operations Research, 22*, 1–12.

Freedman, J., & Sears, R. (1965). Selective exposure. In L. Berkowitz (Ed.), *Advances in experimental social psychology* (Vol. 2, pp. 57–97). New York: Academic Press.

Frey, D. (1986). Recent research on selective exposure to information. In L. Berkowitz (Ed.), *Advances in experimental social psychology* (Vol. 19, pp. 41–80). New York: Academic Press.

Frisch, D., & Baron, J. (in press). Ambiguity and rationality. *Journal of Behavioral Decision Making*.

Galanter, E. (1962). Contemporary psychophysics. In R. Brown, E. Galanter, R. H. Hess, & G. Mandler (Eds.), *New directions in psychology* (pp. 87–156). New York: Holt, Rinehart & Winston.

Galotti, K. M., Baron, J., & Sabini, J. (1986). Individual differences in syllogistic reasoning: Deduction rules or mental models. *Journal of Experimental Psychology: General, 115*, 16–25.

Gardiner, P. C., & Edwards, W. (1975). Public values: Multiattribute utility measurement for social decision-making. In M. F. Kaplan & S. Schwartz (Eds.), *Human judgment and decision processes* (pp. 1–37). New York: Academic Press.

Gardner, H. (1983). *Frames of mind: The theory of multiple intelligences*. New York: Basic Books.

Gelman, R., & Baillargeon, R. (1983). A review of some Piagetian concepts. In P. Mussen (Ed.), *Carmichael's manual of child psychology: Vol. 3*. J. H. Flavell & E. Markman (Eds.), *Cognitive development*. New York: Wiley.

Getzels, J., & Csikszentmihalyi, M. (1976). *The creative vision: A longitudinal study of problem finding in art*. New York: Wiley.

Gewirth, A. (1978). *Reason and morality*. Chicago: University of Chicago Press.

Gick, M. L., & Holyoak, K. J. (1980). Analogical problem solving. *Cognitive Psychology, 12*, 306–355.

Gick, M. L., & Holyoak, K. J. (1983). Schema induction and analogical transfer. *Cognitive Psychology, 15*, 1–38.

Gilligan, C. (1982). *In a different voice: Psychological theory and women's development*. Cambridge, MA: Harvard University Press.

Glaser, R. (1984). Education and thinking: The role of knowledge. *American Psychologist, 39*, 93–104.

Goldberg, L. R. (1970). Man versus model of man: A rationale, plus some evidence, for a method of improving on clinical inference. *Psychological Bulletin, 73*, 422–432.

Gordon, W. J. J. (1961). *Synectics: The development of creative capacity*. New York: Harper & Row.

Gould, S. J. (1981). *The mismeasure of man*. New York: Norton.

Grether, D. M., & Plott, C. R. (1979). Economic theory of choice and the preference reversal phenomenon. *American Economic Review, 69*, 623–638.

Griggs, R. A., & Cox, J. R. (1982). The elusive thematic-materials effect in Wason's selection task. *British Journal of Psychology, 73*, 407–420.

Guilford, J. P. (1967). *The nature of human intelligence*. New York: McGraw-Hill.

Gupta, B. S. (1977). Dextroamphetamine and measures of intelligence. *Intelligence, 1*, 274–280.

Gustafson, D. H., Tianen, B., & Greist, J. H. (1981). A computer-based system for identifying suicide attemptors. *Computers in Biomedical Research, 14*, 144–157. (Reprinted in Arkes & Hammond, 1986, pp. 432–445.)

Haan, N., Smith, M., & Block, J. (1968). Moral reasoning of young adults: Political-social behavior, family background, and personality correlates. *Journal of Personality and Social Psychology, 10*, 183–201.

Hacking, I. (1965). *Logic of statistical inference*. Cambridge University Press.

Hacking, I. (1975). *The emergence of probability*. Cambridge University Press.

Hadamard, J. (1945). *The psychology of invention in the mathematical field*. Princeton: Princeton University Press.

Hammond, K. R. (1955). Probabilistic functioning and the clinical method. *Psychological Review, 62*, 255–262.

Hardin, G. R. (1968). The tragedy of the commons. *Science, 162*, 1243–1248.

Hare, R. M. (1952). *The language of morals*. Oxford: Oxford University Press (Clarendon Press).

Hare, R. M. (1963). *Freedom and reason*. Oxford: Oxford University Press (Clarendon Press).

Hare, R. M. (1975). Abortion and the golden rule. *Philosophy and public affairs, 4*, 201–222.

Hare, R. M. (1978). Value education in a pluralist society. In M. Lipman & A. M. Sharp (Eds.), *Growing up with philosophy* (pp. 376–391). Philadelphia: Temple University Press.

Hare, R. M. (1981). *Moral thinking: Its levels, method and point*. Oxford: Oxford University Press (Clarendon Press).

Harris, R. J. (1969). Dissonance or sour grapes? Post-"decision" changes in ratings and choice frequencies. *Journal of Personality and Social Psychology, 11*, 334–344.

Harris, R. J., & Joyce, M. A. (1980). What's fair? It depends on how you phrase the question. *Journal of Personality and Social Psychology, 38*, 165–179.

Hayes, J. R. (1985). Three problems in teaching general skills. In S. F. Chipman, J. W. Segal, & R. Glaser (Eds.), *Thinking and learning skills: Vol. 2. Research and open questions* (pp. 391–405). Hillsdale, NJ: Erlbaum.

Heckerman, D. E. (1986). Probabilistic interpretations for MYCIN's certainty factors. In J. F. Lemmer and L. N. Kanal (Eds.), *Uncertainty in Artificial Intelligence* (pp. 167–196). Amsterdam: North Holland.

Heckerman, D. E. (1988). An axiomatic framework for belief updates. In J. F. Lemmer and L. N. Kanal (Eds.), *Uncertainty in Artificial Intelligence, Vol. 2* (pp. 11–22). Amsterdam: North Holland.

Hempel, C. G. (1966). *Philosophy of natural science*. Englewood Cliffs, NJ: Prentice-Hall.

Henle, M. (1962). On the relation between logic and thinking. *Psychological Review, 69*, 366–378.

Herrnstein, R. J., Nickerson, R. S., de Sánchez, M., & Swets, J. A. (1986). Teaching thinking skills. *American Psychologist, 41*, 1279–1289.

Hill, P. H., Bedau, H. A., Chechile, R. A., Crochetiere, W. J., Kellerman, B. L., Ounjian,

494   *References*

D., Pauker, S. G., Pauker, S. P., & Rubin, J. Z. (1978). *Making decisions: An interdisciplinary introduction*. Reading, MA: Addison-Wesley.

Hobhouse, L. T. (1901). *Mind in evolution*. New York: Macmillan.

Hoch, S. J. (1985). Counterfactual reasoning and accuracy in predicting personal events. *Journal of Experimental Psychology: Learning, Memory, and Cognition, 11*, 719–731.

Hogarth, R. M., & Kunreuther, H. C. (in press). Risk, ambiguity, and insurance. *Journal of Risk and Uncertainty*.

Hornstein, H. A. (1976). *Cruelty and kindness*. Englewood Cliffs, NJ: Prentice-Hall.

Horton, R. (1967). African traditional thought and Western science (pts. 1–2). *Africa, 37*, 50–71, 155–187.

Horwich, P. (1982). *Probability and evidence*. Cambridge University Press.

Hovland, C. I. (Ed.) (1957). *The order of presentation in persuasion*. New Haven: Yale University Press.

Hovland, C. I., & Mandell, W. (1957). Is there a "Law of primacy" in persuasion? In Hovland, C. I. (Ed.), *The order of presentation in persuasion* (pp. 13–22). New Haven: Yale University Press.

Humphrey, G. (1951). *Thinking: An introduction to its experimental psychology*. London: Methuen.

Hunt, E. B. (1978). Mechanics of verbal ability. *Psychological Review, 85*, 109–130.

Ingram, D. (1971). Transitivity in child language. *Language, 47*, 888–910.

Irwin, F. W. (1971). *Intentional behavior and motivation: A cognitive theory*. Philadelphia: Lippincott.

Janis, I. L. (1982). *Groupthink: Psychological studies of policy decisions and fiascoes* (Revised edition of *Victims of groupthink: A psychological study of foreign-policy decisions and fiascoes*, 1972). Boston: Houghton-Mifflin.

Janis, I. L., & Mann, L. (1977). *Decision making: A psychological analysis of conflict, choice, and commitment*. New York: Free Press.

Jencks, C., Smith, J., Ackland, H., Bane, M. J., Cohen, D., Gintis, H., Heyns, P., & Michelson, S. (1972). *Inequality: A reassessment of the effect of family and schooling in America*. New York: Basic Books.

Jenkins, H. H., & Ward, W. C. (1965). Judgment of contingency between responses and outcomes. *Psychological Monographs, 79* (1, Whole No. 79).

Jennings, D. L., Amabile, T. M., & Ross, L. (1982). Informal covariation assessment: Data-based versus theory-based judgments. In D. Kahneman, P. Slovic, & A. Tversky (Eds.), *Judgment under uncertainty: Heuristics and biases* (pp. 211–230). Cambridge University Press.

Jensen, A. R. (1969). How much can we boost IQ and scholastic achievement? *Harvard Educational Review, 39*, 1–123.

Jensen, A. R. (1982). The chronometry of intelligence. In R. J. Sternberg (Ed.), *Advances in the psychology of human intelligence* (Vol. 1). Hillsdale, NJ: Erlbaum.

Jervis, R. (1976). *Perception and misperception in international politics*. Princeton: Princeton University Press.

Johnson, D. M., Parrott, G. L., & Stratton, R. P. (1968). Production and judgment of solutions to five problems. *Journal of Educational Psychology Monograph Supplement, 59*, 1–21.

Johnson, E. J., & Tversky, A. (1983). Affect, generalization, and the perception of risk. *Journal of Personality and Social Psychology, 45*, 20–31.

Johnson, R. H., & Blair, J. A. (1983). *Logical self-defense* (2nd ed.). Toronto: McGraw-Hill Ryerson.

Johnson-Laird, P. N. (1983). *Mental models: Towards a cognitive science of language, inference, and consciousness*. Cambridge, MA: Harvard University Press.

Johnson-Laird, P. N. (1985). Logical thinking: Does it occur in daily life? Can it be taught? In

S. F. Chipman, J. W. Segal, & R. Glaser (Eds.), *Thinking and learning skills. Vol. 2: Research and open questions* (pp. 293–318). Hillsdale, NJ: Erlbaum.

Johnson-Laird, P. N., & Bara, B. G. (1984). Syllogistic inference. *Cognition, 16*, 1–61.

Johnson-Laird, P. N., Legrenzi, P., & Legrenzi, M. S. (1972). Reasoning and a sense of reality. *British Journal of Psychology, 63*, 395–400.

Johnson-Laird, P. N., & Steedman, M. (1978). The psychology of syllogisms. *Cognitive Psychology, 10*, 64–99.

Johnson-Laird, P. N., & Wason, P. C. (1970). Insight into a logical relation. *Quarterly Journal of Experimental Psychology, 22*, 49–61.

Kagan, J., Rosman, B. L., Day, D., Albert, J., & Phillips, W. (1964). Information processing in the child: Significance of analytic and reflective attitudes. *Psychological Monographs, 78* (1, Whole No. 578).

Kahane, H. (1980). *Logic and contemporary rhetoric: The use of reason in everyday life* (3rd ed.). Belmont, CA: Wadsworth.

Kahneman, D., Knetsch, J. L., & Thaler, R. H. (1986). Fairness and the assumptions of economics. *Journal of Business, 59*, S285-S300.

Kahneman, D., & Tversky, A. (1972). Subjective probability: A judgment of representativeness. *Cognitive Psychology, 3*, 430–454.

Kahneman, D., & Tversky, A. (1973). On the psychology of prediction. *Psychological Review, 80*, 237–251.

Kahneman, D., & Tversky, A. (1979). Prospect theory: An analysis of decisions under risk. *Econometrica, 47*, 263–291.

Kahneman, D., & Tversky, A. (1984). Choices, values, and frames. *American Psychologist, 39*, 341–350.

Katona, G. (1940). *Organizing and memorizing: Studies in the psychology of learning and teaching*. New York: Columbia University Press.

Keeney, R. L., & Raiffa, H. (1976). *Decisions with multiple objectives*. New York: Wiley.

Keinan, G. (1987). Decision making under stress: Scanning of alternatives under controllable and uncontrollable threats. *Journal of Personality and Social Psychology, 52*, 639–644.

Keller, L. R. (1985). The effects of problem representation on the sure-thing and substitution principles. *Management Science, 31*, 738–751.

Kelly, C. W., III, & Barclay, S. (1973). A general Bayesian model for hierarchical inference. *Organizational Behavior and Human Performance, 10*, 388–403.

Kempton, W. (1986). Two theories of home heat control. *Cognition, 10*, 75–90.

Keren, G., & Wagenaar, W. A. (1985). On the psychology of playing blackjack: Normative and descriptive considerations with implications for decision theory. *Journal of Experimental Psychology: General, 114*, 133–158.

King, P. M., Kitchener, K. S., Davison, M. L., Parker, C. A., & Wood, P. K. (1983). The justification of beliefs in young adults: A longitudinal study. *Human Development, 26*, 106–116.

Kitchener, K. S., & King, P. M. (1981). Reflective judgment: Concepts of justification and their relationship to age and education. *Journal of Applied Developmental Psychology, 2*, 89–116.

Klayman, J. (1984). Learning from feedback in probabilistic environments. *Acta Psychologica, 56*, 81–92.

Knetsch, J. L., & Sinden, J. A. (1984). Willingness to pay and compensation: Experimental evidence of an unexpected disparity in measures of value. *Quarterly Journal of Economics, 99*, 508–522.

Knight, F. H. (1921). *Risk, uncertainty, and profit*. Hart, Schaffner, & Marx.

Kohlberg, L. (1963). The development of children's orientations toward a moral order. I. Sequence in the development of human thought. *Vita Humana, 6*, 11–33.

Kohlberg, L. (1970). Stages of moral development as a basis for moral education. In C. Beck & E. Sullivan (Eds.), *Moral education* (pp. 23–92). University of Toronto Press.

Köhler, W. (1917). *The mentality of apes*. London: Kegan Paul.

Kolb, D. A. (1965). Achievement motivation training for underachieving high-school boys. *Journal of Personality and Social Psychology, 2*, 783–792.

Kolm, S.-C. (1986). The Buddhist theory of 'no-self.' In J. Elster (Ed.), *The multiple self*. Cambridge University Press.

Koriat, A., Lichtenstein, S., & Fischhoff, B. (1980). Reasons for confidence. *Journal of Experimental Psychology: Human Learning and Memory, 6*, 107–118.

Kourilsky, M., & Murray, T. (1981). The use of economic reasoning to increase satisfaction with family decision making. *Journal of Consumer Research, 8*, 183–188.

Krantz, D. H., Luce, R. D., Suppes, P., & Tversky, A. (1971). *Foundations of measurement* (Vol. 1). New York: Academic Press.

Krebs, D. (1975). Empathy and altruism. *Journal of Personality and Social Psychology, 32*, 1134–1146.

Kris, E. (1952). *Psychoanalytic explorations in art*. New York: International Universities Press.

Kruglanski, A. W., & Ajzen, I. (1983). Bias and error in human judgment. *European Journal of Social Psychology, 13*, 1–44.

Kruglanski, A. W., & Freund, T. (1983). The freezing and unfreezing of lay inferences: Effects on impressional primacy, ethnic stereotyping, and numerical anchoring. *Journal of Experimental Social Psychology, 19*, 448–468.

Krzysztofowicz, R. (1983). Strength of preference and risk attitude in utility measurement. *Organizational Behavior and Human Performance, 31*, 88–113.

Kuhn, D., Amsel, E., & O'Loughlin, M. (1988). *The development of scientific thinking skills*. New York: Academic Press.

Kuhn, D., Phelps, E., & Walters, J. (1985). Correlational reasoning in an everyday context. *Journal of Applied Developmental Psychology, 6*, 85–97.

Kulik, J. A. (1983). Confirmatory attribution and the perpetuation of social beliefs. *Journal of Personality and Social Psychology, 44*, 1171–1181.

Laboratory of Comparative Human Cognition. (1982). Culture and intelligence. In R. J. Sternberg (Ed.), *Handbook of human intelligence* (pp. 642–719). Cambridge University Press.

Lakatos, I. (1978). Falsification and the methodology of scientific research programmes. In I. Lakatos, *The methodology of scientific research programmes* (J. Worrall & G. Currie, Eds.) (pp. 8–101). Cambridge University Press.

Lancaster, K. (1963). An axiomatic theory of consumer time preference. *International Economic Review, 4*, 221–231.

Langer, E. J., & Abelson, R. P. (1974). A patient by any other name . . .: Clinician group differences in labeling bias. *Journal of Consulting and Clinical Psychology. 42*, 4–9.

Larkin, J. H. (1981). Enriching formal knowledge: A model for learning to solve textbook physics problems. In J. R. Anderson (Ed.), *Cognitive skills and their acquisition* (pp. 311–334). Hillsdale, NJ: Erlbaum.

Larkin, J. H., McDermott, J., Simon, D. P., & Simon, H. A. (1980). Expert and novice performance in solving physics problems. *Science, 208*, 1335–1342.

Lazar, I., Darlington, R., Murray, H., Royce, J., & Snipper, A. (1982). Lasting effects of early education: A report from the consortium for longitudinal studies. *Monographs of the Society for Research in Child Development, 47* (2–3, Serial No. 195).

Lenat, D. B. (1983). Toward a theory of heuristics. In R. Groner, M. Groner, & W. F. Bischof (Eds.), *Methods of heuristics* (pp. 351–404). Hillsdale, NJ: Erlbaum.

Lepper, M. R., & Greene, D. (Eds.), (1978). *The hidden costs of reward*. Hillsdale, NJ: Erlbaum.

Levin, I. P., Johnson, R. D., & Farone, S. V. (1984). Information integration in price-quality tradeoffs: The effect of missing information. *Memory and Cognition, 12*, 96–102.

Levine, M. (1971). Hypothesis theory and nonlearning despite ideal S-R reinforcement contingencies. *Psychological Review 78*, 130–140.

Lichtenstein, S., Earle, T. C., & Slovic, P. (1975). Cue utilization in a numerical prediction task. *Journal of Experimental Psychology: Human Perception and Performance, 104*, 77–85.

Lichtenstein, S., & Fischhoff, B. (1977). Do those who know more also know more about how much they know? *Organizational Behavior and Human Performance, 20*, 159–183.

Lichtenstein, S., Fischhoff, B., & Phillips, B. (1982). Calibration of probabilities: The state of the art to 1980. In D. Kahneman, P. Slovic, & A. Tversky (Eds.), *Judgment under uncertainty: Heuristics and biases* (pp. 306–334). Cambridge University Press.

Lichtenstein, S., & Slovic, P. (1971). Reversal of preferences between bids and choices in gambling decisions. *Journal of Experimental Psychology, 89*, 46–55.

Lichtenstein, S., & Slovic, P. (1973). Response-induced reversals of preference in gambling: An extended replication in Las Vegas. *Journal of Experimental Psychology, 101*, 16–20.

Lichtenstein, S., Slovic, P., Fischhoff, B., Layman, M., & Combs, B. (1978). Judged frequency of lethal events. *Journal of Experimental Psychology: Human Learning and Memory, 4*, 551–578.

Lindley, D. V. (1982). Scoring rules and the inevitability of probability (with discussion). *International Statistical Review, 50*, 1–26.

Lipman, M. (1974). *Harry Stottlemeier's discovery*. Upper Montclair, NJ: Institute for the Advancement of Philosophy for Children.

Lipman, M. (1985). Thinking skills fostered by Philosophy for Children. In J. W. Segal, S. F. Chipman, & R. Glaser (Eds.), *Thinking and learning skills: Vol. 1. Relating instruction to research* (pp. 83–108). Hillsdale, NJ: Erlbaum.

Lipman, M., Sharp, A. M., & Oscanyan, F. S. (1980). *Philosophy in the classroom* (2nd ed.). Philadelphia: Temple University Press.

Lindley, D. V., Tversky, A., & Brown, R. V. (1979). On the reconciliation of probability assessments. *Journal of the Royal Statistical Association A. 142*, 146–180 (with commentary).

Lloyd, J., & Barenblaatt, L. (1984). Intrinsic intellectuality: Its relations to social class, intelligence, and achievement. *Journal of Personality and Social Psychology, 46*, 464–654.

Loewenstein, G. (in press). Anticipation and the value of delayed consumption. *Economic Journal*.

Loewenstein, G., & Linville, P. (1986). *Expectation formation and the timing of outcomes: A cognitive strategy for balancing the conflicting incentives for savoring success and avoiding disappointment*. Unpublished manuscript, Center for Decision Research, Graduate School of Business, University of Chicago.

Loomes, G. (1987). Testing for regret and disappointment in choice under uncertainty. *Economic Journal, 97*, 118–129.

Loomes, G. (in press). Further evidence of the impact of regret and disappointment in choice under uncertainty. *Economica*.

Loomes, G., & Sugden, R. (1982). Regret theory: An alternative theory of rational choice under uncertainty. *Economic Journal, 92*, 805–824.

Lopes, L. L. (1987a). Procedural debiasing. *Acta Psychologica, 64*, 167–185.

Lopes, L. L. (1987b). Between hope and fear: The psychology of risk. In L. Berkowitz (Ed.), *Advances in experimental social psychology* (Vol. 20, pp. 255–295). New York: Academic Press.

Lord, C. G., Lepper, M. R., & Preston, E. (1984). Considering the opposite: A corrective strategy for social judgment. *Journal of Personality and Social Psychology, 47*, 1231–1243.

Lord, C. G., Ross, L., & Lepper, M. R. (1979). Biased assimilation and attitude polarization: The effects of prior theories on subsequently considered evidence. *Journal of Personality and Social Psychology, 37*, 2098–2109.

Lowin, A. (1967). Approach and avoidance: Alternative modes of selective exposure to information. *Journal of Personality and Social Psychology, 6*, 1–9.

Luchins, A. (1942). Mechanization in problem solving: The effect of Einstellung. *Psychological Monographs, 54* (6, Whole No. 248).

Luchins, A. S. (1957). Primacy-recency in impression formation. In Hovland, C. I. (Ed.), *The order of presentation in persuasion* (pp. 33-61). New Haven: Yale University Press.

Luchins, A. S., & Luchins, E. H. (1959). *Rigidity of behavior: A variational approach to the effects of Einstellung*. Eugene: University of Oregon.

Luria, A. R. (1968). *The mind of a mnemonist* (L. Solotaroff, Trans.). New York: Basic Books. (Original work published 1965)

Lytle, S. L. (1982). *Exploring comprehension style: A study of twelfth-grade readers' transactions with text*. Unpublished doctoral dissertation, School of Education, University of Pennsylvania, Philadelphia.

Machado, L. A. (1980). *The right to be intelligent* (M. C. Wheeler, Trans.). Oxford: Pergamon.

Machina, M. (1987). Decision-making in the presence of risk. *Science, 236*, 537–543.

Marcia, J. E. (1966). Development and validation of ego identity status. *Journal of Personality and Social Psychology, 3*, 551–558.

McClelland, D. C. (1960). *The achieving society*. Princeton, NJ: Van Nostrand.

McCloskey, M. (1983). Naive theories of motion. In D. Gentner & A. L. Stevens (Eds.), *Mental models* (pp. 299–324). Hillsdale, NJ: Erlbaum.

McCord, M., & de Neufville, R. (1985). *Eliminating the certainty effect problem in utility assessment: Theory and experiment*. Unpublished manuscript, Ohio State University, Columbus, OH.

McGuire, W. J. (1960). A syllogistic analysis of cognitive relationships. In M. J. Rosenberg, C. I. Hovland, W. J. McGuire, R. P. Abelson, & J. W. Brehm (Eds.), *Attitude organization and change*. New Haven: Yale University Press.

McLuhan, M. (1964). *Understanding media*. New York: McGraw-Hill.

Medin, D., Altom, M. W., Edelson, S. M., & Freko, D. (1982). Correlated symptoms and simulated medical classification. *Journal of Experimental Psychology: Learning, Memory, and Cognition, 8*, 37–50.

Medin, D., Dewey, G., & Murphy, T. (1983). Relationships between item and category learning: Evidence that abstraction is not automatic. *Journal of Experimental Psychology: Learning, Memory, and Cognition, 9*, 607–625.

Mednick, S. A. (1962). The associative basis of the creative process. *Psychological Review, 69*, 220–232.

Meehl, P. E. (1954). *Clinical versus statistical prediction: A theoretical analysis and a look at the evidence*. Minneapolis: University of Minnesota Press.

Messer, S. B. (1976). Reflection-impulsivity: A review. *Psychological Bulletin, 83*, 1026–1052.

Messick, D. M. (1985). Social interdependence and decision making. In G. Wright (Ed.), *Behavioral decision making* (pp. 87–109). New York: Plenum.

Messick, D. M., Bloom, S., Boldizar, J. P., & Samuelson, C. D. (1985). Why we are fairer than others. *Journal of Experimental Social Psychology, 21*, 480–500.

Mill, J. S. (1863). *Utilitarianism*. London: Collins.

Miller, G. A. (1956). The magical number seven, plus or minus two: Some limits on our capacity to process information. *Psychological Review, 63*, 81–97.

Mischel, H. H., & Mischel, W. (1983). The development of children's knowledge of self-control strategies. *Child Development, 54*, 603–619.

Mischel, W. (1974). Processes in delay of gratification. In L. Berkowitz (Ed.), *Advances in experimental social psychology* (Vol. 7, pp. 249–292). New York: Academic Press.

Mischel, W. (1984). Convergences and challenges in the search for consistency. *American Psychologist, 39*, 351–364.

Modigliani, F. (1986). Life cycle, individual thrift, and the wealth of nations. *Science, 234*, 704–712.

Montgomery, H. (1984). Decision rules and the search for dominance structure: Towards a process model of decision making. In P. C. Humphreys, O. Svenson, & A. Vari (Eds.), *Analysing and aiding decision processes*. Amsterdam: North Holland.

Morgan, C. Lloyd. (1894). *An introduction to comparative psychology*. London: Scott.

Morgan, J. J. B., & Morton, J. T. (1944). The distortion of syllogistic reasoning produced by personal convictions. *Journal of Social Psychology, 20*, 39–59.

Moscovitch, M., Winocur, G., & McLachlan, D. (1986). Memory as assessed by recognition and reading time in normal and memory-impaired people with Alzheimer's disease and other neurological disorders. *Journal of Experimental Psychology: General, 115*, 331–347.

Murphy, A. H., & Winkler, R. L. (1977). Can weather forecasters formulate reliable probability forecasts of precipitation and temperature? *National Weather Digest, 2*, 2–9.

Mynatt, C. R., Doherty, M. E., & Tweney, R. D. (1977). Confirmation bias in a simulated research environment: An experimental study of scientific inference. *Quarterly Journal of Experimental Psychology, 29*, 85–95.

Mynatt, C. R., Doherty, M. E., & Tweney, R. D. (1978). Consequences of confirmation and disconfirmation in a simulated research environment. *Quarterly Journal of Experimental Psychology, 30*, 395–406.

Nagel, T. (1970). *The possibility of altruism*. Princeton: Princeton University Press.

National Commission on Excellence in Education. (1983). *A nation at risk: The imperative for educational reform*. Washington, DC: Government Printing Office.

Neill, A. S. (1964). *Summerhill: A radical approach to child rearing*. New York: Hart.

Neisser, U. (1982). *Memory observed: Remembering in natural contexts*. San Francisco: Freeman.

Nel, E., Helmreich, R., & Aronson, E. (1969). Opinion change in the advocate as a function of the persuasability of his audience: A clarification of the meaning of dissonance. *Journal of Personality and Social Psychology, 12*, 117–124.

Newcomb, T. M. (1929). The consistency of certain extrovert-introvert behavior patterns in 51 problem boys. *Contributions to Education, 382*. New York: Teachers College, Columbia University.

Newell, A. (1983). The heuristic of George Polya and its relation to artificial intelligence. In R. Groner, M. Groner, & W. F. Bischof (Eds.), *Methods of heuristics* (pp. 195–243). Hillsdale, NJ: Erlbaum.

Newell, A., Shaw, J. C., & Simon, H. A. (1958). Elements of a theory of human problem solving. *Psychological Review, 65*, 151–166.

Newell, A., & Simon, H. A. (1972). *Human problem solving*. Englewood Cliffs, NJ: Prentice-Hall.

Newman, J. R. (Ed.). (1956). *The world of mathematics*. New York: Simon & Schuster.

Nickerson, R. S. (1986). *Reflections on reasoning*. Hillsdale, NJ: Erlbaum.

Nickerson, R. S. (in press). On improving thinking through instruction. *Review of Educational Research*.

Nickerson, R. S., Perkins, D. N., & Smith, E. E. (1985). *The teaching of thinking*. Hillsdale, NJ: Erlbaum.

Nilsson, N. J. (1971). *Problem solving methods in artificial intelligence*. New York: McGraw Hill.

Nisbett, R. E., Fong, G. T., Lehman, D. R., & Cheng, P. W. (1987). Teaching reasoning. *Science, 238*, 625–631.

Nisbett, R. E., Krantz, D. H., Jepson, D., & Kunda, Z. (1983). The use of statistical heuristics in everyday inductive reasoning. *Psychological Review, 90*, 339–363.

Nisbett, R. E., & Ross, L. (1980). *Human inference: Strategies and shortcomings of social judgment*. Englewood Cliffs, NJ: Prentice-Hall.

Nisbett, R. E., & Wilson, T. D. (1977). Telling more than we can know: Verbal reports on mental processes. *Psychological Review, 84*, 231–259.

Nozick, R. (1974). *Anarchy, state, and utopia*. New York: Basic Books.

Olton, R. M. (1979). Experimental studies of incubation: Searching for the elusive. *Journal of Creative Behavior, 13*, 9–22.

Orbell, J. M., van de Kragt, A. J. C., & Dawes, R. M. (in press). Explaining discussion-induced cooperation in social dilemmas. *Journal of Personality and Social Psychology*.

Osborn, A. F. (1953). *Applied imagination*. New York: Scribner's.

Osherson, D. N. (1974). *Logical abilities in children: Vol 2. Logical inference: Underlying operations*. Hillsdale, NJ: Erlbaum.

Osherson, D. N., & Markman, E. (1974–75). Language and the ability to evaluate contradictions and tautologies. *Cognition, 3*, 213–226.

Pareto, V. (1971). *Manual of political economy* (A. S. Schwier, Trans.). New York: Augustus M. Kelley. (Original work published 1909)

Parfit, D. (1984). *Reasons and persons*. Oxford: Oxford University Press (Clarendon Press).

Pascal, B. (1941). *Pensées* (W. F. Trotter, Trans.). New York: Modern Library. (Original work published 1670).

Patrick, C. (1935). Creative thought in poets. *Archives of Psychology* (no. 178), R. S. Woodworth (Ed.). New York: Columbia University.

Patrick, C. (1937). Creative thought in artists. *Journal of Psychology, 4*, 35–73.

Paul, R. W. (1984). Critical thinking: Fundamental for education for a free society. *Educational Leadership, 42*, (September) 4–14.

Payne, J. W. (1976). Task complexity and contingent processing in decision making: An information search and protocol analysis. *Organizational Behavior and Human Performance, 16*, 366–387.

Payne, J. W., Bettman, J. R., & Johnson, E. J. (in press). Adaptive strategy selection in decision making. *Journal of Experimental Psychology: Learning, Memory and Cognition*.

Payne, J. W., Braunstein, M. L., & Carroll, J. S. (1978). Exploring pre-decisional behavior: An alternative approach to decision research. *Organizational Behavior and Human Performance, 22*, 17–44.

Pearl, J. (1982). Reverend Bayes on inference engines: A distributed hierarchical approach. In *American Association for Artificial Intelligence, Proceedings of the Second National Conference on Artificial Intelligence* 133–136. Los Angeles: Kaufman.

Perkins, D. N. (1981). *The mind's best work*. Cambridge, MA: Harvard University Press.

Perkins, D. N. (1985). *The nature of shortcomings in everyday reasoning*. Unpublished manuscript. Harvard University, Graduate School of Education, Cambridge, MA.

Perkins, D. N. (1986). *Knowledge as design: Critical and creative thinking for teachers and learners*. Hillsdale, NJ: Erlbaum.

Perkins, D. N., Allen, R., & Hafner, J. (1983). Difficulties in everyday reasoning. In W. Maxwell (Ed.), *Thinking: The expanding frontier* (pp. 177–189). Philadelphia: Franklin Institute.

Perkins, D. N., Bushey, B., & Faraday, M. (1986). *Learning to reason*. Unpublished manuscript, Harvard Graduate School of Education, Cambridge, MA.

Perry, W. G., Jr. (1971). *Forms of intellectual and ethical development in the college years: A scheme*. New York: Holt, Rinehart & Winston.

Peterson, C. R. (1980). Recognition of noncontingency. *Journal of Personality and Social Psychology, 38*, 727–734.

Peterson, C. R., & DuCharme, W. M. (1967). A primacy effect in subjective probability revision. *Journal of Experimental Psychology, 73*, 61–65.

Piaget, J. (1929). *The child's conception of the world*. New York: Harcourt, Brace, & World.

Piaget, J. (1932). *The moral judgment of the child*. Glencoe, IL: The Free Press.

Pintner, R. (1931). *Intelligence testing: Methods and results* (2nd ed.). New York: Holt.

Pitz, G. F. (1969). An inertia effect (resistance to change) in the revision of opinion. *Canadian Journal of Psychology, 23*, 24–33.

Pitz, G. F., Downing, L., & Reinhold, H. (1967). Sequential effects in the revision of subjective probabilities. *Canadian Journal of Psychology, 21*, 381–393.

Platt, J. R. (1964). Strong inference. *Science, 146*, 347–353.

Poincaré, H. (1913). *The foundations of science* (G. B. Halstead, Trans.). New York: Science Press.

Polya, G. (1945). *How to solve it: A new aspect of mathematical method*. Princeton: Princeton University Press.

Popper, K. R. (1962). *Conjectures and refutations: The growth of scientific knowledge*. New York: Basic Books.

Poulton, E. C. (1979). Models for biases in judging sensory magnitude. *Psychological Bulletin, 86*, 777–803.

Pruitt, D. G. (1967). Reward structure and cooperation: The decomposed prisoner's dilemma game. *Journal of Personality and Social Psychology, 7*, 21–27.

Putnam, H. (1975). The meaning of "meaning." In *Philosophical papers*, Vol. 2, *Mind, language, and reality* (pp. 215–271). Cambridge University Press.

Putnam, H. (1981). *Reason, truth and history*. Cambridge University Press.

Quattrone, G. A., & Tversky, A. (1984). Causal versus diagnostic contingencies: On self-deception and the voter's illusion. *Journal of Personality and Social Psychology, 46*, 237–248.

Quiggin, J. (1982). A theory of anticipated utility. *Journal of Economic Behavior and Organization, 3*, 323–343.

Quinn, R. J., & Bell, D. E. (1983). *A preliminary test of a reference-point model of risky choice*. Unpublished manuscript, Harvard University, School of Public Health, Cambridge, MA.

Rachlin, H., Logue, A. W., Gibbon, J., & Frankel, M. (1986). Cognition and behavior in studies of choice. *Psychological Review, 93*, 33–45.

Raiffa, H. (1968). *Decision analysis*. Reading, MA: Addison-Wesley.

Ramsey, F. P. (1931). Truth and probability. In R. B. Braithwaite (Ed.), *The foundations of mathematics and other logical essays by F. P. Ramsey*. New York: Harcourt, Brace.

Rawls, J. (1971). *A theory of justice*. Cambridge, MA: Harvard University Press.

Rawls, J. (1980). Kantian constructivism in moral theory. *Journal of Philosophy, 77*, 515–572.

Read, J. D., & Bruce, D. (1982). Longitudinal tracking of difficult memory retrievals. *Cognitive Psychology, 14*, 280–300.

Read, S. J. (1983). Once is enough: Causal reasoning from a single instance. *Journal of Personality and Social Psychology, 45*, 323–334.

Reber, A. S. (1969). Transfer of syntactic structure in synthetic languages. *Journal of Experimental Psychology, 81*, 115–119.

Reber, A. S. (1976). Implicit learning of synthetic languages: The role of instructional set. *Journal of Experimental Psychology: Human Learning and Memory, 2*, 88–94.

Reed, S. K. (1987). A structure-mapping model for word problems. *Journal of Experimental Psychology: Learning, Memory, and Cognition, 13*, 124–139.

Regan, D. (1980). *Utilitarianism and co-operation*. Oxford: Oxford University Press (Clarendon Press).

Reitman, W., Malin, J. T., Bjork, R. A., & Higman, B. (1973). Strategy control and directed forgetting. *Journal of Verbal Learning and Verbal Behavior, 12*, 140–149.

Rest, J. R. (1975). Longitudinal study of the Defining Issues Test of moral judgment: A strategy for analyzing developmental change. *Developmental Psychology, 11*, 738–748.

Richards, D. A. J. (1971). *A theory of reasons for action*. Oxford: Oxford University Press (Clarendon Press).

Riker, W. H., & Ordeshook, P. C. (1968). A theory of the calculus of voting. *American Political Science Review, 62*, 25–42.

Rips, L. (1983). Cognitive processes in propositional reasoning. *Psychological Review, 90*, 38–71.

Robinson, L. B., & Hastie, R. (1985). Revision of beliefs when a hypothesis is eliminated from consideration. *Journal of Experimental Psychology: Human Perception and Performance, 11*, 443–456.

Rokeach, M. (Ed.). (1960). *The open and closed mind*. New York: Basic Books.

Rosch, E. (1973). On the internal structure of perceptual and semantic categories. In T. E. Moore (Ed.), *Cognitive development and the acquisition of language* (pp. 111–144). New York: Academic Press.

Ross, M., & Sicoly, F. (1979). Egocentric bias in availability and attribution. *Journal of Personality and Social Psychology, 37*, 322–336.

Rumelhart, D. E., & Norman, D. A. (1981). Accretion, tuning, and restructuring: Three modes of learning. In J. W. Cotton & R. Klatzky (Eds.), *Semantic factors in cognition* (pp. 37–60). Hillsdale, NJ: Erlbaum.

Russell, B. (1945). *A history of western philosophy and its connection with political and social circumstances from the earliest times to the present day*. New York: Simon & Schuster.

Sabini, J., & Silver, M. (1981). *Moralities of everyday life*. Oxford: Oxford University Press.

Samuelson, C. D., Messick, D. M., Rutte, C. G., & Wilke, H. (1984). Individual and structural solutions to resource dilemmas in two cultures. *Journal of Personality and Social Psychology, 47*, 94–104.

Samuelson, P. (1950). Probability and the attempts to measure utility. *Economic Review, 1*, 167–173.

Savage, L. J. (1954). *The foundations of statistics*. New York: Wiley.

Scarr, S., & Carter-Saltzman, L. (1982). Genetics and intelligence. In R. J. Sternberg (Ed.), *Handbook of human intelligence* (pp. 792–896). Cambridge University Press.

Scheerer, M. (1963). Problem solving. *Scientific American, 208*, 118–128.

Scheffler, I. (1965). *Conditions of knowledge: An introduction to epistemology and education*. Chicago: Scott, Foresman.

Schelling, T. C. (1978). *Micromotives and macrobehavior*. New York: Norton.

Schleser, R., Meyers, A. W., & Cohen, R. (1981). Generalization of self-instructions: Effects of general versus specific content, active rehearsal, and cognitive level. *Child Development, 52*, 335–340.

Schmitt, N. (1976). Social and situational determinants of interview decisions: Implications for the employment interview. *Personnel Psychology, 29*, 79–101.

Schoemaker, P. J. H. (1979). The role of statistical knowledge in gambling decisions: Moment vs. risk dimension approaches. *Organizational Behavior and Human Performance, 24*, 1–17.

Schoenfeld, A. H. (1985). *Mathematical problem solving*. New York: Academic Press.

Schroeder, H. M., Driver, M. J., & Streufert, S. (1967). *Human information processing*. New York: Holt, Rinehart & Winston.

Schustack, M. W., & Sternberg, R. J. (1981). Evaluation of evidence in causal inference. *Journal of Experimental Psychology: General, 110*, 101–120.

Schwalm, N. D., & Slovic, P. (1982). *Development and test of a motivational approach and materials for increasing use of restraints* (Final technical report PFTR-1100–82–3). Woodland Hills, CA: Perceptronics, Inc.

Schwartz, B. (1982). Reinforcement-induced behavioral stereotypy: How not to teach people to discover rules. *Journal of Experimental Psychology: General, 111*, 23–59.

Schwartz, B. (1986). *The battle for human nature: Science, morality, and modern life*. New York: Norton.

Schwartz, B. (in press). The experimental synthesis of behavior: Reinforcement, behavioral stereotypy, and problem solving. In G. H. Bower (Ed.), *The psychology of learning and motivation: Advances in research and theory* (Vol. 22). New York: Academic Press.

Schwartz, S. M., Baron, J., & Clarke, J. R. (1988). A causal Bayesian model for the diagnosis of appendicitis. In J. F. Lemmer and L. N. Kanal (Eds.), *Uncertainty in artificial intelligence, Vol. 2* (pp. 423–434). Amsterdam: North Holland.

Scribner, S. (1977). Modes of thinking and ways of speaking: Culture and logic reconsidered. In P. N. Johnson-Laird & P. C. Wason (Eds.), *Thinking: Readings in cognitive science* (pp. 483–500). Cambridge University Press.

Segal, U. (1984). *Nonlinear decision weights with the independence axiom.* UCLA Working Paper No. 353, University of California at Los Angeles, Department of Economics.

Selz, O. (1935). Versuche zur Hebung des Intelligenzniveaus: Ein Beitrag zur Theorie der Intelligenz und ihrer erziehlichen Beeinflussung. *Zeitschrift für Psychologie, 134*, 236–301.

Shafer, G. (1976). *A mathematical theory of evidence.* Princeton: Princeton University Press.

Shafer, G. (1981). Constructive probability. *Synthese, 48*, 1–60.

Shafer, G. (1982). Lindley's paradox. *Journal of the American Statistical Association, 77*, 325–351 (with commentary).

Shafer, G. (1986). Savage revisited. *Statistical Science, 1*, 463–501 (with discussion).

Shafer, G., & Tversky, A. (1985). Weighing evidence: The design and comparison of probability thought experiments. *Cognitive Science, 9*, 309–339.

Shaklee, H., & Fischhoff, B. (1982). Strategies of information search in causal analysis. *Memory and Cognition, 10*, 520–530.

Shaklee, H., & Mims, M. (1982). Sources of error in judging event covariations. *Journal of Experimental Psychology: Learning, Memory, and Cognition, 8*, 208–224.

Shaklee, H., & Tucker, D. (1980). A rule analysis of judgments of covariation between events. *Memory and Cognition, 8*, 459–467.

Sharp, D., Cole, M., & Lave, C. (1979). Education and cognitive development: The evidence from experimental research. *Monographs of the Society for Research in Child Development, 44* (1–2, Serial No. 178).

Shweder, R. A. (1977). Likeness and likelihood in everyday thought: Magical thinking in judgments about personality. *Current Anthropology, 18*, 637–648.

Shweder, R. A., Mahapatra, M., & Miller, J. G. (1988). Culture and moral development. In J. Kagan (Ed.), *The emergence of moral concepts in young children* (pp. 1–83). Chicago: University of Chicago Press.

Shweder, R. A., & D'Andrade, R. G. (1979). Accurate reflection or systematic distortion? A reply to Block, Weiss, and Thorne. *Journal of Personality and Social Psychology, 37*, 1075–1084.

Simon, H. A. (1957). *Models of man: Social and rational.* New York: Wiley.

Simon, H. A. (1969). *The sciences of the artificial.* Cambridge, MA: M. I. T. Press.

Simon, H. A. (1978). Information processing theory of human problem solving. In W. K. Estes (Ed.), *Handbook of learning and cognitive processes* (Vol. 6, pp. 271–295). Hillsdale, NJ: Erlbaum.

Simon, H. A., & Newell, A. (1971). Human problem solving: The state of the theory in 1970. *American Psychologist, 26*, 145–159.

Singer, P. (1979). *Practical ethics.* Cambridge University Press.

Skov, R. B., & Sherman, S. J. (1986). Information-gathering processes: Diagnosticity, hypothesis-confirmatory strategies, and perceived hypothesis confirmation. *Journal of Experimental Social Psychology, 22*, 93–121.

Slovic, P. (1975). Choice between equally valued alternatives. *Journal of Experimental Psychology: Human Perception and Performance, 1*, 280–287.

Slovic, P., & Fischhoff, B. (1977). On the psychology of experimental surprises. *Journal of Experimental Psychology: Human Perception and Performance, 3*, 544–551.

Slovic, P., Lichtenstein, S., & Fischhoff, B. (1984). Modeling the societal impact of fatal accidents. *Management Science, 30*, 464–474.

Slovic, P., & Tversky, A. (1974). Who accepts Savage's axioms? *Behavioral Science, 14*, 368–373.

Smedslund, J. (1963). The concept of correlation in adults. *Scandinavian Journal of Psychology, 4*, 165–173.

Smetana, J. G. (1982). *Concepts of self and morality: Women's reasoning about abortion*. New York: Praeger.

Smith, E. E., & Medin, D. L. (1981). *Categories and concepts*. Cambridge, MA: Harvard University Press.

Snow, R. E., & Yalow, E. (1982). Education and intelligence. In R. J. Sternberg (Ed.), *Handbook of human intelligence* (pp. 493–585). Cambridge University Press.

Snyder, M. & Swann, W. B. (1978). Behavioral confirmation in social interaction: From social perception to social reality. *Journal of Experimental Social Psychology, 14*, 148–162.

Solnick, J. V., Kanneberg, C. H., Eckerman, D. A., & Waller, M. B. (1980). An experimental analysis of impulsivity and impulse control in humans. *Learning and Motivation, 11*, 61–77.

Solomon, R. L., & Corbit, J. D. (1974). An opponent-process theory of motivation. *Psychological Review, 81*, 119–145.

Spearman, C. (1904). "General intelligence" objectively determined and measured. *American Journal of Psychology, 15*, 201–293.

Spyropoulis, T., & Ceraso, J. (1977). Categorized and uncategorized attributes as recall cues: The phenomenon of limited access. *Cognitive Psychology, 9*, 384–402.

Standing, L., Bond, B., Smith, P., & Isely, C. (1980). Is the immediate memory span determined by subvocalization rate? *British Journal of Psychology, 71*, 525–539.

Staw, B. M. (1976). Knee-deep in the big muddy: A study of escalating commitment to a chosen course of action. *Organizational Behavior and Human Performance, 16*, 27–44.

Stein, M. (1975). *Stimulating creativity: Individual differences* (Vol. 2). New York: Academic Press.

Steinlauf, B. (1979). Problem-solving skills, locus of control, and the contraceptive effectiveness of young women. *Child Development, 50*, 268–271.

Stern, W. (1912). *Psychologische Methoden der Intelligenz-Prüfung*. Leipzig: Barth.

Sternberg, R. J. (1985). *Beyond IQ: A triarchic theory of human intelligence*. Cambridge University Press.

Stevenson, H. W., Parker, T., Wilkinson, A., Bonnevaux, B., & Gonzalez, M. (1978). Schooling, environment, and cognitive development: A cross cultural study. *Monographs of the Society for Research in Child Development, 43* (3, Serial No. 175).

Stewart, R. H. (1965). Effect of continuous responding on the order effect in personality impression formation. *Journal of Personality and Social Psychology, 1*, 161–165.

Stroop, J. R. (1935). Studies of interference in serial verbal reactions. *Journal of Experimental Psychology, 18*, 643–661.

Strotz, R. H. (1955). Myopia and inconsistency in dynamic utility maximization. *Review of Economic Studies, 23*, 165–180.

Suedfeld, P., & Rank, A. D. (1976). Revolutionary leaders: Long-term success as a function of changes in conceptual complexity. *Journal of Personality and Social Psychology, 34*, 169–178.

Suedfeld, P., & Tetlock, P. E. (1977). Integrative complexity of communications in international crises. *Journal of Conflict Resolution, 21*, 169–184.

Sugden, R. (1986). New developments in the theory of choice under uncertainty. *Bulletin of Economic Research, 38*, 1–24.

Svenson, O. (1979). Process descriptions of decision making. *Organizational Behavior and Human Performance, 23*, 86–112.

Svenson, O. (1981). Are we all less risky and more skillful than our fellow drivers? *Acta Psychologica, 47*, 143–148.

Sweeney, P. D., & Gruber, K. L. (1984). Selective exposure: Voter information preferences and the Watergate affair. *Journal of Personality and Social Psychology, 46*, 1208–1221.

Sweller, J., & Gee, W. (1978). Einstellung, the sequence effect, and hypothesis theory. *Journal of Experimental Psychology: Human Learning and Memory, 4*, 513–526.

Sweller, J., Mawer, R. F., & Ward, M. R. (1983). Development of expertise in mathematical problem solving. *Journal of Experimental Psychology: General, 112*, 639–661.

Terman, L. M. (1916). *The measurement of intelligence*. Boston: Houghton-Mifflin.

Tetlock, P. E. (1979). Identifying victims of groupthink from public statements of decision makers. *Journal of Personality and Social Psychology, 37*, 1314–1324.

Tetlock, P. E. (1983a). Cognitive style and political ideology. *Journal of Personality and Social Psychology, 45*, 118–126.

Tetlock, P. E. (1983b). Accountability and the perseverance of first impressions. *Social Psychology Quarterly, 46*, 285–292.

Tetlock, P. E. (1984). Cognitive style and political belief systems in the British House of Commons. *Journal of Personality and Social Psychology, 46*, 365–375.

Tetlock, P. E. (1985). A value pluralism model of ideological reasoning. *Journal of Personality and Social Psychology, 50*, 819–827.

Tetlock, P. E., & Kim, J. I. (1987). Accountability and judgment processes in a personality prediction task. *Journal of Personality and Social Psychology, 52*, 700–709.

Thaler, R. H. (1980). Toward a positive theory of consumer choice. *Journal of Economic Behavior and Organization, 1*, 39–60.

Thaler, R. H. (1985). Mental accounting and consumer choice. *Marketing Science, 4*, 199–214.

Thaler, R. H., & Shefrin, H. M. (1981). An economic theory of self-control. *Journal of Political Economy, 89*, 392–406.

Thomas, J. C., Jr. (1974). An analysis of behavior in the Hobbits-Orcs problem. *Cognitive Psychology, 6*, 257–269.

Thorndike, E. L. (1898). *Animal intelligence; an experimental study of the associative processes in animals* (Contributions of the Department of Philosophy and Psychology, Columbia University, vol. 4, no. 3). New York: Macmillan.

Thorndike, E. L., & Woodworth, R. R. (1901). The influence of improvement in one mental function upon the efficiency of other functions. *Psychological Review, 8*, 247–261.

Thurstone, L. L. (1938). *Primary mental abilities*. Chicago: University of Chicago Press.

Toulmin, S. E. (1958). *The uses of argument*. Cambridge University Press.

Trivers, R. L. (1971). Evolution of reciprocal altruism. *Quarterly Review of Biology, 46*, 35–57.

Tschirgi, J. E. (1980). Sensible reasoning: A hypothesis about hypotheses. *Child Development, 51*, 1–10.

Tulving, E., & Thomson, D. M. (1973). Encoding specificity and retrieval processes in episodic memory. *Psychological Review, 80*, 352–373.

Turiel, E. (1983). *The development of social knowledge: Morality and convention*. Cambridge University Press.

Tversky, A. (1967). Additivity, utility, and subjective probability. *Journal of Mathematical Psychology, 4*, 175–202.

Tversky, A. (1969). Intransitivity of preferences. *Psychological Review, 76*, 31–48.

Tversky, A. (1972). Elimination by aspects: A theory of choice. *Psychological Review, 79*, 281–299.

Tversky, A., & Kahneman, D. (1973). Availability: A heuristic for judging frequency and probability. *Cognitive Psychology, 5*, 207–232.

Tversky, A., & Kahneman, D. (1974). Judgment under uncertainty: Heuristics and biases. *Science, 185*, 1124–1131.

Tversky, A., & Kahneman, D. (1980). Causal schemas in judgments under uncertainty. In M. Fishbein (Ed.), *Progress in social psychology* (pp. 49–72). Hillsdale, NJ: Erlbaum.

Tversky, A., & Kahneman, D. (1981). The framing of decisions and the psychology of choice. *Science, 211*, 453–458.

Tversky, A., & Kahneman, D. (1982). Evidential impact of base rates. In D. Kahneman, P. Slovic, & A. Tversky (Eds.), *Judgment under uncertainty: Heuristics and biases* (pp. 153–160).

Tversky, A., & Kahneman, D. (1983). Extensional versus intuitive reasoning: The conjunction fallacy in probability judgment. *Psychological Review, 90*, 293–315.

Tversky, A., Sattath, S., & Slovic, P. (1988). Contingent weighting in judgment and choice. *Psychological Review, 95*, 371–384.

Tweney, R. D. (1985). Faraday's discovery of induction: A cognitive approach. In D. Goodring & F. James (Eds.), *Faraday rediscovered: Essays on the life and work of Michael Faraday* (pp. 189–209). London: Macmillan.

Tweney, R. D., Doherty, M. E., & Mynatt, C. R. (Eds.). (1981). *On scientific thinking*. New York: Columbia University Press.

Van Avermaet, E. (1974). *Equity: A theoretical and empirical analysis*. Unpublished doctoral dissertation, University of California, Santa Barbara.

Van Lehn, K., & Brown, J. S. (1980). Planning nets: A representation for formalizing analogies and semantic models of procedural skills. In R. E. Snow, P.-A. Federico, & W. Montague (Eds.), *Aptitude, learning, and instruction* (Vol. 2). Hillsdale, NJ: Erlbaum.

Vernon, P. E. (1950). *The structure of human abilities*. London: Methuen.

von Neumann, J., & Morgenstern, O. (1947). *Theory of games and economic behavior* (2nd ed.). Princeton: Princeton University Press.

von Winterfeldt, D., & Edwards, W. (1986). *Decision analysis and behavioral research*. Cambridge University Press.

Vosniadou, S., & Brewer, W. F. (1987). Theories of knowledge restructuring in development. *Review of Educational Research, 57*, 51–67.

Voss, J. F., Tyler, S. W., & Yengo, L. A. (1983). Individual differences in the solving of social science problems. In R. F. Dillon & R. R. Schmeck (Eds.), *Individual differences in cognition* (Vol. 1, pp. 205–232). New York: Academic Press.

Wagner, D. A. (1974). The development of short-term and incidental memory: A cross-cultural study. *Child Development, 45*, 389–396.

Wagner, D. A. (1978). Memories of Morocco: The influence of age, schooling and environment on memory. *Cognitive Psychology, 10*, 1–28.

Wallach, M. A. (1976). Tests tell us little about talent. *American Scientist, 64*, 57–63.

Wallas, G. (1926). *The art of thought*. New York: Harcourt, Brace.

Walster, E. (1966). Assignment of responsibility for an accident. *Journal of Personality and Social Psychology, 3*, 73–79.

Walster, E., Walster, G. W., & Berscheid, E. (1978). *Equity: Theory and research*. Boston: Allyn & Bacon.

Wason, P. C. (1960). On the failure to eliminate hypotheses in a conceptual task. *Quarterly Journal of Experimental Psychology, 12*, 129–140.

Wason, P. C. (1968a). "On the failure to eliminate hypotheses. . ."–a second look. In P. C. Wason & P. N. Johnson-Laird (Eds.), *Thinking and reasoning* (pp. 165–174). Harmondsworth: Penguin.

Wason, P. C. (1968b). Reasoning about a rule. *Quarterly Journal of Experimental Psychology, 20*, 273–281.

Wason, P. C. (1977). Self-contradictions. In P. N. Johnson-Laird & P. C. Wason (Eds.), *Thinking: Readings in cognitive science* (pp. 114–128). Cambridge University Press.

Wason, P. C., & Evans, J. St. B. T. (1975). Dual processes in reasoning? *Cognition, 3*, 141–154.

Watson, S. R., & Buede, D. M. (1987). *Decision synthesis: The principles and practice of decision analysis*. Cambridge University Press.

Waugh, N. C. (1970). Associative symmetry and recall latencies: A distinction between learning and performance. *Acta Psychologica, 33*, 326–337.

Wegner, D. M., Coulton, G. F., & Wenzlaff, R. (1985). The transparency of denial: Briefing in the debriefing paradigm. *Journal of Personality and Social Psychology, 49*, 338–346.

Weinstein, N. (1980). Unrealistic optimism about future life events. *Journal of Personality and Social Psychology, 39*, 806–820.

Weisberg, R. W., & Alba, J. W. (1981). An examination of the alleged role of "fixation" in the solution of several "insight" problems. *Journal of Experimental Psychology: General, 110*, 169–192.

Weisberg, R. W., & Suls, J. (1973). An information-processing model of Duncker's candle problem. *Cognitive Psychology, 4*, 255–276.

Wertheimer, M. (1959). *Productive thinking* (rev. ed.). New York: Harper & Row (Original work published 1945).

Wheeler, D. D. (1979). A practicum in thinking. In D. D. Wheeler & W. N. Dember (Eds.), *A practicum in thinking*. University of Cincinnati, Department of Psychology, Cincinnati.

Whimbey, A., & Whimbey, L. S. (1975). *Intelligence can be taught*. New York: Dutton.

White, R. W. (1959). Motivation reconsidered: The concept of competence. *Psychological Review, 66*, 297–333.

Williams, B. (1981). *Moral luck*. Cambridge University Press.

Wissler, C. (1901). *The correlation of mental and physical traits* (Contributions of the Department of Philosophy and Psychology, Columbia University, vol. 9., no. 2). New York: Macmillan.

Wittgenstein, L. (1958). *Philosophical investigations* (2nd ed.), (G. E. M. Anscombe, Trans.). Oxford: Blackwell Publishers.

Wolf, S. (1982). Moral saints. *Journal of Philosophy, 79*, 419–439.

Wollman, W., Eylon, B., & Lawson, A. E. (1979). Acceptance of lack of closure: Is it an index of advanced reasoning? *Child Development, 50*, 656–665.

Woodrow, H. (1927). The effect of type of training upon transference. *Journal of Educational Psychology, 18*, 159–172.

Woodworth, R. S., & Schlosberg, H. (1954). *Experimental psychology*. New York: Holt.

Woodworth, R. S., & Sells, S. B. (1935). An atmosphere effect in formal syllogistic reasoning. *Journal of Experimental Psychology, 18*, 451–460.

Wright, G. N., & Phillips, L. D. (1980). Cultural variation in probabilistic thinking: Alternative ways of dealing with uncertainty. *International Journal of Psychology, 15*, 239–257.

Wright, G. N., Phillips, L. D., Whalley, P. C., Choo, G. T., Ng, K. O., Tan, I., & Wisudha, A. (1978). Cultural differences in probabilistic thinking. *Journal of Cross-Cultural Psychology, 9*, 285–299.

Yaari, M. E. (1985). *Risk aversion without diminishing marginal utility and the dual theory of choice under risk*. Research Memorandum No. 65, Center for Research in Mathematical Economics and Game Theory, Hebrew University, Jerusalem.

Yamagishi, T., & Hill, C. T. (1981). Adding versus averaging models revisited: A test of the path-analytic integration model. *Journal of Personality and Social Psychology, 41*, 13–25.

Yamagishi, T., & Sato, K. (1986). Motivational basis of the public goods problem. *Journal of Personality and Social Psychology, 50*, 67–73.

Zajonc, R. B., & Markus, G. B. (1975). Birth order and intellectual development. *Psychological Review, 82*, 74–88.

Zigler, E., & Seitz, V. (1982). Social policy and intelligence. In R. J. Sternberg (Ed.), *Handbook of human intelligence* (pp. 586–641). Cambridge University Press.

Author index

Subject index

accountability, 279–80

active open-mindedness, 30–2, 99; and attentional bias, 247; beliefs about, 265–70, 463–6; and conflict, 284, 466; and creativity, 129; and decision biases, 350; examples of, 31; and fallacies, 159–61 and four–card task, 146; and hindsight bias, 214; and hypothesis testing, 218–19, 240–1; and naturalistic fallacy, 377; and overconfidence, 204; and personal plans, 455; and probability biases, 217; and reflection impulsivity, 120–2; and representativeness, 209; and social dilemmas, 427; and thinking assignments, 476–9; and thoughtlessness, 421; and total discrediting, 262; and tutorial method, 472–6; *see also* selective exposure

admission decisions, 208, 353–9; and interviews, 361–2

Allais paradox, 327–30, 332, 333

altruism, 408–11

analogy, 14–15, 78–9, 371–2

artificial intelligence, 51, 67–8, 194–7

averaging, 215–16, 366–8

beliefs: as causes of good thinking, 265–70, 463–6; as object of thinking, 4, 10–13; rationality of, 37–40

biases, 217; anchoring and adjustment, 214–15; attentional (contingency), 247–9; attentional (correlation), 245–7; averaging, 214–15, 367–8; certainty effect, 331–2; confirmation, 229–36; conjunction fallacy, 208–9; endowment effect, 436–8; gambler's fallacy, 209; "halo effect," 251–4; hindsight, 213–14; illusion of control, 247–51; illusory correlation, 251–4; information, 236–40; intransitivity, 320–1; neglect of priors, 205–8; outcome, 342; overconfidence, 200–4, 361–2; polarization effect, 263–5; primacy effect, 259–62; representativeness, 205–9, 368–70; self-deception, 270–1; sunk-cost effect, 433–6; temporal myopia, 445–6; total discrediting, 261–2; voter's illusion, 419–20; wish-

ful thinking, 271–2, 448; *see also* active open-mindedness; single–mindedness

bootstrapping, 358–9

calibration of probability, 183–5, 200–4

categorizing, 75–8, 226–9, 370–2

certainty effect, 331–2, 342

classification, *see* categorizing

cognitive dissonance, 272–7

cognitive style, 120–2; teaching of, 469–72

coherence of probability, 182–3, 187n, 188; justification of, 191–2

commitment: and identity, 453–4; and primacy effect, 261

concepts, *see* categorizing

creativity, definition, 123–4

critical (moral) thinking, 384–8

cross-cultural studies: goals, 468; intelligence, 115–17; modes of cooperation, 424–7; moral thinking, 391–2, 395–6; probability, 200–1; social dilemmas, 422–3

decision analysis, 289–80, 302–4; amniocentesis, 308–10; cataract, 314–15; vs. cost-benefit analysis, 302–3; and MAUT, 312–15

descriptive models, 16–25

development: of identity, 451–5; of knowledge, 86–8; of learning, 82; of moral thinking, 390–7; of reflective judgment, 256–8; of self-control, 447

diagnosis, 10; *see also* medical examples; psychological diagnosis

disappointment, 344–6

elimination by aspects, 321–4

emotion: control of, 447; effect of, on probability judgment, 212; effect of, on thinking, 280; and intertemporal choice, 449–50; and rationality, 36–7, 345–6; *see also* disappointment; fear; regret

envy, 411–17

evidence, *see* search-inference framework

exchangeable propositions, 176–7, 348

expected-utility theory, 288, 290–4; and ax-